COURT MARTIAL PROCESS

Empirically Studied

DEDICATION

With all the reverence, love and very rich memories,

this book

is dedicated to my late parents,

Lala Makkhan Lal

and

Smt Ram Pyari Devi,

who,

notwithstanding their own academic limitations,

beckoned me always

to

'tamaso ma jyotirgamaya.'

COURT MARTIAL PROCESS

Empirically Studied

Brigadier(Retd) Dr Rama G Vidhu

Vij Books India Pvt Ltd
Ansari Road, Daryaganj, New Delhi

Published by

Vij Books India Pvt Ltd
(Publishers, Distributors & Importers)
2/19, Ansari Road, Darya Ganj
New Delhi - 110002
Phones: 91-11-43596460, 91-11- 65449971
Fax: 91-11-47340674
web : www.vijbooks.com
e-mail : vijbooks@rediffmail.com

ISBN: 978-93-80177-36-6

CONTENTS

Foreword

Rama G Vidhu, the author of this book, and I have been friends for the last about two decades. Besides a common bond of ex- servicemen's comradery between the two of us, he has been with me on the editorial board of a quarterly defence journal and also assisted me in the publication of some military books that I have authored. It gives me now pleasure to write a Foreword to his work on Court Martial Process.

The process of Court-Martial is a concern of every commander as a functional tool of his troops' discipline. Its practical application may, however, be differently seen by different people, depending on their perception of the system. Douglas of the US Justice Department feels that "Court- Martial strikes terror in the heart of the accused," while nearer home, Justice Wadhwa finds that the procedure prescribed for a Court-Martial is equally fair, if not more, than a criminal trial provides to an accused. It is in the light of such diverse views, that Rama decided to undertake a study of the attitudes that the people of different sections of our society have towards Court-Martial.

In his study, the author examines , besides other parameters, whether the procedure prescribed for Court-Martial trial is, in fact, equally fair if not more than that provided for a criminal court; does Court- Martial imparts speedy justice within the confines of the existing legal system; does Court-Martial suffer from an over-riding "pull" exerted by the command system and also suffers from pre-determined decision-making; are there enough checks and balances in-built in the Court -Martial system to make up for the inability of the accused to appeal against Court-Martial decisions; etc. Except that the last question has now become irrelevant, with the Armed Forces Tribunal having since been created to hear such appeal, in addition to certain other powers, all these are some very pertinent questions with a visible bearing on the validity of the military justice system. The author can rightly claim credit for a pioneer attempt to seek their answers with objectivity of an empirical research.

In the early part of the book, Rama outlines the methodology adopted for his research. Then, after discussing, in detail, the data collected on various aspects of his topic, he sums up the entire discussion. Finally, the author comes up with some "out of the box" suggestions for improvement of the military justice system, which need expert unbiased evaluation.

I feel that the book is an excellent overview of the existing military system of Court-Martial and should be studied by all "Legal Eagles" of the Armed Forces. It provides timely and definitive advice, in its contents, to the military command and staff hierarchy, from Commanding Officers to Corps Commanders and their 'A' and 'JAG' staff, on all aspects both legal and procedural, of the conduct and laws governing the Court-Martial system. The data and the conclusions drawn in the book should also provide legislative direction for corrective measures to be incorporated in our military justice system.

A supportive work indeed.

Meerut (India)
01 Oct 2010

(Mathew Thomas)
Lt Gen (Retd)

Lt Gen Mathew Thomas (Retd) is a much respected scholarly General of 1948 commission, with half a dozen books on military subjects to his credit. He took part in several operations, set up Counter Insurgency and Jungle Warfare School (CIJWS) in Mizoram, commanded an Infantry Corps, is formerly Commandant, Indian Military Academy, and has an uncommon distinction of being decorated with all the three distinguished service awards of PVSM, AVSM, VSM.

- Publishers

Preface

It is rather unconventional to begin the preface of a work on military law with a segment of Vedic prayer *'idannamama* इदन्नमम' (the offering is for the deity, 'not for me'). And yet, this is being done here, not with any intention of taking " my job as spiritual work" like Chief Justice S H Kapadia (CJ's speech while releasing Veerappa Moily's treatise on the Ramayan), but to present to the reader, at the very outset, the distinguishing feature of the book. Being based on a project of legal research, it is purported to be marked with an uncompromised objectivity, dedicatedly strived for by eliminating 'me' — 'mine' element, in the spirit of the words of BA Worstley, who, in his address before the Society of Public Teachers of Law, at the University of Manchester, on 24 Sep 1965, had this to urge:-

> *However difficult, and sometimes even dangerous, it may be to express truth (toute v'erite ne'st pas bonne a' dire) the scholar will at least, like the judge and the honest witness, attempt to do this, as Aristotle would say "for truth's own sake," rather than from fear of the opprobrium resulting from being found out in deliberate lie or expression of bias.* **(viii Journal of the Society of Public Teachers of Law, 1964-65, pp 249-260, reprinted as "some Reflections on Legal Research" in Silver Jubilee number(1982) of Journal of Indian Law Institute)**

The research project was conducted by me under the aegis of the University of Delhi, for the doctoral degree of Ph D, on the decision-making process of court- martial.

The institution of court-martial is presently there in all military systems the world over, with minor variations of designation, jurisdiction, composition or procedure on national level. However, it severely suffers a loss of image and is systemically called in question for such cases as that of 18 year old Midshipman Philip Spencer and two others, who were tried, convicted and hanged for mutiny, on board the USS *Somer,* in 1842, even without being brought before the officers trying them or knowing that they were being tried. The US military law has since undergone a sea-change, and Justice Walter T Cox III of the US Court of Military Appeals assures " both to the civilians who cry ' drumhead justice' and to military members who cry that the system is too civilianized, ...that .....there may be tactical errors and an occasional injustice as the system malfunctions, but the grand strategy is sound." However, can we say the same of our own military legal system? Perhaps, not; even after the Armed Forces Tribunal has been recently established for appeal against court-martial decisions. We still have to go a long way to be truly awakened to the 'changed value' system, for which the apex court had exhorted our Parliament, in 1984, in PPS Bedi's case. To achieve this objective, "our system of military justice cannot be viewed solely from the vantage point of the military, it must also be viewed from the perspective of the people and the politicians", as Justice Cox would suggest. Accordingly, the project aforesaid was taken up to study the attitudes not only of those who are directly involved in the system but also of conscientious civilian citizens with some level of awareness of the military legal system.

It was a first ever empirical study of the court-martial decision- making process as a whole and the end-product of the study is being published in the form of this book. The reader will find here scientifically analyzed and logically interpreted data collected from a little over 200 individuals interviewed on a total of 22050 possible responses to the questions and sub-questions in the Interview Schedule appended at the end of the book. The respondents include Governor (1), High Court Judges (5), law officers from the Ministry of Law and the Law Commission (6), and advocates practising in superior and lower courts (4), in addition to the serving and retired personnel of the Army, Navy, Air Force, Coast Guards and BSF, of various ranks from Lieutenant General down to Sepoy or equivalent ranks. Some of them are highly decorated with awards like Param Vishisht Seva Madel and Mahavir Chakra, etc. Most of them also possess high academic or professional qualifications, there being Ph D(9), M Phil(1), LLM(5), Barrister of Law(1) and so on. However, there were some (7) below Matriculation too.

The book comprehensively covers the subject, expanding the concept of the decision-making process of court-martial, for the reasons contextually explained, to include not only the decisions of court-martial proper on various issues before it, but also the pre and the post- trial matters, including investigation of the reported offence and review of the trial proceedings. Some of the specific questions designed to cover the subject relate to highly debatable and sensitive issues, such as the desirability of extending the court-martial jurisdiction to all civilian offenders in terrorism-struck areas like J&K. Similarly, much controversial Service issues, like command influence, human right violations by armed forces personnel, advisibility of continuing with summary court-martial in the Army, the court-martial verdict being a foregone conclusion and the trial procedure mere formality, the requirement of providing for bail and plea bargaining in the court-martial procedure et al, have been included in those questions or taken up in detail while interpreting the primary or secondary data.

The entire work is divided into nine chapters. The first three chapters are essentially theoretical, dwelling upon the historical, legislative and the methodological aspects of the subject respectively. The methodology adopted to meet the needs of an empirical study inter alia explains the compulsions which determined the choice to fall on quota sampling for the study. The rest of the chapters discuss the data at hand in the context of the different stages of court martial cases, including pre-trial custody, court of inquiry, summary of evidence, hearing of the charge by the commanding officer, the trial proper by the officers constituting the 'courts-martial' and the post-trial review by the military authorities and, if approached, by the Armed Forces Tribunal and the constitutional courts. The issue of the efficacy of the process of court-martial has been devoted one full chapter (Ch-8), with all the available related data being discussed there. The last chapter sums up all that had been earlier taken up in the preceding eight chapters, draws final conclusions and makes recommendations based on the primary and secondary data, adding further certain suggestions which do not emerge from the primary data alone.

Efforts have been made to achieve a graphic understanding of the subject by spreading the data on as many as 54 Tables and 10 Charts. Further, while delineating various aspects of the subject- matter of each chapter, all the relevant decisions of our own superior courts and foreign judicial decisions have been liberally cited to support the perspective emerging therefrom. Classical treatises, such as those of Clode, Simmons, Pratt and Winthrop, to name only a few out of the whole lot, as also the modern works like those of Judge JW Rant, Federico Andreau- Guzman, Wade & Philip, Rear Admiral Dr OP Sharma, Maj Gen AC Mangala et al and a host of foreign and Indian articles and papers (including some unpublished ones) have also been suitably referred to, in addition to the related basic provisions of the principal and subordinate legislations governing the three Services in India and in the countries like the UK, the USA, France , China, Germany , Canada, Australia and the Netherland etc. In some contexts, even the provisions of the legal systems like that of Pakistan, Argentina, Peru, Chile and Chad have also not been ignored.

The net result of all this may, perhaps, be summed up in the words of Professor Deepak Pental, the Vice Chancellor of the University of Delhi, who, while awarding me the degree of Ph D, observed," It must be an interesting subject." Obviously, I felt elated and hope that the book will equally arouse the interest of the reader.

Before closing this, I must place on record my deep gratitude to Lieut Gen Mathew Thomas, PVSM, AVSM, VSM, for graciously sparing his precious time to write a Foreword to this book, in spite of being very busy in various commitments. He has always been kind to me.

My thanks are due to Brig PK Vij (Retd), Managing Director, M/S Vij Books India Pvt Ltd, and his team too, for the pains taken to bring out this title so well-bound. I would also gratefully acknowledge here the selfless gesture of my friend Wg Cdr(Retd) Dr U C Jha , who introduced me to the publishers.

There are some others too, to whom I owe a debt of gratitude for their very valuable contribution in my successful completion of this project. In fact, any study like the present one is a cooperative collaboration in which everyone associated with it, in whatever capacity, is a share-holder. But for the paucity of space, I would have liked to specifically make a mention of each one of them. May God bless them all. Amen!

-Rama

Acknowledgements

"Our song is the voice of desire, that haunts our dream", says Robert Bridges. Likewise, these acknowledgements are wordy representation, albeit within the usual linguistic limitation, of how intensely I feel indebted to those who have helped me over the past five years, in my bid to come up to the expectations of a researcher.

Professor Dr M.P. Singh, an old friend from my college days, indulgently guided me on how to go about enrolling myself for research work with the Faculty of Law of the University of Delhi. I gratefully acknowledge his kind gesture of putting me on the track.

Professor Dr S.C. Raina, as my research supervisor, maintained his stance of giving me a patient hearing and providing all necessary help, extending also his unhesitated support for whatever and whenever required, at all stages of the project. It will be a poor attempt on my part to give words to what I feel about the benefit I derived from his technical expertise and scholarly guidance. I would, therefore, only repeat the end-part of a Sanskrit couplet "***tasmai shree gurve namah***" (I bow to my revered teacher).

Dr S.K. Gupta, formerly an executive at the UNESCO research wing, and his lady wife Dr Mrs. Sangeeta Gupta of Meerut College, Meerut, provided me constructive guidance in preparing the Interview Schedule. Major General KTG Nambiar, VSM, Colonels SK Aggarwal and YR Sharma, in addition to the 200 individual respondents, made their valuable contribution in the data collection. Wing Commander UC Jha, VSM, Commodore P K Goel, AVSM, VSM, and Shri A P Agarwal rendered their immeasurable assistance to secure the literature on the subject. Shri Agarwal, in fact, also accorded to me much needed administrative help in computerization of the data and preparing the report, apart from benefiting me with inspiring ideas from the store of his rich experience, initially as a lecturer at the law faculty of a post-graduate college and later as a Legal Adviser at the Ministry of Law in the rank of Joint Secretary. Words will fall short to express my gratitude to all of them for what they have done to help me out.

I am also grateful to Major General Nilendra Kumar, AVSM, VSM, the then Judge Advocate General (Army), and Group Captain PC Grover, VSM, the then Judge Advocate General (Air), for supplying to me the official statistics in respect of the Courts Martial held during the past few years under their respective jurisdiction. I am also thankful to the JAG (Army) for the access to the Departmental library so graciously allowed to me.

I would also reverentially acknowledge the debt of Rear Admiral (Dr) OP Sharma, AVSM, VSM, for sparing time to discuss with me the present project at its budding stage and Major General BR Parashar, PVSM, AVSM, who had earlier injected in my mental make-up the need to strive for professional excellence in the matters of military justice. And now, a very solemn note of acknowledging the *rishi rin* (sacred debt) that I owe to the old masters. They include Thomas Frederick Simmons who authored his all-time great treatise in 1830 on the constitution and practice of courts-martial, Colonel William Winthrop who is often described as the Blackstone of the American military law, and a host of other great military jurists like Adye, Sullivan, Grose, McArthur, Clode, Pratt and several others. The debt is equally due to the high exalted judicial personalities whose pronouncements served as the principal light-house in the trackless waters of military jurisdiction. To express my feelings in the context, I can only borrow words from an English poet, R Southe, to say "The mighty minds of old; / My never failing friends are they / ..... And while I understand and feel / How much to them I owe, / My cheeks have often bedew'd/ with tears of thoughtful gratitude."

Finally, I should also acknowledge the contribution of my kith and kin, Mrs. Indu Bala Sarraf, my wife, Dr Prachur Vidhu, my son, his wife Dr Meenakshi and my grand children Angela (Deeksha) and Ojasvee. But for the support they extended and the tolerance they showed, all through the five years of my continuous Sabbath from home management and at times even to my throwing tantrum for no fault of theirs, it would have been impossible for me to meet the challenges of the daunting task.

- Rama

ABBREVIATIONS

1.	AA	Army Act, 1950
2.	AAR	Army Act Rules, 1950
3.	AF	Air Force/ Armed Forces
4.	AFA	Air Force Act, 1950
5.	AFAR	Air Force Act Rules, 1950
6.	AFR	Air Force Rules, 1968
7.	AFSPA	Armed Forces (Special Powers) Act, 1958.
8.	AFTA	Armed Forces Tribunal Act, 2009
9.	AFT	Armed Forces Tribunal
10.	AI	Army Instructions
11.	AJAG	Assistant Judge Advocate General
12.	AO	Army Orders
13.	AR	Army Rules, 1954
14.	BSF	Border Security Force
15.	BSFA	Border Security Force Act, 1968
16.	BSFR	Border Security Force Rules, 1969
17.	BrAFA'6	British Armed Forces Act, 2006
18.	CG	Central Government
19.	CO	Commanding Officer
20.	COAS	Chief of the Army staff
21.	CONS	Chief of the Naval Staff
22.	C of I	Court of Inquiry
23.	CM	Court Martial
24.	Cr PC	Code of Criminal Procedure, 1973
25.	DAJAG	Deputy Assistant Judge Advocate General
26.	DC	Disciplinary Court
27.	DCM	District Court Martial

28.	DJAG	Deputy Judge Advocate General
29.	DFDA	(Austratlian) Defence Force Discipline Act, 1958
30.	DPCM/ CM process	Decision-making Process of Court Martial
31.	ECHR	European Court of Human Rights
32.	GCM	General Court Martial
33.	GOC	General Officer Commanding
34.	GOC in C	General Officer Commanding in Chief
35.	GREF	General Reserve Engineering Force
36.	H of C	Hearing of the Charge
37.	IAA	Indian Army Act, 1911
38.	IAAR/IAFAR	Indian Army Act Rules, 1912/Indian Air Force Act Rules 1933
39.	IEA	Indian Evidence Act, 1872
40.	IPC	Indian Penal Code, 1860
41.	JA/TJA	Judge Advocate/Trial Judge Advocate
42.	JAG	Judge Advocate General
43.	JAG's Dept	The Department of the Judge Advocate General
44.	JCO	Junior Commissioned Officer
45.	JO	Judicial Officer
46.	Joint JAG	Joint Judge Advocate General
47.	MA	Mutiny Act
48.	MCM	(US) Manual of Court Martial
49.	MIML/MML	Manual of Indian Military Law/Manual of Militay Law
50.	NA	Navy Act, 1957
51.	NCO	Non-Commissioned Officer
52.	NDPS	Narcotic Drugs and Psychotropic Substances Act
53.	N Regs II(S)	Defence Services Regulations (Regulations for the Navy, 1965), Vol II (Statutory)
54.	OR	Other Ranks

55.	PM	Provost-Marshal
56.	PO	Presiding Officer
57.	PW	Prisoner of War
58.	QR	(British) Queen's Regulations/King's Regulations
59.	RA	Defence Services Regulations (Regulations for the Army), 1987
60.	RAF	Defence Service Regulations (Regulations for the Air Force), 1964
61.	RAI	Regulations for the Army in India - Reprint 1945
62.	RAT	Report on Application for Trial
63.	RCM	(US) Rules for Court Martial
64.	RI	Rigorous Imprisonment
65.	RP	(British) Rules of Procedure
66.	RT	Report on Trial
67.	SAI	Special Army Instruction
68.	SAO	Special Army Order
69.	SCM	Summary Court Martial
70.	SGCM	Summary General Court Martial
71.	S of E	Summary of Evidence
72.	SRO	Statutory Rules and Orders
73.	WO	Warrant Officer

LIST OF TABLES

List of Charts

LIST OF CASES

Title and Citation **Page No.**

I

J

K

S

Chapter - 1

COURT MARTIAL PROCESS : A HISTORICAL PERSPECTIVE

While no written military codes remain from the times of the Greeks or Romans, some of the principal military offences familiar to our present law, as desertion, mutiny, cowardice, the doing of violence to a superior, and the sale or appropriation of arms were recognized in their armies; and, of the punishments inflicted by them, while a portion, such as decimation, denial of sepulture (in connection with the death penalty), maiming, exposure to elements, taking of meals standing, & c, have long ceased to be known, others, such as dishonorable discharge, expulsion from the camp ... have come down to our day without substantial modification. [1]

- Winthrop

1.1 Introduction

Innumerable battles fought from the distant age of the Rigvedic warrior king Divodasa to our own times of the Gulf War II present a compelling evidence to support the Hobessian thesis of man being a fighting animal. As a consequence of the inevitability of war, some sort of rudimentary norms would have been formulated to regulate the conduct of soldiers at an early stage of human civilization, almost contemporaneously with the evolution of state sovereignty. With the advent of standing army (which in the case of India was sometimes in the middle of the 6th century BC during the days of Bimbisara[2] and of Britain in the later half of the 17th Century AD in 1660 though formally sanctioned by Parliament later through the first Mutiny Act, in 1689[3]), more elaborate codes would have been formed to define expected standards of military discipline and suitable mechanism to punish their breaches. The modern system of court-martial

---

1 William Winthrop, Military Law and Precedents, 2nd ed, 1920 (First Published 1886), Washington, Government Printing Pr ess, p 17 .

2 Sarva Daman Singh, Ancient Indian Warfare, 1st ed, 1965, Delhi, Motilal Banarsidass, p 145; read with Raychowdhuri HC, Political History of India, 1938, Calcutta, p 155.

3 Holdsworth, Sir Wi lliams, Essay in Law and History, 1946, p 6.

(hereinafter referred to as 'CM') is one such a measure evolved over the centuries since its seminal existence in the Aula Regis of William, the conqueror (1066-1087 AD).

1.2 Historical Background of Court Martial

Law treated historically becomes an entertaining study, says Lord Karnes[4]. The lure of such a treat through a glance at the justice dispensing agencies in different military legal systems of ancient times has to be, however, resisted in the present context which is essentially concerned with our British legacy only. The starting point there would be a Supreme Court called Aula Regis under the direction of Chief Justicier who led the forces and also administered the laws. This court comprised of great officers of the state including the Lord High Constable of England, the King's General, and the Earl Marshal[5], the lord responsible for the mustering of the army. The High Constable and the Earl Marshal presided over the jurisdiction of the Court of Chivalry blended in the Aula Regis in matters of honour and arms, determining according to whatever was then considered the law military and the law of nations. The court was popularly known as the Court of Marshal or Court Marshal, from which the 'courts martial' derive their name, the spelling of 'marshal' having been affected by a 'false etymology' as 'Mars' of 'Martialis' under Roman influence. The change was first noticed in the commission dated 14 February 1640 authorizing Algernon, Earl of Northumberland, Captain General of the Army, to hold "military or marshal or martial courts" as quoted in Rymer, XX, 369. However, this thesis is disputed by some military writers on the ground that both the spellings 'marshal' and 'martial' are still in vogue and military and 'martial' are found in some of the old records as being synonymously used[6].

(a) **Court of Chivalry**

When Edward I subdivided the Aula Regis into separate courts in the later part of the 13th century, one of the new courts was designated as the court of chivalry under the High Constable and the Earl Marshal. Both of them presided jointly while the court

---

4 Cit in Dr. (Rear Admiral) OP Sharma, Military Law in India, 2nd ed, 1990, Bombay, NM Tripathi, p. 15.

5 Earl' is a Norman equivalent of 'ealdorman' who was one of the three principal officers of a shire in the Anglo-Saxon England, the other two being the bishop and the shire-reeve (sheriff); See AKR Kiralfy, Potters' Historical Introduction to English Law 4th ed, 1958; London, Sweet and Maxwell, Ch.1. As for 'marshal'; the etymology of the word (mare= a female horse + 'shall' = governor) along with 'chivalry' (Fr, cheval = horse) is suggestive of a probability of Marshal's courts having been introduced at very remote periods, because of the peculiar honour being traditionally bestowed on the basis of dexterous management of horses in Greece, Rome, monarchies of Asia and among the savage warriors of Seythia and Germany; John McArthur Principles and Practice of Naval and Military Courts Martial, 4th ed, 1805, London, Butterworth, Ch II.

6 Thomas Frederick Simmons, The Constitution and Practice of Courts Martial 6th ed, 1873, London, John Murray, p 1, footnote 1

exercised a criminal jurisdiction over pleas of life and member, arising in matters of arms and deeds of war, but when it served as a military court or court of honour, the Earl Marshal alone held the court.[7] In times of war, the court followed the army and punished summarily according to the Articles of War. In the time of King Henry IV (1399-1413), the court was known as curia militaris[8]. Later, the courts of chivalry came to exercise extended jurisdiction, both civil and criminal, taking cognizance even of contractual matters. After the attainder and execution of the High Constable Stafford Duck of Buckingham in the thirteenth year of Henry VIII (1507-1547), there was appointed no permanent High Constable of England (only stop gap arrangement was made for occasions like coronation) and with this lapsed all the criminal jurisdiction of the court. Marshal alone held a court occasionally on purely civil matters. Gradually, the court became extinct even though it was never formally abolished.

(b) **Military Justice by Commanding Generals**

Upon the decadence of the court of chivalry, justice was administered in military matters by the General in command of the troops on the basis of special commission issued under the royal prerogative. His deputies would also hold trials on being so authorized by him. The decisions of these councils of war were based on the existing continental military jurisprudence[9]. However, the law administered, specially during the reign of the Tudors (1485-1603) and the Stuarts (1603-1714) more nearly resembled the martial law than the military law of modern times; trials of civilians by CsM, and the imposition by the same of the death penalty being sanctioned in cases in which the law of the land did not. Blackstone described it as "no law but something indulged rather than allowed as law. The power excised was plenary and the sentence carried into execution without the confirmation required under the present law."[10]

(c) **Mutiny Act**

This state of military justice continued until the first Muting Act passed by British Parliament in 1689, under an unprecedentedly grave politico-military environment, emphatically required that "noe man may be forejudged of Life or Limb or Subjected to

---

7 The corresponding jurisdiction in the Navy was exercised by the Lord High Admiral; please see Pilcher Committee's Report (cmd 8094), No vember 1950, London, HM' s Stationary Office, p . 7.

8 Simmons, The Constitution and Practice of Courts Martial ,op cit, n 6, p 1.

9 In olden days foreign military law was recognized in the British Services. The Dutch "Laws and ordinances touching Military Discipline" decreed at Arnhem on 13 August 1590 by the Council of State as printed in English at the Hague, were reprinted in 1691 as order in council, together with the Scotch Articles printed by order of King Charles II; Simmons, loc cit, p 2, footnote 5.

10 Lieut. Colonel Sisson C Pratt, Military Law - Its Procedure and Practice, 19 th ed, 1915, London, Kegan Paul, Trench, Trubner & Co , p 6.

any Kind of punishment by Martill Law, or in any other manner than by the judgement of his Peers, and according to the Knowne and Established Laws of this Realm" and that "noe Court Martill ... shall consist of fewer than thirteen, whereof none to be under the degree of Captaines".[11] This may be said to have paved the way for the constitution of the present day CsM including those under our own Service laws.

1.3 Military Justice in India : Evolution of CM System

The task of tracking the traditions of military justice in India from early ages is rendered stupendous by lack of war literature produced in ancient India despite her history of Dig-vijayas and later heroic resistance posed to periodical incursions by foreign military adventurers and migratory tribes from the 5th century BC onwards. However, some relevant references are found scattered in sacred texts and the accounts of foreign travellers like Magesthanes. Thus, there existed a rule that a deserter from the ranks might be killed or even burnt to death. There was also an injunction that the king should, in time of war, put to death those men who opposed his orders, the soldiers who ran away and did not keep their weapons, avaricious Generals who fought treacherously and men who did not face the enemy, fought against each other, deceitfully informed the enemy the king's designs, gave way to the enemy or rejoiced in the king's misfortune. A punishment of death was prescribed for disobedience of military regulations and a requirement of such regulations being communicated to soldiers every eighth day was also laid down[12] However, none of the known references speak of any institution with even a far resemblance to a CM of the current military legal system. A council of war does find mention in several passages of ancient texts[13] but contextually it appears to be more in the nature of a command instrumentality rather than a body with any judicial function.

(a) Import from British Military Law

Thus, our present military justice system does not seem to be embedded in the early

11 This was a far cry from the General sitting alone deciding on the life and limb even of civilians arbitrarily. The constitution of a court martial prescribed under the first Mutiny Act seems to have drawn inspiration from the Articles of King Gustavous Adolphus of Sweden, 1621, providing for 'Courts of Warre' at two levels: one; 'Marshall Court' presided over by the King's General and the other at the level of the Regiments. The former was held by the President with five of his associate General Officers and all available Colonels while the latter was constituted of officers who "together with the President ... may be to the number of thirteen at the least"; Winthrop, Military Law and Precedents , op cit, n 1.

12 Santiparva (97.20-22); Vaishampayana, Nitiprakasika (VII, 60-63); Sukraniti (IV. 2 pp 763-778) all cit in PC Chakravarti, The Art of War in Ancient India, 1941, Delhi, Low Price Publications, p. 83.

13 Atharva Veda (XV- 9.2, speaking of sabha cha samitischa sena cha); KP Jayaswal, Hindu Polity, p 20; and Satpatha Brahmana (VIII- 6.1.16) and Mahabharata 5.149, all cit in Sarva Daman Singh, Ancient Indian Warfare, op cit, n 2, pp 144-147 .

jurisprudential ethos of India. On the other hand, the historical evidence abundantly shows it to be a direct import from the British military law, which was first applied to the guards enrolled for the protection of the factories or trading posts established by the East India Company at Surat, Masulipatam, Armagon, Madras, Hoogly and Balasore in the first half of the 17th century. In some cases, special restrictions were placed by treaty on their strength so as to prevent them from acquiring any military importance. Gradually, however, the organisation of these guards was improved and from them sprang the Company's European and Indian troops. The Company was incorporated initially for 15 years, on 31 December 1600, by a charter of Queen Elizabeth-I, under which the General Court (constituted of all members) of 'the Governor and Company of Merchants of Landon Trading into the East Indies' was authorized to make laws for the good government of itself and its servants and impose simple punishments for their infringement. The laws were not to deviate from the principles of English law.

These legislative powers apparently being inadequate, King's Commission was granted to the Commander-in-Chief of each voyage to inflict punishment for offences like murder and mutiny, putting into execution 'the law martial'. Under one such commission, the first trial was held on 28 February 1616 on board the 'CHARES' lying at the Surat Port. The offender Gregory Littington was convicted of murder of Henry Barton at Surat and was condemned to death. In 1623, powers were granted to the Company itself to issue similar commission. In 1616, a new charter was granted by Charles II creating a judicial system of sort empowering the Governor and Council of each factory to punish not only company's servants but also the natives living in the Company's settlements in accordance with English law.

Further charters were issued from time to time to improve legislative strength of the Company in its sway which, by the 18th century, though restricted to the three Presidency towns, included the territories surrounding these towns and known as 'mofussils',[14] Statutory provision was first made in 1754 by an Act (27 Geo II, Cap 9) which empowered the Crown to make Articles of War, by its Sec 8, for "punishing Mutiny and Desertion of officers and soldiers in the service of" the Company. Despite the terms of the Act, the language of the Articles of War made by the Crown showed that those were intended for Europeans only. However, the Governments of Bengal, Madras and Bombay adopted those Articles, with certain modifications, to apply to the Indian troops maintained by

14 MP Jain, Outlines of Indian Legal History,1972, Bombay, NM Tripathi, Ch. II. During the early part of the 19th century, the jurisdiction of a CM under the British Military law was extended in India at a distance of 120 miles from the Presidency cities; Simmons, Constitution and Practice of Courts Martial, op cit, n. 6,.

them[15]. The legality of such a course was questionable for the native troops were the subjects of the Indian princes, the Company having acquired no sovereignty by then. To remove doubts, provisions were inserted in the Act (53 Geo III, Cap 155, ss 96, 97), passed in 1813, to extend the Company's privileges for a further term, which legalized the existing system and gave power to the Government of the three Presidency towns to make laws, regulations and Articles of War for the government of all Indian officers and soldiers in their respective services. In 1824, another Act (4 Geo, Cap 81, s. 63) provided that such legislation would apply to the Indian troops of each Presidency, wherever serving, and whether within or beyond His Majesty's dominions. Accordingly, Presidency formed a military code for own troops on the pattern of the Articles of War applicable to their Europeans, making death, dismissal, suspension and reprimand awardable to native officers and death and corporal punishment to soldiers; imprisonment and transportation were kept out.

(b) **Government of India Act, 1833, to Indian Army Act, 1911**

The Government of India Act 1833, (3 & 4 Will IV, Cap 85) came as a land-mark in the history of the British Indian military law. It gave power to the Governor General in Council to legislate for the whole native army officers and soldiers wherever serving. Under this authority, Act XX of 1845 enacted by the Governor General in Council made first (Indian) Articles of War which however, were replaced two years later by Act XIX of 1847. Frequent amendments followed and the Act was finally replaced by Act XXIX of 1861, which too was repealed and replaced by "the Indian Articles of War" of Act V of 1869 covering "native officers, soldiers and other persons in Her Majority's Indian Army", the last expression recognising what later came to be known as 'followers'.[16] The three native armies of the Presidency towns being amalgamated into one in 1895, the Indian Articles of War were altered through various amending Acts from 1894 to 1905 but the code originally designed to serve the requirements of three separate local forces could not adequately meet the needs of the new development, despite the

15 A trial held under this arrangement was that of Sep Ramjee Warring of Bombay Native Infantry. He was charged with desertion and tried at Poonah (now Pune) on 12 December 1803 by a CM. Convicted of "the crime exhibited against him and the same being to the prejudice of good order and military discipline and contrary to the rules and Articles of War", he was sentenced to "suffer death by being blown away from the gun". The proceedings were confirmed but the sentence remitted; please see Dr OP Sharma, Military Law in India, op cit, n 4, p 24.

16 The followers, European as well as native and of both sexes were subject to the East India Company's Mutiny Acts and subsequently, after 1863, to the British Mutiny Act. At a GCM held at Meerut on 06 August 1825, Hannah Fitchet, wife of Private Joseph Fitchet, 14th Foot, was tried for murder and, being found guilty of manslaughter, was sentenced to 2 year imprisonment which was later mitigated to 3 month imprisonment by Gen Sir Edward Paget, the C-in-C in India; Simmons, The Constitution and Practice of Courts Martial, op cit, n 6, p 33.

patchwork of those amendments, which, on the contrary contributed to confusion and gave rise to difficulty of understanding. A project to make further amendments therein was therefore abandoned in 1908 and a fresh draft Bill was prepared to consolidate the existing laws and add such provisions as experience had shown to be required. The Bill was passed on 16 Mar 1911 as the Indian Army Act, 1911 (hereinafter referred to as 'IAA'), which came into force on 1 Jan 1912. Amendments were subsequently made to this Act by Acts of Governor General in Council in 1914, 1917, 1918, 1919, 1920 (twice), 1923, 1930, 1934 and 1935. Among these amendments is also included the provision made for the suspension of sentence, as a temporary measure of war necessity in 1917. Being found useful, the measure was made permanent by Act XX of 1920.

(c) **Post-Independence Era**

The need for a general revision of IAA and the rules made thereunder as Indian Army Act Rules, 1911 (hereinafter referred to as 'IAAR') was felt for some time, some of the provisions having become out-dated for the modern requirements. This need, however, became imperative after Independence for obvious reasons. A Bill to consolidate and amend the law relating to the government of the regular Army was therefore introduced in the Constituent Assembly of India on 21 Dec 1949. This was passed into law by Parliament on 20 May 1950 as the Army Act, 1950 (Act XLVI of 1950) (hereinafter referred to as 'AA') and came into force on 22 Jul 1950 on receiving the assent of the President.[17] Subsequent amendments made by amending Acts of 1955, 1957 and 1992 and laws adopted by 2 ALO 1956 are now part of the AA. Under the provisions of AA s. 191, the Central Government framed the Army Act Rules, 1950[18] which were later replaced by the Army Rules, 1954[19] (hereinafter referred to as 'AAR' and 'AR' respectively). The Air Force Act, 1950 (hereinafter referred to as 'AFA') similarly replaced the Indian Air Force Act, 1932. It has provisions similar to those of the AA, with certain Service-specific modifications. The Navy Act, 1957 (hereinafter referred to as 'NA'), has replaced the Indian Navy (Discipline) Act, 1934, which was modelled on the corresponding British legislation. In 1950, when the AA and the AFA were passed, the revision of the British Naval Code was being examined by a committee headed by Honourable Sir Gonne St Clair Pilcher, MC. The NA takes into consideration the recommendations of that committee as well as the provisions of the AA and AFA, differing

17 SRO 120 of 22 July 1950 in Gazette of India, Part II, Sec 4, p 86. The day acquired added significance when '22 July' was later adopted, in 1984, as the Corps Day of the Department of Jugde Advocate General(Army). In 1996, however '21 December' replaced it as the Corps Day of the JAG's Dept.

18 SRO 125 of 22 July 1950 in GOI.

19 SRO 484 of 27 November 1954 in GOI.

wherever necessary in view of the conditions and usages of the Indian Navy. The amendments made in the NA by amending Acts of 1960, 1970, 1974 and 1982 are now incorporated in the Indian Naval law. However, some significant amendments made in the AA and AR in 1992 and 1993 respectively have not so far been adopted in the NA nor in the AFA either.

(d) **Present Military Tribunals**

The current military code of India has four kinds of the CM under the AA. These are: General Court Martial (hereinafter referred to as 'GCM'), Summary General Court Martial (hereinafter referred to as 'SGCM'), District Court Martial (hereinafter referred to as 'DCM') and Summary Court Martial (hereinafter referred to as 'SCM'). Under the AFA there are three kinds of the CM namely, GCM, SGCM and DCM; the SCM being Indian Army specific. The NA provides for only one kind of the CM for all offences and all personnel subject to the NA. Additionally, it has a 'disciplinary court' (hereinafter referred to as 'DC') for a trial in time of war or on active service in respect of certain specified offences committed by officers and punishable in lesser degree. In other armed forces like Border Security Force, (hereinafter referred to as 'BSF'), General Reserve Engineering Force (hereinafter referred to as 'GREF'), there are similar fora for trial of defaulting personnel with more or less similar procedure as adopted under the AA and the AR, even though those fora are differently named. For instance, the BSF Act, 1968 provides for four kinds of Security Force Courts corresponding to the aforesaid CsM under the AA. In addition to the provisions of the respective Acts, elaborate regulations made under the concerned Act also govern the procedure adopted by the CM which, generally speaking, is that of a jury trial though with significant variations in certain respects. The over all procedure of the CM may, however, be said to be comparable to that followed by civil courts of criminal jurisdiction at sessions level.

(e) **Evolutionary Process**

It may be seen that the constitution and procedure of a present day CM is not some thing that came up over-night. It took centuries and various influences to bring them up to what they are today. It will be beyond the scope of the instant discussion to deal with the historical development of each aspect of the CM. However, the number of officers presently required to constitutive a GCM may be taken up to illustrate how the forces of evolution work in such matters. In ancient times, military offenders were punished instantaneously by the king or the commander all by himself. In Rome, justice in military matters was administered by magistri militum and legionary tribunes either as sole judges or with the assistance of councils. Similarly, in Germany, much before militargerichts (German Version of CM proper which is earliest traceable to the Articles of Frederick III of 1487 vintage), this was done by Duke or military chief through the priest accompanying the army. Later, courts of regiments held by the Colonel or an officer invested by him with 'mace' (called 'regiment') and the trials of high commanders by courts of bishops or noblemen came in. In France, military personnel were subjected to the jurisdiction successively of Mayor of the Palace, the Grand Seneschal, the Constable and the Provost Marshal, before counseils de guerre (French equivalent of CM)were introduced in 1655[20]. In the case of England, there is no trace of multi-member CM before the Articles of Gustavus[21] which provided for a 'Court of Warre' at Regiment level to consist of at least 13 members. In the time of James II, 'the concil of war or court-martial' was to consist of seven at least, which Sir James Turner describes as the French practice. From the first Mutiny Act, 1689, to the year 1868, GCM consisted at home (England), as at first, of 13 commissioned officers but in 1868 the number was reduced to 9 with a proviso that each of the members shall have a commission from Her Majesty for 3 years before assembly of the court. The minimum number fixed by the Articles of War of 1868 was nine in the East Indies, Malta and Gibraltar. It was fixed at 7 in the case of Nova Scotia or Bermuda and reduced to 5 in any other colony or outside the Queen's dominions and all GCM were to be necessarily attended by a Judge Advocate. By the time of the enactment of the IAA, the constitution of a GCM was stabilized to a number of not less than five British officers or Indian commissioned officers each of whom had held a commission for not less than three whole years and of whom not less than four were of a rank not below that of captain[22]. The AA has retained this position verbatim in its s. 113.

1.4 Judge Advocate

CsM being composed of Service officers, who, irrespective of their rank and experience in military affairs, may be merely lay persons in the field of law, the concerned Acts provide for the trial to be attended by a professional known as the Judge Advocate (hereinafter referred to as 'JA', compulsorily at the highest level court, i.e., GCM[23] or the Naval CM and advisedly at SGCM and DCM too. The designation of the JA, comprising of the words denoting two entirely different functions, appears to be somewhat curious, more so in view of its incumbent being factually neither a judge nor an advocate - judging no matter, advocating for none. However, a close look at the related historical

---

20 Bruce Insts, 295-300; Adam R oman Ant, 300; V on Mol itor, Kriegsgerichte Und Mil itarstrafen, 11; cit in Winthrop, Military Law and Precedent, op cit, n 1, pp 45-48 for the Roman System; Koppmann, Militarstraf-gesetzbuch for the German system and Le F aure, p 141 and F oucher, Code de la Justice Militaire p 3, f or the French system.

21 Code of Articles of King Gustavus Adolphus of Sweden (1621). In olden days, foreign law was recognised as authority in the British Services; Simmons, The Constitution and Practice of Courts Martial, op cit, n 6, p 2.

22 IAA s 57.

23 AA s 129

facts would suggest several possible explanations, the most agreeable one being in the description of the JA by Carnwoth as 'judex advocates' i.e., a judge called in (advocates) to advise the court though forming no constituent of it.[24] Slightly in a different sense, the expression may as well be taken to suggest an adjudication forum related appointment from professional cadre as distinguished from other non-professional appointees on the forum. This gets support from a 17th century fact of the Indian legal history. The appointment of Sir John Biggs on the Court of Admiralty on 10 July 1686, under the Charter of 1663, carried the designation of 'Judge Advocate', while made in response to a requirement projected by the Governor and Council for the assistance of "a person better skilled in law and formalities", in view of the difficulty they were experiencing in discharging judicial duties under the Charter of 1661, being laymen as far the law was concerned. The other judges appointed on the court alongwith sir John Biggs were simply merchants.[25] Returning to the CM, the charter of duties of the JA included some functions which had earlier been the preserve of advocates and at the same time the place was assigned to him with the CM members. This fact would have also contributed to the coinage of this designation.

The story of the office of the JA in England is marked with a constant struggle between the forces representing the monarchical traditions, on the one hand, and the democratic ideal of judicial independence, on the other. It appears that from early times, the court of the Constable and Marshal was assisted by a civilian lawyer to superintend the procedures of the trial and advise the court as to the provisions of the civil laws. He was called the Judge Marshal or by the old Roman name the Praetor. His attendance at the Marshal's court would have been clearly an accepted thing about 50 years before Francis comes to describe him, in 1622, as "a renowned and reverend officer"[26]. The Articles of War put out in 1629, 1639 and 1662-1663 speak of the Marshal's Court "to hear and judge", the "Council of war and Advocate of the Army" and the "Judge Advocate of the Forces" respectively. In 1666, Samual Brown was appointed to be the first holder of the office of Judge Advocate General (hereinafter referred to as 'JAG'). The reverend officer of Markham's times, with a role of judicial nature, was however, saddled with the task to "inform the court and prosecute", by the Articles of War, 1673 and required thereafter to combine the functions of prosecutor and legal adviser to the court until the Articles of War, 1860 were amended to expressly provide that the JA would not prosecute and should be completely impartial. In his capacity as

24 The Army and Air Force Court Martial Committee Report, cmd 7608 (1949) at p 7 .

25 M Rama Jois , Legal and Constitutional History of India, 1984, Bombay, NM Tripathi Pvt. Ltd., Vol II, p 6.

26 Francis Markham, Five Decades of Epistles of Warre, 1622, p 100, cit in Stuart-Smith, James, 'Military Law: Its History, Administration, and Practice', Law Quarterly Review, Vol 85, 1969, pp 478-504 , at 481. Please also see the Code of Articles promulgated by Gustavus in 1621. Swedish King Gustavus Adolphus was the first commander to appoint a JA to his staff.

adviser of the court, the JA continued to retire with the members of the CM and sum-up in the closed court, when they considered their finding, until the Lewis committee's recommendations[27] inter alia against this practice were implemented on 1st October 1948. Some other recommendations of this report also led to the JAG ceasing to be responsible to the Service Ministers and becoming responsible instead to the Lord Chancellor. Further, although the JAG was no more prosecuting after 1860, he was not relieved of his responsibility for the preparation of the prosecution until the recommendations of this report were implemented in 1948 by transferring to the Directorates of Army Legal Services and Legal Service Air Ministry the functions performed by the Military Departments of the JAG's office. The said Departments were formed in 1923 to undertake the prosecuting functions independently under a Dy JAG in each case. Lastly, the turbulent years of the 19th century had also connected the JAG to the political sphere. In 1806, he had become a member of the Privy Council, with personal access to the Throne and sharing with the Secretary of the State for War the responsibility of answering for the Army in Parliament. This involved inappropriateness of the holder of a judicial office being constantly altering with each change in the administration. In 1893, the office was removed from the political sphere. Later, in 1905, it was decided to fill the office as a paid appointment by a person of suitable legal attainment subject to the orders of the Secretary of State for War. This continued until the JAG became responsible to the Lord Chancellor in 1948.[28]

Charged with the administration of military justice, there is a JAG separately for each of the three Services in the UK, the USA and in India. In the UK, the JAG Navy is designated as the Judge Advocate of the Fleet and is appointed from among the practising barristers. Under our own system, the JAG Navy is appointed by the Central Government and may not necessarily be a person in the uniform. The JAG Army and the JAG Air Force are appointed like any other General Officer of the Service from among the commissioned officers. He is, in the case of the Army, the legal advisor of the Chief of the Army Staff (hereinafter referred to as 'COAS') in matters of military, martial and the International Law in its fighting service aspect[29]. He has his deputies at the Army

---

27 Lewis Committee (appointed in 1946) Report of the Army and Air Force Court Martial Committee, cmd 7608, (1948); His Majesty's Stationery Office.

28 Stuart-Smith, James, "Military Law : Its History, Administration, and Practice', Law Quarterly Review, Vol 85, 1969, pp 478-504 , at 481-484 . The various aspects of the institution of the J A stand dealt with at length in Simmons, The Constitution and Practice of Courts Martial, op cit, n 6, pp 194-200; in Winthrop, Military Law and Precedents, op cit, n 1, pp 179-195; in OP Sharma, Military Law in India, op cit, n 4, pp 99-104. Please also see R v Linzee (1956) 3 All ER 980; Major Sansar Chand v UOI,, 1980 (3) SLR 125 (HP); RS Bhagat v UOI, AIR 1982 Del 191; Trilochan Joshi v UOI, 1983 Cr L J NOC 109 (Del); Mohan Rao Nayak and Others v UOI, CWP No. 400 of 1988, Raj HC (Jaipur) (DB) order dated 26 May 1988; Major Taj Mohammed Sheikh v UOI, 61 (1996) DLT 197 and UOI v Charanjit S Gill, AIR 2000 SC 3425.

29 Defence Services Regulations (Regulations for the Army), Revised Edition, 1987, (hereinafter referred to as 'RA') para 33.

Headquarters, Command and Corps levels holding the permanent appointments of Joint JAG, Deputy JAG, Assistant JAG and Deputy Assistant JAG (hereinafter referred to respectively as 'Joint JAG', 'Dy JAG', 'AJAG' and 'DAJAG'). Irrespective of the nomenclature of their permanent staff appointment, their designation at the CM trial is 'JA' in the case of the Army and the Air Force and 'Trial Judge Advocate' in the case of the Navy.

1.5 Military Codes

The mainspring of the CM system is the code that governs it. It includes the three Services Acts, the rules and regulations made thereunder, the instructions and orders issued by the concerned authorities and the custom of the Service. Passing from the time when the spoken word of the king or the commander was sufficient to execute a military offender to the time of written military law, the first authentic instance one comes across in Europe is the Salic Code, originally made by chiefs of the Salinas at the beginning of the 5th century and revised and matured by the successive Frankish Kings. The laws of the Western Goths, the Lombards, the Burgundians and the Bavarians existing in the 9th century belong to this period and were all civilians as well as military laws, the civil and military jurisdiction being scarcely distinguished and the civil judges being also military commanders in war time. The laws of the Merovingian and Carlovingian Franks, however, had reached their full development in 1532 in the elaborate penal code, the Constitutio Carolina Criminalis of Emperor Charles V, which has been viewed as the model of the existing military codes of continental Europe, including the elaborate Articles of Gustavus Adolphus framed in 1621.[30] The constitution of the CM prescribed under the first (British) Mutiny Act 1689, was well comparable with that of the 'Courts of Warre' under those articles of Gustavus.

Before the first Mutiny Act (hereinafter referred to as 'MA'), the ordinances and articles of war were issued to govern the troops during their engagement in hostilities. The earliest available such articles were those issued by Richard II on the occasion of war with France in 1385. The ordinances and articles ceased to have effect on the disbandment of the army at the close of the war. In 1688, there was no war and no articles of war in force but there was an unprecedented politico military environment with a state of constant conflict between Parliament and the King over the attempt of the later to enforce military law in peace time to meet the needs of discipline of an unsanctioned army which was riddled with soldiers disloyal and disobedient[31] to the reigning monarch William III. The MA was enacted to legalize the standing army as a

30 Winthrop, Military Law and Precedents, op cit, n 1, p 18;

31 The King's preference for the Dutch troops had generated dissatisfaction among the British Regiments. The Duke of Monmouth commanding Scottish regiments of Dunbarton openly declared his adherence to James II, the abdicated prince. On a message f orm William III and Mary, suggesting the suspension of

necessary evil and to provide a law in peace time to bring to "more exemplary and speedy punishment than the usual forms of Laws will allow" all such soldiers who shall "mutiny or stir up sedition or shall desert"[32]. Accordingly, the MA prescribed punishment of "death or such other punishment as by a court martial shall be inflicted" for all such cases and keeping intact at the same time the Royal prerogative of making articles for governing troops in time of war.

(a) **Army, Air Force and Navy Acts**

The MA proved to be a high water-mark of the British military law, not only by changing the age old tradition of restricting the application of military law to war times but also by introducing a practice of an annual renewal of the Act of Parliament dealing with military discipline. The inconvenience of the Army being governed partly by an Act of Parliament and partly by Articles of War led to a consolidation of the two into the Army Discipline and Regulation Act 1879, which was repealed and re-enacted as the Army Act 1881, again with a stated life of one year. Thereafter, the Army Act was required to be brought into operation every year by an Army (Annual) Act[33] so as to "securing the constitutional principle of the control of Parliament over the discipline requisite for the government of the Army"[34]. A select committee was appointed by the House of Commons in 1952 for suggesting amendments in the Army and Air Force law and advising on the desirability of making two permanent Acts separately. Pursuant to the recommendations of the committee, two new Acts, i.e., Army Act 1955 and Air Force Act 1955 came into force in 1957, both being essentially of one year life-span but having provisions to continue these by Order in Council for a period not exceeding 5 years.

There have been various amendments in the Army Act from time to time on every fifth yearly renewal, comparatively more important ones being through the Armed Forces Acts 1966, 1971 and 1976, 1997, 2001 and 2006. Certain other independently framed Acts of Parliament have also added to the administration of military justice. One such Act of great importance is the Court Martial (Appeals) Act 1951 (later amended in

Habeas Corpus Act in these circumstances, a debate was held in the House of Commons, underwriting the need for a measure to regulate the Army. On 13 Mar 1689, leave was given to bring in a Bill to punish the mutineers. At this time 800 men enlisted under James II, who had been under orders for embarkation for Holland, mutinied at Ipswich and refused to go there, marching instead northwards and declaring that James II was their rightful king. This expedited the Bill which, introduced in the House of Commons, was passed by both the Houses on 28 Mar and received Royal Assent on 30 Apr.

32 Pratt, Military Law - Its Procedure and Practice, op cit, n 10, p 3.

33 Army (Annual) Act 1881 was a consolidation of the Army Mutiny Act, the Marine Mutiny Act, the Articles of War and the Army Enlistment Act of 1870. Later, the Army (Annual) Act was designated as the Army and Air Force (Annual) Act from 1917 onward.

34 Pratt, Military Law - Its Procedure and Practice, loc cit, p 9.

1968) that established an appellate court for appeals against the decision of the CM as recommended in the Lewis Committee Report 1948.

The development of the Naval law, however, followed a separate course in England. The earliest example of a code for the governance of a Naval force there appears to be the ordinance of Richard I issued in 1190 to prevent disputes between the soldiers and soldiers in their voyage to the holy land of Jerusalem as a part of the fleet raised for crusade. In early times, regulations were issued for each expedition with summary powers granted to the commander of the ship. However, no institution like the CM was introduced for keeping discipline in the Naval forces until the 17th century in spite of a standing Royal Navy having been instituted in the reign of Henry VII (1425-1509), though Councils of War for advising the General in more serious cases do figure in the 16th century record. A three tier system of courts on the line of the Army system was instituted by commissioners appointed for managing the affairs of the Admiralty and the Navy by an ordinance in 1653. Eight years later, Articles of War 1661 were passed by Parliament for the enforcement of discipline "among the crews in actual service aboard men of war at sea or in the main stream of the great rivers below the bridges", which provided for "Court-Martials, consisting of Commanders and Captains". These articles having been amended on several occasions were consolidated in 1749. Under the Act of 1749, Admiral Byng was tried in 1756 for "not having done his utmost to take and destroy the ships of the enemy" and, having been found guilty of the offence, he was awarded the mandatory punishment of death and executed. This raised a storm of protest among the Naval officers but it was not until 1779 that the words "or such other punishment" were added in the penal provisions. In 1847, the severities of the old Act were removed for all but two capital offences. A fresh Act in 1860 was passed, followed by its later editions in 1861 and 1864 and finally the Navel Discipline Act 1866 came into existence, which was later replaced by an Act of same title in 1950. The latter one was also replaced in 1955 by another Naval Discipline Act. The new Act of 1955 carried the provisions which were designed to implement the recommendations of the Pilcher Committee[35].

On the line of Lewis Committee and Pitcher Committee, a committee was set up in India too, vide Govt. of India, Min of Def UO No 9/1/61/D (AG-1) dated 01 Apr 1965 for drafting a unified code for the three Services. The Committee prepared a draft unified code but its adoption was shelved on the recommendations of the Chiefs of Staff Committee in 1979, on the ground that the three Services themselves remained ununited and the working problems of each were different and should, therefore, continue to be governed by respective Acts. Thereafter, a large number of amendments was suggested for incorporation in the three Services Acts in order to modernize their provisions on

35 Pilcher Committee Report, op cit, n 7, pp. 7-9

the lines of the developments in military laws of other advanced countries. However, only a very few amendments were finally made by the Army (Amendment) Act, 1992 and the Army (Amendment) Rules 1993. These are yet to find place in the other two Services Acts.

(b) **Rules of Procedure and Indian Army Rules**

For the purpose of carrying into execution the various provisions of the British AA so far as those relate to the investigation, trial and punishment of offences, Rules of Procedure (hereinafter referred to as 'RP') were made by the Sovereign under the hand of the Secretary for State. The power to frame such rules was first contemplated by the Army Discipline and Regulation Act which had substituted the MA and Articles of War on 24 July 1879. Two years later, in 1881, when the statute was designated as the Army Act (or 'Army Annual Act'), the RP were fully revised. These rules have since been updated from time to time to incorporate such provisions as found desirable on the basis of experience gained over the years. Their equivalent on the Indian side at present are Army Rules, 1954.[36] As subordinate legislation these rules are purported not to contain anything inconsistent with the provisions of the Act under which those have been framed. When not so inconsistent, those shall have "effect as if enacted in this Act" and may be judicially noticed. Such rules are required to be laid before Parliament as soon as practicable and AR were so laid in the mid-nineties.

(c) **Regulations**

Regulations are administrative rules or directions as contrasted with enactment. The authority for army regulations is to be sought primarily in the distinctive functions of the President as the Supreme Commander of the Defence Forces of the Union, under which he would be authorised to issue personally or through his military subordinates such orders and directions as are necessary and proper to ensure order and discipline in the army. However, executive power to make rules and regulations, in the case of India, is vested in the Central Government [37].

---

36 IAAR were issued under the late Army Department notification No 911 dated 3 November 1911. Their current descendants are the AR issued under SRO No 484 of 27 Nov 1954 which have been amended form time to time (twenty one times in all) the last amendment being published in Gaz. of Ind. (Extraordinary) Part II Sec 4, Min of Def SRO No 17E dated 6 Dec 1993.

37 Constitution of India, Article 53 (2). Please see also Winthrop, Military Law and Precedents, op cit, n 1, p 27 wherein the US President's powers as commander-in-chief and as Executive have been cited as authority for the President to issue regulations for the Army. Under the latter authority, the US President may, personally or through the Secretary of War, prescribe rules for the due execution of the statutes relating to the military establishment. Since the Executive powers, in the case of India, are vested in the Central Government and not the President the rules and regulations are to be both made by that Government under AA ss 191 and 192 respectively.

Under the British system, King's Regulations or Queen's Regulations,[38] as the case may be, (hereinafter referred to as 'QR') deal with organisation and command of the Army, appointments and responsibilities of its officers, and detailed instructions for the maintenance of discipline, the interior economy, military training and general duties of troops in peace time. In addition to QR, there are also the Royal Warrants, which are issued by the Crown, through the Secretary of State as responsible to Parliament, from time to time. Royal Warrants lay down the permanent regulation as to the government, pay, promotion and conditions of service in Her Majesty's forces. Prior to 1888, monthly General Orders and Army circulars were issued respectively by the Commander-in-Chief as the Crown representative and the Secretary of War representing Parliament. Army Orders are issued by the Army Council to promulgate these warrants, orders, regulations and instructions to Army. The, Orders in Council are regulations issued by the Crown with the advice of the Privy Council to meet cases which cannot be conveniently dealt with Royal Warrants or Army Orders.[39]

On the Indian side, approximate current equivalent to RP, QR and Royal Warrants are AR, RA and Statutory Rules and Orders (hereinafter referred to as 'SRO') respectively. Regulations issued for various subjects include Pay and Emoluments Regulations and Pension Regulations issued apart from RA. RA 1987 were issued to replace RA 1962 which in turn had superseded Regulations for the Army in India - Reprint 1945 (hereinafter referred to as 'RAI'), RAI Instructions Reprint 1945 issued by the Commander-in-Chief and Queen's Regulations 1940 Edition. SROs are issued by the Central Government through the respective Ministry. For instance, while the Army (Amendment) Act, 1992 (Act 37 of 1992) was published by the authority of Ministry of Law, Justice and Company Affairs (Legislative Department) in the Gazette of India, Extraordinary, Part II- Section 1, on 7 Sep 1992, SRO 17 E of 6 December 1993 which amended AR 1954 was published in Gazette of India (Extraordinary) Part-II- Section 4, by the Ministry of Defence. RA were issued by Secretary to the Government of India, Ministry of Defence. RA Vol 1 has 13 chapters on various aspects of organisation, control and training. Its Part II on 'Discipline' inter alia covers the CM in Chapter X. Vol 2 is on administration with Chapters XIV to XXXVI. RA are non-statutory while Regulations for the Navy (Part II) (hereinafter referred to as 'N Regs II (S)') are statutory. Further, we also have Army Orders (hereinafter referred to as 'AO') and Army Instructions (hereinafter referred to as 'AI'), general and special, issued respectively by the COAS and the Ministry of Defence and covering more or less the same grounds as the Army Orders, General Orders and Orders in Council under the British system.

---

38 Simmons, The Constitution and Practice of Courts Martial, op cit, n. 6. Preface to the Sixth Edition, refers to the publication of the 'Queen's Regulations and Orders for the Army' in 1868.

39 Pratt, Military Law - Its Procedure and Practice, op cit, n 10, p 11.

(d) **MML**

Since very little guidance was available in the form of judicial precedents for the application of military law, an official publication called Manual of Military Law, (hereinafter referred to as 'Br MML') was brought out by the British War Office on 1 Oct 1882 to assist all concerned in the conduct of the CM and day-to-day functioning of the Army. It was prepared by seven different writers and revised by JAG.[40] This furnished the model on which the Manual of Indian Military Law, 1912 (hereinafter referred to as MIML) was compiled, the ruling contained in the MML being largely drawn upon in its preparation in the Judge Advocate General's Department. It was divided into four parts. Part I contained a history of the law relating to His Majesty's Indian Forces, with a general account of that law and its application under the IAA 1911 along with the law of evidence applicable to the CM, such offences against the ordinary criminal law of India as were likely to engage the attention of the CsM and other legal matters a knowledge of which might be useful to officers and soldiers of the Indian Army. Part II consisted of a reprint of the IAA and IAAR with copious notes which would materially help in the administration of Indian military law. Part III had the texts of certain analogous Acts. The last Part contained various notifications issued by the Governor General in Council under the IAA and also the forms for use in the preparation of court martial warrant under that Act. The first edition of the MIML appeared on the IAA coming into force on 1 January, 1912. Its next important edition was the 3rd edition brought out in 1937 updating the publication upto July 1936 with important changes in Parts I and II in view of the amendments in the IAA and IAAR in 1934. This remained in vogue almost for half a century with only a few reprints in 1961, 1967, 1971 and 1976. A crying need was, however, being felt for a thorough revision of the MIML, more particularly because the provisions of AA 1950 and AR 1954, even though incorporated in the reprints, had to be interpreted and understood with the help of notes appended to the provisions of the IAA and IAAR. The stupendous task of revising the MIML was accordingly started in March 1977 and the revised manual was finally published in 1983 in diglot form in three volumes. Volume I consists of eight chapters dealing with a brief history of military law in India, outline of the AA, arrest and investigation of charges, courts-martial, evidence, civil offences, duties in aid of civil power and service privileges. Volume II contains the AA 1950 and AR 1954 with explanatory notes, forms and appendices. Volume III contains the texts or relevant extracts from certain Acts of Parliament and Ordinances in addition to the extracts from the Constitution of India. Some of the Acts include the Armed Forces (Special Powers) Act, 1958, the Assam Rifles Act 1944, the Official Secrets Act, 1923, the Indian Evidence Act, 1872 and the Indian Penal Code, 1860. This volume also contains some notifications and warrants

40 Winthrop, Military Law and Precedents, op cit, n 1, 'Explanation of References'.

issued under the AA, 1950. These warrants inter alia include 'A-1' Warrant by COAS to certain officers granting power to convene a GCM, 'A-2' Warrant from the Central Government authorising the COAS to confirm the finding and sentence of any GCM, 'A-3' Warrant from the COAS to certain officers to confirm the finding and sentence under their command and 'B-1' Warrant authorising Brigade and equivalent commanders to convene a DCM and confirm its finding and sentence.

1.6 Classical Treatises

Even though not a hot pursuit of legal research and academic writing, "military law, from its early origin and historical association, its experience of many wars, its moderation in time of peace, its scrupulous regard of honor, its inflexible discipline, its simplicity and its strength[41]" attracted a sizeable number of classical authors and later day writers. Some of the well known military writers, who are usually cited simply by name, include Mathew Sutcliffe, Bruce, Adye, Sullivan, Grose, Williamson, Tytler, McArthur, Samuel, Delafons, Mc Naghtan, Simmons, Harcourt, Griffiths, Kennedy, Napier, Hughes, Hickman, D' Aguilar, Prendergast, Thring, Tulloch, Franklyn, Gorham, Jones, O'Dowd, Brackenbury, Pratt, Story, Tovey, Worsley, Macomb, Malthy, O'Brien, DeHart, Coppee, Benet, Lee, Harwood, Ives, Birkhimer, Clodes, James, Warren, Rymer and Winthrop. Unfortunately very few classical treatises on military law are now available, most of them being out of print. A reward of $ 1000 was being offered sometime back for a copy of Clode's Administration of Justice under Military and Marshal Law from any private possession. In India, libraries of the Departments of the Judge Advocate General Army, Navy and Air Force are the only source for the availability of some of these works. Among the works of military writers in India at present are included C Sanjeeva Row Nayudu, Hand Book of Military Law, 1951, Dr OP Sharma, Military Law in India, 1973, Major General AC Mangala, Commentary on Military Law in India, 1992, Col GK Sharma and Col MS Jaswal, Study and Practice of Military Law, 2006, and Major General Nilendra Kumar & Rekha Chatuvadi, Law Relating to the Armed Forces in India, 2006 and RP Sharma, Manual of BSF Law, 1971.

To conclude this historical introduction to military justice system, one may join with Colonel William Winthrop to say that "there is a military code of greater age and dignity and a more elevated tone than any existing American civil code, as also a military procedure which, by its freedom from technical form and obstructive habit that embarrass and delay the operations of the civil courts, is enabled to result in a summary and efficient administration of justice well worthy of respect and imitation."[42]

41 Winthrop, Military Law and Precedents, n 1, 'Preface to First Edition' 1886

42 Winthrop, ibid

Chapter - 2

OUTLINE OF COURT MARTIAL PROCESS

Military justice is a system of law created to enforce certain standards of behaviour some of which are identical to standards enforced in civil life. These standards have importance in maintaining discipline in the armed forces and public respect for those forces.[1]

- Captain De Vico

2.1 Scope

The word 'process' implies "connected series of actions, changes, etc"[2]. The CM Process or decision-making process of CM would therefore cover the entire series of actions involved in the proceedings before a CM and also those which lead thereto or flow therefrom. In the present context, this would include various steps taken by the concerned agencies from the time the fact of an offence having been committed in the area of their responsibility comes to light and until the case is finally closed, on all legal remedies having been exhausted on the decision of the CM under the related code. Further, within the defined scope of the project at hand, the process to be taken note of would be as obtaining in the system that governs the Army of the Union of India. The process under the AA and AFA is more or less same. Under the NA, however, it varies at times, which will be pointed out where necessary.

As explained in the previous chapter, the military code that regulates the conduct of the Army personnel consists of the AA, the AR, the RA and various AI and AO issued from time to time, along with the relevant civil laws, the Indian Penal Code, 1860 (hereinafter referred to as 'IPC') and the Indian Evidence Act, 1872 (hereinafter referred to as 'IEA'). At a CM trial, any other civil laws, such as the Official Secrets Act, 1923, may also be brought in, if relevant to the charge.

1 Captain De Vico, AJ, US Navy, "Evolution of Military Law" The JAG Journal, (Dec 1966- Jan 1967) p. 67.

2 AS Hornby and others, The Advanced Learner's Dictionary, 1965, London, OUP, p. 223.

2.2 Jurisdiction of CM Process

All officers, junior commissioned officers (hereinafter referred to as 'JCO'), warrant officers (hereinafter referred to as 'WO'), non-commissioned officers (hereinafter referred to as 'NCO') and other enrolled persons (hereinafter referred to as 'OR') variously designated in the regular Army, and their counterparts belonging to the Territorial Army and Reserved Forces, in specified circumstances, are subject to the AA irrespective of their location - they are so subject even when they are on leave far away from their Army unit. The civilian camp followers, contractors, press correspondents etc., who accompany the forces on the line of march or when on active service are also subject to the AA.[3] They all may be tried by a CM for an offence under the AA, though, as a matter of policy, the civilians so subject to the AA are not tried by a CM without prior sanction of the Central Government.

2.3 Pre-trial Procedure

CM Process sets in motion with the proper military authority taking cognizance of an offence that has come to light. If the offender is not identified at this stage, a Court of Inquiry (hereinafter referred to as 'C of I') may be ordered to pin-point the responsibility for the offence.

(a) **C of I**

C of I is an assembly of officers, or of JCOs, or of officers, JCOs, WOs or NCOs, to collect evidence and if so required, to report with regard to matters referred to them and may consist of any number of officers etc. However, when the character or military reputation of an officer is likely to be a material issue, the presiding officer of the C of I, wherever possible, will be senior in rank and other members at least equivalent in rank to that officer.[4] Any officer in command of troops is competent to assemble a C of I.

(b) **Arrest**

From the finding of the C of I or otherwise, when the offender is identified, he may be taken into military custody, which means arrest or confinement of a person according to the usage of the Service. Arrest is either 'close' or 'open', the difference lying mainly in the nature of restrictions imposed. In close arrest one cannot, while in open arrest one can, for specified purposes, leave the place of detention. In either case, one remains under surveillance at all times - NCOs and above under an escort of equal rank and

---

3 AA s. 2. Under the NA s. 2(2), every person ordered to be received or taking passage on board an Indian Naval ship or Air Craft, whether in the uniform or civilian is also subject to the NA.

4 AR 177 as amended by SRO 8-E of 23 Jun 2003, read with RA para 518.

Sepoys under guard commander or section commander. Detailed provisions[5] exist to cover various aspects of arrest, such as the authority competent to order arrest, the formalities to be observed on arrest in matters of communicating the grounds of arrest to the detenu, report to superiors in command and sanctions of prescribed authorities for continuation of arrest beyond specified time limits and release without prejudice to re-arrest. Certain irregularities in arrest or confinement are made severely punishable under the AA. It is important to note in this connection that the arrest of an offender is not a legal necessity under military system.

(c) **Investigation**

The charge against every person taken into military custody is required to be investigated within 48 hours from the time his committal is reported to his commanding officer[6] (hereinafter referred to as 'CO'), unless investigation within that period is impracticable, in which case the reason for the delay is required to be reported to the specified superior authority. The investigation is primarily the responsibility of the CO but in the case of a JCO, WO or OR a preliminary investigation is generally made by his squadron, battery or company commander [7] before he is marched to the CO.

(d) **Hearing of the Charge**

Every charge against a person subject to the AA, whether an officer, JCO, WO or OR, shall, unless already disposed by his company etc commander within his power of punishment, be heard by the CO in the presence of the accused.[8] Except a charge for an offence in relation to the enemy and punishable with death (AA s. 34), mutiny (AA s. 37), a civil offence (AA s. 69) or an offence against the officer hearing the charge, which all require a prior-reference to a superior officer, the charge brought before the CO may be either dismissed by him or further proceeded with. The former course may be adopted in either of the two circumstances: one, when the evidence does not show that an offence

5 AA s. 3 (xiii), 50, 101-103, AR r. 27 and RA paras 391-396, for analogous provisions under the Naval law, please see NA ss 83-85.

6 AA s. 3 (v) for definition of 'CO', which, in practical term, signifies the legal status of an officer to exercise powers and duties under the AA by virtue of being in command of a separate portion of the Army. Usually it refers to an officer commanding a Battalion or Regiment but would as well cover a General Officer or any other officer appointed as the CO of the personnel belonging or attached to a Formation Headquarter or the headquarter of an Establishment. The expression 'Officer Commanding', on the other hand, signifies factual state of commanding a separate portion of the Army but usually refers to sub-unit commanders like company commander though, again, may be used even for a General Officer Commanding (GOC) a Formation, the main difference between 'CO' and 'OC' being that of legal and factual signification respectively.

7 RA para 403 (6) and MML Vol I, p 106, para 12.

8 AR r. 22 as amended by SRO 17E dated 6 Dec 1993.

under the AA has been committed; and two, when the CO is satisfied that the charge ought not to be proceeded with. The discretion is obviously to be used purely on objective considerations, when, for instance, the accused has already been acquitted or convicted by a civil court or a CM on the same charge, or the charge has been dismissed or summarily dealt with earlier, or the evidence is doubtful, or the offence is trivial, or a compelling Service interest so requires, or any other similar reasons, including the expiry of the limitation period of 3 years in applicable cases or pardon or condonation[9] of the offence by competent military authority. In the event of the CO deciding to proceed with the case, four courses are open: one, the disposal of the case under AA s. 80 with punishments like 28 days imprisonment, detention or confinement to lines, extra guards or duties, 14 days' pay fine or severe reprimand etc by the CO; two, reference by the CO to the proper superior military authority; three, adjournment of the case with an order for recording the Summary of Evidence (hereinafter referred to as 'S of E'); and, four, ordering a trial by an SCM if the accused is below the rank of WO.[10]

---

9 Condonation is permissible only by specific prior sanction of the COAS; please see AO 288/72 and SAO 1/S/2002/DV-Court Martial, para 45.

10 The rank-structure in the Army is as under (RA paras 131 and 733):

Rank		Appointment
(a) General	-	Chief of the Army Staff (COAS)
(b) Lieutenant General	-	(i) General Officer Commanding-in-Chief of an Army Command (GOC-in-C Command or Army Commander), (ii) Principal Staff Officer (PSO), (iii) GOC Corps or (iv) Commandant IMA etc.
(c) Major General	-	GOC Division or GOC Area or other appointments.
(d) Brigadier	-	Brigade or Sub Area Commander or other appointments.
(e) Colonel	-	Battalion Commander or other appointments.
(f) Lieut Colonel	-	2nd in Command of Battalion or other appointments.
(g) Major	-	Company (Coy) Commander, Battery (Bty) or Squadron (Sqn) Commander.
(h) Captain, Lieutenant	-	Platoon commander.
(j) JCOs	-	(i) Subedar Major or Risaldar Major; } (ii) Subedar or Risaldar; } Platoon Commanders (iii) Naib Subedar or Naib Risaldar. }
(k) WO Class I or II		
(l) NCO	-	Havildar/Dafadar, Naik/Lance Dafadar, Lance Naik/Acting Lance Dafadar: Section Commander.
(m) Sepoy, Sowar, Gunner, Sapper, Signalman, Rifleman.		

(e) **S of E**

If the CO has adjourned the case for the purpose of having the evidence reduced to writing, the evidence of all material witnesses, whether called during the hearing of the charge or not, is taken down in writing in the presence and hearing of the accused. This is done either by the CO himself or by such officer as he directs. The accused is afforded an opportunity to cross-examine witnesses, make a statement if he so desires (after a caution is given to him that such statement may be used in evidence) and call his witnesses, if any. At S of E, the witnesses are not sworn or affirmed and their evidence is recorded in a narrative form but the questions put to them in cross-examination thereafter are recorded verbatim alongwith the answer in each case. The evidence of each witness, including cross-examination, is read to him and interpreted, if needed, in the language he understands and then it is signed by him. The CO is empowered to issue a summons to procure the attendance of a civilian witness. In certain cases, a signed statement of evidence may be accepted, with the officer recording the S of E certifying the reason therefor.[11]

After the S of E has been taken down, it is required to be considered by the CO, who again has the earlier stated options open to him, including the re-hearing of the case and dismiss or dispose the charge in view of fresh material, if any[12]. Apart from this, S of E has a number of other uses.

2. 4 Trial by CM

(a) **Application for Trial**

On consideration of the S of E, if the CO remands the accused for trial by a CM, the CO is required either to assemble an SCM, after a due reference to specified authority, if need be under AA s. 120 (2), or apply to the proper military authority to convene a CM when a trial by GCM, SGCM or DCM is intended. The format IAFD-937 (Revised) for such an application is given in Appendix III, Part I (A) to AR[13], which also lists out the documents to be sent along, including S of E in original and its copies.

---

11 AR r. 23; N Regs II(S), reg 149.

12 AR r. 24; The option of awarding minor punishment under AA s. 80 is available to the CO before as well as after the S of E but summary disposal, under AA s. 85, in the case of a JCO, is possible only after the S of E, since the procedure laid down in AR r. 26 for this purpose requires a copy of the S of E to be delivered to the accused at least 24 hours before the disposal.

13 MML, Vol II, p 402.

(b) **Convening of CM**

The kinds of CM under the AA, the power to convene them, their composition, and power and other related matters such as prohibition of second trial, period of limitation for trial, liability of offender who ceases to be subject to the AA and choice between a civil court of criminal jurisdiction and CM are stated in Chapter X of the AA. Accordingly, on a reference made by the CO, or on receipt of his application for trial, a superior officer may convene the appropriate kind of CM, if he has power [14] to do so, or dispose the case summarily under AA ss 83 to 84, or direct the disposal of the case by SCM, or refer the case to the next superior officer.

Before convening a GCM or DCM, the officer empowered to do so is required to satisfy himself, from the documents accompanying the application for trial, about the legal validity of the charges, adequacy of the evidence thereon and the jurisdiction of the kind of the CM to be convened[15] depending upon the rank of the accused and severity of the offence. While GCM and SGCM are empowered to try any person subject to the AA and inflict any punishment awardable thereunder, a DCM can try only WOs, NCOs and Sepoys and award a maximum punishment of imprisonment for 2 years or less punishment except that it cannot award any imprisonment to a WO. An SCM can try only NCOs and below and award the maximum punishment of one year imprisonment.

While satisfying himself, the convening officer is also required to take into consideration the legal advice on the case. The application for trial is, therefore, routed through the Dy JAG command who himself or his AJAG or 'DAJAG' prepares a report on application for trial (hereinafter referred to as 'RAT') advising the convening officer on these aspects and attaching thereto a draft charge-sheet and the points to be borne in mind by the prosecutor at the trial.[16] On being so satisfied on the afore-stated aspects, the convening officer endorses his sanction for trial by the proposed CM under the charge-sheet, ensuring that the charge-sheet is in accordance with the draft charge-sheet of the RAT and signed personally by the CO of the accused. Thereafter, a convening order is issued, appointing or detailing the officers to form the court, some waiting officers, an interpreter if need be, the prosecutor and the JA as nominated by the Dy JAG. The convening order is required to be signed by the convening officer personally or 'for' him by a staff officer authorised by the custom of the Service to sign his orders, or

14 Power either directly given under the Act or through appropriate warrant (A-1 or B-1) under the AA ss 109-110.

15 AA s 118, 119, 120 AR r .37 and RA par a 459.

16 RA T is a confidential document in terms of RA par a 471 and is meant only f or the addressee. However, 'at the trial' points are extr acted from it and given to the pr osecutor for his guidance.

by a staff officer as such[17], while the endorsement for trial under the charge-sheet must be signed by the convening officer personally or 'for' him.

The convening officer shall furnish to the senior member of the court with the original charge-sheet and, where no JA is appointed, a copy of the S of E and the convening order. All other members are sent copies of the charge-sheet and the JA, when appointed, is given a copy of the charge-sheet and a copy of the S of E.[18]

(c) **Warning of the Accused and Preparation of Defence**

On a decision having been made for the trial of the accused by a CM, he shall be informed of every charge for which he is to be tried and given a copy of the charge-sheet along with a translation thereof, if he so desires, in a language he understands. A list of the names, rank and corps of the officers to form the court shall also be given to him alongwith similar details of officers in waiting, if any. Further, the charges shall be read and explained to him, if necessary, and he will also be informed that on his giving the names of witnesses whom he desires to call in defence, reasonable steps will be taken to procure their attendance. All this is required to be done not less than 96 (on active service 24) hours before his arraignment at the CM[19]. At this time, the accused shall also be given free of charge a copy of the S of E, if not already given on being remanded for trial by a CM. He shall also be explained his rights under the AR as to preparing his defence and being assisted or represented at the trial by an officer assigned to him by the convening officer if he (accused) wishes and states so in writing. This, in fact, is a part of the right of the accused to prepare his defence, which includes an uncensored communication between him and his legal adviser whose names he should inform his CO alongwith any distinctive mark that the correspondence between him and such adviser would bear. A written statement from any of his defence witnesses may also be procured for him by his CO in a closed envelope, which shall be given to him unopened. Further, if he gives to his CO the names of his defence witnesses, no person shall interview them with reference to the charges except in the presence of the accused. Similarly, the accused too may interview a prosecution witness but only in the presence of an officer detailed by the CO. The accused has the right also to address an application to the DJAG Command, if he is not given full liberty for preparing his defence or is kept under

17 A convening order is formally known as the order for the assembly of the court-martial; please see IAFD – 916 in MML V ol 2, pp 403-404 .

18 AR r. 37(4).

19 AR r. 34; If the accused is intended to be tried jointly with certain other accused persons (s), a notice to this effect is also required to be given to him at this time. The accused may then claim a separate trial, either by notice to the convening authority or when arraigned before the court, on the ground that the evidence of one or more of the joint accused will be material to his defence or that otherwise he would be prejudiced or embarrassed in his defence. If the claim is allowed, the accused shall be tried separately.

arrest longer than 48 days without being brought to trial. In addition to a defending officer assigned to the accused, as stated above, he (accused) may engage a civil counsel too for his defence at a GCM or DCM trial, giving a notice to the convening officer to this effect so that a civil counsel may be engaged for prosecution, if need be. A similar notice is required to be given to the accused if the services of a counsel are obtained for prosecution without such notice from him. An accused may also engage a counsel at Government expenses, on prescribed rate of fee, if the charge is punishable with death.[20]

(d) **Administrative Arrangements**

CM being an ad hoc body constituted every time a trial is to be held, necessary administrative arrangement are made, on the trial being ordered, for arranging the court-room, the accommodation and transportation of out-station personnel arriving at the venue of the trial, the detainment of the accused and his medical examination to certify his fitness to undergo the trial etc. This responsibility is usually shouldered by the unit of the accused or the unit to which he is attached for trial. The trial is generally held at the place of the offence.[21] The Formation to which the unit belongs or forms part of, or any other local Formation in the event of the former being located away from the station where the trial is to be held, supervises the administration. The said Formation issues an administrative order assigning various related responsibilities to different local units or establishment[22] and laying down general instructions on such matters as dress to be worn while attending the court.

The provisions of RA cater for such administrative matters as a ban on the transfer of personnel involved in breach of discipline, securing attendance of Service witnesses, summons to civilian witnesses, orders for witnesses not to leave station after application for CM, junior officers to attend CM for instruction, escort for accused, medical examination of the accused on the morning of each day the court is to sit for his trial and psychiatric examination of the accused where defence of insanity is, or is likely to

---

20 AR r. 33 read with rr 95-101 and RA par a 479.

21 This is not a legal necessity since a person subject to AA who commits an offence against it, may be tried and punished at any place whatever; please see AA s. 124 and RA para 452(c).

22 In practical terms, 'unit' signifies a separate body of troops like a Battalion or Regiment under the permanent command of an officer of the rank usually of Colonel or Lieut Colonel and Formation 'signifies' an organisation comprising of specified number of units or lower Formations. 'Establishment', on the other hand, signifies a static organisation like military hospital, military prison, regimental centre etc. A Battalion consists of sub units known as companies. In Armoured Corps, Corps of Signals, Corps of Engineers and the Corps of Artillery, the equivalent of a Battalion is called Regiment and its sub-units are Batteries or Squadrons which are equal to Companies. The designation Formation applies to organisations like Brigade, Division, Corps, Command, Area, Sub-Area etc.

be, raised[23]. There is nothing in the AR on the seating arrangement of a court-room but by custom of the Service, the lay-out given here in Chart 2.1 is followed, being convenient in practice.[24]

23 RA paras 453, 454, 455, 456, 457, 461, 462 and 463 respectively.

24 MML Vol II p 403. There is a little variation in the lay-out of the CM room under the Naval law, for which please see infra, ch 7.1.

Chart 2.1

Lay-Out Plan of Court Room for Court Martial

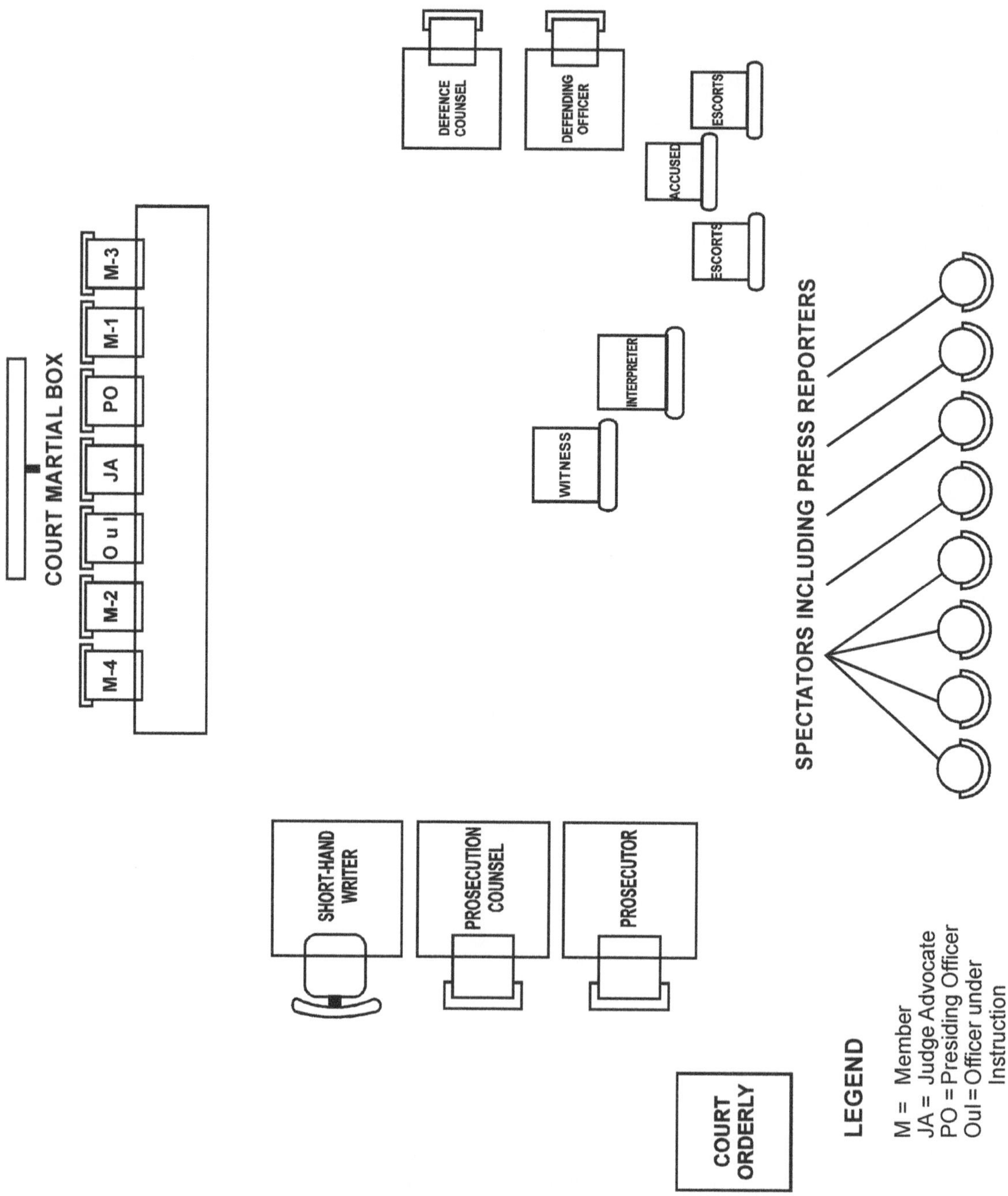

(e) Composition of CM

All CsM except SCM are multi-member courts. GCM, under the AA and AFA and CM under the NA have 5 members at the minimum and SGCM and DCM of the Army and Air Force and DC of the Navy have 3, though a larger number of officers, usually 7 or 9, is detailed for a GCM if the circumstances of the case so require. Under the AA, each member of a GCM should have at least 3 year commissioned service to his credit which in the case of a DCM and SGCM is 2 and 1 year respectively, with preference in selection to officers with 3 year service for SGCM, if available. A further embargo in the case of a GCM is that at least four of the members should be of the rank of Captain or above and even where the number detailed is more than 5, not more than one should be a subaltern, i.e., Lieutenant. As far as practicable, the officers of different corps or department, and in no case exclusively of the corps or department of the accused, should be detailed and they should generally not be of a rank lower, than that of the accused. Lastly, when the CO of a corps is to be tried, as many members as possible will be officers who have held or are holding commands equivalent to that held by the accused. The presiding officer of a GCM should be not less than a Colonel and of DCM a Major but if the accused is a Lieut Colonel or Colonel, the presiding officer should respectively be a Brigadier and Major General[25]. Analogous provisions exist in the Air Force and Naval law with an added requirement that majority of the members of Naval CM or DC shall be from the Executive Branch.[26] These general provisions are further qualified by provisions as to ineligibility and disqualifications of individuals. For instance, an officer is not eligible for serving on a CM if he is not subject to the concerned Service Act and is disqualified for this purpose if he is the provost-marshal (hereinafter referred to as 'PM') or a prosecution witness etc. Further, no technical officer, particularly, medically qualified officers from the Army Medical Corps or Remount and Veterinary Corps should be detailed as members lest they should sub-consciously apply their technical knowledge to the case without the accused having opportunity to cross-examine them.[27]

---

25 AA ss 113-115; AR rr 40, 151, 153; RA para 460 and AHQ letter No. 35418/PS-1 dated 21 July 1971. It may be seen that the term 'Corps' has been used here in the sense of a unit such as a Battalion, the two other uses of the term being (a) an active Formation consisting usually of three Divisions, and (b) a still larger organisation based on professional specialty such as Armoured Corps, Corps of Artillery, Infantry etc. Further it may be noted that an SGCM is essentially an active service forum. Further, it may be noted that the Department of the Judge Advocate General is alone known as a department in the Army, all others are Corps or Regiment.

26 NA ss 96 and 97 and N Regs II(S) regs 160 and 174.

27 AR r. 39 read with AHQ letters No. 2081/2/43-44/1 AA dt 18 Oct 1944 and No. 47588/JAG dt 29 Jun 1949.

2.5 Procedure at GCM & DCM Trial

(a) **Assembly of the Court**

Pursuant to the convening order, the officers appointed to form the court, the waiting members, the JA, the prosecutor, the civil counsels, if any, and the accused with his escort(s) report at the place of trial, on the specified date, at the time appointed by the administrative authority in consultation with the senior most officer detailed as member. The members of the court take their seats in accordance with their seniority, with the senior-most occupying the place in the centre as the presiding officer (hereinafter referred to as 'PO'), the next senior sitting to his left and the JA to his right as shown in the layout of the court-room. At this stage, no one except the members, the JA, if appointed, the officer-under-instruction and the waiting members should be in the court-room. The order convening the court, the charge-sheet and the S of E are then placed before the court by the JA, if any, or, in his absence, by the PO whom those would have been forwarded by the convening officer.[28]

(b) **Closed Court Inquiries**

A CM is said to be sitting in closed court while on deliberation amongst the members in the presence of the JA and officer(s)-under-instruction, if any, without the prosecution and defence representatives or anybody else.[29] In closed court at the outset, the CM will examine the convening order and the charge-sheet to satisfy itself that the members, the waiting members and the JA are those mentioned in the convening order, or, if not named in that order, are of the ranks and units stated therein, that the court has been convened in accordance with the provisions of the AA and AR, that each of the officers so assembled is eligible and not disqualified for serving on that CM, that the accused is subject to the jurisdiction of the court and that the charge (s) is/are framed in accordance with the AA and AR and is/are so explicit as to enable the accused to readily understand what he has to answer. The action to be taken on various situations related to these inquiries are stated in AR 38 to 41 and explanatory notes thereunder. If the convening order appears, on the face of it, to be in accordance with the format IAFD-916 and appears to be duly signed, the court will have fulfilled its duty to satisfy itself that it is convened validly, provided its composition reflected in the convening order is in accordance with the provisions explained in the foregoing (as are also explained by the JA on the spot). The eligibility and disqualification of each individual member and JA may be checked by PO questioning him in the light of the provisions of AR r. 39 read with r. 102.[30]

28 AA s. 128, AR rr 41 & 75 read with IAFD 906 footnote.

29 AR r. 80.

30 AR rr 38-41 and 102, MML V ol II pp 403-404 .

(c) **Court Opens**

The court being satisfied on the inquiries stated above, it shall cause the accused to be brought before it.[31] The prosecutor, the defending officer and the counsels, if any, follow and take their respective seats on the court, i.e., PO or JA on behalf of the court, asking them to do so. The accused and his escort are also asked to take their seats. The spectators, if any, also similarly enter thereafter and take their seats, the CM now being open[32] like any other court of justice.

A word about the role of the prosecutor and defending officer at a CM trial would be pertinent here. Like the JA, they are also functionaries of the court and irrespective of their allegiance to the party they represent, they are expected to maintain an upright stance vis-a-vis the interests of justice almost like the JA. The JA is responsible for informing the court of any informality or irregularity in the proceedings. Further, whether consulted or not, he shall inform the convening officer and the court of any informity or defect in the charge or in the constitution of the court. He also has the duty of summing up the evidence and giving opinion upon the legal bearing of the case before the court proceeds to deliberate upon its finding. Further, he is required to be careful to maintain an entirely impartial position and expected to render proper advice to the prosecutor and accused, if consulted by them, on any questions of law relative to the charge or trial.[33] Similarly, the object of the prosecutor, "like that of the court, should be simply justice and he has no right to sacrifice this to any pride of professional success".[34] As a general rule, he is the officer who had recorded the S of E and has a working knowledge of AA, AR and laws of evidence. However, in a difficult case, the convening officer will select a specially qualified officer to act as prosecutor, more specially where the accused is, or is likely to be, represented by a legally qualified officer or a civil counsel. The law requires the prosecutor to bring all the facts of the case before the court, without taking an unfair advantage of or suppressing any evidence in favour of the accused. In view of the onerous duty he is thus to discharge, the task is entrusted, almost invariably, to an officer even

31 AR r. 43 read with r. 80-A. As a custom of Service, a Sepoy is marched by an NCO or a JCO along with two escorts but an ac cused of superior r ank i.e., NCO or abo ve enters into the court -room accompanied by his escort wi thout any marching order. In either case, he is not in chain etc. nor does his escort ha ve any weapons while inside the court-room. Security measures if any required, may be arranged out side the court-room. The accused only stands erect and does not salute, being without his belt in close arrest (which ordinarily is ordered before commencement of trial even if the accused was not under arrest earlier; please see RA para 392), while his escort and every body else salute every time on appearing before the court or leaving the court-room, and civilians observe the requirement of paying respect to the court in accordance with traditions of the civil courts.

32 AR r. 80-A

33 AR 105.

34 Hurd v People, 25 Mi ch, 416.

though any "person subject to the AA" will fit in the rule position. Despite this, if the prosecutor refers to any matter not relevant to the charge or indulges in any undue violence of language or exhibits any want of fairness, the court in general and the PO and the JA in particular are charged with the responsibility of stopping him. The various duties of the prosecutor spelt out in different provisions of the AR stand summarized in paras 36 to 38 of the Memoranda for Guidance of Officers concerned with Courts Martial at pages 443 to 445 of MML Vol II.[35] As for the defending officer at GCM, SGCM or DCM, unlike his counterpart (friend-of-the-accused) at SCM, he is required to be an officer, not just any person subject to the AA, and is invested with the same rights and duties as the accused himself in relation to addressing the court or calling or examining any witnesses or raising any plea. The accused cannot claim, as a matter of right, the services of any particular officer to represent him at the trial but due consideration is given to his choice. However, if the officer assigned for this duty, is not acceptable to the accused, the latter may carry out his defence himself or engage a civil counsel. The counsel shall conform strictly to the rules of criminal courts in India as well as the provisions of AR, including r. 77 (3) which requires the accused to refrain from any contemptuous or disrespectful remarks towards the court and any coarse or insulting language towards others. Subject to this, the court shall allow great latitude to the accused in defence and shall not stop his defence merely on ground of irrelevance, even though could caution the accused in this regard. The counsel for the accused as well as the defending officer have the same powers and duties. Either of them may have a right of audience with the court, in accordance with the wishes of the accused, when both of them are present.[36] These provisions relating to the availability of the services of a counsel or defending officer to the accused may, in certain circumstances, be suspended, but this is rarely done. Further, the appearance of a counsel at a GCM or DCM, both for the accused and the prosecutor may be disallowed by a declaration of the convening officer in respect of a particular place or any particular CM.[37]

---

35 AR rr 43, 77 (1) and (2), RA paras 458 and 464 read with AHQ letter No. 61967/JAG dated 24 Mar 1966 along with the duties of the PO and the JA respectively in AR rr 76 and 105 to ensure that the accused does not suffer any disadvantage in consequence of his position as such or his ignorance. In the context of the onerous duty of the JA, the experience of Earnest W Gibson may be cited with applause. He was Law Officer and Member of a GCM which acquitted a coloured man on a moral charge, while the Commanding General wanted him convicted, though the evidence did not warrant it. Gibson was called down and told that if he did not convict in a greater number of cases, he would be marked down in his Efficiency Rating. Gibson, however, "squared right off and said that wasn't my conception of justice and that they had better removed me, which was done forthwith"; Willis, "The United States Court of Military Appeals : Its Origin, Operation and Future", Military Law Review, Vol 55, 1972, p 39, n 3.

36 AR rr 95 to 101, 77 (3), RA para 479, and AHQ letter No. 30143/AG-22 dated 23 Feb 1943 and A/04358/PS-1 (Vig) dated 9 Sep 1965.

37 AR r. 36 and proviso to r. 96 as amended by SRO 17E dated 6 Dec 1993.

(d) **Challenge to Members**

Since a CM is constituted of the peers of the accused as distinguished from the professional judges in the civil judicial system, it is possible that some of the officers appointed to form the court might be carrying some prejudice against the accused or may be disqualified, on some count within the knowledge of the accused though not known to the convening officer. To remedy such a situation, the law provides for challenge by the accused to any of the officers detailed as members of the court to try him.[38] No such right is, however, available at SCM since none other than the CO is legally competent to hold that court. Soon after a GCM, SGCM or DCM is open, the order convening the court and the names of the PO and the members are read over to the accused by the JA, or in his absence by the PO, and he (accused) is asked whether he objects to being tried by any officers sitting on the court as members. The accused has no right to object to the JA or the prosecutor [39] since this has not been provided for in the AA or AR. The objection by the accused to any member is resolved in the light of the procedure laid down in AR r. 44 in the case of GCM and DCM and AR r. 154 in the case of SGCM. If the objection of the accused is allowed, the concerned officer retires forthwith, an officer from among the waiting officers taking his place subject to the right of the accused to similarly object to him as well. If the accused makes no challenge, or the vacancy of every officer successfully challenged has been filled by another to whom no objection is made or allowed, the court shall proceed with the trial.

(e) **Swearing of the Court**

As soon as the court is constituted after the challenge procedure, if any involved, is over, the members of the court, the JA and the officer-under-instruction, the short-hand writer and the interpreter, if any, are sworn or affirmed in accordance with the provisions of law[40] after an opportunity given to the accused to object to the person appointed as a short hand writer or an interpreter.

---

38 AA s. 130 and AR rr 44 and 154.

39 MML Vol II, p 290, Note 4 to AR r . 44.

40 AA s. 131 read with AR rr 45-47 and 90 (3) and notes ther eunder. Christians and Sikhs ar e generally sworn while the Hindus and Muslims are affirmed, all placing their right hand on their respective religious scripture. An atheist may also be affirmed in a form as the court may ascertain to be binding on his conscience as explained in Br MML 1972, p 398. The wordings of the oath or affirmation in the case of members requir e them to administer justice according to the AA without partialit y, favour or af fection and if any doubt shall arise then according to their conscience, the best of their understanding and the custom of w ar in l ike cases. Further, they also swear or af firm not to disclose the v ote or opinion of an y particular member unless required to give evidence thereof in a court of justice or CM.

(f) **Arraignment**

On the oath ceremony being over, the accused is arraigned on each of the charges against him. This involves the charge being read and, if necessary, translated to him by the interpreter, and the accused then being required to state whether he pleads guilty or not guilty thereto.[41] In the event of two or more persons being tried together or one accused being tried on more than one charge-sheet, each accused is separately arraigned and each charge-sheet taken up in an order provided for in the AR.[42]

At this stage, before pleading to the charge(s), the accused may object to the charge on the ground that it does not disclose an offence under the AA or that it is not framed in accordance with the requirements of the AR. He may also raise a plea to the general jurisdiction of the court to try him on the ground, for example, that the court is improperly constituted in matter of the number of members or that he is not amenable to the jurisdiction of the court, not being subject to military law or not subject to that description of the court, for instance, in the case of an officer or a JCO being brought before a DCM. While pleading to the charge, the accused may also raise a plea in bar of the trial on the ground of having been previously convicted or acquitted of the offence or dealt with summarily, or the charge having been dismissed by the CO, or the offence having been pardoned or condoned, or the limitation of period of 3 years having elapsed and not extended, or his liability for trial after ceasing to be subject to the AA having been over. The procedure to deal with all these pleas or to amend the charge, if necessary, is given in AR rr 49 to 53. If the accused raises no such pleas, or the pleas when raised by the accused are disallowed or resolved in a manner that involves no adjournment or dissolution of the court, or if the court reassemble pursuant to adjournment, or when a fresh court is convened after dissolution[43] has reached the stage where the accused makes a general plea of 'Guilty' or 'Not guilty', the court is set to record such plea in accordance with the procedure explained in the following two sub-sections.

(g) **Plea of Guilty**

If the accused clearly pleads "Guilty", the PO or the JA, on behalf of the court, explains to the accused the meaning of the charge(s) to which he has pleaded "Guilty"

---

41 AR r. 48.

42 AR rr 78 and 79 r ead with note 1 to r . 48.

43 AA s. 117 r ead wi th AR r . 83 under which a CM ma y be dissolv ed on being r educed below the minimum number of officers required to form that kind of CM or on the trial having become impossible to continue for the reason of the illness of the accused (including insanity) or its continuance appearing to the convening officer to have been rendered impossible or inexpedient by military exigencies or the necessities of discipline. The accused may then be retried. Please see also NA s. 123 (1).

and ascertain that the accused has understood the nature thereof in each case[44]. The accused is also informed of the general effect of the plea and the difference in procedure such a plea would make. The court, after having satisfied itself that the accused understands the charge(s) and effect of his pleas of "Guilty" thereto, separately in respect of each charge, accepts the plea, records it accordingly, and also records a finding of "Guilty" on those charges. If the accused pleads "Guilty" to the first of the two or more charges laid in the alternative, the prosecutor may, after that plea is accepted by the court and before the accused is arraigned on the alternative charge(s), withdraw such alternative charge(s) without requiring the accused to plead thereto. To cater for such eventuality, the most serious charge of the two or more alternative charges is placed first in the charge-sheet. In such event, the accused will not be entitled to a verdict on the alternative charge(s) so withdrawn since he will not be arraigned thereon.[45]

Where the charge-sheet has more than one charge and the accused pleads "Guilty" to some while "Not Guilty" to other(s), the court will first proceed with the charges to which he has pleaded "Not Guilty", without recording the finding of "Guilty" on the former charges. After proceeding with the latter charges, to which the accused pleaded "Not Guilty", upto finding on those charges, the court will be re-opened and the charge (s) on which a plea of "Guilty" had been entered will be read again to the accused. Thereafter consolidated findings on all the charges against the accused will be recorded[46] and announced.

After the record of the plea 'Guilty' and findings according to the above stated procedure, the court shall receive any statement which the accused desires to make in reference to the charge and shall read the S of E and annex it to the proceedings. If there is no S of E or the S of E does not contain sufficient evidence to enable the court to determine the sentence and the convening officer to know all the circumstances connected with the case, the court shall record the requisite evidence in the manner provided in the AR on a plea of "Not Guilty". Thereafter, the accused may make a statement in mitigation of punishment and call witnesses, if any, as to his character or to prove any

44 If the ac cused does not plead intel ligibly, the plea is to be r ecorded as "Not Gui lty". The plea is also recorded as "Not Guilty" when the accused pleads in a language not understood by the court, or when he refuses to plead or offers a qualified plea of guilty which is not acceptable under the law or to the convening officer, or pleads "Not Gui lty" to the mor e serious one of the char ges laid in the al ternative, or pleads "Guilty" to an offence punishable with death or when his plea of guilty seems to be the result of misunderstanding as noticeable from his subsequent statements or from the contents of the S of E read afterwards; AR r. 52(1) and (4) and notes (1) to (9) ther eunder.

45 AR r. 52 and notes ther eunder.

46 AR r. 54 (1) r ead with 'Instruction' under "Pr oceeding on Plea of Gui lty" in MML V ol II p. 410.

fact stated in mitigation of punishment.[47] This is to be followed by the procedure for awarding the sentence.

If from the statement of the accused or from the S of E or otherwise it appears to the court that the accused did not understand the effect of his plea of "guilty", the court shall alter the record and enter a plea of "Not Guilty" and proceed with the trial accordingly. For instance, if Sepoy 'A', having pleaded 'Guilty' to a charge for desertion, not being desertion to avoid a particular service, states with reference to charge or in mitigation of punishment, "I always meant to come back," the plea of 'Guilty' would be required to be altered to 'Not Guilty'. Before doing so, however, the court may remove their doubt, if any, by questioning the defending officer in this regard. Any question put by the court in this connection and answer thereto should be recorded in the proceedings. If the inconsistency gets resolved, being due to misunderstanding or inadvertence, the plea need not be altered.[48]

In the same way, the accused may initially plead 'Not guilty' but later withdraw his plea and plead 'Guilty'. In that situation too, the court will inform the accused of the general effect of his new plea and the difference it will make in procedure, as required under AA s. 52(2) and follow the procedure of AR r. 54 explained above.[49]

(h) **Plea of 'Not Guilty'**

The proceedings on a plea of 'Not Guilty' involve the recording of the testimony of witnesses in accordance with the provisions of the IEA, subject to the modification or addition, if any, by the relevant provisions of the AA and AR[50]. Even though the court is required to continue the trial from day to day[51], adjournment(s) in between the various steps of the proceedings may be necessary, since no court shall usually sit for more than 6 hours in any one day and that too not before six in the morning nor beyond six in the afternoon nor on a Sunday or a holiday.[52] Adjournments may also be inevitable for the reason of military exigencies or unforeseen situations like ill-health of members, the JA or the accused or non-availability of an indispensable witness etc. The authorities competent to adjourn and the procedure to be followed for this purpose are laid down in AR r. 82.

---

47 The procedure being a post-findings procedure is to be followed after consolidated findings on all the charges are recorded. Please also see AR r . 54(7).

48 AR r. 54 (5) r ead wi th AO 250 of 1972.

49 AR r. 55.

50 AA s. 133.

51 AA s. 82 (1).

52 Ar r. 81

(i) **Opening Address**

On a plea of 'Not Guilty', the very first step of the procedure may lead to an adjournment, depending on the decision of the court when the accused seeks time to prepare his defence, in response to a specific question by the court in this regard in accordance with the requirement of AR r. 56 (1) and (2). However, if no such adjournment is sought or allowed, the prosecutor may, if he desires and shall, if so required by the court, make an opening address, stating therein the substance of the charges(s) against the accused and the nature and general effect of the evidence which he proposes to adduce in support thereof. In a case of complicated nature, the prosecutor would always make an opening address, so that the members of the court have a clear understanding of the nature of the allegation. If the opening address is in writing, as it usually is, it will be read by him and handed to the court for attachment to the proceedings.[53] If it is made orally, its salient points may be noted in the proceedings alongwith such matters in the address as the accused may require specifically in accordance with AR r. 92 (4).

(j) **Prosecution Evidence**

The evidence for the prosecution may be taken thereafter. Each witness is to be examined, cross-examined and re-examined in accordance with the provisions of Chapter X of IEA (ss 135-166) subject to AR rr 134 to 143. These modifications cater to the Service-specific needs, such as the calling of a witness whose evidence is contained in the S of E and whom the accused desires to cross-examine, even if the prosecutor does not otherwise intend to call him (AR r. 134), or the requirement of a prior notice to the accused along with an abstract of the proposed evidence when the evidence of a witness is not contained in the S of E (r. 135), or the procuring of the attendance of civil witnesses by summons issued by the CO etc and served through the magistrate of competent jurisdiction (AA s. 135 read with AR r. 137 and RA para 455) etc. Similarly, provisions exist in the AA and AR to supplement the provisions of the IEA in respect of the documentary evidence, judicial notice, questioning of witnesses by the court and the JA etc and the examination of witnesses on commission where necessary[54]. Further, the prosecutor may examine himself as a witness for prosecution, if need be. He should do so after his opening address and this would be subject to the provisions of the IEA the same way as any other witness.

---

53 AR r. 56 r ead with note 4 ther eunder and AR r . 144.

54 Please see AA s. 134 for judicial notice, ss. 136, 140, 141 and 142 for documentary evidence, ss 137 and 138 for examination of witnesses on commission and AR rr 141, 142 and 143(1) for questioning of witnesses. Similar provisions exist under NA ss.132 (judicial notice) 133 (documentary evidence), 135 and 136 (commission) and N Regs II (S), regs 179 to 181 (questioning of witnesses).

During the course of the examination of witnesses, if any objection is raised to any piece of evidence proposed to be given or on any matter of law, evidence or procedure, the opposite party has a right to answer and the party raising the objection has a right of reply. The JA then advises the court. Finally, the matter is decided in a closed court by majority vote, the opinion being taken by word of mouth, in succession beginning with the member lowest in rank.[55]

The members who were sworn to constitute the court are required to be present through out. A member who has been absent while any part of the evidence is taken can take no further part in the trial and no officer is allowed to be added to the court after the arraignment of the, accused.[56] In view of this legal stringency, the court, if constituted of bare minimum number required, will have to carefully balance the unforeseen eventualities like illness etc, or the military exigencies like the operational requirements with the diktats of law. Some of the situations like death or illness of accused, death retirement or absence of the PO, and substitute on death, illness or absence of the JA have been covered by the provisions of the AR.[57] Wherever desirable or necessary, an adjournment of suitable duration may be allowed at the request of the accused or the prosecutor to save the situation. If, however, an adjournment is not likely to meet the requirement, the court may have to be dissolved and thereafter the accused may be tried before another CM.[58]

(k) **Plea of No case**

At the close of the case for the prosecution, the accused may submit that the evidence adduced on behalf of the prosecution, in respect of any one or more charges, has not established a prima facie case against him and he should, therefore, not be called upon to enter into defence thereon. The prosecutor may address the court in answer and the accused may reply. The JA may advise the court, avoiding opinion on the facts and pointing out to the court the possibility of any special finding under the related law. It is, however, important to note that a plea of no case means that there is no evidence at all, and not that the evidence is not sufficient or trust-worthy. The plea shall then be considered in a closed court. The decision of the court, when the plea is allowed, shall be recorded as a finding of "Not Guilty" on the charge or the charges, with brief reasons and shall be announced as subject to confirmation. Even though it is not expressly provided in the related rule, it is understandable on the analogy of the provisions relating to plea of 'Guilty', that where the plea of no case is raised or allowed in respect of some

55 AA s. 132 and AR rr 87 , 88 and 105.

56 AR r. 86.

57 AR rr 84, 85 and 104.

58 AA s 117 and AR rr 82 and 83.

charges in the charge-sheet but not in respect of others, the finding of 'Not Guilty' on the concerned charge(s) need not be recorded in a formal manner at this stage and may be recorded in a consolidated form later alongwith the findings on the remaining charges. In that event, the decision of the court may be announced and the court may proceed with the trial. If the plea, however, is over-ruled, no recording of the decision as a finding is involved and the decision will merely be announced and the court will proceed.

Even if the accused does not raise a plea of no case but the court finds, at the close of the case for the prosecution, that the evidence on the record does not establish a prima facie case on any charge against the accused, it may, of its own motion, take similar action as stated above. The JA may sua sponte advise the court on the meaning and implication of the fact that no case has been made out by the prosecution.[59]

(l) **Defence by Accused**

The plea of no case having been over-ruled or otherwise when the court proceeds with the trial, after the close of prosecution case, the court or the JA shall question the accused generally, before he is called upon for his defence. The purpose of such questioning is to enable the accused personally to explain any circumstances appearing in evidence against him. The accused shall not be liable to punishment by refusing to answer any questions put to him under this provision or by giving answers to any of those questions which he knows not to be true. All this will be explained to the accused and he will not be sworn or affirmed before such questions, which alongwith their answers shall be recorded verbatim.

Thereafter, the PO or the JA if any, shall explain to the accused that he may make an unsworn statement, orally or in writing, giving his account of the subject of the charge(s) against him or, if he wishes, he may give evidence as a witness, on oath or affirmation, in disproof of the charges against him or against any of his co-accused at the trial. In the latter case, he shall be examined as the first witness for defence and shall be liable to cross-examination or question by the court, like any other witness. On the other hand, if he does not appear as a witness, this shall not be made the subject of any comment or adverse presumption against him or against his co-accused. The accused may then make an opening address and call his witnesses thereafter.[60]

---

59 AR r. 57 as amended by SRO 17E of 6 Dec 1993 read with AHQ letter No 100/2/43-44 IAA date 5 Feb 1944 and para 40 (E) of the Memorandum in MML Vol II, p 446. As for the question of a special finding in such cases, please see AA s.139 and AR r. 62 under which the accused may be found guilty of an offence other than that charged, or guilty of committing an offence in circumstances involving a less degree of punishment or guilty subject to certain exceptions or variations in matters of facts averred in the charge.

60 AR r 58 as amended by SRO 17-E of 6 Dec 1993.

(m) **Recalling of Witnesses and Viewing of Place**

Any witness examined earlier for the prosecution or defence may also be recalled by the leave of the Court[61] and the court may also view any place of evidentiary interest at this stage alongwith the accused etc.[62]

(n) **Closing Addresses and Summing Up**

After the evidence of all the witnesses, the prosecutor may make a closing address and the accused may reply thereto. Where any point of law is raised by the accused in his address, the prosecutor may, with the permission of the court make his submission thereon.[63] At a joint trial of more than one accused, the prosecutor makes only one address in respect of all the accused.

The closing addresses are followed by the summing-up of the JA, briefly discussing the law relating to the charges (s) and important features of the evidence along with the related provisions of law. Even though the summing-up as well as the closing addresses may legally be made either orally or in writing but, in practice, the summing-up is invariably in black and white, read in open court and attached to the proceedings. After the JA's summing-up no other address to the court is allowed.[64]

(o) **Findings of the Court**

After the summing-up, the court-room is cleared to enable the members of the CM to deliberate upon their findings in closed court in the presence of the JA.[65] The presence of the JA is purported to ensure that the discussion among the members, if any, on the evidence, with reference to ingredients of the charges(s), is uninfluenced and the opinion of each member is taken in accordance with the requirement of the law, i.e., by word of mouth, starting from the junior most and proceeding to the next senior, the PO being the last to vote.[66] If need be, the court may record special finding on any charge in terms

---

61 AR r. 143, the wi tness, on r ecall, is questioned only thr ough the court.

62 AR r. 82(2) and MML V ol 1, p 39.

63 AR rr 59 (as amended) and 78.

64 AR r. 60(2).

65 AR r. 61. Under the Na val la w, the J A is not to si t wi th the court during this del iberation. Further, there is no break between the summing-up and the announcement of findings by the CM. This is as in a jury trial. However, although such a br eak should be a voided, there is nothing in the la w to prevent a CM, while sitting in closed court to consider its findings, from adjourning for some proper purpose and resume deliberation after the adjournment for unlike a juror who is under the charge of the trial judge, each member of the CM is a judge and not under the J A; please see R v Linzee and R v O'Driscoll, All ER, Vol 3, 1956, p 980 at 984-985.

66 AA s. 132 (1) read with AR rr 61 and 87; in case there is equality of vote (when the CM was constituted of 7 or 9 members and one of them is unavailable for whatever valid reason), the decision shall be in favour of the accused.

of AA s.139 and AR r. 62(4) and (5), finding the accused guilty of an offence other than that charged in specified cases or guilty of the charge with certain exceptions or variations. The insanity of the accused at the time of the commission of the offence or at the time of the finding would require a finding accordingly recorded, following the procedure prescribed in AA ss 145 to 149 and AR r 145 and similar provisions in NA ss 143 and 144. After recording the finding on each charge, the court is also required to give brief reasons in support thereof.[67]

In the case of a 'joint trial' of more than one accused by the same CM, the findings in respect of each accused person are recorded separately on a different page of the proceedings. The provisions in the AR also cover various other eventualities relating to the findings such as the accused pleading 'Guilty' to some and 'Not Guilty' to other charges in the same charge-sheet, or the accused being tried by the same court on more that one charge-sheet or at a joint trial some accused pleading 'Guilty' while others 'Not Guilty' to a joint charge[68] or when the court is doubtful whether the facts proved show the accused to be guilty.[69]

After the findings are recorded, the court shall be open again, the accused, the prosecutor, the defending officer and the counsels, if any, are called in and all except the accused and his escort (s) take their seats. The findings are then announced as subject to confirmation.[70]

If the findings on all the charges are 'Not Guilty, the PO shall date and sign the findings and such signature shall authenticate the whole of the proceedings. Thereafter, the proceedings being signed by the JA shall be transmitted for confirmation.[71]

On the other hand, if the accused is found 'Guilty' of one or more charges, the court shall proceed, after the trial in respect of all the charges or charge-sheets is complete, to take evidence of the general character, age, service, rank, recognised acts of gallantry, distinguished conduct, previous conviction and pre-trial custody etc of the accused. For this purpose, the Adjutant of the concerned unit or any other witness produces before the court IAFD-905 which is a 'Statement as to Character and Particulars of Service of the Accused', containing extracts from the Regimental Books or other official records alongwith the defaulter-sheet (Schedule of Convictions by CM or Criminal Court and

67 The requirement was added by SRO 17 E dated 6 Dec 1993 and is presently applicable to a finding under the AA only .

68 AR rr 54 (1) and (6), 79, 35. Please see MML V ol II, p 442, par as 27-29;

69 AR 62 (3) and (8) for reference to confirming officer in such a case.

70 AA s.153 and AR r .62(10). Under the Naval la w, no confirmation is r equired and pr oceedings are transmitted to the JAG Navy; please see NA s.118 (5)

71 AR r.63.

of Summary Awards under ss 83, 84 or 85 of the AA), certified under the hand of the CO, the officer having custody of the said Regimental or other records. The witness producing AFD-905 orally states on oath that the person named in the statement is the accused whom he identifies, that he (the witness) has compared its contents with the said record and that those are true extracts of that record and the defaulter sheet is a fair and true summary of the entries in the record. The witness may be cross-examined thereafter by the accused who may also address the court and also make statement in mitigation of punishment.[72]

(p) **Sentence**

The court is thereafter closed for consideration of the sentence, the JA again being present and deliberation and voting being carried out the same way as in the case of the finding, with an additional requirement that every member must give his opinion as to the sentence notwithstanding that he had given his opinion in favour of acquittal.[73] Irrespective of the number of the offences of which the accused has been found guilty, or even if the trial has proceeded on more than one charge-sheet, only one sentence shall be awarded, though the sentence may consist of more than one punishment. The punishments awardable by a CM are laid down in AA s. 71 in a graded scale, from the punishment of death on top and stoppages of pay at the bottom. In between are the punishments of imprisonment for life, and some punishments of military nature such as cashiering (ignominious form of dismissal) or reduction in rank or reprimand etc. The punishment of fine is not expressly stated there but may certainty be awarded for a civil offence carrying this punishment under the civil law. This is implied in the provision of AA s. 69 which allows a CM to award, for a civil offence, the punishment inter alia assigned under the related law but not whipping. In the event of the said punishment being death, the CM must award that punishment alongwith a direction that the offender shall suffer death by being hanged by the neck until he be dead or by being shot to death and may also award additionally such less punishment as mentioned in the AA. In any other case, the CM may award either the punishment assigned in the related civil law,

72 AR r.64; NA s.119. In the case of SCM, similar information may be placed on record of the proceedings by the CO f rom his own knowledge; please see AR r .123.

73 AR rr 65, 80(1) and 87 . Unlike the deliberation on finding, NA s.120(2) r equires the JA to be pr esent during consideration of sentence. The factors to be borne in mind during deliberation on sentence are enumerated in MML Vol I, Ch IV, p 42 (para 84). In this context, it may be noted that a sentence of death may be passed only by 2/3 majority in the case of a GCM and the concurrence of all the members in the case of SGCM; please see AA ss 132 (2), (3). Further , the court is also empower ed to mak e a recommendation to mercy by giving its reason therefor and entering in the proceedings the number of opinions by which such r ecommendation is adopted. Howev er, in view of the discr etion of the court in the matter of awarding a sentence, a recommendation to mercy will be made only in exceptional circumstances as stated in Note 2 to AR r . 66.

or imprisonment upto 7 years or such less punishment as mentioned in the AA.[74] There are certain consequential punishments specified in the AA and NA. Cashiering in the case of an officer before being awarded death, imprisonment for life or imprisonment for 14 years or less and reduction to the ranks in the case of a WO or NCO who has been awarded life imprisonment, imprisonment for a specific term or dismissal are such punishments.[75] To avoid an anomalous situation in the execution of a sentence carrying certain punishments, AA s. 73 provides what all punishments are permitted to be combined.

After the sentence is determined, the court is opened again and the sentence together with recommendation to mercy, if any, is announced as subject to confirmation; the sentence having already been signed and dated by the PO to authenticate the whole of the proceedings and also signed by the JA[76]. A copy of the proceedings is then made available to the accused.[77] Administrative instructions also exist to regulate the matters relating to the continuation of close arrest or release of the convict and his leave, depending upon the quantum and quality of the punishments included in the sentence awarded to him.[78]

(q) **Review**

On conclusion of the trial, the proceedings duly signed and dated are forwarded to the Dy JAG or AJAG of the Command in the case of a GCM and direct to the confirming officer in the case of a DCM or SGCM, unless the sentence awarded by the DCM is dismissal or above in which case the proceedings are to be routed through the Dy JAG or AJAG. The proceedings are reviewed by the Dy JAG or AJAG and necessary advice

---

74 AA s.69 and NA s. 77. The sentence of death by shooting should normally not be awarded except in operational area where hanging is impracticable; please see Army Headquarters Letter No. 30285/AG – 22 dt 21 Jul 1943).

75 AA ss74 and 77. Cashiering differs from dismissal in as much as an officer who has been cashiered is thereby disqualified from ever serving the Crown (Central or State Government in our case) in any capacity, civil or military, whereas dismissal does not entail such disqualification; Clode, Military and Marshal Law, cit in Simmons, The Constitution and Practice of Courts Martial, op cit, ch 1, n 6, p 280. Under the Naval law, the punishment of cashiering does not exist and 'dismissal with disgrace' occupies its place in the graded scale of punishments stated in NA s.81. However, unlike cashiering, this punishment is not restricted to officers in the NA.

76 AR r.67. Under the Naval law, the court is dissolved after the announcement of the sentence which, unlike the sentence by a GCM, SGCM or DCM under the AA or AFA, is not subject to confirmation and cannot be revised by the court.

77 AR r.147 as amended permits a copy of the proceedings to be given to the accused, on demand, after the sentence is announced and the proceedings are signed and dated by the PO and the JA. A copy of the revision proceedings if any, may be given to him later.

78 RA 392 (l) and (m).

rendered to the confirming officer in the form of a report known as report on trial (hereinafter referred to as 'RT'). If a revision is advised in the RT and the court re-assembles accordingly by the order of the confirming officer, the proceedings are forwarded to the Dy JAG or AJAG again, after the revision proceedings and a further report is issued with suitable advice on the further course of action.[79] It may be noted that under the AA and AFA, no hearing is accorded to the accused during the review, which is based purely on the record of proceedings. Under the Naval law, however, elaborate provisions exist for a judicial review of the proceedings of a CM or DC by the JAG Navy, either on his own motion or on an application made, within 20 days by an aggrieved person, who is then given an opportunity of being heard either in person or through a legal practitioner or an officer of the Indian Navy (IN). The JAG Navy reports to the Chief of the Navel Staff (CONS) with his recommendation, if any, in review. In the case of capital punishment having been awarded by the CM or the CM having been ordered by the President of India under the NA (not provided under the AA or AFA) such report and recommendation are to be further transmitted by the CONS to the Central Government. An order to acquittal by the CM, however, cannot be set aside nor can even be recommended by the JAG to be set aside.[80]

(r) **Revision**

At times the finding and sentence of the court may have a flaw which cannot be remedied in review and confirmation. In such a case, the finding or sentence of a GCM, SGCM or DCM may be once revised by the CM on re-assembly by an order of the confirming officer. If so directed by the confirming officer, additional evidence may be taken before deliberation on the revision order. The revision proceedings are considered to be an extension of the trial, the court comprising of the same officers as were present when the original decision was passed. If any of those officers are unavoidably absent, the court would proceed with the revision provided the number of those present is not less than 5 in the case of GCM and not less than 3 in the case of SGCM or DCM. The procedure to be followed for the purpose of revision is prescribed under the AR. The court may adhere to its former finding or sentence, as the case may be, or revoke its former finding and sentence, where the finding is sent back for revision, and record a new finding and pass fresh sentence if the new finding so requires. In the event of the revision being ordered only for sentence, the finding shall not be revoked. The court

---

79 AR rr 69 and 162.

80 NA ss 160 and 161. It is doubtful whether the review by the JAG Navy, under NA s 160, may be validly described as a 'judicial review', with powers of the JAG to make only recommendations to the CONS, since a judicial power necessarily implies a binding and authoritative decision, whether subject to appeal or not; please see the Australian High Court decision in Huddard Parker, (1909) 8 CLR 330 at 357, per Griffith, CJ.

being open thereafter, the decision is announced as subject to confirmation and the proceedings being duly dated and signed are transmitted to the confirming authority through Dy JAG or direct as may be required by the provisions relating to review.[81]

2.6 Post-Trial Matters

Under the AA, post-trial matters, after revision, if any, would include confirmation, petitions by the accused, promulgation and execution of sentence.

(a) Confirmation

No finding and sentence of a GCM, SGCM and DCM is valid until confirmed by the concerned specified authority and in a prescribed manner.[82] The Central Government (hereinafter referred to as 'CG') and an officer holding 'A-2' or 'A-3' warrant (both issued by the CG, the former to the COAS and the latter to officers commanding Formations like the army command, corps or division) are authorised under the AA to confirm the finding and sentence of a GCM except where the sentence of death has been awarded, in which case the proceedings are to be transmitted to superior authority, i.e., CG. An 'A-3' warrant holder is authorised to confirm the finding and sentence of a GCM in respect of a person under his command, again with an exception of a case involving death sentence which in all cases needs confirmation by the CG. Both the 'A-2' and 'A-3' warrant holders may also reserve confirmation for superior authority in any other case. Accordingly, RA further restrict the power of confirmation of 'A-3' warrant holders in certain cases based on the rank of the accused and severity of punishment or gravity of the offence in the event of acquittal and also on the ground of involvement in investigation of the case.[83] Further, the provisions of AR also debar a member of the CM or its prosecutor from confirming its finding or sentence if they later assume the position which would entitle them to exercise the powers of the confirming officer in that case as 'A-2' or 'A-3' warrant holder.[84] Similar provisions exist in the AA for confirmation of the finding and sentence of a DCM or SGCM.[85] Upon receiving the proceedings, the confirming authority may, based on the advice of the Dy JAG in RT, or otherwise, confirm or refuse confirmation or reserve confirmation for superior authority,

---

81 AA s.160 and AR r .68. It may be noted that the proceedings of SCM need no conformation and hence connote be revised. Further, there are no provisions under the NA for revision since the finding and sentence passed by a Naval CM need no confirmation.

82 AA ss153-159 and AR rr70-74 . Similar provisions exist under the AF A but the Na val law, as pointed out earlier, requires no confirmation of finding and sentence of CM or DC.

83 Texts of 'A-2' and 'A-3' Warrants in MML V ol III, p. 753 and RA par a 472.

84 AR r.74.

85 AA ss155 and 157 respectively read with RA para 472.

entering an appropriate minutes to that effect in the proceedings.[86] The net result is that if a finding of 'Guilty' or 'Not Guilty' is not confirmed, there is no conviction or acquittal to debar a subsequent trial of the accused on the same charges, though it is a different matter as to whether or not a retrial, which is rarely resorted to, would be ordered depending upon the circumstances of the case.[87]

While confirming the sentence of a CM, the confirming authority may mitigate or remit the punishment or commute that punishment for any punishment lower in the scale or may vary the form of an informally expressed sentence or a sentence carrying a punishment in excess of that authorised by law.[88]

(b) **Promulgation**

After confirmation, the charge, finding and sentence and any recommendation to mercy together with the confirmation or non-confirmation are required to be promulgated in such manner as the confirming authority may direct; and if no direction is given, according to the custom of the Service which may be said to now stand codified in the provisions of the RA. The requirement is three-fold. Firstly, the charge, finding, sentence, recommendation to mercy, the confirmation or non-confirmation minute etc. are to be read out to the accused on parade or otherwise, as may be directed by the confirming officer or by the CO in the case of an SCM trial. Secondly, the result of the CM trial is to be published in the orders of all Formations in which the notice of the convening of the CM had appeared and also in the order of the concerned unit, in Part I in the case of officers and in Part – II in the case of others. Thirdly, in the event of the accused being a deserter before promulgation, the publication of these particulars is to be made in the unit Part I or Part II orders as the case may be and communication thereof is made to the accused on his being apprehended or on his surrender. If the sentence awarded to the accused includes cashiering or dismissal in the case of an officer, and dismissal or reduction to the ranks or to a lower rank or grade in the case of others, the accused will be stripped off his badges of rank and all regimental insignia. It may be noted that promulgation is a legal necessity to complete confirmation - the finding and sentence shall not be held to have been confirmed until promulgated.[89]

---

86 AR r.70.

87 Note 3 (a) to AA s.153, notes 1 to 3 to s. 21 and note 3 to AR r . 149.

88 AA s.158 and AR r .73.

89 AR r.72 and RA par a 473.

(c) **Execution of Sentence**

(i) **Death Sentence:**

A person sentenced to death may, pending confirmation or execution, be committed to a civil prison for safe custody, if the CO thinks fit. During promulgation, after confirmation, he is informed of his right to petition to the proper military authority under AA s.164(2) and the period specified by the confining authority within which it may be submitted. The sentence is not carried out until the expiry of such period or until the final disposal of the petition, if filed, by the competent authority. The sentence may finally be carried out in a civil prison or under the arrangement of the military authorities in accordance with general or special instructions issued from time to time. The committal of the convict to civil prison or his withdrawal therefrom as well as the execution of the sentence takes place on the authority of the appropriate warrant issued by the competent authority. An officer not below the rank of Lieut Colonel or a PM is nominated by the authority issuing the death warrant for the responsibility of ensuring due execution of the sentence and report thereafter through 'Return of Warrant' to the officer who had issued the warrant. As noted earlier, an officer is sentenced to cashiering before be is awarded death sentence and cashiering takes effect on his being received in civil prison. A JCO or OR, however, will not be dismissed or discharged on being sentenced to death but will be struck off strength of his unit on the date the sentence of death is carried out.[90]

(ii) **Imprisonment for Life and Imprisonment of a Term:**

The sentence of imprisonment for life awarded by a CM or when the sentence of death is commuted to imprisonment for life is undergone in a civil prison. The Prisoners Act, 1900 (Act III of 1900) renders unnecessary an elaborate scheme of provisions in the military law for the execution of such a sentence. All that is required is to arrange for the transmission of military convicts and prisoners to a suitable civil prison (generally in the home district of the prisoner as required by related administrative orders). The officer making the committal order informs the superintendent of police of the district in which the prisoner is in custody at that time about the proposed committal and the latter provides an escort to convey the prisoner to the concerned jail.

A person sentenced by a CM to imprisonment, or whose sentence awarded by a CM has been commuted to imprisonment for a specific term, may be directed to undergo his sentence in military custody, military prison or civil prison, the first and the second options being available in the case of an OR only, and not in the case of an officer, JCO

90 AA ss 123(4) and 166, AR rr 168 to 170, 170- A and Forms 'H', 'I', 'I-A' and 'I-B' in Appendix V to AR at pp 454 on ward of MML V ol II as amended b y SRO 17E dated 6 Dec 1993 and RA par a 166(c).

or WO. Further, the sentence of imprisonment may be undergone in military custody or military prison only when the term of imprisonment does not exceed 3 months or 18 months respectively. Cashiering, in the case of an officer convict and dismissal in the case of others, if combined with imprisonment, take effect on their being received into a civil prison though even thereafter the AA applies to them during their term of imprisonment or during their sentence to life imprisonment, for the limited purpose of being kept, removed, imprisoned and punished for the offences committed earlier.

Both the imprisonment for life and the imprisonment for a specific term awarded by a CM commence on the date on which the proceedings were originally signed by the PO even if such sentence was pronounced on revision and not at original proceedings.[91] Further, both the imprisonment for life and imprisonment for a term, whether accompanied by dismissal or not, may be suspended by the CG, the COAS or any officer empowered to convene a GCM or SGCM. On suspension of the sentence, the offender is released but the sentence continues to run.[92] The suspension may, if considered desirable, be revoked subsequently.

(iii) **Other Punishments:**

The execution of the sentence involving other punishments, namely, cashiering, dismissal, reduction to the ranks or to a lower rank, etc. involves an entry in the related service or personal documents. The service conditions, official standing or financial position of the offender may accordingly be affected.

(d) **Petition Against CM Orders, Finding or Sentence**

After confirmation, a petition may be made to the CG, COAS or any officer superior in command to the confirming officer. The petition may be addressed by an aggrieved person either personally, or if he is no longer in service, through a representative appointed by a power of attorney. The said authority may pass such order thereon as it thinks fit.[93]

(e) **Preservation of Proceedings**

After promulgation, the proceedings of a CM are forwarded to and are to be preserved[94] as follows:

---

91 AA s.167 and Notes ther eunder.

92 AA ss182 to 188.

93 AA s.164, RA par a 365. This concludes the CM process. The proceedings in AF T, High Court or Supreme Court, i f any, in r espect of CM or der, finding or sentence, ar e held under the r elated la w, and the AA, AF A,NA.

94 AR r. 146.

(i) GCM for 7 years at the office of the JAG

(ii) SGCM and DCM for 3 years – at the office of the JAG

(iii) SCM for 3 years – at the office of the Record Officer of the Regiment to which the accused belongs.

2.7 Procedure at SGCM

The rules relating to the procedure to be adopted at a trial by SGCM forms a separate section in Chapter V of the AR. AR r. 164, however, enumerates a large number of earlier rules as applicable to SGCM. The whole idea is to cut down detailed procedure as far as possible without sacrificing the spirit of natural justice. However, in practice almost the entire procedure of a GCM trial is adopted at SGCM trial. Thus, in practical terms, SGCM differs from GCM only in respect of the authorities empowered to convene it, the format of the convening order and the composition of the court.

The system of SGCM being primarily tailored for active service conditions, such a court may, on active service, be convened, firstly, by the officer commanding the forces in the field or any officer empowered by him, and, secondly, by an officer commanding any detached portion of the regular Army when, in his opinion, it is not practicable, having due regard to the exigencies of the Service, to try the offender by a GCM. Such opinion is required to be recorded in the convening order. During peace time, it may some time be necessary to convene SGCM at a remote station where a sufficient number of officers to constitute a GCM may not be available.

The minimum number of officers to constitute an SGCM is three as against 5 in the case of GCM. Unlike the latter, for which each officer to be appointed as a member is required to have held a commission for not less than 3 whole years (2 years for DCM), no length of commissioned service is laid down as a requirement for a member of an SGCM. However, AR r. 115 requires that the officer to be appointed as a member of SGCM should have held commission for not less than one year but if officers who have held commission for 3 years are available, they should be selected in preference to those of less service.[95] Further, no officer is disqualified for appointment if he is not a PM or prosecutor or a prosecution witness.

The law does provide for an abbreviated procedure to be followed at a trial by SGCM. In practice this means that in the charge, the statement of offence may be made briefly in any language sufficient to describe or disclose an offence under the AA.[96]

---

95 AA s.115 and AR r .151.

96 AR r.152.

Further, only a brief record of the evidence of the witnesses and of the defence of the accused is a legal necessity in the case of SGCM and that too may be dispensed with if it appears to the convening officer that military exigencies or other circumstances prevent compliance with this requirement. For this, necessary direction will have to be given in the convening order along with a brief statement about those exigencies or circumstances.[97] However, this is rarely done and evidence of all witnesses is recorded at full length in the same manner as at a GCM trial.

In rest of the matters the procedure to be adopted at an SGCM trial will be the same as in the case of a GCM, the power of punishment and jurisdiction over persons subject to the AA in both the cases being the same. Interestingly, SGCM and GCM were clubbed together in a letter by the Joint JAG, while furnishing to this researcher, the data of the CsM held during the past five years. However, a subsequent letter disclosed that SGCM (70) shared almost equal space with GCM (79) in matters of CM trials under the AA during the years 2003 and 2004.[98] Further, it seems to reflect upon the nature of SGCM, essentially as a field service tribunal, that no SGCM trials were held under the AFA during the years 2002, 2003 and 2004, while the number of GCM and DCM trials during the same period, under the AFA, were 54 and 158 respectively.[99]

2.8 SCM and its Procedure

Unlike the other three kinds of multi-member CM, an SCM is a one-man show and may, to that extent, be said to be a relic of the ancient system under which the will of the king or the commander alone decided the fate of a military offender. However, the present day SCM is based on the British experience during the Great Uprising of 1857. While the discipline in the British Indian Army was in a bad shape, the state of discipline in the irregular Corps and the Sikh and other levees was much better because of the paramount authority lodged in the hands of COs to exercise judicial powers either directly or by means of panchayats on the basis of "established usages of the service", which secured recognition in the Mutiny Act 1863, Sec 1.[100] The union of functions of

97 Ar r. 160. If the evidence recor d is dispensed with, the only record of the trial will be av ailable in the Schedule annexed to the convening order (IAFF-956) and a certificate of the PO r egarding assembly, the plea, finding and sentence alongwith the record of the swearing of the court, of witnesses as Part 'B' and confirmation and promulgation of P arts 'C' and 'D'. Please see Appendix III of the AR at at p. 431 of MML V ol II.

98 Department of Judge Advocate General, Army Headquarters, New Delhi, Letters no. 05742/2003/JAG dated 25 Nov 2003 (Appendix A) and no. 05742/AR/CM/2005/JAG dated 27 Sep 2005.

99 JAG (Air) Letter No. Air HQ/20059/78/Lgl dated 18 Oct 2005

100 Simmons, The Constitution and Practice of Courts Martial, op cit, Ch 1, n 6, p5. The CO of the Punjab Irregular Forces had almost absolute powers to deal promptly and effectively with all military offenders by holding trial and issuing warrant for execution whereas the commandants of the Regular Regiments occupied position of insignificance. Please see RP Sharma, Manual of BSF Law, 1979, New Delhi, Joshi Publications, p 93.

deputy commissioner, political officer and military commandant in one and the same person which was frequent those days on the Frontier, facilitated the success of the experiment of similarly strengthening the hands of the regimental COs in the regular British Indian Army organized on the ruins of the old Bengal Army which had practically disappeared during 1857 uprising. The CO, as such, would convict and sentence a military offender and issue warrant for the execution of the sentence which would be respected by the civil and prison officials as emanating from him in his civil and magisterial capacity. This led to the introduction of SCM tentatively at first, and firmly established later by Act V of 1869. The utility of SCM as a military justice tribunal is evident from the fact that out of 7856 CM trials held under the AA during the years 1998 to 2004, the number of the trials by SCM was 7234 (92%).[101]

Under the present provisions, the CO of a unit (be it corps, department or detachment) alone constitutes the SCM, though the proceeding thereof are required to be attended through out by two other persons who shall be officers or JCOs or one of either. The CO is sworn but the two persons attending the proceedings are administered no oath. They may be consulted by the 'Court' but perform no function of their own during the proceedings.[102] There are no provisions for any legal back-up to the court or the accused. There is no civil counsel or defending officer to represent the accused even though the accused is allowed to have a 'friend-of-the-accused', who may be any person, including a civil lawyer. He may advise the accused on all points and suggest questions to be put by the accused but cannot examine witnesses or address the court on behalf of the accused.[103] The court itself examines the witnesses for prosecution and the accused is allowed to cross-examine them, make a statement and lead evidence for defence.[104] The general procedure followed at the SCM is more or less the same as applicable to DCM, including, the swearing of the court, the interpreter and the witnesses, the arraignment of the accused, objection by accused to the charge, amendment of the charge, general pleas of 'Guilty' or 'Not Guilty' and record of finding, procedure on acquittal, procedure on conviction, sentences, signing of proceedings, promulgation of finding and sentence and review of proceedings.[105]

101 Data furnished by Army Headquarters letters, op cit, n 98.

102 AA s.116.

103 AR rr 95 (1), (4) and 129.

104 AR r 118.

105 AR rr 106 to 133.

However, unlike the other three types of CM, there is no provision of challenge or objection by the accused against the officer holding the court, since the CO alone is empowered to hold SCM. At the same time, an inbuilt safeguard against the possible misuse of the forum by the CO is provided in AA s.120(2) which requires a reference to be made to the officer empowered to convene a DCM or, on active service, SGCM, before the CO holds an SCM in any ease involving an offence against that officer himself or an offence under AA ss 69 (civil offence), 34 (offences in the face of the enemy and punishable with death) or 37 (mutiny).[106] Then, the Service ethos enjoins upon the CO to conduct himself as a father figure vis-à-vis the men he commands. The ill consequences of any failure in this regard by reason of immaturity or inexperience on the part of the CO stand reduced by certain safeguards provided by the law, such as the detailed guidelines provided by Regulations in matters of the award of punishment by the SCM for different offences and different circumstances, the limit imposed on maximum punishment power of the CO below the rank of Lieut Colonel[107], the requirement of approval (except on active service) by an officer commanding not less than a Brigade before the sentence is carried into effect in case the officer holding the trial has less than 5 years service and the sentence of dismissal being required to be accompanied by a memorandum giving reasons therefor. The final and most important check, of course, is review of the proceedings by the specified authority after scrutiny thereof by the Dy JAG.[108] Within this perimeter, an SCM operates in its jurisdiction of trying NCOs and below for any offence under the AA with its maximum power of punishment being 1 year imprisonment.

The post-trial part of the decision making process of CM in the case of an SCM or SGCM would remain, with marginal variations, the same as in the case of a GCM or DCM which has since been discussed earlier. Some variations, such as no need of confirmation, in the case of SCM have been brought out above. Other variations would include the authority empowered to deal with petitions against finding or sentences of an SCM.[109]

---

106 AA s 120(2). This requirement may be dispensed with only when there is a grave reason for immediate action and reference cannot be made without detriment to discipline. In such circumstance, an explanatory memor andum is r equired to be at tached to the pr oceedings, please see AR r .132.

107 AA ss120, 161(2), AR rr 131 and 132, RA para 448.

108 AA s 162 read with AR rr 133 and 200.

109 Any authority superior in command to the reviewing authority; RA para 365.

2.9 Conclusion

The CM process is at times improperly interfered with, either under ignorance or deliberately, though not necessarily with a questionable motive. This would include the cases of resorting to administrative termination of services of the accused or summarily disposing his case or closing the case by awarding censure or warning or in some other way, contrary to the legal requirements. For instance, an offence involving moral turpitude, fraud, theft etc, which is required to be tried by a CM or prosecuted before a criminal court, in accordance with RA para 432, may be inadvertently or otherwise disposed by awarding minor punishment under AA s. 80 or by summarily disposing the case under ss 83 to 85, preferring the charge under s. 63 for an act prejudicial to good order and military discipline. It should be realised that any such action in itself is subversive of military discipline and may be said to be as wrong as the getting rid of an inconvenient man by awarding him imprisonment in a civil jail, coupled with dismissal, for a minor offence.

2.9 Conclusion

[illegible]

CHAPTER - 3

RESEARCH METHODOLOGY

This is a civilization in which decisions are increasingly based upon scientific fact, and those who cannot understand how the facts are reached will be unable to separate fact from speculation and wish.[1]

—Goode, W.J. and Hatt, P.K.

3.1 Statement of Problem

Law has been variedly seen in the social context, from being eulogized as the 'King of Kings'[2] to being mocked as 'an ass',[3] and its purpose has also been contemplated in equally diverse terms from 'divine dispensation' to 'social engineering'[4]. In such a perceptional ambience, it should be interesting as well as rewarding to peep into the functioning of a judicial forum that "strikes terror in the heart of the prisoner to be tried",[5] according to some legal luminaries, but, according to others, is "equally fair if not more than a criminal court trial".[6] This legal institution 'of the Army, by the Army, for the Army' rules over the destiny of a huge mass of men and women numbering around 1.2 million[7] in India alone and also enjoys the distribution of a global presence in relation to the man who being "good enough to shed his blood for his country is good enough to be given a square deal".[8] Known as the CM, it is the very symbol of the rigour of military discipline. Deriving its strength from the law contained in the AA in the case

1 Goode and Hatt, Methods in Social Research, 1952, New York, McGraw - Hill Broke Company, p.1

2 Brihadaranyak Upanishad, 1.4.14.

3 Charles Dickens, Oliver Twist, (Mr. Bimble's statement)

4 Roscoe Pound, Social Control through Law, p. 132 cit in George Whitecross Paton, A Textbook of Jurisprudence, 4th ed, 1972, London, ELBS & OUP, p 38.

5 Justice William O Douglas, "Tough Test for Military Justice," Time Magazine, 3 Oct 1969, pp. 42-43, quoted by Justice DA Desai in PPS Bedi v UOI, AIR 1982 SC 1413, at 1437.

6 UOI v Maj A Hussain, AIR 1998 SC 577.

7 Times of India, (hereinafter referred to as 'TOI') Late city Delhi ed, 31 December 2001, p. 9 "India has military edge over Pakistan" quoting the report of the Center of Strategic and International Studies.

8 Theodore Roosevelt.

of the Indian Army personnel, it wields its sway over them "wherever they may be"[9] in all matters of life and death, including even those which are generally regarded as purely personal such as eating or not eating food.[10] This seems to amply bring out the desirability of scientifically studying how sound is the decision making process of the CM. Since justice should not only be done but should manifestly and undoubtedly be seen to be done, as Lord Justice Hewart would say, the existing theoretical position of DPCM may be examined for the purpose in the light of how the concerned people take it. The starting point in this regard would be an attitudinal study of DPCM.

DPCM is one of the three channels available under military law for dealing with delinquent personnel of the Armed Forces, the other two being the administrative disposal of cases (including termination of service) and the infliction of punishments without the intervention of the CM.[11] As distinguished from these two other channels, DPCM involves a full fledged trial by a quasi-judicial tribunal of ad hoc nature, in a procedure broadly analogous to that of a Judge and jury trial. As a course of necessity, the pre-trial investigation through C of I, the hearing of charges by the CO and recording of the S of E[12] and post-trial review by specified authorities also form part of DPCM. An attitudinal study of DPCM would seek to find out the settled mode of thinking or behaving, on the part of the connected people, in relation to such extended scope of DPCM.

With a view to appreciating the reach of such a study, it may be noted that Leonard Doob was of the view that "attitude" had no systematic status as a scientific construct and suggested that it should be replaced with learning theory constructs like drive etc.[13] However, referring to various approaches on the subject, such as those of Allport (1935), Erich Fromm (1940), Blumer (1955) et al, David L Sills concludes that "the confused status of the concept can be best corrected not by abandoning it, but by subjecting it to continued critical analysis ...". [14] In the context of social science, 'attitude' may be seen as a "relatively enduring organisation of beliefs around an object or situation predisposing one to respond in some preferential manner".[15] Asch, Solomon E, also underlines the

9 AA s.2 (1), simi lar provisions also exist under the AF A and NA.

10 Ranjit Thakur v UOI, AIR 1987 SC 2384 at 2392. With reference to charge under AA s.41 for disobedience of lawful command, the SC observ ed: "A disregard of direction to accept food might assume complexion of disr espect and ev en defiance of authori ty."

11 AA ss 19, 20 and 80-85.

12 Supra 2.3(a), (d) and (e).

13 Doob Leonar d, "The B ehaviour of A ttitudes", Psy chological R eview (1947), V ol 54 135:156, quoted in International Encyclopedia of the Social Sciences, 1968, Macmi llan Company and the Free Pr ess, Vol I, p 4 .

14 International Encyclopedia of the Social Sciences, loc cit, n 13, p 449.

15 Ibid, p 450.

enduring nature of attitudes saying that attitudes "are particularly enduring sets formed by past experience".[16] There may well be a possible hereditary basis, but all writers agree that attitudes are acquired through the principles of learning. In an empirical study, "an attitude can be approached from many different angles, and this explains why a series of questions is needed to measure it ... a sample of beliefs covering a range of aspects of the attitude needs to be obtained and the set of answers combined into some form of average" for the purpose of measuring a person's more general attitude, reducing the effects of idiosyncrasies of the particular respondent in respect of particular aspects of the attitudes.[17] Accordingly, those who have acquired attitudes towards DPCM as enduring sets by past experience have been subjected to the present study. Such persons include those who have been tried by the CM or those who have constituted the forum as members or JA or dealt with the CM cases as Judges, counsels, academicians and so on. Their beliefs about functional validity of the CM, which would pre-dispose them to respond in some preferential manner in the context of DPCM, have been studied by putting them a series of questions on such aspects of the CM as an ad hoc body rather than a permanently static forum, its capability to arrive at impartial and legally valid decisions, its suitability to the needs of the Armed Forces and also the desirability of extending its jurisdiction to civilian accused persons in terrorism struck areas and so on.

3.2 Review of Literature

Even though the profession of soldiering is traceable to the ancient texts like the Vedas[18], the need for some code to regulate the conduct for fighting troops was felt much later when standing armies were introduced on the political scene. However, the law remained mostly unwritten and justice administered summarily by the king or the military chief in those times. There is no reference to any institutions like the present day CM in our ancient literature. As for Europe, the Articles of Emperor Fredrick III (1487) have the earliest mention of 'militargerichts', followed by the 'Constitutio Carolina Criminalis' of Charles V (1532) speaking of 'spear' courts which were defined more accurately in the Articles of Maximilian II (1570), and the elaborate Articles of Gustavus Adolphus (1621) finally shaping the system of the CM. An Ordinance of 1655 in France introduced conseils de guerre thereafter in that country. Since then, private publications in the form of treatises on military law and CM practices and official publications in the

---

16 Asch, Solomon E, Social Psychology,1959, New Jersey, Prentice - Hall, p 585.

17 CA Moser and G Kalton, Survey Methods in Social Investigation, 1971, London, English Language Book Society and Heinemann Educational Books Ltd, p 351.

18 Priyavrata Vedavachaspati, A study in Vedic Polity, 1999, New Delhi, Meerut, Meenakshi Prakashan, Vol 3, Ch 2; Dr. Deva Vrat Acharya, Dhanurveda, 1999, New Delhi, Vijaya Kumar Govindram Hasanand, p 20.

form of enacted legislations, rules and regulations framed by the executives and manual published by the dealing ministry or department have been brought out almost in all the countries including the UK[19], the USA and the countries of the Indian sub-continent. Further, the Service litigation having found its way to the superior courts of the state judiciaries, some well researched judicial pronouncements from the Indian as well as the foreign courts on various aspects of DPCM, are also available. Similarly, journalistic publications also contain useful material on the subject in the form of articles by professionals and academicians. All these will find place in the bibliography to be appended to this Report. A special mention is, however, required of some of the classical treatises[20] on the subject. Unfortunately the majority of them are not now available in India (or perhaps even elsewhere) even in the library of the JAG. No work of lasting value is found on military law from the later half of the 20th century, perhaps because of the two world wars having kept engaged those who had the first hand experience of military law in practical terms and could have otherwise brought out an authentic work on the subject. The only recent publication that this researcher came across on the British system of DPCM is a 'Court Martial Handbook',[21] which too was not available for a personal copy even from the Delhi office of its publisher.

As for the Indian publications, perhaps Dr. (Rear Admiral) OP Sharma's book[22], based on his Ph.D. thesis, is the only well researched work published on the subject. It has the distinction of having been relied upon by a High Court in its decision on a writ petition by an Army Officer. Among other works, Nayudu's book is by far the first publication on the subject after the enactment of AA by our Parliament. Colonel GK Sharma's book is a practical guide for Army personnel on the lines of Simmon's treatise

19 Mathew Sutcliffe, The Practice and Lawes of Armes, 1593, was the first treatise in English on military law, though the first Englishman to write on the subject was Nicholas Upton who had seen several campaigns in France and elsewhere and authored De studio militari; please see Simmons, The Constitution and Practice of Courts Martial, op cit, Ch 1, n 6, pp 90-91 (s 197). The first official publication, i.e., the first edition of the British Manual of Military Law was brought out in 1882.

20 supra Ch 1.6.

21 Judge JW Rant, Court Martial Handbook: Practice and Procedure, 1998, New York, John Wiley and Sons. The second edition of the book has now been published in 2003 by OUP as Courts Martial, Discipline, and The Criminal Process in the Armed Services.

22 Dr. OP Sharma, Military Law in India, op cit, Ch 1, n 4; other works include C Sanjeeva Row Nayudu, Handbook of Military Law, 1951, Delhi, Metropolitan Book Co. Ltd.; Lt Col AC Mangala, Regimental Officers' Handbook on Military Law, 1976, New Delhi, Army Law Publishers; Col GK Sharma and Col MS Jaswal, Study and Practice of Military Law, 6th ed, 2006, New Delhi, Deep and Deep Publications Pvt. Ltd.; Maj Gen Nilendra Kumar & Rekha Chaturvedi, Law Relating to the Armed Forces in India, 4th ed, 2005, New Delhi, Universal Law Publishing Co. Pvt. Ltd.; Maj Gen Nilendra Kumar, Case Study on Military Law, 2003, New Delhi, Universal; Maj Gen AC Mangala, Commentary on Military Law in India, 1992, New Delhi, Eastern Law House; DC Jain, NK Indrayan & CG Goel, Military Law in India, 1984.

on the British military law. In a recent article by an American writer, this book was referred among "excellent foreign works on military law".[23] Then, there is Major Gen. Nilendra Kumar and Rekha Chaturvedi's very first effort on compilation of judicial decisions on military law in India. Major Gen. Mangala's commentary is marked for a comparative study of the three Services' Acts and Major Gen. Nilendra Kumar's case study, though rudimentary, has the distinction of being the first ever attempt on case study in the field. A mention may also be made of 'Military Law Journal' published by the Institute of Military Law, Kamptee; 'Air Force law Reviews' and 'Civil and Military Law Journal' for articles found useful for the present study. Some articles in 'Sainik Samachar', an official periodical of the Indian Armed Forces, like Brig RP Singh's article on the "Rights of an Accused" and an article by the present researcher with a title 'Court Martial; How far Court and How far Martial' (both the articles in Vol 37 Nos. 28 and 29 of July 1990) and 'Command Influence in Military Justice' (Sainik Samachar, Vol 39, No. 7) by this researcher were also useful though reflecting largely the official view on the subject. The reports of certain committees like a committee set up by the Government of India vide G of I, M of D, UO No. 9/1/61/D/AG-1 dated 01 Apr 1965 to draft a uniform code and of seminars on 'The Relationship of Military Law and Discipline with the Judicial System of the Country', held at Vigyan Bhawan, Delhi on 26 Feb 1982, on 'The Role of Civil and Military Judicial System in the Maintenance of Discipline in the Armed Force' held on 21 July 1991 at Usman Officers' Institute, Jammu and on 'Human Rights and Armed Forces' held on 28 and 29 Nov 2003 at Surya Defence Auditorium, Lucknow were also found to be revealing. There were also some articles published in AIR Journal Section, Civil and Military Law Journal, India Today, Tehelka and national dailies like Times of India and Hindustan Times by various authors like Wing Commander UC Jha, Lieut Gen Harvant Singh, Major A K Upadhyay, Paramjit Kaur, Dhananjaya Mahapatra, Rakesh Bhatnagar et al which were relevant to the matters within the scope of the present study and accordingly find place in this report in the chapters to follow. None of the works and references cited in the foregoing are, however, based on an empirical study.[24]

---

23 Eugene R Fidell, "A World-Wide Perspective on Change in Military Justice", The Air Force Law Review, Vol 48, 2000, pp 195-209 at 207 (n. 73)

24 This author has not come across any title relating to an empirical study on any aspect of DPCM except Lermack "Summary and Special Courts Martial : An Empirical Investigation", St Louis University Law Journal, Vol 10, Spring 1974, p329 and Major James Kevin Lovejoy, "Abolition of Court Member Sentencing in the Military", Military Law Review, Vol 142, Fall 1994, pp 1-66; partially based on a Thesis Survey conducted by him for his dissertation for the Master of Laws degree, to gain insight into the current attitudes and opinions of those affected by the sentencing process, collecting data from defence counsels (54), prisoners (68), Law course students (25), convening authorities (47), military judges (15) and staff JAs (68). Major Lovejoy also refers in his article to a survey conducted by the Advisory Commission to the Military Justice Act of 1983.

3.3 Objectives of the Study

For the reasons discussed earlier, there is apparently a felt need for the study of what attitude people related to DPCM, directly or indirectly, have towards it. Since an empirical approach is best suited to an attitudinal study, a non-doctrinal research for the project at hand has been undertaken. The non-doctrinal research typically takes either some aspect of the legal decision process, or the people or institutions supposedly regulated by law and the field work is resorted to. Legal doctrines may be included in a non-doctrinal study but are treated simply as one of the variables affecting the decision, or the practices and attitudes of people or affecting the operation of institution. However, much legal research falls in between the doctrinal and non-doctrinal research. This researcher having dealt with DPCM, while serving in the Army, and closely watched all its nuances, including those which draw flaks, is generally aware of the doctrinal aspects of the problem. An empirical study was therefore, undertaken as a step towards discharging the responsibility of "auditing the extent to which such legal processes serve the needs of the community that aspire to be democratic ..."[25] Thus, the immediate objective of the project was to study empirically the attitudes towards DPCM. On drawing logical conclusions from the data, it was intended to examine the related provisions of law in the light of those conclusions and offer appropriate suggestions in a reformative spirit, if feasible. If any further investigation appeared to be desirable, the aspects of DPCM which need such investigation were intended to be identified for the benefit of future researchers. The 'aim plus' was to contribute to the treasure of scientific thought in the sphere of law, however humble be such contribution, in the cause of striking a balance between the demands of military discipline and justice as an undeflectable path of Dharma as exhorted by the Hon'ble Supreme Court at the close of their celebrated pronouncement in SP Gupta v Union of India.[26]

3.4 Hypotheses

Stating the hypotheses involved in the present study, it may be useful to begin with 'fact', which may be described as "an empirically variable observation". The "relationship between facts" or "the ordering of them in some meaningful way" is termed as 'theory'. On logical analysis of the various facts in a theory, relationships other than those stated in the theory can be deducted. At this point there is no knowledge as to whether such deductions are correct. The formulation of such deductions constitutes a hypothesis. If verified, it becomes a part of a future theoretical construction.[27] Thus, hypothesis is a

25 Earnest Jones, "Some Current Trends in Legal Research", JILI, Vol 24, 1982, pp 197-198

26 ' न्य्यात् पथः प्रविचलंति पदं न धीराः ' ('nyayat pathah pravichalanti padam nah dhirah' - the prudent do not deflect from the path of justice.) quoted at the end of judgment in AIR 1982 SC 149.

27 Goode and Hatt, Methods in Social Research, op cit, n 1, ch 2 and 6 "Science, Theory and Fact" and "Basic Elements of the Scientific Method – Hypotheses".

statement, which is plausible but needs to be tested through field studies in a scientific manner.[28]

The formulation of hypotheses is irrelevant to - and impossible for - many fact collecting inquiries. To insist that a sociologist must not collect facts until he has a hypothesis would merely encourage the use of arbitrary hypotheses, which can be as bad as indiscriminate fact-collecting.[29] However, a hypotheses does help in keeping a research project intact, saving it from becoming a "random empirical wandering"[30] since the function of hypotheses is to direct our research for the order among facts.[31] In the light of this, the following hypotheses were formulated for the instant research project:

(a) The procedure prescribed for CM trial is equally fair if not more than a criminal trial provides to the accused;

(b) CM imparts speedy justice within the framework of the rule of law and suit the needs not only of the Armed Forces but also those of civil administration of justice in terrorism struck areas;

(c) The entire system of DPCM is fraught with command influence at all stages;

(d) The decision of a CM is pre-determined and the procedure followed at the trial is a mere legal formality;

(e) The in-built checks and balances of the CM system sufficiently make up the absence of the provisions for appeal against CM decision.

3.5 Operationalisation of Concepts

The word 'concept' is derived from Latin 'conceptum' meaning an 'abstract idea' or 'idea underlying a class of things; general notion'.[32] Concepts are foundation of all human communication and thought but since science requires greater precision in communication, the process of communication must be more consciously a part of science than is the case for most common sense and every day contexts.[33] Each concept

---

28 Young, PV, Scientific Social Surveys and Research : an introduction to the back ground, content, method, principles and analysis of social studies, 4th ed, 1966, New Jersey, Prentice Hall, p 104.

29 Moser and Kalton, Survey Methods in Social Investigation, op cit, n 17, p 4.

30 Goode and Hatt, Methods in Social Research, op cit, n 27, Chapter 6.

31 Cohen, Morris R, and Ernest Nagel An Introduction to Logic and Scientific Method, 1934, New York, Hercourt Brace & Co., p 100, quoted in unpublished Ph D thesis by Makhan Singh, Police and Custodial Violence, 2000, University of Delhi, p 233.

32 Compact Oxford Reference Dictionary, 2003,OUP, p. 169; The Advanced Learner's Dictionary of Current English, 1965, OUP, p. 196.

33 Goode and Hatt, Methods in Social Research, op cit, n 27, Ch 5 "Basic Elements of Scientific Method: Concepts".

communicates a vast amount of experience, abstracted and clarified for those who understand the term. Thus, the concepts are the 'short hand' of science; precise and basic to easy communication. It should be noted that 'concept', as a term of research methodology, is merely a symbol and not the phenomenon that it symbolizes. To confuse the concept with the phenomenon is an error known as 're-ification'. Secondly, a term used to denote a particular concept may have different meaning in other frames of reference or different terms may have been used to refer to the same phenomenon by different researchers. Lastly, the terms used for certain concepts may be so contrived by using Latin or Greek roots or the name of the inventor etc that they may have no referent outside the scientific frame of reference.

The variables used in the present research project have been operationalised to assign them meaning in terms of the concepts stated below:

(a) **Active Service**

In common parlance, the expression seems to suggest the pre-superannuating phase of employment. However, for the purpose of this research, the concept denotes the time during which a person subject to the AA is attached to or forms part of a force which is engaged in an operation against an enemy, or is in military occupation of a foreign country, or the time during which such a person is engaged in military operation in or is on the line of march to a country or place wholly or partly occupied by an enemy. Apart from this, a person or class of persons may also be deemed to be on active service, if the Central Government so declares by notification with reference to the area in which they may be located or with reference to any provisions of law.[34] A person on active service is liable to greater punishment for certain offences like desertion and incurs the curtailment of certain safeguards and rights otherwise available.

(b) **Attitude**

As a favorable or unfavorable mind-set towards DPCM in the context of the present study, an attitude may be seen as a relatively enduring organisation of beliefs around an object or situation predisposing one to respond in some preferential manner. 'Belief' here has three components: (i) cognitive, i.e., knowledge held with varying degrees of certitude about what is true or false, good or bad etc, (ii) affective, because the belief is capable of arousing effect of varying intensity around the objects of belief, around other objects, individual or groups, taking a positive or negative position with respect to the object of belief or around the belief itself where its validity is questioned, and (iii) a behavioral component, i.e., it must lead to some action when it is suitably activated. The

34 Based on AA ss3(1) and 9. Similar provisions also exist in AF A but NA provides for deemed active service only, i.e., by declaration by the CG.

affective component will not become manifest under all conditions. Only when the belief is somehow challenged by the attitude object or by someone else or when the preferential action towards which one is predisposed is some how blocked, the affective component reacts itself. But the affective component must be assumed to be there and it will become activated when the belief becomes a matter of controversy. A preferential response towards an attitude object must necessarily be elected within the context of some social situation about which we have attitude. We may conceive attitude object as a figure and the situation as the ground. Most psychologists agree that attitudes are acquired through the principles of learning, the heredity playing little part. Further, an attitude is not a basic irreducible element within the personality but represents a cluster or syndrome of two or more inter-related elements. In the definition conceived here, the elements are beliefs or cognition or expectations or hypotheses. It is in this connotation that the expression 'attitude' appears in such titles as "Article 33, Armed Forces and the Judicial Attitude: an Appraisal"[35] and is also to be understood in the context of the present study accordingly.

(c) **Cashiering**

The expression originalities from the French word 'caisssier' and denotes the act of dismissing from the Armed Forces because of serious wrongdoing.[36] Under the AA, various punishments awardable by a CM include cashiering in the case of an officer. The punishment is an ignoble form of dismissal from the service under the AA and the AFA and may be broadly equated with 'dismissal with disgrace' awardable under the NA.[37] The punishment entails a disqualification for employment in the public service after release from the Army. The promulgation parade for the punishment includes the convict being stripped off his badges of rank and other regimental insignia, with a bayonet, by his Formation commander in the presence of his CO and other officers.[38]

(d) **Civil Offence**

An offence may be said to be a legally punishable act or omission. Two categories of offences are punishable under the AA; those purely of military nature which can be punished exclusively under the penal scheme of the AA, i.e., by the CM or summarily by specified military authorities and secondly, those which are offences punishable under AA as well as by a court of ordinary criminal justice. The latter are termed as 'civil

35 An article by P aramjit K aur, R esearch Scholar, Department of Laws, Punjab Universit y, Chandigarh, published in Civil and Military Law Journal, 1988, p 175.

36 Compact Oxf ord R eference Dictionary, supr a, p 127 .

37 AA s. 71 (d), AF A s. 73(e), NA s.81(e).

38 RA para 373(a)(i)

offences'[39] and may be tried by a CM or punished summarily under the AA, except an offence of murder, culpable homicide and rape against a person not subject to military, Naval or Air-Force law. However, even these three offences may be tried by a CM if committed by a person subject to the AA on active service or at a notified frontier post or outside India.[40]

(e) **Commanding Officer**

Literally speaking, the expression would mean an officer who is commanding a particular person or class of persons. However, for the purpose of this research project, it refers to an officer who has either been specifically so appointed in respect of a person or class of persons, or who is in immediate command of the unit to which such person or persons belong (s) or is/are attached for discipline; and is, by virtue of his appointment as the unit commander, empowered under the RA or by the custom of the Service to discharge the functions of a CO in matters relating to DPCM under the AA.

(f) **Corps/Army Corps**

The expression attracted much controversy in some writ cases. Commonly it is used in three senses, namely, (i) the fighting formation of the Army hierarchy between Command and Division, (ii) certain Army organisations historically raised on functional basis for the entire Indian Army, such as the Corps of Engineers, and lastly, (iii) a separate body of persons subject to the Army Act as set out in sub-rule (3) of Rule 187 of the AR. For all the provisions relating to DPCM, the expression 'corps' signifies the last category of a separate body of persons, while the expression 'army corps' denotes the hierarchical Formation of the first category. This research study uses these two expressions accordingly.

(g) **Court of Inquiry**

Contrary to any linguistic suggestion, a C of I is merely an inquiry or investigation under the AA/AR and not a court or adjudicatory forum. In this research project, the expression is accordingly used as an assembly of military officers etc ordered to collect evidence, by an officer in command of troops, and to report, if so required, with regard to any specific matters. The proceedings and record thereof carried out by the assembly of such officers is also known as C of I.

---

39 AA s.3(ii);

40 AA ss 69 and 70; simi lar provisions exist under AFA and NA.

(h) **Court Martial and Process of Court Martial**

CM is a quasi-judicial forum under military law to adjudicate upon an offence committed by a person subject to military law or a civilian subject to the jurisdiction of the CM under that law. As for DPCM, it will include not only the decision of a CM on various issues, its finding(s) on the charge(s) and the sentence but also pre-trial matters like hearing of the charge by the CO, and post-trial matters like confirmation, petitions etc under the AA.

(i) **Criminal Court**

The definition of the expression given under AA[41] has been adopted for the purpose of this study. Accordingly, it denotes a court of ordinary criminal justice in any part of India. It may be interesting to note that the definition of "criminal court", as it originally stood, excluded the courts in the State of Jammu and Kashmir. The words "other than the State of Jammu and Kashmir" have since been omitted from that definition by Air Force and Army Laws (Amendment) Act, 1975, as a follow up action of certain judicial pronouncements in respect of civil offences committed by military personnel in the state of Jammu and Kashmir.

(j) **Desertion**

Desertion is a typical military offence consisting of an unauthorised absence from duty, either with no intention to return to the Service or with an intention to avoid an important military duty, such as proceeding overseas or carrying out a military operation like attacking the enemy defenses. If committed on active service or while under orders for active service, it is punishable with death or lesser punishment provided by the AA.

(k) **Enemy**

In the context of military forces, a layman would generally take the expression 'enemy' to mean a soldier belonging to hostile foreign forces. However, for the purpose of an offence under military law, it is widely construed. Accordingly, the three Service Acts define and this research study uses the expression 'enemy' to include all armed mutineers, armed rebels, armed rioters, pirates and any person against whom it is the duty of any person subject to military law to act. Very severe demands of military discipline may at times require a soldier to shoot down his own kith and kin in the present day scenario of terrorism, hence such a wide connotation of the expression 'enemy'.

---

41 AA s. 3(viii).

(l) **Forces**

Irrespective of several connotations that the word 'force' or 'forces' has in the every day usage, for the purpose of this study, the word 'forces' stand for the regular Army, Navy and Air Force or any part of any one or more of them.

(m) **Judge Advocate**

In the present study, as also under the provisions of the AA, it refers to an officer from the JAG's Dept. appointed as the legal advisor of the CM, with the designation of JA, to discharge the duties and functions assigned to him as such under the provisions of the AA, AR and RA.

(n) **Lawful Command**

For the purpose of this study, the expression signifies, an order given by a superior officer individually to a person subject to AA, which is capable of individual execution by the person to whom it is addressed, is justified by military law, relates to a military duty and is not contrary to any Indian or international Law. Such a command must also have an implied or express reference to time at or by which it is to be carried out and disobedience to it must tend to impede, delay or prevent a military proceeding.

(o) **Service**

The dictionary meanings of the word 'service' included the position as a servant, government employment or the employment in a department or branch of public work. However, in the present study, as also in military parlance, the expression 'the Service' stands for the Army, Navy and Air Force or any one of them as the case may be.

(p) **Superior Officer**

The expression 'superior officer' would literally exclude a person other than an officer from its ambit. However, under the military law and in the present study, when used in relation to a person subject to the AA, it means not only an officer but also a JCO, WO and NCO who is senior in rank to that person or who, though not so senior, is entitled under the AA, the RA or by the custom of the Service to give a command to that person and also includes persons of corresponding ranks in the Navy or Air Force as regards the Army personnel under their orders.

(q) **Unbecoming Conduct**

In the context of the present study, the expression unbecoming conduct of an officer, JCO or WO implies a conduct other than what is usually associated with an officer, JCO or WO as befitting his rank and status and may be of military or social character.

All other expressions used in the present study have meaning assigned to them under the AA or, when not defined in the AA, the meanings assigned under the IPC. When defined neither under the AA nor the IPC, those expressions have to be understood as per their ordinary dictionary meanings. However, the term 'India', irrespective of its definition in the IPC as excluding the state of Jammu and Kashmir, is to be taken as India including Jammu and Kashmir.

3.6 Methodology Adopted

The growing methodological sophistication and technical skill of sociologists are the direct outcome of their realization of their having the same foundations as any other science. An application of the fundamentals of science accordingly to the field of sociology is what we mean by 'method'. 'Techniques' comprise the scientific procedures by which sociologist gathers and orders his data prior to their logical or statistical manipulation. Operations or formulas of any other science may not be blindly applied but continuous adaptation of such methods has resulted in the growth of sociological techniques - cross-fertilisation among various sciences.[42]

The normative character of law as a social science and the desirability of stability and certainty in the sphere of law make the doctrinal research to be of the primary concern to a legal researcher.[43] However, ever since the Curriculum Committee Report, 1946 of the Yale Law School emphasized the "need for a combined approach in the study of social problems ... in law", it is being increasingly realised that "the distinction between doctrinal and non-doctrinal research does not truly reflect the distinction between legal and social science research. Legal research is as much non-doctrinal as social science research is doctrinal. The techniques adopted in legal research and social science research are not opposed to each other but complementary. The main distinction between the legal and social scientific pursuits is that of prescriptive and descriptive. The arm-chair type of research is not acceptable when, for instance, the requirement is that in order to enact purposeful legislation, attitudinal studies of those whose legal position is sought to be modified must be taken into account.[44] Keeping this in mind, suitable methodology has been adopted for the present study as may be seen from the discussion to follow.

---

42 Goode and Hatt, Methods in Social Research, op cit, n 1, Ch 1 "New sociology" .

43 S.N. Jain, "Doctrinal and Non-doctrinal Legal Research", JILI, Vol 24, 1982, p 341.

44 D N Saraf, "Reference and Utility of Empirical Research in Law", JILI, Vol 24, 1982, p 611.

(a) **Universe of the Study and Survey Population**

The serving soldiers of the Army numbering around a little more than one million make a formidable size of the jurisdiction of DPCM under the AA. Ex Servicemen of a strength of about six lakhs have also had a close association with DPCM during their service period of two decades as an average. Apart from this, the entire country of one billion population has an indirect stake in DPCM for the reason of national security being linked with the discipline of the Armed Forces. There are also certain sections of the society like lawyers, Judges, academicians, media persons and sociologists who are concerned with DPCM as interest groups. A study of the attitude of all these people towards DPCM would be beyond individual capabilities for a researcher. Further, considering that many of them may not be available for study, it would be a waste of time and resources to take all of them for a study. Lastly, the present researcher having on Army background was likely to handle more effectively the theoretical facts under the AA. In view of this, the present study was restricted to attitudes towards DPCM under the AA and the attitude to be studied was confined to that of a survey population[45]. The said survey population comprised firstly, those who had been tried by the CM; secondly, those who served at the CM as members or JA, and thirdly, commanders and staff associated with DPCM at pre-trial, at the trial and post-trial stages. The Judges of the civil judiciary who pronounced on or remained concerned otherwise with any aspect of DPCM and others actively interested in DPCM as lawyers, academicians et al were also included in the survey population covered for the study. Finally, the locale of the present study was the region where the presence of the Army is comparatively more prominent, i.e., the States of J & K, Punjab, Himachal Pradesh, Rajasthan, National Capital Region, Assam, Manipur and West Bengal. It is in this region that other interest groups are also comparatively more active.

(b) **Sampling**

A sample is a smaller representation of a larger whole. Its utility lies in the fact that the observation of the whole phenomenon and analysis of its data are cumbersome and time consuming, if not a sheer waste of time when sample can as well serve the purpose. Money and time saved by resorting to sampling can be utilized for more intensive analysis of fewer cases and other investigation.[46] The basic requirements of a sampling procedure

45 The term 'population' is used in its statistical sense, i.e., to denote the aggregate of units to which the survey results are to apply. An alternative term is 'universe'. The population for which the results are required is know as target population' and the population actually covered, the 'survey population'; Moser and Kalton, Survey Methods in Social Investigation, op cit, n 17, p 53.

46 Goode and Hatt, Methods in Social Research, op cit, n 1, Ch 14 "Probability sampling".

to be adopted in an empirical study are, firstly, that the sample should be representative of the whole 'universe' and, secondly, that it should be adequate. There are several types of sample designs, such as random, purposive, stratified, quota, multi-stage, convenience sampling or accidental sampling, self-selected sampling, bluster or area sampling, element sampling and snow-ball sampling.[47] Random sampling is one sure way of avoiding bias arising through the sampling method and greater precision may be achieved by stratification of the population and then select random sample from each strata. Random sampling gives an equal probability[48] of selection to each member of the population. The two basic procedures adopted for the purpose of achieving randomness are the 'lottery method' and the use of sample numbers whereby the members of the population are numbered from 1 to 'N'[49] and 'n' numbers are selected in any convenient and systematic way. In the latter case, every tenth number, for example, may be selected. However, even these procedures may at times fail as a result of unsatisfactory mixing up of the discs in the lottery method and the list itself not being in a random order in the latter case. Irrespective of this possibility of failure, the existence or availability of a sampling frame[50] is apparently a condition precedent for the working of the either of the two procedures of random sampling.

Considering the high reliability of random sampling, the possibility of adopting stratified random sampling was explored for the present study at the planning stage. However, it was realised that the circumstances in which the universe of the study was set, no sampling frame was likely to be available. Constituted of 'N' units comprising the serving and the retired or released service personnel alongwith those indirectly concerned with DPCM and hence having developed attitudes towards it, the population of the present study was not borne on any consolidated or unconsolidated list(s) or record that could form a sample frame for 'n' units to be picked up for random sampling. The Service Lists of the Forces contained the details of gazetted personnel only and none about the OR. Similarly, the names of the JCOs and OR on the long rolls maintained by Record Officers of different Regiments and Corps, even if made available crossing all barriers of supposed security concerns, would not meet the entire requirement; those indirectly concerned in DPCM being out of the preview thereof. Any attempt to list out

47 K.D. Gangrade, "Empirical Methods and Tools of Research", JILI Vol 24, 1982, p 635.

48 In American literature the term 'probability sampling' is used in place of random sampling; Moser and Kalton, Survey Methods in Social Investigation, op cit, n 17, p 80.

49 'N' symbolises the units of the target population while 'n' units stand for the units actually picked for investigation i.e., individuals interviewed in the present case.

50 Sampling frames are the lists, indexes, maps or other population records from which the sample can be selected at each sampling stages ; Moser and Kalton, Survey Methods in Social Investigation, op cit, n 17, p 154 .

those lawyers, Judges and academicians who have had an association with or interest in DPCM would itself be a separate research project. The Shakespearian dilemma of 'to be or not to be' could easily lead to abandoning the project research but the lure of a first ever empirical study on DPCM was too much to allow such a course. In this scenario, there was no alternative but to settle for quota sampling which, according to Moser and Kalton "may be the only method of sampling a population for which no suitable frame is available"[51]. Even if "some experts hold the quota method to be so unreliable and prone to bias as to be almost worthless", others think that "although it is obviously less sound theoretically than probability sampling, it can be used safely on some subjects."[52]

Quota sampling is a method of stratified sampling. The first step in quota sampling is to stratify the target population. It is common, although not necessary, for quota samples to employ random selection procedures at the initial stages of selection the same way as probability samples.[53] The essential difference between probability and quota samples lies in the selection of the final sampling units, say individuals. Once the general breakdown of the sample is decided (e.g. how many men and women, how many people in each group it is to include in a survey based on a quota sample), the choice of the actual sample units is left to the interviewers, specifying how many of them are to be with men and how many with women, how many with people in various age groups, social classes and so forth.

The kind of factor to be chosen as a quota control is partly determined by its usefulness as a stratification factor. A second consideration in the choice of controls is that the resulting strata should, as far as possible, be homogeneous with respect to their member available for interview. Once the controls and quotas have been fixed, the next step is to give interviewer his assignment. The two common assignment schemes are 'independent' and 'inter related' schemes. In the former only the marginal quotas for sexes, ages, social-class groups are set, while in the latter, these are formally related to each other to ensure, for instance, that a given number of interviews in each group is with women and a certain number with men. Thus, with inter-related controls, the numbers to be interviewed in all these sub-groups are assigned. The two schemes may be illustrated by the following hypothetical assignments.[54]

51 Moser and Kalton, ibid, p 135. Please also see supra n 24 for similar methodology adopted by Lovejoy to gain insight into the current attitudes and opinions of those affected by the sentencing process.

52 Moser and Kalton, ibid, p 127.

53 When a selection of cities or areas is chosen purposively, i.e., because they have certain characteristics believed to be typical, the method is known as 'purposive sampling'. Some precincts, states or cities are used because election results in them coincide with national results, or because economic patterns show up there before they do in larger area, or they seem to be key region in other respects; Goode and Hatt, Methods in Social Research, op cit, n 46, Ch 14 "Probability and Sampling".

54 Source : Moser and Kalton, Survey Methods in Social Investigation, op cit, n 17, pp 129-130.

Chart - 3.1

Independent Controls					
Sex		**Age**		**Social Class**	
Male	9	20 - 29	4	**Highest**	2
Female	11	30 - 44	6	**Middle**	4
		45 - 64	7	**Lowest**	14
		65 +	3		
Total	**20**	**Total**	**20**	**Total**	**20**

Independent controls are simpler for the interviewer and, on the whole less costly; they are also easier to set accurately since a statistical basis is more readily found for the marginal zones than the sub-groups. But they are less likely to ensure representativeness.

Chart - 3.2

Inter-related Controls								
Social Class								
		Highest		**Middle**		**Lowest**		**Total**
Age	**Sex >**	**Male**	**Female**	**Male**	**Female**	**Male**	**Female**	
	20 - 29	1	-	-	1	1	1	**4**
	30 - 44	-	1	-	1	3	1	**6**
	45 - 65	-	-	1	1	2	3	**7**
	65 +	-	-	-	-	1	2	**3**
	Total	**1**	**1**	**1**	**3**	**7**	**7**	**20**
		2		**4**		**14**		

Attempts have also been made to combine random and quota sampling. Many quota samples, for instance, use design in which each interviewer is assigned exact instructions on how to proceed. (S)he may be asked to call out every second house and interview every one or one person in the house until her quota is filled. Such a design restricts the interviewer's influence. Moser and Kalton quote Sudman describing the use of a prescribed travel pattern for the interviewers and calling it 'probability sampling with quotas'.[55] Goode and Hatt emphasize the need of describing the technique in detail, particularly statistical and sampling procedure, in a research report, since "some writers use 'random' in technical sense but at times it is used only to show absence of bias and nothing more."[56]

Whether 'random' or 'quota' or any other, the "sample design is decided upon in the light of what is practically feasible as well as of what is theoretically desirable ... due regard must be paid to the purpose of the survey, the accuracy required in the results, the cost, time and labour involved, and other practical considerations".[57] Accordingly quota sampling was adopted as the sampling design, within the constraints of the present study, in the light of what was practically feasible and theoretically permissible. The interviewers were assigned control scheme, i.e., by assigning the number of the members from each stratum to be interviewed. The sample size was fixed as 200 units from four strata of the accused, the members, the JAs and others, with 50 interviewees of each stratum. No control of age, sex or social status was relevant to the factors of stratification, no female having ever been subjected to the jurisdiction of DPCM under the AA ever since its enactment in 1950, although instances of CM trial in respect of females during the British days do exist[58]. Similarly, no boys Battalions exist any more in the Indian Army and social status as an officer or Sepoy is not considered to decide as to whether or not an accused be subjected to DPCM jurisdiction.

(c) **Research Tools used for Collection of Data**

The word 'data' is the plural of the Latin word 'datum' and stands for facts or statistics used for reference or analysis.[59] The data collected directly from respondents in an empirical study are called 'primary data' and the data from published or unpublished material are termed as 'secondary'. Thus, the primary data are those assembled for the specific purpose of solving a particular research problem while the

55 Moser and Kalton, Survey Methods in Social Investigation, op cit, n 17, p 137.

56 Goode and Hatt, Methods in Social Research, op cit, n 46, Ch 21 "Preparing the Report".

57 Moser and Kalton, Survey Methods in Social Investigation, loc cit, n 56, p 41.

58 Supra Ch 1, n 16 for the trial of Mrs. Hannah Fitchet. Two cases of CM in respect of female officers have taken place subsequent to this decision on quota control. Those are, however, inconsequential for the present study.

59 Compact Oxford Reference Dictionary, 2003, p 208.

secondary data are those already recorded for some other purpose and subsequently used in a research project. There are four methods of obtaining data about a group of people: documentary sources, observation, mail questionnaire and interviewing. In the present study, the primary data were collected from respondents through interviews.

(i) **Primary Data Collection**

An Interview Schedule was prepared to provide a standardized tool (Appendix 'A'). It was divided into three parts. Each part had a number of questions and sub-questions, mostly structured ones with possible answers listed underneath, except the last question in each part being open-ended for detailed suggestions and the first question seeking personal data. The first part was meant for those who had been either a member or the JA at a CM trial. The questions in the second part were to be answered by those who had been tried by a CM and convicted or acquitted. Care was taken to ensure that the questions in this part were suitably worded so as to avoid an emotionally coloured response. The questions in the third part were to be answered by all respondents including those of the assorted category of commanders, Judges, lawyers, academicians et al and also by those who had already responded to the questions of Part 1 or 2. While devising the questions for each of the three parts, it was borne in mind that an attitude can be approached from different angles. Further, although a belief on a specific issue tends to suggest an attitude, a particular individual's belief on that issue way be heavily weighted by an idiosyncratic component which makes his belief untypical of his more general position. A worker may reasonably believe, for example, that the mangers are well qualified for the task, and yet he may still have a generally unfavourable attitude to management. The earlier referred requirement to reduce the effect of idiosyncrasies[60] of the respondents was, therefore, kept in mind and the set of statements for ascertaining beliefs was chosen.

Individual attitudes towards the CM system, widely varying for psychological reasons, could be approached by a social psychologist, employing a suitable scaling method. Such an exercise would, however, be more conducive to obtain a measure, and a reasonably reliable one, of his actual position on the attitude continuum, instead of learning whether or not a respondent is favourably inclined on any issue. Instead of differences in kind, this would measure differences in degree.[61] Further, too little sociology leads away from the law but much sociology leads back to it just as a little law leads away from sociology but much law leads back to it.[62] An individual research scholar, like this researcher, would have his own limitations of time, energy and resources which

60 Supra, n 17.

61 Moser and Kalton, Survey Methods in Social Investigation, op cit, n 17, p 358.

62 Maurice Harion cit in Upendra Baxi, "Socio-Legal Research in India – A Programschrift", JILI, Vol 24, 1982, p 416.

may be required to bring in "much sociology" to lead back to law. The approach was adopted here, therefore, to measure the respondents' attitude by combining the answers to a set of opinion questions into some sort of deduction.

As for the method adopted for respondents' interview in each case, the interview was conducted at a place and time convenient to each respondent. The interviews were mostly conducted by the researcher himself. However, wherever distances involved did not make it feasible, an officer well versed in the theoretical aspect of DPCM was assigned the task of interviewing the respondent according to independent control scheme explained earlier. Before starting the interview, effort was made to make the respondent at ease. The notes given in the Interview Schedule before the personal data column were explained by the interviewer, making it absolutely clear that the responses were sought purely for academic research and the respondent was not obliged to answer the questions or any particular inconvenient question and was free to maintain anonymity as well. A brief resume of DPCM theoretical provisions was also given wherever required to refresh the memory of the respondent about them. For the mode of answering, it was explained that the respondent could pick up an answer from the given possible answers or could give entirely a different answer. The respondents were also impressed upon the need of being forthright, frank and faithful to their belief and that no 'right' or 'wrong' aspect was involved, the requirement being only of a true response. In addition to the answer of a question, any further explanation or suggestion in general or in the context of a particular question was welcome and could be noted down in the given space or on a separate sheet or chit to be attached to the response(s). Due effort was made to maintain a sense of participation and interest on the part of the respondent by exhibiting proper respect to his views. Further probe, wherever needed, was done without giving an impression of grilling the respondent and all reactions of the respondent in the form of words or changes in the facial expressions were noted down, without editing even for grammatical accuracy. The interview was ended smoothly with an expression of thanks to the respondent.

(ii) **Secondary Data**

In addition to the information available in various libraries or otherwise from published works on the subject, the statistics obtained from official record in the Department of the JAG (Army) and JAG (Air Force), as supplied by them have been used as secondary source of data. Further, personal notes made by the present researcher during the course of his service in the Army in respect of unclassified information have also been taken into consideration. Lastly, a significant source of the secondary data also comprised of the case law reflecting the attitude of the Judges towards DPCM. For this purpose, all the decisions of the Supreme Court in the Service litigation, from 1951 to 2007 and land mark decisions of various High Courts, including important decisions during Pre-Independence period, and of the US and the UK superior courts have also been gone through as a supplementary study of judicial attitude to DPCM.

(d) **Processing of Data**

The processing of data involved four steps. Firstly, the record of the responses on the Interview Schedules was checked. This required the editing of the Schedules for completeness, accuracy and uniformity and filling the gap, if any, created by inadvertent omission of record, with the help of answers to other questions or notes made in the margin or by recalling interview details, if possible, relevant to the gap. As a second step in the data processing, the answers were coded with a view to classifying the answers to a question into meaningful categories so as to bring out their essential pattern in the case of each question, the whole point of coding being to summarize the data with a view to reducing the mass of details to manageable proportions. Thereafter the data were put together by means of statistical tabulation. This was an attempt to render the data clear and comprehensible with the help of simple but effective statistical tables and charts.

The data having been summarized, the task of analyzing and interpreting them was taken up by the researcher's own judgment and skill, carefully under the able guidance to the Research Supervisor. This consisted of two procedures; one, statistical description, i.e., describing the features of the research study aggregate, and secondly, inference, i.e., estimating the population characteristics from those of the sample. In addition to this, effort was also made to seek an explanation, by analytical methods, of how the demonstrated relationship comes about. In other words, this required the investigation of meaning of the relationship between two or more variables, i.e., the attempt to make cause-effect inferences or an attempt at understanding of the causal mechanisms from a causal model in which the connection between several variables appeared simultaneously. Lastly, summation and suggestions based on the conclusions drawn from the data have also been put forth.

(e) **Difficulties Faced**

This being a pioneer empirical study on the subject, an uncultivated ground had to be cleared of several pit-falls and stumbling blocks with assiduous efforts. The convergence of the little known branch of law in academic circles, as the military law is at present in our country, and the technical needs of an empirical study was a daunting task. The challenge was met at the planning stage with the encouragement and constructive guidance provided by Prof. M.P. Singh of the Law Faculty, who has since retired, Rear Admiral O P Sharma, formerly JAG Indian Navy and Maj Gen B R Parashar, formerly JAG Army. Dr. Sushil Gupta, an ex-UNESCO executive located at Meerut also rendered valuable help in preparing the Interview Schedule. However, in spite of all this guidance and cooperation from my academic superiors, a number of difficulties raised their heads at the stage of the data collection. The support of erstwhile colleagues from the Services that I was rightfully banking upon unexpectedly fell prey to a mistaken notion of proverbial secretiveness in defence related matters.[63] The worst was that for the reason of personal regards for me, they would not expressly come out with their constraints in extending the support. The result was that the Interview Schedules issued in October 2003 with a request to do the needful, within a period of about 6 months, remained unreturned altogether despite telephonic assurances of compliance at the other end of the communication. Alternative channels had to be adopted for the task, on learning the true position from a well-wisher that my former colleagues had been advised to be 'discreet' in the matter. The non-response from the individuals selected to form 'n' units of sample was equally disheartening. Two instances, are those of an ex DG Tihar Jail and a Divisional Commander located at Meerut. This researcher personally met the former and handed him over the Interview Schedule, which he promised to complete and return but never did so despite several telephonic reminders. In the second case, the General Officer promised to give an appointment every time I telephonically approached him but finally proceeded on posting and promotion, having remained unable to do the needful over a period of 3-4 months. Two of the High Court judges expressed their inability to grant an interview on the subject which could come some day for their decision and an expression of views thereon in advance could embarrass them when required to pronounce thereon in the discharge of their duty. In several other cases, the individuals felt shy of speaking on a matter which they were supposed to be well aware of as a part of their profession but were actually not confident. Similarly, in many cases they declined on the ground that they never had a tryst with DPCM, even though it was a part of their command function as officers in the Army.

Non-availability of latest published material as well as old treatises on the subject, both in the libraries and the open market compounded the difficulty faced in getting an access to the related material from the official records and archives. However, the needed material was collected from related websites. Making a way through the maze of such difficulties, I have striven to make the study a successfully completed project on an empirically untouched subject. To claim a last word in the matter would obviously be

---

63 Judge Advocate General John Gillison, "Evolution actuelle de la justice militaire – Rapport general" in Huitieme Congres International Ankara, 11-15 Oct 1979, L'Evolution actuelle de la justice militaire, Recueils de la Societe internationale de droit penal militaire et de droit de la guerre, VIII, Vol I,Brussels, 1981, p. 28 [French original, free translation would read: "the issue of military justice is shrouded in the secrecy that enshrouds the whole military organization"]

an antithesis to the very spirit of scientific research. This should, however, open a door to future researcher, hopefully with an unhesitatingly active support from the Services, which would make his effort not only more rewarding to the researcher but also more useful to the users of the CM Process, i.e., the Servicemen themselves.

(f) **Report**

The chapters to follow alongwith the present Chapter 3 and the two preceding it, are the outcome of my engagement with the data in the pursuit of the objectives of the research project.

CHAPTER - 4

SOCIO-INTELLECTUAL PROFILE OF RESPONDENTS

> *...Social background of many judges and the attitude of detachment to which they are conditioned during their formative years at the Bar, can produce difficulties of communication and understanding between them and people of lesser privilege and education who appear before them.*[1]
>
> -Justice RK Abichandani

An attitude being a predisposition acquired through the process of learning rather than an innate trait, it is axiomatic that the social background and intellectual attainment of an individual would substantially contribute to the shaping of his attitudinal make-up. The social and economic environment of his upbringing, the direction and level of his academic pursuit, the professional preferences tried and adopted by him at the cross-road of life, the career finally chosen along with the pattern of advancement therein and the stakes he comes to have in the politico-economical structure of the society, all go to influence his attitude towards different objects, institutions and situations. Several such contributory factors were intended to be studied in the present research project in respect of the respondents. Certain added factors were also planned to be tapped in the case of those respondents who were being or had been tried by a CM. These included the places where the respondents lived before joining the armed forces, their father's (or guardian's) occupation, educational background, income, size and the structural nature (joint or nuclear) of the family, the type of entry in the Services, the institution of the initial training and gallantry award/foreign courses or assignment. The additional factors, however, seemed to tilt the balance of the study disproportionately to the sociology of law extending the boundary off jurisprudence almost to absurd length of making it "merely a branch of sociology", as Paton would speak of Ehlrich theory.[2] These factors were, therefore, later ignored, while interviewing the respondents.

---

1 Justice RK Abichandani, "How to Groom Better Lawyers and Better Judges", AIR 2003 Journal 20.

2 George Whitecross Paton, A Textbook of Jurisprudence, op cit, Ch 3, n 4, pp 29-30.

Total 208 respondents were interviewed from four strata[3]. During the course of editing, it was noticed that some of the respondents had left unanswered quite a few questions from the Interview Schedule. In all such cases where it was not possible to deduce from the existing data as to what the missing answer(s) should have been, the Interview Schedules were abandoned as suggested by Moser and Kalton.[4] The remaining 200 Interview Schedules have been relied upon for this study report. The socio-intellectual profile of the respondents as it emerges from the concerned data is projected in the statistical tables to follow.

TABLE - 1

Profession-wise Classification of Respondents

		Response	Frequency					
Sl No.	Professional Status	Member	JA	General	Accused	Total	%	Remark
1.	Governor	00	00	1	00	01	0.5	A retired Lt. Gen.
2.	Judges	00	01	04	00	05	2.5	Incl. two serving HC CJs.
3.	Academicians	00	01	03	00	03	1.5	Incl. a Head Univ. Law Department
4.	Law Officers	00	01	05	00	06	3.0	Incl. Secy. Law Comm.
5.	Civil Servants	00	00	01	00	01	0.5	Retired IAS Officer
6.	Advocates	00	00	04	00	04	2.0	Incl. an Advocate on Record at SC
				Total Civilians		20	10	
7.	Armed Forces Pers.	50	48	32	50	180	90.0	
	Total	50	50	50	50	200	100.0	

3 Supra, Ch 3.6(b)

4 Moser & Kalton, Survey Methods in Social Investigation, op cit, Ch. 3, n 17, p 411.

It may be seen from Table-1 that 180 (90%) respondents are retired/released or serving Armed Forces personnel and 20 (10%) are civilian gentlemen. Strictly speaking, all retired or released persons, notwithstanding their past association with the Armed Forces should be termed as civilians but for the purpose of this study-report, only such Armed Forces personnel who acquired some prominent civil office after their retirement or release from the Forces, have been placed in the civilian group alongwith those who never had any active association with the Armed Forces. The rest have been all clubbed together simply as Armed Forces personnel. The respondents from the Armed Forces apparently have had an active interaction with the CM system. The rest of the respondents too have had occasions to come in contact with it, some having practically participated in it while others having with it only an academic association. It may be interesting to note that 18 out of the total 20 (90%) civilian respondents have never been associated with the CM system. This is in sharp contrast with their British or American counterparts, most of whom would have personal association with the Armed Forces at some stage or the other of their life, having thereby significant difference in the attitude towards military institutions like CM. In the present study, one Judge and one Law Officer reflected in Table - 1 under category 'J' performed the duty of JA at CM during the course of their service in the Army.[5] Similarly, the respondent who is presently occupying the high office of a Governor had been the convening officer and confirming officer in several CM cases before he retired as a Lieut General. The remaining civilian respondents had no military background. However, two of the four Judges have dealt with the CM cases both at the Bar and the Bench. One of them appeared at GCM as defence counsel in some cases and the other dealt with the CM cases as Advocate General of a HC before elevation to the Bench. From among the academicians, one respondent had read a paper on "Military Judicial System and Rule of Law" at the Northern Command Legal Seminar 1991. As for the 180 (90%) respondents from the Armed Forces background, each one of them has had a direct involvement in the system as a person subject to the Services law. One of them, who is presently a practising lawyer at the Supreme Court, with a Ph.D. degree in military law, also had an unpleasant experience of being tried and convicted by an SGCM. All this association of the respondents with the CM system should have gone a long way in the development of whatever attitude they have towards the DPCM.

---

5 The respondent who later became a Judge of the Gauhati and Assam HC, was the first Indian Judge Advocate General. He served in the Army from 1945 to1957. The Law Officer (Addl. Solicitor General of Uttaranchal) too retired as a Colonel from the Army after putting in 30 yr service there, which included his attachment to the JAG's Dept for some time.

TABLE -2

Services-wise Classification of Armed Forces Respondents

Sl No	Service	Response Frequency					
		Member	Judge Advocate	General	Accused	Total	%
1.	Army	48	40	31	49	168	84.0
2.	Navy	00	03	00	00	03	1.5
3.	Air Force	01	02	01	00	04	2.0
4.	BSF	01	00	00	01	02	1.0
5.	Coast Guards	00	03	00	00	03	1.5
	Total AF Pers	50	48	32	50	180	90.0
	Civilians	00	02	18	00	20	10.0
	Total	50	50	50	50	200	100.0

Table-2 shows that 180 (90% of the total 200) respondents form a broad group of serving and retired or released personnel of the Armed Forces, which consist of 175 respondents from the three Services, i.e., the Army, Navy and Air Force and 5 respondents from BSF and Coast Guards. The term 'Services' does not traditionally cover the armed forces like BSF and Coast Guard. For the purposes of this study, however, the respondents from the BSF and Coast Guards have been placed together with the respondents from the Services since the disciplinary codes of the BSF and Coast Guards are modelled on the three Services Acts. The attitudinal make-up of the BSF and Coast Guards respondents in respect of the decision-making process of their own tribunal should, therefore, be well comparable to the subject matter of this study. Further, the proportional margin between the respondents from the Army 168 (93%) and the other Service respondents should be taken as normal, since the area of study proposed for the present research project is essentially the regular Army of India.

TABLE -3

Class-wise Distribution of Armed Forces Respondents

Sl No	Service Class	Response Frequency					
		Member	Judge Advocate	General	Accused	Total	%
1.	Officers	50	48	30	10	138	76.7
2.	JCOs	00	00	02	01	03	1.7
3.	NCOs	00	00	00	13	13	7.2
4.	Sepoys	00	00	00	26	26	14.4
5.	Total	50	48	32	50	180	100.0

In Table - 3, the largest number of respondents 138 (77.2%) is from the officers class of the Armed Forces. This is due to their greater exposure to the functional face of the system. Under our military law, they alone are eligible, while the JCOs, NCOs and Sepoys are not, to sit as members or JA at CM trials and are also associated more closely with pre and post-trial matters of DPCM in their administrative and executive capacities. Their superior academic standard further makes them more articulate on questions covered in respect of the general category of the respondents. This accounts for their numerical lead in categories 'M', 'J' and 'G' responses and shapes their position in the Table despite their percentage in the last category 'A' being comparatively smaller, i.e. 10, (20% in that category of 50 respondents) and Sepoys, NCOs and JCOs being respectively 26 (52%), 13 (26%), JCOs 1 (2%).

TABLE - 4
Rank-wise Classification of Armed Forces Respondents

Srl No	Rank	Response Frequency					
		M	J	G	A	Total	%
1.	Lieut Gen/Vice Admiral/Air Marshal	00	00	02	00	02	1.1
2.	Maj Gen/Rear Admiral/Air Vice Marshal	01	04	01	01	07	3.9
3.	Brig/Commodore/Air Commodore/DIG	06	04	03	00	13	7.2*
4.	Col/Captain (Navy)/Gp Captain (Air Force) Commandant (BSF and Coast Guards)	20	09	06	02	37	20.6
5.	Lt Col/Commander/Wing Commander/Dy. Commandant	12	09	11	03	35	19.4
6.	Major/Lt. Commander/ Squadron Leader	10	13	05	01	29	16.1
7.	Capt/Flight Lieut/Lieut/Sub Lieut/Flying Officer	00	03	01	01	05	2.8
8.	Subedar Major	00	00	02	00	02	1.1
9.	Subedar/Naib Subedar	00	00	00	01	01	0.6
10.	Havildar/Head Constable (BSF)	00	00	00	05	05	2.8
11.	Naik/Lance Naik	00	00	00	08	08	4.4
12.	Sepoy	00	99	00	16	16	8.9
13.	Anonymous Officers	01	06	01	02	10	5.6
14.	Anonymous OR	00	00	00	10	10	5.6
	Total	**50**	**48**	**32**	**50**	**180**	**100.1 (100.0)**

* Remark: DIG of Coast Guards.

Table 4 reflects the same data as Table 3 does, but through the prism of rank structure of the Armed Forces. Srls 13 and 14 in Table 4 show the number of the respondents who have not disclosed their identity but their class status and ranks wherever possible to discern from their other responses have been included in the concerned data. It is interesting to note that the maximum number of the anonymous officers-respondents is from category 'J'; 6 out of 10 (60%) anonymous officers-respondents being from this category. In the case of OR, anonymous respondents 10, are all from category 'A'. In the context of the rank structure of the respondents from the four categories, i.e., 'M', 'J', 'G' and 'A', it is also worth noticing that 'Maj. General' was the highest rank among the respondents who have been tried by a CM and Lieut. General among the respondents of category 'G'. The highest rank held by a respondent of the remaining two categories, i.e., 'M' and 'J' was also Maj. General. The lowest ranks of the respondents in categories 'M', 'J', 'G' and 'A' respectively were 'Major', 'Captain', 'Subedar Major' and 'Sepoy'.

TABLE-5

Decoration-wise Classification of Service Respondents

Srl No.	Rank	Response Frequency					
		M	J	G	A	Total	%
1.	PVSM, AVSM, VSM	00	00	02	00	02	1.1
2.	PVSM, AVSM	00	01	00	00	01	0.6
3.	PVSM, VSM (Bar)	00	00	01	00	01	0.5
4.	MVC	00	00	01	00	01	0.6
5.	AVSM, VSM	00	03	00	00	03	1.7
6.	AVSM	01	00	00	00	01	0.5
7.	VrC	01	00	01	00	02	1.1
8.	SM, VSM	00	00	01	00	01	0.6
9.	VSM	00	02	02	01	05	2.8
10.	COAS Commendation	00	01	00	00	01	0.5
11.	No decoration	48	41	24	29	162	90.0
12.	**Total**	**50**	**48**	**32**	**50**	**180**	**100.0**

Medals and decorations are awarded to Armed Forces personnel in recognition of their service. They may, on the one hand, be suggestive of the mental make-up (attitude included) of the concerned individual, at the time of the award, and may, on the other, influence the direction of his thinking and beliefs in time to come.

Medals may be awarded to commemorate certain events or conditions of service. For instance, Indian Independence Medal 1947 was instituted for all personnel serving in the Armed Forces on 15 August 1947, Nava Varsha Dirgha Seva Medal is awarded to individuals on completion of their nine year service in the Armed Forces, and Poorvi Star was meant for all ranks who participated in operations in and around Bangladesh. Decorations, unlike medals, are individual specific, signifying an act of gallantry on his part or distinguished service rendered by him.[6]

In Table 5, Param Vishisht Seva Medal (PVSM), Ati Vishisht Seva Medal (AVSM), Vishisht Seva Medal (VSM), irrespective of the word 'medal' in their nomenclatures, are the awards earned individually for distinguished service of the most exceptional order in the case of PVSM, distinguished service of an exceptional order in the case of AVSM, and distinguished service of a high order in the case of VSM.[7] During the course of service, one may earn one or more of them, one after the other. If an individual is entitled to the same award, say VSM, again, the word 'Bar' is mentioned after the award or an asterisk is marked there. Table 5 shows that two respondents of category 'G' stand awarded all the three awards of distinguished service series and one from the same category PVSM and VSM with Bar. Some of the respondents have also been decorded with gallantry awards: one with Mahavir Chakra (MVC), two with Vir Chakra (VrC) and one with Sena Medal (SM). MVC is awardable for acts of gallantry in the presence

---

6 RA, Vol.2, Ch xvi, pp 275-296. Common medals and individual decor ations both are displayed on the uniform in the shape of a metallic medal suspended with a riband, the metallic medal and riband being differently designed to prescribed specifications for each category of award.

7 RA, p 278. Distinguished service of an exceptional order may be differentiated from acts of bravery for which gal lantry awards are bestowed. To illustrate the former, respondent No.J-77-A-2 was awarded AVSM on 26 January 1977 for the reason that "During his tenure as Deputy Judge Advocate General, justice in the Command has been dispensed not only with speed and efficiency but also with marked impartiality and honest y. Highly qualified and expert in scientific management, he brought to bear his talent on the affairs of his department. He also extended his willing help and cooperation in matters which were not strictly within the orbit of his professional duties. With his literary bent of mind and amiable temperament, he has also enriched the social and cul tural cir cles of the station" . The lat ter may be illustrated from the citation of the gallantry award MVC in the case of respondent 'G-121-A-3' who, on 21 November 1971 had "directed his troops with great courage and confidence. With utter disregard for his personal saf ety, he mo ved from one company local ity to another, inspiring his junior commanders and troops, while occupying a defended position in the ar ea Garibpur-Jagannathpur on the Eastern Fr ont and the Battalion under his command faced the enemy attack with two infantry battalions and a squadron of tanks...."

of the enemy and is the second highest gallantry award (the highest one being Param Vir Chakra) of the Indian Armed Forces. VrC is next to MVC in lower order of precedence.

The respondents have also been classified on the basis of their professional/ academic distinction. The data is presented in Table 6 below.

TABLE 6

Academic/Professional Distinction-wise Classificatin of Respondents

Srl No	Academic/Professional Distinction	Response Frequency						Remarks
		M	J	G	A	Total	%	
1.	Ph. D	00	02	06	01	09	4.5	6 in Law, 2 in Sociology and 1 Hony.
2.	M Phil	00	01	00	00	01	0.5	Actual M Phil 3(1.52) but 2 not incl here since already incl with Ph.D (Sociology).
3.	LL.M.	01	01	03	00	05	2.5	Actual LLM are 11 (6.5%) but not incl here since already incl in Ph. D (Law).
4.	Barrister in Law	00	01	00	00	01	0.5	From the Middle Temple in 1945.
5.	M.A., M.Sc., M Com.	05	00	02	01	08	4.0	Actual M.A., MSc, M.Com. 31 (15.5%) but 22 not incl. here since already incl in Ph. D, M Phil, LL.M and LL.B.
6.	M Tech, ME, MEd AMIE, BE B.Tech.,MD, MBBS, BDS, MBA, PSC Dip in Engineering	12	00	10	03	25	12.5	Actual number of respondents with such qualifications is 33 (16.5).
7.	LLB	09	45	13	01	68	34.0	Total LLB 80 (40 %) but 11 respondents with LLM and one with M Phil not incl here. Twenty are with MA, MSc, M Com & rest with BA, BSc, B Com. One of them obtained LLB in 1942.
8.	Graduate	14	00	14	07	35	17.5	(Those with graduation as their highest degree are shown here)
9.	FA/Intermediate/-Matric SLC, Army Spl.	05	00	00	12	17	8.5	
10.	Below Matriculation	00	00	00	07	07	3.5	
11.	No response	04	00	02	18	24	12.0	
	Total	50	50	50	50	200	100.0	

Table - 6 reflects all shades of intellectual standards in academic/professional terms from Ph D downwards to under Matriculation. The professional distinctions of the respondents included M Tech/ME 1, BE, B Tech, AMIE 5, MBBS-1 PSC ('passed staff college'), a professional qualification of Armed Forces officers recognized by certain Universities[8] as equivalent to M Sc in Defence Studies and so on.

TABLE-7

Sex-wise Classification of Respondents

Srl No.	Sex Denomination	Response Frequency M	J	G	A	Total	%
1.	Male	50	50	48	50	198	99.0
2.	Female	00	00	02	00	02	01.0
	Total	50	50	50	50	200	100.0

Unlike the Western countries, the females in our Armed Forces are restricted only to officer class. In fact about a decade back, they were found only in the Medical Corps and Nursing Services. During the last 13 years, a symbolic presence of female short-service commissioned officers has been introduced[9] in non-Arms Services like Supply and Transport Corps, Ordnance Corps, Judge Advocate General's Department and so on. The first ever Court Martial trial of a female was recently held in the case of Flight Lieutenant Anjali Gupta of the Air Force[10]. The females are generally non-responsive to questions of a research study, more particularly the one on lesser known issues like DPCM. All these factors account for a fractional presence of respondents in the present study with merely two female respondents, one from the Army and the other from academic field.

8 TOI, 25 Oct 05, p-4 "Garhwal Varsity's stand stuns retired Colonel, "criticising H N Bahuguna University for not recognising PSU which was recognized by Madras University as equivalent to M Sc in defence studies and informing Colonel M N Gulati (retired) to this effect 4 years after he was registered for M Phil with HNBU.

9 'Dainik Jagaran' (Hindi daily), 15 Jan 2006, p 16, Army Day special feature 'Jharokha' stating inter alia that 25 female officers were first inducted in the Army on 06 March 1993.

10 TOI, 10 Dec 2005, p .7 "Anjali Gupta : First woman of ficer court martial led".

TABLE - 8

Age-wise Classification of Respondents

Srl No.	Age-Group	M	J	G	A	Total	%
		— —Response Frequency— —					
1.	20-35	05	13	01	30	49	24.5
2.	36-50	22	18	20	13	73	36.5
3.	51-65	14	09	18	06	47	23.5
4.	66-80	08	10	11	00	29	14.5
5.	81-95	01	00	00	00	01	0.5
6.	No response	00	00	00	01	01	0.5
	Total	50	50	50	50	200	100.0

The data in this Table (Table-8) show that the maximum number of the respondents 73 (36.5%) is from the age-group of 36-50 years and the minimum number, i.e, 01 (0.5%) is from the age group 81 years and above. The second highest number 49 (24.5%) is from the age-group 20-35 years, closely followed by the age group of 51-65 with its total number 47 (23.5%). From this, it may be inferred that the data collected in the present study is from well matured mind not adversely affected by any senility of advanced age. It is also worth noting that out of 50 respondents of category 'A' (accused), 30 (60%) are from comparatively tender but hot-headed age-group of 20-35 years.

The data collected in respect of marital status, religion and income of the respondents have been found to be prima facie neutral on their attitude toward DPCM and hence not being tabulated here.

An overall picture of respondents that emerges from Tables 1 to 8 is that majority of them (90%) consists of Armed Forces personnel of all ranks from Lieut. General or equivalent rank down to Sepoy or equivalent rank. The civilian respondents who form 10% of the total are from cross-section of the elite of society including politicians, judges, civil servants, academics and lawyers. Thus, all the respondents were likely to be well concerned with DPCM. Their academic status ranges from Ph D downwards to under-Matric and majority of them are married males of different age-groups from 20 years onward.

CHAPTER-5

PRE-TRIAL CUSTODY

I know not whether Laws be right,
Or whether Laws be wrong,
All that we know who lie in gaol
Is that the wall is strong,
And that each day is like a year,
A year whose days are long.[1]

Oscar Wilde.

5.1 Introduction

The law of arrest is one of balancing individual rights, liberties and privileges, on the one hand, and individual duties, obligations and responsibilities on the other; of weighing and balancing the rights, liberties, and privileges of the single individual and those of the individuals collectively.[2] Pre-trial military custody is a link in the chain of this balancing exercise. Any person subject to the three Services Acts, who is charged with an offence, may be taken into military custody by the order of any superior officer or even by the order of an officer of inferior rank, if engaged in a quarrel, affray or disorder.[3] The word 'charged' here does not mean the requirement of being given a formal written charge such as the one on which an accused is arraigned before a CM; it

---

1 "The Ballad of Reading Gaol" by Oscar Wilde.

2 Joginder Kumar v State of UP , AIR 1994 SC 1349 (1349, par a 11)

3 AA s 101; NA s 84; AFA s 102. Such an arrest is permitted under the Naval law only in the case of an offence punishable with death, or imprisonment for life or imprisonment for a term which may extend to 14 years Further, since the expression 'Superior Officer' includes a JCO, WO, NCO and persons of equivalent ranks in the Navy and Air Force, as defined in AA s3 (xiii) and corresponding provisions of NA and AFA, any military offender may be arrested by any such person of superior rank or of the same rank but greater seniority. Historically arrest by a person of inferior rank was not restricted to the cases of quarrel, affray or disorder. Brevet Lieut. Col. Alexander Hog was arrested by Capt. Elligood for being drunk on duty when under arms inspecting the guards and picquet of the 55 regiment of foot, at Playmouth on or about 9 Oct. 1819, tried by CM, and cashiered on conviction. While confirming the finding and sentence, His Royal Highness found it justifiable. Simmons, The Constitution and Practice of Courts Martial, op cit, ch 1, n 6, p 150 (s 357). Other persons empowered to arrest a military offender include a provost marshal, a police officer and a Magistrate in appropriate cases; AA ss 104 , 105, 107, NA s 89 (3), AF A ss105, 106, 108.

Contd/-

simply means an accusation or complaint that he has committed the offence.[4] It may, however, be clarified that it is not obligatory in every case that a person accused of an offensive act must be placed in military custody.[5]

5.2 Military Custody

Military custody "means the arrest or confinement of a person according to the ussage of service and includes naval or air force custody". In literal terms, this should be the definition of the 'forces' or 'service' custody as distinguished from the custody under ordinary criminal process. Even though the word 'military', in its usual dictionary meaning, signifies the armed forces of a country,[6] in the Indo-British martial traditions, it stands for the regular Army as distinct from the Navy and the Air Force, and is to be accordingly understood in the term 'military custody'. Such custody is therefore essentially a custody according to the usages of the Army. However, by a legal fiction, 'military custody', as defined in the AA, also includes the Naval or Air Force custody so as to cater for an eventuality of a person subject to the AA being kept in the custody of either of the other two Services. The definition of the Naval custody and the Air Force custody in the respective Service Acts is to be similarly construed.[7]

(a) Custody, Arrest and Confinement

The word 'custody' has originated from the Latin word 'custos' meaning 'guardian'.[8] In the present day usage, it stands for 'duty of caring for' or 'guarding' and in the common man's legal perception, it denotes the state of being in the charge of the police or in prison awaiting trial.[9] Essentially custody implies physical control[10] with or without arrest which is only one of several possible modes of taking a person into custody. In

---

contd/-

However, a military offender shall ordinarily not be placed under arrest by an authority other than his CO unless the needs of discipline so require; RA, para 392(b).

4 MML, Vol II, p.199, Note 2 to AA s 101; cf Gian Chand v UOI, 1983 Cr L J 105 (Delhi) para 35 where similar interpretation was given to 'charge' for the purpose of "hearing of charge" by the CO during pre-trial investigation under rr 22 and 23 of the AR. This is unlike the position under British military law where a person is treated as charged with an offence on being provided with a copy of the charge-report (AF B-252) and different procedure is followed for custody review on his being so charged and a different one prior to that.

5 MML, Vol I, Ch III, p 13 (para 1); cf C. Sanjeeva Row Nayudu, A Handbook of Military Law, op cit, Ch 3 n 22, p 6 (Ch III, para 3). For similar practice under the British and the US laws, please see Stuart-Smith, James, 'Military Law : Its History, Administration, and Practice', op cit, ch 1, n 26, p 493.

6 Compact Oxford Reference Dictionary, op cit, ch 3, n 32, p 533.

7 AA s 3 (xiii), NA s 3 (xii), AFA s 4 (v).

8 Compact Oxford Reference Dictionary, loc cit, n 6, p 201.

9 The Advanced Learner's Dictionary, op cit, ch 2, n 2, p 240.

10 Krishna Iyer, J., in Niranjan Singh v Prabhakar Rajaram Kharate and Others, 1980 Cr L J 426.

relation to detention of a person, custody implies restraint upon the movements of the person concerned, denying him freedom to move about according to his volition.[11] Arrest, on the other hand, is derived from the Latin word 'restare' meaning 'remain, stop'.[12] In legal parlance, it is used for the restraining of the liberty of man's person to compel obedience to the order of a court of justice, or to prevent the commission of a crime or to ensure that a person charged or suspected of a crime may be forthcoming to answer it.[13] The essential elements to constitute arrest in legal sense are that there must be an intent to arrest under the authority, accompanied by a seizure or detention of the person in the manner known to law, which is so understood by the person arrested.[14] Halsbury's Laws of England insist upon "the actual seizure or touching a person's body with a view to his detention" as an essential of arrest.[15] However, under enlightened modern conditions, it seldom becomes necessary for any police officer or authority empowered to make arrest to actually seize or even touch a person's body with a view to his restraint. Utterance of a word or sound, a gesture of the index finger or hand, the sway of the head or even the flicker of an eye are enough to convey the meaning to the person concerned that he has lost his liberty.[16] Briefly put, arrest is essentially a legal process whereas custody is a mechanism of physical control achieved through arrest or otherwise. In every arrest there is custody but not vice versa. Custody may amount to arrest in certain cases but not in all cases.[17] Custody may amount to confinement when its physical control element is translated into physical restraint, the former being the power to influence behaviour[18] and the latter being the so controlled behaviour[19] To distinguish 'confinement' from 'custody', it may be stated that custody is the restraint which is imposed by apprehension (the US military law equivalent of 'arrest') and which may be, but is not necessarily, physical. Confinement, on the other hand, is necessarily physical restraint, imposed by order of competent authority, depriving a person of freedom pending disposition of offences.[20]

---

11 Law Commission of India, 152nd Report (1994) para 2.1.

12 Compact Oxford Reference Dictionary, op cit, n 6, p 40.

13 Legal Glossary', 1988, New Delhi, Ministry of Law and Justice, Government of India, p.6.

14 Roshan Bibi v Joint Secretary, Government of Tamil Nadu, 1984 Cr L J 134, para 16.

15 Halsbury's Laws of England, 3rd ed, 1955, Vol 10, p342.

16 Kaisar Omar's Case 1981 Cr L J (NOC) 208, p 104 .

17 Roshan Bibi, Loc cit, para 29.

18 Compact Oxford Reference Dictionary, loc cit, n 12, p 178.

19 Ibid, p.712.

20 Manual of Court Martial, United States, 2000 Edition (hereinafter referred to as 'MCM') Pt II, Rules for Court Martial (hereinafter referred to as 'RCM'), RCM 304-305 'Discussion' .

Applying this conceptual discussion to the Forces or Service Custody, it may be said that the physical control or power to influence, as the essence of custody, in the case of Military, Naval or Air force custody, lies primarily in the authority of the Service law which manifests in the exercise of the power given to the CO and others in that regard. Such an exercise of power would take either the form of arrest or confinement, made through the practices established by the related usages of the Service.

(b) **Usages of the Service**

The usages of the Service form part of lex non-scripta, which consist of certain established principles and usages peculiar or pertaining to the military status and service recognized as means for guidance where written law is silent.[21] In general terms, a usage may be described as a long standing practice uniformly observed in a community to determine the pattern of conduct on a particular subject. Its closest kin is 'custom' from which usage is distinguishable mainly in so far as a custom should have existed from time immemorial whereas usages of recent growth may also be given effect to if well established.[22] A ministerial officer cannot institute a usage but the same must be built up out of a series of precedents. So also a custom cannot be created by isolated or occasional instances or by the practice of a particular command or commander, but must be a usage of the army at large or of some separate or distinct branch of the military establishment.[23] In the field of military custody, the Service usages are at the root of the kinds of arrest as 'close' or 'open' and the related matters,[24] the conditions applicable in the matters of dress to be worn, the restrictions on social activities and the nature of the duties to be performed while in arrest. The fact that confinement is not

---

21 Winthrop, Military Law and Precedents, op cit, Ch 1, n 1, p.41.

22 SP Dwivedi, Jurisprudence and Legal Theory, 1985, Allahabad, Central Law Agency, Allahabad, p 205.

23 U S v Babcock 4 Mc Lean 113; U S v Buchanan, O Howard 102; Greenwich Insurance Co v Waterman, 54 Fed 839.

24 Open arrest is an arrest during which the person arrested has his movements restricted to a certain limited area, such as camp area or unit lines. He would not be under the escort of any one. Close arrest, on the other hand, would mean that the person arrested is either confined (as in the case of a Sepoy) or is placed in the custody of another person (preferably of his own or superior rank) subject to military law, so that a person in close arr est would always have an escort accompanying him. An officer, JCO, WO or NCO, while under arrest, will not wear sash, sword, belt or spurs but will appear in uniform whenever outside his quarter or tent. Explaining the custom of an officer under arrest not wearing sword with his uniform, Simmons notes that on being placed in arrest, an officer delivers his sword to the person imposing it. If this form be sometimes omitted, it is considered, nevertheless, to have taken place, and hence the custom. Capt. Jervis was tried on an additional charge and found guilty of his having refused to deliver his sword when under arrest at Simla (India); Simmons, The Constitution and Practice of Courts Martial, op cit, n 3, p 148). In close arrest, an officer will not leave his quarter or tent except to take such exercise under supervision as the medical officer considers necessary or when permitted to go out by

applicable to an officer, JCO, WO or NCO, though he may be placed in custody, if circumstances so require, under the charge of a guard, piquet, patrol, sentry or provost-marshal, and that a Sepoy under close arrest will be placed in confinement, usually accommodated in the guard detention room, also originated from the service usages. These all are now governed by the provisions of the RA, N Regs II(s) and Regulations for the Air Force (hereinafter referred to as 'RAF). The conversion of a usage into regulation is rather consequential. A conventional custom or usage, unlike a legal custom, "does not possess absolute authority".[25] Dicey referred to "conventions, understanding, habits or practices", saying, "though they may regulate the conduct of the several members of the sovereign power... are not in reality laws at all since they are not enforced by the courts".[26] In any case, usages of the Service and the custom of war are to provide guidance only in the absence of written law as noted earlier. Regulations, on the other hand, if published in the Official Gazette, shall have the effect as if enacted in the main Act which empowers the specified authority to make the regulations. Even when not so published and therefore, being not statutory, they have the status of "general instructions affecting all the officers (and all the Other Ranks if and when affected) similarly situated and form the conditions of service of such officers protected by Article 16 of the Constitution. They can, therefore, be enforced by a writ petition".[27]

5.3 Research Data

Q 2.6(a) in the Interview Schedule was designed to seek data relating to the pre-trial military custody in the case of the respondents of 'A' (accused) category consisting

---

competent authority in any eventuality. On being under open arrest, he may take exercise at stated periods and within stated limits which will usually be the precincts of the barracks or camp of his unit. He will not appear in any place of amusement or entertainment or at public assemblies. Whether under close or open arrest, he will not perform any duty other than personal routine and such duties as may be necessary to relieve him from his charge of cash or stores etc. A Sepoy under close arrest will remain confined but while in open arrest, he will attend parades and may be ordered to perform all duties. Under close arrest, a Sepoy will not be required to perform any official duty. On active service, an NCO under arrest or a Sepoy under close arrest may be ordered to bear arms, attend parades and perform all such duties as may be required of him; MML, Vol I, p 15, paras 7 and 8; RA paras 394-396. It may be noted that the classification of arrest into 'open' and 'close' has since been done away with in the British Army. One is there now either in 'military custody' or simply at liberty with, if need be, conditions imposed by the CO, in his inherent power, which the accused must observe while awaiting trial or other order. Please see Rant, Courts-Martial, Discipline, And the Criminal Process in the Armed Services', op cit, Ch 3, n 21. Such a state of liberty with specified conditions is comparable to 'open arrest' under the Indian system and also with the US concept of 'restriction in lieu of arrest' or of 'conditions on liberty' when imposed separately from other forms of restraints; RCM 304 (a) (1) and (2).

25 Dwivedi, Jurisprudence and Legal Theory, op cit, n.22, p.284.

26 AV Dicey, The Law of Constitution, p.24, cit in ECS Wade and G Phillips, Constitutional Law, 9th ed, 1980, London, ELBS and OUP, p.16.

27 Col Shyam Kumar v Union of India, 1981 (2) SLJ 337 Del.

of 50 persons of different ranks and services who had been tried by the CM or similar forum in para military forces or were being so tried at the time of the interview. The data obtained are reflected in Table-9 below:

TABLE - 9

Duration of Pre-trial Custody

Srl No.	Custody Period	Response Frequency — — Number	Percentage	Remark
1.	Nil	22	44	Incl. all ranks
2.	Less than one month	08	16	
3.	1 - 6 months	02	04	
4.	6-12 months	05	10	Incl. one Maj.Gen.
5.	12-18 months	02	04	Incl. one Major
6.	18-24 months	06	12	
7.	24-30 months	03	06	
8.	30-36 months	01	02	
9.	No response	01	02	
	Total	50	100	

5.4 Zero Pre-trial Custody

The data at Srl 1 of Table 9 disclose that as many as 22 (44%) of the total number of the respondents who were tried by CM spent no time whatsoever in custody before their trial. This seems to be in sharp contrast with the practice followed in the civil system of criminal law to arrest routinely every suspect for investigation of the offence.

So much so, a trial court refused to accept the CBI charge-sheet in a case on the ground that the accused was not arrested during the course of such investigation. When the matter came up before the High Court, Justice J D Kapoor of the Delhi High Court not only held the trial court order as prima facie illegal but also had to issue a caution that "the liberty of a citizen's Constitutional guarantee cannot be incised and therefore, the police or investigation agency should not remain under the impression that in every cognizable and non-bailable offence they should invariably arrest the offender.[28] The High Court, however, conceded that arrest becomes necessary if the offence alleged was of grave nature and prescribes serious punishment.

(a) **Nature of Charges in Nil-Custody Cases**

Seriousness of the offence is also one of the considerations before the concerned commander, while deciding the desirability of arrest of the offender or otherwise, in a case. Having no expressly specified criterion for taking an offence as a serious one, unlike the British military laws,[29] the seriousness of the offence may be identified with the punishment prescribed in its penal clause for the purpose of the present analyses. Where a respondent was charged with two or more offences, the offence carrying the severest punishment in quantitative or qualitative terms is alone to be taken into consideration. Table 10 on the next page reflects the nature of the offences charged against those who remained in no pre-trial custody and also shows in each case, within brackets, the number of those respondents who did undergo some pre-trial custody while facing the same charge. The class status of the respondents as an officer, JCO, NCO or Sepoy is also being included in the Table.

---

28 TOI dated 02 F eb 04, p 5 " Avoid arrests until very necessary, rules HC".

29 (British) Code of Practice, para 104, Note 2(g) defines 'serious service offence' as an offence under any of the Service Discipline Acts (Br AA, Naval Discipline Act, 1957, and AFA 1955) which cannot be dealt with summarily, or which appears to an interviewing service pol iceman to be serious. The of fences which can be summarily dealt with have been listed out in Custody and Summary Dealing (Army) Regulations 2000 (CDSAR'00) reg 9.

TABLE-10

Nature of Offences Charged against Respondents with Zero/Some Custody

AA Sections	Officer	JCO	NCO	Sepoy	Anony- -mous	Sub- totals	Grand Total
37	–	–	02	04	–	06	06
38	–	01	–	(02)	–	01(02)	03
39			02	02(04)	02(03)	06(07)	13
41	–	–	–	–	01	01	01
52	03	–	(01)	–	–	03(01)	04
54	–	–	–	–	(01)	(01)	01
57	01(02)	–	–	–	–	01(02)	03
63	01	–	–	–	–	01	01
69	02	–	(07)	(06)	(02)	02(15)	17
NR	01	–	–	–	–	01	01
Total	08(02)	01	04(08)	06(12)	03(06)	22(28)	50

Note: 1. The respondents included in the charge under AA s 63 and 'NR' (No response) were anonymous but from their other responses they appeared to be officers.

2. AA s 37 Mutiny, punishable with death or less punishment.

38 Desertion, punishable with death or less punishment on active service and 7 years imprisonment or less elsewhere.

39 Absence without leave (AWL) punishable with 3 years imprisonment or less.

41 Disobedience to superior punishable with 14 years imprisonment or less on active service and 5 years imprisonment or less elsewhere.

52 Property offences like theft, misappropriation, fraud etc., punishable with 10 years imprisonment or less.

54 Making away with equipment etc., punishable with 10 years imprisonment or less.

57 Falsification of official documents, punishable with 14 years imprisonment or less.

63 Act prejudicial to good order and discipline punishable with 7 years imprisonment or less.

69 Civil Offence punishable with the punishment prescribed in Indian Penal Code 1860 (IPC) (or other Statute as the case may be) or 7 years imprisonment or less.

3. Civil Offences : Details

(a) Officers : IPC ss 392 and 354 (one each)

(b) Others : IPC ss 302, 304, 375, 304-A and Official Secrets Act totaling respectively as 6, 2. 1. 2. and 4, i.e. 15 (in all).

As may be seen from the data in Table 10 and notes 2 and 3 thereunder, 13 respondents with no pre-trial custody (59% of the total number of 22 of such respondents) were charged with the offences which were punishable with 10 to 14 years imprisonment. These were 3 cases of property offences (AA s 52), 1 each case of disobedience to superior officer (AA s 41), falsification of official documents (AA s 57), and robbery (under AA Sec 69 read with IPC s 392), and 6 for mutiny under AA s 37 and one for desertion under AA s 38. The rest of the nine cases, except one where the respondent did not specify the charges against him, were punishable with 3 to 7 year imprisonment (including 6 cases of AWL under AA s 39 and 1 each case of act prejudicial to good order and military discipline under AA s 63, and outraging the modesty of a woman under AA s 69 read with IPC s 354). The punishment less than the maximum punishment prescribed in all these cases could be imprisonment for any lesser period or any other punishment lower in the scale of punishment given in AA s 71. The seriousness of the charges involved in these 22 cases is evident not only from the penalty prescribed for them but also from certain other related factors. One, 15 out of these 22 cases were such as are expressly excluded from the jurisdiction of ordinary criminal jurisdiction[30] and were thus triable exclusively by CsM which are considered to be tough forum. Two, those 15 cases also included the cases of mutiny and desertion which are punishable

30 IPC s. 139 read with Criminal Courts and Courts Martial (Adjustment of Jurisdiction) Rules, 1978, published in SRO 488 of 1978 and reproduced in RA para 418.

with death, are free from any limitation period and are to be dealt with only by GCM.[31] Three, like the offences of 'mutiny' and 'desertion', the offences involving moral turpitude, fraud, theft, dishonesty and culpable negligence are also to be tried by CM and not disposed summarily and the punishment in such cases is also required to be deterrent.[32] The cases of the respondents charged with the offences under AA ss 52, 57 and 69 read with IPC ss 354 and 392 would fall in this category.

(b) **Why Nil Custody Despite Serious Offences**

The foregoing discussion in respect of the 22 respondents with zero pre-trial custody brings out that all of them, except those six who were charged with AWL and the one who did not disclose the nature of the charges levelled against him, had carried serious liability of heavy punishments from 7 years RI to death punishment, depending upon the charge in each case. The available data may be further examined to see why the respondents were not taken into custody at the pre-trial stage despite such serious charges pending against them. At the outset, while examining this aspect, one may proceed with the presumption of 'omnice proesumuntur rite et solemniter esse acta' (all acts are presumed to have been rightly and regularly done) in respect of judicial and official acts.[33] Official acts by military authorities, in particular, also have, in this regard, the support of a judicial pronouncement. When an apprehension was expressed that the military authorities might let go scot-free six persons subject to the AA who had been handed over to them for trial by the CM on the charges of robbery, house trespass and criminal intimidation, the High Court of Jammu and Kashmir rejected the "uncharitable submission" and emphasized that Parliament having, in its wisdom, "entrusted them (military officers) with certain powers and duties and charged them with certain responsibilities", they "must be trusted to exercise these powers properly, to discharge those duties honourably and carry out those responsibilities creditably". The High Court was "not able to see even a vestige of justification to apprehend any deliberate lapse or intentional omission on their part".[34] In the case of the 22 zero pre-trial custody cases, the personal data of the respondents also reveal that all of them, except six charged with mutiny, were under the command of different COs who took a decision of not placing them under arrest despite the nature of the offences against each. If the same decision was taken by different officers holding the senior rank of

---

31 AA ss 37 , 38, 122(2), Arm y Headquarters New Delhi, let ters No. 42331/PS-1 dated 5/10 F eb 1976 and No. 01086/122/AG/DV-1(P) dated 12 Apr 2001; cf Maj Gen AC Mangala, Commentary on Military Law in India, op cit, Ch 3, n 22, pp 54-55 and Simmons, The Constitution and Practice of Courts Martial, op cit, n 3, pp 86-87 .

32 RA para 432. cf Army Headquarters New Delhi, letter No.32908/AG/DV-1 (P) dated 16 Oct 2000 (para 3) insisting upon CM trial for disposal of such cases.

33 IEA, s 114, Illustration (e).

34 Bimla Devi v Capt. G L Bakshi and others , AIR 1960 J&K 145 (148).

Colonel and commanding about 1000 men in each case, it will be logical to infer that the decision was based on merit rationally considering that there was little possibility of the accused absconding, interfering with evidence and so on, which have been the age-old considerations for arriving at a decision on placing or not placing an accused under arrest. The situation would have been assessed in each case, keeping in mind the security arrangements of the unit, the known character of the accused, his social circle and the particulars of the act, neglect or omission constituting the offence on factual level of the case. It is not possible, from the data at hand, to reconstruct the circumstances of each individual case, nor perhaps is this the need of the present project. However, the punishments meted out to the respondents would suggest suitable inferences in this regard. With this in view, the punishments actually awarded to these 22 respondents, except in the cases of acquittal and of trial not concluded by the time of their interview, are shown in Table 11 below.

TABLE-11

Punishments Awarded in Zero Custody Cases				
Sl. No	Punishment	Response Frequency	Percentage Out of 22	Remark
1.	RI: 1-3 Months	04	18.18	Only 24 days RI in one case.
2.	RI: 3-6 Months	00	00	
3.	RI: 6-9 Months	01	04.5	
4.	RI: 9-24 Months	00	00	Not applicable in the present context.
5.	RI: 24-27 Months	01	04.5	
6.	RI: quantum not disclosed	01	04.5	
7.	Cashiering/Dismissal	03	13.6	Other than mandatory punishment[35]
8.	Other punishments as reduction in rank etc.	04	18.18	-
9.	No punishment	01	04.5	Acquittal
10.	Not known	06	27.29	Trial not concluded
11.	No response	01	04.5	
	Total	22	99.75 (100)	

35 An officer shall be sentenced to be cashiered before he is awarded any of the punishments of death,

The data in Table 11 disclose that only 7 respondents were awarded imprisonment as punishment. Out of these 7, only two were awarded imprisonment for a period of 6 months or more, 1 being awarded exactly 6 months imprisonment and one 24 months imprisonment. One respondent was awarded imprisonment but the quantum of imprisonment has not been specified by him. The remaining 4 respondents were awarded imprisonment for a period varying from 1 month or less to 3 months in each case. From the rest of the respondents, three were dismissed from the Service or cashiered and four were awarded much milder punishments like forfeiture of service for promotion etc. Thus, the punishments actually awarded to these 22 no pre-trial custody respondents stand nowhere in comparison to the maximum liability of punishment prescribed for the offences they were charged with. This fact apparently suggests that the factual particulars of the offences in their cases were either not significantly grave or there existed some important extenuating circumstances in all these cases to treat the offences as much less serious than the general nature of the offence conceptually expected. This state of things would have prompted the concerned authorities not to take the respondents into custody. The authorities would have been guided by the spirit that the existence of the power to arrest is one thing, the justification for the exercise of it is quite another.[36]

5.5 Other Cases

For the justification of power to arrest vested in the commanders, the data given within brackets, in Table 10, to show the number of respondents who were kept in military custody before their trial may be examined. It is interesting to note that the number of those who remained in custody and of those who did not, vary by just one in most cases except in the cases of the civil offences. This may be briefly shown as under (excluding the offences involving only one category, i.e., either only custody or only 'no custody' in all the cases of the offence in question):

---

contd/-

imprisonment for life or any imprisonment for 14 years or less (AA s 74). A JCO, though not covered with this mandate, is also generally awarded dismissal in such a case except when sentence to death (RA para 167). A WO, NCO or Sepoy is also similarly awarded dismissal when awarded imprisonment for life or imprisonment more than 3 months which is carried out in civil prison. A WO or NCO sentenced by CM to imprisonment for life or dismissal shall be deemed to be reduced to the ranks but in practice he is formally awarded such reduction in such a case (AA s 77 and note thereunder).

36 Joginder Kumar v State of UP op cit n.2; p1353 (para 24).

TABLE -12

Offence-wise Data of Custody and No Custody Cases

	Army Act sections of Offences					IPC ss302	304	375	304A	OSA
	38	39	52	75	69					
Custody	02	07	01	02	15	06	02	01	02	04
No Custody	01	06	03	01	02	IPC ss 392	01	IPC ss 354	01	

Thus, almost equal number of the respondents charged with an offence (other than civil offence) remained in custody and free from custody awaiting trial for the same offence. The details of the length of pre-trial custody, in the available data, show that it varied from 02 days to 3 years. The punishment awarded to the respondents who did remain in pre-trial custody also widely varied from 24 days for AWL to 14 years RI in a case under Official Secret Act and imprisonment for life in all cases of murder. This is understandable in view of the gravity of the offence involved in the cases of murder and the offence of AWL being comparatively a much milder offence.[37] What, however, is important to emphasize here is that the respondents involved in the offences of murder, culpable homicide not amounting to murder, rape and the offences under Official Secrets Act were all kept in pre-trial custody. The offences commonly shared by those kept in custody and those not so kept, as displayed in Table 12, were the offences under AA ss 38, 39, 52, 57 and 69 only technically, the actual acts or omissions involved in those offences being different. The punishments awarded to the accused respondents of the two categories on these shared offences (except the civil offence cases which cannot be compared since those involved different individual offences) may be comparatively shown as in Table 13 on the next page.

---

37 The offence of AWL, which is punishable with 3 years imprisonment at the maximum, and the offence of desertion, which may be punished with death on active service or less punishment and with 7 year imprisonment or less punishment elsewhere, both involve unauthorized absence, i.e. , the absence from the place where the offender knew or ought to have known, that his duty required him to be. The distinction between the two "must depend on the animus. If there is animus desrendi, the absence is straightaway :desertion"; Capt. Virender Kumar (through his wife) v Chief of the Army Staff, AIR 1986 SC 1060. In other words, desertion is absence without leave accompanied with an intention "either to quit the Service altogether or to avoid some particular duty for which he would be required"; Army Order 43/ 2001/DV-DESERTION. The absence of any such intention in the case of the offence of AWL prevents it from being a very serious offence of desertion and it remains a mild offence of absence without leave simplicitor.

TABLE - 13

Comparative Data of Punishments Awarded to Respondents in Custody and in No Custody

Sl No	Offence	Punishments Awarded to Respondents With Pre-trial Custody	 With no Pre-trial Custody
1.	Desertion (AA s 38)	Two cases: both dismissal.	One Case: forfeiture of service for pension.
2.	AWL (AA s 39)	Seven cases: Dismissal (2), RI 1-3 months (4), acquittal (1).	Six cases: Dismissal (1), RI 1-3 months (4), Reduction (1).
3.	Property offences (AA s 52	One case : RI - 2 year and dismissal	Three Cases: RI 1-6 month (1), Forfeiture of pension (2).
4.	Falsification of Official Documents (AA s 57)	Dismissal (1), trial not yet concluded (1).	One case : Dismissal

On the charge of desertion, two respondents remained in pre-trial custody and on conviction they were both sentenced by CM to dismissal from the Service whereas one respondent, who was kept in no pre-trial custody on the same charge, was, on conviction, awarded mere forfeiture of one year service for the purpose of pension. In the former case, both the respondents were Riflemen (equal to Sepoys) but the latter respondent was a JCO. On the charge of AWL, the punishments awarded to seven respondents (three Riflemen/Gunner all equal to Sepoys, one NCO holding the rank of Naik and three anonymous) who remained in custody included dismissal in two cases, imprisonment from 1-3 months in four cases and no punishment in one case, the accused being acquitted. More or less the same punishments were awarded to the six respondents who remained free from pre-trial custody, except that there was no acquittal and one respondent holding the rank of Hawildar was reduced to the ranks. In the case of property offences, there was only one respondent who remained in pre-trial custody. He was a Head Constable in the Border Security Force (equal to the status of NCO in the Army) and was charged under BSF Act 1968, s. 30(b) for dishonest misappropriation of property belonging to the Government, and s. 19(b) for AWL. On conviction by a General Security Force Court (equal to GCM), he was awarded 2 year imprisonment and dismissal from the Service. The three respondents who remained in no pre-trial custody while similarly charged for the property offence under AA s. 52, along with charges for certain other offences, were all Army Officers. One of them was awarded 6 month imprisonment and cashiering. The sentence of imprisonment in his case was set off partially against the custody period during the trial and remaining portion thereof was remitted by the

Confirming Officer who also commuted cashiering to dismissal. The other two were awarded forfeiture of service for pension. Lastly, the two respondents convicted on the charge of falsification of official documents, one having remained in pre-trial custody and one having been kept in no such custody, were both dismissed from the Service. In the case of one respondent who also remained in pre-trial custody facing the same charge, the trial by CM was not yet concluded by the time of his interview. This comparative analysis of punishments awarded on a charge for the same offence in the case of those who remained in pre-trial custody and those who did not, brings out no significant difference in the punishments awarded in the two cases. This suggests that in the cases of offences other than civil offences, the gravity of the offence involved in the charge and the nature of the act, neglect or omission constituting the offence could be a sufficient condition for placing the offender in pre-trial custody but it would not be a necessary condition. Certain other variables seem to cause the effect of a decision on pre-trial custody in such cases.

The decision to place in pre-trial custody in the remaining 26 cases also appears to have been made pragmatically. Six of them (22.2% of 27 pre-trial custody cases) were charged with the offence of murder, 2 (7.4%) with culpable homicide not amounting to murder, 1 (3.7%) with rape and 4(14.8%) under the Official Secrets Act. All these charges being severely punishable, the decision to place the concerned respondents in military custody would be in conformity with the requirement that if "the charge is a serious one, such as, murder, mutiny, and other similar serious offences, close arrest in the case of officers, junior commissioned officers and non-commissioned officers and confinement in the case of others may generally be regarded as the proper action to take, whereas in the case of minor offences, open arrest is normally resorted to. At the same time, there may be cases where the circumstances may not justify any placing under arrest at all."[38]

5.6 Need to make Example

The need to make an example by an immediate arrest of the offender to meet the ends of discipline[39] is one of the considerations for a military authority to decide whether to take an offender into military custody or not, on his being charged with an offence. Such a decision for making an example would generally be taken with reference to circumstances other than those connected with the individual offender. When there is a

38 Nayudu, Handbook of Mi litary Law, op ci t, n 5, p 6, (The author, holding the r ank of Major, was an officer in the JAG's Department in India during pre-Independence era. He later joined the Navy and subsequently became the Chief Justice of Assam High Court; 'History of the Department of Judge Advocate General', 2001, New Delhi, Lancer Publ ishers and Distributors, p 14).

39 Ibid. The prevalence of offence is similarly a criterion for awarding a severe punishment to make an example, for an offence which would otherwise receive a more lenient punishment. This is done from the point of view of the effect which it will produce on the force to which the offender belongs than the offender himsel f; MML V ol I, p42 "Consider ations af fecting sentence".

general prevalence of offences or of the offence of a particular kind, an example may be necessary. On factual level, any controlled or uncontrolled observation of the Service life will bring out that the commonly committed offences in the Armed Forces are AWL, desertion, act prejudicial to good order and discipline and offences towards superiors. Under the influence of our present day socio-economic environment, the offences relating to Government and regimental property are also on fast increase in the Services.[40] This may be borne out from five year figures (1985-1989) of ten military offences tried by CM as presented in Table - 14.

TABLE- 14

Ten Main Offences Tried by CM 1985-89

Sl No	Offences	Year Wise Incidence of Offences					Total	%
		1985	1986	1987	1988	1989		
1.	Mutiny (AAs.37)	252	42	01	02	05	302	03.32
2.	Desertion (AA s. 38)	1046	471	382	313	268	2480	27.22
3.	AWL (AA s.39)	582	605	599	550	752	3088	33.89
4.	Striking, insubordination, disobedience of superiors (AA ss 40 &41)	110	120	114	101	114	559	06.14
5.	Intoxication (AA s.48)	30	29	34	28	40	161	01.77
6.	Property Offences (AA s.52)	121	163	129	128	112	653	07.17
7.	Act prejudicial to good order and mil. discipline (AA s.63)	564	194	133	184	138	1213	13.32
8.	Murder and Culpable Homicide (AA s.69 read with IPC ss.302 and 304)	11	14	03	14	14	56	00.61
9.	Vehicular 'accident' causing death by rash or negligent act (AA s.69 read with IPC s.304-A)	91	97	93	100	124	505	05.54
10.	Sexual Offences (AA s. 69 read with IPC ss 354, 376 and 377)	09	15	28	20	21	93	01.02
	Total	2816	1750	1516	1440	1588	9110	(100.00)

40 Lt. Col R.G. Vidhu "Common Service Offences", Sainik Samachar (Military Justice Special) 15 & 22 July 1990, pp 9-11.

The data at Srl No.1 in Table 14 show that the offence of mutiny is not an offence of general prevalence. Its share in the total number of 9110 cases tried by CM on ten main offences over a period of five years is just 03.32%. In fact, this would have been much less but for a disproportionately large number of 252 mutiny cases in the year 1985, with a spill over to the next year too in 42 cases, and the incidence thereafter going down to a single digit in the three years to follow. Any student of the military history of India would easily see the reason for such an inflated incidence of this offence in the year 1985 which followed the Operation Blue Star. As an aftermath, there was unrest in four Sikh army units (out of 400) and some men mutinied.[41] This, however, seems to be a subdued statement on the subject. According to an eminent defence observer of the present day military activity in India, no single event in the modern Indian history has so affected the armed forces as the Sikh/Punjab crisis of 1983-84.[42]

The six respondents of the present study who were charged with the offence of mutiny had no connection with the Operation Blue Star being so far off in terms of time. They, however, all belonged to one unit, i.e., 3 Arty Bde Signal Company, as usually happens in the case of mutiny. The CO of the accused respondents might have felt no need to place them under arrest to make an example since the offence of mutiny, though very serious, is not an offence of general prevalence. Then, at entry no. 2 of Table 10 is the respondent JCO charged with desertion but placed in no custody. His other responses in the Interview Schedule disclose that he pleaded 'Guilty' to the charge, the CM thereafter sentencing him lightly to mere one year forfeiture of service for the purpose of pension. As for the two respondents of Sepoy rank charged with the same offence of desertion but kept in pre-trial custody, one for 18 days and the other for 20 days, both were finally dismissed from the Service by the CM that tried and convicted them. It appears that in their cases, their respective COs, i.e., the officer commanding 12th Battalion of the Assam Rifles in one case and the officer commanding 21st Battalion of the Assam Rifles in the other, were guided in their decisions (to place them under arrest, try them by SCM within a short period of less than one month and award them heavy punishment of dismissal,) by the need to make an example in the interest of unit discipline and deter thereby other unit personnel from committing the offence. The same does not seem to be the case in respect of 13 respondents charged with the offence of AWL. Six of them remained in no pre-trial custody and seven remained in such custody for various lengths of time from 2 days to 3 months. Their trials by CM resulted into acquittal in one case and various punishments being awarded in the remaining cases as discussed earlier in detail. The pre-trial custody in the case of these seven respondents does not seem to

---

41 Lt Gen E V V as, Fools and I nfantrymen, 1995, Meerut, K artikeya Publ ications, p 271.

42 Stephen Cohen, "The Mi litary in I ndia's Democracy", in Atul Kohli, India's Democracy : An Analysis of the Changing State & Society Relations, 1988, Princeton Press, p 135.

have been ordered to make an example since the offence of AWL is taken lightly, the preferred forum for the offence being summary disposal, if the duration of absence involved is short, and SCM if the duration is longer. The details of the remaining cases also do not disclose the need of making an example having been involved therein. An interesting aspect of the data concerning these cases is that the respondents kept in military custody were all OR, whereas none of the officer respondents remained in pre-trial custody except two officer respondents involved in the charge of the falsification of official documents along with a few more charges. In this situation, the first reaction that one would have is to feel curious as to whether any rank discrimination was at the root of the matter.

5.7 Rank Discrimination in Pre-trial Custody

In the Armed Forces, where rank is characteristic feature of the system, being a command necessity, complaints of rank discrimination could be frequently heard in whispering speech, if not loudly. The European Court of Human Rights (hereinafter referred to as 'ECHR') was approached by five Dutch Soldiers with a complaint of rank discrimination in the matters of arrest. They were subjected to 'aggravated arrest' by their CO under disciplinary proceedings, which, according to the complainants was discrimination in violation of Articles 5 and 6 (freedom from unlawful detention and right to fair trial, respectively) of the European Convention on Human rights, since 'aggravated arrest' could be imposed on Other Ranks (OR) but not on officers under the Dutch system.[43] ECHR, however, ruled that such a provision was not objectionable since each rank bore different responsibility and distinct methods suited to each category were necessary.[44] In our own case, the Supreme Court upheld the 'distinction' between officers and other persons made by the erstwhile rules 22-25 of the AR by requiring a mandatory hearing of the charge by the CO in the case of the latter but not the former. Rejecting the contention of a violation of Article 21 of the Constitution by such provisions in the case of officers, the apex court ruled that "an officer would be a person belonging to the upper bracket of the Armed Forces ... the necessary presumption being that he is highly educated, knowledgeable, intelligent" and therefore, such a hearing being conducted in his case "if the officer so requires" is "quite rational and understandable".[45]

43 The Dutch Military Discipline Act, 1903, provides for 'aggravated arrest' for which the offender would be locked in a cell and prevented from performing his normal duties or was confined to a disciplinary unit. In the 'light arrest' which is applicable to all ranks, a soldier is confined to barracks and an officer to his quarter but both are not excluded from performing their normal duties; Peter J Rowe, "Military Justice within the British Army"', Military Law Review, Vol 94.1981, pp 99-134 , p 123.

44 Judgment of 8 June 1976, Series A, No.22 cit by Peter J Rowe, ibid, pp 121-124.

45 Lt. Col Prithi Pal Singh Bedi v UOI, AIR 1982 SC 1413 (1434); cf . UOI v Hav/Clk SC Bagari, AIR 1999 SC 1412, upholding the availability of study leave to officers but not OR and observing that "legislature while creating different classes of officers (like commissioned officers, JCOs and NCOs) has classified them

Perhaps for the same consideration, officers have traditionally been privileged of being generally placed under 'open arrest' while others are kept in 'close arrest'. The theory advanced to explain this practice is that in the case of an officer "the possession by him of a commission, which would be in danger of being forfeited if he violated his parole and escaped, is sufficient security answering to bail at the criminal law, for his not withdrawing himself from military custody and for his appearance before the Court for trial at the appointed time.[46] Thus, the officer gives bail in the value of his commission.[47] In the case of a soldier, military superior, if liberty allowed to the prisoner, would not have that security against his escape.[48] Such a security, however, is no more available in the case of an officer when the practice of buying commission in monetary terms, which was prevalent in England in olden days, has become a history. What, however, still holds good as a check against escape from custody, in the case of officers, is an imponderable value of the pride and honour attached to the status as a commissioned officer of the Armed Forces and the officer-like quality (OQ). Any dereliction of "an officer for not being also a gentleman" "is to be looked down upon in his social circle, apart from also attracting the jurisdiction of a CM which has traditionally been known as a "court of honour" [49] for the reason of punishing a dishonourable conduct, " a dereliction not being cognizable by any other specie of tribunal".[50] A fear of social condemnation serves as some sort of a security against escape in the case of commissioned officers. The surmise gets support from the fact that there have been hardly any cases of officers escaping from military custody except one odd attempt to exhaust limitation period.[51]

All this discussion suggests that the status of the eight officers respondents (80% of the total 10 officers) included in the category of the 22 respondents who were not placed

---

on the basis of the r equirement of Armed F orces and this classi fication cannot be said to be arbi trary.... We are, therefore, of the opinion that there is no question of violation of provisions of Articles 14 and 16 of the Consti tution."

46 Winthrop, Military Law and Precedents, op cit, n.21, p 114.

47 Clode, Administration of Justice under Military or Martial Law, 1874, p 113 cit in O P Sharma, Military Law in India, op cit, Ch 1, n 4, p 115.

48 Winthrop, Military Law and Precedents, loc cit, n 46, p 124.

49 Ibid, p 54.

50 Nott J, in Fletcher v US, 26 Ct C l563.

51 UOI v Maj Gen ML Y adav (Rtd.), AIR 1996 SC 1340. Ha ving retired on 31 A ug 1987, the officer was in open arrest for his trial to commence on 25 Feb 1987 when he escaped on 16 Feb 1987 and surrendered two weeks later on 01 Mar 1987 . On his peti tion against his trial to commence after the expiry of the prescribed 6 month period of limitation (now 3 years after AA amendments of 1992), the Bombay HC allowed his petition but the Supreme Court held that the CM trial must be deemed to have commenced the moment the GCM assembled on 25 Feb 1987 and examination of the charges was undertaken.

in military custody during pre-trial investigation might have made its own contribution to the decision against their arrest, despite the nature of the charges they were facing with liability of punishments ranging from 7 years to 14 years imprisonment. In one case, even the concerned respondent was amazed enough at the situation to remark, "This was a great CM where the accused was neither placed under closed or open arrest...." However, it appears that in addition to the status of the respondents, there were certain other factors too which influenced the decision in each case. For instance, one such respondent,[52] who was charged under AA s. 69 read with IPC s. 392 and was later tried by SGCM for having committed robbery on 11 Dec 1971 at Hajiganj while serving in Bangla Desh, had taken a plea in defence that he was motivated with a desire to deprive the enemy of the resources. This might have led to a perception that he was moved by a false sense of patriotism and bravado rather than any criminal intention while committing the offensive act and hence no need of arrest might have been felt in his case. His present status as an advocate and his high academic achievement of Ph D in Military Law would perhaps vindicate the decision of trusting him. However, irrespective of the trust generally reposed in an officer accused for refraining from a dishonourable conduct of escaping from lawful custody, he would not enjoy any immunity from arrest merely on the basis of his status as an officer, if other circumstances warrant his detention in custody. This is evident from the data in Tables 9 and 10 which include two officer respondents (20% of the total ten officers respondents tried by CM) who were kept in pre-trial custody for varying lengths of time. One of them held the rank of Major General and remained in pre-trial custody for nine months.

Thus, there seems to be no rank discrimination involved in the matters of pre-trial custody of the respondents. Whatever consideration appears to have been given to their status as officers in the case of some respondents, who were placed in no pre-trial custody, would be justifiable for the reasons given by ECHR and our own Supreme Court to uphold a distinct treatment to be given to the officer class.

5.8 Constitutional Perspective

As already discussed, 22 (44%) of the total 50 respondents tried by CM remained free from any pre-trial custody altogether. From the remaining 28, another 8(16%), included in the data at Srl 2 of Table 9, spent in custody less than one month in each case, the actual periods ranging from 2 to 20 days. Thus, 60% of the undertrials interviewed in the present study remained either absolutely free or spent insignificantly short period in pre-trial custody. From the rest of them only one (2%) was detained in such custody for the longest period of 36 months while others charged with serious offences like murder, culpable homicide and rape etc. or numerous Service offences

52 Respondent No.A-186-A-7.

were in such custody for 1-6 months in two (4%) cases, 6-12 months in 5(10%) cases, 12-18 months in 2 (4%) cases and 18-24 months in 6(12%) cases. This state of pre-trial military custody does not seem to be worrisome when compared with the state of pre-trial custody under the system of our ordinary criminal law where 60% of the arrests were found to be either unnecessary or unjustified.[53] An "appalling" fact of over one lakh undertrial languishing in pre-trial confinement having been noted by the Eighth Law Commission,[54] our apex court underlined the need for a radical change in approach of enacted and administered law, more than two decades back, and directed the release of all such persons who had been in jail for a period longer than the maximum punishment provided in the law for the offence charged.[55] A provision has also since been incorporated in the Cr PC for release of anyone who has been in custody awaiting trial for half of the maximum period of sentence laid down for the offence in its penal clause.[56] And yet one would still come across cases such as that of Armagam Munnaswami Kounder who spent long agonizing eleven years in Yerawada Central Jail Pune, five at pre-trial stage and six thereafter, on his conviction in April 2000, before he was released on the direction of the Bombay High Court taking cognizance, in October 2006, of a suicide note by police inspector Iqbal Bargir that Kounder was falsely implicated by the Police on a charge of murder and rape of six year old girl in June 1995.[57] A still worse case is that of Yakub Punaiya Nadar, who in his youthful age of mid-twenties, would go insane in Arthur Road Jail, Bombay, awaiting trial for the last five years on a charge of murder[58] or the case of those who have been in custody for the last thirteen years in connection with Bombay blasts of 1993 and are not as lucky or well connected as the actor Sanjaya Dutt who could get out of the pre-trial detention after 16 months of arrest for various offences in relation to the same blasts.[59] However, one should guard against any statistically inspired complacence from the comparative data in respect of pre-trial custody under the military system. Statistics, they say, are like Bikini which conceals the vitals and reveal the trivial. It will be meet, therefore, to have an integrated view of the Constitutional perspective involved in the cases under study.

---

53 Third Report of the National Police Commission, January 1980.

54 Law Commission of India, 78th Report, 1979, on congestion of under-trial prisoners in jails.

55 (a) Hussainara Khatoon v Bihar, AIR 1979 SC 1369, (b) Hussainara Khatoon v Home Secretary Bihar, AIR 1979 SC 1819 (C) Hussainara Khatoon v State of Bihar, AIR 1979 SC 1377 (d) Veena Sethi v Bihar AIR 1983 SC 339.

56 CrPC s 436-A.

57 Gitesh Shelke, "Innocent man freed after 11 yrs in jail", TOI, 17 Oct 2006, p 6.

58 Kartikeya, "Undertrial goes insane waiting for case to end", TOI, 16 Oct 2006 p. 6.

59 "He's No Khalnayak – Apply Sanjay Dutt yardstick to all TADA, POTA accused", TOI, 29 Nov 2006, p 16, Editorial-1.

(a) **Length of Custody Period**

If life means something more than mere animal existence, as Field, J[60], would say, personal liberty would claim the first place among the constituents of such life. It is personal liberty that makes for the worth of the human person.[61] Life and personal liberty are therefore bracketed together in the Constitutional mandate that no person shall be deprived of his life or personal liberty except according to procedure established by law.[62] The 'procedure' contemplated here means a fair and not merely a formal procedure and 'law' would stand for a reasonable law and not any enacted piece. This makes the words "procedure established by law" by and large synonymous to the "procedural due process" of the US Constitutional law.[63] Applying this to the duration of custody period, the first requirement would be to insist that an arrested person is not kept in custody a minute longer than is necessary for the investigation[64] or for other lawful ends such as prevention of interference with the evidence etc.

With a view to properly regulating pre-trial arrest and custodial period, the Service law requires that the investigation of the charge thereafter should take place "without any unnecessary delay" within 48 hours[65] beyond which the fact of detention together with reasons thereof "shall be reported" by the CO to the prescribed superior authority.[66] When an accused person is remanded for further investigation or for trial by CM, it is the duty of the CO to decide whether the accused may be released, without prejudice to re-arrest, until trial or until further orders.[67] In case the accused is detained in custody

---

60 94 US 113 (1877).

61 Krishna Iyer J in Maneka Gandhi v Union of India, AIR 1978 SC 597.

62 The Constitution of India, Article 21.

63 Krishna Iyer J, in Maneka Gandhi's case, loc cit, n 61.

64 State v Ram Autar Chaudhary, 1955 Crl J 394 (Allahabad).

65 NA ss 85, 86; the latter provision further requires that "as soon as may be, either the proceedings shall be taken for the trial or such person (detainee) shall be discharged from custody". The period of 48 hours figures in such context not only in our three Services Acts but also under Br AA s 75 C in respect of custody review and under the US Law probable cause review by a neutral and detached officers under RCM 305(c)(1).

66 AA s 102; AFA s 103; a similar report by CO to the convening authority alongwith reasons is required beyond 48 hours under the Australian law too; Wing Commander Frank B Healy, "Australian Military Justice System", Air Force Law Review, Vol 52, 2002, pp 93-136 (108) and the Defence Force Discipline Act, 1982 (hereinafter referred to as 'DFDA') (c th) s 95(4).

67 RA para 392 (j); In the case of an officer, once the arrest has been reported to superior authority, it would not be proper to order the release without the sanction of such superior authority. Further, if an officer is released unconditionally, i.e., not without prejudice to re-arrest, he will normally not be re-arrested on the same charge unless circumstances have changed and some new conditions have arisen which justify his re-arrest, Nayudu, Handbook of Military Law, op cit, n.5 pp 7, 8.

beyond 8 days, the CO shall make a special report, at intervals of every 8 days, to the officer empowered to convene a GCM or DCM until a CM is ordered in the case or the case is summarily disposed or the accused is released[68] by the CO or by an order of the superior officer to whom such report was addressed and who has the responsibility of satisfying himself, on receipt of the report, as to the necessity for the offender's continuance in custody.[69] A copy of such report, on or after the 48th day of custody shall be sent direct to the Dy JAG of the Command.[70] In case an accused is to be detained beyond two months, without a CM having been ordered, the prior sanction of the COAS and for beyond three months such sanction of the Central Government are required unless the accused is on active service.[71] No ex post facto sanction can cure the negligence of not taking sanction before hand in every such case and a lapse in this regard may be punishable under the AA and AFA when it amounts to unnecessarily detaining a person in arrest or confinement without bringing him to trial or without investigating the case.[72] The latest addition to these pre-trial custody regulating measures are the guidelines issued by the Army Headquarters in matters of discipline relating to women officers which inter alia require that a woman officer may be ordered under close/open arrest by any officer but it will be effected by two persons one of which shall be a woman officer. While under close arrest, she shall, all the time be under an escort of another

---

68 AA s 103 read with AR r 27; AFA s 104 read with AFR r 23. Similar 8 days report is required from the CO to the convening authority under DFDA, s 95(5). The period of 8 days also figures in Br AA s75F in the context of custody to be authorized by a Judicial Officer (JO). Similarly RCM 305(c)(2) under the US system also requires a 7 day review of pre-trial confinement by a neutral and detached officer. This military law universality of 7-8 days period in the context of pre-trial custody appears to be based on such period being generally considered adequate to resolve the conflicting interests of individual liberty and the security of collective community.

69 RA para 408 (a).

70 AR 27(3) and AFR 23(2). The powers of the Dy JAG to be exercised on receipt of a copy of the report are not defined under the Indian military law. He may use his inherent power and duty to suitably advise the General Officer Commanding-in-Chief of the Command concerned and seek his intervention, if need be, to secure the release of the accused or to expedite the further disciplinary proceedings. Under the British law, however, the JOs appointed by the JAG play a direct role in the custody review under Br AA s 75G read with Army Custody Rules, 2000, rr 18-23.

71 AR r 27(3) and AFR rr 2(2) & (3); Under the Australian law, the convening officer must notify the reasons for delay beyond 30 days to a Chief of Staff who must order the release of the person unless satisfied that it is proper to let him continue in custody; DFDA, s 95(8) (9).

72 AA s 50(a); AFA s 50(a); RA para 208(b); AHQ letter No8426/AG/DV-1 dated 19 Jan 1993 cit in Maj Gen Nilendra Kumar, Case Studies in Military Law, 2003, Delhi, Universal Law Publishing Co. Pvt. Ltd., p 102; cf Bhuneshwar Singh v UOI, AIR 1993 SCW 3072 holding that the authorities could not be permitted to deal with the liberty of a person subject to AA in a casual manner and awarding Rs.30000/- as compensation to the petitioner kept under pre-trial custody illegally beyond 3 months, despite the Court finding no cause to interfere with the proceedings which followed such detention; cf Br AA s 53 for stringent provision to ensure that no person is kept in arrest unreasonably and without justification.

woman officer and will under no circumstances be kept under a male escort.[73] These instructions may not have the status of law as contemplated in Article 21 of the Constitution[74] but being in conformity with the directions of the Bombay High Court passed in the case of Jarina Adam[75] in 1996 (which have since been modified by the Supreme Court in 2003) should keep the matters well within control in relation to the pre-trial military custody of women offenders in the Army. Similar instructions issued from the Air Headquarters were put into practice when Flying Officer Anjali Gupta was taken into custody on 28 April 2005 so as "to prevent her from harming herself."[76] With these checks and balances in place, even one case of a long pre-trial custody of 3 years and six cases of 18-24 months custody, two of 12-18 months and five of 6-12 months, apart from two cases of 1-6 months custody, as reflected in Table 9, would arouse curiosity for reasons behind them. To begin with the 3 years long custody case, the available data disclose that the respondent was an NCO from 501 Survey Engineering Group who was arrested by the UP Police in November 2000 for passing information to foreign agents. At the time of interview by this researchers, he had been in custody for about 3 years and was attached with the Rajputana Regimental Centre, Delhi Cantt, alongwith three other co-conspirators for investigation and trial under the AA. The trial was, however, stayed at that time under an order of the Delhi High Court on a writ petition. One of them was tried by a GCM from 12 December 2001 onwards on a charge under AA s 69 read with Official Secrets Act 1923, s 3(1)(c) and his trial concluded on 06 November 2003 after the stay order was vacated. He was convicted of the charge and sentenced to 14 years rigorous imprisonment alongwith reduction to the ranks and

73 AHQ letter No. A156102/AG/DV-1 dated26 June 1996; A/56102/AG/DV-1(P) dated 18 Aug 1997 and 5424/AG/DV-1 (P) dated 21 A ug 2000, the last two ci t in Maj Gen Ni lendra Kumar, Case Studies, ibid p 113 and the first cit in Col G.K. Sharma, Col M S Jaswal, Study and Practice of Military Law, 2006, New Delhi, Deep & Deep Publ ications, Pvt. Ltd. , pp 347-349.

74 Departmental instructions without any statutory authority not held to be law within the ambit of Art 21, Kharak Singh v UP, AIR 1963 SC 1295.

75 Jarina Adam was molested by the police when she went to inquire about her husband Junious Adam Illamatti who had been arrested by the Crime Branch of Nagpur Police on 23 June 1993 and had died in custody. While dealing wi th the case, B ombay High Court issued directions that no f emales would be detained or arrested without a woman constable's presence, specially after sunset. Pronouncing in a case on 16 Oct 2003, the SC modified the direction to the effect that woman constable's presence was not mandatory for the police to arrest a woman at any time of the day or night if it felt that securing her presence would delay the process but the arresting officer in that case would be required to record the reasons for not securing a woman constable' s presence; "Lady cop's presence not must; SC", TOI 17 Oct 2003, p 5. At a workshop on conditions of women in detention organized by Asian Women's Fund at Penang in Jan 03, it emerged that women in detention face multiple discrimination of varying degrees and are particularly vulnerable to human right abuses. This is an almost universal phenomenon not confined to any particular country or r egion; Soli J S orabjee, "Women prisoners & whist le blowers", TOI, 19 Jan 2003.

76 TOI, 20 Apr 2005, "IAF har assment case; Gupta put in custody" , p 7; cf Sugata Sriniv asaraju, "Flight of the Do ve", Out look, 13 Jun 2005, p 30.

dismissal from the Service. Thus, by the time his case concluded, he had been in pre-trial military custody for three years or so. It is to be noted that the respondent and his co-conspirators were not on active service and all the afore-stated checks meant to control pre-trial custody, including the requirement of prior sanction for detention beyond the specified periods of 2 and 3 months were applicable to his case and yet his pretrial custody could spread over three years,[77] which, even after taking into consideration the time during which the disciplinary proceedings remained stayed by an order of the High Court, seem to be quite excessive. The respondent under discussion was somewhat reticent but his co-accused, respondent A-175-A-10 felt, a need to suggest that "during or before a remand[78] for trial by CM, the accused should be produced before some judicial authority or a responsible Service officer. Nobody, including my CO, took notice of me during the three month long remand" and that he felt aggrieved but could do nothing since he "was not allowed to meet anybody". There is yet another suggestion by another respondent which has a bearing on the 9 month long pre-trial custody that he underwent. The suggestion is that the attachment of an accused should be ordered only after charges are finally framed against him and not when the case is still pending for a decision on charges.[79] With these suggestions and the discussed facts, one need not go into individual data of the rest of the detainees to conclude that there is a felt need for review of the existing provisions and instructions to make them practically effective rising above the state of mere an exercise in reports and returns.

(b) Bail and Military Custody

While looking for a mechanism to cut down the length of pre-trial custody under the military system one may stumble over the absence of any provision for bail in military law. The three Services Acts in India are silent altogether on the subject. There is no equivalent of bail under the British military laws[80] either. However, some human rights

---

77 No sanction was required under AR r 27(3) for his detention in custody once the trial by CM had been ordered. This, however, does not affect the human right aspect of such a long custody period before conviction.

78 Remand is "to send a prisoner back to the custody to be kept until the hearing is resumed or the trial comes" such an order being passed "after a preliminary hearing or partial hearing before a Court or Magistrate"; Aiyer's Law Lexicon, 2nd ed, 1997 , Nagpur, Wadhwa & Co ., p1650.

79 Respondent A-208-A-2.

80 Stuart-Smith, James, 'Military Law : Its History, Administration, and Practice', op cit, ch 1, n 26, p 492; Bishop, "Civilian Judges, and Military Justice : Collateral Review of Courts-Martial Convictions", Columbia Law Review, Vol 40, 1961, pp 40-71, at 56; and Gorden D Henderson, "Courts-Martial and the Constitution : The Original Understanding" , Harvard Law Review, Vol 71, 1957 , pp 293-324 at 315-316, make it abundantly clear that bail has never been known to the military law. Please see US ex rel. Watkins v Vissering, Misc No . 722 Ed. V a., 10 Jun 1960; Levy v Resor, 17 CMA 135; 37 CMR 399 (1967) and De Champlain v Lovelace, 23 CMA, 35, 48 CMR 506 (1974) and Hon'ble Walter J Cox III, "The Army, The Courts, and the Constitution: Evolution of Military Justice", Military Law Review, Vol 118, 1987, pp 1-30 at 26 for inapplicability of bail to military justice. Also see Winthrop, Digest of Opinions of the Judge Advocates General (1895-1912), 1912, Washington, Government Printing Office, p 481.

enthusiasts have lately suggested the need of incorporating the provision of bail in the military law,[81] without, of course, elaborating the pros and cons of the proposal.

(i) **Ordinary Criminal Law Concept**

The word "bail" stands for setting an accused person free before he is tried, often on condition that a sum of money is promised to the court to make sure he attends the trial, or for money paid by such a person.[82] The basic provisions of our ordinary criminal law as to bail and bonds are laid down in the Code of Criminal Procedure, 1973 (hereinafter referred to as the 'Cr PC').[83] Broadly speaking, the provisions cater for releasing on bail the persons accused of bailable, non-bailable and capital offences by a prescribed police officer, court of sessions and High Court respectively, on or without conditions. In the case of a bailable offence such a person shall, and in other cases may, be released if he is prepared to give bail. Thus, there is no right for the court or the police to refuse bail in bailable offences[84] whereas in non-bailable cases the question of the grant of bail is to be decided in the light of further considerations such as nature and seriousness of the offence, the character of the evidence, the circumstances which are peculiar to the accused, reasonable possibility of the presence of the accused not being secured at the trial, reasonable apprehension of witnesses being tampered with, the larger interest of the public or state and similar other circumstances.[85] There also exist the provisions for anticipatory bail[86] which were not in the old Cr PC 1898 but were introduced in the Act No. 2 of 1974 (the current Cr PC) at the recommendations of the Law Commission of India.[87] Unlike a post-arrest order of (usual) bail, anticipatory bail is " a pre-arrest legal process which directs that if the person in whose power it is issued is thereafter arrested on the accusation in respect of which the direction is issued, he shall be released on bail.[88] Cr PC also has a provision worth adopting by the military legal system straightaway with suitable adaptations to avoid prolongation of pre-trial custody on default. It provides for a mandatory release on bail any under-trial in judicial custody in whose case the police has not been able to complete investigation and file a

---

81 Wing Commander UC Jha (Rtd), "Military Justice System in India", USI Journal, April-June 2006, p 220-232 (221) and "Military Law needs reform", AIR 2003 J 108.

82 Compact Oxford Reference Dictionary, op cit, n.6, p.55; cf Kali Dass v SO, Police Station, 1979 Cr L J 345 (350) (J&K) "to set free or liberate a person arrested or imprisoned, on taking security for his appearance".

83 Cr PC Ch XXIII (ss 436-450).

84 Abdul Habbi Khan v Emperor, 29 Cr LJ 450; cf Balsara, " Bail and not Jail – empty the Prison", 22 JILI 341 (1980)

85 MP Jayaraj v State of Karnataka, 1977 Cr L J 1724.

86 Cr PC s 438(2).

87 Law Commission of India, 41st Report 1969.

88 Gurbaksh Singh Sibbia v State of Punjab 1980 Cr L J 1125 (1130) (SC).

charge-sheet within 90 days if the offence is punishable with death, imprisonment for life or imprisonment for a term not less than 10 years and within 60 days, in other cases and who is prepared to furnish bail.[89] The object is "to expedite the investigative process so that the accused does not have to languish in jail… while the police goes on with their investigation lethargically.[90] Indeed it is a release on bail on the default of the prosecution in filing charge-sheet within the prescribed period and "may be termed as an order on default". [91]

The statutory provisions in the Cr PC seem to create a limited right to bail. However, keeping in mind the need to be cautious while depriving an accused of his Constitutionally guaranteed right to liberty, the courts have generally adopted a liberal attitude on granting bail, the apex court ruling that an accused should be released on bail if he is indigent and there is no substantial risk of his absconding.[92] In fact a norm evolved in this regard is that bail is the rule and jail an exception in most cases.[93] This approach has influenced even the common man's expectations, including the media, to the extent that the Times of India devoted one full editorial to criticize as "unconscionable" the attempt of the Delhi Police to oppose the bail in the case of Iftikhar Gilani, insisting that "bail should only be denied in the most serious cases."[94] There is a plethora of judicial pronouncements, both from the foreign as well as the Indian courts on different approaches, liberal, strict and balanced, on the question of granting bail, which need not be gone into details in the present context. Suffice to note that the Supreme Court set aside the Allahabad High Court order[95] and also the order of the Orissa High Court[96] granting bail cryptically, in the cases of murder and dowry death respectively, asking the courts to exercise their discretionary power to grant bail in a judicious manner, discussing the reasons for granting bail a little more elaborately. The apex court laid down a three-point guideline for a court seized of a bail plea, which briefly speaking included the nature of accusation alongwith the likely punishment and available evidence, the possibility of the accused tampering with the evidence alongwith an apprehension in the mind of the witnesses and the complainant on threat from the

89 Cr PC s 167 (2) (a)(i)(ii).

90 Feroz v State, 1986 Cr L J 409 (Pat).

91 Rajnikant Jivanlal Patel v Intelligence Officer, Narcotics Control Bureau, 1990 Cr L J 62 (SC).

92 Hussainara Khatoon v Home Secretary, AIR 1979 SC 1360.

93 Rakesh Bhatnagar, "The bail – acquittal syndrome", TOI, 05 April 2004, p5.

94 "Bail for Gilani", TOI, 11 Nov. 2002, ed page, p14 .

95 "SC: Follow directions while granting bail", TOI, 22 Sep 2005, p .6, on Anwari Begum's petition against bail granted by Lucknow Bench of Allahabad HC to Sher Mohammad who had shot dead her husband.

96 Dhananjay Mahapatra, "SC : No easy bail for serious offences"; TOI, 06 Oct 2006, p 7 .

accused and lastly the seriousness of the offence alongwith prima facie case thereon against the accused. Similar considerations were suggested by the National Police Commission for justification of arrest during the investigation of a cognizable offence, enumerating them as, firstly, the case involves a grave offence like murder, dacoity etc and it is necessary to restrain the movements of the accused to infuse confidence among the terror stricken victims; secondly, the accused is likely to abscond and evade the process of law; thirdly, the accused is given to violent behaviour and is likely to commit further offences unless his movements are brought under restraint, and finally, the accused is habitual offender and is likely to commit similar offences again unless kept in custody.[97]

(ii) **Military Justice Aspect**

The guidelines of the Supreme Court and the considerations suggested by the National Police Commission make an interesting comparison with the considerations of the military authorities governing the decision on the arrest in a particular case as pointed out earlier.[98] Both the set of factors being more or less the same, this would mean in practical terms that an accused will not be taken into military custody, in the first instance, in the circumstances in which his counterpart, on commission of a cognizable offence, need not be arrested by the civil police and, if arrested, would be released on bail. Further, if already under arrest but the circumstances do not require the continuation of his detention, the accused in military custody will be released, without prejudice to re-arrest if need be, or the status of his arrest may be changed from 'close' to 'open' arrest[99], identically the way his counterpart under the civil law would be granted bail. The detention of a person subject to AA while in "open arrest is something like bail on certain conditions. In view of Article 33 of the Constitution, the exercise of power under the provisions of Cr PC with reference to bail is not applicable to persons subject to the Army Act." With this premise, the Madras High Court turned down the prayer of the petitioner for ordering the military authorities to release him on bail, bond or guarantee, while under his extended liability for trial by CM, under the AA s. 123.[100]

---

97 The National Police Commission, Third Report, op cit, n 53, p 32; cf Criminal Code of Canada, s 495 prohibiting a Police Officer from arresting a person if having regard to all the circumstances, i.e., the need to establish identity of the person, secure or preserve evidence relating to the offence, prevent the continuation or repetition of the offence or the commission of another offence, he or she behaves on reasonable grounds that public interest may be satisfied without arresting him and has no reasonable grounds to believe that he will fail to attend court.

98 Supra, 5.4 (b); please also see n 39.

99 RA para 392 (j).

100 Lt. Col S P Sharma v Union of India, unreported order dated 06 Feb 1990 in Cr WP No. 754 of 1990 cit in Maj Gen Nilendra Kumar and Rekha Chaturvedi, Law Relating to the Armed Forces in India, op cit, Ch 3, n 22, p 95. The Madras High Court has based its decision on the power of Parliament to modify the

The Services laws all over the world are indifferent to the civil concept of bail because any such provision would not only be redundant but also incongruous in the context of a military system in view of its peculiar ethos. On the redundancy aspect, it may be stated that unlike the civil system where 60% of the arrests were found to be unjustified, suggesting thereby that arrest in ordinary criminal process is perceived, though erroneously, as a necessary adjunct of the investigational process of an offence and hence gives rise to the need of bail in all those cases, a CO in the military system will not as a rule, place an offender under arrest without investigation of the complaint or the circumstances tending to incriminate him. [101] This is evident from the data in the present study bringing out that 8 out of the total 10 officers respondents (i.e., 80%), as reflected in Table 10, remained free from pre-trial custody. Similarly, in the case of a JCO, WO, or NCO, the arrest may be delayed when there is some doubt as to the commission of the offence, and if the offence is not serious, it may be disposed without previous arrest.[102] The data in Table 10 corroborate this too, by disclosing that out of 31 JCO, OR cases, pre-trial custody was ordered only in 20 (64.5%) cases and further details in the responses reveal that 14 out of those 20 (70%) were charged with serious offences like murder (5), culpable homicide (2), rape (1), spying under Official Secret Acts (4) and causing death by rash or negligent act (2). These were the offences, except the last one, in which bail would not be easy to get under ordinary criminal law either and the Supreme Court would expect the trial court to discuss the reasons for granting bail a little more elaborately in all such cases as noted earlier.[103] Briefly put, the arresting authority in the military system generally does not place an accused in pre-trial custody in a case which would attract the provision of bail if tried under the ordinary criminal system. Further, our Service law also includes in the term 'military custody' a kind of arrest, i.e., open arrest which is something like bail, as brought out by the Madras High Court in an earlier referred case[104] and which is comparable to the US concept of restrictions in lieu of arrest.[105] On the other hand, 'close' arrest is normally employed only in the circumstances corresponding to those in which an ordinary criminal court would refuse bail for similar reasons. Nor is an accused kept in open arrest unless it is for some reason felt necessary

---

contd/-

Fundamental Rights in their application to forces etc under Article 33. However, it may be respectfully submitted that the provision of Cr PC with reference to bail is not applicable to persons subject to the AA for the reason of the 'saving' Section 5 of the Cr PC itself, under which nothing contained in the Cr PC "shall... affect any special or local law... or any special jurisdiction".

101 MML, Vol I, p.14, para 3.

102 Ibid, p 15, para 6.

103 Supra n 96.

104 Supra n 100.

105 Supra n 24.

to maintain a limited measure of control over his movements. In the majority of cases, the accused soldier or airman is not placed in arrest at all, or if he has been arrested in the first instance, is released as soon as possible, being merely ordered to present himself at the appropriate place at the appropriate time for such inquiries and proceedings as may be held.[106]

Thus, the provisions and practices of military law leave little room for the introduction of anything like bail in it. The services ethos also makes it redundant from a different angle. "Stone walls do not a prison make", was rightly said by Richard Lovelace. The extent and nature of restraint on the personal liberty and their effect on the prisoner's mind, in the case of military custody, are much different from those in the police custody or civil prison. The usual bonds of Olive Green comradery between the arrester and the arrestee, the escort or guard and the prisoner, and the attitude of the CO as the pater familias towards his subordinates and their family members, wherever they may be, change the very complexion of arrest in the case of the Service personnel. Except arrest related restrictions on movements of the prisoner, nothing drastically changes for him. He puts on the same uniform, eats the same food and chats with the same colleagues, as earlier before his arrest. He also continues to get his pay and allowances as in normal times, subject of course, to deduction thereof on conviction, if any, subsequently.[107] While in custody, he is also not deprived of an opportunity to prepare his defence.[108] Men detained in military custody do even normal military training and are given opportunity for preparation of professional examinations necessary to promote their career interests. All this would keep a person in military custody in a frame of mind much different from that of a suspect in police lock-up or an undertrial in judicial custody in a prison where "Pale Anguish keeps the heavy gate/And the warder is Despair".[109] These differences in the conditions prevailing in the military custody and those in arrest under civil law suggest that the provisions of bail may be much needed under the ordinary criminal law but will be of mere cosmetic value if imported in the military system.

Further, the existing concept of bail would be at odds in the general working conditions of military life. Bail involves the release of an arrested person on monetary security for his appearance to attend criminal investigation or trial against him. In the case of a military offender, the demand of any such security would not only be superfluous but also illogical when he faces, under the military law, grave consequences for the

---

106 Supra n 5, pp.492-493.

107 AA ss 90 (b), 91(b); AF A ss 91(b), 92(b); NA ss 28(2), 29(2).

108 AR r. 33; AFR r. 39; N Regs Pt II (s) reg 172.

109 Oscar Wilde, "The Ballad of Reading Gaol", op cit, n.1.

disobedience of a lawful command[110] that may be given to him for such appearance or the consequences of desertion by escaping to avoid such an important military duty.[111] Additionally, there is also monetary loss to be suffered by him in the form of deductions of pay and allowances for every day of absence[112], if any, involved in his attempt to avoid such appearance. Then, on the grant of bail under the civil system, the offender is free to return home to seek solace in the bosom of his kith and kin from the trauma of incarceration and it also enables him to resume his economic occupation and restart social life. In the case of a military offender released from military custody, none of these would apply. The usual restrictions of military life will not allow him to proceed to his home for emotional comfort. Even if he applies for leave, he will have to wait for its sanction which may or may not come forth depending upon his turn in the leave roster, the state of personnel on parade in the unit[113] and so on. Nor will there be in his case any such thing as resumption of occupation since he was not far from it even while in custody.

Irrespective of the above, the concept of bail under the Cr PC may provide a direction for relief in such cases as the one involved in the earlier referred Madras High Court decision. Like the petitioner in that case, a respondent in the present research project has, while being tried by a CM after his retirement as a Lieut. Colonel, also voiced his concern for the plight of a superannuated soldier who is no more entitled to the privileges of a serving military man and yet in military custody, under his extended liability, to face the proceedings for some allegations related to his past Service life. The respondent suggests that "no restrictions should be imposed on the movements of the accused either by way of putting him under arrest or non-grant of leave during the pendency of the disciplinary case except when an attempt to desert is apprehended on his part and in such a case reason be placed on record for the restrictions imposed." In view of the foregoing discussion, the suggestion needs no further consideration in the context of a serving soldier but is certainly thought provoking for some provision like bail in the case of an ex-service-man so that he can freely engage a counsel for his defence and arrange for funds with the help of his friends and relations. In this regard, he should in fact be

---

110 AA s 41 prescribing 14 years RI for offence on active service and 5 years elsewhere.

111 AA s 38 providing death punishment on active service and seven year imprisonment otherwise and the liability of trial by CM for desertion continuing without any time limitation under AA ss 122 and 123.

112 Supra n 107.

113 Gorden D Henderson, "Courts-Martial and the Consti tution : The Original Understanding" , op ci t, n 80, p 316, expresses a similar view to argue the inapplicability of the Eighth Amendment of the US Constitution (right against excessive bail) to soldiers, citing in his support the views of Ady e, A Treatise on Courts- Martial, 1979, p 139-140 and T ytler, An Essa y on Mi litary Law and the Pr actice of Courts Martial, 1814, p 202 to the effect that bail has never been granted, to members of the military awaiting trial by CM.

treated at par with any offender under the ordinary criminal law, subject, of course, to the limitations of jurisdiction in the case of purely military offences, and be released on bail on suitable monetary security given by him or any other person as under the Cr PC. The three Services Acts may be amended to incorporate appropriate provisions in this regard. Another provision of the Cr PC that may be imported in the military law for application to all cases of pre-trial military custody is the provision for statutory requirement of release, in the case of a person who has been in military custody for a specified period, say 90 days, without prejudice to re-arrest and on the risk of some stringent punishment, like forfeiture of all pay and allowances or service for specified period et al, for default in being available for the proceedings under the military law without any valid reasons. As brought out earlier, provisions already exist in the Services Acts and regulations for release without prejudice to re-arrest. Those may be invested with teeth by providing for compulsory release on the line of the provision of the Cr PC. It may be noted in this context that the Armed Forces Tribunal Act, 2007, does have power to grant bail to any person accused of an offence who is in military custody, except in the cases of the offences punishable with death or imprisonment for life. [114]

(c) **Custody Review**

The bail proceedings followed under the Cr PC may also be utilized with suitable adaptation for use at custody hearing that may be introduced in the Indian military system, on the pattern of the related provisions under the three Services Acts of the United Kingdom as modified by the Armed Forces Act, 2006,[115] so as to ensure that the procedure to be adopted to deprive a person of his life or personal liberty must be "right and just and fair" and "not arbitrary, fanciful or oppressive, otherwise it would be no procedure at all and the requirement of Article 21 would not be satisfied".[116] The existing provisions in our military law in this regard are overly vague and do not set out any narrow and precise circumstances for the release of the accused and also fall short of the test of a fair procedure since the accused has no opportunity to urge any reasons against his continued pre-trial detention. As against this, the British, the US and the Canadian systems elaborately provide for pre-trial custody review. The British law provides to the accused a right to apply in writing to the person who arrested him, or to his CO after the latter has received a report of his arrest, for his release explaining why he thinks he should be released. Accordingly, once the CO has received the arrest report and considers it necessary to keep the accused in custody before charge, the accused

114 The Armed Forces Tribunal Bill, 2005, cl 15(3) and Standing Committee on Defence (2005-2006), Tenth Report, May 2006, Chapter 10, pages 32 and 33.

115 The Armed Forces Act, 2006, will provide the disciplinary mechanism for all the three Services as a combined legislation and has come into force in 2008.

116 Bhagwati J. in Maneka Gandhi op cit, n 61

can make an application to the CO for his release. Generally within 48 hours, and in every case within 96 hours, from arrest, the accused is to be taken before Judicial Officer (hereinafter referred to as ('JO'),[117] either in person or by video teleconferencing, for a decision on further custody, if the CO so applied, prior to which the CO must inform the accused of his intention to so apply, in writing with reasons therefor. The accused has a right to be present at a hearing before JO and also has a right to be legally represented at the hearing. The CO may also be legally represented. The JO has the power to order the continuation of custody maximum upto 96 hours, from the arrest or surrender, before the charge or to order the release or direct that the accused be charged. After the charge, the CO has to apply to the Court Administration Officer (an officer or other person, independent of command, appointed by the Defence Council to convene GCM and DCM and perform other prescribed functions, including the arranging of custody hearing by JO) for hearing with the JO, giving again a notice to the accused of his intention and the grounds therefor alongwith relevant information on the rights of the accused at the hearing. The accused or his legal adviser, arranged by him independently or under the Service legal aid scheme (which would provide him the services of a civilian lawyer or counsel from the Royal Navy or Royal Air Force), may address the JO at the hearing. At the first hearing after the charge, the JO may allow the accused to be kept in custody for a maximum period of 8 days or less, if he is satisfied on any of the grounds specified in the Act expressly, or may refuse the CO's application in which case the accused is to be released without delay. If the custody continues, the case is to be reviewed not later than the period for which the custody was authorised, i.e., 8 days or less. If the accused, in the presence of his lawyer, states that he does not wish the review to be made after every 8 days, the JO may agree to review the custody after 28 days or may agree to release the accused if the CO feels that the reasons for the custody no more apply. If the case proceeds to CM trial, similar rules apply for custody review thereafter, except that the decision is made by the JA[118] instead of the JO earlier. The US law also provides for reviews of pre-trial confinement in military custody by 'a neutral and detached officer' appointed in accordance with regulations prescribed by the Secretary concerned. The first review is made within 48 hours of the imposition of confinement to

---

117 The JO is a legally qualified person, usually a civilian but at times a Naval Judge Advocate, appointed a JO b y the or der of the Judge Adv ocate Gener al under B r AA & AF A, s 75 L(1)(2) and NDA s 47A -K. Armed Forces Act 2006 assigns this task to Judge Advocates in place of JO and devotes its entire Part 4, with full three chapters therein to deal with custody and its review, retaining practically the earlier legal position in this regard with minor changes.

118 Br AA & AF A ss 75- A, 75-B, 75-C, 75-F , 75-G, 75-H and Custody and Summary Deal ing (Arm y) Regulations, 2000 rr 9, 20 and 21 and Sch 2; Army Custody Rules 2000, rr 11, 13, 14, 15 and 19 and (Royal Air Force) Regulations 2000 and NDA ss 47A-K; Rant, Courts-Martial, Discipline, And the Criminal Process in the Armed S ervices', op ci t, n 24 , pp36-53 and 308; Armed F orces Act 2006, ss98-111.

determine the adequacy of probable cause to continue such confinement. Thereafter, if the accused is still in confinement, there will be a review of the confinement on every 7th day. Once the charges are referred for trial, the military judge shall review the propriety of pre-trial confinement upon motion for appropriate relief.[119] The prisoner and his counsel shall be allowed to appear before the 7-day reviewing officer and make a statement, if practicable. The procedure of review and representation in cases of pre-trial military custody also exist in the Canadian military system, which inter alia provides for the review of pre-trial custody by a custody review officer. His decision to allow the continuance of custody is further reviewable by a military judge and his decision for release may be reviewed by an officer in the chain of command, with an opportunity to be heard given to both the sides, i.e., a representative of the Canadian Force and the person released. It is now being recommended that the latter review of the decision should also be made by military judge. [120] Suitable provisions for the custody review may also be incorporated in our military law, taking into account our own Constitutional requirements of Article 21, the salutary provisions of our Cr PC Sec 167 (2)(a)(i)(ii) and the experience gained in other military systems in respect of their provisions relating to custody review.

(d) **Information to Kin**

Every person who is arrested and detained in custody has a right to consult, and to be defended by, a legal practitioner of his choice. [121] Such a right being the only ray of hope to regain his personal liberty by showing the illegality of his arrest is by far the most important right available to him during his detention but will be of no avail if he is not aware of it or of the course to be adopted to materialize it or has no access to the assistance of his friends and relations to select, contact and engage a suitable lawyer for this purpose. A dismissed NCO of the Pioneer Corps (respondent A-178-A-10), who was undergoing imprisonment for life in the Tihar Jail, lamented over his having been denied an access to anyone from his family or any lawyer while in pre-trial custody on a charge of murder. Though a civil counsel was engaged, at government expense, to represent him at his trial by a GCM, he felt that he was unjustly convicted since, according to him, even the lawyer, who was a retired Colonel, did not listen to him. Another

119 RCM, R. 305 (c) (d)(1)(2) and (j).

120 The First Independent Review by the Right Honourable Antonio Lamer, PC, CC, CD, of the provisions and operation of Bill C-25, An Act to amend the National Defence Act and to make consequential amendments to other Acts, required under Section 96 of Canada 1998 C-35, submitted to the Minister of Defence, September 3, 2003 (hereinafter referred to as 'Lamer, Independent Review of Bill 'C-25'), website www/forces.gc.ca/site/reports/reviews/en/report_e.pdf, p 52; (Canadian) National Defence Act, 1950 (as last amended 1998), ss 158 and 159. Military judges have at least 10 years' standing at the bar of a province as a pre-requisite for appointment and are appointed by the Ministry of National Defence.

121 Constitution of India, Article 22 (1).

respondent, as noted earlier, has also complained that he was not allowed to meet anybody while in custody on charges under Official Secrets Act and hence could make no representation about certain irregularities in pre-trial proceedings of which he felt aggrieved. These cases may not be representative of such a state of helplessness, while in pre-trial military custody, being only 2 (4%) out of total 50, but certainly illustrate the violation of important rights "inherent in Article 21 and 22 (1) of the Constitution" that " an arrested person being held in custody is entitled, if he so requests, to have one friend, relative or other person, who is known to him, or is likely to take an interest in his welfare, told as far as practicable, that he has been arrested and where is being detained.[122]" The police officer, (analogically the arresting officer under the Service law) is charged with the responsibility of informing the arrested person of this right and the Magistrate before whom he is produced (the CO, under the Service law) to satisfy himself that these requirements have been complied with. Further, these requirements are directed to "be followed in all cases of arrest till legal provisions are made in this regard" and these rights" to be recognized and scrupulously protected." Such a right of the arrested person is well recognised in England under the ordinary criminal law.[123] In the military law, the Treatment and Questioning Code, provides that a person arrested and held in close arrest by or at the request of the Service police, may have one person, known to him or who is likely to take interest in his welfare, informed at public expense, of his whereabouts, as soon as practicable. If the person, he selects, cannot be contacted, he may choose upto two substitutes. He should also be allowed to send a letter and speak telephonically to one such person for a reasonable time, except when the Service policeman considers that this may result into interference with evidence on a serious Service offence or physical harm to others or the alerting of other suspects yet not arrested or hindrance in the recovery of a property obtained through the offence. The suspect must be told of these rights at the time of his arrest or as soon as practicable afterwards and must be permitted to exercise the rights within 36 hours from the time of his arrest and his CO must be informed of his arrest as soon as practicable.[124] Under the Australian military law too, a person in custody in respect of a Service offence is entitled to communicate with a friend or relative and also with a legal practitioner of his choice.[125] These provisions of the foreign military laws may serve as guidance while giving effect to the directions of the apex court, noted earlier, by incorporating in our military law a

122 Joginder Kumar v State of UP, supra n 2, p 1354 paras 25-29; cf DK Basu v State of West Bengal, AIR 1977 SC 610 for similar observations.

123 Police and Criminal Evidence Act, 1984 , s 56(1); cf Richard Clayton and Hugh Tomlinson, Civil Actions Against the Police, p313, cit in Joginder Kumar, ibid, at p 1354 .

124 Rant, Courts-Martial, Discipline, And the Criminal Process in the Armed Services', op cit, n 24, pp 67-68 (ss 3.142-3.148) and 311 (s 9.20).

125 DFDA, s 101 E(1).

provision for right of the arrested person to have a friend or relation informed of his arrest and allow such friend or relation to contact the arrested person so as to render him necessary assistance in his defence.

(e) Legal Assistance

The friend or relation of an arrested person, after being informed of his arrest, may not turn up or may have his own limitations in the task of assisting him in his defence, being not aware of the legal requirements of the military justice. In fact, awareness of military law in general is found to be deficient even among those who are, or are expected to be, otherwise well informed of legal matters. Question 2.2 in the Interview Schedule fetched in this regard the data displayed in Table – 15 collected from the accused category respondents as to whether or not they were, before the trial, aware of the provisions of law and procedure relating to a CM.

TABLE - 15

Pre-trial Awareness of Related Law and Procedure

Srl. No.	State of Awareness	Response frequency Detained	Not Detained	Total	%	Remark
1.	Aware	04	07	11	22	Inc. 9 Officers and 2 NCOs.
2.	Partially aware	01	00	01	02	Aware of right to def. officer only.
3.	Not aware	22	15	37	74	Incl. 2 Officers
4.	No response	01	00	01	02	
	Total	28	22	50	100	

As may be seen from the above tabulated data, as many as 37(74%) out of 50 respondents who were tried by CM had no awareness of the provisions and procedure to be followed in the CM system at its different stages including pre-trial investigation. This also includes two accused persons of the officers' rank, taken to be "highly educated, knowledgeable, intelligent[126]," which fact underlines the need of some mechanism to be

126 Lt Col PPS Bedi v UOI, supra n 45, p.1434.

adopted to make an arrested person aware of his rights in respect of pre-trial military custody. Under the British system, a CO is required to ensure that an accused, before being put to him as charged with an offence, is issued with a standardized pamphlet (Army Code No. 12730) on the "Rights of a Soldier Arrested For or Charged With An Offence Under the Army Act, 1955)" if he is a WO, NCO or Private (equivalent to Sepoy in the Indian Army). If he is in doubt about the contents or his rights generally, the pamphlet advises him to ask for an officer, WO or Senior NCO to assist him. He can also ask for a lawyer to represent him when his case is being investigated by the Royal Military Police or special Investigation Officers in the event of the charge being a serious one. Further, he may as well consult a legal adviser of his own choice, the duty solicitor (where available) or a legal adviser selected by him from a list of persons indicating that they are available for the purpose of providing legal advice. Lastly, the right of the accused to be legally represented at a custody review, as noted earlier, also allows the arrested person to apply for legal aid for the purpose of appointing a person as his "legal adviser" to act for him in connection with such hearing. The person to be so appointed should have a general qualification within the meaning of Courts and Legal Service Act 1990, or should have other prescribed qualification as advocate or solicitor.[127] The US Military law also provides for the right of an accused to retain a civilian counsel at no expenses to the US or to request for the assignment of military counsel, upon being placed in pre-trial confinement and also for his right of being "promptly" informed of such right.[128] Under the Australian military law, a person in custody in respect of a Service offence is entitled to communicate with a legal practitioner of his choice and may also ask for the services of a legal officer, if available, to represent him at CO's hearing.[129] Similarly, the Canadian law also provides for an assisting officer to be appointed as soon as possible after the charge has been laid against a Service personnel[130]. In India, the right of an arrested person to consult and to be defended by a legal practitioner of his own choice has been ruled to arise "as soon as the arrest takes place" and not to be lost on bail.[131] It extends also to an accused "in circumstances of near

---

127 QR 6.0041 for legal aid and Army Custody Rules, 2000, rr 19,20; Air Force Act, 1955 s 75 C(3) and NDA s 47 A-K for custody hearing legal representation.

128 RCM 305(e) (3); the Sixth Amendment of the US Constitution and pronouncements of the US Supreme court in cases like Miranda v Arizona (1966) 384 US 436 and Edward v Arizona (1981) 451 US 477 make it a fundamental right of accused to have his counsel present during custodial interrogation. In US v Tempias, 16 USCMA 629, the US Court of Military Appeal held that the rule of Miranda was fully applicable to the military.

129 DFDA, s 101 E(1).

130 Lamer, Indpendent Review of Bill C-25, op cit, n.120, pp 59-60.

131 M.P. v Shobharam, AIR 1968 SC 1910; Khatu v Bihar AIR 1981 SC 928.

custodial interrogation", though not formally under arrest or custody.[132] However, the legal aid under our criminal law is restricted to trial proceedings and not extended to an accused in pre-trial custody.[133] Similarly, the laws relating to the Army and Air Force have no provision for any legal assistance to an accused during the pre-trial custody. In the case of the Navy, the assistance of an officer or other person in the ship, who may or may not be law qualified, is, however, afforded at the practicably earliest possible stage to an accused, at his request, if the offence is one which may be brought before the CO. If no such request is made, it shall be the duty of the Divisional Officer or such other officer as the CO may detail, to advise the accused at all stages, including the identification parade, if any, and to cross-examine the witnesses on behalf of the accused at investigation of the offence.[134] Similar provisions for "a non-legally-trained officer or other person from the ship" to be provided to the accused for his assistance exist in the British Naval law.[135]Even though the differences between the provisions relating to the Army and the Air Force on the one hand and those under the Naval law on the other, "stem, essentially, from the continuing need for Captains of ships, which still sometimes spend months on isolated service, to maintain discipline, [136] the Constitutional requirements of Article 22(1) read with Article 39A for equal justice and free legal aid , in India, make a strong case for incorporating in the laws relating to all the three Services free legal assistance to an accused at all stages, including pre-trial custody.

(f) **Right against Torture**

Q. 2.5 in the Interview Schedule was designed to collect data relating to force etc, applied to extract confession, if any made. The data obtained is tabulated in Table 16 given on the next page.

---

132 Nandini Satpathi v PL Dani, AIR 1978 SC 1025, DK Basu v State of West Bengal, supra n 122. The presence of the counsel during police interrogation was held to be a 'substantial guard against improper and illegal practices of police procedures.'

133 Cr PC ss 303, 304.

134 N Regs II(S) regs 26, 31 and N Regs I (Non Statutory), reg 1014.

135 Rant, Courts-Martial, Discipline, And the Criminal Process in the Armed Services', op cit, n 24, p312 (s 9.21).

136 Ibid, p.18 (s 1.44).

TABLE- 16

Whether Confession was Made under Threat etc.

Srl. No.	State of Confession	Response Frequency Number	%	Remark
1.	Not made	34	68	
2.	Made Voluntarily	08	16	
3.	Made on threat etc.	04	08	Dictated and made to sign (2 cases)
4.	Any other	01	02	Confession being falsely attributed to me.
5.	Can't say/No response	03	06	
	Total	50	100	

As disclosed from the data in Table 16, only 12(24%) of respondents made confession and 35(70%), stated to have made no confession. Out of those 12, only 4 (33.3%) claimed to have made the confession under duress, two of them stating that they were forced to sign a confession dictated to them on a charge under the Official Secrets Act, 1923. The said Act brings down the standard of proof required for conviction on a charge of spying,[137] and provides thereby a temptation to the prosecution to extract a confession, though unjustifiably indeed. The fact that 70% of respondents made no confession also indirectly suggests the absence of any pressure for confession in the military system. Thus, the present study hardly brings out any cause for alarm on the score of the use of torture for extracting confession under the DPCM. There have been, however, numerous complaints of human right abuses by the Armed Forces in respect of people taken into military custody in the areas covered by the Armed Forces (Special Powers) Act, 1958[138] (hereinafter referred to as the 'AFSPA'). Even if those cases need not engage attention in the present discussion, being not concerned with DPCM, there do exist on record some

137 Official Secrets Act, 1923, s 3(2).

138 In addition to a large number of complaints regarding disappearance of civilians taken into custody by the Assam Rifles troops, during the past three decades, there have been, in recent years, numerous complaints of human right abuses, including the alleged sexual assault and death in custody of a woman Thangjan Manorama in Imphal. Following Manorama's death, thirty two civil society organizations in Manipur

cases of custodial violence in respect of military offenders under investigation connected with DPCM too. In a case of notorious publicity, the wife of an Army Havildar approached the Delhi High Court with a prayer for a CBI investigation in the alleged custodial death of her husband during interrogation by military intelligence personnel and claiming compensation of rupees fifteen lakhs. The officer commanding of her late husband, one Major RK Midha, in his affidavit before the High Court, stated that the deceased had in fact been tortured to death by Major SC Jolly (later rose to the rank of Brigadier) and Capt Sudhir of the Military Intelligence, while interrogating him in some cases of military intelligence leakage. The respondents, however, denied any torturous act on their part, attributing his death to drug addiction and explaining 39 injurious on his body as having been caused as a result of his violently rolling over the floor in his craving for the drug. The High Court dealt at length with the law relating to custodial death and torture, including a reference to Article 5 of the Universal Declaration of Human Rights in 1948 that "no one shall be subjected to torture or to cruel, inhuman or degrading treatment or punishment". While conceding that "freedom of an individual must yield to the security of the State", the High Court held that the "action of the State, however, must be right, just and fair. Using any form of torture for extracting any kind of information would neither be right, nor just nor fair and therefore would be impermissible, being offensive to Art 21 ... Challenge of terrorism must be met with innovative ideas and approach. State terrorism is no answer to combat terrorism .... The State must, therefore, ensure that various agencies deployed by it for combating terrorism act within the bounds of law and not become law upto themselves. Need therefore is to develop scientific methods of investigation and train the investigators properly to interrogate to meet the challenge." On the specific case at hand, the High Court, however, noted that an "inquest" having been done in "terms of Regulation 529 of Army Service Regulations" the clear position is that death was custodial. It has to be noted that the matter was investigated under the Army Act and finding has been recorded that nobody is responsible for the death of the Havildar. It would not be desirable to doubt the authenticity of the report submitted and ask any other agency to undertake the investigation". The Court thus rejected the prayer of the petitioner for an inquiry by the Central Bureau of Investigation (CBI) in the case.[139]

---

contd/-

formed a coalition Apunba Lup to protest and seek repeal of the Act and there have been extreme protests in the North East region, including self-immolation, fasting until death and protest march of naked women. During his visit to Manipur in November 2004, the Prime Minister promised to look into the peoples' grievance and this led to the appointment of a five member committee under Justice B P Jeevan Reddy which submitted its report in June 2005. In his visit to Manipur on 02 Dec 2006, the Prime Minister has agreed to amend the Act suitably but not to repeal it; TOI, 04 Dec 2006, " ASPA based on British model", p 8.

139 Angoori v UOI, 2001 Crl L J 3697 (Del).

The incidence of such known cases of torture in military custody as the one discussed in the preceding paragraph is rather trifle and the data in the present study too disclose only a meager percentage of cases in which confession was forcibly extracted, as noted earlier. Irrespective of this, the track-record of our own soldiers acting under AFSPA and the recent inhuman treatment of prisoners at Guantanamo Bay and Abu Ghraib by the US soldiers[140] suggest that military uniform is no guarantee of better behaviour towards the in-custody lot than the khaki of the civil police, which is generally taken as a brand-name of custodial violence. The unprecedented award of death punishment to a senior police officer Rishi Prakash Tyagi by a Delhi additional Sessions Judge, on 15 Dec 2006, for having tortured to death Mahender Kumar and Ram Kumar at Vivek Vihar Police Station, Delhi, in 1987[141] speaks volume of the civil police way of working in such matters. In view of this, any discussion on pre-trial military custody will remain incomplete without a brief deliberation on torture and its relevance to such custody.

(i) **Torture as Human Right Violation**

The use of torture in custody is not specific to any country or times. Throughout history, rulers and governments of all political shades have used torture when it was expedient for them to do so, whether it is Egyptian, Babylonian, Hebrew, Greek or Roman or whether it is Oriental.[142] In terms of time, the drawings of the twelfth dynasty tombs (2000 BC) in Beni Hassan, Egypt, may be cited as the earliest available record of torture, depicting a man being beaten with a stick by a policeman-like figure, with three others holding his arms and legs and an official supervising the proceedings.[143] In our own case, Kautilya's Artha Sastra speaks of 18 kinds of torture[144] prevalent in the Mauryan domain.

The wide spread of torture to all times and all lands, however, cannot hide its ugly face. It "is a wound in the soul so painful that sometimes you can almost touch it but is also intangible that there is no way to heal it."[145] The Universal Declaration of Human

140 TOI, 16 Jan 05, "US soldier found guilty in Abu Ghraib prison abuse case",p.1. Please also see Rasul v Bush, President of the United States, 159 L.Ed. 2d 548 (2004), wherein the US Supreme Court has recently upheld the right of the detainees at Guantanamo Bay to invoke habeas corpus relief from the US courts despite being aliens and held outside US sovereign territory at a US Naval Base (Guantanamo Bay, Cuba).

141 TOI, 16 Dec 2006, "Retired top cop to hang" ,p.1.

142 Encyclopedia Britannica, 1973, Vol 22, p .100.

143 Franklin Charles, Third Degree, 1970, London, Robert Hale, p.15.

144 VA Smith, The Oxford History of India, 4th ed, pp.108-109, cit in GK Sharma, Study and Practice of Military Law, op cit, n 73, p19.

145 DK Basu v State of West Bengal, AIR 1997 SC 610 quoting Adrina P . Bartow.

rights in 1948 which marked the emergence of a world-wide trend to protect and guarantee certain basic rights, therefore stipulated in its Article 5 that "No one shall be subjected to torture or to cruel, inhuman or degrading treatment or punishment". This article 5 is the basis of the general prohibition of torture under the international law from which many international instruments have originated. Most explicit in this context is the UN Convention against Torture (1984), which lays down detailed provisions for State parties to fulfill and also provides an internationally accepted definition of 'torture'.[146] Accordingly, 'torture' stands defined as 'any act by which severe pain or suffering, whether physical or mental, is intentionally inflicted on a person for such purposes as obtaining from him or a third person information or confession, punishing for an act he or a third person has committed, or intimidating or coercing him or a third person or for any reason based on discrimination of any kind, when such pain or suffering is inflicted by or at the instigation of or with the consent or acquiescence of a public official acting in the official capacity.[147] Briefly put, a conscious and concerted movement for eliminating the inhuman phenomenon of torture is an important development of the second half of the present century. According to one survey, torture is prohibited, for example, expressly or by necessary implication by the constitutions of 55 nations, including the United States and there is universal abhorrence with which torture is viewed but elimination of torture in all its facets is yet a distant dream. One third of the UN Member States either practice or tolerate it,[148]the usual refrain being the compulsions of state security (salus republicae est suprema lex). In a study[149] conducted with 741 respondents who were members of Indian Medical Association, the data revealed that 533 (71.7%) of them had, as a doctor, come across a case of torture/suspected torture. In spite of 664 (89.4%) agreeing that physicians have an ethical duty to be active in efforts to prevent the practice of torture, majority of the respondents 427 (57.6%) justified coercive techniques to elicit information from non-cooperative suspects. When elite professionals like medicos were found to hold such views, it is no wonder that in a study[150] on 200 policemen, 122 (61%) spoke affirmatively on the necessity of the use of third degree methods during the investigation, giving reasons as follows:

---

146 Ibid, at para 11.

147 U Gener al Assembly, Resolution No.39/46 [annex, 39 UNGA OR Supp (No .51) at 197, UN Doc A/39/ 51(1984)]

148 Justice A.S. Anand "T orture-Negation of Human Rights and Digni ty", JIMA (Journal of the Indian Medical Association) V ol 98, Number 6 (June 2000) pp 296-298 (296).

149 Jagdish C Sobti, BC Chapperal, Eric Hoist "Study of Knowledge, Attitude and Practice concerning Aspects of T orture", JIMA V ol 98 Number 6 (June 2000), pp 334-339.

150 Makhan Singh, Police and Custodial Violence, op cit, Ch 3, n 31, p 263.

-Accused will not divulge merely by questioning	: 91 (74.6%)
-Pressure from senior officers	: 05 (04.1%)
-Pressure from complainant	: 05 (04.1%)
-There is no way of obtaining the correct information	: 15 (12.3%)
-It is an effective method of investigation	: 06 (04.9%)
Total	: 122 100%)

Similarly, after a three-day course on human right education, when certain personnel from subordinate prison staff were interviewed about their reaction, they were still generally opposed to human right concept on the ground that it gave an upper hand to the prisoners.[151]

The net result of this attitude to human rights in general and torture in particular, is that the police torture cases are on the rise in our country despite all the right noises by human right activists. There were 94 cases of custodial death in 2004 with 04 policemen punished for involvement therein. The corresponding statistics for 2005 were 144 and 12 respectively.[152] This is partly attributable to an extraordinary protection enjoyed by guilty policemen in the procedure for inquiry in such cases under Cr PC Sec 176 and to the social climate shaped by media, films and political discourse that sanction police excesses ostensibly to root out terrorism.[153]

The attitudinal problems relating to human rights violations, including torture, would generally need mechanisms, firstly, to positively transform attitudes and beliefs about human rights, through informing and educating at every level, and through the creating of societies that are democratic, just and equitable, and secondly, to have credible deterrent by setting up the right legislation and enforcing accountability through national and international courts. On the second aspect, we have, on our national level, the constitutional guarantees provided in Articles 20, 21 and 22. Torture adversely affects one's right to life and therefore it comes within the ambit of Article 21. Further, the Supreme Court, in D.K. Basu's case, laid down certain requirements to be fulfilled in all cases of arrest or detention as the rights of the arrested person flowing from Articles 21 and 22, including the requirement that every 24 hours a person under arrest shall be medically examined by medical practitioner on approved panel. Then, there are

151 Tomas Martin "Carr ots or Sticks? –Experiences of Human Rights Education b y the Subor dinate Staff of an I ndian Prison", JIMA, V ol 98 Number 6 (June 2000), pp 309-311.

152 Dainik Jagaran (Hindi), Meerut ed, 17 Dec 06, "Hir asat mei maut ki saja",p.14.

153 TOI, 20 Dec 06 " Ardh Satya", (Edi torial II), p .16.

constitutional remedies provided in Articles 32 and 226 for appropriate writs or orders to be issued on infringement of any Fundamental Rights, including those covering torture. In addition to the provisions of the Constitution, there also exist certain legislative provisions relevant to the ill of torture. Cr PC ss 54, 162, 164, 176; IPC ss 330 and 331 and IEA ss 25 and 26 are some such provisions. Lastly, the Human Rights Act, 1993, provides for constitution of the National Human Rights Commission, State Human Right Commission and Human Right Courts for protection of human rights and other connected matters with special jurisdiction and authority for relief in case of violation of one's right to life, liberty, equality and dignity by a public servant.[154]

(ii) **Torture and DPCM**

All the provisions of the International Law relating to torture and those of our Constitutional and statutory law discussed in the preceding paragraph, except the provisions of the Cr PC, are equally applicable to military custody. Further, any act of causing hurt or grievous hurt to extort confession will also constitute an offence, not only under AA s. 69 as a civil offence, but also under AA s. 40(a) as an act of using criminal force to a superior officer, or under AA s. 47 as using criminal force to a subordinate, depending upon whether the victim was of a rank superior or inferior to that of the accused. Then, if the act in question involved in the torture reflects a very low type of perversion of character - a conduct which is below human dignity or is repugnant to human nature or is a disgraceful conduct of a cruel, indecent or unnatural kind, it will also constitute an offence under AA s. 46(a). Disgraceful conduct "implies confirmed vice and all unnatural propensities, indecent assault, ... ferocity in having maimed other soldiers or persons ... tampering with eyes .... Where the conduct is proved to be so irreclaimably vicious as to render the offender unworthy to remain in the Army."[155] As regards, the procedural provisions of the Cr PC which will not apply to any proceedings relating to DPCM, the equivalents thereof do exist in the provisions of the rules and regulations made under the three Services Acts. For example, Regulations for the Army require investigation by a Court of Inquiry when an officer, JCO, WO, OR or nurse, whether on or off duty is injured except by wounds received in action.[156] The regulations also provide for similar inquiry when a court of inquest is to be held under the arrangement of the Service authorities on the occurrence of any unnatural death, including custodial death.[157] Both these provisions put together would meet the requirement of an inquiry envisaged in Cr PC s. 17. The provision of Cr PC s. 162 also

154 Justice Chittatosh Mukherjee (Chairman, WB Human Rights Commission) "Torture from Legal Viewpoint in the Eyes of Human Rights Commission", JIMA Vol 98 Number 6 (June 2000), pp 327-331.

155 Lord Hardinge, the then Secretary of War, Circular No.649 dated 23 Nov 1929.

156 RA para 520.

157 Ibid, para 529.

has its equivalent in AR r. 182 restricting the use of the C of I statements to only against the person making it for his cross-examination at his trial or for proving a charge of willfully giving false evidence.[158] Any parity with the civil system in respect of the provisions dealing with the malaise of torture cannot, however, be a reason for complacency for a military jurist. In the very nature of things, the use of military jurisdiction to try members of the Armed Forces and police who have committed gross human rights violations is considered to be incompatible with international human rights law. "The reality is", says Federico Andreu-Guzman, Senior Legal Adviser, International Commission of Jurists, "that, on the whole, as far as ensuring that justice is dispensed independently and impartially is concerned, military courts do not adhere to general principles and international standards and their procedures are in breach of due process."[159] Several factors said to contribute to such incompatibility, include subordination of the members of military court to senior military commanders who, in many cases, are directly or indirectly responsible for human right excesses, absence of legal qualification in most of the members, the military justice system being a part of the executive and not the judiciary of the country, the military jurisdiction being often used as a means of escaping the control of the civilian authority and consolidating military as a power within the society, and the tendency of military courts to hand down harsh sentence when the offence concerns the internal police or armed forces relations but the situation being different when the offence was against a civilian.[160] Given the unlawful criminal nature of human rights gross violations, the right to have access to a court falling within the domain of criminal law and the independence and impartiality of the judiciary being more a human right of the consumers of justice than the privilege of the judiciary for its own sake, it is felt that the dispensation under ordinary criminal system would give greater consumer satisfaction. It needs objectivity of an impartial mind to concede that most of these factors do apply to the CM convened under our three Services Acts. To remedy the situation, the three Services Acts may be amended suitably. The amendments in this regard may be envisaged, firstly, to incorporate in the defining sections of the Army, Navy and Air Force Acts a suitable definition of the term "torture". For this purpose, the definition of "torture" adopted by the UN Convention against Torture (1984), as brought out earlier, may be imported with due adaptation into our Services law. The provisions may also be made for a mandatory investigation by a Court of Inquiry, on the line of an inquiry into absence without leave under the AA. On the C of I declaring it to be a case of "torture" and the directions thereon by the proper military authority directing it to be a case falling within the definition of "torture", the accused

158 AR r 182 as amended by SRO 17-E of 06 Dec 1993.

159 Federico Andreau-Guzman, Military Jurisdiction and International Law, 2004, Columbian Commission of Jurists, Vol 1, p.10.

160 Ibid, pp 28, 83, 92-93, 108.

may be handed over to the criminal court for trial. With a view to placing an offence of torture beyond the jurisdiction of the CM, AA s. 70 and the corresponding provisions in the other two Services Acts may be amended to incorporate the offence of torture in the list of those offences which are not triable by a CM, with an explanation that the exceptions of active service etc. made in the case of other offences of such category would not apply to torture cases. The course of action suggested here may appear to be rather drastic. In its defence, however, one may repeat only what an eminent jurist of International Law said: "Let us be clear that, for human rights to have true legal protection, it is not enough - on the contrary; it is dangerous - simply to satisfy formal legal requirements (and) maintain a semblance of legal protection which reduces vigilance and, what is more, only gives the illusion of justice."[161]

5.9 Law of Arrest to be consolidated

Despite an unambiguous unanimity of thinking on the part of all concerned that the existence of power to arrest is one thing and the justification for its exercise is quite another, a wide gap often remains in the theory and practice, mainly because the conditionality of such exercise does not presently stand precisely defined authoritatively. On the civil side, there is a move to undertake suitable amendments in some provisions of the Cr PC such as s. 41(i)(a) which permits a police officer to arrest, without an order from a Magistrate and without a warrant, any person who has been concerned in any cognizable offence or against whom a reasonable complaint, credible information or reasonable suspicion exist of having been so concerned. While 'cognizable offence' is an objective ground, the rest of the provision is fraught with unbridled subjectivity of assessment. It is proposed to specify the offences which call for an arrest without warrant and also other circumstances requiring such arrest, with an additional mandate for the concerned police officer to record in his diary the reasons for such arrest.[162] Certain other provisions of the Cr PC are also proposed to be subjected to scrutiny for the desirability of amendment. In the case of military law, the guiding principles of arrest at present lie scattered in Chapter III of MML Vol. I and RA para 392 and corresponding provisions of the Naval and Air Force laws. Further, the problem of subjectivity, as pointed out in the case of Cr PC, is equally present in these guiding principles which are so very sketchy. Being almost mere reprint of pre-Independence law, these do not sufficiently cater for the need of our constitutional guarantees related to arrest and

161 Dalmo De Abreu Dallari " Jurisdicciones nacionales y derechos humanos" in Jornadas Internacionales contra la Impunidad, Comision Internacional de Juristas y Comision Nacional Consultiva de Derechos Humanos de Francia, Geneva, 1993, p.209 (Spanish original, free translation in Federico Andreu-Guzman, ibid p.9)

162 Subodh Ghildiyal "Police arrest power may shrink", TOI, 21 Oct 2006, p .11.

detention. The safeguards provided or proposed to be provided in the civil law and in other modern system of military law may be studied and suitably incorporated in the statutory provisions of the three Services Acts themselves so as to properly regulate, in such matters, the existing absolute discretion. A comprehensive legislation covering all the aspects of the deprivation of liberty by way of arrest, including the rights of the detainee and codifying the related customary practices should be brought out as 'Law of Arrest' for the benefit of the concerned authorities as well as the arrested person.

5.10 Conclusion

The three Services Acts and the rules and regulations made thereunder provide for the power and procedure of taking into military custody a person subject to military law who is charged with an offence. The data in the present study, however, disclose an attitude of military authorities to generally avoid a recourse to such power unless the circumstances of a case so require. This is in sharp contrast with the practice of the civil police of routinely arresting an accused for investigation. The reason for a different tendency in the case of the Service authorities is that an accused is easily available for pre-trial investigation under the Service law. The arrest of an offender is therefore, governed by the probability of his absconding or harming to himself or tampering with the evidence or seriousness of the offence or the disciplinary requirement of an immediate arrest to make an example. Officers are trusted for not escaping to avoid trial and hence are generally not taken into custody but placed in open arrest. These arrest and custody related provisions of military law are presently lying scattered in AA, AR, RA and MML notes. It will be desirable to have them all put together as consolidated law of arrest.

CHAPTER - 6

INVESTIGATION OF CHARGES

More than one student of society has expressed the view that not the least significant test of the quality of civilization is its treatment of those charged with crime. [1]

- Frankfurter, J.

1.1 Introduction

Unlike the ancient times when military offenders were summarily punished with instantaneous execution[2], all modern systems of military justice provide for an elaborate procedure of investigation upon receipt of information that a member of command is accused or suspected of committing an offence. The formal investigation may, if need be, preceded by an inquiry[3] to crystallize the linking details, before the CO, who is the key figure in the whole disciplinary process, takes over.

6.2 Parallel to Civil System

The needs of discipline In the Armed Forces and the nature of their duties make it inevitable to have somewhat different norms for their governance.[4] In the dispensation of criminal justice, this translates into a separate code of substantive and procedural laws for them, all over the world. Accordingly, in our legal system, the Cr PC is not applicable to a special jurisdiction like CM trial and related pre and post trial proceedings of the system.[5] The space vacated by the inapplicability of the Cr PC is filled, in the pre-

1 Irwin v Dawd, 366 US 717 (1961), Frankfurter J. Concurring, p 729.

2 Nitiprakashika, (VII, 60-63), cit in PC Charkravarti, The Art of War in Ancient India, 1941, Delhi, Low Price Publication, p 85.

3 Such as a C of I.

4 Parker v Levy, 417 US 733, (1974), describing mi litary as a "special ized society separate from civilian society" (p 473) and observing further that "The fundamental necessity for obedience and the consequent necessity for imposition of discipline may render permissible within the military that which would be constitutionally impermissible outside i t (p758)."

5 Cr PC, s 5; cf Dev Anand Singh v UOI, 1987 Cr L J 8 (J&K), observing that at a trial by CM, "procedure under Criminal Procedure Code and section 133 Evidence Act are not required to be followed in view of the

trial investigation by the CO. The pre-trial investigation by the CO "in many respects is analogous to those by which an alleged offence is investigated and tried by the civil courts" and "the function undertaken by the magistrate of himself disposing of minor charges and conducting preliminary investigation of those to be brought before a superior court is undertaken by the commanding officer".[6]

6. 3 Coverage of Interview Schedule

Questions 2.3, 2.4 and 3.3 in the Interview Schedule of the present study were designed to assess the attitude of the concerned respondents towards various aspects of the pre-trial investigation. Questions 1.2 and 2.2 also covered some aspects thereof. Briefly speaking, these questions were related to the conduct of C of I, the hearing of the charge by the CO and the recording of S of E, together with the satisfaction level of the affected respondents in respect of these proceedings and suggestions for improvements, if any, in the sphere.

6.4 Court of Inquiry

(a) Provisions and Practice

Though not mandatory, C of I is the first formal investigation into the allegation of an offence having been committed. Its designation is somewhat misleading in so far as it tends to suggest any judicial functions being performed at its proceedings. It is in fact a "rather council than a court, of which any officer in command may take advantage to assist him in arriving at a correct conclusion on any subject on which it may be expedient for him to be thoroughly informed."[7] In the present day technologically oriented phraseology, it may be described as a "management tool in the hands of a formation commander or a commanding officer. He makes use of it when, in his view, such a course of action will assist him in administration of the organization or administration of justice".[8] Considering from this angle, the designation 'Board of Inquiry' (hereinafter referred to as 'BOI') given to the corresponding proceedings under the Naval law[9] appears

---

special comprehensive procedure prescribed by Army Act and duly supported by the rules framed thereunder."

6 James, Stuart-Smith, "Military Law: Its History, Administration and Practice", op cit, Ch 1, n 26, p 493; cf RP Dwivedi v COAS, MP High Court decision of 03 Jul 1998 in WP No. 4430 of 1997 observing that the preliminary investigation in respect of charges framed against the petitioner was akin to the investigation of Magistrate doing a preliminary inquiry in respect of a criminal offence.

7 Simmons, The Constitution and Practice of Courts-Martial, op cit, ch 1, n 6, p 136, (s 334).

8 Army Headquarters, New Delhi, Letter No. 46440/AG/DV-1(P) of 03 May 2001.

9 N Regs II(S), regs 197-209. N Regs II(S) not only adopt the designation ' Board of Inquiry' alternatively suggested by Simmons for C of I but also interestingly borrow from him the expression "to be thoroughly informed" while describing the purpose of convening a B of I.

to be more appropriate. The expression 'Board of Inquiry' may, however, cause some confusion if adopted in the Army or Air Force, since there also exists another similarly sounding procedure 'Board of Officers' which differs from C of I in that a Board of Officers is convened to inquire into matters involving no point of discipline[10] whereas a C of I may investigate any matters of importance[11], including disciplinary cases. Being a functional necessity in the absence of a standing investigational agency[12] in the Services on the pattern of the civil police, C of I is a military law universal. It was sanctioned by the custom of the Service before Queen's Regulations (hereinafter referred to as 'QR') 785 - 787 of 1868, in the British system.[13] The three Services of the UK had separate Boards of Inquiry and lower level inquiries such as regimental or unit inquiries but are now going to have a uniform provision of 'Services inquiries' under the Armed Forces Act, 2006.[14] The US military law similarly provides for courts of inquiry to investigate any matter and to be convened by any person authorized to convene a GCM or by any other person designated by the Secretary concerned for that purpose".[15] Under the Canadian law, military judges may be appointed, with the approval of the Chief Military Judge, to constitute a 'board of inquiry', which assignment, however, as Chief Justice Lamer advises, should be accepted by a military judge after carefully considering the terms of reference and the effects on judicial independence in each case.[16]

In India, the three Services have provisions for C of I in their respective laws. With marginal differences in the matters like composition and power to convene, the procedure works similarly in the Army, Navy, Air Force and para-military forces like the Border Security Force (hereinafter referred to as 'BSF'). A significant difference in the case of the Army and Air Force, on the one hand, and the Navy on the other, is that Army or

---

10 RA, para 517.

11 Sanjeeva Row Nayudu 'Handbook of Military Law', op cit, Ch 3, n 22, p 17 .

12 The duties of Provost Martial, assigned to him under ' AA', s 107 , AFA, s108 and NA, s. 89, do not include the investigation of offenses. The personnel of the Corps of Military Police, which is headed by the Provost Marshal accordingly are not formally entrusted with the investigation of offenses as their preliminary duty, unlike the civilian police personnel. Under the British system, however, there is now an increasing trend of the Royal Military Police handling the investigation of criminal offenses much the same way as the civil police would do; please see Rant, Courts Martial, Discipline and the Criminal Process in the Armed Services, op cit, Ch 3, n 21, pp 5-6 (s 1.13).

13 Simmons, The Constitution and Practice of Courts-Martial, loc cit, n 7, p 134.

14 (British) Armed Forces Act, 2006, s 243.

15 Uniform Code of Military Justice, 1950, (hereinafter referred to as 'UCMJ'), Art 135.

16 National Defence Act of Canada, 1985, s 165 as amended by Bill C-25 of 1998; Lamer, Independent Review of Bill C-25, op cit, Ch 5, n 120, p 30 (para 17).

Air Force C of I is not, whereas a Naval BOI may be, composed of inter-service element.[17] Yet another point of difference between the two is that a Naval BOI is required to sit with closed doors unless otherwise ordered[18] whereas no such provisions exist in the case of an Army or Air Force C of I, which may, otherwise be held 'in camera' to investigate into loss of secret documents[19] or in any other case where a need is felt for keeping it a closed door affair. The provisions in other matters are mostly similar. The important common features of C of I/BOI under the three Services laws may be listed below:

(i) It is not a standing body; it is convened each time by a separate written order. Depending upon the nature of the subject matter of inquiry and the authority to convene it, a C of I may be unit C of I, Formation C of I (popularly known as staff C of I) or Departmental C of I.[20]

(ii) The presiding officer is to be senior in rank and other members at least equivalent in rank, wherever possible, to the officer whose character or military reputation is likely to be a material issue before a C of I.[21]

(iii) It may consist of any number of persons as its members but usually it is composed of three members, the senior most of whom presides over it.[22]

(iv) No oath or affirmation is taken by members nor administered to witnesses except that in the case of a recovered prisoner of war (hereinafter referred to as 'PW') a declaration is made by each member upon his honour for duly and impartially inquiring and giving opinion as to the circumstances of his becoming PW and except that witnesses are examined on oath at C of I on PW, illegal absence or when so directed by the convening authority.[23]

(v) Save in the case of a PW who is still absent, whenever any inquiry affects the character or military reputation of a person subject to the concerned Services Act, the presiding officer is required to ensure that full opportunity is given

17 AR, rr 177(3) and (1) respectively as amended by SRO 8E of 23 Jun 2003; AFR, rr 154(2), (3) and N Regs II (s), r egs 197, 198

18 N Regs II (S), r eg 203(4), cf Simmons, op ci t, n 7, p 139 (s 338).

19 RA para 525.

20 Army Headquarters letter op cit n 8, paras 18-22.

21 RA para 518 and N R egs II(S), r eg 198(5). Howev er, not being mandatory, these pr ovisions may be deviated whenever it is not practicable to observe them; please see Lt Col GS Dhillon v UOI, 1987 Lab IC 1264 (Gauhati HC) and Col MPS Ghuman v UOI, J&K High Court order dated 27 Feb 1996 in SWP No. 497 of 1994.

22 AR, r 177(2); N Regs II(S), reg 198(1); AFR, r 154(3)

23 AR, rr 178, 181; N Regs II (s), regs 201, 206; and AFR, rr 156(3), (5).

to such person of being present throughout the inquiry and making any statement and of giving any evidence he may wish to make or give, and of cross examining any witness whose evidence, in his opinion, affects his character or military reputation.[24]

(vi) It may be re-assembled as often and with such change in its composition,[25] as the officer who assembled it may direct, for the purpose of examining additional witnesses, or further examining any witness, or recording further information.[26] If need be an entirely fresh C of I / BOI may be convened on the same subject by the same or a different authority.[27]

(vii) Its proceedings or any confession, statement or answer to a question made or given thereat are not admissible in evidence against a person subject to the Army, Navy or Air Force laws, nor shall any evidence respecting such proceedings be given against any such person except upon his trial for willfully making false evidence.[28] This applies to summary trial as well as trial by CM and cannot be relaxed even with the consent of such person.[29]

(viii) Any person subjected to the Services law is entitled to a copy of the proceedings of the C of I /BOI, if he is tried by a CM in respect of anything reported by the said C of I /BOI or if his character or military reputation is affected by anything in the evidence or the report thereof.[30]

---

24 AR, r 180; N Regs II (S), regs 205(1) and (2); and AFR, r 154 (1).

25 N Regs II (S) Reg 203(5). The corresponding Army and Air Force provisions do not expressly provide for any change in composition on the re-assembly of a C of I though in practice such change is allowed, if needed. A C of I being only a fact finding body with no adversarial proceedings, such a mid-stream change is inconsequential and legally unobjectionable unlike in the case of a CM trial where such change is not permissible under AR, r 86 (2).

26 AR, r 179(5); N Regs II(S), reg 203(3); AFR, r 154(7); cf Gurnam Singh v UOI, 1984 Cr L J 718 (Cal) upholding the legality of the re-assembly of a C of I.

27 Col Sarvajit Singh v UOI, 2002(5) SLR 711 (P&H), holding that "there is no bar to a matter being inquired into for a second time ... which may be in the nature of re-investigation as contemplated under section 173(6) of the Code of Criminal Procedure ... the principle of double jeopardy would not be available at C of I stage ...."; cf Lt Col Ramesh Mohan v UOI, J&K HC, order dated 25 Aug 1995 in SWP No. 276 of 1995 and order dated 02 Sep 2002 in LPA No. 54 of 1995.

28 AR, r 184; N Regs II(S), reg 207; AFR r 156(6).

29 Special Army Order (hereinafter referred to as 'S AO') 1/s/2002/DV—'Court Martial', paras 70-71.

30 AR, r 184; N Regs II(S) reg 209; AFR 156(7). The Army, Navy and Air Force provisions are identical so far as the entitlement is restricted to the two categories of persons and the broad nature of the entitlement. However, the provisions of the three Services differ on the question of the entitlement to the report made by the C of I. From the very beginning, the Naval provisions excluded the report from

(b) **Research Data on Questions 2.3 and 2.4**

Questions 2.3 and 2.4 were put to 50 respondents who had been, or were being, tried by CM. The data fetched in response to the information on the following aspects of C of I:

(i) Whether a C of I was held in the case of respondent?

(ii) Whether the respondent was given an opportunity, at the C of I, if any, to cross examine witnesses , make a statement and produce witnesses in his defence?

(iii) Whether the respondent in any way felt aggrieved of anything related to the C of I; and if he did, what action, if any, was taken by him and to what result?

The data collected in respect of aspect (i) along with the main charges on which the respondents were tried are displayed in Table 17 on the next page:-

---

contd/-

such entitlement while the Army and the Air Force provisions originally included such report in the entitlement but the Army provision was amended vide SRO 44 of 24 Jan 1985 to restrict the entitlement only to a copy of such statements and documents as are relevant to prosecution or defence of the applicant at his trial by CM or as have a bearing on his character or military reputation. The power of the Service chief to deny the entitlement, for a specific reasons, to a person whose character or military reputation is affected and the requirement of payment at prescribed rate, as given in the original text, was done a way with. The Air F orce pr ovisions, however, ha ve remained unchanged in respect to the report with the Service chief's power to deny entitlement and the requirement of payment since the original text is sti ll unamended in i ts entirety. In Maj Gen I nderjit Kumar v UOI, (1997) 9 SCC 1 and UOI v Maj A Hussain, AIR 1998 SC 577 , the apex r ejected the contention that on a cop y of the r eport of the C of I ha ving been denied to the peti tioner, the subsequent pr oceedings of the CM trial wer e vi tiated, observing further that there is no provision for supplying the accused with a copy of the report of the C of I nor was this necessary as a part of natural justice requirement since C of I was a preliminary inquiry to which the rules of natural justice would not be attracted though adequate protection was otherwise given by Rule 180 at C of I. Howev er, where an administr ative action was taken against the peti tioner by way of awarding a censure to him on the basis of the findings of a C of I and the petitioner urged that he was denied an adequate opportunity to submit his defence in reply to a show cause notice by reason of the non-furnishing to him a copy of the finding and opinion of the C of I, HP High Court allowed the petition. In the order passed on 09 Jul 2003 in Avtar Singh v UOI in CWP No. 101 of 2003, the High Court felt unhappy that "a person is sought to be proceeded against on the basis of proceedings of a Court of Inquiry and y et the findings of the Court of I nquiry are withheld from his perusal."

TABLE - 17
Whether C of I was Held

Srl No.	Charge	Response Frequency Held	Not Held	No Response	Total	%
1.	Mutiny (AA s 37)	06	00	00	06	12 *
2.	Desertion (AA s 38)	03	00	00	03	6 **
3,	Illegal Absence (AA s 39)	12	01	00	13	26
4.	Disobedience to superior (AA s 41)	01	00	00	01	02
5.	Property Offences, theft, fraud etc. (AA s 52)	04	00	00	04	08***
6.	Losing equipment by neglect (AA s 54)	00	00	01	01	02
7.	Falsifying official documents (AA s 57)	02	01	00	03	06
8.	Violation of good order and military discipline (AA s 63)	01	00	00	01	02 #
9.	Civil Offences (AA s 69)					
	a. Murder	06	00	00	06	12
	b. Culpable Homicide	01	00	00	01	02
	c. Causing death negligently or rashly (MT Accident)	02	00	00	02	04
	d. Outraging modesty	01	00	00	01	02 @
	e. Rape	02	00	00	02	04
	f. Robbery	00	01	00	01	02 $
	g. Spying	00	04	00	04	08
10.	No response on nature of charge	01	00	00	01	02
	Total	42	07	01	50	100

* All from same unit ** Include one JCO *** Include three officers

\# Officer @ Accused a medical officer $ Officer

(c) Holding or not Holding of C of I

It is noticed from Table 17 that in 42 (84%) cases out of 50, C of I was held, in 7 (14%) cases, no C of I was held, and in 1 (2%) case it is not known whether or not it was held. Before analyzing the data further, it will be desirable to note when a C of I is a required to be held and when it need not be.

Though technically not a part of formal pre-trial investigation under the AA[31], NA or AFA, C of I under DPCM, is in the nature of criminal investigation which may be seen as "a lawful search for people and things useful in reconstructing the circumstances of an illegal act or omission and a mental state accompanying it, ... a probing from the known to the unknown backward in time ... to determine truth as far as it can be discovered in any post-factum inquiry".[32] The function of a C of I is in the nature of a fact finding body (whose parallel in civil law is a preliminary inquiry).[33] During a combined hearing on three writ petitions, when it was contended that it was obligatory upon the authorities concerned to appoint a C of I whenever an inquiry was likely to affect the character and military reputation of a person subject to the AA, the Supreme Court rejected the contention, holding that except in certain cases expressly specified by law, "Rule 180 cannot be construed to mean that whenever in any inquiry or an inquiry before a commanding officer under Rule 22 or a convening officer under Rule 37 or the trial by a court-martial, character or military reputation of the officer concerned is likely to be affected, a prior inquiry by the Court of Inquiry is a sine qua non."[34] Under the existing provisions of the law and the specific requirements of certain general and special instructions or orders, the cases specified in the Army for investigation by C of I are the cases of absence without leave for 30 days or more, a loss of a weapon or part thereof, ammunition and range accident, PW, assault and affray between persons subject to the AA and the personnel of the other two Services or civilians not subject to the Service law, collective insubordination, military transport 'accidents' resulting in death or serious injury, suicide attempt or suspected, murder and rape when triable by CM, loss of secret documents, fatal or grievous injuries, loss of stores, outbreak of fire or explosion, loss of documents of JCOs, WOs or ORs, loss or straying or destruction of animals, death due to enemy action or counter-insurgency (when an element of doubt exists as regards the circumstances of death), loss of identity card of officers, and JCO/OR unless C of I is

31 Major Hussain's case supra, n 30 (para 18).

32 Paul W Weston and Kenneth M Wells, Criminal Investigation – Basic Perspective, 1974, New Jersey, Prentice Hall Inc. Englewood Cliff, p 1.

33 Lt Col GS Dhillon v UOI, 1987, Lab IC 1264 (Gau).

34 Lt Col PPS Bedi v UOI, AIR 1982 SC 1413 (p 1436, para 41); cf Maj Gen DSC Rai v GCM Fort St George Madras, Madras HC decision date 25 Apr 1984 and Lt Col Karam Jit Singh v UOI, Raj HC, Jaipur (DB) order dated 08 Mar 1989 in CWPs No. 1709 of 1988 and 3287 of 1987, both unreported.

dispensed with by a competent authority and the suspected loss or damage to a company or corporation when claim against the government is anticipated.[35] Additionally, a C of I may be held in any other case where it is considered necessary or desirable. Generally speaking, it should be assembled when a prolonged examination of witnesses or documents is required or lengthy investigations are expected or the identity of the persons involved is not yet clearly made out.

(d) **Data Analysis**

Turning to the data in Table 17, it is noticed that Cs of I were held in 12 out of 13 cases of illegal absence and in all the three cases of desertion. In the case of respondent A-190-A-11 who was charged with the offence of absence without leave, to which he pleaded 'Guilty' at his trial, no C of I was held. Even though no explicit reason is given for a C of I having not been held in the case, it appears from the punishment of less than three months rigorous imprisonment (hereinafter referred to as 'RI') awarded to him, that the duration of absence might have been less than 30 days and hence no C of I. Thus, the action taken to hold C of I in 15 cases and not to hold in one case involving the offences of absence without leave and desertion, both of which are the cases of illegal absence in generic terms, was in conformity with the requirements of AA s 106 read with AR r 183.[36]

Cs of I were also held, in accordance with the reuirements of RA, in all the six cases of murder, one case of culpable homicide which is treated at par with murder for the purpose of the requirement to order a C of I, two cases of rape and two cases of MT accidents. In all the six cases of mutiny, the respondents have replied in the affirmative to the question whether a C of I was held in their cases but it was only one respondent who was allowed to remain present throughout the C of I proceedings. The offence of 'mutiny' is understood to imply extreme, and more strictly speaking, collective

35. AA, ss 89, 106; AR, rr 181, 183, 185; RA par as 520, 522, 525, 623, 903(d), 957 , 1195; AOs 19/2002 MT, 2/2000; S AO 14/s/76 and Arm y Headquarters, New Delhi, Let ter No. 46440/AG/DV-1(P) of 30 Jan 2003, para 6.

36 AA, s 106 requires a C of I to be held, and AR r 183 lays down the procedure to be followed when a person subject to the AA has been illegally absent for 30 or more days. A prolonged absence prima facie suggests an inference of the absentee's intention not to return to the Service. Such an intention is the gravamen of the offense of desertion. A C of I assembled under AA, s 106, on being satisfied of the absence in question being without due authority or other sufficient cause, is required to declare such absence, the period ther eof and the deficiency , if any, in the pr operty of the Go vernment ha ving been entrusted to the absentee bef ore he absented himsel f. A r ecord of the declar ation is enter ed by the CO of the absentee in the unit CM Book and the original proceedings destroyed. A certified copy of this record may later be given as a proof of the absence etc. as contained in the record; cf Simmons, The Constitution and Pr actice of Courts Martial, op ci t, n 7, p 144 (s 346) f or simi lar procedure of C of I on illegal absence under British Articles of War 1673.

insubordination, or rising against or resisting military authority in combination or simultaneously.[37] A C of I was a mandatory requirement in all the six cases of mutiny in terms of RA para 522(b)(i). Further, it is noted from the personal data of the concerned respondents given in the related Interview Schedules that all the six of them were posted at 3 Artillery Signal Company when the incident of collective insubordination occurred and all of them were involved in one and the same incident of mutiny. Even if one or more of them were given no opportunity to be present throughout the C of I set up to investigate the occurance, it would not be a violation of the requirement of RA para 522(b)(i) though may attract the violation of Rule 180 noted earlier.

The other cases in which Cs of I were held related to disobedience to superior, property offences, falsifying official document (in two out of three cases), violation of good order and military discipline and outraging the modesty of a woman (Srls 4, 5, 7, 8 and 9-d of Table 21). It was not a mandatory requirement of law under any provisions of AA, AR and RA etc. to order a C of I in any of these cases. Apparently, the discretionary power of ordering a C of I in any case where it is considered desirable was used.

No C of I was held to investigate the cases at Srl. 7. A C of I not being a mandatory requirement of law in any of such cases, it may be assumed that the concerned military authorities did not find it to be necessary or expedient to order a C of I in any of these cases.

It turns out from the discussion so far that out of 50 respondents tried by the CM, a C of I was a mandatory requirement in 32 cases (64%) in term of various provisions listed out earlier and those were accordingly investigated by Cs of I. Out of the remaining eighteen cases, in one case (A-188-A-12) the nature of charges is not known and hence it cannot be made out as to whether or not a C of I was mandatory though a C of I was in fact held in the case. In another one case (A-203-A-12), the charge was under AA s 54 for which a C of I is not a mandatory requirement but it is not known whether or not a C of I was held in the case. In the rest of the sixteen cases in which C of I was not obligatory, as many as 9 (56.25% of 16) cases were still investigated by Cs of I. This incidence of ordering C of I in all but one (99%) case of illegal absence and nine out of sixteen (56.25%) optional cases presents an impressive evidence of the users' confidence in C of I and seems to suggest that the military commanders do order a C of I almost in all the cases where it is a mandatory requirement and also use C of I as a management tool to investigate the cases even when they are not legally obliged to do so.

---

37 The offence of 'mutiny' is otherwise not defined under the AA and AF A. However, NA s 42 does define the offence, adapting for its purpose, the definition given in British Army Act, 1955, s 31(3).

(e) Natural Justice in C of I

Generally speaking, the principles of natural justice are relevant to an investigation that may lead to a binding and adverse decision and not to an investigation conducted with a view to recommending or deciding only on the desirability or otherwise of some other formal proceedings. Further, these rules can operate only in areas not covered by any law validly made.[38] In the case of personnel subject to military law, they are governed by a codified law. There would be hardly any justification for importing the principles of nature justice in a completely codified statute.[39] Even when the concept of natural justice is to apply to any proceedings, the only essential point to be kept in mind is that the person concerned should have a reasonable opportunity of presenting his case and that the administrative authority should act fairly, impartiality and reasonably.[40] Since a C of I is only a fact finding body which is not convened against any particular individual[41], it is possible that no individual is blamed by a C of I investigation. Considering from this angle, the only requirement of natural justice in the case of a C of I would be that whenever any inquiry affects the character or military reputation of a person subject to the Army, Navy or Air Force, he must be afforded an opportunity to be present and to cross-examine witnesses etc. in terms of the related provisions of the Service laws concerned, as noted earlier. To what extent this was done in the case of the respondents interviewed under the present study is reflected in Table 18 on the next page.

38 Kraipak and others v UOI, AIR 1970 SC 150 cit in UOI v Col JN Sinha, AIR 1971 SC 40 (42).

39 Lt Col KNS Sidhu v UOI, 1977 Lab IC 1162 (1164).

40 Keshav Mills Co Ltd v UOI, AIR 1973 SC 389 (393-394).

41 Lt Col Ramesh Mohan v UOI, supr a n 27.

TABLE - 18

Opportunity Afforded Under Rule 180 or Corresponding Provision

Srl No.	Present or not present	Opportunity Offered 1	2	3	4	Total	%
1.	Present throughout	31	00	00	00	31	62
2.	Present during part of proceedings only	00	05	00	00	05	10 *
3.	Not present at all	00	00	06	00	06	12
4.	Not Applicable as no C of I	00	00	07	00	07	14
5.	Can't say/No Response	00	00	00	01	01	02
	Total	31	05	13	01	50	100

* Called to make statement only.

Legend : 1. Cross Examination of witnesses, making statement in defence and producing witnesses in defence.

2. Making statement in defence

3. Not applicable, being not present or there being no C of I

4. No comment

The data in Table 18 disclose that out of 42 cases in which C of I was held, 6 respondents whose character and military reputation was affected by the subject matter of the C of I were not present at all in the proceedings. In another five cases (Srl. No. 2), the respondents were called by the C of I to make statements but otherwise the legal requirement of Rule 180 to afford such persons to be present throughout the proceedings was given a complete go by. It will be interesting to note that historically a person concerned was considered to have "no positive right to be present"[42] at a C of I, which used to "sit with closed door" as presently a BOI under the Naval law does. This remained so until the regret of a CM in this regard was approved by Her Majesty (GO No. 232) and at a debate, in the House of Commons, on a Naval C of I, the absence of accused was admitted by Admiralty as a "grave error", leading to Circular (Admiralty) 08 Sep 1863 requiring that "the party concerned in the result of the inquiry should be present during the whole time that witnesses are being examined. Should he object or refuse to be present, the proceedings would go on in his absence". However, no questions or

42 Simmons, The Constitution and Practice of Courts Martial, op cit, n 7, p 139 (s 338).

production of testimony by accused was permitted but he could make a statement.[43] The denial of being present throughout and to cross-examine the witnesses etc. being the violation of the current codified law on the subject, in their cases, the matter may be examined in the light of the judicial precedents and the relevant legal provisions themselves. In the case of A-198-A-10 too, a C of I was held in his absence. He was later tried by an SCM on a charge of overstaying leave granted to him to which he pleaded 'Guilty'. Apparently it was physically impossible for the C of I to afford him an opportunity to be present. Interestingly, Rule 180 and the corresponding provisions of the other two Services Acts, in their very opening words, expressly allow an exception from their compliance in respect of a PW who is still absent but make no such exception in the case of a person who is absent without due authority. The corresponding provisions of the Indian Army Act Rules, 1911 were also similarly silent in this regard. It seems that no such exception was made since a C of I in illegal absence is required to follow a special procedure provided in Rule 183 and Rule 180 would, therefore, not be attracted in the case of a C of I on illegal absence.

Then, there is the case of the respondents from the BSF who was on leave when a C of I was held in his case. BSF law does not insist upon the presence of an affected person at the C of I proceedings throughout but does require an opportunity to be afforded to him to cross-examine witnesses, make a statement and produce witnesses.[44] However, this was not done in the case of A-182-BSF-10 who had this to say in this context:

> "As soon as I landed at the Rly Station back from leave, I was arrested and pressurized to falsely own up responsibility for loss of money in the Company office where I was a clerk. I was pressurized by the 2 I/C (second-in-command) Shri Hukam Chand, Dy Commandant, and Shri Mahender Singh, Company Commander, BSF 'C' Company, to take responsibility of the loss, failing which I would be killed if I did not make statement as per their wishes."

---

43 Ibid.

44 Border Security Force Act, 1968 (her einafter referred to as 'BSF A') and B order Security Force Rules, 1969 (hereinafter referred to as 'BSFR'). Like a 'closed door' BOI of the Naval law, a C of I under the BSFR, r 173(1) (8) "shall not be open to the public. Only such persons may attend the proceedings as are permitted by the court ... but before giving an opinion against any person subject of the Act, the court will afford that person the opportunity to know all that has been stated against him, cross-examine any witnesses who have given evidence against him, and make a statement and call witnesses in his defence."

Like Respondent A-182-BSF-10, Col Rajbir Singh Khanna was on leave when three Cs of I were held to investigate various allegations against him. His commander had already brought some of the allegations on record in a warning letter and thus there could hardly be any doubt that his character and military reputation were likely to be affected in any inquiry which may be held in that connection. On a writ petition by Col Khanna, J&K High Court ruled in these circumstances, that the C of I "were held in violation of the mandate of Army Rule 180 and to that extent any action taken pursuant thereto, more so on administrative level, gets vitiated and must be invalidated."[45] In another case, the action following the C of I was a trial by the CM, unlike an administrative action in the case of Col Rajbir Singh Khanna. Before the CM trial, two Cs of I were held involving loss of diesel. The first one was held behind the back of the petitioners and in the second C of I too, the procedure of Rule 180 was not followed. The respondents admitted the non-compliance of Rule 180 but submitted that in neither C of I, the character or military reputation of the petitioners were affected. The MP High Court allowed the petition, observing that "looking at the nature of the case, the petitioners were being held responsible in each C of I regarding the deficiency of diesel, their military reputation was bound to be affected.... Subsequently, the findings of the Cs of I were the foundation of framing the charges against the petitioners under section 52 (f) of the Act read with section 34 of the Indian Panel Code and section 63 of the Act. ... Therefore, non-compliance of Rule 180 vitiated the further proceedings of framing of charges as well as holding of GCM on the basis of those proceedings.[46] In the light of these decisions, it may be stated that there has been a flagrant violation of the related provisions of BSFR in the case of respondent A-182-BSF-10 in so far as he was denied an opportunity to know all that had been stated against him at the C of I and to cross-examine the witnesses who had given evidence against him and to make a statement and to call witnesses in his defence. This should have been done before any charge against him was formulated on the basis of the C of I.

Unlike the aforementioned two respondents who were away from their respective units when the Cs of I were held in their cases, respondents No. A-193-A-12 charged with disobedience to superior under AA s 41 and Nos. A-166-A11, A-194-A-11 and A-195-A-10, all charged with the offence of murder, were very much present in the units

45 Col Rajbir Singh Khanna v UOI, J&K High Court order of 31 Dec 1993; cit in Kumar and Chaturvedi, Law Relating to the Armed Forces in India, op cit, Ch 3, n 22, p 246.

46 RP Dwivedi v COAS, MP High Court decision of 03 Jul 1998 in WP No. 4430 of 1997; cf Brig KT Mathew, the JAG's earlier ruling in Army Headquarters Letter No. 25/60/JAG dated 01 Nov 1960 that "if the proceedings, findings or opinion of the courts of inquiry contain any remarks adverse to a person on the basis of which he is l iable to be penal ized in an y manner in the service car eer, the court of inquiry affects his char acter and mi litary reputation."

when the Cs of I were held in their cases. The unit of all the last mentioned three respondents was one and the same, that is, 163 Field Regiment. None of them has added anything as to the circumstances in which they were denied such opportunity. However, from some of their responses, one may gather some clue in this regard. For instance, respondent No. A-193-A-11 has stated that he was not present throughout at his S of E either which was a mandatory requirement under Rule 23. Further, according to him, his trial by the CM was not fair, the members being under command influence. Respondents No. A-194-A-11 and A-195-A-10 were similarly dissatisfied with the outcome of their trial, the former stating that he was being made a scapegoat and the grievance of the latter also being that he was convicted even though he had not killed anybody. As for respondent No. A-166-A-11, he too holds something against the system. Thus, on the face of things, it seems that the requirements of Rule 180 were deliberately ignored in the case of the four respondents of 163 Field Regiment and the concerned authorities should be answerable for the default. However, it will be worthwhile to remember here the decision of the Allahabad High Court in a case, in which the petitioner was in custody but not allowed to be present during the C of I proceedings, though he was subsequently tried and convicted by a CM held in the same case:

> The Court of Inquiry in question was nothing more than a pre-trial investigation for determining what action be taken in the matter. It was not the case of the petitioner that prescribed procedure was not followed at trial ... nor has he claimed causing of any prejudice at trial by General Court Martial. Holding of General Court Martial has nothing to do whether any Court of Inquiry was held or not. The trial by General Court Martial is entirely independent proceeding and want of opportunity to petitioners at Court of Inquiry, even if it is assumed that it was not provided, will not invalidate the General Court Martial."[47]

Passing on to the five cases in which the affected respondents were called by the C of I to make statements only, the authority who assembled the C of I would have been in the knowledge of who all were linked with the incident and should have accordingly given instructions in express terms regarding the requirement of the compliance of Rule 180. The fact that one of the six respondents, namely respondent No. A-180-A-10, was present throughout while others (respondents at Srl 2 of Table 18) were called only to make statements, suggests that the presiding officer who had "the ultimate responsibility of ensuring that they (provisions of Rule 180) are observed in every case[48]" (emphasis

47 Lance Naik Devendra Nath Rai v UOI, All. HC order dated 06 Jan 2000 in CMWP No. 35206 of 1991 cit in Kumar and Chaturvedi, Law Relating to Armed Forces in India, op cit, Ch 3, n 22, p 250.

48 MML, Vol II, p 352, Note to AR, r 180.

added) was aware of the requirement of the compliance of Rule 180 in respect of all the affected individuals but let himself into believing, deliberately or mistakenly, that the five respondents called only to make statements were merely witnesses. This surmise gets support from the precedent of Sub Maj S N Thakur's case, in which the petitioners were examined as witnesses at a C of I investigating the allegations made by certain persons against their superior officer but were later proceeded against.[49] If the respondents in question were in fact examined as mere witnesses, the incident does highlight the need of importing into the AR and AFR the Naval provision explicitly stating that no one charged with an offence shall be bound to make any statement or answer any question and that before examination every witness shall be informed of privilege to refuse to answer any question the answer to which may tend to expose him to any penalty or forfeiture.[50]

Reverting to the figures in Table 18, all the 31 respondents who were present throughout the C of I proceedings, were given due opportunity to make a statement and produce witnesses in defence, if so wished, as well as an opportunity to cross-examine the witnesses. There was no specific complaint by any respondent. Table 19 below reflects the data gathered in response to question no. 2.4 in the Interview Schedule as to whether the respondents felt aggrieved for any reason at the C of I proceedings.

TABLE – 19

State of Being Aggrieved at C of I

Srl	Response	Frequency	Percentage	Remarks
1.	Aggrieved	20	40	4 took action, 1 took no action,15 no response for action taken
2.	Not Aggrieved	11	22	
3.	No Response	19	38	Incl. no C of I and not present cases
	Total	50	100	

The data in Table 19 show that 20 (40%) respondents felt aggrieved at C of I stage on one count or the other, whereas 11 (22%) had no grievance. Respondent A-188-A-12, who kept his identity undisclosed but, considering his other responses, seems

49 Subedar Major SN Thakur v UOI, 76 (1998) DLT 695 (DB).

50 N Regs II(S), reg 203(1) (2).

to be a senior Army officer, had a word of appreciation about the performance of the C of I in his case, stating that it was "conducted fairly".

Turning to those who felt aggrieved, respondent No. A-181-A-9, a JCO who was later tried by a CM on a charge of desertion (AA s 38), complained of "very long delay in the conduct of inquiry." Another respondent, No. A-184-A-5 stated that "cross-examination was not done mainly because of non-specific nature" of the C of I. It may be placed on the record here that the respondent was an officer of the rank of Lt. Col and was later tried by a CM on the charges of falsifying official documents and an act prejudicial to good order and military discipline. The handicap he experienced, despite his intellectual level as an officer "belonging to the upper bracket in the armed forces", to use the words of the Supreme Court, focuses the attention on the absence of any mechanism of legal assistance at C of I and certain other proceedings in DPCM. The point may be reinforced here by quoting from another respondent (A-186-A-7), who is now a practicing advocate but faced the similar predicament during his military service phase of life. He states now, "No legal support being available, I did not have even mental grounding to feel or not feel aggrieved". The situation is aggravated if the authority assembling the C of I, and later the Presiding Officer of CM fail to conscientiously discharge the duties enjoined upon them in the context of the compliance of Rule 180, as soon as it occurs or would occur to a reasonable and prudent person in the given situation, in view of the facts at hand, that the character or military reputation of a person subject to the Army, Navy or Air Force Act is likely to be affected. In the case of respondent A-207-A-11, the compliance of the requirements of Rule 180 after all the witnesses had already been examined, including the respondent himself having been authoritatively questioned as a witness much earlier, was an instance of an utterly perfunctory approach by the presiding officer of the C of I. The respondent was later tried by a GCM on a charge of murder, based on the facts which had been brought out by the very first witness. The correct stage for the compliance of the requirements of Rule 180 was therefore when the first witness had brought out those facts. Unfortunately a letter from Army Headquarters[51] states in this context that after the opportunity ordained in Rule 180 had been provided, "the Rule does not cast any further mandatory duty to ensure participation of the affected person. In other words, once apprised of his rights under the rule ibid, it is for the affected person to avail of those rights." This sounds to be somewhat officious and also at odd with the requirement of adopting a generous attitude when invoking Rule 180 as recommended elsewhere in the same letter. In view of a general deficiency of legal awareness among the servicemen, as brought out earlier, a desirable course of action would be to sincerely ensure that the affected person does understand the nature of his rights under Rule 180 and gets due opportunity to suitably

51 Army Headquarters, New Delhi, letter No. 46440/AG/DV-1(P) dated 15 Dec 2000, para 13.

enforce them, if he so desires. This acquires added importance from the fact that only four out of the twenty aggrieved respondents had resorted to some remedial action. Possibly the rest of them did not know what to do. Two of those four brought the matter to the notice of their superiors, one complained to the Human Rights Commission and the last one filed a writ petition in Allahabad High Court seeking redressal of his C of I related grievances. This calls for a separate discussion on the consequences of the failure at the front of the natural justice mechanism contained in Rule 180.

(f) Legal Consequences of Deficient Compliance of Rule 180

It is axiomatic that a C of I is merely in the nature of preliminary inquiry and cannot be equated with a trial.[52] It is also a truism that the C of I and participation therein are at a stage prior to the trial by the CM and it is the order of the CM which determines the fate of the person concerned and not any earlier proceedings. The Supreme Court has also ruled in this context that the principles of natural justice are not attracted in a preliminary inquiry.[53] However, in relation to C of I as a preliminary investigation prior to a trial by the CM, it may be underlined that unlike the trial by a court of ordinary criminal jurisdiction, a CM trial is an integral part of the same machinery of military administration and ethos as involved in the pre-trial procedures. Any prejudice at the pre-trial stage under the DPCM may as well be reflecting a general prejudice against the accused (seen as a person bringing a bad name to the organization) which is likely to continue all along till the conclusion of the trial by the CM and even beyond, while getting post-trial review by the service authorities. Irrespective of the changes in the individual dramatis personae playing different roles at different stages, all would be working in the spirit of firefighting exercise to save the image of the Service. Considering this, it would be rather spacious to enunciate a blanket rule that since the Supreme Court has observed in PPS Bedi's case that disciplinary proceedings commence from the hearing of the charges and that a C of I is not a sine qua non for such proceedings, "non-compliance with AR 180 will not affect subsequent disciplinary proceedings, specially when the affected person, as accused has fully participated in subsequent disciplinary proceedings."[54] It will equally be an unfair conclusion from "ratio of various judgments of the Supreme Court discussed above (PPS Bedi, Inderjit Kumar, GS Sodhi) and especially in the case of Maj A Hussain"... that such a non-compliance does vitiate an administrative action taken on the basis of such C of I but "would not make a dent on the subsequent Court-martial proceedings".[55] It just could not be the intention of the

---

52 Maj Suresh Chand Mehta v The Defence Secretary, UOI and others, AIR 1991 SC 483, (para 13).

53 Maj Gen Inderjit Kumar v UOI, AIR 1997 SC 2085 (para 8). The Court relied on Maj GS Sodhi v UOI, AIR 1991 SC 1617 .

54 Army Headquarters, New Delhi, letter, op cit, n 51, para 13.

55 Ibid, para 15

Supreme Court to hold that a flagrant violation of the statutory provisions of Rule 180 was inconsequential merely because it came at a stage prior to the trial by the CM. In the case of Maj Gen Inderjit Kumar, no such violation was a fact in issue. A reference to Rule 180 was made in that case only to suggest that "adequate protection" was provided to the accused in the existing provisions relating to a C of I and hence the principles of natural justice could not be involved to claim any additional benefit, such as the report of the C of I, since the C of I proceedings were not adversarial and not a part of the mandatory pre-trial investigation. To deduce from this that Rule 180 too could be ignored in view of such a nature of C of I would be travesty of justice and perversity of logic. Maj Sodhi's case was referred in Inderjit Kumar only to emphasize, by way of reiteration, that C of I and participation therein were at a stage prior to the CM trial and hence natural justice rules independently being inapplicable thereto. As for Maj Hussain's case, the Supreme Court's observations there seem only to strengthen a case of indispensability of Rule 180 requirements and disasterous consequences of their violation, being mandatory provisions, irrespective of the general principle that the "requirement of proper and adequate investigation is not jurisdictional and any violation thereof does not invalidate the court martial unless it is shown that the accused has been prejudiced or a mandatory provision has been violated."[56] (emphasis added). In an old case[57] of British military law, the petitioners succeeded to obtain rule nisi for a mandamus to the Army Council to cause the C of I to reassemble to hear and determine his case according to law when he complained that he had been reverted to half pay on the basis of an inquiry at which regulation 124 under (British) Army Act, 1881 had not been complied with. The said regulation 124 had practically the same provision as presently exists in Rule 180 under the AR. However, the King's Bench Division passed an order to discharge the rule on technical grounds that the court would not interfere in matters of military law and that another and equally appropriate remedy was open to the officer.

The importance of giving adequate opportunity to an affected person to defend himself even at the stage of C of I should be realized from the fact that both under the British[58] and the U.S. military laws, such a person has the right to be represented, irrespective of the C of I proceedings not being adversarial.[59] Without going here into the desirability of introducing in our own system a right to legal representation at C of I stage, it may be further noted that even under the Indian law such opportunity given

56 Maj Hussain's case, op cit, n 30 (para 22).

57 R v Army Council, ex parte Ravenscraft, (1917) 2 KB 504.

58 Br AA, s 135(4), read with Board of Inquiry Rules, r 11.

59 UCMJ, Art 135 (c) requires that any person subject to UCMJ whose conduct is subject to inquiry at a C of I shall be designated as a party and any "person designated as a party shall be given due notice and has the right to be present, to be represented by counsel, to cross-examine witnesses and to introduce evidence."

to an affected person, under AR 180 is treated as effective enough to allow a CO to dispense with the hearing of charge[60] which is indisputably taken as jurisdictional[61]. Thus, the non-compliance or an inadequate compliance of Rule 180 at C of I can not be lightly brushed aside as inconsequential, the legal position being that "if there is any violation of mandatory rules, the necessary benefit of the same should be given to the delinquent and undoubtedly Rule 180 is mandatory."[62] Therefore, non-compliance of Rule 180 of the Rules vitiates the further proceedings ….[63]. To allow the non-compliance of Rule 180 to make no dent on the subsequent CM proceedings would reduce the provision to a mere ceremonial in all the cases of disciplinary proceedings and to a handmaid of administrative action. Thus, being rendered to be almost superfluous in the former kind of cases, the provisions so interpreted would be violative of the basic legislative principles which admit of no redundancy in statutory provisions. Further, in the context of DPCM, this may in fact be much prejudicial to the causes of justice and discipline. Witnesses facing no cross-examination by the affected person at C of I stage are likely to get emboldened to repeat at a later stages, with greater force, such facts as are really not true but stated for whatever reason. Secondly, an opportunity may be lost for the affected person to establish, at the C of I, the earliest version of the incident and contradict and confront the witnesses, if need be, with their former statements in the event of their deviating from those statements at the S of E or trial stage. Lastly, the affected person may suffer an irreparable damage to his military reputation by losing an opportunity of proving his innocence at C of I stage itself and escaping the trauma of having been charged and the ordeal of disciplinary proceedings taken against him thereafter.

It will, therefore, be desirable to develop some sort of mechanism to compensate an accused person at his trial by CM, if any, for any handicap he suffers as a consequence of non-compliance or inadequate compliance of Rule 180 in his case. While arriving at their finding(s) on the charge(s) against the accused and later while determining the sentence, in the event of his conviction, the members of the CM may be required to take into consideration such handicap and its probable adverse effect on his defence. For this purpose, a scheme may be devised to quantify various conviction-quotients and sentence determinants in statistical terms as well as the values of different possible pre-trial handicaps in a digital scale, indicating the handicap of non-compliance or inadequate compliance of Rule 180. An appropriate finding on the charge and sentence, if any required, may be calculated by setting off the points of handicap values from the statistical

60 AR, r 22(1) proviso, inserted in Rule 22(1) by SRO 17E of 06 Dec 1993 vide its r 5.

61 PPS Bedi's case, supra n 34, p 1434; UOI v Nb Sub Baleshwar Ram, AIR 1990 SC 65.

62 Lt Col S Duggal v COAS, AIR 1991 SC 1617 (para 34).

63 RP Dwivedi's case, supra n 46.

values of the related conviction quotients and sentence determinants in the given case. It may be of some interest to note here that the U.S. Federal system and 33 of the American states employ some form of sentencing guidelines for criminal offences.[64]

6.5 Investigation of Offence by Commanding Officer: Hearing of Charge and Summary of Evidence

(a) General

The matters discussed in the preceding section 6.4 essentially related to the pre-charge stage. The details of an untoward occurance having been ascertained through a C of I and the responsibility therein having been pin-pointed, tentative charges are formulated in the concerned Company[65] office against those who appear to have incurred criminal liability. The word 'charge' in this context does not mean a formally

---

64 United States Sentencing Commission, " An Overview of the Federal Sentencing Guidelines" (undated) cit in Major Steven M Immel "Development, Adoption and Implementation of Military Sentencing Guidelines", Military Law Review, Vol 165, Sep 2000, pp 159-231, at 161.

65 A chart roughly showing vertical hierarchy with horizontal equation of Formations, Units and Sub-units of the Army extracted from PPS Bedi's case, supra n 34, p 1427 is reproduced below with minor adjustments:

Supreme Commander : (President of India)

Chief of Army Staff : (Army Chief)

Command : (General Officer Commanding-in-Chief abbreviated as 'GOC-in-C', popularly known as Army Commander for each of the Northern, Central, Eastern, Western, Southern and South Western Commands or armies)

Army Corps	Army Corps	Army Corps	Army Corps	: (GOC Corps/ Corps Commander, Lieutenant General)
Division	Division	Division	Division	: (GOC Division, Division Commander, Major General)
Brigade	Brigade	Brigade	Brigade	: Brigade Commander, Brigadier)
Battalion	Battalion	Battalion	Battalion	: (Commanding Officer, 'CO', Colonel, Infantry)
(Known as Regiment in Cavalry, Artillery, Signal, Engineers)				
Company	Company	Company	Company	(Company Commander, Lieut. Colonel or Major)
(Squadron in Cavalry etc. and Battery in Artillery etc.)				

drafted charge, such as the one on which an accused is arraigned before a CM. The 'charge' here implies only an accusation or complaint about the commission of an offence.[66] Except when summarily dealt with at a lower level, in all cases, whatever be the rank of the offender, a person charged with an offence against military law must, in the first instance, be brought before his CO and the CO must investigate the case in the prescribed manner[67]. Under our system, the investigation of charges by a CO is regulated by the related statutory provisions[68], which stand explained in the case of the Army, in MML, Vol I, Ch III, pp 16 and 17 (paras 10-14), along with the practices to be observed by custom of the Service. Accordingly, it is to be kept in mind that this duty requires deliberation and the exercise of temper and judgment in the interest alike of discipline and justice to the accused. Further, during the course of the investigation proceeding,

---

66 MML, Vol II, p 199, Note 2 to AA, s 101; cf Gian Chand v UOI, 1983 Cri L J 1059 (Del); Flying Officer Sunderajan v UOI, AIR 1970 Delhi 29 (para 37).

67 James, Stuart-Smith, "Military Law: Its History, Administration and Practice", op cit, n 6 p 494 . The requirement of pre-trial investigation by the CO in every case has, however, considerably changed now under the British and American military laws. After the reforms introduced by the (British) Armed Forces Acts 1996 and 2001, the investigation of criminal offenses is carried out by the Royal Military Police. The CO, or a subordinate commander, on the duty being delegated, could summarily deal with mere minor offences. However, the formal process even now is always started by the accused's CO. Once the military police or other investigation is concluded, the matter comes before a CO as a result of a report in the form of a charge (Br AA/AFA 1955, s 76(1). When a charge is referred to him, the CO must investigate it. He has the power to amend the charge and substitute another charge for it and treat the new charge or charges as if they had been referred to him originally. If he takes this course, his power of investigation are the same as for the original charge. After investigation, the CO may dismiss the charge, refer it to higher authority or deal summarily with it. He may not deal summarily if the accused is an officer or WO, or the charge is not capable of being dealt with summarily. Under the U. S. system, the immediate commander is required to make or cause to be made a preliminary inquiry into the charges or suspected offenses upon receipt of information about the offense committed or suspected to have been committed. Such an inquiry is informal but should gather all reasonable available evidence. Each commander has discretion to dispose of offenses by member of that command. He may dismiss the charge or dispose it by awarding a non-judicial punishment or refer the charge to a CM and so on. However, this does not bar a different disposition by a superior authority in respect of the charge already disposed of by inferior commander. Further, irrespective of such preliminary inquiry and disposition, a pre-trial investigation of charge, before it is referred to GCM for trial, is also required unless waived by the accused or an investigation was conducted in respect of the matter before the accused was charged and the accused was afforded on that occasion rights to be present, to cross-examine witnesses and to be represented by counsel; UCMJ Articles 15, 22-24, 30 (b) and 32.

68 AR, r 22; N Regs II(S), regs 25-30 and 149; and AFR, r 24.

the officer conducting it must be careful not to let fall, before he disposes the case, any expression of opinion as to the guilt of the accused, or one which would prejudice him at subsequent proceedings of summary disposal or SCM as judicial disposal of the case under the military law.[69]

The investigation of the charge by the CO consists of the hearing of the charge formally and, if the charge is prima facie made out, the recording of the S of E by him or by any other officer under his order. Both of these proceedings are to be conducted in the presence of the accused, giving him "full liberty to cross examine any witnesses against him and to call such witness and make such statement as may be necessary for his defence."[70]

(b) Procedure at Hearing of Charge

A hearing before the CO is essentially an oral proceeding.[71] The accused is not called upon to plead guilty or not guilty to the charge and advocates are not engaged to represent the prosecution or defence but the accused is given an opportunity to himself cross-examine the witnesses against him.[72]

The hearing of the charge by the CO begins with the nature of the offence charged being made known to the accused. Under the Naval law, immediately after the charge has been read out, the accused is a required to be warned that he should not make any

---

69 MML Vol I, Ch III, pp 16, 17 (par as 13,14)

70 AR, r 22(1) as amended by Arm y (Amendment) R ules, 1993, r. 5 vide SRO 17E of 06 Dec 1993. Before AR, r 22 was amended in 1993, it was not mandatory in the case of an officer subject to the AA that the charge against him be heard in his presence, unless he so required under rule 25. With the omission of the words "other than an officer" from rule 22(1) and of rule 25, the CO's hearing in the presence of the ac cused is mandatory in al l cases in the Arm y as wel l as in the Air F orce. Howev er, by insertion of a new proviso to rule 22(1) to the effect that when the charge arises as a result of investigation of a C of I, wherein the provisions of rule 180 have been complied with in respect of that accused, the CO may dispense with the procedure in rub-rule (1). Art 32 (c) of UCMJ similarly provides for dispensing with pre-trial investigation when at any pre-charge investigation like C of I, the accused was given opportunity to be pr esent, to cr oss-examine wi tnesses and to be r epresented. Howev er, this is subject to the right of the accused to still demand pre-trial investigation under Art 32.

71 Trilochan Joshi v UOI, 1983 Cr L J NOC 109 (Del); The HC f ound no infraction of R ule 22 in the CO hearing the charge orally and then directing that the evidence be reduced to writing. In practice, however, the r ecord of hearing is maintained in the Arm y on a f ormat introduced vide Arm y Order 70/84 (now replaced by AO 24/94) as a result of adverse decision by superior courts in some cases challenging the compliance of Rule 22.

72 James, Stuart-Smith, "Mi litary La w: Its History, Administr ation and Pr actice", op ci t, n 6 p 494 .

statement or give any evidence on his behalf until all the evidence against him has been heard.[73] Even though no such warning is expressly required under the Army and the Air Force provisions, the sequence of events included in the prescribed procedure implies that the accused will have an opportunity to make a statement and call witness in defence after the evidence has been given by all the witnesses intended to support the charge. In our system, those witnesses are not sworn or affirmed,[74] though under the British law the witnesses called by the CO must give their evidence on oath unless the accused agrees that some or all evidence of witnesses may be given from written statements or other documents.[75] The accused must have full liberty to cross-examine any witness examined to support the charge. The CO, after hearing what is stated against the accused will, if he is of opinion that no offence at all, or no offence requiring notice, has been made out, at once dismiss the charge and direct the accused to be released if he was under arrest. On the other hand, if the CO finds that there is a prima facie case against the accused on some or all the charges before him, it would be his duty to ask the accused what he has to say in his defence and whether he has any witnesses to call. The CO will then give to the accused full opportunity both of making a statement and of supporting it by evidence.[76]

After hearing the accused and his evidence, if any, the CO will consider whether the case requires to be proceeded with. He should dismiss a charge brought before him, if, in his opinion, the evidence does not show that an offence under the Act has been committed. He may also dismiss it, if he is satisfied that the charge ought not to be proceeded with, despite the evidence showing that the offence has been committed by the accused.[77] However, the CO is not empowered, under the law applicable to the

---

73 N Regs II(S), reg 27(2).

74 MML Vol II, p 272, Note 2 to AR, r 22

75 'The Rights of a S oldier Arrested For or Char ged With An Of fence Under the Arm y Act, 1955', op cit, Ch 5, n 127 and related text, para 25. S of E is also recorded on oath under the British System; please see James, Stuart -Smith, "Military La w: Its History, Administration and Pr actice", op ci t, n 6, p 495.

76 MML Vol I, ch III, pp 16-17 (par a 13).

77 AR, r 22(2); N Regs II(S), regs 27(4), 28(4); AFR, r 24(2); cf Br AA 1955, s 76(5)(a) and MCM (US) 02, RCM 306(c) for dismissal of charges under the British and the U.S. laws. In UOI v Maj VJ Kharod, the Gujarat HC in SCA No. 497/1981 (which was confirmed in LPA No. 244/1985) quashed GCM orders of finding the accused guilty and sentencing him to dismissal, when the GCM was convened despite the CO, after complying with Rules 22 and 23, had recorded his opinion that the charges against the accused were baseless and stood automatically dismissed and recommended that the accused be exonerated of all the char ges; cf also ex parte B rown, (1892) 37 S ol J 027, wherein certiorari was issued to quash the conviction of Private Brown when the CO had earlier dismissed the charges of embezzlement and neglect inadvertently and without full knowledge of the facts but later had, on orders from his superior officer

Army, to dismiss a charge which he is debarred from trying by SCM without a reference to superior authority,[78] i.e., a charge of an offence in relation to the enemy and punishable with death (AA s 34), mutiny (AA s 37), civil offence (AA s 69), or any offence against the officer holding the court, for which such a reference is the requirement of AA s 120(2) except when there is grave reason for immediate action and reference cannot be made without detriment to discipline.

If the CO does not dismiss the charge, he may dispose the case summarily under his own powers of summary punishments without the intervention of CM.[79] If an award within those powers is not considered adequate to meet the ends of justice and discipline, he may adjourn the case for having the evidence reduced to writing, i.e., for recording the S of E. The S of E shall be necessary if the CO intends to refer the case to proper superior military authority for guidance or with a recommendation for summary disposal

---

contd/-

remanded the accused for trial by CM on those charges. Please also refer James, Stuart-Smith, "Military Law: Its History, Administration and Practice", op cit, n 6 p 493, stating that "... the commanding of ficer, in his capacity as examining magistrate, may dismiss any charge brought before him if he is not satisfied that it is made out; if he does dismiss it, his dismissal is final and the accused may not be tried again on that charge by any military authority (see Army Act, 1955, s 134(1)(b). " Under our own AR r 53(a) and AFR r 61(a), the dismissal of charge by the CO entitles an accused to raise a plea in bar of trial by CM. There is no analogous provision, however, under the Naval law for a plea in bar.

78 Proviso to Rule 22(2) was introduced by the 1993 amendment of the AR. There is no corresponding provision in the Naval or Air Force laws nor are any similar provisions in the Anglo-American military law. However, an increasing trend, under the British system, of withdrawing serious offenses from the investigational jurisdiction of the CO and no finality being attached to the dismissal of charge by the immediate commander under the U.S. system, as noted in supra n 68, provides sufficient check on erroneous dismissal of serious charges by the CO, which seems to be the object of this newly added proviso. The embargo on the dismissal of charge by the CO imposed by the proviso should, under the principle of harmonious interpretation of the statutes, equally applies to the cases of officers, JCOs and WOs which are beyond the jurisdiction rationne personae of SCM. It may be underlined that the wide powers conferred on the CO to dismiss a charge, though having no restrictions in express terms, were in practice expected to be exercised with full sense of judicial responsibility, keeping in mind their unparalled nature, as noted in a minute of 07 Feb 1964 recorded by Colonel NS Bains, the then officiating JAG, on the file of the Ministry of Defence/DS (AG), that there is "no analogy under the Cr PC where a court, if it is satisfied that an offense has been committed, has no power to dismiss a charge even though it may award no punishment" under Cr PC section 562. This peculiarity arises because of the peculiar conditions of service in the Army. Accordingly, the powers were generally used either when the charge was not made out or where no useful purpose would be served in continuing the proceedings for such reasons as double jeopardy, time limitation, doubtful nature of evidence, triviality of the offensive act and the good character of the accused.

79 AR, r 22(3)(a); AFR, r 24(3); N Regs II (s), reg 29(2). However, if the CO intends to summarily dispose a case within his power under AA, s 85, S of E will have to be recorded, to cater for the situation when the attendance of witnesses is dispensed with on the written consent of the accused and S of E is read aloud or the authority dealing summarily with the case informs the accused that he has already perused it, as required vide the direction under Question 3 in Form 1 in Appendix IV to AR.

of the case by that authority or any other superior authority or to apply for trial of the accused by CM or to try him by SCM unless the SCM is intended to be held forthwith without a reference in terms of AA s 120(2).[80]

(c) **Summary of Evidence (S of E)**

Where the case is adjourned for the purpose of having the evidence reduced to writing, the evidence is accordingly taken down on the adjourned hearing, before the CO or such officer as he directs, following the procedure explained earlier.[81] These proceedings of preparing the record of evidence and the record so prepared, both are termed as the 'Summary of Evidence (S of E)'. S of E, though essentially a post-script of the hearing of the charge by the CO[82], is comparatively more important, being a recorded version and taking, in the military system, the place of both the police investigation as well as the preliminary inquiry conducted by the magistrate.[83]

---

80 MML, Vol II, p 273, Note 9 to AR, r 22. No application for trial by SCM is required to be made, though a prior reference to superior authority is required for the trial by SCM on charges of mutiny etc. in terms of AA s 120(2). Therefore, technically S of E need not be recorded before a trial by SCM in non-reference cases or when such a reference cannot be made without detriment to discipline despite being otherwise required. However, it will be advisable to have S of E recorded even in such emergent cases, before holding SCM, since in the event of the accused pleading guilty, there should be material on record to enable the court to determine the sentence and to assist the reviewing authority.

81 Supra, Ch 2, n 9 and related text.

82 Both the hearing of the charge and S of E, though separately provided for in the legal provisions (except in the Air Force law), are so embryonically linked together as investigational proceedings by the CO that they are generally clubbed together for delineation and discussion in administrative instructions (such as AO 217/72, now SAO/1/s/2002/DV-Court Martial, para 6, dealing with the irregularities at the two proceedings and their effect on the validity of subsequent CM trial or summary disposal) and judicial pronouncements (please see PPS Bedi's case, supra n 34, pp 1433-34, paras 37-38 discussing consequences of non-compliance of AR, rr 22, 25) and governed essentially by the same conventions and jurisprudential principles, such as no oath administered to the witnesses (MML Vol II, pp 272-274 , Note 2 to rr 22 and 23), no pleading of guilty or not guilty by accused, no legal representation supra n 72 and MML Vol II, p 274 Note 3 to AR r 23) and opportunity afforded to accused for cross-examination of witnesses etc. (AR rr 22 and 23). The only point of difference between the two, apart from the obvious one of being oral in the case of hearing and written in the case of S of E, is that the order passed by the CO at the conclusion of the hearing is in the presence of the accused whereas the consideration of the S of E, under AR r 24 or the corresponding provisions of the Naval and Air Force laws, and a decision thereon by the CO, may be made in the absence of the accused, who may accordingly be later informed (JAG's Dept Blue Book entry RB 1659 of 06 Mar 1952) about the CO's order. In practice, however, the accused is generally brought before the CO for formal remand.

83 Nayudu, Handbook of Military Law, op cit, n 80, p 29, paras 2, 3 graphically bring out pari materia between the criminal proceedings of the police investigation and inquiry by the Magistrate under the Cr PC and S of E under the military law.

It serves several purposes[84] before, at and after a trial by CM, starting from consideration of the evidence by the CO to determine further course of action to an appropriate decision by the reviewing authority on various questions.

In the light of the experience, the textual provisions relating to S of E had to be glossed over the years by adding some administrative innovations thereto. For instance, in order to meet a challenge subsequently made by the accused to the voluntary nature of his statement, Army Order has been issued to require the presence of an independent witness[85] when the accused is to be given a caution in terms of sub-rule (3) of Rule 23 that he was not obliged to say anything unless he wished to do so, but whatever said by him would be taken down in writing and might be given in evidence. Further, consequent to amendments of 1993 in Rule 22, taking away the option as to the hearing of the charge in the case of an officer, the earlier provision for preparing an abstract of evidence[86] instead of 'S of E', has been done away with by deleting all references to it.

---

84 It is the S of E that determines the direction of the CO in respect of the case, not only on the seminal question whether to proceed further with it but also the nature of the action to be taken if the case is to be proceeded with (please see AR r 24; AFR r 25 and N Regs II(S), reg 152). If the case merits a trial by the CM, a decision as to the type of the CM, i.e., SCM, DCM, GCM or SGCM, is largely to depend upon the evidence in the S of E. On an application for trial by CM, the convening authority considers the S of E to arrive at a decision as to whether or not a trial by CM would be justified. When the convening officer makes a reference to the Dy JAG for advice before trial, the latter renders his advice in the light of the S of E and formulates the charges on which the trial to proceed, if so warranted. Similarly, on a reference to the superior authority for holding SCM on serious charges of mutiny etc. under AA s 120(2), S of E guides the superior authority to suitably dispose the reference. A copy of S of E is given to the accused to facilitate his preparation for his defence. At the trial, S of E is used for contradiction or corroboration of evidence with former statements of witnesses. In the event of the accused pleading guilty in his trial by the CM, S of E is read in the open court so as to enable the court to determine the sentence to be awarded or alter the plea of guilty, if need be. S of E is annexed or attached to the proceedings of CM, depending on the trial having proceeded on a plea of guilty or not guilty, to assist the reviewing authority.

85 SAO 1/s/2002/DV-Court Martial.

86 'Abstract of Evidence' is a set of signed statements taken from the prosecution witnesses or a precis of the evidence to be given by a witness or witnesses when signed statement(s) from him/them is/are not available; please see James, Stuart-Smith, "Military Law: Its History, Administration and Practice", op cit, n 6 p 495.

(d) **Data on Hearing of Charge and S of E**

The data fetched in response to Q. Nos 2.3 and 2.4 in respect of the hearing of the charge and S of E are reflected below in Charts 6.1 and 6.2 respectively showing the number of cases in which the two proceedings were held in relation to 50 respondents subsequently tried by CM.

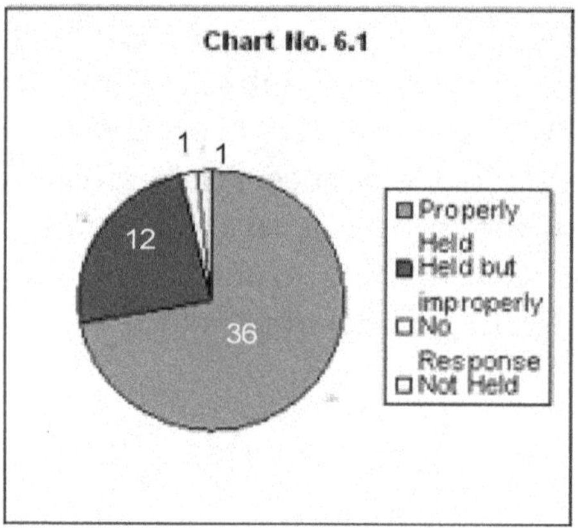

Hearing of the Charge

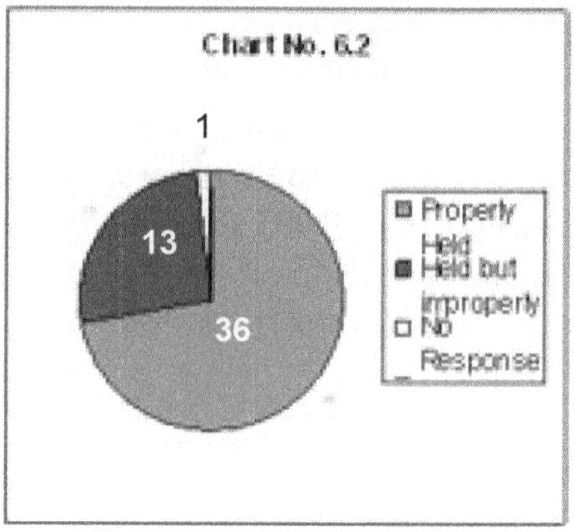

Summary of Evidence

As reflected in Chart 6.1, out of 50 cases of CM trial, the hearing of the charge was rightly conducted in 36 (72%) cases and conducted but not properly in another 12 (24%), making a total of 48 (96%) cases in which the charge was heard by the CO as required by AR r 22. In one (2%) case, the hearing of the charge was not conducted and in another one (2%) case, it is not known whether the charge was heard or not by the CO since the respondent has not replied to the relevant question.

The case in which the charge was not at all heard, the accused was subsequently tried by SGCM on a charge under AA s 69 read with IPC s 392 for robbery at Hajiganj on 11 Dec 1971 while serving in Bangladesh (then East Pakistan). The court assembled for trial on 09 Mar 1972 and subsequent days[87]. Thus, the case pertains to pre-1993 amendment era when it was not mandatory for the CO to hear the charge in accordance with Rule 22 in the presence of the accused officer, unless the accused so required under Rule 25, as ruled by the Supreme Court in PPS Bedi's case.[88] In that case, it was urged by the petitioner's counsel that a precondition to the trial by a GCM by way of the hearing of the charge in the presence of the accused having not been satisfied in the case of the petitioner Lt Col PPS Bedi, the order convening the GCM to try the petitioner was vitiated.

87 Capt Harish Uppal v UOI & others, AIR 1973 SC 258 (para 2).

88 PPS Bedi's case, op cit, n 34, pp 1431-1432 (paras 36 and 37)

The apex court, after going through the entire scheme of the hearing of the charge laid down in AR, rr 22-25, observed that "the opening words of Rule 22 clearly demonstrate the mandatory applicability of the provisions in Rules 22 and 23 in the case of persons subject to the Act other than officers. Any lurking doubt in that behalf is removed by the language of Rule 25 which provides that if an officer is charged with an offence under the Act, the investigation, if he requires, shall be held and the evidence, if he requires it shall be taken in his presence". It was further argued in the same case that to the extent Rule 25 erodes mandatory compliance of the principles of the natural justice as adumbrated in Rules 22, 23 and 24, it would be violative of fundamental rights guaranteed under Article 21 of the Constitution and would be ultra vires the Constitution. Taking support from Lee v Showmen's Guild of Great Britain[89], it was contended that public policy would invalidate any stipulation excluding the application of the rules of natural justice to a tribunal whose decision was likely to result in the deprivation of personal liberty. Therefore, to the extent the application of minimum principles of natural justice enacted in Rules 22, 23 and a 24 depends for its applicability upon the demand of the officer, it would be contrary to public policy which mandates that compliance with rules of natural justice should not be made dependent upon a requisition by the person against whom the inquiry is held but it must be deemed to be obligatory and an integral part of any procedure prescribed for such tribunal. The Supreme Court rejected the contention for three reasons. One, Parliament has power to restrict or abrogate any of the rights conferred by Part III of the Constitution in their application to the members of the Armed Forces so as to ensure the proper discharge of duties and maintenance of discipline amongst them. Secondly, if the procedure established by the law prescribes compliance with principles of natural justice but makes it dependent upon a requisition of the person against whom an inquiry according to such procedure is to be held, it is difficult to accept the submission that such procedure would be violative of Article 21. The Rules have made clear distinction between an officer and any other person subject to the Act. When it comes to an officer, "belonging to the upper bracket in the armed forces, the necessary presumption being that he is highly educated, knowledgeable, intelligent person, compliance with Rules 22, 23 and 24 is not obligatory but would have to be complied with if the officer so requires it. This is quite rational and understandable." Thirdly, while conceding that a body charged with a duty to act judicially must comply with the minimum requirements of natural justice, the Supreme Court pointed out that "in a trial which is likely to result in the deprivation of liberty, the body which has ultimately the power to make an order which would result in deprivation of liberty, must hear the offender offering full participation and that principle cannot be diluted. However, procedure prescribed in Rules 22, 23 and 24 is a stage anterior to trial by Court-martial. It is the decision of the Court-martial which would

89 (1952) 2 QB 329,

result in the deprivation of liberty and not the order directing that the charge be heard or that summary of evidence be recorded or that a court martial be convened. Even in normal trial under the Criminal Procedure Code, it has never been suggested that it is unfair to launch a criminal prosecution without hearing the accused[90]. In another case the apex court went even further, holding that "sub-rule (1) of R 22 ... deals with the charges against a person subject to the Army Act, other than an officer. Admittedly, the petitioner was an officer, and hence, the provisions of R 22 had no application ... It is R 25 which lays down the procedure in respect of the charges against the officers."[91] This explains the legality of the one case of the present study in which the CO did not hear the charges. However, the ground reality in the case of the respondent in question was that he "did not have even the mental grounding to feel or not feel aggrieved" of any non-compliance of such provisions by the CO since no legal support was available, as maybe seen from the response he made to a question as to whether he felt aggrieved of anything at that stage. Considering the state of deficiency in general, among the service personnel in the matters of their legal rights related awareness in the context of DPCM, as brought out earlier[92], this case could not be ignored as an individual-specific problem. Further, the option available to an officer accused to demand or not demand the hearing of his charge in his presence, under the then existing provisions of Rule 25, did not preclude a CO from calling the accused to investigate the case in accordance with the procedure prescribed in Rule 22, if he (CO) deemed necessary[93]. The MP High Court categorically ruled, in the case of Major Subhash Chandra Sarkar, that an order by the CO requiring him to attend the recording of evidence was perfectly valid and a disobedience of such an order would constitute an offence under AA s 41, the order being not violative of Army Rules 25.[94] In view of this, some guidelines should have been laid down to regulate the discretion of the CO as to the conditions in which he would, and the conditions in which he need not, resort to the investigation under Rules 22-24 when no demand was made by an officer accused for such investigation in terms of Rule 25. The cases of Lance Dafedar Laxman[95] and Maj Sarup Singh Sidhu[96], though not directly related to the CO's power to investigate the case of an officer irrespective of

---

90 PPS Bedi's case, op cit, n 34, p 1434 (para 34); please also see Lord Salmon in Cozens v North Doven Hospital Management Committee (1966) 2 QB 330 at p 343.

91 Major Suresh Chand Mehta v The Defence Secretary (UOI), AIR 1991 SC 1483.

92 Supra, Ch 5, Table 15 reflecting the data relating to lack of awareness on the part of the respondents about their CM related rights.

93 MML Vol II, p 276 Note 2 to AR r 25.

94 Major Subhash Chandra Sarkar v UOI, AIR 1973 MP 191.

95 Lance Dafedar Laxman v UOI, 1993 (1) Delhi Lawyer 92, wherein the Delhi High Court ruled that "the decision to proceed with the case further has necessarily to be that of the Commanding Officer ... Army Rule 22 never envisaged that the higher authority should initiate the action and then pass on to lower authority ... The power of commanding officer in this case was usurped by the Brigade Headquarters. The Commanding Officer being subordinate to it could not dare to disobey the order of the superior ...

the erstwhile provision of Rule 25, do highlight the risk involved in the discretionary powers left unbridled, more particularly when those powers are vested in an administrative authority like the CO who has no particular training in discharging quasi-judicial duties and is highly conscious of the need to obey superior orders. However, this is now inconsequential in the present context since the CO is no more left with any discretion in the matter of his duty to hear the charge which, under the new text of Rule 22, after the 1993 amendment, is mandatory in all cases. The law enunciated by the Supreme Court and the various High Courts in relation to the compliance of the mandatory requirements of Rule 22 is to be accordingly understood, subject of course, to the newly added two provisos, one each to sub-rule (1) and sub-rule (2).

Proceeding further with the data reflected in Charts 6.1 and 6.2, it is noted that even though the hearing of the charge and the recording of the S of E were not properly done in 12 and 13 cases respectively, the fact remains that those requisite proceedings were held in a total of 48 (96%) and 49 (98%) cases out of 50 and one case remaining unknown for want of a response. This high percentage of performance at the two proceedings, however, is revealed to be only skin deep on looking into the improprieties or inadequacies reported in the aforesaid 12 and 13 cases. These irregularities may be put into three broad categories of careless handling, infraction of provisions and scuttling of the laid down procedure. The related data is shown in Table 20.

TABLE - 20

Nature of Irregularities in Hearing of Charge and S of E

Srl No.	Proceedings	Careless Handling	Infraction of Provision	Scuttling of Procedure	Not Applicable	Total
1.	Hearing of Charge	03	04	05	38	50
2.	S of E	01	06	06	37	50
	Total	04	10	11	75	100

The last but one column in Table 20 reflects the number of cases in which no irregularities were complained of or no response was offered.

this ... amounted to non application of mind by the commanding officer which is violative of Rule 22 ... there is non-compliance as well as violation of the provision of Army Rule 22 ... hence the entire proceedings ... stand vitiated."

96 Major Sarup Singh Sidhu v UOI, Mil Law Journal 2000 Delhi 34, wherein the High Court allowed the writ petition, holding all further proceedings to be null and void, when the CO had dispensed with the mandatory hearing of the charge on the ground of the matter having already been investigated by a C of I at which the accused was afforded opportunity contemplated in Rule 180, whereas Rule 180 had not in fact been compl ied with in r espect of the petitioner .

In five cases of the hearing of the charge and six of S of E, the procedures prescribed in Rules 22 and 23 respectively were flagrantly scuttled. In four cases, the concerned respondents suffered this fate at both the stages. Respondent Nos. A-172-A-10, A-173-A-10 and A-175-A-10, though originally from different units and regiments, were all attached to Rajputana Rifles Regimental Centre, Delhi Cantt, along with A-174-A-10 involved in the same case. All the three have replied in the negative to the query in Q. 2.3(b) and (c) as to whether they were given an opportunity to cross-examine witnesses, make a statement in their defence and produce witnesses in support of their version of the incident involved in the charge, though those proceedings were held in their cases. Explaining this further, what they individually stated comes to essentially mean that "no witnesses were formally examined" and that they were made to sign the statements prepared before hand and containing untrue facts. They have not stated, as they were not asked, anything about the presence of an independent witness. However, what respondent No. A-174-A-10 stated would suggest that an atmosphere of scare was created at the proceedings to suppress the truth but artificially maintain the required legal technicalities, which would have included the management of a so called independent witness. The respondent, while replying Q. 2.3(b) and (c) about cross-examination of witnesses etc. at the two proceedings had this to say: "Procedure not remembered. I was much scared." The violation of the pre-trial procedure in these cases stands officially documented. In a memorandum attached to the proceedings of the CM trial dated 16 Nov 03, under the provisions of Rule 92(5), the presiding officer brought out that the pre-trial procedure was not properly followed in the case of the accused respondent A-175-A-10 who was tried at that CM trial. Since no witnesses were physically examined at the hearing of the charge, this was essentially a case of non-compliance like the case of Sub Dev Singh.[97]

The other cases under this category include the cases of respondent Nos. A-182-BSF-10 and A-199-A-4 relating to the hearing of the charge and A-166-A-10 and A-188-A-12 from S of E. The first respondent was a Head Constable (BSF equivalent to

---

97 UOI v Dev Singh, Mi l LJ 2003 SC 146. Ha ving been con victed and sentenced to dismissal f rom the Service by a GCM for an offense of outraging the modesty of a woman, the petitioner approached the Delhi HC challenging the CM verdict and sentence as vitiated for non-compliance of Rule 22 by the CO, such compliance being mandatory in his case as a JCO. The contention in the petition was that the CO examined no witnesses physically but merely read their statements to the accused, nor were the names of those witnesses included in the record of the hearing prepared under Army Order 70/1984. The CO had admitted these facts as a witness before the CM. The High Court ruled it to be non-compliance of mandatory provisions of Rule 22 and allowed the petition. An appeal against the decision was also dismissed by the SC on 23 Apr 2003, refusing to interfere in the order of Delhi HC dated 30 Oct 1996. The SC ruled that Maj GS Sodhi's case being the case of an officer was not applicable to the present case but PPS Bedi's case was applicable in so far as it held that Rule 22 was mandatory in the case of a person other than an of ficer.

Havildar) working as a clerk in the Company office. He was on leave when some deficiency of funds was detected in his Company accounts. On return from leave, as soon as he landed at the railway station, he was arrested and pressurized to own up responsibility for the loss of money. At the hearing of the charge under BSFR, r 45, which is in pari materia with AR r 22, only the charge-sheet was read over and nothing more. In the second case some witnesses were not present when the charge was heard, being in a hospital or on leave, and yet their names were included in the record of those examined in support of the charge. The grievance of the third respondent to S of E was that it was not "faithfully recorded". The grouse of the last respondent was that "some defence witnesses were considered non-essential" at both the proceedings of the charge hearing and S of E. Such a refusal to allow some defence witnesses is apparently not in tune with the requirement of "full liberty" being afforded to the accused at the charge hearing, inter alia to "call such witnesses and make such statement as may be necessary for his defence"[98] and that at S of E the accused may "call his witnesses, including if he so desires, any witnesses as to character"[99]. The use of these expressions in the regulating provisions of the two proceedings leave little scope for rejecting defence evidence on the ground of being non-essential. If there were any constraints as to readily procuring the attendance of the witnesses in question, written statements purporting to be signed by the witnesses could be called for and attached to S of E.[100] If this too was not expedient, the accused could have been asked to secure the attendance of those witnesses under his own arrangement instead of the proposed defence evidence being rejected as non-essential. If he had then failed to call those witnesses, the authorities could not be faulted since the responsibility to procure the attendance of the defence witnesses is primarily that of the accused.[101]

Sharply differing from the cases discussed in the foregoing were the cases of some respondents, which reflected a casual attitude adopted by the CO or the officer recording S of E to the procedure to be followed. Respondent No. A-166-A-11, for instance, was facing a charge of murder and yet he missed an opportunity to cross-examine the witnesses or make a statement or produce evidence in defence since "no opportunity (was) specifically given" to him and he was not aware of his entitlement at the hearing of the charge. It may be noted that apart from the text of Rule 22 requiring "full liberty" to be afforded to the accused to cross-examine witnesses and so on, the record of proceedings to be made in accordance with Army Order 24 of 1994 specifically requires, at para 4 of the related format, to state in respect of each witness " whether accused cross-examined

98 AR, r 22(1); AFR, r 24(1); no such words are used in the corresponding Naval provisions.

99 AR, r 23(3). No such expression is used in the related Naval and Air Force provisions.

100 AR, r 23(5); AFR, r 24(8); N Regs II (s), reg 149(4).

101 Brig AK Mahtotra v UOI, Madras HC, order dated 14 Mar 1991 in WP No. 628 of 1991.

the witness or declined to cross-examine ..." Before making such record, the obvious requirement would be to ask the accused whether he would like to cross-examine the witness. Further, under para 5 of the format, the CO is required to declare: "The accused was informed by me that he was at liberty to make any statement and call any witness in defence." If in spite of these clear instructions, the respondent was not specifically given an opportunity to cross-examine witnesses and make statement in defence, the default may apparently be attributed to casual handling of the matter by the CO. The same perhaps would be said of the complaint of respondent A-184-A-5 that a "customary hearing of charge was held, as AR 180 was applied in the C of I, and only one witness was produced who was cross-examined - no other witness was produced, neither a chance to produce any witness was given." It is apparent that the discretionary power given to the CO under the proviso to Rule 22(1), as noted earlier, to dispense with the hearing of the charge was, in this case, mixed up to perfunctorily observe the requirement of the procedure prescribed in Rule 22(1). The manner in which this was done may not be assailable in a strict interpretation of the law to the extent of the subsequent trial by the CM being vitiated for that reason, the CO may certainly be blamed for short-circuiting the procedural requirement of the hearing of the charge to the disadvantage of the accused. The same attitude of paying mere lip service to the procedural requirement was perhaps in the case of respondent A-168-A-11. At the hearing of his charge, he too did not cross-examine the witnesses or make a statement or produce witnesses in defence because he was not aware of his rights to do so, even though facing a very serious charge of 'mutiny' which is punishable with death. The respondent was a Signalman with modest academic background of High School certificate and no legal support presently available to an accused at the pre-trial investigation stage. As noted earlier, even respondents like A-184-A-5 and A-186-A-7 who were from officers cadre admitted their lack of awareness of their legal rights. In the case of a Signalman accused of a grave offence, it was therefore sheer insensibility and carelessness on the part of the CO not to have ensured that the accused was explained his rights before the proceedings of the hearing of the charge and S of E started.

In between the two categories of cases involving a casual attitude towards the procedural requirements and those reflecting a clear-cut attempt of sabotaging the laid down procedure were the cases of some infraction of procedure in letter or spirit or both but displaying no apparent intention to scuttle it. Such cases include the case of respondent A-167-A-11 who was not present over the recording of S of E but the S of E was read back to him and he found it to have been faithfully recorded. The case of respondent A-178-A-10 would also fall in this category. Though facing a murder charge, he was not allowed to meet anyone from his family or even a lawyer and hence could not cross-examine witnesses etc. In the case of respondent A-185-A-6, no witnesses were called at the hearing of the charges (10 charges for various offences like using threatening language to superior, disobedience of lawful command, ill-treating subordinate, falsifying official document etc). No hearing of charge was mandatory in his case since it was a pre-1993 amendment case of an officer. However, it does reflect a half-hearted approach and indecisiveness as to the need to conduct the proceedings fairly. Respondent A-193-A-12 facing a charge of disobedience of lawful command was not present throughout nor was he aware of his entitlements at the recording of S of E against him. Respondent No. A-194-A-11 was present at S of E. He noted that the evidence of the witnesses was not read back to him. In the case of respondent No. A-200-A-5, he was charged with the offence of outraging the modesty of a woman. He was on annual leave at the time of the hearing of the charge and the recording of S of E was, oddly enough, carried out before the hearing of the charge.

It would have been considerably valuable if the irregularities pointed out in the foregoing, or at least those of serious nature, had received a judicial verdict on their legal consequences. However, none of the cases except one, reached the Supreme Court or any High Court and even that one case remained undecided by the time of the interview of the concerned respondent. In fact some of the affected respondents did not even feel aggrieved essentially for the reason of their lack of legal awareness as brought out earlier in the case of respondent A-186-A-7. The cases of those who did feel aggrieved of anything at their pre-trial stage, including S of E, have been reflected in Table 19. The response as to the action taken on the grievance and the relief, if any received thereby, was abysmally low as may be seen from Table 21.

TABLE - 21

Action Taken to Redress Pre-trial Investigational Grievance

Srl No.	Response	Response Frequency Action	%	Relief	%
1.	Brought to notice of superior military authorities	02	04	–	–
2.	Complaints to Human Rights organizations	01	02	–	–
3.	Writs in superior civil courts	01	02	–	–
4.	No action taken	01	02	–	–
5.	No response	45	90	–	–
6.	Relief received	–	–	–	–
7.	Relief awaited	–	–	01	02
8.	Nothing happened	–	–	01	02
9.	No response to relief	–	–	48	96
	Total	50	100	50	100

As may be seen from Table 21, only one respondent stated that no action was taken. Again only one respondent brought the case to the notice of the Human Rights organization by making a complaint and another one filed a writ petition in the High Court, whereas 2 (4%) respondents approached superior military authority in this regard. However, none received any relief. This seems to suggest an utter lack of enthusiasm in the minds of those feeling aggrieved to take up their grievances and expect relief. Some of the reasons for this state of mind would include the absence of any legal support to the aggrieved persons before, during and after the investigational proceedings; non-existence of a specific quasi-judicial mechanism and triviality attached generally to mere irregularities, as distinguished from the non-compliance altogether, of the prescribed proceedings.

(e) **Effect of Non-compliance of Irregularities in Pre-trial Investigation**

On the question of the judicial view to be taken on the non-compliance of or the irregularities committed in the pre-trial investigation by the CO, two mutually opposing approaches were adopted in America. According to one, the scope of the Federal Courts review of military justice was limited to a mechanical testing for the bare essentials of jurisdiction over person and offence and the power to impose a sentence. The other approach would have such a review to approximate, in the breadth and depth, the modern collateral review of the proceedings of civil courts in criminal cases[102]. As an interesting co-incidence, these two different approaches stand illustrated by the decisions of two different District Courts[103] on the same plea of two co-accused convicts, ie, pre-trial investigation by the CO before their conviction at a joint CM trial. As a result, while one went free, the other was summarily denied any judicial intervention on the same facts and pleas[104]. Less than two years later, when a petitioner challenged the CM verdict on the grounds of inadequate pre-trial investigation, the District Court found no merit but the Court of Appeals ordered the writ granted, basing its decision solely on the inadequacy of the pre-trial investigation. The Supreme Court, however, reversed the decision, taking the view that the requirement of pre-trial investigation was not jurisdictional.[105] The next year, the Supreme Court unanimously revised the decision of the lower court, stating that the lower court "was in error in extending its review for the purpose of determining compliance with the due process clause to such matters as the proposition of law set forth in the staff judge advocate's report, the sufficiency of the evidence to sustain respondent's conviction, the adequacy of the pre-trial investigation, and the competence of the law member and defence counsel. The single inquiry, the test is, jurisdiction. In re Grimley."[106] This approach to the collateral review of military cases remained unaffected from the new dimension added by Johnson v Zerbst,[107] until Burn v Wilson.[108] In the Burn's case even though the Supreme Court refused to interfere on the ground that the military courts "have heard petitioners out" and therefore nothing remained for civil courts to do, it was recognized in principle that the "constitutional guarantee of due process is meaningful enough, and sufficiently adaptable, to protect soldiers – as well as civilians." Further, Mr. Justice Frankfurter, who did not share formally the plurality opinion, did make the essentials of his position clear that on an application of habeas corpus challenging the sentence of a military tribunal, the inquiry was not to

---

102 Joseph W. Bishop, JR, "Civilian Judges and Military Justice : Collateral Review of Court Martial Convictions", op cit, ch 5, n 80, at p 43.

103 Anthony v Hunter, 71 F Supp 823 (D Kan 1947) and Arnold v Cozart, 75 F Supp 47 (ND Tex 1948).

104 Private Anthony and Arnold were jointly tried by a CM on 03 Apr 1945 for having raped three German women a month back.

105 Humphrey v Smith, 336 US 695 (1949).

106 Hiatt v Brown, 339 US. The reference cited (In re Grimley) was a 60 year old decision 137 US 147 (1890) wherein the Supreme Court had described the enlistment of a person in the Armed Forces as "a contract between the soldier and the Government which involves, like marriage, a change in his status which cannot be thrown off by him at his will".

107 304 US 458 (1938).

108 346 US 137 (1953). The landmark decision in the case is described as "the principal lighthouse in these trackless waters" of collateral review in court-martial cases; Bishop, "Civilian Judges and Military Justice : Collateral Review of Court Martial Convictions", op cit, n 102, at p 51.

be confined to the legality of its constitution and the spread of its jurisdiction to the person and crime nor was the duty of the civil court over when it found that the sentence had been reviewed by military hierarchy. He also saw no reason for the principle of Johnson v Zerbst as any less applicable to military as the civil courts that the jurisdiction may be lost by a denial of whatever process is due in the circumstances. The general effect of Burn's case on the review of the military cases in the future, being beyond this discussion relating to pre-trial investigation irregularities, the American military legal position on the issue need not be pursued any further, except that the current provisions of UCMJ explicitly declare that a failure to comply with the requirement for a thorough and impartial investigation as a condition precedent to its being referred to a GCM for trial shall not constitute a jurisdictional error.[109]

Like the Americans, the English also believed that by joining the army, a man enters into a compact under which his right becomes the concern only of military men and not of the courts.[110] Accordingly, the High Courts in the UK too have generally been disinclined to exercise control over military decisions. The general approach adopted in judicial review of CM matters has been that the High Court has no jurisdiction over a CM by way of writs of certiorari, prohibition and mandamus (now termed as applications of judicial review) except where the latter has acted without or exceeding its jurisdiction and the civil rights of the soldier are affected. At times, a very narrow interpretation was placed on 'jurisdiction' by declaring that once it is conceded that the petitioner was a soldier, a CM has jurisdiction to try him.[111] This apparently would not cater for situations of 'lost' jurisdiction of the American decision in Johnson v Zerbst. Further, the subjectivity of the person to military cannot be the sole content of the jurisdiction, as may be seen from a plea to jurisdiction that an accused is entitled to make at his trial by the CM. The grounds for this inter alia include that the charge against him has not been investigated by his CO in the prescribed manner[112].

In India, in matters of the judicial review of military decisions, our superior courts have generally remained influenced by the fundamental principles followed in the American and the British courts. Accordingly, it is easy to see that if the jurisdiction of a High Court under Art. 226 or of the Supreme Court under Art. 32 had been invoked

---

109 UCMJ, Art 32 (e). Howev er, it may be underlined that the pre-trial in vestigation under Art 32 is not an investigation by the CO. The investigation under Art 32 seems to approximate, in our case, the duty of convening officer under AR, r 37 to satisfy himself about the desirability of a trial by CM in the given case.

110 Dawkin v Lord Paulet, LR 5 QB 94, 109 (1869).

111 ex parte Martyn, 1 All ER 242 (1949); R v OC Depot Battalion RASC, ex parte Elliot, 2 ALL ER 373 (1949).

112 (British) Manual of Military Law, 1972, 12th ed, P&I p 710, n 2; cf Rex v Thomson, 4 Dominion LR 579 (1946) cit in PPS Bedi's case, op cit, n 48, p 1433.

by respondent A-186-A-7 to challenge his conviction by SGCM and sentence of two years' imprisonment with cashiering, on the ground of non-compliance of the pre-trial investigation in his case, the courts would have refused to interfere as they did refuse a few years later in the case of PPS Bedi and Suresh Chand Mehta. On the other hand, if the respondent had demanded such investigation and yet the CO had not conducted the hearing of the charge in his presence, the subsequent SGCM proceedings would have been declared as vitiated, as in the case of Maj Gen DSC Rai, wherein Madras High Court observed: "If the investigation of charges should not go through the process under Rule 22, a very valuable right of the accused to have the charges dismissed by the commanding officer ... will stand completely crippled. The accused has got every right even at that initial stage, as contemplated by Rule 22, to demonstrate that the charges are futile and baseless and they require rejection ..."[113]

The mandatory hearing of the charge and, in whatever cases it was so required prior to 1993 amendment and in all cases now, has to effectively follow the prescribed procedure and keep the spirit of the related substantive provisions. This is amply evident from the judicial view taken in earlier referred cases of Sub Dev Singh, Lance Dafedar Laxman, Maj Sarup Singh Sidhu, and the case of two OR tried by a GCM with a co-accused JCO in spite of the CO having conducted no hearing of the charge against them since he had found no case in respect of those OR.[114] A mere eye-wash of such a hearing without meeting the requirements of the letter and spirit would be tantamount to non-compliance of the mandatory legal requirement.

Even though the soldier's right to justice flows, in common with a civilian compatriots, from the Fundamental Right enshrined in Article 21 of the Constitution of India, which after Maneka Gandhi's case, is required to be so interpreted as "by and large synonymous with the due process in the USA"[115], covering thereby both of the substantive and procedural law[116], this would, however, not come to a soldier's rescue in his fight against such irregularity or inadequacy because of the judicial attitude in review of military cases and the perception of the civil courts regarding military jurisdiction. Flying Officer Sundarajan was tried and convicted of 31 charges of criminal misappropriation from the Air Force Public Fund Account of various sums totaling Rs. 29000. Charges No. 5 and 6 were not at all heard by the CO, being added subsequently in the charge-sheet. In respect of the remaining charges, a total of seven witnesses were before the CO and all were simultaneously asked what they had to say. Since the evidence of each one was not taken separately, at the CO's hearing, there was no opportunity for

113 Maj Gen DSC Rai v GCM Fort St George Madras, op cit, n 34.

114 UOI v Nb Sub Baleswar Ram, AIR 1990 SC 65.

115 Maneka Gandhi v UOI, AIR 1978 SC 597 .

116 HM Seervai 'Constitutional Law of India' 1983 ed (Supplement 1988), B ombay, NM Tripathi, Ch 24.

the petitioner to cross-examine them. On the other hand, as many as 20 witnesses were examined at the S of E and at the CM trial. Thus, the charges were merely read to the accused (petitioner) without giving him an opportunity to cross-examine the witnesses and without hearing him in defence. This non-compliance with the prescribed procedure under Rule 15(a) of the AFR 1950 (now Rule 24 of AFR 1969) deprived the GCM of the jurisdiction to try him and hence his conviction and detention were illegal. There were the grounds before Delhi High Court in his prayer for habeas corpus under Art. 226 of the Constitution and s 491 of the Cr PC, 1898. His petition was, however, dismissed. The High Court concluded that "any error or irregularity at a stage before the case is adjourned for the purpose of having the evidence reduced to writing will not vitiate the subsequent trial as the guilt of the accused has to be established not on the basis of what the commanding officer might have done or might not have done at the initial stage. Any irregularity in procedure at that initial stage might have a bearing on the veracity of witnesses examined at the trial or on the bona fides of the commanding officer or on the defence that may be set up by the accused at the trial but the irregularity can by no means be regarded as affecting the jurisdiction of the court to proceed with the trial." The court then also added, in the next paragraph, that "In the instant case even if (sic)non-compliance with R 15 in the manner alleged, the non-observance of the Rule is not such as to vitiate the trial and ultimate conviction." As to the non-hearing of charges 5 and 6, the High Court held it to be "of no substance as the charges framed at the proceedings under Rule 15 are not final ... it is only the charge-sheet on which the accused is arraigned before the court which is material as it is that charge-sheet alone which forms the basis of the trial and not any other charge sheet which may have been prepared at the initial stage."[117]

It is important to note that, unlike Rule 22 of AR as it stood prior to 1993 amendment, Rule 15 expressly made no exception, in respect of officers, from the mandatory hearing of the charge by the CO in the presence of the accused. The view taken in Sundarjan's case about non-compliance of Rule 15, or of its compliance in a manner which would virtually be its non-compliance, would not accord with the view taken later by the Supreme Court in respect of the requirements of the corresponding Army provision. In one[118] of those cases, the Supreme Court expressed its reservation about the view taken by the Full Bench to the effect that "Rule 15 is directory and its contravention has no impact on the subsequent trial." The provisions of Rule 15 and its successor Rule 24 of AFR 1969, not having an exception as was applicable in the case of Lt Col PPS Bedi, could clearly not be said to be mere directory and had to be taken as mandatory, for the reason of the word "shall" having been used in the texts of Rule 15(a) and the current

117 Flying Officer S Sundarajan v UOI & others, AIR 1970 Del 29 (FB).

118 PPS Bedi's case, op cit n 34, p 1433 (para 37).

provision of Rule 24(1). The Supreme Court had an occasion to pronounce more explicitly on the aspect in the case of Maj GS Sodhi v The Chief of Army Staff wherein "the main thrust of the argument" was "only about the violation of Rules 22 to 25." Going through the factual evidence on the record, in respect of the allegations and counter allegations, as to the petitioner having dispensed with the requirement of the charge hearing in his presence, being on annual leave, the court concluded that "... we are unable to find any flagrant violation of any of these rules. Even otherwise if there are some minor irregularities, they do not in any way, affect the proceedings in the General Court-martial during which a regular trial was conducted." In this context, the court referred to its earlier decision in PPS Bedi's case. Disposing Lt Col S Duggal's petition with that of Major Sodhi, the court noted that in this case too "the petitioner did not exercise his option as provided under Rule 25. Therefore, there is no violation of mandatory Rule so far as the petitioner, who is an officer, is concerned, vide Prithi Pal Singh's case." Thereafter, brushing aside certain other contentions of the petitioner for the reason of their inability to appreciate the evidence in the writ petition, the Supreme Court returned to the earlier point to rule that "so far as the procedure is concerned, even assuming that there was a violation of Rules, particularly Rules 22 to 25, we are of the view that by itself it does not affect the whole trial." While dealing with another contention, the court observed with reference to "procedural safeguards" that "it cannot be held that each and every kind of defect in the procedure renders the verdict invalid. The object and effect of the rules should be considered in the context, bearing in mind the general principle whether such an incomplete compliance has caused any prejudice to the delinquent officer. However, if there is any violation of mandatory Rules, the necessary benefit of the same should be given to the delinquent."[119] At the end, the Supreme Court emphasized the need to appreciate that the military officers entrusted with the responsibility to administer justice under the AA were guided, in the discharge of their duty, by factors like exigencies of service, maintenance of discipline in the Army, speedier trial, the nature of offence and the person against whom the offence is committed. Normally having regard to the high office they hold, there should not be any scope to apprehend deliberate lapse or intentional omission on their part."[120] This concluding observation of the Supreme Court would suggest that any irregularity noticed in the hearing of the charge or S of E would generally not be directed against the interest of the accused. However, if it does seriously affect his interest, it cannot be ignored. On the other hand, minor irregularities in the procedure which would not so vitiate the subsequent proceedings may be illustrated from judicial decisions in cases such as that of Maj Gen Inderjit Kumar wherein the investigation under Rules 22 and 25 was carried out on twelve charges, all in the alternative for offences under AA s 52(b) for criminal

119 Major GS Sodhi v The Chief of Army Staff, AIR 1991 SC 1617, (paras 14 and 15).

120 Lt Col Duggal's case disposed with Maj Sodhi's case, para 37.

misappropriation and s 63 for an act prejudicial to good order and military discipline, but after Dy JAG's advice on the same facts, the charge-sheet for his trial by GCM contained nine charges under AA s 52 and three under AA s 63. This ground brought no relief to the petitioner.[121] The recording of additional S of E even though not specifically provided for in the relevant provisions was also held to be no infraction of the related rule, additional S of E being a necessary concomitant of S of E.[122]

In some pre-trial investigation cases, the decision in the judicial review was marked with attitudinal disinclination in the garb of technicalities rather than the consideration of alleged violation of the rule position. In Rajbir Singh's case, the High Court dismissed the petition with a ruling that "the question whether commanding officer failed to comply with the provision of Army Rule 22 cannot be gone into a writ petition, it being purely a question of fact."[123] The petition alleging the non-compliance of Rules 22, 23, 24 and 180, in another case, was dismissed on the ground that the defence counsel did not raise the grievance during the GCM proceedings and the court could not re-appreciate the evidence while exercising powers under Art. 226 of the Constitution and was satisfied from the record that the proceedings of the CM had been conducted in accordance with the Act and Rules in a fair manner.[124] In an appeal against the decision of the Single Judge and of the Division Bench of the Guahati High Court, the Supreme Court too did not allow the petitioner's counsel to argue for the first time the issues of the GCM not being properly convened and the requirements of Rules 22, 23 and 24 along with Army Order 70 of 1984 not having been strictly complied with.[125] To reinforce their view, the court extracted para 23 of their earlier decision in Major Hussain's case that "when there is sufficient evidence to sustain conviction, it is unnecessary to examine if pre-trial investigation was adequate or not. Requirement of proper and adequate investigation is not jurisdictional and any violation thereof does not invalidate the court-martial unless it is shown that the accused has been prejudiced or a mandatory provision has been violated ..." It is difficult to understand how an accused is expected to show that he has been prejudiced when his counsel is not allowed even to raise the issue, merely because the matter was not raised at trial stage despite the well known limitations of a CM trial and legal competence of military accused persons and their defending officers. It is possible that in all such cases even while rejecting the petitioner's contentions on mere technical grounds, the Justices would not have been uncomfortable in their conscience for the reason of their belief that the pre-trial investigation being at preliminary stage,

---

121 Maj Gen Inderjit Kumar's case, op cit, n 53.

122 Gian Chand v UOI, 1983 Cr L J 1059 (Delhi).

123 Rajbir Singh v UOI, 1989 Cri L J NOC 1 (Del).

124 Balwan Singh v UOI, 2001 Cri L J 1293 (Del).

125 UOI v RK Sharma, AIR 2001 SC 3053 (para 11).

the accused still had opportunity to defend himself at the CM trial which would, and not the earlier proceeding, determine his guilt. However, such reasoning fails to take into account that even if a soldier is later acquitted at the CM, the very stigma of having been 'Court-martialled' incalculably damage his military reputation and professional career prospects and that a properly conducted pre-trial investigation does have an in-built opportunity to spare this by way of the dismissal of the charge. Be that as it may, with the present mindset of the superior courts in the matters of pre-trial investigation irregularities, it is difficult to predict what would have been the fate of respondents Nos. A-167-A-11, A-168-A-11, A-178-A-11,A-10, A-185-A-6, A-188-A-12, A-194-A-11 and A-200-A-5 if their earlier discussed cases had been taken up for judicial scrutiny. Such matters often ostensibly being determinable on the jurisdictionality basis, one may only conclude with Lord Denning that so fine is the distinction between an error which entails absence of jurisdiction and an error made within jurisdiction that "in all cases, the choice is that of the court whether to interfere. If it chooses to interfere, it can formulate the decision in terms of jurisdictional error. The court may say that the tribunal below had no jurisdiction to decide this point wrongly as it did. If the court does not choose to interfere, it can say: the court had jurisdiction to decide it wrongly, and it did so."[126]

6.6 Legal Representation at Pre-trial Investigation

Article 22 of our Constitution requires that no person arrested shall inter alia be denied the right to consult, and to be defended by, a legal practitioner of his choice. Being a part of the constitutional scheme of Right to Freedom comprising of Articles 19 to 22, the protection provided in this provision is to be so interpreted as to be available at all the stages in the right to justice which is in-built in protection of life and personal liberty under Article 21. Accordingly, the Supreme Court ruled in Nandini Satpathy v Dani[127] that Article 22(1) does not mean that a person not under arrest or custody can be denied the right to consult and to be defended by a lawyer of his choice. The apex court further ruled that lawyers' services should be available to a an accused under "circumstances of near custodial interrogation" and equally to promote right against self incrimination under Article 20(3). In the true spirit of the Sixth Amendment to the U.S. Constitution, the U.S. Supreme Court held in Powell v Alabama that "a suspect is usually ignorant of the law, he requires the guiding hand of counsel at every step of the proceedings against him" and the Supreme Court defined 'every step of proceedings' to

126 Pearlman v Harrow School (1979) 3 QB 56, per Lord Denning.

127 Nandini Satpathi v P L Dani and Another , AIR 1978 SC 1025; cf . Ecobedo v Il linois, 378 US 478 (1964) which also brings out two things in this connection; first, a suspect during police interrogation is protected by the privilege against self incrimination; and second, he has a constitutional right to counsel during this time.

"include most pre-trial settings"[128]. No such legal support is, however, available to the Army and Air Force personnel in India at pre-trial stage. Even if such a person procures any legal assistance at his own expense, his counsel is not allowed to be present or to represent him at the pre-trial investigations through C of I or by way of the hearing of the charge and S of E, despite the obvious importance of these proceedings as the foundation of subsequent proceedings and as an opportunity for the accused to show his innocence and ward off thereby any disciplinary proceedings against him in respect of the accusation. Q. 3.3 in the Interview Schedule was designed to seek the view of all the 200 respondents on the desirability or otherwise, of allowing some legal assistance or legal representation to the accused at C of I, hearing of charge and S of E. The data collected in this regard are presented in Chart 6.3.

128 Powell v Alabama, 287 US 45 (1932).

Chart 6.3

Desirability of Legal Assistance

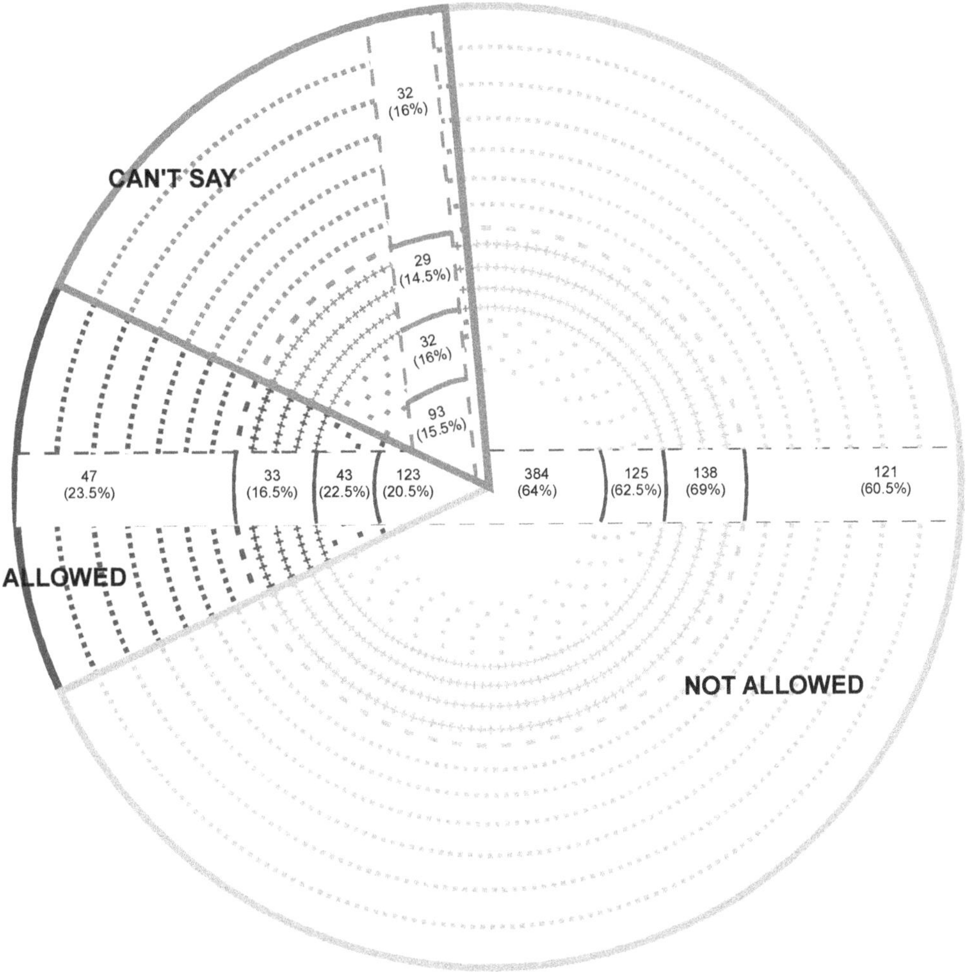

EXPLANATION DATA						
		MEMBERS	JA	GEN CAT	ACCUSED	TOTAL
NOT ALLOWED	S of E	39	41	37	04	121
	H of Ch	48	42	40	08	138
	C of I	44	38	39	04	125
ALLOWED	S of E	09	02	12	24	47
	H of Ch	00	01	10	22	33
	C of I	03	05	10	25	43
CAN'T SAY/ NR	S of E	02	07	01	22	32
	H of Ch	02	07	00	20	29
	C of I	03	07	01	21	32
TOTAL		150	150	150	150	600

As may be seen from Chart 6.3, out of 200 respondents as many as 138 (69%) were opposed to the idea of the counsel being allowed to assist or represent the accused at the hearing of the charge (hereinafter referred to as 'H of C') and 121 (61.5%) and 125 (62.5%) were opposed to the counsel at S of E and C of I respectively. Interestingly, only 4 (8%) , 8 (16%) and 4 (8%) out of 50 accused respondents formed part of these figures of those opposed to counsel at S of E , H of C and C of I respectively. One may feel tempted to infer from these figures that some sort of class bias existed in the minds of these respondents. However, this would perhaps be a hasty inference since 37 (74%), 40 (80%) and 39 (78%) out of 50 respondents from general category, who had never been a part of any CM as a member or Judge Advocate, too opposed the presence of a civil counsel to assist or represent the accused at S of E, H of C and C of I respectively. Though 32 (64%) out of 50 respondents from the general category had a military background, even out of the remaining eighteen respondents who were purely civilians from different professions, a sizable number of 13 (92% of the 18) was opposed to the idea of legal assistance/ representation being allowed at pre-trial investigation stage. One of them (G-109-C-5), a former academician with Ph. D. in Law and then holding the position of Secretary, Law Commission of India remarked: "though lawyers in a criminal trial are must and cannot be dispensed with but in the case of CM it is possible to have no lawyers because of Article 33."

The number of respondents from 'A' (accused) category who were in favor of legal representation at the S of E, H of C and C of I was 24, 22 and 25 respectively. It acquires greater significance since these figures were out of 28, 30 and 30 respectively, the remaining 22, 20 and 20 making no response or making a response of 'can't say'. Thus, 24 out of 28 (86%), 22 out of 30 (73%) and 25 out of 30 (83%) from this category were in favour of legal representation at pre-trial investigation stage, which is a very high percentage.

Some respondents did qualify their response while some others gave reasons for the view held by them either for or against the presence of a lawyer at pre-trial investigation proceedings. The reasons against the presence of a lawyer may be broadly categorized into three: one, the causation of delays; two, improper attitude of lawyers in general; and three, inadequate understanding of military law on the part of most of the civilian lawyers. On the first count, respondent No. M-6-A-3 feels that the presence of lawyers may at times result into resolution of the case at the preliminary stage but in most cases that stage itself will prolong unreasonably because of the obstructionist attitude of the lawyers. Five other respondents expressed the same view in different words. Respondent No. G-110-C-6, a retired IAS officer, has this to say in rather hard hitting words:

"Ideally speaking, the role of a civil lawyer is to assist the court in reaching a just and truthful finding in the case. But in practice the ennobled profession of lawyer is being prostituted to earn money only and the best skills and genius of the profession work as hired harlots of the rich and those who can pay, resulting into most anti-social manifestations. Hence, appearance of a civil lawyer at any preliminary stage ... will simply be a stumbling block."

A new dimension is added to this view by what respondent A-186-A-7 states. Having himself been tried by a CM and now being a practising lawyer with a Ph. D. degree on a military law related topic, his line of thinking cannot be easily brushed aside when he stays that there is no use of having a lawyer at any of these stages (C of I, H of C and S of E) unless lawyers knowledgeable in the military law are available. Presently the lawyers and even the officers from the JAG's Department, according to him, are disappointingly deficient in the knowledge of military law.

Irrespective of such an adverse impression, some respondents find it a felt need that legal assistance be available to the affected person since "such advice is available to prosecution/ administration from the staff officers" (M-31-A-5). The requisite assistance may be procured from a legally qualified officer (M-31-A-5 and J-100-A-6) or an officer from the JAG's Department (G-105-C-5 and G-133-A-5) or a civil counsel (J-94-A-6). Some respondents, however, had a compromising solution to suggest that a civil counsel generally need not be allowed at a pre-trial investigation but an exception could be made in "very serious cases when persons affected don't have much of legal sense" (five respondents). Respondent No. G-112-C-4, a senior practising lawyer suggested an objective criterion that a lawyer could be provided to the accused at government expense in serious cases punishable with imprisonment for more than ten years. Similarly some respondents recommended the lawyer to be allowed at S of E only "which forms the basis for subsequent trial" (six respondents). One of them suggested that a civil lawyer be allowed both at S of E and at SCM, not for or against the accused but only to advise the officer recording the S of E or the CO holding the SCM. Yet another suggestion was that counsel be allowed to the concerned person at his own expense but only for consultation and not for representation. The view came full circle with respondent A-183-A-5 suggesting that the counsel be allowed for C of I and S of E but not for H of C and SCM and respondent G-147-A-9 recommending a counsel for the very first stage, i.e., C of I, adding that the counsel's presence at that stage will stabilize things.

To sum up, out of the 200 respondents, only 30 elaborated upon their response on the issue. Their views may be reflected in Table-22 on the next page:

TABLE - 22

The Elaborations on Response to Counsel's Appearance at Pre-trial Investigation

Srl	Elaborated Points	ResponseFrequency	Percentage
1.	Why no Counsel	13	6.5
2.	Counsel at part of pre-trial stage such as S of E only	04	2.0
3.	No counsel but alternate legal assistance	03	1.5
4.	Counsel in serious cases only	05	2.5
5.	Counsel only for consultation	01	0.5
6.	Counsel only for advice to officer recording S of E	01	0.5
7.	Counsel or legally qualified officer be allowed to accused since legal advice available to prosecutor	02	1.0
8.	Counsel's presence if dispensed, not legally objectionable	01	0.5
9.	No elaborating comments	170	85.0
	Total	200	100

If the responses of those who have gone through the mill of the CM suggest that the wearer knows where the shoe pinches, the responses of the others equally represent a genuine concern for the institutional interest, untainted with any personal bias. Wading through the two sets of conflicting demands, one has to reach the golden gate of justice and equity by striking at a solution that meets the needs of both the individual and the organization. While no legal support whatsoever is available to the Army and the Air Force accused personnel, even the mechanism available to a sailor under the Naval law, as brought out earlier in the context of pre-trial custody, seems to fall short of the requirement of effectual legal assistance, since the person appointed to assist the accused thereunder "may or may not be law qualified"[129], whereas at the corresponding civilian criminal proceedings by a magistrate, the offender and the prosecutor both have a right to legal representation. Under the British military law, an affected person at the C of I has a right of "being present and represented[130]" and legal assistance is also not missing

129 N Regs II (S), reg 26,

130 Br AA, s 135(4) read with Board of Inquiry Rules, r 11.

all together at the CO's hearing, at which no advocates as such appear for the prosecution or the accused. A mechanism exists to ensure that the accused does not suffer in his defence for want of a right to be legally represented at the investigation by the CO.[131] The U.S. system has similar provisions in respect of legal support to an accused at inquiry by his immediate commander and at C of I.[132] Under the Australian military law, if an accused person requests for representation by a legal officer at the hearing before the CO or a superior summary authority, the legal officer's services are permitted to him, if such officer is available and the leave is given by the CO or superior military authority.[133] In the Canadian system, an assisting officer is appointed, as in our Naval system, to assist an accused as soon as possible after the charge has been laid. The accused is also afforded an opportunity to consult with the counsel about the choice, if he is to make, between summary trial and a trial by CM. In a survey conducted for the office of the JAG, accused persons were found to have contacted a lawyer about such choice in 32.6% cases.[134]

Keeping in mind the innovations adopted in various modern military systems to strike a balance between the military need of upholding the CO's authority and the requirements of the human rights and natural justice, our current provisions of pre-trial investigation need to be suitably modified. While it may not be desirable, for various reasons, such as the needs of expedient disposal and so on (and also in view of the responses of over 60% respondents in the present study against the induction of lawyer at C of I, H of C and S of E), to allow a civil counsel to represent the accused at the pre-trial investigation proceedings, the accused should not be left high and dry altogether

---

131 The pamphlet 'Rights of A Soldier ...' is issued to a WO, NCO or Private before he is put up to the CO for investigation of charge. At the summary hearing, if any to be conducted, which is permissible only in the case of a serviceman below the rank of WO, is entitled to be assisted by an 'Accused's Advisor' (normally an officer, WO or SNCO available for consultation and also having the power to make a statement about the background of the accused or in mitigation of punishment to be awarded to the accused and can also assist the accused to prepare questions for witnesses). If the CO does not dismiss the charge but refers the case to the higher authority, the latter may in turn, refer the case to the prosecuting authority. The Prosecuting Authority has the power to order a 'preliminary examination' which is to be conducted in the army by an officer of the legal services branch of any corps of the regular forces and in accordance with a prescribed procedure (Br AA 1955, s 83A read with pamphlet 'Rights of a Soldier ...' paras 24-25). In the case of criminal offences, the matter is investigated by the Royal Military Police at which investigation, the accused is entitled to a lawyer to represent him. These provisions have been modified to some extent, under the Armed Forces Act, 2006 but not to the disadvantage of the accused.

132 The U.S. military law has no provision for the accused to be legally represented at preliminary inquiry by the immediate commander but does have a right to legal representation at the pre-trial investigation before trial by GCM and also at C of I under UCMJ Articles 32 and 135 respectively.

133 The Defence Force Discipline Act, 1982 (Cth), s 198.

134 Lamer, Independent Review of Bill C-25, op cit, Ch 5, n 120, pp 59-60.

without any support even at that stage of DPCM. Accordingly, the related legal provisions may be amended to ensure that when the involvement of a person subject to the Services law is brought out, his legal care should be allocated to an officer with sufficient service and experience to his credit; preferably from his own Company, Battery or Squadron. Such officer should be charged with the responsibility to ensure that the necessary infrastructure of administrative as well as legal support is not wanting in the defence of the accused as his ward. Either the said officer himself or some other officer or a civil lawyer with adequate grounding in military law should be available to guide the accused in his defence throughout the pre-trial stage, including custody hearing (if any, introduced in accordance with the recommendations made in the last chapter) and the proceedings before the CO and at S of E. It should be ensured that the intended legal support is not allowed to degenerate into mere tokenism. This will require firstly, that the related rules, regulations and administrative instructions issued by the Government or the Services headquarters are meticulously amended to institutionalize the approach. Secondly, the selection and availability of the right person will have to be ensured in a true spirit of comradery towards the accused, along with an unbiased attitude of treating a person innocent until he is proved to be guilty. Lastly, no compromise should be made on the question of competence of the person to legally assist the accused. He could be a law qualified officer with at least ten years service to his credit or a sufficiently senior officer of the rank of at least Lt Col who has done DSSC or an officer who, even though of a junior rank and service, has been an instructor in military law at a Service training institution for a period of at least two years. If a civilian lawyer is engaged for this purpose, he should be unhesitatingly asked about his experience of military cases before he is retained, unless he had military law as one of the papers for his university law degree.

CHAPTER - 7

TRIAL BY COURT MARTIAL

> *"It has rightly been said that Court-martial remains to a significant degree a specialist part of over-all mechanism by which the military discipline is preserved ..... Court martial discharges judicial function and ... has also the same responsibility as any court to protect the rights of the accused charged before it."* [1]
>
> - Justice D. P. Wadhwa

Even though the time when the Army could rationally be described as a "separate community" with a separate system of government[2] is long past[3], the special needs for which the military justice system is designed inevitably make it a tailor-made exercise. The ad hoc nature of CM, the process required to set up such a body, its composition, the trial procedure prescribed for it, its power of punishment, the authority wielded by superior commanders over its pronouncements and a limited judicial review of its decisions, are all dictated by those special needs and are manifestly different, in a degree varying from aspect to aspect, from their counterparts under the ordinary criminal justice. A bird's eye view of the CM system has been presented earlier in Chapter - 2. The data collected in response to questions in the Interview Schedule will be examined here to see as to what attitudes are adopted at various stages of the CM trial.

7.1 Convening of Court-Martial

CM being an ad hoc body, an appropriate kind of military tribunal out of the ones available in the related law is selected and convened every time a person subject to the concerned Services Act is to be tried under the military justice system. This is done by an

1 Justice D.P. Wadhwa in UOI & Others v Major A Hussain, AIR 1998 SC 577 .

2 Carter v Mc Claughry, 183 US 365, 389 (1902), wherein Chief Justice Fuller thought that this apartheid was "essential to the maintenance of discipline which renders the Army efficient in war and morally progressive in peace."

3 Bishop, "Civilian Judges and Military Justice: Collateral Review of Court Martial Convictions", op cit, Ch 5, n 80, at p 70.

order[4] issued by an authority specified in the concerned Service Act as empowered to convene a CM of the specific kind of CM, if the said authority in the particular case is holding a warrant ('commission' in the Naval terminology) to do so. The officer convening the CM is generally a Brigade or equivalent commander or an officer superior to him, in the channel of command of the accused, who holds the necessary warrant.

(a) **As Source of Command Influence**

Since the basic aim of military justice is the maintenance of discipline[5], "one of its dominant features has always been control by the commander. But such control carries with it the serious danger that the commander may use his influence improperly. The temptation is certainly great."[6] Several checks and balances are adopted under the modern military justice systems to keep away the command influence flowing through the process of convening CM. Under the British system, for instance, the responsibility of convening the GCM and DCM now lies with the court administration officer, who is appointed by the Defence Council. He also has the duty of selecting the members for the CM from outside the accused's immediate chain of command, so as to ensure that there is no suggestion of the command pressure.[7] The National Defence Act of Canada similarly has now a Court Martial Administrator who is responsible for convening the CM, appointing members of GCM and Disciplinary Court Martial panels and performing other administrative functions associated with the convening of a CM.[8] In America, when the UCMJ was first enacted, Congress acknowledged the need to address both

---

4 The order is known as 'convening order' in the Army and Air Force. In the Navy, it is called 'Warrant for Assembly of the Court Martial'. It is on a prescribed form in the case of GCM/DCM (IAFD-916) and SGCM (IAFF-956). No convening order is issued for SCM which is held by the CO of the accused by endorsing an order to that effect on the Offence Report (IAFD-901) itself. The convening order contains all necessary details such as the kind of the CM being convened, the details of the accused to be tried, the names and ranks of the officers to constitute the CM as members, along with the officers in reserve (known as 'waiting members'), the particulars of the JA and the Prosecutor, the interpreter and the short hand writer (but not the particulars of the defending officer and the defence counsel) and the date and place for the assembly of the CM. Judge JW Rant remarks, perhaps lightly, that a convening order of a CM may be regarded as a 'birth certificate'; Rant, Courts Martial, Discipline, And The Criminal Process In The Armed Services, op cit, Ch 3, n 21, p 9 (1.20). However, this would not be an accurate statement and may even create jurisdictional error if a convening order is issued after the 'birth' of the CM as birth certificate issued after the child is born.

5 Clode, Military Forces of the Crown, Vol. II, p. 361, cit in Winthrop, Military Law and Precedents, op cit, ch 1, n 1,p 49.

6 Joseph Di Mona, Great Court Martial Cases, 1972, New York, Grosset & Dunlop, pp vii to xi (Introduction by Hon'ble Birch Bayh)

7 Rant, loc cit, pp9,147, see also Armed Forces Act 2006, s.154(4) requiring members other than the JA being specified by or on behalf of the court administration officer.

8 Lamer, Independent Review of Bill c-25, op cit, ch 5, n 120, pp. 31-32

actual and apparent unlawful command influence[9] and provided in general terms inter alia that no authority convening general, special or summary CM, nor any other commanding officer may censure, reprimand or admonish the court or any member, military judge, or counsel thereof, with respect to the findings or sentence adjudged by the court or with respect to any other exercise of it, or his functions in the conduct of the proceedings.[10]

In our system, however, the CM is still convened by a superior military authority commanding a Formation which the unit of the accused forms part of or commanding a similarly placed military establishment or training institution.[11] This brings in more vigorously the possibility of the command influence, directly or indirectly, since "the members of the court martial must look to the appointing officer for promotions, advantageous assignments and efficiency ratings – in short, for their future progress in the service."[12] In view of this, all the 200 respondents were asked what they felt about the authorities of the same army command convening the CM, appointing the members and the JA for the CM, reviewing the CM proceedings and confirming, in most cases, as well as taking on the pre-confirmation petition. The multiple choices of response inter alia included the out-sourcing to different army commands any of these responsibilities. The related question (Q. 3.3(c)) of the Interview Schedule fetched the data reflected in Table 23.

---

9 United States v Cruz, 20 MJ 873, 880 (ACMR 1985) (en banc) reviewed on other grounds, 25 MJ 326 (CMA 1187)

10 UCMJ , Art 37(a)

11 AA ss 109, 110 and 112 ; AFA ss 110,111 and 113; Powers to convene GCM, DCM, SGCM respectively in the Army and the Air Force.

NA ss 97 and 95. Power to order CM lies with the President or any officer empowered in this behalf by commission of CNS. The officer having the power to order CM may order a Disciplinary Court to be constituted instead of a CM if he considers that the nature of the offence is such as not to necessitate trial by CM, in the case of an of ficer, in time of w ar or on activ e service, and the of fence is one of those specified in NA s. 95.

12 Reid v Covert, (1957) 1 L. Ed 2d. 1148: 354 US 1, per Justice Black at p 1174 of L Ed.

TABLE - 23

Whether Different Army Command be Involved in CM Process

Sr. No.	Options	M	J	G	A	Total	%	Remarks
		Response Frequency						
1	No Change in present provision/practice	30	25	24	09	88	44.0	
2	Members be drawn from outside command	06	01	02	04	13	06.5	
3	Different Commands be involved in---							
	(a) Appointing members	01	00	00	11	12	06.0	
	(b) Making RAT	01	00	02	01	04	02.0	}Advised by }Dy JAG
	(c) Making RT	01	02	01	01	05	02.5	
4	Any other suggestion	08	15	19	02	44	22.0	
5	No comments/can't say/no response	03	07	02	22	34	17.0	
	TOTAL	50	50	50	50	200	100.0	

As many as 88 (44%) out of 200 respondents saying 'No' to any change in the present practice of convening a CM within the same army command to which the accused belongs or is attached gives an impression of a conservative attitude on the part of the respondents on the issue. However, a somewhat different picture would emerge from the suggestions and explanations given by different respondents. Before adverting to those suggestions, it may be noted that 13 respondents (6.5%) are in favour of the members of the CM being drawn from outside the army command and 12 (6%) would like to have the appointment of such members being given to an army command other than that where the CM is being convened. Further, 4 (2%) respondents are for outsourcing the task of preparing pre-trial legal advice (RAT) to a different army command and yet another 5 (2.5%) have the same recommendation to make in respect of post-trial legal advice (RT), both of which are presently rendered by Dy JAG of the army command in which the trial is held or by officers posted under him. Thus, a total of 34 (17%) respondents are in favour of change in the present practice. Some of these respondents have suggested more than one change. Their explanations and suggestions, given in addition to specific response to the question, reveal that 39 (19.5%) respondents voted for the combination of the options at serials 2,3, 4 and 5. For instance, Respondent

M-32-A-5 who, being a legally qualified officer, has held a staff appointment dealing with disciplinary cases, at Area Headquarter level, was of the view that CM should be convened by a commander other than a Formation commander in the channel of command of the accused so as to avoid influence on witnesses. Further, the respondent would also not like to have members drawn from the same Formation except in minor cases. More or less the same was the view of respondent A-200-A-5, an officer from the Army Medical Corps. who, having been convicted of the offence of outraging the modesty of a woman, felt that "CM should invariably be held outside the command so as to avoid command influence which is always there since members are dependent on such senior officers for their career prospects..." Respondent G-132-A-5 suggests that pre-trial advice be obtained from some independent civil agency. Respondent G-104-C-5, an Additional Legal Adviser in the Ministry of Law and Justice, was generally for no change but an exception could be made, according to him, involving serious charges as was done in the fake enemy encounter case from Siachin in which the trial was held in a different command.[13] Respondent No. N-19-A-4, a 1942 law graduate and 1943 commissioned veteran, wanted the presiding officer to be invariably from a different army command, a pre-trial and post-trial legal advices to be rendered by a staff officer other than from the JAG's Department so that the JAG's Department's officers, while performing the duty as a JA at a CM, are totally free from all prejudice, direct or indirect. Respondent No. G-110-C-6, a retired IAS officer with university degree in law, felt the need of different army command headquarters being involved in the appointment of members and dealing with petitions relating to CM, so as to neutralize the command influence, but the rest of the related matters may continue to be dealt within the same army command so as to have expeditious disposal of cases. G-136-A-5 would like the same army command being involved in the prosecution but not sitting in judgement so as to avoid the influence of preconceived view on the guilt, arisen from prior information, and being partisan as a party to the matter or making no application of mind as a result of acting on the advice of somebody else.

Rest of the explanations and suggestions are in support of 'no change' for various reasons such as, likely delay in disposal, erosion of the GOC-in-C's command, making the Dy JAG's position suspect and the present system being time tested, which all reasons would not deserve to be lightly ignored. The academic standard of our men being what it is, they are guided more by instincts and emotions than by rationality and reasoning

13 Major Surender Singh of 5/5 Gorkha Rifles was charged under Army Act s. 63 (an act prejudicial to good order and military discipline) for having staged fake encounters with the enemy in August 2003 on Point 5469 in Siachin glacier . He w as tried b y a 7 member GCM f rom Sep. to Dec. 2004 . In order to achieve transparency, the GCM was convened by GOC 12 Desert Corps and assembled at Jodhpur. He was being defended by ex-Major R.S. Randhawa, now a Judge of P&H High Court, but was convicted and sentenced to 3 year RI and dismissal from the Service on 21 Dec. 2004.

and hence are more regimentally oriented than the European soldier. As a result, the dispensation of justice within the same command may prove to be more effective in their case, from the discipline and command needs point of view, as an extension of regimental spirit. However, this would certainly need, especially in the changing social environment, reciprocity, in equal measure, on the part of those in the 'upper bracket of the armed forces', i.e., the officers class. For this, the latter will have to rise above their age old class prejudice and rank consciousness and come down to sympathetically understand the problems and aspirations of their men as members of the Service family without, of course, sacrificing the interest of the organization and the call of duty. Lastly, while interpreting the data on 'no change', it should not be overlooked that a sizable number of 22 out of 50 (44%) persons tried by the CM remained non-responsive to the question, which may not necessarily be reflective of their position as fence sitters. However, the irony of the situation is that one cannot take it as something adding strength to either side too.

(b) **An Administrative Law Perspective**

Administrative law, at its most fundamental, is about power and its allocation, operating at two levels - horizontal and vertical, the former involving the description of powers and their exercise by the concerned authority and the latter being concerned with the distribution of the power between the court and any one of the bodies exercising public law functions, keeping in mind the sovereignty of Parliament, the rule of law and an implicit view of the purposes of a legal system.[14] However, administrative law being often criticized for terminological inexactitude, one may, in the present context, move on to the laid down powers of the convening officer and his related responsibility, without indulging in the controversy of their classification as quasi-judicial or administrative.

On receipt of an application for trial from the CO, or from any such officer as empowered under the Naval law to apply for a CM in the given circumstances,[15] the convening officer is required, before convening a CM, to satisfy himself about the legality of the charge, its justifiability in the face of the evidence in the S of E (and the facts stated in the circumstantial letter in a case under the Naval law[16]) and that the case is proper one to be tried by the kind of the CM he proposes to convene.[17] If not so satisfied, the convening officer will take an appropriate decision, including a decision to release

14 PP Craig,Administrative Law, 1983, London, Sweet & Maxwell, Ch. 1.

15 N Regs II (S), reg 148 (2) to (5).

16 Ibid, reg 153(1).

17 On being so satisfied, he con venes an appropriate kind of CM under AA or AF A, as the case ma y be. Under the Naval law, there being only one kind of CM, the convening authority satisfies itself that a CM is required to be convened. If the nature of the offence does not necessitate a trial by CM, he may order a Disciplinary Court to assemble in the case of an officer who committed, in time of war or on

the accused when the offence discloses no offence having been committed by the accused.[18] Various options available to a convening officer under the AA, as a superior officer, are; one, that he may refer the case to the next superior; secondly, he may direct the disposal of the case summarily or by SCM if legally feasible; thirdly, he may convene a GCM or DCM depending upon the rank of the accused and the gravity of the charge made out from the evidence, and finally, he may dispose of the charge summarily under AA ss 83 or 84, if he has the legal powers to do so.[19] The details of other connected duties of the convening officer are laid down in the provisions of the rules made under the AA and AFA and the regulations made under the NA.[20] These duties are expected to be performed by the convening officer by keeping in mind the general requirement of administrative law relating to discretionary powers.[21] Since absolute discretion, like corruption, marks the beginning of the end of liberty, as Justice Douglas observed,[22] various checks are laid down in the rules, regulations and administrative instructions.[23] For instance, the law requires that the members of a CM for the trial of an officer accused shall be of a rank not lower than that of the accused officer unless, in the opinion of the convening officer, the officers of such rank, having due regard to the exigencies of the Service, are not available and that in no case shall an officer below the rank of Captain be a member of a CM for the trial of a field officer. Further, such opinion of the convening officer is required to be recorded in the convening order.[24] Thus the convening officer's power to appoint members to constitute the court is subject to the checks laid down in

active service, any of the offences listed in NA s 95. When the convening officer is satisfied, on the other hand, that a CM "ought to be convened" and that all the documents received by him are in order, he issues a warrant, together with a copy of the charge-sheet, to the officer nominated by him as president of the CM, directing him to assemble a CM at the place and date stated in the warrant; N Regs II (S), reg 159. Other duties of a convening officer under the Naval law are laid down in regs 160-165, 167 and 168.

18 AR, r 37 (1); AFR r 43(1).

19 RA para 449 (a). A convening officer under the AF Regs, 1964, has similar duties and powers except that disposal by SCM is not available under the AF law.

20 AR, r 37 read with MML Vol. II, p 286, Notes 1 to 7 to Rule 37; cf SAO 1/S/2002-DV-Court Martial; AFR, r 43; N Regs II (S) regs 156-165, 167, 168 read with Guide on Naval Law, 1990, Judge Advocate General, Naval Headquarters, New Delhi, pp 34-36

21 Discretionary power is a power with choice between alternative courses of action and may be distinguished from ministerial powers, prescribed in certain and specific terms, leaving nothing to the choice; Keir and Lawson, Cases in Constitutional Law, (5th ed) 1967, Oxford University Press, p 402; cf Hirday Narain v ITO, AIR 1978 SC 209.

22 New York v USA, 342 US 882.

23 Squadron Leader G N Raju v OC 48 Squadron, AIR 1974 All. 362, upholding the power of the Service authorities to issue instructions which are not inconsistent with the Services Acts or the rules or regulations made thereunder and the obligation of Servicemen to carry them out.

24 AR, r 40 (2), (3); AFR r 46 (2), (3); NA s 97 (7), (13) – (17) for the rank of the officer to be appointed as president of CM in different kinds of cases. The president appoints other members by following the procedure prescribed in s 97(19) and AR r 102.

this rule. In Charanjit S Gill's case, an officer, junior to the accused was appointed to perform the duty of the JA, at his trial by GCM. An officer who is disqualified for sitting on a CM as its member is also disqualified for acting as a JA at the CM. In view of this, the Supreme Court held that the JA appointed with the CM should not be an officer of a rank lower than that of the officer facing the trial unless the officer of such rank is not (having due regard to the exigencies of public services) available and the opinion regarding non-availability is specifically recorded in the convening order. The Supreme Court dismissed the appeal, upholding the decision of the High Court which had quashed the convening order and the sentence of the CM on the ground of an officer junior to the accused having been appointed as the JA.[25] Various other checks to regulate the powers of the convening officer and the exercise of discretion by him thereunder relate to the appointment of presiding officer of an appropriate rank,[26] the need of a reference by the convening officer to the Dy JAG Command or DJAG Corps in all cases of indecency, fraud, theft (except ordinary theft) and civil offences except simple assault before ordering a trial by GCM, and the debarring of a superior officer from convening the CM if he has been the CO of the accused at any time between the date on which the cognizance of the offence was taken against the accused and the date on which the case is taken up for disposal by ordering CM etc.[27]

In addition to the legislative control exercised over the discretionary powers of convening officers, in the form of rules, regulations and instructions, a significantly important measure for keeping them in check is judicial control. The latter works at two levels: one, compelling the legislation to desist from conferring too broad or uncabined discretionary power; and secondly, through post-decisional review by courts or institutional tribunals and ombudsman. In the present context, only the post-decisional review by courts is available, the judicial control of uncabined discretionary power having already been exercised in the context of the cases like Ram Sarup v UOI[28] on the issue of repugnancy between Fundamental Rights and the provisions of the AA,NA or AFA. There are several instances of the superior courts intervening in matters relating to exercise of the convening officer's powers, upholding in some cases the action taken under these powers and quashing the concerned orders in others. When the petitioner prayed for the quashing of his conviction on the ground that a member of the CM was from his own corps., it was held that Rule 40(1) would be violated only if all the members of the GCM belonged to the corps. to which the petitioner belonged.[29] In another case, it

25 UOI & another v Charanjit S Gill, AIR 2000 SC 3425, para 23.

26 RA para 460 (a), (c); AFR, r 46; NA s 97 (13) to (16).

27 RA para 459 and 449 (b).

28 AIR 1965 SC 247 .

29 Nb Risaldar Rohiteshwar Singh v UOI, 1982 (2) SLR 236 (Del).

was held by the Supreme Court that the term 'corps.' in such a context would not be synonymous to the expression 'Army Corps.' – it must receive a restricted construction with a narrow connotation of 'every battalion' within the meaning of AR r 187(3).[30]The requirement of AR r 37(1) for the convening officer to satisfy himself about the legality of the charges was held to have been met where the convening officer convened the GCM agreeing with the Dy JAG's pre-trial advice and without giving a hearing to the accused (petitioner).[31] On the other hand, where the convening authority, after taking the decision to bring to trial Sergeant Saheb Dayal Sharma of Air Force Station Samba, left to the staff officer the task of appointing officers to form the CM, Rule 43(3) of the Air Force Rules, 1969 was held to have been violated.[32] In another case, however, the Supreme Court, in appeal, interfered in the decision of the Delhi High Court ,which had set aside the punishment imposed by the CM and directed a compensation of rupees five lakhs, agreeing with the contention that the convening authority had neither applied its mind to the charges or the evidence available, nor exercised the personal power in appointing the members of the CM, in view of the facts that Brigadier Raj Kumar Singh was the convening officer whereas the convening order was signed by Lt. Col. R N Singh. The apex court remitted the case to the High Court with a direction for considering all points raised by the respondent except the plea regarding the violation of Rule 37, noting that the proposal for the assembly of the GCM together with the details of the ranks of the presiding officer and the members to constitute it was in fact approved by the then General Officer Commanding on 2nd April 1987 and thereafter the convening order was signed by Lt. Col. R N Singh on 7th May 1987, the officiating GOC Brig. Raj Kumar Singh having empowered him to do so.[33] The Supreme Court distinguished this case from their earlier decision in Harish Chandra Goswami's case in which such empowerment, though alleged, was not borne out from any record nor was the form for assembly of the CM found to be contemporaneous to the alleged oral order making such empowerment of the staff officer.[34] The last three cases noted here are essentially based on the important principle of the administrative law that the delegated powers cannot be further delegated unless so authorized expressly by the parent Act (delegatus non potest delegare). The rules and regulations containing the powers of the convening officer have been made by the Central Government under the authority of the Services Acts.[35] The superior courts have accordingly upheld or rejected the powers exercised thereunder on the basis as to whether or not the act in question was physically or

30 Lt Col Prithi Pal Singh v UOI, AIR 1982 SC 1413, pp 1428-1429 (paras 26, 27).

31 Major SN Purandare v UOI, 1988 Cri L J 714 (Del).

32 Saheb Dayal Sharma v UOI, (1987) Lab I C 843 (845).

33 UOI & Ors v Gurnam Singh, JT 2004 (4) SC 280 (283-286).

34 UOI & Ors v Harish Chandra Goswami, JT 1999 (3) SC 322: AIR 1999 SC 1940 (para 7).

35 AA s 191; AF A s 189; NA s 184 .

constructively done by the authority empowered by these rules and regulations.

In addition to the primary duty of convening a CM, the convening authority is also assigned various other responsibilities and entrusted with certain other powers such as suspension of certain rules on the ground of military exigencies or the necessities of discipline,[36] action on reference by the CM in the situation of doubt on question before it,[37] power to allow the CM to sit on Sunday or any other holiday[38], dissolving the CM where its continuation is inexpedient or impracticable in the event of the CM having been reduced below the minimum number of officers required by the Act[39] and so on. With such varied powers conferred on the convening officer, an accusation of command influence directly or indirectly incidental thereto cannot be outrightly rejected notwithstanding the control measures being in place. In fact the command influence in the sense of a lawful participation in the process is a "necessary and predominant feature" of the military justice system[40]. The data collected in the present study on the question of command influence in DPCM will be taken up in the next chapter.

On a decision of the convening authority to order the CM, an administrative order is issued by the concerned staff officer to the unit or Formation assigned the administration of the impending trial.[41] Under the Naval law, an officer of the court is appointed by the convening authority to undertake the task of "the due transaction of the administrative business of the court"[42], in addition to a general notice of the CM issued by the convening authority.[43] The unit responsible for arrangement and administration makes all necessary preparation for a smooth functioning of the CM, catering for requisite men, material and funds and arranging the court-room according to the required prescribed lay out of CM.[44]

---

36 AR r. 36.

37 AR r 88 and also on specific pleas such as the one under AR r 51.

38 AR r 81.

39 AA s 117.

40 Major Deena MC Willis "The Road to Hell is Paved With Good Intention: Finding and Fixing Unlawful Command Influence", The Army La wyer, 3 (August 1992).

41 Supra, Ch 2.4 (d).

42 N Regs II (S), reg 165.

43 Ibid, reg 166.

44 Lay- out for the CM under the AA and AFA is described in Ch 2. A CM under the Naval law has a slightly different lay out. The trial JA does not sit on the table where the president and members have their seats. He sits at a separate table, but on the same level at the raised platform, on the left of the court table. The members si t in or der of seniori ty, the of ficer next senior to the pr esident si tting on his right and the second next on his left. The spare (waiting) members shall stand at one end of the court table. Facing the court table, two tables are placed, one f or the ac cused and def ence representativ es at the left of the president and the other for prosecution. The witness box is placed on the right of the court;

On the day the CM is to assemble, the accused shall be medically examined for his fitness to undergo a trial, well before he is brought to the court-room. This is done every day except when the CM is adjourned, for whatever reasons, as a departure from the general requirement of its continuing the trial for day to day.[45]

7.2 Court-Martial Ceremonials and Formalities

Whatever be a psychological explanation, ceremonials have always been an integral part of the military activities. There are numerous references in ancient Indian war treatises about every charioted warrior carrying his brand counch to blow as a token for the commencement of the battle, Krishna's Panchajanya and Arjuna's Devadutta being well known counches. In the context of a highly formal institution of law, it came natural to the military justice system, therefore, to develop indigenous ceremonial formalities to accompany its various proceedings. Even the procedures like the execution of the sentence were marked with specified drills in the olden days. While whip-lashes were to be administered as a punishment awarded to a deserter, for instance, it was traditional to place the unit drum in the centre of the proceedings. Then the unit drummer was called upon to administer the "cat-O'-nine-tails" to the convicted man. From this, military justice came to be criticized as 'drum-head justice' with perceived irrationality. Most of such weird practices have since ceased to exist and others are in the process of fading away.

Until some time back, bugle was sounded to mark the commencement of the CO's orderly room proceedings. The prisoner[46] was taken for the orderly room, with an escort ceremonially dressed and holding an uncovered bayonet upward at chest level and marching ahead and another escort following the prisoner. No such ceremonial practices are now in vogue in the Army for a CM trial. However, under the Naval regulations, the president, along with the trial JA, is responsible to ensure not only that the trial is conducted in accordance with the legal provisions but also that the customary ceremonial

---

N Regs, Appx III, para 2(d) & (e). cf Simmons, The Constitution and Practice of Courts Martial , op cit, Ch 1, n 6, p 492 (s 211). The seating arrangement of CM as described by Simmons, citing QR 771-g

as authority, resembles with the CM lay out currently in vogue in the Navy. However, in the case of Lt. Col. Crawley in 1863, a new arrangement was tried on experimental basis, after a decision at a high power conference of the C -in-C and the S ecretary of State f or War. On being f ound convenient, it was adopted in the Army and later became the basis for the current CM lay out in the Army and the Air Force.

45 The day to day continuation of the trial may be disrupted when it appears that adjournment is necessary for the ends of justice, or that such continuance is impracticable. Otherwise the trial is to continue, between six in the morning and six in the afternoon, every day except Sundays and holidays; AR rr 81, 82.

46 An accused was formerly addressed as 'prisoner' before CM. The custom is still retained in the Navy; Simmons, The Constitution and Practice of Courts Martial, op cit, ch 1,n 6, p 230 Note (2).

is observed[47]. The National Flag is required to be hoisted when a CM is sitting or is about to sit and it shall be hauled down on the court adjourning for the day. A gun is also to be fired each day of the sitting. At the trial of an officer, his sword in scabbard shall be laid on the table opposite to the president so that neither the hilt nor the point is towards the accused. After the evidence and arguments, when the court has considered its findings, the sword shall be so laid, before the court reopens, that the point is towards the accused if he has been found guilty of any of the charges. In the event of his being acquitted on all the charges, the hilt shall be towards him.[48]

Befitting the solemnity of the occasion, those attending the CM in whatever capacity, are required to be ceremonially dressed with full medals, the officers wearing peak caps, the court orderly wearing sash and carrying cane[49]. The accused, however, being in custody, shall be without his belt[50]. The armed escorts of the accused are not to carry their weapons inside the court- room[51] and the accused not to be handcuffed unless this is absolutely necessary to prevent his escape or restraining his violent conduct.[52]

7.3 Assembly of the Court and Proceedings before the Court Opens

At the time and place fixed for the assembly of the CM, the Naval law requires that Captain(s) and Commanders (equivalent to the Army ranks of Colonel and Lieut Colonel respectively) are received by a Petty Officers' (equivalent to JCO in the Army) guard presenting arms to the president of the court ('presiding officer' in the Army terminology). The trial JA shall receive the president at the entrance of the court-room and then introduce the other members of the court to him.[53]

---

47 N Regs II (S), reg 175.

48 Ibid, Appx III, para 5(a).

49 Rant, Courts Martial, Discipline, And The Criminal Process In The Armed Services, op cit, n 7, p 12 (s 1.28).

50 Cf Lieut Col Sisson C Pratt,Military Law – Its Procedure and Practice, op cit, Ch 1, n 10, pp 73-82: Dress GCM-Review Order, DCM – Undress Order, RCM – Drill Order; Dress Regulations for the Army, 1961, prescribe the pattern and occasions of the dress to be worn on different occasions including the occasion of attending CM. A Sam Brown belt or cross belt still worn in the British Army is no more worn by the officers of the Indian Army. Further, the JA at a British CM wears a bench wig, bands and a black full length gown with a red, blue and black girdle, being a civilian advocate appointed as JA. In our case JA is a commissioned officer of the regular Army, Air Force or Navy and accordingly puts on a Service uniform. The accused does wear his cap in India unlike there in the UK.

51 Ibid

52 RA para 461

53 N Regs II (S), Appx III, paras 2 (a) and (k). No corresponding provisions in the Army and Air Force laws. All concerned, however, are expected to reach the court -room in time.

After the members and the JA have taken their seats in the court-room, the order convening the court, the charge-sheet and the S of E are laid before the court and the court satisfy themselves as provided by AR, rr 41 and 42, including their jurisdiction to try the accused, the legality of their constitution, the amenability of the accused to trial by CM, the validity of the charges and so on.[54] If not satisfied or if the full number of officers detailed are not available to serve, by reason of non-availability, disqualification or otherwise and there are not sufficient number of officers in waiting to take their place, the court shall ordinarily adjourn and report the matter to the convening officer. However, if the court is of an opinion that in the interest of justice and for the good of the Service, it is inexpedient to adjourn, it may, if not reduced in number below the legal minimum, proceed after recording its reasons for so doing.[55] The insistence for ordinarily not to proceed with less number of members than appointed, even if not reduced below the legal minimum of five in the case of GCM and three in the case of SGCM or DCM, is based on the assumption that the convening officer in detailing the given number had in mind the desirability of submitting the issue to the arbitration of a larger tribunal in the circumstances of the case, or the need to avoid dissolution of the CM on being reduced below the legal minimum in the wake of unforeseen events occurring during a prolonged trial. It may be kept in mind that once the trial has begun, fresh members cannot be appointed.[56] A trial is said to have commenced when the accused is arraigned.[57] On the other hand, if the court is satisfied on what all it is required to satisfy itself, it will have the accused brought before it. His defending officer and the defence counsel, if any, shall also accompany him, followed with the prosecutor and the prosecution counsel,

---

54 AR rr 41 and 42; AFR r 49 and 50; No corresponding provisions in the Naval law

55 AR r 38 (1); AFR r 44; No corresponding provisions exist in the Naval law since it is only the president of the CM who is appointed by the convening officer and the other members are appointed by the president in the manner provided in NA s 97(19) read with N Regs, regs 167 and 168. The difference between the Naval provisions and the provisions of the other two Services is attributable to the reason that the CM system in the Navy needs to support the sea going operations in which ships sometime spend several months in isolated service leading to discipline related ramifications; Rant,Courts Martial, Discipline, And The Criminal Process In The Armed Services, op cit, n 4, pp 18 and 305-306.

56 MML Vol, II, pp 286,287, Note 4 to AR r 37 and Notes 1 to 3 to r 38

57 Ibid, Note 3 to AR r 38. Under the British military law also the trial is deemed to commence, by virtue of Courts-Martial (Army) Rules, 1997, r 42 (1), immediately after the last court member has been sworn. This was also the view taken by the Assam High Court in Gulab Nath Singh v Chief of the Army Staff, 1974 Assam L R 260. The Bench that took this view included Justice (formerly JAG Army in the rank of Brigadier) D M Sen. However, the decision has been overruled by the Supreme Court in UOI v Maj. Gen. Madan Lal Yadav, AIR 1996 SC 1340, holding that the trial must be deemed to have commenced the moment the GCM assembles and the examination of the charge is undertaken (para 21). The decision, however, would not affect the power of convening authority to appoint fresh members when the court is reduced below the legal minimum "before the accused is arraigned" (but not afterwards) as contemplated in AR r 38.

if any. They will take their seats on being asked by the court to do so.[58] Further proceedings of the CM shall take place in the open court except when the court is closed for deliberation[59] or the proceedings are held 'in camera'.[60]

7.4 Preliminary Proceedings

Before the court proceeds with the examination of the witnesses, there are certain preliminaries to be conducted in the open court as "integral and inseparable parts" of the trial.[61] These include, one, objection of the accused to any members; two, swearing of the members, the JA and other court officials like interpreter and short-hand writer; three, arraignment of the accused and his general plea to the charge as 'Guilty' or 'Not guilty'; four, objection, if any, of the accused to the charge(s); five, special plea to general jurisdiction; six, recording of the accused's plea of 'Guilty' or 'Not guilty' and finally, the plea in bar, if any, raised by the accused.

Q. 2.8 in the Interview Schedule was put to the 50 respondents tried by the CM in respect of those preliminaries as to whether the respondent in each case or his defending officer or counsel had raised any of those pleas and to what result. The data collected in response are reflected in Table 24.

---

58 AR r 43; AFR r 51; N Regs II (S), Appx III, para 5(a).

59 AR r 80-A inserted vide SRO 58 of 22 Feb. 1985; AFR r 87; NA s 100; analogous criminal law: Cr PC s 327. However, deliberation on a question for the decision of the court is to be invariably conducted in a 'closed court', which expression implies the exclusive presence of the members, the JA and the officer-under-instruction, if any; AR r 80. An 'open court', on the other hand, functions in the presence of all concerned, including the accused and is accessible to public and the media.

60 AR rr 80 (1), (2) and 80-A inserted by SRO 550 of 1985; AFR, r 87; NA, s 100. Similar provisions also exist in Cr PC s 327 and the US military law vide UCMJ Art 39 (b). Special provisions, however, require that a witness, other than the prosecutor, shall not, except by the special leave of the court, be present in court while under examination; please see AR, r 139; AFR, r 117. For inherent power of a court to sit in camera, if necessary for the proper administration of justice, please see Naresh Sridhar Mirajkar v Maharashtra, AIR 1967 SC 1.

61 Major Gen. M L Yadav's case, op cit, n 57, para 21.

TABLE 24

Preliminary Objections at CM Trial

Srl. No.	Whether or not objection made, and, if made, to what result	-Objection to-				
		Member	Charge	Jurisdic-tion	Limitati-on	Any Other
1.	Made and was allowed	06	08	01	01	01
2.	Made but was rejected	00	08	06	04	03*
3.	Not made, having no ground	30	23	27	31**	25
4.	Not made being not aware of right	05	02	06	04	04
5.	Not made, considering it futile	01	02	02	01	08
6.	Can't say	01	01	01	01	00
7.	Not applicable, as pleaded guilty	03	03	03	03	03
8.	No response	04	03	04	05	06
	Total	50	50	50	50	50

* Objections to evidence was made but rejected.
** No ground for plea in bar on any count

(a) Objection to Members

The objection to members is the first major event on the accused having been brought before the court and the prosecution and the defence representatives having settled down for the proceedings of the CM. It is such an important procedural safeguard that the law requires the court to take the initiative of inviting any objection that the accused may have against being tried by any officers sitting in the court whose names have been read over to him from the convening order. When the court failed to do so, the Supreme Court ruled that "the participation of respondent 4(the CO presiding over the SCM) rendered the proceedings coram non-judice"[62]. Under the present study, six (12%) out

62 Ranjit Thakur v UOI, AIR 1987 SC 2386 (2391). Referring to the related provision of the substantive law on the subject, the court held that "the non-compliance of the mandate of s. 130 is an infirmity which goes to the root of the jurisdiction and without more, vitiates the proceedings" (page 2389) Accordingly, the apex court concluded that the "proceedings of the Summary Court Martial are rendered infirm in law..." On a review petition pointing out that the provision of AA s 130 was restricted to GCM, DCM and SGCM and was not applicable to SCM, the apex court, on 10 Aug. 1988, corrected the error but

of 50 respondents have stated to have raised objection to members at their trials. As may be seen from the data reflected at Srl. 1 in Table 24, the objection was allowed in all the six cases. Thirty (60%) respondents had no ground to raise such an objection. Five (10%) respondents could not make any objection in this regard because they were not aware of their right to do so and one (2%) respondent raised no such objection because he considered it to be futile. The response to the question in one (2%) case was 'can't say' and there was no response in five (10%) cases while such objection was not applicable in the cases of three (6%) respondents. It may be noted that the right to object to members is not available to an accused while being tried by SCM. This is due to the legal requirement of the CO alone being empowered to hold SCM and also being its lone constituent.[63] No person other than the CO being eligible to do so, there is no alternative available to preside over the CM in the event of an objection being sustained; hence no provision for an objection by the accused at SCM. Further, a right to object to members is available, under the Army and Air Force laws, to the accused only. Under the Naval law, such a right is assigned to the prosecutor as well[64]. Lastly, the accused has no right to similarly object to the JA[65] or the prosecutor, but he is entitled to object to interpreter and short-hand writer[66].

---

maintained its earlier decision of reinstating the petitioner, on other grounds. Irrespective of the judicial faux pas, various observations of the Supreme Court generally confirmed to their earlier pronouncements on the issue in P P S Bedi's case, op cit, n 30, p 1431 (para 33) that the "provision (AA s 130 read with AR r 44) conferring a right on the accused to object to a member of the Court-martial sitting as a member and participating in the trial ensures that the charge of bias can be made and investigated against individual members composing the Court-martial. This is pre-eminently a rational provision which goes a long way to ensure a fair trial".

63 AA s 130 providing for an objection to members forms part of Ch. XI of the AA which deals with GCM, SGCM and DCM only, in addition to the fact that the said provision itself expressly speaks of only these three kinds of CM and not SCM. Rule 44 dealing with the procedure to resolve such objection also forms part of 'Section-2 General and District Courts Martial' under Ch V of the AR. Section 3 of this Ch dealing with SCM has no such provision whereas Section 5 on SGCM has Rule 154 for such challenge on the line of Rule 44. Additionally, it may be noted that AA s 116 runs as under:

> *116. **Summary Court-martial.** (1) A summary court-martial may be held by the commanding officer of any corps, department or detachment of the regular Army, and he shall alone constitute the court. (2) The proceedings shall be attended through out by two other persons who shall be officers, or junior commissioned officers or one of either, and who shall not as such be sworn or affirmed.*

64 NA s 101 (4), (5). The old British law also allowed such challenge "both by prisoner and by the Judge Advocate or prosecutor on the part of the crown. " Mutiny Act later provided for challenge by prisoner only; please see Simmons,The Constitution and Practice of Courts Martial, op cit, n 46, p 213 (s 495) Note (9) "Qualified Challenges".

65 MML Vol. II, p 290, Note 4 to AR r 44. Under the British law, the JA being a member of CM after 1996 amendments (please see Rant, Courts Martial, Discipline, and the Criminal Process in the Armed Services,op cit, n 7, p 137, s 5.53) is subject to objection by the accused under Br AA s 92 (1) as a member. An officer under instruction being not a member cannot, however, be objected to (Rant, loc cit, p 141, s 5. 71)

66 AR r 90 (3); MML Vol II, p 320, Note 5 to r 90 suggests that the same procedure as in the case of a member may be adopted for resolving the objection to a short-hand writer or an interpreter.

Broadly speaking, while availing his right to object to members, an accused must make each objection separately; he cannot object to the entire court collectively. Should he however persist in objecting to the court collectively[67], the objection should be resolved as an objection made to all the members individually. The procedure laid down in AA s 130 read with AR r 44 and corresponding provisions in the other two Services is to be followed meticulously in all such cases. The procedure inter alia provides for the remaining officers of the court to vote, in the absence of the challenged officer, notwithstanding that objections have been made to any of those officers. This procedure was upheld by a Division Bench of the Delhi High Court observing that "There is a great sense in these provisions because otherwise an accused, by merely objecting to all officers constituting the court could completely dislodge the court."[68]

The provision for objection to members by the accused indirectly entails several other side issues. It is, for instance, suggested that an officer objected to on grounds of personal enmity, prejudice or malice or of having formed or expressed an opinion on the case, should, unless the objection is obviously groundless, request and be permitted to retire.[69] A legitimate further query in this context would be as to whether there could be any other equally important ground for similar action needed on the part of the member and the court. On jurisprudential level, there could be various other points for thought, such as, the desirability of prescribing certain other qualifications, in addition to the existing ones, for an officer to be detailed as a member of the CM, or the desirability of having, as the constituent of the CM, personnel other than officers in the case of trial

---

67 MML ibid, p 290, Note 3 to 44. Simmons recalls that in July 1871 a GCM was held at Woolwich for the trial of Private Williams of the Rifle Brigade on a charge of insubordinate conduct before a Regimental Court Martial at which, he had, when asked whether he objected to be tried by any member of the court, violently kicked the court table and ex claimed, "I object to the whole lot of y ou." He was convicted for contempt of the court and sentenced to two year imprisonment; please see Simmons, op cit, n 64, p 180 (s 434). It should, howev er, be understood b y the ac cused and the court that an objection to the entire court could more appropriately be dealt with under a different provision of the plea to general jurisdiction laid down in AR r 51. If "the court is not constituted in accordance with the Act and the Rules, Rule 44 (the provision presently under discussion) would hardly assist, because ... if ... each officer was disqualified from being a member of court -martial, there is none left to dispose of the contention .... "; please see P P S Bedi's case, op cit, n 30, p 1431.

68 Capt Ram Kumar v Chief of the Arm y Staff, AIR 1985 Del 374 (DB). The ac cused had objected to the presiding officer Brig Faridoon Noshir Bilimoria and the junior most member Maj Sarabjit Singh Dhillon at his trial by GCM. His counsel raised the point before the High Court that since he had objected to two members, one of them could not participate in the decision on the objection to the other . The High Court rejected the contention and justified the provision of an objected member participating in the decision on objection against some other member , though not at the disposal of the objection against himself.

69 MML, Vol II, p 290, Note 5 to r 44; cf Simmons, The Consti tution and Pr actice of Courts Martial, op cit, n 46, p 215 (s 500). "In general an officer objected to on the score of prejudice or malice, requests permission to wi thdraw and the court or dinarily feels disposed to assent when i t can do so consistent ly."

of any person below the rank of an officer. These and many other possible questions should lead to the consideration as to what was the initial objective sought to be achieved by the provision for such objection. It is noted in this context that the trial by the CM being analogous to jury trial in many ways, and as the law allowed of challenge against the jury, the right was initially secured to the military offender as a practice of the Service. In 1847, the practice was transformed into a statutory provision of military law by introducing it, for the first time, in the Mutiny Act passed by the British parliament that year[70]. It is based on the premise that the object of all interested in the administration of military justice is to obtain a competent and impartial tribunal, actuated neither by partiality, favour or affection and that the members are all of competent rank with no professional or pecuniary interest in the result of the case.[71] Accordingly, the provision exists in the Anglo[72]-American[73] military law and all other military legal systems modeled thereon, including the Indian system. However, the Indian law on the subject remains antiquated whereas a frog leap of developments in this field has been attained elsewhere. For instance, an accused is entitled to receive variedly extensive information about the members under the American law so as to enable him to effectively exercise his right to object the members.[74] Under our system, an accused, while being warned for trial, is inter alia required to be given a list of the members, rank and corps of the officers of the officers who are going to form the CM in his case and this is to be given to him at least

70 Simmons, ibid, pp 214-216 (ss 488-504) quoting Blackstone (3, Commentaries 360) on the principal causes to challenges to jurors, Simmons notes that there are four heads for such challenges in general law: proper honoris respectum, proper defectum, proper effectum and proper delictum of which only the second and the third are applicable to the CM and observes that "it is equally necessary, as on juries, that members of a court-martial should be omni ex ceptione majores". Hence the practice and later the law in 1847 for challenge of members.

71 Clode, Military and Martial Law, 1874, p 120, cited in O.P. Sharma, Military Law in India, op cit, Ch 1, n 4, p 129.

72 British Army Act, 1955, s 92 (1) for the right to object to an original or replaced member "on any reasonable ground". Sub-sections (2) to (6) provide for the procedure to be followed on such objection to a member officer or WO, the president and the J A. Court Martial (Army) Rules, 1997, r 40 lays down the procedure in detail, the JA being solely responsible for deciding this issue sitting on his own.

73 Under the US Military law, RCM 912 together with UCMJ Art. 41 deal with various aspects of the challenge of selection of members and challenge for cause against any member. The procedure inter alia includes the examination of the member (called 'voir dire') and presentation of evidence in this regard. These provisions also provide for peremptory challenge to one member by each party. Any member so challenged shall be excused. Generally no reason is necessary for a peremptory challenge. [US v Calley, 46 CMR 1131, 1162 (ACMR), affirmed 23 USCMA 534: 48 CMR 19 (1973) but see US v Harris, 13 MJ 288 (CMA 1982) and US v Curtis 33 MJ 101 (CMA 1991)]

74 Each member may be requested to furnish the information as to his date of birth, sex, race, marital status, home address, civil and military education along with areas of study, name of school or university and number of dependents, along with unit, rank, past assignments, awards, decorations and whether acted as accuser, investigating officer etc. in the case and any additional information to facilitate effective voir dire.

96 hours (24 hours on active service) before his arraignment, along with certain other documents. However, in practice scant attention is paid to this requirement as may be seen from the data collected in the present study in response to Q. 2.6 in the Interview Schedule. A full length discussion on the data will be undertaken later but it may be stated here that only 13 (26%) out of 50 respondents were furnished the details of the officers appointed to constitute the CM at their trials, even though 43 (86%) were given other requisite documents like charge-sheet and S of E. We may hope that the spirit of the Right to Information Act, 2005 will improve the record on the issue, the Army Headquarters having taken due notice of the Act.[75]

(b) **Swearing of the Court**

On the objection to members having been resolved or if there is no such objection, the members, the JA, the officer(s)-under-instruction, if any, and the interpreter as also the short-hand writer, if any, are sworn or affirmed in the prescribed manner.[76] An oath is an outward pledge given by the person who takes it that his attestation or promise is made under an immediate sense of his responsibility to a Divine Being, who according to his belief will be displeased at being called upon to witness the utterance of a falsehood. The form may and more often does, contain a virtual or a direct expression of accountability; and this is the least notion of Deity which is consistent with the nature of an oath in that sense in which alone it can be administered as legally binding in any court of justice, where the necessity of the sanction is imperative by act of Parliament.[77] Thus, the oath or affirmation, though taken or made in somewhat religious terms, has the sanction of the statute.

The oath or affirmation administered to the members of the court, the JA and the officer under instruction includes a vow to administer justice without partiality, favour or affection, in the case of the members, and to carry out his duties to the best of his ability in the case of a JA. An additional vow is included, in the case of all of them not to disclose vote or opinion of any particular member unless required to give evidence thereof in due course of law. The latter part of the oath is a functional necessity of an institution like CM[78] whereas the former one is in tune with their capacity as jurors, in the case of

---

75 Army Headquarters, New Delhi, Letter No. 17732/6/Info Act – DV -1(c) dated 18 Nov. 2005.

76 AR, rr 45-47 and MML Vol. II, pp 291-293, Notes 1-8 to AR r 45 and Notes 1-2 to r 47 . AFR, rr 53-54 and NA, ss 103 (2), 104

77 Simmons,The Constitution and Practice of Courts Martial, op cit, n 46, p 185 (s 444)

78 Clode, Military and Martial Law, p 127 cited in O.P. Sharma, Military Law in India, op cit, n 71, p129

"Constituted as a court-martial is, and employed in the discharge of a duty so individious as to decide between brother officers or between a soldier and an offended General, it would be hopeless to expect impartial justice unless the secret voting was, in such a case, continued."

the members.[79] As the manner in which a thing is done has often a far greater influence upon the generality of mankind than the real character of the thing itself, the mode of administering an oath becomes a subject of very great importance.[80] Accordingly, "decent solemnity"[81] is customary to be observed at the CM while oath is being administered. The person taking the oath places his palm on the religious book according to his faith and every body else present in the court room stands erect with his cap on (except the accused at a Naval CM). Further, it is customary to have all witnesses present in the court-room on such occasions but they should withdraw before the arraignment.[82]

Irrespective of the solemnity that marks the oath taking, no legal consequences flow therefrom except that it symbolizes the activation of an ad hoc tribunal appointed for the trial. The Supreme Court decision in Maj Gen Yadav's case crystallizes the legal position even under traditional view that the oath taking of the CM members represents the commencement of the trial by the CM.[83] There also exists a legislative clarification in the AR that where any finding and sentence are otherwise valid, they shall not be rendered invalid by reason only of a failure to administer oath or affirmation to the

---

79 Simmons, op cit, n 77, p 183 (s 440). Until the revolution of 1688, members of all CM were required by Articles of War to perform the duty of judges "under the sanction of an oath" . Thereafter, Mutiny Act prescribed only the jurors oath and that too only in cases of offences punishable with death. Further, the oath of secrecy was initially without any limitation (exception) which was added later in the form of "unless required to give evidence ...". However, it will be erroneous to much emphasize any comparability between a jury trial and the one by a CM. Further the members' oath also includes a vow to administer justice "in accordance with the Army Act" (Air Force Act in the case of an AF court-martial) or "according to law" (in the Navy). The jury element in their oath manifests more visibly while covering the situation of doubt for which they pledge to be guided by their "conscience, the best of my understanding and the custom of war in the like cases".

80 Tylor on Oaths, (1836), 47; cit in Simmons, The Constitution and Practice of Courts Martial, loc cit, n 46, p 188 (s 450).

81 Simmons, ibid, N Regs II (S), Appx III para 5(c). In fact, before the president and the members are administered oath and after the objections to members, if any, have been duly disposed of, the trial JA is required to announce: "The court has been duly constituted. Gentelmen, off caps, if you please"; please see Appx III, ibid, paras 10 and 11.

82 MML Vol. II, p 336, Note 1 to AR r 131.

83 MML Vol. II, p 441, Memoranda for the Guidance of Officers concerned with Courts-Martial, para 16, for the traditional view and for Maj Gen Yadav's case, please see n 57 . Dwelling upon the place of the oath taking by the members of the CM, in the whole scheme of CM Process, the apex court observed: "The members get right, power and duty to try an accused only on appointment and the same ends with the close of the particular case. Therefore, Rule 45 insists on administration of oath in the prescribed manner. For a judicial officer , the act of appointment gives power to try the offender under Criminal Procedure Code; warrant of appointment by the President of India and the oath taken as per the form prescribed in Schedule III of the Constitution empowers the High Court/Supreme Court Judges to hear the petition or appeals. For them, need to take oath on each occasion of trial or hearing is obviated. Therefore, the occasion to take oath as per the procedure for GCM and the right of the members of the

interpreter or short-hand writer.[84] This clarification may be reasonably extended to similar failure of the administration of oath to the members in view of the same provision making it explicitly clear that when a CM has jurisdiction and there is legal evidence or a plea of guilty to justify any finding, such finding and any sentence shall be valid notwithstanding any deviation from the rules. In the present study, respondent A-196-A-4 had brought out in his petitions to the Service authorities under AA s 164 as well as writ petition filed in Allahabad High Court that the JA at the revision proceedings was required to take oath, being newly appointed, but failed to do so until the very fag end of the proceedings. However, the revised findings and sentence were confirmed by the prescribed authority, ignoring this contention.

(c) Arraignment and Objection to the Charge

After the members of the court and other persons are sworn or affirmed, the accused is arraigned on the charges against him. The arraignment consists of two parts: one, the charge(s) being read out, and if necessary, being translated to the accused, and two, the accused being required to plead separately to each charge.[85] When required to plead to the charge(s), an accused may object to the charge on the ground that it does not disclose an offence under the Act, or that it is not in accordance with the rules.[86]

It may be seen from Table 24, serials 1 and 2 that 16 (32%) out of 50 respondents had raised objection to the charge(s). Chart 7.1 represents details in this regard.

---

contd/-

GCM arises, with their empanelment as GCM and they get power to try the accused the moment they assemble and commence examination of the case, i.e. , charge-sheet and the record. The trial, therefore, must be deemed to have commenced the moment the GCM assembles.... " (para 21) Interestingly, the American system does contemplate of Secretarial regulations for a one time basis administration of oath to certified legal personnel; please see UCMJ Art. 42 (a) as amended by Pub L 90-632 in 1968.

84 AR, r 149.

85 AR, r 48, AFR, r 56; NA, s 105 (1); cf Colonel Bedi, "accidenta destinalis" 1992, (unpublished memoirs) pp 9-10. At his first CM as JA, in 1946, at the East Indies, the author read the charge to the accused, one Private Browne of the Paratroops, for having robbed a local Chinese of certain items like watch etc and asked, in arraignment, whether he was "Guilty" or "Not Guilty" of the charge. "That's your job to find out, Sir, why ask me", replied the accused, keeping a straight face with no trace of trying to be cheekie or clever. The members let out a gaf faw of laughter and the JA was crest-fallen, not knowing what to do .

86 AR, r 49; AFR, r 57; there is no corresponding provision under the Naval law.

Chart 7.1

Objection to Charges

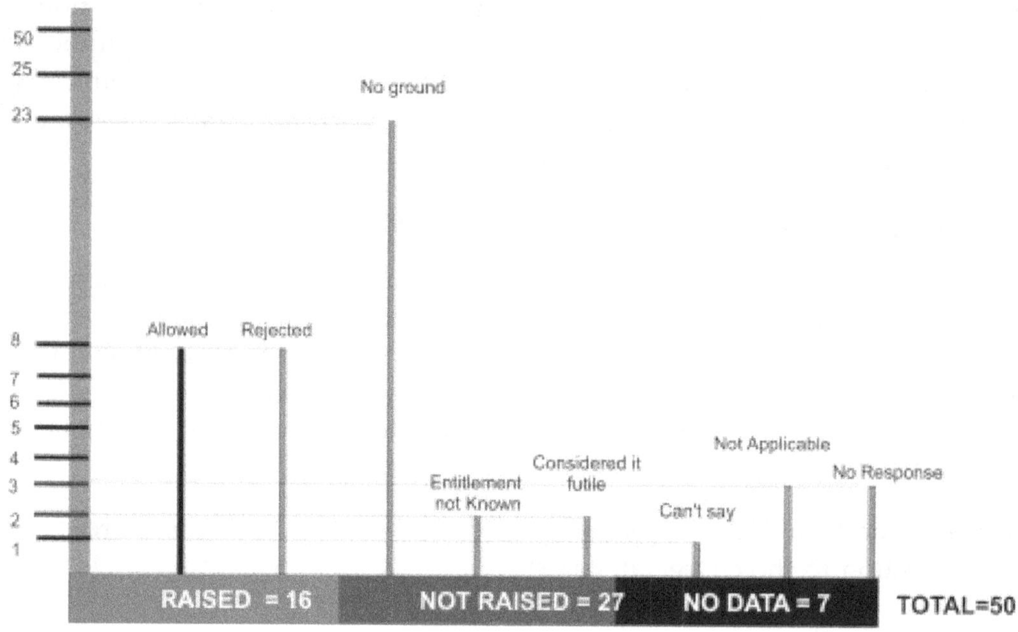

Before proceeding to analyze the data, it may be clarified that the term 'charge' here, unlike a charge at the pre-trial stage, denotes a formal charge contained in a charge-sheet that the concerned person subject to the related Act has been guilty of an offence.[87] Each charge is divided into two parts: one, the statement of offence, and the second, a statement of the particulars of the act or omission constituting the offence.[88] Elaborate guidance is available how a charge is to be framed, what all should be avoided while framing a charge, the lay out of the charge-sheet and the authority legally competent to sign the charge-sheet, along with the action on the part of the convening officer to

87 AR, r 28 (2); AFR, r 34(2). The term 'Charge' does not stand formally defined in the Naval law.

88 AR, r 30 (2); AFR, r 36(2); N Regs II (S), reg 155 (9), (10). The two parts of a charge are similarly termed under the British military law too; please see the Court Martial (Army) Rules, 1997, Sch. I. However, in the American mi litary la w terminology, the term 'char ge' is used f or the first one, i.e. , 'statement of offence' and 'specifications' for the statement of particulars; please see MCM, Appex 4, DD Form 458 that provides a format for charge-sheet.

ensure that the trial is ordered on a legally valid and evidentially sustainable charge.[89] In the context of the statement of offence, it may be noted that the AA "creates new offences with specified punishment, imposes higher punishment to pre-existing offences, and enables civil offences by a fiction" to be treated as offences under the Act.[90]

The new offences in all the three Services Acts are the Service specific offences for acts which either relate to the very essence of the military duty, or acquire criminal character in the context of a soldier, unlike his civilian counterpart. The former may be illustrated by 'offences in relation to the enemy', such as shamefully abandoning any post etc. committed to the charge of the offender. The latter would include offences like absence without leave or using insubordinate language to a superior. The second category of offences may be termed as 'hybrid offences' which, though primarily of the same nature as the offences under the ordinary criminal law, assume greater severity in the specific circumstances of the Service life and hence are made punishable much more severely under the Services Acts than under the criminal code of the land. Theft of Government property or the property belonging to a person subject to military law or to any military Mess, band etc. will, for example, attract upto 10 year imprisonment, while the maximum punishment for the offence of theft under the IPC is 3 year imprisonment.[91] Lastly, any civil offence, i.e., an offence triable by a criminal court meaning thereby a court of ordinary criminal justice in any part of India,[92] except the offences specifically excluded,[93] may be tried either by a CM or by a criminal court[94] and so also may be tried hybrid offences[95]. Any conflict of jurisdiction between the CM and the criminal court in respect of such offences may be resolved in the light of the rules made by the Central Government for this purpose.[96]

---

89 AR, rr 28-30, 37, MML Vol. II, pp 278-287, Notes to rr 28-32, and pp 364-366 Notes to the Forms of Charges and Appex II (Forms of Charges), Notes on Indian Military and Air Force Law, 1942, pp 3-33 (paras 12-89); and RA paras 451, 452, 459.

90 Major E.G. Barse v State of Bombay, AIR 1961 SC 1762; cf AA ss 34-69; AF A ss 34-70 and NA ss 34-77 for offences under the three Services Acts. Under the NA, those are called as 'Articles of War'. Please also see Delhi Special Police Establishment v Lt Col SK Loraiya, AIR 1972 SC 2548, for three-fold scheme of offences in the AA, i.e., the offences exclusively triable by CM, those exclusively triable by the ordinary criminal courts and the offences triable by both.

91 AA, s 52 and IPC s 379

92 AA, s 3 (ii) read with (viii)

93 Murder, culpable homicide not amounting to murder and rape, committed against a person not subject to AA, NA or AF A and committed while not on active service or at a place outside India or at a notified frontier post; AA, s 70; AF A, s 72, NA, s 78 (2)

94 AA, s 6 read with s 126; AF A, s 71 read with s 124; NA, ss 77 , 78 (1)

95 RA para 419 (a) , (b)

96 AA, ss 125, 126; AFA, ss 124, 125; Cr PC, s 475 read with rules made thereunder vide the Government of India, Ministry of Home Affairs, Notification No. 488 dated 09 Feb. 1978, applicable to all the three Services and reproduced in RA para 418.

Irrespective of the foregoing delineation of the nature of 'charge', as conceived under the military law, it may be added that one is not bound by the technical formalities which prevail in other courts of law, but there is this essential principle in every charge before any court that exists in the civilized world that the charge should be sufficiently specific to enable the person to know what he is to answer and to enable the court to know what they are called to enquire into.[97] Keeping in mind that the charge is at the very root of the trial, it is necessary to ensure that no defects exist in the charge or the charge-sheet which might necessitate the quashing of the proceedings.[98] However, when it appears that a CM had jurisdiction to try the accused and that there is legal evidence or a plea of guilty to justify the finding, the said finding and any sentence that the CM had jurisdiction to pass thereon may be confirmed and shall be valid notwithstanding that the charge-sheet has not been signed by the CO or the convening officer, provided that the charge had in fact been approved by the CO and the convening officer before the trial or notwithstanding any defect or objection, technical or other, unless it appears that any injustice has been done to the accused.[99]

Returning to the data on objection to the charge, it is noticed from the data reflected in Table 24 and Chart 7.1 that there is equal distribution of objection being allowed and being rejected, 8 (16%) being the number involved in both situations. In 6 (12%) cases, there was no response, the provision being not applicable in 3 (6%) cases in view of the pleas of 'Guilty', and in the remaining three cases, the respondents having made no reply to the question. In one (2%) case, the response was 'can't say'. In the rest of the 27 cases (54%), the respondents raised no objection to the charges: 23 (46%) having no ground to object to the charge, two (4%) being not aware of their entitlement to do so and the remaining two (4%) having considered it to be futile to do so. It is not clear from the available data why those two respondents considered it to be futile. It could be either way. It is possible that they had some doubt about the charge but raised no objection, thinking that the authority would not have erred in that regard since an expert legal advice would have been taken in accordance with the usual practice or with the mandatory requirement of RA para 459, depending upon the nature of the offence. It is equally possible that they desisted from raising any such objection, assuming that the result of any such exercise was forgone rejection of the submission.

97 The JAG on the trial of Col Quentin cit in Simmons, The Constitution and Practice of Courts Martial, op cit, n 46, pp 160-161 (s 386 on'Framing of Charges')

98 Nayudu,Handbook of Military Law, op cit, Ch 3, n.22, p 23

99 AR, r 149; AFR, r 128; no specific corresponding provision in the Naval law.

It may be pointed out that in the 8 cases in which the objections to the charge were allowed, the convening authority would have either amended or dropped the charge and ordered the court to proceed with the trial after due notice to the accused or would have directed new trial by freshly convening a CM.[100]

(d) **Special Plea to General Jurisdiction**

Before pleading "Guilty" or "Not guilty" to the charge as it finally stands, whether amended or not, the accused may offer a special plea to the general jurisdiction of the court.[101] In the context of a judicial or quasi judicial tribunal, the term 'jurisdiction' may be conceived to denote the area over which the legal authority of the court or other institution extends.[102] The jurisdictional powers of military courts may be broadly classified as ratione materiae, ratione personae, ratione loci or ratione temporis. Accordingly, a special plea to the general jurisdiction may be raised to contend, firstly, that the offence in question is not triable by a CM or that the offence being triable both by a CM and a criminal court, the latter has exclusive right to try the offence in the given circumstances of the case; secondly, that the accused is not a person subject to the law under which the CM stands convened or that the kind of the CM convened has no power to try the accused; thirdly, that the offence has been committed at a place to which the jurisdiction of the CM does not extend and, finally, that the offence is time-barred either in terms of the ordinary limitation period under the Act or being beyond

---

100 AR, r 50; AFR, r 58; N Regs II (S) reg 182. The Army and the Air Force provisions identically allow amendment of the charge subject to two conditions: one, any mistake in the name or description of the accused in the charge-sheet may be amended by the court at any time during the trial; secondly, any addition to, omission from or alteration in the charge, if required in the interest of justice, will have to be reported by the court to the convening authority before it has begun to examine the witnesses. The convening authority may either amend the charge and order the trial to proceed after due notice to the accused or may direct the new trial to be commenced. Pending decision by the convening authority, the court will remain adjourned. Under the Naval law, the trial judge advocate may amend the charge after the court has been sworn and before the finding. This may be done only to cater for a variance in "inessential details" between the charge and the evidence, subject to three conditions: one, no evidence which could not have been given in support of the original charge shall be given in support of the substituted charge; two, the accused shall not be substantially prejudiced by such amendment, and finally, the court shall adjourn, if so requested by the accused, for a reasonable time to enable him to meet the amended charge.

101 AR, r 51; AFR, r 59; NA, s 103 providing for "any further objection" in general terms but otherwise there is no corresponding provision to AR, r 51 in the Naval law.

102 The Compact Oxford Reference Dictionary; cf Ujjam Bai v State of UP, AIR 1962 SC 1621, wherein 'jurisdiction' was held to mean "authority to decide" and explained that to have jurisdiction is to have power to inquire into the facts, to apply the law and to declare the punishment in a regular course of judicial proceedings. It was further observed that the question whether a tribunal has jurisdiction depends not on the truth or falsehood of the facts but upon their nature and it is determinable at the commencement, not at the conclusion, of the inquiry.

the time-extent of the post-release responsibility of the accused as a person who has since ceased to be subject to the related law.

The first and the third of these contentions may possibly be combined in the case of an offence excluded under AA s 70 from jurisdiction of the CM and committed at a place not outside the territory of India nor located at any notified frontier post. This may be illustrated by a case study of No. 1550999 Acting Naik Driver Military Transport Baldev Singh of 270 Engineer Regiment. He was tried by a GCM that assembled on 04 Feb 1989 at Trincomalee (Sri Lanka) for his trial on eight charges, out of which five were for murder under AA s 69 read with IPC s 302, involving death of five civilian citizens of Sri Lanka caused by the accused by shooting them down with his Service rifle in the city bazaar area, on 21 Nov 1987, and three charges were for attempt to murder another three persons of the same general description, on the same date and place. The defence counsel provided to the accused under the provision of RA para 479, took special plea to the general jurisdiction of the court on two grounds; firstly that a trial under an Indian law could not be held on a foreign territory and any court holding such trial would lack jurisdiction; and, secondly, that the offences with which the accused stood charged could not be tried under the AA. The JA pointed out, in his advice to the CM, that under AA s 70, the jurisdiction of a CM could technically be challenged inter alia for an offence of murder but not the offence of an attempt to murder. Even in the case of murder, a CM would have jurisdiction if the offence was committed outside the territory of India, on active service or a frontier post notified in the Official Gazette. In the case at hand, the Indian troops had been declared to be on active service, within the meaning of AA s 9, vide SRO 20 - E of 09 Nov 1987 and, further, the offence involved in each of the charges was alleged to have been committed beyond India. The defence counsel also argued that a CM was also a criminal court within the meaning of AA s 3(viii) and therefore Cr PC s 188 would not allow a CM trial beyond the Indian Territory. The JA explained that this was prima facie a fallacious contention in view of the definition of 'Criminal court' in AA s 3(iii). Further, Cr PC s 188 empowered the courts in India to try offences committed outside India in specified circumstances but did not affect the liability of the offender in such cases to be dealt with in the territory of a foreign country wherein the offence was committed. This would mean that an offence committed by a member of the Indian Peace Keeping Force, could, depending upon the understanding between Indian and Sri Lanka Governments, be tried by the local courts or any other court held in Sri Lanka, such as a CM which under AA s 124, could be held "in any place whatever" for the trial of a person subject to the Act. In relation to the defence counsel's remark that the principle of sovereignty would not permit, on the territory of a state, the trial by a court constituted under a foreign law, it was clarified that in the modern age of internationalism, the principle of sovereignty admitted of its erosion on various counts such as diplomatic immunities. In the case of foreign troops permitted by a State on its territory, the internal discipline of the troops was the exclusive preserve of the commander of the troops. As regards the cases affecting the nationals or property of the host State, the local courts did have jurisdiction but the international law did not debar either the jurisdiction of a court constituted under the military law of the troops. In the light of the legal and factual positions of the matter at hand, the special plea to the general jurisdiction raised on behalf of the accused was over-ruled by the CM.[103]

The procedure to be followed on such a plea inter alia requires that the court would proceed with the trial if it over-ruled the plea. On the other hand, if it allows the plea, the court records its decision and its reasons for it and reports the matter to the convening authority and adjourns. Such a decision of the CM does not require confirmation but the convening authority either orders the release of the accused or forthwith convenes another court. In the case of Subedar Major Bishamber Ram, the special plea to the general jurisdiction was allowed by the CM on the ground that the trial had commenced after the expiry of six months (now 3 years after 1992 amendment) laid down in AA s 123 from the time the accused had ceased to be subject to the AA. The convening officer having convened another court for the trial, the accused approached the J&K High Court for the issue of a writ of certiorari and also a writ of mandamus. The High Court, however, dismissed the petition. Though observing that the language of Rule 51 is not happily worded, the clause that "such decision shall not require any confirmation" was "intended to indicate that the court martial while taking its decision as to the want of jurisdiction to try the accused is not required to get a confirmation of its decision to that effect from the convening authority, but it is free to take its decision independently of the convening authority. But (it) is open to the convening authority either to accept or not to accept the decision of the court-martial. The convening authority...is fully entitled to convene another court-martial.... In the instant case, the convening authority had still another very good reason to ignore the decision of the first court-martial. Sub-rule 3 of Rule 51 makes it imperative for the court-martial to record its reasons for its decision when it allows the special plea as to jurisdiction, but the court-martial has given no reason whatsoever for its decision.... The convening authority, for this reason alone, could be entitled to convene another court for the trial of the petitioner."[104]

The expression "general jurisdiction" in the provision would suggest that a plea relating to "lost" jurisdiction might not be admissible under the provision. The concept of lost jurisdiction envisages that the original jurisdiction of the CM in respect of a person subject to the Act for an offence triable by the CM may be lost within the meaning

---

103 The present author was the JA at the trial.

104 Subedar Major Bishamber Ram v General Officer Commanding 26 Inf Div, WP No. 407 of 1967, order passed by the High Court at its winter location of Jammu on 12 Jan 1968.

of the decision in the famous English case of Anisminic Ltd.[105], wherein the House of Lords held that the decision of the Commission was a nullity, being based on an inquiry which the order-in-council did not empower it to make. Lord Reid elaborated further how certain factors would deprive a body of jurisdiction and render its decision a nullity even though it had jurisdiction initially. The concept had been introduced in the American civil law in Johnson v Zerbst[106] and recognized by Justice Frankfurter in Burns v Wilson[107] as equally applicable to military courts. Irrespective of the wordings of AR r 51, the decisions of the (Indian) Supreme Court in the cases of Major A Hussain[108] and Sub Dev Singh[109] would leave little room for doubt that the pleas of lost jurisdiction could as well be entertained under the provision for special plea to the general jurisdiction. In both the cases, the findings and sentence of the CM were challenged on the ground of the violation of the provision relating to the hearing of the charges by the CO at the pre-trial stage. In the case of Sub Dev Singh, the apex court upheld the decision of the High Court of quashing the order of dismissal of the petitioner on the ground of violation of the mandatory Rule 22 and dismissed the appeal. With reference to the reliance placed by the appellant on Major Hussain's case, wherein the petition was dismissed even though made on the same ground, the Supreme Court observed that in that case no objection was taken as to the violation of Rule 22 at the CM proceedings. The concerned officer (accused) went through the CM proceedings and cross-examined the witnesses without raising objection to the jurisdiction of the CM on the ground of the violation of Rule 22. Therefore, the apex court, relying on Rule 149, came to the conclusion that whatever irregularity that was before the stage of initiating the GCM proceedings and because the said proceedings were in accordance with the law, the irregularity, if any, in the preliminary proceedings would not prejudice the delinquent officer. The decisions in these two cases disclose that the issue of lost jurisdiction along with its grounds must be raised at the trial stage, so as to enable the military court to drop the proceedings if so required by the related law and facts. If the CM had no occasion to consider the objection, the respondent could not contend before the superior court that the lacuna was rectified in subsequent proceedings.

---

105 Anisminic Ltd. v The Foreign Compensation Commission, (1969) 2 AC 147.

106 Johnson v Zerbst, 304 US 458 (1938)

107 Burns v Wilson, 346 US 137 (149-151) per Frankfurter J. Please see supra Ch 6.5 (e) in general and the text related to nn 107 and 108 in that chapter in particular.

108 Union of India v Major A Hussain, 1998 (1) SCC 537 (para 21).

109 Union of India v Subedar Dev Singh, CA No. 5978 of 1997, Order of the Supreme Court dated 23 Apr 2003.

Moving on to the analysis of the relevant data, it is seen from Table 24 that a special plea to the general jurisdiction was raised in 7 (14%) out of 50 cases. It was allowed in one (2%) case and rejected in the remaining 6 (12%) cases. No such plea was raised in 38 (76%) cases for various reasons. In one (2%) case the response was 'can't say' while there was no response at all in 4 (8%) cases. The related data may be depicted as under in Chart 7.2:

Chart 7.2

Plea to General Jurisdiction

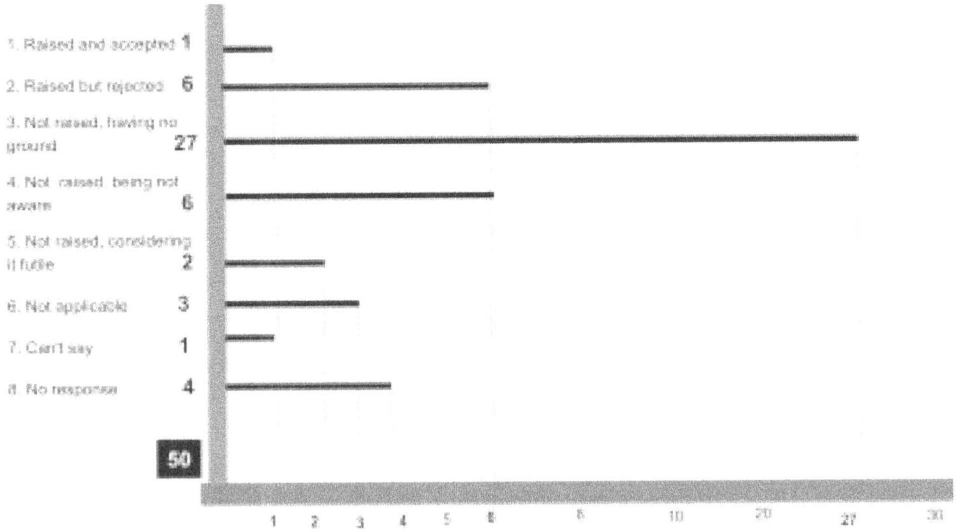

The graph at point 3 reflects that the respondents had no ground to raise the plea in 27 (54%) cases whereas in six (12%) cases it could not be raised because of unawareness of their right to do so on the part of the respondents. In two (4%) cases it was considered to be futile to raise the pleas, while in three (6%) cases it was not applicable, there being plea of "Guilty" to the charge.

The data suggest that in the majority of cases it is sufficiently ensured by the convening authority that the accused is brought to trial by a CM only when the CM has undoubted jurisdiction to try him on the charges in question. If a plea to jurisdiction is nonetheless raised, it may be accepted or rejected, depending upon the view taken by the court on the merit of the plea. It is mostly rejected since the plea lacks merit, the jurisdictionality of the CM having been carefully considered in the light of the legal advice and a final decision taken to convene the court only on being satisfied in this regard. No such plea is understandably applicable if the accused pleads "Guilty" to the charge(s). In some cases, the accused may suffer the handicap of not being aware of his right to raise such a plea or understand the requirement to do so. This would mostly happen in the case of the SCM. Though the provision of AR r 114 caters for such a plea at a trial by the SCM, the accused has no defending officer or defence counsel to advise him suitably and act on his behalf to meet the requirement. A friend-of-the-accused, within his limitations of legal awareness and incapability to represent the accused before the court, would usually fail to even guide the accused in this regard.

(e) **Plea in Bar**

The Army and the Air Force Rules also provide for the accused to raise objection to his trial by the CM on certain other grounds, all put together by the law under a collective head of 'plea in bar'. The grounds in question include, one, double jeopardy; two, pre-trial dismissal of the charge; three, pardon or condonation of a charge; and, four, the expiry of the post-release period of liability.[110] Such pleas may in a way be said to be part of a plea to the jurisdiction of the court.[111] However, unlike the special plea to the general jurisdiction, a plea in bar, when allowed by the court, is subject to confirmation.[112]

Out of the four grounds of a plea in bar, the pre-trial dismissal of the charge by the CO and the legal consequences of such dismissal have been discussed earlier in Ch- 6.[113] The ground of limitation period being a special feature of DPCM, will be discussed in Ch- 8. The law relating to this ground will, however, be also briefly touched later in the present chapter so as to facilitate analysis of the related data on the plea in bar. The issue of double jeopardy may, therefore, be immediately considered here along with condonation.

(i) **Double Jeopardy**

The concept of double jeopardy prohibits a trial of a person after he was previously convicted or acquitted of the offence by a competent criminal court or a CM or has been summarily dealt with for the same offence.[114] The military law provisions in this regard reflect the constitutional guarantee against a person being prosecuted and punished for

110 AR, r 53 (1); AFR, r 61(1); No corresponding provisions in the Naval law though NA s 79 does lay down the general limitation of time.

111 Simmons,The Constitution and Practice of Courts Martial, op cit, n 46, pp 232-234 (ss556-560) deal under the'plea in bar' a plea to the jurisdiction of the court and special plea stating reason why the prisoner be not called on to answer the charge, including inter alia the ground of time limitation. Also see the last one among the grounds for special plea to general jurisdiction as enumerated in the preceding sub-section (e).

112 AR, r 53 (4).

113 Ch. 6, nn 77 and 78 and the related text.

114 AA, s 121; AFA, s 120; Similar provisions exist in the US and the British Military laws for which please see UCMJ Art. 44 and B r AA 1955, s 133 r espectively.

the same offence more than once.[115] However, as an exception, AA did have, until 1992 amendments, and the AFA still has, a provision for the trial of a person by a criminal court for the same offence, or on the same facts, with the previous sanction of the Central Government, after the said person has been convicted or acquitted by a CM.[116] The exception was introduced in the military law by the Mutiny Act, 1721, in order to afford protection to civil authorities against soldiers being unduly protected by own peers in clashes with civilians.[117] A justification given for the provision is that the offender in such a case is two distinct persons, each of whom has committed a distinct offence.[118] Such a legal fiction apparently cannot stand in the modern times of scientific thinking as is evident from the repeal of the similar provisions in the British Army Act by the Armed Forces Act, 1966. On the home front, it was contended in Ram Sarup's case that AA s 127 was ultra vires of Art 20 of the Constitution but the Supreme Court did not consider it necessary to decide the question since the petitioner was not subjected to a second trial.[119] However, in the cases of Lt Col Loraiya and Maj SK Sharma[120], the Supreme Court made a reference to the provision in positive terms as an instrument to save the cause of justice. Irrespective of this, the very facts that the Naval authorities never experienced any difficulty without any such provision, and that there never was an occasion for the use of the provision over a century long span of period since it was first enacted as s 71 of the Indian Army Act, 1911, amply justify the removal of this legal fossil from the AA and suggest an instantaneous need for similar action in respect of the AFA provision.

---

115 Constitution of India, Art. 20 (2), cf Roman law doctrine 'nemo debet bis vexari pro una et eadem causa' (no man ought to be twice v exed for one and the same cause). It ma y however, be seen that the Fundamental Right under Article 20 of our Constitution does not include the principle of 'autre fois acquit' within its ambit and embodies only'autre fois convict' from the English common law rule which comprises both. The Supr eme Court observ ed in V enkataraman v UOI, (1954) SCR 1150, that i t "seems that our constitution makers did not think it necessary to raise one part of the common law to the level of a fundamental right and thus make it immune from legislative interference. This has been left to be regulated by the general law of the land". Cr PC s 221 (2) ac cordingly caters for left out portion autr e fois acquit as well as autr e fois convict and so do AA s 121 and AF A s 120.

116 AA, s 127 [since omi tted by the Army (Amendment) Act, 1992, s 11]; AF A, s 126; No corr esponding provision in NA. It is probable that these principles originated in the seventeenth century fear that the army might be used as an instrument of pol itical r epression. If, f or example, a soldier who had shot a civilian could be court-martialled and acquitted by a court composed of his fellow officers, and that acquittal could be pleaded as a bar to the soldier 's subsequent trial bef ore a civi l court f or murder, there would be a danger of the civi l authorities losing the contr ol over the intimidation of civi lians by the arm y.

117 R V Aughet, cit in Bernard Starkman ,"Canadian Military Law: The Citizen as Soldier", Canadian Bar Review, Vol 43 (1965), pp 423-424:

118 Winthrop,Military Law and Precedents, op cit, Ch 1, n 1, p 94 (Note 65) quoting a number of authorities in support.

119 Ram Sarup v UOI, AIR 1965 SC 247 (para 6)

120 Delhi Special Police Establishment v Lt Col S K Loraiya, AIR 1972 SC 2548 (para 10); Maj S K Sharma v UOI, AIR 1987 SC 1878, p 1883.

Returning to the doctrine of double jeopardy, it may be noted that the Fifth Amendment of the US Constitution inter alia mandated that "nor shall any person be subject for the same offence to be twice put in jeopardy of life or limb". The words "life or limb" are reminiscent of the period of their origin when all considerable offences were felonies punishable capitally or by dismemberment.[121] Capital punishment in the USA now applies only to such offences as murder, treason and piracy and dismemberment has been consigned to legal history. The words 'put in jeopardy' in the judicial context would, therefore, practically mean the same as 'tried'. Construing the constitutional provision in this light, the US courts have viewed the provision as covering in principle all crimes and prohibiting a person to be tried more than once for the same offence in all cases.[122] Article 102 d of Articles of War of the American military law reflected this by declaring that "No person shall be tried a second time for the same offence." It is, however, important to note in this context that unless the case has proceeded at least to an acquittal or conviction, it would be taken that there has been no trial and no jeopardy.[123] Further, conviction or acquittal does not necessarily relate to sentence or legal sentence adjudged nor has the accused been less 'tried' where the finding has been formally disapproved by reviewing authority.[124] Within the perimeter of this line of reasoning, the word 'tried' in the provision is to be interpreted as meaning duly prosecuted before a CM to a legal conviction or acquittal. Going a step further, Bishop held the view that "though for any causes mentioned, the trial may not have been a legal one, yet if the accused, having been convicted thereon, has undergone a

---

121 People v Godwin, 18 Johns 200.

122 US v Gi lbert, 2 Summner, 38, 42, wher ein it was also pointed out that the pr ovision was based on common law maxim recognizable in Magna Carta and traceable in the precept of the Roman civil law 'non bis in idem'

123 Hartung v People, 26 NY 182.

124 This is a hotly contested issue. Winthrop vigorously argues in support of this view, observing that the finding is no less a consummation in law of the trial, though from a cause beyond the control both of the accused and the court, such finding has been rendered ineffectual. Quoting Macomb 72, O Brien 277 and others in favour of his view, he disagrees with a contrary ruling of the Secretary of War in the case of Lieut DC Buell on the ground that a disapproval renders a finding inoperative. Winthrop feels that this would "subject an officer or a soldier to be tried a second time or an indefinite number of times at the will of his commander, where he was acqui tted when the latter thought he should be convicted, or if convicted, was not, in commander 's opinion, punished with suf ficient sev erity. But the Articles of W ar, while making an approval by the commander necessary to the execution of the judgement of the court (Art 104) have not provided that such action shal l be essential to complete a trial. " [please see Winthr op, Military Law and Practice, op cit, n 118, p 261 (s 391)] The tone and texture of these words of Winthrop almost literally echoed in the decision of the J&K High Court (DB) in Surat Singh v The Chief Engineer Project Beacon, AIR 1970 J&K 179: Though every finding of a General Court Martial, whether of acquittal or gui lt, cannot be r egarded as v alid unless i t is confirmed b y the competent authori ty, the Legislatur e could not have reasonably intended that an officer convening a General Court Martial can go on dissolving such Courts Martial and reconstituting them ad infinitum until he obtained a verdict or a finding of his own liking. Such a position would not only be against public policy and the ancient maxim'nemo debet bis

sentence thereupon adjudged, he is not again amenable to trial for the same offence".[125] In brief, to sustain a plea of double jeopardy, six conditions should be met: one, the former trial must have been before a competent court having jurisdiction; two, the charge must have been legally sufficient; three, the proceedings must have been without any fatal defect such as less number of officers than the minimum required to constitute the court; four, the finding must have been complete and valid in itself; five, the proceedings must not have been discontinued before finding; and, six, the offences at the former and the pending trial must be identical or so related that an acquittal or conviction of the one necessarily puts the accused in jeopardy of the other. The usual test for determining their identity is to determine the question whether the same evidence will support both. The offences related to the same subject matter or transaction may yet be different.[126]

The situations discussed in the foregoing will, however, have to be distinguished from the proceedings of the former trial having been set aside by a court in judicial review. It was held in the case of Hav Ram Adhar Tiwari that when the Single Judge has set aside the SCM, it cannot be said that the conviction of the accused is still standing. Section 121 contemplates those acquittal and conviction which have attained finality. When the court quashes the conviction, section 121 cannot be said to be attracted.[127] Section 121 of the AA would also not be attracted to the reassembly of the CM for the revision proceedings ordered by the confirming officer under section 160 for the purpose of the reconsideration of the finding or sentence or both. In Kukreti's case the Allahabad High Court described such a course "in the nature of an exception to the law laid down in Section 121."[128] The traditional view, however, has been that the revision proceedings are mere extension of the original trial and not a fresh trial since "the sentence of a court-martial is interlocutory and inchoate until confirmed."[129] After confirmation or even when the findings are not confirmed, if a fresh trial is ordered by annulling the proceedings so that the accused does not escape punishment merely on the basis of legal technicalities, the course of action adopted would be barred.[130] However, an administrative termination of service was held to be an unobjectionable course of action

---

vexari pro una et eadem causa' (no man ought to be twice vexed for one and the same cause) but would also reduce the provisions of the Army Act to a mockery and give an appearance of mala fides. In such a case, the proper course for the confirming authority would be to refer the case to its superior authority for confirmation.

125 Bishop, 1 C L $ 1023; Com v Loud, 3 Met 328, both cit in Winthrop, Military Law and Practice, op cit, n 118, p 261 (s 391)

126 Winthrop, ibid.

127 UOI v Hav Ram Adhar Tiwari, Allahabad High Court Order dated 20 Aug 2002 in Special Appeal No. 726 of 1997 .

128 Maj D P K ukreti v COA S, 1978 SL J 266 (Al l): 1978 Lab IC 9.

129 Mills v Martin, 19 John Rep, p 30.

130 Manohar Lal v UOI, (1971) 1 SLR 717 (P&H).

and the notice under AR 14 for such termination of service was held to be justified, when the finding of the CM was not confirmed, since even on revision the CM had adhered to the finding of 'Not guilty' and the finding in the view of the confirming authority was against the weight of evidence on record. In appeal in the Kukreti's case, the Supreme Court observed that "in such circumstances, to order a fresh trial by Court Martial would be both inexpedient and impracticable and therefore it is open to the Chief of the Army Staff to take action under Army Rule 14 despite the fact the officer was tried by Court Martial and was acquitted."[131] The court reversed the Allahabad High Court decision wherein the confirming officer had been held to be "bound to confirm second verdict of Court Martial consequent on a revision under Section 160 (1) of the Act so that it had validity." One may have reservation on equitability of the Supreme Court decision allowing administrative termination of service in the instant case, but the decision nonetheless clearly establishes the principle enunciated in GB Singh's case[132] that even though CM finding and sentence are subject to confirmation, under the Army and the Air Force laws, yet, if the accused has been tried once, a fresh court martial cannot be ordered in his case by withholding confirmation or dissolving the CM.

(ii) **Limitation Period**

In the present study, double jeopardy was not the ground for the plea in bar raised by any respondent. As may be seen from Table 24, a plea in bar was raised by 5 (10%) respondents on the ground of the limitation period having expired. It may be noted that irrespective of the law of the land providing no limitation period for most of the offences, the limitation period under the military jurisdiction is laid down in all the three Services laws in India and is almost a universal phenomenon.[133] Accordingly, no trial by CM of any person subject to AA, NA or AFA shall be commenced after the expiration of the period of three years from the date of commission of an offence. The embargo shall, however, not apply to a trial for an offence of desertion, fraudulent enrolment or mutiny.[134] Limitation period of three years in the AA and six months in the NA and AFA is also provided for the trial to commence from the time of release in the case of a person who ceases to be subject to the concerned Act.[135] The general limitation period of three years

---

131 COAS v Maj Dharam Pal Kukreti, AIR 1985 SC 703

132 G B Singh v UOI, 1973 Cr L J 485 (with reference to AF A s 120 which is in pari materia with AA s 121).

133 AA, s 122; AF A, s 121; NA, s 79; B rAA s 161; UCMJ Art 43; (Australian) Defence Forces Discipline Act, 1982, s 96 (1).

134 AA, s 122(2); AF A, s 121 (2); NA, s 79.

135 AA, s 123; AF A, s 122; NA, s 80.

is related to a plea in bar while the post release liability may be covered in a plea to general jurisdiction as is evident from earlier discussed case of Sub Major Bishambher Ram (supra, n 104). Out of four (8%) respondents who raised the plea in bar on the ground of the limitation period having expired, the plea was allowed in one (2%) case and rejected in the remaining three. In 31 (62%) cases, no plea in bar was raised, there being no ground for raising such a plea. In 4 cases the respondents raised no plea in bar, being not aware of their right to do so. In three (6%) cases, no such plea was applicable since the trial had proceeded on a plea of 'Guilty'. It was decided in an American case that by pleading 'Guilty' or 'Not guilty' at the trial without interposing the special plea in bar, and having waived thereby his right to raise such a plea, the accused cannot raise the matter in general issue except the limitation period plea.[136] Bishop justifies provision for waiving the right to raise a plea in bar for the simple reason that the plea is essentially for the benefit of the accused.[137] On the basis of the same logic, the Delhi High Court had ruled that the period of limitation was for the benefit of the accused and would not come in the way of an accused who is ready to undergo a trial after the expiry of such period.[138] The decision, however, has since been overruled in a later case by the Division Bench of the same High Court.[139] Returning to the data in Table 24 on plea in bar, one respondent did not raise the plea, considering it futile to do so and in yet another case, the response was 'can't say'. The rest of the five respondents made no response to the question.

(iii) Pardon and Condonation

The grounds of pardon and condonation have not been involved in the response of any respondent. However, for academic interest it may be brought out that pardon and condonation are generally rare occurrences. Pardon is an act of grace and mercy presupposing the commission of an offence. Under the plenary power conferred by the Constitution,[140] the President, while not often exercising such power before conviction, may legally pardon an offender in advance of trial. There are, however, no known instances of a plea having been taken at arraignment for an accused having been individually pardoned, though proclamation of general amnesty, after a war, is not

---

136 State v Barnes, 32 Maine 530 cit in Winthrop, Military Law and Precedents, op cit, n 118, p 268-269.

137 Bishop, 1 C L $ 992, cit in Winthrop, ibid.

138 Maj Harbhajan Singh v UOI, 1982 AISL J Vol 12 p 120 (Del).

139 Lt Col (TS) HC Dhingra v UOI, 1988 (2) Delhi Lawyer (DB) 109. Please also see Maj Radha Krishan v UOI, (1996) 3 SCR 837 and Nb Sub Niranjan Singh v UOI, Delhi High Court decision dated 07 Aug 1997 in WP No. 3603 of 1990.

140 Constitution of India, Article 72. The President has the power to grant pardon in all CM convictions, all cases of the sentence of death and so on.

very uncommon, as was done by the American President after the termination of the Black Hawk War in 1832 when many soldiers had deserted from the dread of the cholera. Similarly, constructive pardon may take place by a promotion or appointment to a new office while an officer under arrest is awaiting trial for the commission of certain offences. If a plea in bar made on any such ground is sustained, the court should proceed, as required by AR 53(3), to notify its finding on the plea to the confirming authority for confirmation or otherwise rather than acquitting the accused, since the pardon was based upon the theory of his guilt.[141] Condonation, as distinguished from pardon, is overlooking of an offence by a superior, having an authority to dispose the case, with the knowledge of circumstances. Condonation would be construed only when the offence has advisedly overlooked or forgiven by competent authority and not under a wrong impression as to the extent of the misconduct or without due authority, or without any authority.[142] In the case of the Indian Army, no authority is competent to condone an offence triable by CM so as to bar trial except with prior specific sanction of the COAS.[143]

7.5 General Plea of 'Guilty' or 'Not Guilty'

The arraignment of the accused, interrupted by various preliminary objections raised by him, if any, is resumed if a decision of the court on any such objection has not led to an inchoative end of the trial. The accused is asked again whether he is guilty or not guilty of the charge, the question being repeated in respect of each charge separately if there are more than one charge in the charge-sheet. Based on his reply, the plea of the accused against each charge shall be recorded. If he refuses to plead or does not plead intelligibly or pleads in some language not understood by the court, the plea shall be recorded as 'Not guilty' against the concerned charge. Further, a plea of 'Guilty' shall not be accepted when the accused is liable, if convicted, to be sentenced to death. If such a plea is offered, a plea of 'Not guilty' shall be recorded and the trial shall proceed accordingly. [144]

---

141 Winthrop,Military Law and Practice, op cit, n 118, p 272.

142 Simmons,The Constitution and Practice of Courts Martial, op cit, n 46, p 236; cf JAG Ruling Book entry no. 6336 dated 01 Sep 1944 and MML Vol II, p 298, Note 3 to AR r 53 citing custom of Service as authority.

143 Army Headquarters, New Delhi, Special Army Order 1/S/2002/DV-COURT MARTIAL, para 45.

144 AR, r 52 (1) and (4); AFR, r 60 (1) and (4); NA, s 105 read with N Regs II (S) reg 177 for recording plea of guilty but with no other details. Formerly, in the case of a prisoner, standing mute when required to plead, the plea was recorded as 'Guilty'. This was done in the case of Surgeon Harrison of the 17th Foot at Ghazipoor in 1816 in conformity with the custom of the common law courts before the Statutes 7 and 8 Geo 4, C. 28, s 2, that allowed a court to order a plea of 'Not guilty' to be entered in such circumstances. Ancient Indian traditions also treated silence to be suggestive of admission (***maun svikriti lakshanam***). Blackstone (4 Com 524) described it as a "point undermined whether death could be

(a) **Plea of Guilty**

A plea of 'Guilty', being treated as a "conclusive admission of guilt",[145] the procedure to follow does not envisage the examination of any witnesses to prove the charge and the finding of 'guilty' is recorded by the court on the basis of the plea offered by the accused. However, certain safeguards are required to be followed before the court records such finding so as to prevent any miscarriage of justice by the court. The presiding officer, or the JA, shall, on behalf of the court, ascertain that the accused understands the nature of the charge to which he has pleaded guilty, and shall inform him of the general effect of that plea, and, in particular, of the meaning of the charge and the difference in procedure which will be made by the plea, and shall advise him to withdraw that plea if it appears from the S of E that the accused ought to plead 'Not guilty'. If any charges are laid in the charge-sheet as alternative to the charge to which the accused has pleaded guilty, such alternative charges may be withdrawn by the prosecutor before the accused is arraigned on any of them after the court has recorded the finding of 'Guilty'.

After the record of the plea of 'Guilty' on a charge and if the trial does not proceed on any other charge on which the procedure of 'Not guilty' is to be followed, the court shall receive any statement which the accused desires to make in reference to the charge and shall read the S of E and annex it to the record of the proceedings. If there is no S of E, the court shall take and record sufficient evidence to enable to determine it the sentence and confirming officer to know all the circumstances connected with the offence. This evidence shall be taken in the manner in which it is taken on a plea of 'Not guilty'. Thereafter, the accused may make a statement in mitigation of punishment and may call witnesses as to his character. If from the statement of the accused or from the S of E or otherwise, it appears to the court that the accused did not understand the effect of his plea of 'Guilty', the court shall alter the record and enter a plea of 'Not guilty' and proceed accordingly.[146]

---

awarded one who had never pleaded and who can say nothing in arrest of judgment"; Simmons, The Constitution and Practice of Courts Martial, op cit, n 46, p 232 (s 555).

145 AR, r 52 (2) as amended by SRO 17E of 1993, and (3); AFR, r 60 (2) and (3); NA, s 105. The amended Rule 52(2) requires the court to record the fact of it having satisfied itself in the manner stated in newly inserted sub-rule (2A). In the Naval court-martial the circumstantial letter is read before accepting the plea of 'Guilty' offered by the accused. Simmons, ibid, p 231 (s 553). Under the Naval law, the application for trial consists of a formal letter by the CO of the accused's ship and addressed to the convening authority. It is known as cir cumstantial let ter and i ts aim is to f urnish the con vening authori ty with a clear idea what the of fence is, how it was commi tted, and briefly , how it came to l ight. It is accompanied with the charge-sheet, list of prosecution witnesses, S of E, list of exhibits and certified extracts of the service records of the accused.

146 AR, r 54 (3), (4) (5); AFR, r 62 (3) (4) (5); NA, s 105. During the trial the ac cused may, if he thinks fit, withdraw his plea of 'Not gui lty' at an y time and of fer a plea of 'Gui lty'. In that case, the court wi ll at

It may be noted that a plea of 'Guilty' is to be taken to the extent to which it is pleaded. On a charge of losing by neglect a number of articles, if the accused pleads 'Guilty' in respect of some of those articles only, the court may accept such a qualified plea of guilty, if it is satisfied of the justice of such a course and if the concurrence of the convening officer is signified by the prosecutor, and come to a special finding under AR r 62 (4) and (5).[147] However, a qualified plea that negatives a plea of guilty to the charge cannot be accepted. Thus, an accused may except, from the application of his answer of guilty, certain words or allegations against him in a qualified plea of 'Guilty' or may plead 'Guilty' to a lesser offence included or involved in the charge and his qualified plea may be accepted but it cannot be accepted when it takes the form of a demurrer which admits the facts of the case but issue is joined on some point of law to insist that the facts as stated do not constitute the offence charged. Such a plea is admitted in civilian courts but not at CM, though, on a plea of 'Not guilty', this may be argued.[148]

The legal effect of a plea of 'Guilty' is that it waives any defects of forms in the charges and by it, the accused admits his own identity as the person described therein as the offender and other particulars of the charges such as time and place of the occurrence. A substantial defect, however, going to the sufficiency of the charge as statement of a military offence is not waived. Nor, of course, can any such radical defect as an illegality in the constitution of the court or an absence of jurisdiction of the offence or the person, be done away with or lessened by the plea.[149]

(b) **Plea of 'Not Guilty'**

Academically the 'trial proper' begins with the plea of 'Not guilty' or 'Guilty';[150] previous to the jury being charged with prisoner, everything done is mere preliminary.[151] However, full majesty of law manifests only on the proceedings progressing on a plea of 'Not guilty'.

---

once, subject to the requirement of satisfying itself in terms of AR r 52 (2) and not accepting such plea in a capital offence, will record a plea and finding of 'guilty' and shall, so far as is necessary, proceed in the manner directed by r 54. After recording the finding of 'guilty' pursuant to the accused pleading guilty, the court shall follow the procedure on conviction provided in AR r 64 and then proceed to deliberate on the sentence to be awarded.

147 MML Vol II, p 296, Note 4 to AR, r 52.

148 Simmons, The Constitution and Practice of Courts Martial, op cit, n 46, p 231 (s 553).

149 Winthrop,Military Law and Precedents, op cit, n 118, p 275 (s 414).

150 Winthrop, loc cit, p 280.

151 Mc Faddin v Com, 23 Pa St, 12, cit in Winthrop, ibid.

(c) Data on Plea of 'Guilty' or Not Guilty'

Table 25 below reflects the data relating to the pleas of 'Guilty' or 'Not guilty' offered by the respondents (50), who were tried by CM.

TABLE - 25

Pleading to Charges by Accused Respondents

Srl. No.	Plea	Response Frequency	Percentage
1.	Guilty	10	20
2.	Not Guilty	37	74
3.	No Response	03	06
	Total	50	100

The data at Srl. No. 1 in Table 25 show that 10 (20%) respondents out of 50 pleaded 'Guilty' to the charge(s). Interestingly, the data in Table 24 at Srl 7 reflect 3 respondents having raised no preliminary pleas for the reason of such pleas being inapplicable in case of plea of 'Guilty' to the charge. It may be clarified that since preliminary pleas are raised before the accused pleads to the charge on which he is being arraigned, the accused may or may not raise those pleas irrespective of his intention to later plead 'Guilty'. If he considers futile to raise any such pleas in view of his yet-to-be-offered plea of 'Guilty' to the charge, he would not raise any preliminary pleas. On the other hand, nothing stops him from raising such pleas and take a chance thereon.

As shown at Srl. No. 2 of Table 25, as many as 37 (74%) respondents pleaded 'Not guilty' to the charge(s). Such a high percentage of the plea of 'Not guilty' need not be read as an adverse reflection on working of the CM system, since pleading 'Not guilty' does not necessarily mean the denial of the commission or omission of the act charged; his assertion being only to the effect that the same does not amount to offence or that the evidence on record in the S of E does not prove his guilt beyond reasonable doubt. By so claiming to be 'Not guilty', he is also not resorting to any falsehood or deception, since the plea is merely a legal issue and not a moral disclaimer.[152] In other words, by pleading 'Not guilty' to the charge, the accused is only translating into practice his right

152 MML, Vol II, p 296, Note 6 to AR, r 52, cf Wintrhop , loc cit, p 276 (s 415):"The plea is thus a legal issue, not a mor al disclaimer, it commits the party r esorting to i t to no f alsehood or deception. Ev en where every material averment in the charge is admitted to be true, and no defence to the same exists

to be treated as innocent until proved otherwise by cogent and reliable evidence in the true spirit of a great jurisprudential adage.

The data in Table 25 also present an opportunity for peeping into another interesting comparability. The plea of 'Guilty', as already noted, was offered by 10 (20%) of the respondents. A plea of 'Guilty' being "conclusive admission" of guilt by the concerned individuals, it will be interesting to consider here, for the sake of comparison, the data collected through Q 2.5 of the Interview Schedule, on the voluntary nature of the confession, if any, made by the respondents.

(d) Comparison with Confessional Data and Possibility of Plea Bargaining

As may be seen from the data in Table 16, no confession was made by 34 (68%) out of 50 respondents. Eight (16%) respondents made confession voluntarily, at the pre-trial investigation. However, 10 respondents pleaded 'Guilty' to the charge at their trial as reflected in Table - 25 at Srl - 1. The details of the respondents who pleaded 'Guilty' at their trial and those who confessed their guilt voluntarily at the pre-trial stage show that the individuals were not the same. Respondent Nos. A-157, 160, 165, 177, 181, 190, 192, 197, 201 and 204 pleaded 'Guilty' to the charge, eight of them under AA s 39 (absence without leave), one under AA s 38 (desertion) and one under AA s 69 read with IPC s 304-A for causing death by rash and negligent act of driving. Four of them including respondent Nos. A-181 charged with desertion and A-197 charged with causing death by a rash or negligent act of driving (driver by trade) and A-190 and 192 charged for absence without leave had made no confession. They all appear to have pleaded 'Guilty' to avoid harassment involved in a CM trial and with an expectation of getting lesser punishment or at least avoiding protracted proceedings on a plea of 'Not guilty'. The additional remarks of respondents A-181 (very long delay in the conduct of enquiry) and A-197 (pleaded 'Guilty' so as to avoid harassment of not getting leave etc. even though I was not really at fault) and the punishments received by respondents A-190 (less than 3 months imprisonment in military custody) and A-192 (one month imprisonment in military custody) are suggestive of such probability. It is possible that some sort of unofficial 'plea bargaining' took place in these cases between the accused and the disciplinary authorities, for which there is no provision under the Indian military law, unlike the American law expressly providing for pre-trial agreements for such purpose.[153] On the other hand, respondents No. A-171, 189, 191 and 202 had made voluntary confession of their guilt at pre-trial investigations but chose to plead 'Not-

contd/-

on merits, this plea is always justifiable, since it is in general only through this legal form that all the circumstances surrounding the offence, and which, taken together may very considerably extenuate its criminality, can be br ought out ...."

153 RCM 705 provides for a promise by the accused to plead guilty and promise by convening authority, in a pre-trial agreement, to refer the charge to certain types of court-martial or refer a capital offence as

guilty' at the trial. In the case of respondents A-178 and 189, a plea of 'Guilty' could not be accepted since the offence charged (murder) was punishable with death. Thus, there may be occasions for variation between confession at pre-trial stage and plea of 'Guilty' or 'Not guilty' offered by the accused. It may be possible to somehow account for such variations and yet those variations may not be acceptable to a court in judicial review. In Ramalingam's case, the accused pleaded 'Guilty' to a charge of gang-rape and asked for mercy, owning full responsibility for his serious lapse. A GCM then sentenced him to suffer rigorous imprisonment for ten years and to be dismissed from the Service. Later, he approached the Madras High Court, contending that his confessional statement had been extracted by threat, coercion and use of force and that he did not know English and the translated copy of the proceedings was not provided to him. The High Court dismissed his petition, holding that when the petitioner had himself pleaded guilty before the Army court, he could not wriggle out and argue that his statement had been obtained by force, coercion and threat.[154]

(e) Greater Precaution Taken by CM than under Cr PC

The discussion in the foregoing reveals that much greater precaution is prescribed by legislation for being taken under the military law to proceed on a plea of 'Guilty' than under the ordinary criminal law, to avoid miscarriage of justice. On the accused pleading guilty, the Cr PC requires the Judge in a matter of fact approach, simply to record the plea and 'in his discretion' to 'convict him thereon'. If the accused is not so convicted or refuses to plead or does not plead or claims to be tried, a judge shall straightway go to fix the date for the examination of witnesses.[155] As against this, AR r 52 (r 116 in the case of SCM) elaborately lays down what all the CM has to do to ensure that the accused understands the nature of the charge and the substantive and procedural consequences of his plea of guilty thereon, and also to proceed in a procedure applicable on a plea of 'Not guilty', despite the accused having pleaded 'Guilty', if considered desirable. In a recently decided case, it was brought to the notice of the Supreme Court that in spite of the accused having pleaded guilty to the charge of absence without leave, the CO holding SCM for his trial "had proceeded in terms of Section 116 of the Act (holding SCM) on the premise as if the delinquent officer (*sic* soldier) had not pleaded guilty."[156] The provision being obtainable in military law the world over,[157] may be

non-capital or withdraw one or more charges. The provision is intended to prevent informal agreements and protect the rights of the accused and the interest of the Government; Santobello v New York, 404 US 257 (1971).

154 Ramalingam A v UOI, Madras High Court Order of 26 Jul 2001 in WP No. 1225 of 1999.

155 Cr PC, ss 229 and 230;

156 Sheel Kr Roy v Secretary M/o Defence , JT 2007 (7) SC 485 at p 489.

157 MCM 2000, RCM 910 (e); The (British) Court Martial (Army) Rules, 1997, r 46.

explained as a measure of extra care being due when lay commanders are entrusted with the onerous duty of dispensing justice, in a system which is an amalgamation of a jury trial and a trial by Judge, without the counterparts of the jurors and the Judge having powers of the originals, and saddled with an unenviable responsibility of such widely apart interests as those of military discipline and justice traditionally being blindfolded.

7.6 Onset of Trial Proper : Inquiry by Court as to Defence Preparedness

The procedure prescribed for the trial to proceed on a plea of 'Not guilty' is "in the nature of regular trial before a criminal court in as much as courts-martial are bound to follow the provisions of the general law of evidence contained in the Evidence Act subject to certain modifications."[158] To begin with, the court ascertains from the accused whether he needs, and grants if convinced of such a need, an adjournment on the ground that any of the rules relating to procedure before trial have not been complied with and that he has not had sufficient opportunity to prepare his defence.[159] If no such adjournment is requested or granted on the court reassembling pursuant to such adjournment, the prosecutor makes an opening address followed with the examination of prosecution witnesses and so on.

(a) Documents for Preparation of Defence

On the issue of the accused having not had sufficient opportunity to prepare his defence, it is relevant to examine whether he had received the documents required to be given to him for the preparation of his defence. Table – 26 presents the data, collected in response to Q. 2.6 in the Interview Schedule, in respect of the documents given to the respondents before their trial to enable them to prepare their defence.

158 Major G S Sodhi v The Chief of Army Staff, AIR 1991 SC 1617, (para 10).

159 AR, r 56 (1) and (2). No corresponding provision under the Air Force or Naval laws. Under N Regs II (S), reg 178(5), however, an accused may ask for time when he is called upon for his defence. For the accused's right to prepare his defence, please see AR, r 33; AFR, r 39 and N Regs II (S), reg 172 and earlier discussion at 2.4 (c). Accordingly, he is entitled to receive a copy each of the charge-sheet, S of E, relevant statement and documents from the C of I and names of the officers to constitute the CM, under AR rr 33(7), 34 and 184(1).

TABLE - 26

Documents Given for Preparation of Defence

Srl No	Documents	Response Frequency	%	Remarks
1.	Charge-sheet and S of E.	14	28	24 -96 hours before trial in 24 cases, less than 24 hours before trial in 2 cases and 5 - 10 days before trial in 14 cases and no time specified in 3 cases.
2.	Charge-sheet, S of E, C of I.	16	32	
3.	Charge-sheet, S of E, C of I. and details of members	13	26	
4.	No documents given.	02	04	
5.	No Response.	05	10	
	Total	50	100	

It is noticed from Srl 3 of Table 26 that only 13 (26%) out of 50 respondents received their full entitlement of the documents required to be given to an accused to enable him to prepare his defence. No names of the officers appointed to constitute the CM and as waiting members were given in 32 (64%), cases as reflected against Srl 1, 2 and 4 of the Table. It may be seen that a prior information of names etc. of the members or waiting members appointed would enable the accused to decide, before hand, as to which of them he would object under AA s 130 read with AR r 44, as discussed earlier, and to plan evidence to support his objection. The importance of such information is directly proportionate to the accused's right to object to members. Further, it may be recalled that under the American law,[160] an accused is entitled to several other details in addition to those given under Indian provisions. However, classical military jurists have a difference of opinion on the issue of furnishing such details to the prisoner.[161] The Indian

160 Please see supra n 74.

161 Simmons, The Constitution and Practice of Courts Martial, n 46, p 177. Simmons cites Tytler observing in his treatise on 'martial law' that it was necessary to furnish the prisoner with a correct detail of the members of the CM but Simmons finds it opposed to the custom of Service, even though conceding that such information may help the prisoner in challenge proceedings.

Naval law also does not provide for furnishing such details to the accused, though it does confer a right on the accused, as well as on the prosecutor, to raise an objection to members.[162] However, since none of the 50 respondents was subject to the Naval law, they were all entitled to such details in respect of the members, except those who were tried by an SCM, the challenge of members being inapplicable to the SCM. Accordingly, the number of respondents who were entitled, but not furnished, these details will be reduced considerably from earlier calculated number of 32. Similarly, the number of respondents who were not provided the relevant statements and documents from the C of I, as reflected at Srl 1 of Table 26, will be reduced from 14 to 7, since no C of I was held in the case of other 7 respondents, as may be seen from Table 16 in Chapter - 6. Finally, a charge-sheet and S of E having been received by the respondents in 43 cases (86%), as is evident from data at Srls 1 - 3 of Table 26, and there having been no response in 5 cases, it may be concluded that the general attitude of military commanders has been to provide to the accused with sufficient information as to charges against him and evidence thereon to enable him to prepare his defence. Two cases in which no documents were furnished to the accused may, thus be treated as an abrasion to the generality of a positive approach being adopted in this regard by the officers given the duty to convene the CM.

The other three sub-questions of Q. 2.6 relating to the accused's preparation of his defence were concerned with the defence witnesses being called at the government expense, the accused being informed of his right to engage counsel and notice of joint trial, where applicable. The data collected in response to those sub-questions are reflected in Table - 27 on the next page.

162 NA, s 102 for right to object to members and N Regs II (S), reg 169 for what all documents are to be given to the accused.

TABLE - 27

Matters Related to Preparation of Defence

Srl No.	Preparatory Matters	Response Frequency				
		Yes	No	Any Other	No Respon-se	Total
1.	Were witnesses called at Government expense ?	35	08	02*	05	50
2.	Was respondent accused informed of his right to engage counsel ?	31	11	03**	05	50
3.	Was respondent accused given notice of intended joint trial ?	00	10	32***	08	50

* Chose to call no witness. ** Not applicable, as SCM trial
*** Not applicable, as no joint trial

(b) Calling of Defence Witnesses

The data at Srl 1 show that in 35 (70%) out of 50 cases, the witnesses were called at the government expense. In 8 (16%) cases, the witnesses were called by the accused respondents under own arrangements and in 2 (4%) cases, the respondents chose to call no witnesses at all in defence. Five (10%) respondents made no response to the question. It may be brought out that the law provides for the CO, the convening officer, and the presiding officer of the CM after the assembly of the court, to procure the attendance of the witnesses whom the prosecutor or the accused desires to call.[163] The person requiring the witness may be asked to defray the cost, which provision is essentially meant to prevent an unreasonable demand, but would not be allowed to interfere with the calling of a witness who appears to be material. This, however, is not an altruistic gesture or charity. The absence of a material witness might afterwards be held to invalidate the proceedings of a CM, though even if the witness had been called, the court would probably have arrived at the same decision.[164] Travel Regulations provide

163 AA, s 135 read with AR, r 137 and MML Vol II, p 335, Notes 1 to 5 to AR, r 37; RA para 454-456; AFA, s 134; and NA, s 134.

164 MML, ibid, Note 5 to r 139.

for the conveyance of civilians in the government service in a civil department or in the defence services, the cadets and the civilians not in the government service, who attend a military court and also for their traveling and subsistence allowance. A witness who is not in government service is required to be advanced, through the Magistrate or direct, whatever be the mode of calling him, a sufficient sum to cover his traveling expenses, and pay similarly for his return journey, before he leaves the station to which summoned.[165] Those who are subject to AA may be ordered by the proper authority, without formally issuing summons, to attend before a CM. If no summons has been issued, however, he cannot be dealt with, in the event of default, under AA s 59 for an offence relating to the CM, but may be charged under a AA s 41 (disobedience to superior officer) or s 63 (violation of good order and discipline). In the case of a civilian witness, more particularly one who is not in the government service, the summons issued under the hand of the CO etc. shall be sent to the Magistrate within whose jurisdiction the witness may reside or may presently be located.[166] The Magistrate is required to give effect to the summons as if the witness were required in the court of the said Magistrate. These words in the provisions are not to be narrowly understood to mean that the Magistrate is to play merely an assisting role in executing the summons. Since the presiding officer of the CM has no jurisdiction to issue the summons and warrant to the non-military personnel, the Magistrate, upon such request, has to issue the summons or warrant as if issued by him, with a direction to appear or produce documents before the CM. The Karnataka High Court accordingly directed the Magistrate in a recent case to issue a warrant for the arrest of a defaulter and that the execution of the warrant of arrest be entrusted to the Army authorities in terms of Cr PC s 72.[167] These provisions and the data at Srl. 1 in Table 27 suggest that an accused under DPCM is generally in a sound position to effectively prepare a defence in relation to the witnesses required to give evidence in support of his version of the case and is not left to suffer for any lack of pecuniary resources.

(c) Legal Assistance and Right to be Represented

The rights of the accused to prepare his defence also include his right to be assisted or represented at the trial. The officer giving him a copy of charge-sheet and of the S of E is also required to ask him to state in writing whether or not he wishes to have an officer assigned by the convening officer to represent him at the trial.[168] The officer

165 Defence Services Regulations – Travel Regulations (TR) 1976, par a 131.

166 MML, Vol II, p 217 , Note 6 to AA s 135.

167 India v XI Additional Chief Metropolitan Magistrate, Bangalore in Cr WP No. 481 of 2002, cit in Col G K Sharma & Col M S Jaswal,Study and Practice of Military Law, 6th ed, 2006, New Delhi, Deep and Deep Publications P Ltd. , p 184 .

168 AR r 33 (7); AFR r 102 (2).

representing the accused at a GCM or DCM is called 'defending officer'.[169] For the trial by GCM or DCM, he may also engage a counsel to represent him.[170] In the case of an offence punishable with death, the convening officer may also employ a civil counsel for the defence of the accused, if the accused himself is unable to do so owing to the lack of pecuniary resources.[171] The data relating to the accused being informed of the right to have a counsel to represent him at the trial, placed at Srl. 2 in Table 27 show that 31 (62%) respondents were so informed. In 3 (6%) cases, the right to be represented by a counsel was not applicable, this being a trial by the SCM. At an SCM trial, the accused is entitled to have only the friend-of-the-accused, there is no prosecutor either. In a case recently decided by the Supreme Court, it was noted with 'grave concern' that the petitioner "was tried in a Summary Court-Martial proceeding held ... only for an hour ... the commanding officer himself was the Prosecutor and also the Judge."[172]

In the context of the right to be represented by a counsel of once own choice, it may be pointed out that historically the military system has been reluctant to afford to an accused such a right at the CM trial.[173] The wordings of AR r 96, before its recent amendment in 1993, and the corresponding provisions under the Air Force law (but not under the Naval law) even at present reflect such reluctance. In the case of Ram Sarup who had been sentenced to death by a GCM without such legal representation being allowed to him, the Supreme Court had an opportunity to pronounce on this aspect of the GCM. However, the apex court did not go into this aspect, relying on the affidavit filed by the military authorities that no request for such representation was made by the accused and thus there was no violation of his fundamental right guaranteed by Art. 22 (1) of the Constitution.[174]

(d) **Joint-Trial Notice**

Table - 27 at Srl 3 reflect the data relating to joint trial notice being issued to the accused when he is informed of the charge.[175] Any number of accused persons may be charged and tried jointly, for an offence committed by them collectively or for offences not charged jointly but their commission having been abetted by others, and the offences being based on the same facts or forming part of a series of offences of the same or

169 AR r 95 (1); AFR r 102 (1); N Regs II (S), reg 173 (1).

170 AR r 96, as amended by SRO 17-E of 6 Dec 1993; AFR r 103; N Regs II (S), reg 173 (1).

171 RA para 479.

172 Sheel Kr Roy's case, op cit, n 156, p 488 (para 9).

173 Simmons, The Constitution and Practice of Courts Martial, op cit, n 46, p 202

174 Ram Sarup's case, op cit, n 119, (para 7).

175 AR, r 35 (4).

similar character.[176] Any of the accused persons intended to be tried jointly may claim, either by notice to the convening authority, or to the court at the time of arraignment, that he or some other accused be tried separately, basing the claim on the ground that the evidence of one or more of the other accused persons will be material to his defence or that otherwise he would be prejudiced or embarrassed in his defence.[177] The claim may be accepted or rejected after due consideration. The related data in Table - 27 show that in 32 (64%) cases, no such notice was warranted, since it was not a joint trial. In 10 (20%) cases, even though it was a joint trial, no such notice was received by the respondents. Out of those 10 cases, the offence of mutiny was involved in six (12%) cases, which were all from the same unit, i.e., 3 Artillery Brigade Signal Company and the respondents were co-accused persons. In the case of conspiracy to cause or joining in mutiny, the essence of charge is combination between the accused persons. In such a case, the nature of the charge may not admit a separate trial.[178] Thus, even if a request had been made by these accused respondents (A-168, 169, 170, 171, 179 and 180) for a separate trial, it might not have been acceded. Nonetheless, a notice of the intention of joint trial was a legal requirement and a failure to issue such a notice was clearly the violation of such a requirement. The other accused persons (respondents No. A-166, 189, 194 and 195) were from 163 Field Regiment, being jointly tried for the offence of murder. The nature of the offence as such could certainly admit of a separately trial, and thus, in the absence of any further details of the circumstances of the case being on record of the related Interview Schedules, these four cases would be described as an infraction of the provisions in AR r 35. However, the same provision expressly lays down that where any such claim for a separate trial has been made but disallowed, either by the convening authority or by the CM, the disallowance will not be a ground for refusing confirmation of the finding or sentence, unless, in the opinion of the confirming authority, substantial miscarriage of justice has occurred thereby.[179] This renders the requirement of the notice to be directory and not mandatory. In any case, it is not known what finally happened in these cases at post-trial review. As regards the 8 (16%) no-response cases, the details of other responses from the concerned respondents disclose that they were not jointly tried and hence no such notice was required in their cases.

No data were collected in the present study as to whether or not any adjournment was in fact sought by any respondent on the ground of inadequate opportunity to prepare defence. However, general attitude of the CM on any such request usually is not to deny any such adjournment.

---

176 Ibid, r 35 (1), (2), (3).

177 Ibid, r 35 (4).

178 MML Vol II, p 284 , Note 6 to AR r 35.

179 AR, r 35 (4).

7.7 Examination of Witnesses

The examination of witnesses is the most prominent feature of the proceedings on a plea of 'Not Guilty' and follows immediately the prosecution opening address. The witnesses are examined in accordance with the provisions of the IEA in general and its Chapter X in particular, interpreted in the light of the case-law developed over the years and modified to suit the Services specific peculiarities catered by the provisions of the concerned Act, Rules and Regulations.[180] For instance, in variance of s 135 of the IEA as to the order of production and examination of witnesses, the officer performing the duty of the prosecutor, if required to give evidence on the facts of the case, shall give such evidence soon after his opening address, going through the steps of examination-in-chief, cross examination and re-examination, after being sworn or affirmed, like any other witness.[181] Similarly, a CM may also take judicial notice of any matter within the general military knowledge of the members,[182] in addition to the facts listed in s 57 of IEA. Thus, evidence need not be given, before a CM, as to the relative ranks of officers, their general duties, authorities and different matters of the Service or generally as to any matter which an officer, as such, may reasonably be expected to know,[183] but not any matter of Special service knowledge which one might acquire as a member of a particular arm or branch of the Service. This, however, does not prevent a member putting questions to a witness which are based on his special knowledge.[184] Similarly, even though the provisions of the Cr PC do not apply to a special procedure,[185] such as that of the CM, any Cr PC provisions may, in the appropriate circumstances, be used for guidance in regard to any matter not specifically provided for in the Service laws, since competent military authority is empowered to do such thing or take such action in such a situation as appears to be just and proper.[186]

Upon any point of law or procedure which arises at the trial, the court is required to be guided by the opinion of the JA and not to disregard it except for very weighty reasons.[187] Any information or advice given to the court by the JA, on any matter before

180 Supra, Ch 2, n 54 and related text.

181 AR r 56(5) r ead with IEA ss 137 , 138.

182 AA s 134 , AFA s 133; NA s 132.

183 MML Vol II, p 217 , Note to AA s 134 .

184 Br MML, 1972, p 394 read with Br AA, s 99(3).

185 Cr PC s 5.

186 AR r 6; AFR r 6; N Regs II (S), reg 6; cf Simmons, The Constitution and Practice of Courts Martial, op cit, n 46, p 244, citing Capt John Williamson, The Elements of Military Arrangements, 1783, Vol II, p 67 (note 113) stating, on the authority of Major Adye (an eminent classical military jurist) that "where the act of Parliament and Articles of War are silent, courts-martial must in their proceedings conform to the practice of the established courts of judicatur e."

187 MML Vol II, p 326, Note 1 to AR, r 105.

the court, shall, if he or the court desires it, be entered in the proceedings. The court, following the opinion of the JA on a legal point may record that it has decided the issue in consequence of that opinion.[188] However, all questions of fact and law are to be decided by the members of the court after due deliberation in a closed court.[189] The procedure to be followed in specific situations such as objection to the charge etc., has been specifically provided. However, there also exists a blanket provision for procedure on incidental matters such as admissibility of a particular piece of evidence, propriety of any question put to a witness and so on. The procedure consists of three steps: one, the ground being spelt out by or on behalf of the party raising the objection; two, answer by the opposite party or its counsel, and three, a right of reply vested in the party raising it.[190] After the advice of the JA on the legal aspect of the question, the court closes for its deliberation and arrives at a decision thereon by simple majority[191] of votes, the voting being by word of mouth and beginning from the junior-most member and the JA being present in the closed court but not entitled to vote.[192]

The presiding officer of a CM is responsible for the trial being conducted in proper order, and in accordance with the Act and the Rules made thereunder and in a manner befitting a court of justice. It is his duty to see that justice is administered, that the accused has a fair trial and does not suffer any disadvantage in consequence of his position as a person under trial, or of his ignorance, or of incapacity to examine or cross-examine witnesses or otherwise.[193] The same duty in respect of the accused equally devolves upon the JA, in addition to his duties of informing the court and the convening officer of any infirmity or defect, whether consulted or not, and of rendering advice to the prosecutor and the accused if such advice is sought, whether inside the court or outside, on any question of law relative to the charge or trial and to be entirely impartial in fulfilling his duties.[194] Further, the court is required to stop the prosecutor from referring

---

188 AR, r 105 (4), (5); AFR, r 111 (d), (f).

189 AR, r 80, for the meaning of 'closed court' and r 87 for the requirement of voting by every member on every question which the court has to decide. AFR, rr 87 and 94 correspond to those provisions. The Naval law (NA s 114) howev er, casts upon the J A the dut y to decide al l questions of la w arising in the course of trial and ma y, if desirable, advise the pr esident for the court to r etire or the J A may hear the arguments in some other convenient place in the absence of the members.

190 AR, r 88; AFR, r 95.

191 AA s 132 (1); AR, r 87 (1), (2); AF A, s 131 (1).

192 AR r 80, f or the J A's presence in a close court and AR, r 105 f or the J A's power and duties which do not include any decision to be made by him.

193 AR r 76; AFR, r 83, NA, s 175.

194 AR r 105; AFR, r 111. Such insistence upon the "entirely impartial" posture on the part of the JA is a great development from the times of the B ritish Articles of W ar, 1673, under which he w as required to "inform the court and prosecute" and, later in the 18th Century and part of the nineteenth, required to combine the functions of prosecutor and legal advisor to the court;" Stuart-Smith James, "Military Law: Its History, Administr ation and Pr actice",op cit, Ch 1, n 26, at 483.

to any matter not relevant to the charge but allow great latitude to the accused in making his defence, restricting itself from stopping his defence solely on the ground of irrelevance even though cautioning him in this regard, if need be.[195] In the same spirit, the court also restrains itself from interfering with the prosecution or defence and reserves all questions until after examination of a witness is finally concluded[196] by the parties to the trial, as a part of the modification of law of the land by special provisions of the military law.[197] Special care is also taken to make a record of any objection taken to any question or to proposed evidence, and dealt with as earlier brought out,[198] but rejected by the court[199] and a record of the correction, if any, made by a witness in his evidence when read over to him at the close of his examination.[200]

The trial proceedings, after the arraignment of the accused, must continue from day to day[201] and with the same officers as members,[202] on all days except Sundays or holidays, the court sitting ordinarily not more than six hours a day, from six in the morning and six in the afternoon, unless an adjournment is necessary for the ends of justice or such continuance is impracticable.[203] Similarly, if a JA has been appointed to a

---

195 AR, r 77 (3); cf Simmons, The Constitution and Practice of Courts Martial, op cit, n 46, p 242, quoting the advice of J AG Mr. Mowbray, dated 06 Mar 1867 , to Lt Gen Sir Storks that the prisoner be "restricted as little as possible in the examination of his own witnesses, or in the cross-examination of those called by the prosecutor, as an error in this respect by the court may invalidate the whole proceedings." As for the prosecutor 's conduct, the military law charges him with the responsibility of bringing the whole of the transaction before the court, behaving impartially, and not to take any unfair advantage of, or suppress any evidence in favour of the accused; AR, r 77 (1), RA para 464; AFR, r 84 (1); cf Daryao Singh v State of Punjab, AIR 1965 SC 332 at p 333.

196 AR r 142 (1); AFR, r 120 (1); MML Vol II, p 338, Note 2 to AR r 142; cf Simmons, The Constitution and Practice of Courts Martial, op cit, n 46, p 242:"The court and each individual member ought to reserve all questions until after the examination of a witness is finally concluded by the parties to the trial."

197 IEA s 165, AA s 133.

198 Supra n 190.

199 AR, r 92(3), AFR, r 98 (3). Question with decision of the court be recorded if requested by the prosecutor or the accused or if the court thinks it fit to do so. cf Simmons, ibid: "Where the court exercises it authority in refusing to allow a question to be put to a witness the question so rejected still appears in the proceedings, accompanied by a statement of the objection to it in order that it might be known to the convening authority whether the court has exercised its authority according to law."

200 AR, r 141 (2), (3); AFR, r 119 (2), (3); Simmons, loc cit, pp 242-243: "No erasure or obliteration is, in any circumstances, admitted, as it is essentially necessary that the authority which has to review should have the most ample means of judging, not only of any discrepancy in the statement of a witness, but of any incident which may be made a subject of remark by either party in addressing the court."

201 AR, r 82, AFR, r 89;

202 AR, r 86 (2); AFR, r 93 (2).

203 AR, r 81; AFR, r 88.

CM, which is a legal necessity in the case of a GCM and is desirable in the case of SGCM,[204] the JA must be present at the trial and the court shall not proceed in his absence. However, unlike a member, a JA may be replaced except at a Naval CM.[205] The presence of the accused through out the CM proceedings is also a mandatory legal requirement under the Indian military law.[206] Further, since no new member may be added to a CM after the members are sworn,[207] it has to be dissolved if the number of the members present falls below the minimum number required to constitute that particular kind of the CM convened under the AA or AFA or below four under the NA[208]. It will also have to be dissolved in the event of a prolonged illness or death of the accused[209] or of the officer performing the duty of the trial JA under the Naval law.[210]

7.8 Defence of Accused

The rules on examination of witnesses apply alike to the defence case. It is a principle to be scrupulously observed in a military trial that the accused, whatever be his rank, is not only to be deprived of no right but is also to be accorded every proper privilege is in no manner to be embarrassed or placed at a disadvantage, but in every reasonable degree facilitated in making his defence. Accordingly, before he takes up the examination of his witnesses, if any, two valuable procedures are provided for in the military law. Firstly, at the close of the case for the prosecution, the accused may offer a "plea of no case", suggesting that the evidence led on behalf of the prosecution, in respect of any

---

204 AA, s 129; AFA, s 128; NA, s 99 (1) for legal necessity of a trial JA to attend a Naval CM.

205 AR, r 82 (4); AFR, r 89 (3); The related provisions prohibit any change, replacement or addition of an officer appointed as a member, after the commencement of the CM trial but no similar provisions exist in any of the three Services laws in the case of JA. The grounds for dissolution of a CM in all the three Services Acts inter alia include alike the illness of JA. The mandatory requirement of a JA attending a GCM and a CM under the NA is also the same. And yet while an officer appointed as a trial JA is never changed in the Navy and a CM is eventually dissolved if the same individual is no more available to perform the duty of the JA, in corresponding situation under the Army and the Air Force, an individual officer performing the duty of the JA may be freely replaced by another. The only legal authority therefore may be traced in the different custom of the concerned Service.

206 AR, r 84; AFR, r 91; NA, s 123 (b) suggesting inter alia that the trial cannot proceed in the absence of the accused. However, under the US law (RCM 804) the accused is mandatorily required to be present at certain specified initial proceedings. He can also be excluded from the proceedings after warning by the military judge (corresponding to JA) on the ground of disruptive conduct on his part.

207 Supra, n 202.

208 AR, r 85; AFR, r 92; NA, s 122 (2), proviso.

209 Supra, n 206.

210 Supra, n 205.

one or more charges, has not established a prima facie case against him and that he should not, therefore, be called upon to make his defence to that charge or the charges. Following the prescribed procedure, if the court allows the plea, it shall record a finding of 'Not Guilty' on the charge(s) to which the plea relates and announce it as subject to confirmation. If the plea is over-ruled, the court shall proceed with the trial. The prosecution evidence disclosing no case against the accused, the court may also record a finding of 'Not guilty' suo motu even in absence of a plea by the accused.[211] The second procedure to be observed by the court at this stage is based on the principle that every man ought to have an opportunity of being heard before he is condemned.[212] It is, therefore, required that in every trial, for the purpose of enabling the accused personally to explain any circumstances appearing in evidence against him, the court or the JA may, at any stage, without previously warning the accused, put such questions to him as he considers necessary, and shall after the close of the case for the prosecution and before he is called on for his defence, question him generally on the case. No oath shall be administered to the accused nor shall he render himself liable to punishment by refusing to answer the question or by giving answer to them which he knows not to be true.[213] The amendment to AR brought in 1993 makes a significant procedural departure from the old procedure[214] under which such questions were, and under the AFR still are, put after the unsworn statement, if any, made by the accused. The said statement, having been prepared in writing by the accused in consultation with his counsel or defending officer would leave much less room for the court to put questions to the accused and would impart much more confidence to the accused to answer the questions by the court, if still asked. Thus, the new provision is less in tune with the original spirit of facilitating the defence, and, on the contrary sounds to be somewhat aggressive in the very tone of the language used. In practice, many times questions are so framed by the court, with the help of the legal expertise of the JA, that the accused is pushed into a 'catch – 22' situation of being embarrassed in his defence either way, by replying to the question or by opting not to reply. The provision, thus becomes a counter-productive safe-guard, being misused as an underhand exercise in cross-examination of the accused. As a remedial measure, it may be provided, on the pattern of the proviso to AR r 58 (2), as substituted by 1995 amendment, that the accused shall not be questioned under the provision except on his own request in writing and his failure to offer himself for such

---

211 AR, r 57 as amended by Army (Amendment) Rules, 1993, r 14; AFR, r 65; NA, s 111 (1) to (5).

212 King v Gaskin, 8 T er Rep p 210, ci t in Winthr op, op ci t, n 126, p 135.

213 AR, r 58 as substituted by Army (Amendment) Rules, 1993, r 15 (SRO 17-E of 1993).

214 AR, rr 58 (2)(a) and 59 (b); AFR, r 66 (3).

questioning shall not be made the subject of any comment by any of the parties or the court or give rise to any presumption against him.

If the trial survives a plea of no case or where no such plea has been raised, the accused or his legal representative may make an opening address and examine his witnesses, if any, including himself as the first witness. His failure to examine himself as a witness shall not be made a subject of any adverse comments or inference.[215]

7. 9 Data Related to Evidential Matters

Q. 2.8 in the Interview Schedule had four sub-questions on different aspects of evidence related matters at the CM trial in the cases of the respondents. The data collected in response have bearing on the general trend of the CM decisions on the defence pleas or submissions, and on the submissions of the prosecution representative, on opportunity to cross-examine witnesses, making a statement, calling witnesses and their being satisfactorily examined. Tables 28 and 29 reflect respectively the data on the general trend of CM decisions and those on the remaining aspects.

---

215 AR, r 58 (3) as substituted by SRO 17 - E of 1993.

TABLE - 28

General Trend of CM Decisions on Prosecution/Defence Submissions

Srl No	CM Response to Submission	For Prosecution		For Defence	
		Frequency	Percentage	Frequency	Percentage
1.	Heard and				
	(a) Mostly accepted	21*	42	10**	20
	(b) Mostly rejected	00	00	10	20
	(c) Decided on merits (accepting or rejecting as deserved)	18	36	17	34
2.	Not heard	01	02	03	06
3.	Not applicable	04	08	04	08***
4.	Can't say	01	02	01	02
5.	No response	05	10	05	10
	Total	50	100	50	100

* "Not mostly but always" says A - 188; ** "Trend changed at revision" says A-182.
*** Plea being 'Guilty'

The data presented in Table - 28 may be more effectively examined along with the data on natural justice related matters displayed in Table - 29.

TABLE - 29

Natural Justice Related Matters During CM Trial

Srl.	Natural Justice Requirements		Response Frequency					Total
			Yes	No	NA	Can't Say	NR	
1.	Cross examination		36	01	05	02	06	50
2.	Making statement		34	04	05	01	06	50
3.	Producing Witness		33	03	05	03	06	50
4.	Was there any witness who could not be called because of -							
	(a) High status	03						
	(b) Service conditions	03						
	(c) Pecuniary limitations	01						
	(d) Non-cooperation of adm. authorities	02						
	(e) Any other reason	03						
	Sub-total	12	12	27	05	00	06	50
5.	Was there any witness who could not be properly examined because of -							
	(a) Frequent interruption or interference by JA or the members	01						
	(b) Being won over by the prosecutor	01						
	(c) Any other	01						
	Sub-total	03	03	36	05	00	06	50
	Total		118	71	25	06	30	250

Legend: NA = Not Applicable NR=No Response

As may be seen from the data at Srl 1 of Table – 28, the submissions made in respect of evidence were duly heard by the CM in 39 (78%) cases out of 50 when made by the prosecution and in 37 (74%) when made on behalf of the accused. It was only in one

(2%) case from the prosecution and 3 (6%) from the defence that the submissions were not heard by the court. Thus, both the sides were given almost equal opportunity of being heard. However, when it came to decision, 21 (42%) respondents felt that the prosecution submissions were mostly accepted. In fact, respondent No. A-188-A-12 added that the prosecution submissions were accepted and defence ones rejected not only 'mostly' but 'always'. However, 10 (20%) respondents also had a satisfying experience of the defence submissions having been accepted in most of the cases. There was no respondent who witnessed the prosecution submissions having been mostly rejected. On the other hand, 10 (20%) respondents did have the rude shock of the defence submissions having mostly been rejected. However, an almost equal number of the respondents reported such submissions having been rejected or accepted purely on merit both in respect of the prosecution (18, i.e., 36%) and the defence (17, 34%). Rest of the data in Table - 28 is self-explanatory and hence no elaboration.

Some of the respondents also chose to further add to their responses. Respondent No. A-175-A-10, whose trial by GCM lay stayed by an order of the Delhi High Court at the time of his interview by this researcher, stated in respect of the trial proceedings before the stay that the questions put by the defence counsel to prosecution witnesses were not permitted as leading questions, whereas all sorts of questions were allowed to be raised by the prosecution counsel. The said respondent was being tried under the Official Secrets Act and had a retired Army Officer from the JAG's Dept to represent him as a civil counsel, who must be knowing his rights to put leading questions in cross-examination of the prosecution witnesses. In view of this, it appears that the respondent did not present here a true picture of the trial.

Turning to the data in Table - 29, it is noticed that 36 (72%) respondents stated to have cross-examined the prosecution witnesses, 34 (68%) had made statements in their defence and 33 (66%) had produced witnesses in defence. It was only in one (2%) case that the prosecution witnesses were not cross-examined by the accused. Even though an abysmally low percentage, yet it cannot be lightly ignored, considering that the "exercise of this right (the right to cross-examine) is justly regarded as one of the most efficacious tests which the law has devised for the discovery of the truth."[216] The denial of this right to the respondent in question will, therefore, not only arouse curiosity for its reason but would also make the proceedings rather suspect of being a mere eye-wash. The concerned respondent, No. A-186-A-7, was charged for bank robbery during Bangladesh war. At his trial by SGCM, he did make a statement and also produced defence witnesses but did not cross-examine any prosecution witnesses for which he gave no reason. In the context of pre-trial procedure of the S of E, he had stated that no

216 Tylor, 12th ed, s 1428, p 910 cit in Ratanlal Ranchohoddas and Dhirajlal Keshavlal Thakore, The Law of Evidence, 16 the ed, 1973, B ombay, Bombay Law Reporter Pvt. Ltd. , p 298

legal support being available, he did not have even mental grounding to feel or not feel aggrieved. In a different context, he has also stated that in his view, the lawyers or even officers from the JAG's Dept are deficient in their knowledge of military law. It is possible that he failed to cross-examine prosecution witnesses at his trial for the reason of an unsatisfactory state of legal support. As for a possible explanation for the response "can't say" in two (4%) cases, what comes to one's mind in the chain of association, is the strongly worded innuendos of Justice Douglas about CM.[217] Any criminal investigation, much less of a full fledged trial by a military tribunal, adversely affects the nerves of the person facing it, particularly if he is not a habitual offender. Simple soldiers, whose valour is essentially restricted to the battle field or the events of simulating nature, often find it difficult to keep their wits about, while in the presence of their superiors and more so in connection with disciplinary proceedings. No wonder if the CM proceeding, with all its solemn formalities and ceremonials, numbed the faculty of understanding in the case of the related respondents as to what all was going on there in fluent English loaded with legal jargon.[218] Then, the six (12%) no-response cases include the three cases in which the trial proceedings were stayed and another three cases of plea of 'Guilty'.

Moving to the data at Srls. 4 and 5 in Table 29, it is noticed that in 27 (54%) cases, there was no witness who could not be called while the accused was desirous of calling him. Similarly, in 36 (72%) cases, there was no witness who could not be properly examined because of any undue interference or interruption. However, in 12 (24%) cases, the attendance of some of the witnesses, whom the accused wanted to call, could not be procured. This was due to service conditions in 3 (6%) cases, high status of the witnesses in another 3 (6%) cases, pecuniary limitations in one (2%) case, administrative non-cooperation in 2 (4%) cases and some other unspecified reason in 3 (6%) cases. One of these respondents, No. A-188-A-12, growls that some witnesses, in his case, could not be called quoting service conditions for the inability to procure their attendance but actually this was due to non-cooperative attitude of the JAG's Branch which advised for not calling them. His responses to certain other questions also bring out the dissatisfaction with the entire process of the dispensation of justice in his case, and among the factors responsible therefor, he has inter alia listed "playing with evidence by JA". While it is difficult to say how far his attitude towards the JAG's Dept is or is not justifiable, the remark of respondent No. A-178-A-10 with the same import lends support to him. The latter is equally sore about the attendance of some witnesses having remained

217 O Callahan v Parker, 395 US 258, 1969, at 262-269.

218 AR r 92 (1); AFR, r 99 (1) requiring the proceedings of the CM trial to be recorded in English. The Army Amendment Rules, 1993, r 20 substitutes the words "Hindi or English" for the word "English". In practice, however, the proceedings are still held in English only as contended by the petitioner in Ramalingam's case, supra, n 154.

elusive for the reason of "not being considered relevant by the JA (Major Paramjit Kaur)" and the respondent feeling to have been "erroneously convicted" on the charge of murder, getting "almost no opportunity to defend". Without probing further into the question of justifiability of these comments, the need of the proceedings to be not only fair but also to look to be fair may always be underlined. Having said this, it may be noted that the JAG, his Dept. and his officers are often chosen for pot-shot by the accused and his counsel, mostly out of grudge for frustrating their efforts to cleverly manipulate justice in their favour at the CM constituted of lay commanders. Further, in the absence of due cooperation by the administrative authorities, the attendance of witnesses could be procured by the accused under his own arrangement, if those witnesses were really important for defence.

The data at Srl 5 of Table - 29 bring out frequent interruption or interference by members or JA in 1 (2%) case; the witness having been won over in yet another one case and some unspecified reason in still one more case leading to the cross-examination of the witness being unsatisfactory. Respondent No. A-200-A-5 had the grievance against much interference by the JA during the course of the examination of some defence witnesses. This certainly would be termed as a violation of the requirements of the members and the JA generally reserving their questions "until after the examination of a witness is finally concluded by the parties" and the prisoner being "restricted as little as possible in the examination of his own witnesses, or in the cross-examination of those called by the prosecutor" as noted earlier. In the case of respondent No. A-196-A-4, some witnesses could not be satisfactorily examined because one of the prosecution witnesses, who had been the 2nd-in-command of the accused respondent, had some professional grudge against him and was influencing witnesses against him outside the court and was also hobnobbing with the members of the court in private. The respondent, who was holding the rank of a Colonel before he retired shortly preceding his trial by GCM, should have brought this to the notice of the presiding officer so as to enable him to discharge his duty of ensuring that the trial was conducted "in a matter befitting a court of justice" and that "the accused has a fair trial."[219] The same may be said of the complaint of respondent No. A-208-A-2 (who was holding a very senior military rank of Major Gen. before his trial) that the prosecution witnesses could not be satisfactorily cross-examined since the court (presided over by a Lieut Gen.) appeared to be "in a great hurry".

219 Supra, n 193.

7.10 Closing Addresses and Summing-Up

After the examination of the witnesses both for the prosecution and the defence, if any, including any witnesses recalled or called to rebut any unforeseen matter[220], the closing addresses by the prosecutor and the defence representative may be made in the prescribed order.[221] These are generally written addresses, though there is nothing to prevent the prosecutor and the accused or their counsels, if any, from arguing their cases orally, in part or in entirety, as done under the ordinary criminal procedure[222]. Another distinguishing feature of closing addresses, or for that matter any address, at a CM trial, is that by custom of the Services, counsels address the court from behind their table, and are not to wander about[223] while making their addresses or examining witnesses.

---

220 AR, r 143; AFR, r 121; NA, s 137 (1); cf Simmons, The Constitution and Practice of Courts Martial, op cit, n 46, p 258, (s 600) for the prosecution evidence in reply being allowed when the defence has "examined witnesses" to points "not touched in the prosecution" or "reflecting on the credibility of the prosecutor's evidence" and also "on any points which, in their nature, he (prosecutor) might not have foreseen previous to the def ence of the prisoner ",and hence pr evented "on an y points not introduced by the prisoner". Please see MML, Vol II, p 339; Note 3 to AR, r 143 f or action on new mat ter introduced by a witness in rebuttal.

221 AR, r 59 as substi tuted by r 16 of Arm y (Amendment) R ules, 1993; AFR, rr 67 , 68; NA, s 111 (a). Before the 1993 amendments, the order of the closing addresses in the AR was, and in the AFR and in the NA still is, that on calling a witness on facts of the case, the accused would make a closing address and the pr osecutor would ha ve a right to r eply. The ac cused would ha ve a right to r eply only when he called no def ence wi tness on f acts. This w as, howev er, not in tune wi th the custom of the S ervice for the prisoner to ha ve the "right to the last wor d", which custom was first deviated from by a general order issued on 09 Nov 1866 and the deviation later incorporated in QR 722, bringing the order of addresses at CM trial at par with the corresponding practice at the ordinary criminal trials, under Denman's Act (28 Vict c 18). The Change of 09 Nov 1866 is criticized by Simmons stating that "courts martial ... are held in very different circumstances, especially as the services of experienced officers as judge advocates and member are not alw ays a vailable ..." Based on this, "courts martial ha ve constantly admi tted the prisoner 's claim from the trial of Lord George Sackville in 1760, down to the trial of Ensign Cullen" who was allowed a rejoinder on 03 Dec 1866 after the general order of 09 Nov 1866 had been issued at the Horse Guards and before it was promulgated at Jamaica. "This has been done, not in ignorance of the fact that a rejoinder was a deviation from the rule in ordinary criminal courts, but because it had been recognized as a pecul iarity of Engl ish mi litary jurisprudence" f ounded upon the "custom of w ar in l ike cases". Simmons quotes from Capt John Wi lliamson, The Elements of Mi litary Arrangement, 1783, Vol. II, p 67 (Note 113) in support, how Major Ady e held it to be "r egular and legal" , despite Ady e himself being otherwise in favour of a CM conforming to the practice of the established courts where the Act of Parliament and Articles of War were silent. Williamson is quoted to conclude that the rejoinder derives its force of law, despite being deviant f rom the pr actice followed in the common la w courts, f rom the "customs of w ar, lex non scripta of the army to which the common law is correspondent as the statute law is to the written rules and articles of war"; Simmons, op cit, n 220, pp 244-245 (s 581).

222 Cr PC, s 314 provides for oral arguments only but with a memorandum which may be submitted setting forth the arguments concisely to form part of the record.

223 Rant,Courts Martial, Discipl ine, and the Criminal Pr ocess in the Armed S ervices, op ci t, n 7 , p 12, (s 1.29)

The last address to the court at a CM trial, before the court is closed for deliberation on findings, is the summing-up by the JA, if one appointed. Like the addresses of the prosecution and the defence representative, the JA's summing-up too may be given orally or in writing but in practice it is required to invariably be in writing and read in open court,[224] summing up the evidence and advising the court upon the law relating to the case.[225] Accordingly, the contents of the summing-up will differ from case to case, but in its style, it takes after a summing-up by the Judge at the jury trial. However, since a JA at the CM trial is not in the same position as a Judge at the jury trial, the pattern of the summing-up to be made at a CM in India developed independently over the years, under the guidance of the JAsG like Col Maisey, whose instructions given on the subject in 1874, are still preserved in the Blue Book of the JAG's Dept in India. Briefly speaking, "the summing-up is adequate if it states fairly the facts for the prosecution and states fairly the nature and evidence of the defence". In every summing up, "if one goes through it with a magnifying glass, some sentence can be found of which one can say that it is not quite accurate or that something else ought to have been said." However, "one would not look at the summing-up in that way. The summing-up must be taken as a whole and it must be seen that there is no misstatement of law .... It must then be seen whether, in those cases where a long-standing practice has become established of requiring certain warnings or directions to be given, the warnings or directions have been given" but one "should not expect the judge advocate necessarily to address the court-martial in the same way in a particular case as a judge exercising his discretion might direct a jury." Nonetheless, "if there was no evidence to support a conviction, he should say so".[226]

7.11 Findings of the CM

Immediately after the summing-up by the JA, the court is closed for deliberation over their findings on the charge. Generally it is ensured that there is no break between the summing-up and announcement of the findings though any such break would not render the findings invalid, since a CM trial is for keeping the traditions of a jury trial,different.[227]

---

224 AR, r 144; MML V ol II, p 339, Note to AR r 144; AFR, r 122.

225 AR, r 60; AFR, r 69; NA, s 112.

226 (Combined judgment) R v Linzee , R v O 'Driscoll, [1956] 3 All ER 480 (482, 484).

227 Ibid, p 485:... there is no true analogy between a court-martial, a jury or a bench of magistrates. It is a court which is sui generis ... it is certainly not a court in which the old common law rule of jury closure and jury retirement would be applied .... A jury is in an entirely different position. Since the earliest days, as soon as a judge has furnished his charge to the jury, they are given in charge of the bailiff, who is sworn to keep them in a private place and suffer no one to speak to them, except to ask whether they have agreed in their v erdict, without the lea ve of the judge. S ee Halsbury 's Laws of England (3r d ed)V ol 10, p 431, para 795.

(a) **Legal Provisions**

The related provisions in the Act, the rules and connected notes in the MML afford guidance on the procedure to be followed by the CM to consider and arrive at their findings[228] and the format in which the findings are to be expressed in various contingencies,[229] such as the special finding of guilty on less serious analogous offence though not guilty of the offence charged,[230] and the requirement of giving reasons in brief for the findings[231]. It may be pointed out that before the Army (Amendment) Rules, 1993 amended AR r 62 (1) so as to require a CM to record brief reasons for its finding, the finding in the case of a CM under the AA was, and that under the other two Services laws is still, recorded simply as "Guilty" or "Not guilty".[232] No reasons for the finding(s) are recorded by the CM under the British and US systems either.[233] The amendment of 1993 in AR r 62 (1) is clearly in the nature of a follow-up action on the recommendation of the Supreme Court in the case of Major S N Mukherjee. The apex court, though

---

228 AA, s 132, AR, r161 r ead with rr 80 and 87; AF A, s 130, AFR, rr 70, 87 , 94; NA, ss 116-118. The finding, like any other decision of the court, is arrived at by an absolute majority of vote, the opinion of each member given by word of mouth on each char ge separately. Decision, in case of equal ity of votes is given in favour of the accused, there being no casting vote available in the matters of challenge, finding or sentence. (AA, s 132); cf K ennedy 205 and De Hart 187, cit in Winthrop, Military Law and Precedents, op cit, n 118, p 377 . In the findings as final ly made and r ecorded, whatever they ma y be and howev er small may be the majority by which they were arrived at, the court acts as a unit. In law, the finding is its act, not the act of certain members. S o neither the majori ty, nor an y member or members can pr otest against a finding after it has been reached by a majority vote; Winthrop, ibid page (s 575). During deliberation on the findings, the JA is present in the closed court under the Army and the Air Force provisions but he does not vote. Under the Naval law, the trial JA withdraws before the members deliberate on the findings and returns only to assist the court to draft the findings after the court has arrived at the findings. Under the present British military system, the JA is a full fledged member of the CM, and v otes ac cordingly, ex cept on the finding (B r AFA06, ss154(a) and 159(2).)

229 AR, r 62 r ead with MML, Vol II, p 418 (f or the format of r ecording and announcement of findings subject to confirmation). Please also see AHQ letter no. 35418/AG/DV dated 01 Mar 1994; AFR, r 71; NA, ss 117, 118. The findings of a Na val CM ar e not subject to confirmation.

230 AA, s 139, AR, r 62 (4), (5); AF A, s 138, AFR r 71 (4) (5); NA, ss 125-127 .

231 AR, r 62 (1) as amended by Army (Amendment) Rules, 1993, r 18.

232 AR, r 62 (1) as it stood before amendment by Army (Amendment) Rules, 1993; AFR, r 71 (1); No provisions exist under the NA or the N Regs II (S) for recording any reasons in support of the findings except that the reasons are required for findings in navigational cases; please see N Regs II (S), reg 185-A; cf Shanmugam v OC 65 Coy ASC, Madras, 1984 (1) SLR 108 ruling that it is not necessary to set out elaborately the evidence on the basis of which the conclusion is arrived at by a CM.

233 BrAA, s 96; The Court Martial (Army) Rules, 1997; British Armed Forces Act, 2006, s 160; UCMJ Art 50; MCM 2000, RCM-921. Please also see In re Roberts, Times 11th Jun 1879, in which Captain Roberts applied for certiorari on the ground that the sentence of the CM dismissing from the Service was invalid, in that it simply sentenced him to be dismissed without stating the cause for dismissal. The court rejected the application, relying upon In re Mansergh, (1861) 1 B &S 400, and stating that the rights referred to for the petitioner were purely military in nature and dependent upon military status and regulation and hence no interference by the court was needed.

holding that under the then existing law, a CM was not required to give reasons for its findings or sentence, had stated, after surveying the legal position in various countries on the requirement of reasons being recorded by an administrative authority and taking note of the 14th Report of the Law Commission of India on the reforms of Judicial Administration[234], that in the case of administrative decisions, provisions should be made that they should be accompanied by reasons. An important consideration for such an approach was that the reasons, if recorded by an administrative authority exercising judicial function would enable the courts to effectively exercise the appellate or supervisory power. Further, this will, firstly, guarantee proper consideration of the matter by concerned authority; secondly, will introduce clarity in the decision, and lastly, will minimize chances of arbitrariness in the decision making. The Supreme Court concluded: " ... therefore, the requirement that the reason be recorded should govern the decision of an administrative authority exercising quasi judicial functions, irrespective of the fact whether the decision is subject to appeal, revision or judicial review. It may, however, be added that it is not required that the reasons should be as elaborate as in the decision of a court of law ... what is necessary is that the reasons are clear and explicit so as to indicate that the authority has given due consideration to the points in controversy."[235]

The newly introduced requirement of the reasons to be given by a CM is undoubtedly a welcome progressive initiative. What, however, has always been and will ever remain a perennial requirement that "Absolute impartiality ought most clearly to be the paramount object of the court collectively, and of every individual member. There should be no wish for the guilty to escape or for the innocent to suffer. No false pity, no undue severity, should influence their judgment. Nor should there by any hasty indolent or hasty adoption of the opinion of another, however, classified or experienced, but careful investigation and patience in deliberation should be the aim of each member for himself and so characterize the judgment of the whole.[236]

---

234 Law Commission of India, 14th Report 1958, on Reforms of Judicial Administration, p 694.

235 Major S N Mukherjee v UOI, AIR 1990 SC 1984, p 1995.

236 Simmons, The Constitution and Practice of Courts Martial, op cit, n 46, p 263, (s 611); cf Locke, cit in Simmons, ibid page:We should keep perfect indifference for all opinions; nor wish any of them true, or try to make them appear so; but being indifferent, receive and embrace them according to evidence, and that done, give the attestation of truth. He that, by any indifference for all but truth, suffers not his assent to go f urther than his evidence, nor bey ond it, will learn to examine, and examine f airly, instead of presuming.

It was presumably this line of thinking that also might have been at the back of mind in doing away the epithets like "honourably", "most r espectfully" or "f ully and honour ably" etc. to describe the acqui ttal by the CM while recording the finding. QR of 1868 replaced such provisions and required that the finding be recorded simply as "Not guilty" in all the cases of acquittal. The Duke of Wellington, in his order in the Peninsula justified the decision on the ground that it was difficult to define in what all cases an honourable acquittal was applicable. For instance, in a case in which any part of the transaction was disgraceful, an

(b) **Data on Findings**

Q. 2.10 in the Interview Schedule was intended to fetch data on the outcome of the trial in the case of 50 respondents who were tried by CM. The data collected in respect of the CM verdict as to the guilt of the accused on the charge(s) laid against them in each case are presented in Table – 30 below:

TABLE - 30

CM Verdict as to Guilt of Accused Respondents

Srl. No	Verdict	Response Frequency	Percentage	Remarks
1.	Acquitted of the charge/all charges	02	04	
2.	Convicted of the charge/all charges	33	66	
3.	Acquitted of some but convicted of remaining charges	05	10	
4.	Finding of "Not guilty" originally but revoked and finding of "Guilty" recorded on some or all charges, in revision	02	04	
5.	Finding of "Not guilty" adhered to on some or all charges, in revision	01	02	
6.	Revision ordered but not yet took place	01	02	A-194 Revision of Sentence
7.	No outcome, trial being not concluded	06	12	
	Total	50	100	

contd/-

honourable acquittal cannot be mentioned without exciting the feeling of disgust. He had, therefore, recommended in letter to the President of the GCM, Lisbon, 12 Oct 1809 – Wellington Despatches (1838), Vol 221-222 to omi t the word 'honourable' in the sentence. Simmons, howev er, criticizes the decision as an honourable acquittal could contribute to the desirability of keeping up in all ranks of the Army a proper feeling and a high sense of honour; please see Simmons, ibid, p 271 (s 624). This criticism does not seem to be entirely groundless since a "court martial has been often called a 'court of honour' for the reason that it punishes dishonorable conduct where the same affects the reputation or discipline of the arm y". Winthrop,Military La w and Pr ecedents, op ci t, n 118, p 54 (s 62) and the honour should, therefore, be restored or reaffirmed on acquittal in appropriate cases. In view of this, the practice of 'honuorable' acquittal continued in the form of a letter accompanying the finding of "Not guilty" in suitable cases of of ficers only under RP 66 (2)(b); B r MML, P&I, (12th ed) 1972, p 727 .

The data at Srls 1 and 2 in Table - 30 show that in 33 (66%) cases out of 50, the respondents were convicted of the charge/all charges and it was only in 2 (4%) cases that the CM gave a verdict of clean acquittal. In another 5 (10%) cases, as noted against Srl No. 3, the concerned respondents had been found "Not guilty" of some but "Guilty" of the remaining charges on which they were tried. In yet another 2 (4%) cases, the finding of "Not guilty" pronounced at the original trial was revoked and a verdict of "Guilty" took its place in the revision proceedings held by the CM which was reassembled by the confirming officer under the provisions of AA s 160. In one case, the revision was pending against the sentence though the respondent was convicted on the charge of murder and awarded imprisonment for life which was considered inadequate by the confirming authority in the circumstances of the case. Thus, in a total of 41 (82%) cases, the findings recorded by the CM were "Guilty". It will be of some interest to recall that 37 (74%) accused respondents had pleaded "Not Guilty" to the charges on which they were arraigned, as shown at Srl 2 of Table - 25. It was brought out in that context that the plea of "Guilty" or "Not guilty" was no measure, in fact, of the guilt or otherwise of the person offering that plea. The manner in which the trial proceeds and the mindset of the functionaries of the court may be said to be the true determinants of the efficacy of the findings of the court, in addition to the professional competence of the justice delivery mechanism. In the present case, the accused persons were allowed the facility of calling witnesses at the Govt. expense in 35 (70%) cases as reflected at Srl 1 in Table - 27. Further, in 37 (74%) cases (Srl 1 in Table - 28), the submissions for defence were heard without any dissatisfaction in that regard felt by the accused-respondents. Table - 29 shows that the number of cases in which the accused cross-examined prosecution witnesses made statement in defence and produced defence was at 36 (72%), 34 (68%) and 33 (66%) respectively. From this, it appears that the findings arrived at the CM trial are generally in conformity with the members' oath of administering justice according to the Army Act without partiality, favour or affection and according to their conscience, the best of their understanding and the custom of war in the event of any doubt arising.

(c) **Procedures on Acquittal and on Conviction**

Reverting to the trial proceedings, after the CM has arrived at its findings, in case the accused is found "Not guilty" of all the charges, the presiding officer shall date and sign the findings, authenticating thereby, the whole of the proceedings. The JA, if any appointed, shall then also sign the proceedings,[237] which, having been announced as subject to confirmation in the case of the findings recorded under the AA or AFA, shall be transmitted for confirmation. Since no confirmation is required under the Naval law,

---

237 AR, r 63; AFR, r 72; NA, s 118 (4).

the court is dissolved after the announcement of the findings and the proceedings transmitted to the JAG for judicial review and further action, as provided in NA ss 118(5) and 128.[238] On the other hand, if the accused is found "Guilty" of the charge or any of the charges, the court shall, whenever possible, take evidence of his military character, acts of gallantry and distinguished conduct, his total reckonable service, his pre-trial custody period, previous convictions by the CM or summary punishment awarded to him in the past and so on. The accused is entitled to cross-examine the witness producing such evidence, and make a statement in mitigation of sentence.[239] If it is not practicable to take such evidence, the CM must record in the proceedings the reasons therefor.[240] The provision for taking evidence of previous conviction was originally introduced in the civil in England in 1827 in order to more severely punish a previously convicted person.[241] It was brought to the Army in 1829 and was originally applicable to soldiers only and not to officers[242] until the Mutiny Act.[243]

7.12 Sentencing of the Convict

The procedure on conviction requiring the court to take evidence of certain matters, as stated in the preceding paragraph and allowing the accused not only to cross-examine the witness who produces such evidence but also to address the court in mitigation of punishment, is analogous to the procedure required under the provisions of the ordinary

238 AR, r 63; RA para 470; AFR, rr 72, 101; NA ss 118 and 128.

239 AA, s 144, AR, r 64 r ead with RA par as 171 and 465- A for the assessment of char acter; AFA, s143, AFR, r 73; NA, s 119.

240 MML, Vol II, p 307 , Note 2 to AR r 64; AO 255/1972.

241 7 & 8 Geo 4, c 12, s 11.

242 Articles of W ar, 1829, Art 88

243 Mutiny Act, 1847 empowering the court to receive such evidence against "any person" which expression was replaced in 1857 wi th "any person subject to the articles. " The enquiry w as confined to general character and particular offences could not be referred; Simmons, The Constitution and Practice of Courts Martial, n 46, pp 271 and 274 (ss 626-627 and 635).Under the current (British) Court Martial (Army) Rules, 1997 , r 76, the evidence to be taken bef ore sentence includes, in addition to matters listed as required under the Indian law, the details of pay of the accused, terminal benefits and his future pension entitlement and whether the CO of the accused wishes to retain the accused in his unit. These matters, however, may be pr esented to the court b y the pr osecutor merely as inf ormation and need not be adduced as evidence unless the accused so desires. The court shall consider any pre-sentence report concerning the accused in possession of the court administration officer and a record of antecedents signed by the accused may also be accepted in evidence of previous convictions. The evidence may also be given on behalf of the ac cused in mi tigation of sentence and as to his char acter. Under the US la w, in addition to all such matters in evidence, the court is also required to be given instructions on sentence, by the military judge, on such aspects as maximum authorised punishment and mandatory minimum punishment, a statement of the effect any sentence announced will have on the accused's entitlement to pay and allowances; a statement of procedure to be adopted for deliberation and voting and a statement that the members should consider all matters in extenuation, mitigation and aggravation whether introduced before or after finding; RCM 1001 and 1005.

criminal jurisdiction for the judge to hear the accused on the sentence if he is convicted.[244] It was held by the Supreme Court that the enactment of the said provision satisfied dual purpose. It satisfies the rule of natural justice by according the accused an opportunity on the question of sentence, and, at the same time, helps the court to choose the sentence to be awarded. The sentencing court must approach the question seriously and must endeavour to see that all the related facts and circumstances bearing on the question of sentence are brought on record. Only after giving due weight to the mitigating as well as the aggravating circumstances placed before it, the court must pronounce the sentence.[245]

(a) Procedure

As in the case of the findings, the decision as to the sentence to be awarded to the accused is made in a closed court after due deliberation in the presence of the JA. Under the Naval law, the trial JA who was not present during the deliberation on the findings remains present while the court is considering the sentence to be awarded and is required to assist the court in the determination of the sentence but shall not vote thereon.[246] For the decision on the sentence a member is required to vote even if during the voting on the findings he had voted for acquittal.[247] Every member must give his opinion by word of mouth and the opinions of the members shall be taken in succession, beginning with

---

244 Cr PC, s 435(2).

245 Allaudiin Mian v State of B ihar, AIR 1989 SC 1456.

246 NA s 120 (2) expressly provides for the trial JA to sit with the court while they are considering the sentence. No provision under the Army and Air Force laws expressly speaks about it but the deliberation on the sentence as mentioned in AR, r 64 (1), when read with the requirement of AR, r 80(1) for the presence of the JA during deliberation in a closed court by the members, pre-supposes the JA sitting with the members during such proceeding under the Army or the Air Force laws too though not voting or in any way influencing the decision. Under the US system, a military Judge is not present during deliberation and voting on the sentence just as he was not present during the decision on the findings; Please see RCM – 1006 (a) on sentence. Howev er, under the Br military law, the JA is now a member of the CM (B r AA 1955, s 84-B(1) and being not expressly excluded from voting on sentence, unlike in the case of finding, will be entitled to vote and will also have a casting vote in the case of an equality of votes on the sentence; Br AFA '6 s.159; cf Dennis L Bird "The British Court Martial System", Contemporary Review , Vol 271, (Sep 1997) p 47 (at p 49).

247 AR, r 87; AFR, r94; NA, s 120(1). The US military law has the similar provision in MCM 2000, RCM – 1006 (d)(1); cf Simmons, The Constitution and Practice of Courts Martial, op cit, n 46, pp 275, 276. Simmons urges that the majority in every case binds the minority; the opinion of the majority is the opinion of the court. He further presents a legal fiction, saying that as a CM acts in two fold capacity of judge and jury, the court having performed the duty of jurors in finding a v erdict, is imperatively required by the law to proceed in the character of judges, acting independently of their votes as jurors, to award a punishment. Last ly, Simmons also r eminds that the members sworn to administer justice ac cording to the Articles of War, on conviction having been reached by the laid down procedure must award punishment prescribed by the Articles of War on conviction. In 1834, an officer was tried by a CM for having refused

member lowest in rank.[248] The decision on the sentence shall be passed by an absolute majority and where there is equality of vote, the decision shall be in favour of the accused, the presiding officer having no casting vote in a decision on sentence. No sentence of death shall be passed, however, by a GCM without the concurrence of at least two thirds of the members and be passed by a SGCM without the concurrence of all the members.[249] If the court makes a recommendation to mercy, it shall give its reasons and the number of opinions by which the recommendation is adopted or rejected may be entered in the proceedings.[250] Finally the law requires that the court shall award only a single sentence in respect of all the charges of which the accused is found "Guilty" and such sentence shall be deemed to be awarded in respect of the offence in each charge in respect of which it can be awarded, and not to be awarded in respect of any offence in a charge in respect of which it cannot be legally given.[251]

---

to vote on the punishment after he had voted for a finding of "Not guilty" at a Regimental Court Martial. The CM acquitted him but the C-in-C at the presidency disapproved it. The matter was referred to the C-in-C in India, Sir H Fane. The General C-in-C Lord Hill obtained the view of the JAG who held the view that the finding of Guilty "must be deemed the finding of the whole; and the member who voted for the acquittal may be called upon to vote on the punishment". cf Winthrops view at supra n 228.

248 AR, AFR, rr ibid. Under the US law, the proposed sentence shall be voted on by secret written ballot and all members shall vote on each proposed sentence in its entirety, beginning with the least sentence and continuing, as necessary, with the next least severe, until a sentence is adopted by the concurrence of the number of members required. The junior member shall collect the ballots and count the votes. The president shall check the count and inform the others. Please see RCM 1006 (d)(2), (3) (A),(B).

249 AA, s 132; AFA, s 131; NA, s 124. The US law too requires a death sentence to be "adjudged only if all members present vote for that sentence"; RCM – 1006 (d)(4) and UCMJ Art 52 (b)(1). Br AA, s 96 (4) too had the same provision which however, has since been repealed under the Armed Forces Act, 2000, the liability for a sentence of death and the power to impose it having been effectively repealed by the Human Rights Act, 1998, s 21 (5). Under NA, s 124, the number required to pass a death sentence is 4 when the CM is constituted of 5 members and in all other cases 2/3 majority of the members may pass such sentence and the same number of votes is required for finding on an offence carrying death sentence as the only punishment awardable.

250 AR, r 65; AFR, r 74; No provision under the Naval law. Br AA 1955, s 97 (3) does speak of recommendation for mercy. Reasons are required to be given by the president of the CM for any such recommendation; Br CM (A) Rules, 1997, r 80 (4); cf MML Vol II, p 308, Notes 1-3 for when such recommendation may be made.

251 AR, r 65; AFR, r 74; No provision in NA; Br CM (A) Rules, 1997, r 79 also requires only one sentence; cf Halsbury's Laws of England,4th ed, 1983 s 505 inter alia to the effect that one sentence in respect of all the offences is to be given which may, however, include more than one punishment.; cf Carter v Mc Claughry, 183 US 365 for similar observations under military usage. This saves CsM from pronouncing sentences which approximate fantasy, such as, for instance, 450 years imprisonment recently awarded by an Israeli Tribunal to a member of Hamas; please see Hindustan (Meerut ed.) 27 Nov 2007, p 15 (website www.hindustandainik.com)

(b) Considerations

Keeping in mind the procedure to be followed, the members shall deliberate and vote to decide the sentence. The deliberations may properly include full and free discussion of the sentence to be imposed.[252] While deliberating on the sentence, the CM should analyse the sentence on the record taking into consideration the requirements of discipline, degree of criminality of the act, premeditation, provocation, previous convictions and the prevalence of the offence. The proper amount of punishment to be inflicted is the least amount by which discipline can effectively be maintained; occasionally the exigencies of discipline, apart from the circumstances of the case, may render a severe sentence necessary. While taking into consideration the degrees of criminality, an NCO should be dealt with more severely than a Sepoy. Similarly, an accused who has clearly made long preparation to commit the crime should be more severely punished than one who acted on the spur of the moment. As for provocation, though it may be no defence to a charge, except when it reduces the offence of murder to culpable homicide not amounting to murder under Expl. 1 to s 300 of the IPC and in the case of certain other offences like causing hurt, grievous hurt, assaulting, or using criminal force under IPC ss 334, 335, 352, 355 respectively, the CM will take it into consideration in determining the punishment to be awarded. Habitual offenders and the cases of a general prevalence of offences or offences of a particular nature are also required to be more severely punished with a view to setting an example.[253]

(c) Punishments

The words 'punishment' and 'sentence' are used synonymously in common parlance. However, as a part of DPCM jargons, 'sentence' may be conceived as an award by the CM assigning one or more punishments laid down under the concerned Service Act, to meet the ends of justice and discipline, in the case of a person found guilty of the charge(s) tried by the said CM. It is a rule according to military usage that in the case of conviction on charges and specifications embracing several distinct offences, a CM must impose a single sentence as an entirety regardless of any differences in the character of the offences

---

252 MML Vol II, pp 304 and 306 f or procedure of del iberation finding and sentence. Note 2 to AR, r 61 and Note 6 to AR r 63.

253 MML Vol I, p 42: Consider ations af fecting sentence – cf RA par a 468; also K autilya's Arthasastr a, Books IV and V wherein the king, before awarding the sentence is required to take into consideration the nature of the offence, its time and place, ability and motive of the offender and such other factors as consequences, the present effect, strength, age, conduct, learning, monitory position and frequency; cit in VK Singh and AB Bajela, Military Justice System in Dock, 1993, Lucknow, Institute of Judicial Training and Research, p 435 (unpublished).

or in the manner in which they may be punished.[254] The law expressly accords validity to the sentence carrying punishments some of which stand prescribed for some of the offences charged and proved but are not awardable for some other offences of which the accused has been convicted.[255] If, for example, an accused has been found guilty by a GCM on a charge of desertion on active service and also on a charge of making away with arms and equipment, a sentence of death awardable in respect of the first charge will be valid although a sentence of 10 year imprisonment is the maximum sentence which could have been awarded upon the second charge. Further, more than one punishment may be included in the sentence under the scheme of punishments contained in AA ss 69-77 and corresponding provisions in the Naval and Air Force laws.[256] In the case of a civil offence, the punishment to be awarded is governed by two additional determinants: firstly, that if the offence is punishable with death or imprisonment for life under any law in force in India, the accused shall be liable to suffer the punishment assigned for the offence by that law **and** such less punishment as mentioned in the AA, AFA or NA, as the case may be; and secondly, in any other case, his liability will be to suffer any punishment, other than whipping, assigned for the offence by the concerned civil (criminal) law **or** imprisonment for a term which may extend to seven years, or

---

254 Carter v Mc Claughry, 183 US 365; Jackson v Tylor 353 US 569 cit in Carl T Drechster , Henry C Lind, et al edi tors, American Jurisprudence, 2nd V ol, 1971; New Y ork, The Law yers Cooperative Publ ishing Company, Rochester, p 91 (s 254).

255 Supra, n 273

256 The penal clause of almost every statutory provision defining an offence under the three Services Acts lays down the maximum punishment awardable therefor accompanied with an alternative "or such less punishment as is in this Act mentioned;" (AA and AF A) or slightly di fferently worded expression practically to the same effect (NA). AA, s 72 too provides that in the case of military offences (other than civil offence) the CM may either award the punishment prescribed in the dealing section of the offence or, in l ieu thereof, any one of the punishments lower in the scale set out in AA s 71 (AF A, s 73 and NA, s 81). Thus whenever there is a power to a ward a less or lesser punishment under the AA or AF A or 'such other punishment as is hereinafter mentioned' under the NA, a lesser punishment is determined by the ranking as set out in AA, s 71, AFA, s 73, and NA, s 81, which list out punishments in a graded descending order starting from 'death' on top and coming down to 'stoppage of pay and allowances' at the bottom in the AA and AF A and 'minor punishments ... ac cording to the custom of the na vy' at the same posi tion under the NA. Some of those listed punishments are purely military specific punishments, such as 'cashiering' or 'reduction to the ranks' while some others are analogous to civil service penalties such as 'dismissal' or 'reprimand' and yet others are imported from the ordinary criminal law, such as 'death' or 'imprisonment' for life or for specified term. More than one such lesser punishments may be awarded as a result of the combination of punishments permissible under the AA, s 73 or consequential punishment required under AA, ss 74 and 77, i.e., cashiering to be awarded to an officer before sentencing him to death, imprisonment for life or for imprisonment for a term and reduction to the ranks in the case of a WO or NCO sentenced to imprisonment for life or for a term or dismissal from service. 'Cashiering' is not provided as a punishment under the NA. There is "dismissal with disgrace' in its place but awardable to all ranks in specified cases as a mandatory consequential punishment and otherwise in other cases.

such less punishment as in the Act mentioned.[257] Thus, when a person is convicted of a civil offence under the AA, he may be awarded 7 years RI, even if the maximum punishment prescribed under the ordinary criminal law for the same offence is imprisonment for just 24 hours or a fine of Rs. 10 under IPC s 510 for the offence of misconduct in public by a drunken person. In practice, however, the punishment to be awarded by a CM shall not be disproportionate to the gravity of the offence.[258] Further, an express averment in the penal clauses of the offence defining sections as to the punishment prescribed therefor prevents the CM from awarding any unauthorized punishment[259] and the court must always award such punishment, out of the prescribed ones, as the members consider to be just and proper and must not presume that the convening authority, in sending the case for trial, took a more serious view of the facts.[260] Where the court can award only one punishment under the related legal provision but feels inclined to take a lenient view in the circumstances of the case, it may make recommendations for mercy.[261] The sentence so awarded shall be announced in the

257 AA, s 69; AF A, s 71 and NA, s 77 . Under NA, s 77 , the maximum punishment a wardable for a civil offence, other than one punishable by death or life imprisonment, is 3 years in place of 7 years or imprisonment assigned for the offence by the concerned law in the civil.

258 AHQ New Delhi let ter No. 3548 dated 03 No v 1967.

259 Unlike this requirement of the military law and practice of military tribunals under the AA, a young man Deepak Gupta recently did community service as a traffic cop for three days at Nehru Place and two youths did Kar Sewa by cleaning utensils and plates and polishing shoes at Gurdwara Bangla Saheb in Delhi under orders of sentence passed by courts at Delhi; Nikhila Pant and Pallavi Pasricha, "Serves them right", TOI, 08 A ug 2007, p 2. The article also mentions of Naomi Campbel l, the supermodel , to ha ve worked as a cleaner with the sanitation department for throwing a mobile phone at her maid. Irrespective of this, it may be pointed out that the US military law prohibits cruel and unusual punishments like flogging, branding, marking or tattooing on the body; UCMJ – Art 55. In fact, early Articles of War in England and contemporary code of Gustavus Adolphus prescribed punishments such as decimation (Art 8 of James II and Arts 60, 67 , 73 of Gusta vas code), beheading (Arts 2, 7 , 10, 20, 21 of Richar d II), to be drawn to death (Arts 2, 9, 17 of Richard II), to be drowned or buried with the body of the person killed (ordinance of Richard I as punishment for homicide), to have the tongue perforated with a red hot iron (Art 1 of sec 1 of Charles – I for blasphemy) and so on; Winthrop,The Constitution and Practice of Courts Martial, op cit, n 118, p 437. Further instances of weird and savage methods of imposing death penalty on criminals in human history included throwing the convict into a pit of hungry lions, or a blazing furnace (Babylon), wrenching the prisoner's body tied to four horses driven apart (medieval times), beheading by guillotine (France, 1780 onwards for 180 years), electrocution by electric chair (America, 06 1890 onward), gas chamber (Germany in Hitler's time), strangulation by garrothe (Spain), stoning to death (Islamic countries) and throwing before a mad elephant (India – Moghul times). Simmons also speaks of a British statute (since repealed) under which the body of every murderer was to be dissected or hanged in chains after execution. Simmons, The Constitution and Practice of Courts Martial, op cit, n 46, p 278. All these practices would be outlandish from the modern standards of penology and have no place in the present day military law in an y civilized society, including India, where even field punishment has been recently abolished on the same ground vide SRO 17-E of 1993.

260 MML Vol I, p 42 (s 84).

261 ibid p 43 (s 85).

open court as subject to confirmation[262] and the record of the trial proceedings on being dated and signed by the presiding officer and the JA, if any, shall be transmitted to the Dy JAG command in cases of trial by GCM and direct to confirming authority in cases of trial by SGCM or DCM.

(d) Data on Sentence

The various punishments awarded to the 50 respondents in the present study are reflected in Table - 31.

262 ibid (s 87) and supra n 261. In the case of death sentence, even Naval law requires confirmation by the Central Government except in the case of mutiny in time of war or on active service; NA, s 82 (2). For transmission of proceedings in the case of SGCM, please see AR, r 162 and AFR, r 142.

TABLE - 31

Punishments Awarded as CM Sentence to Respondents

Srl.No.	Punishments	Response Frequency	Percentage	Remarks
1.	Life Imprisonment	06	12	Alongwith dismissal as part of sentence.
2.	Imprisonment for a term:			
	(a) less than 1 month	04	08	By SCM and to be undergone in military custody.
	(b) 1 - 3 months	04	08	-do-
	(c) 3 - 6 months	01	02	
	(d) 6 - 9 months	02	04	Incl an officer awarded cashiering and forfeiture of service for pension in addition to imprisonment.
	(e) 9 - 12 months	01	02	
	(f) 1 - 5 years	03	06	2 year RI and dismissal in each one of the 3 cases.
	(g) 5 - 10 years	02	04	Both awarded 7 years RI and dismissal.
	(h) Over 10 years	01	02	Under Official Secrets Act (14 years RI)
3.	Cashiering	01	02	Cashiering alone
4.	Dismissal from service	07	14	Dismissal alone
5.	Any other	04	08	Forfeiture of service for pension with severe reprimand in 3 cases, reduction to the ranks in 1 case
6.	No Sentence	13	26	Incl. acquittal in 2 cases, sentence remitted in 1 case and trial not complete in 10 cases
7.	No Response	01	02	
	Total	50	100	

No death sentence was awarded to any of the respondents included in the present study. However, it may be pointed out that while awarding the death sentence, the CM is also required to add the direction as to the mode of its execution, requiring the accused to be hanged by the neck until he be dead or to be shot to death.[263] Further, detailed provisions exist in the rules, regulations and administrative instructions prescribing related procedure and clarifying other connected matters in relation to the execution of the sentence of death,[264] which still continues to remain on the statute in our case though abolished in several countries. Its legality has been debated by our legislature and judiciary, alongwith the question of its desirability, a number of times from 1956 onward when a Bill was first introduced in the Lok Sabha for abolition of death sentence. On the question being referred to the Law Commission of India, the Commission expressed the view that we could not risk the experiment of abolishing capital punishment.[265] Relying on the Commission's report, a Constitution Bench of the Supreme Court also rejected the plea for its abolition[266] and upheld its legal validity later in a number of cases, including Bachan Singh v Punjab[267] (rarest of rare cases criterion being laid down) and Kehar Singh v UOI,[268] the latest being the cases of Afzal Guru.[269]

The second highest punishment awardable under the three Services Acts, i.e., imprisonment for life, was, however, awarded to six soldiers of various ranks, other than officer or JCO, in the case of the present study, as may be seen from the data at Srl 1 in Table – 31. In the case of an officer, the accused is required to be awarded the punishment of cashiering before he is awarded a sentence of death, imprisonment for life or imprisonment for a specific term, but there is no requirement in the cases of other ranks and JCOs for similarly being awarded any mandatory consequential punishment of dismissal from the service to an accused tried under the AA or AFA, though the NA does require mandatory dismissal or dismissal with disgrace to accompany the punishment of imprisonment[270]. However, in practice a person, other than an officer,

263 AA, s 166; AF A, s 163; NA, s 147 . However, an old let ter from the Arm y Headquarters, No. 30285/ AG-22 (c) dated 21 Jul 1943 requires that the sentence of death by shooting should not ordinarily be awarded.

264 Ibid letter and AR, rr 170, 170-A, 170-B, RA para 166 (c); AFR rr 147-150; NA, ss 148-149.

265 Law Commission of I ndia, 35th R eport, 1967.

266 Jagmohan Singh v Ut tar Pradesh, AIR 1973 SC 947 .

267 AIR 1980 SC 898.

268 AIR 1989 SC 653.

269 The death sentence of Mohammad Afzal Guru a warded by the Special PO TA Court on 18 Dec 2002 and maintained by Delhi High Court was confirmed by the Supreme Court on 04 Aug 2005. A warrant was issued for its ex ecution accordingly by an addi tional sessions judge. Howev er, before the scheduled ex ecution on 20 Oct 2006, a mercy petition was made to the President of India. The petition is awaiting decision as on date in Aug 2010, though the Home Ministry has already recommended its rejection in Jun 2010.

270 AA, s 74; AF A, s 76; NA, s 82 (3), (4) put together r equire dismissal wi th disgrace to be a warded mandatorily in all cases of imprisonment for a term exceeding 2 years and dismissal with disgrace or dismissal in all other cases of imprisonment. In the case of officers any sentence of imprisonment not exceeding 2 years shall involve dismissal unless dismissal with disgrace has been awarded.

while awarded the sentence of imprisonment for a period of more than 3 months, is also invariably awarded dismissal from the Service. Hence, dismissal from the Service in addition to imprisonment for life, in the cases of the data at Srl 1[271].

Cashiering[272] unaccompanied with any other punishment was awarded in one case while dismissal so unaccompanied was awarded in 7 (14%) cases. In four (8%) cases, the respondents were given punishments like forfeiture of service for pension etc. in 3 cases and reduction to ranks in one case and no other punishment was additionally awarded to them.

The sentence awarded to the respondents interviewed under the present study, were all in conformity with the related provisions of the military law. However, there have been several cases in which extraordinary sentences were passed by the CM. Lt Col Walcot of 5th Horse was tried, during the American war, for striking a subaltern Ensign Patrick. He was awarded suspension from pay and allowances for six months. Additionally Ensign Patrick was ordered to draw his hand across the face of the accused officer before the whole garrison in return for the insult he had received.[273] One of the

---

271 MML Vol II, p 125, Note 3 to AA s 20 f or administrative dismissal, if dismissal is not a warded by CM alongwith imprisonment. It is not considered desirable to retain in service a person who has remained in contact with hard-core criminals in civil prison. Therefore, all persons who are to undergo their sentence of imprisonment in civil jail are also awarded dismissal by a CM. It may be noted that the sentence of imprisonment awarded to an officer, JCO or WO has to be under gone in civil prison in all cases but in the case of NCO and below, the sentence of imprisonment upto 3 months may be directed to be undergone in military custody in accordance with AA, s 169 (3) and upto 18 months in military prison (RA para 494). Any sentence of life imprisonment or imprisonment ma y, in appropriate cases, be suspended under AA, s 182. If not so suspended, the sentence which cannot be undergone in military custody or military prison will attract administrative dismissal and therefore dismissal in such cases is awarded by CM itself. In Saubhagya Chandra Patnaik v UOI, AIR 1969 Orissa 169 (DB), the petitioner, having been convicted of an offence of over-staying leave and sentenced to 6 months RI and dismissal from the service, challenged the sentence on the ground that the offence was punishable with imprisonment only and he could not, therefore, be dismissed from the service. The High Court, howev er, found the sentence legally valid in view of AA, s 73 which provide for combination of punishments. Broadly speaking, the same view was taken in Ranjit Singh Chaurasia v UOI AIR 1976 All 405 (DB), and R Shanmugam v The Officer Commanding, 1984 (1) SLR 108 (Madras) (DB). Similarly, the legality of the mandatory punishment of cashiering w as recognized by Delhi High Court in the case of M R Saini v UOI, 1985 Cr L J 1263 (Delhi) para 7 while upholding the validity of revision order to bring the sentence of 14 years RI and dismissal awarded by the CM to the accused, who was an officer, in conformity with the AA in view of its s 74. Further, in the case of life imprisonment, the applicability of Cr PC s 433-A (the requirement of the accused undergoing at least 14 years of imprisonment excluding remissions earned in jail) to a person convicted by the CM was insisted by the Supreme Court in UOI v Sadha Singh, AIR 1999 SC 3833, referring to Maru Ram v UOI, (1981) 1 SCR 1196: AIR 1980 SC 2147: 1980 Cr L J 1440.

272 Cashiering is an officers specific punishment under the AA and AF A. The punishment of dismissal with disgrace awardable under the NA, in place of cashiering is, howev er, not restricted to officers. But both are ignominious form of dismissal.

273 Simmons,The Constitution and Practice of Courts Martial, op cit, n 46, p 280.

punishments in the US Navy in the 1800's was 'drumming out' of the convicted soldier, under which the soldier was marched out of garrison at bayonet point after his rank and insignia had been stripped and his head shaved, all to the tune of "Rogues March".[274] There is little room now for such macabre punishments and practices to be carried or adopted by CM, because of the elaborately laid down procedure and the mandatory presence of the JA at a GCM under the Indian law or of his counterpart military judge under the American system. However, there is an inbuilt danger in the penal clauses of the offence defining provisions themselves, in most cases, in the form of wide discretion, working out sometimes into disproportionately harsh or lenient sentence being awarded to a convict by amateur judges of the military tribunals, for considerations other than the requirement of justice or even of discipline in some cases. This calls for some scheme of objective criteria to be developed as a guide[275] for sentencing by the CM.

7.13 Regulation of the Finding and Sentence: Post Trial Mechanism

The mechanism presently in place to take care that the finding and sentence of a CM are legally valid and to regulate the punishment awarded, consists of the statutory requirement of the confirmation of such finding and sentence by the confirming officer and the powers enjoyed by him. He has the power to mitigate, remit or commute or suspend the sentence or to vary the form of the sentence if informally expressed, or vary the amount of it if it awards a punishment in excess of the punishment authorized by law.[276] However, the confirming officer too has his own limitations and cannot amend a wholly illegal sentence or a legally unsustainable finding of "not guilty". In such a situation, he can only direct the court to reassemble, reconsider the finding or the sentence or both as the case may be and take an appropriate decision on such reconsideration.[277] The verdict of a CM under the Naval law, however, needs no confirmation, except in the case of the sentence of death, which is required in all cases to be confirmed by the CG before being inflicted on any offender. The sole exception to the requirement of such confirmation under the Naval law would be a case of mutiny in time of war or on active service.[278] As a result, there is no provision for any revision proceedings either, under the Naval law. After the finding, where the accused is found "Not guilty", and after the sentence in the event of his conviction, a Naval CM is dissolved.[279] The National Flag

274 E Cofferman,The Old Arm y, A P ortrait of the American Arm y in P eacetime, 1784 – 1898, ci t in Hon'ble Walter T Cox III, "The Army, The Courts, and the Consti tution: The Evolution of Military Justice"; Military Law Review, 1987, Vol 118, pp 1 -30, at p 8.

275 Infra, Ch 9.5(b)(vii).

276 AA, ss 153–159; AR, rr 70, 72, 73 and 74 r ead with MML Vol II pp 229–231 and 310–312, Notes to these provisions. There are similar provisions under the AF A and AFR.

277 AA, s 160 and AR, r 68 as amended by SRO 17–E of 1993.

278 NA, s 82(2).

279 NA, s 118 (4) and 121 (3).

which remains hoisted when a CM is sitting shall then be hauled down and the president of the CM shall wait on the convening authority or the senior officer present; as a Naval convention to mark the conclusion of the CM trial.[280]

(a) **Related Data**

The data at Srls 4, 5 and 6 in Table 30 disclose that revision was ordered in 4 (8%) out of 50 cases of the respondents included in the present study as persons tried by CM. In two cases (4%), the original finding of "Not guilty" was revoked and finding of "Guilty" recorded. In one case where the accused was a high ranking officer (Maj General), and the GCM was presided over by an officer of the rank of Lieut General, the accused had been found "Not guilty" of eleven but "guilty" of seven out of eighteen charges on which he was tried. He was awarded a sentence of forfeiture of 3 year service for the purpose of pension. The court was reassembled to reconsider its finding of "Not Guilty" on one of the eleven charges and the sentence awarded. However, the court having considered the finding and sentence in the revision proceedings adhered to its original finding and sentence. In the last case out of the four cases of revisions, by the time of the interview of the concerned respondent, the revision had been ordered but had not taken place.

Apart from revision, the convening officer used his powers of commutation, mitigation, or remission in three (6%) cases. In one case, the unexpired portion of the sentence of six month RI to the accused Colonel was remitted and the sentence of cashiering was commuted to dismissal. In another case, the sentence of dismissal of a Major was converted into release at confirmation stage, resulting into his acquiring entitlement to pension. Interestingly, similar relief was recently provided by the Supreme Court to Signalman Sheel Kumar Roy of 2 Corps Air Sp Signal Unit by declaring him to have been discharged from the date of conviction, 7 Sep 1991.[281] In the case of another respondent, who, from the details furnished, appears to be a Sepoy, a sentence of 3 months RI awarded under AA s 69 read with IPC s 304-A is stated to have been remitted by the confirming officer. However, in view of the fact that he had been in pre-trial custody for more than 3 months, it seems that he was in fact ordered to be released by setting off of pre-trial custody against the sentence in accordance with newly inserted provisions in the AA.[282]

280 N Regs II (S), Appendix III, paras 2, 20 and 21.

281 Sheel Kr R oy v S ecretary, M/o Def ence, JT 2007 (7) SC 485 at 491

282 AA, s 169-A inserted by sec. 17 of the Army (Amendment) Act, 1992. Before this amendment the Supreme Court had ruled that a person convicted or sentenced by a GCM under AA was not entitled to the benefit of Cr PC s 428 to have his pre-trial detention set off against the sentence of imprisonment, the AA being a special enactment applicable to persons covered under section 2 thereof; Ajit Kumar v UOI, AIR 1988 SC 283.

7.14 Post-trial Review

Before Armed Forces Tribunal Act, 2007, came into force, the post-trial review of the finding and sentence of CM in India stood fossilized, over a period of almost a century, as restricted to an arm chair review of the GCM proceedings by the JAG and the consideration of the pre and post trial petitions, if any, by the specified military authorities and the Central Government.[283] There was no right of appeal against the decision of a CM[284] nor were and still are not , the constitutional benefits of the High Court's power of superintendence over subordinate courts and the appeal to the Supreme Court by special leave available against the CM proceedings and verdict[285]. The only avenue open to a soldier for seeking relief against anything done to him under DPCM, outside the antiquated Service mechanism, were writ petitions under Articles 32 and 226 of the Constitution. Thus, in the wake of ever-increasing load of the apex court and the High Courts in writ jurisdiction, the timely relief was a far cry for the soldier in such matters.

In the present study, 5 (10%) out of the 50 respondents knocked at the door of the superior courts for their DPCM related grievances. Respondent A - 196 - A - 4 after exhausting the service channel for relief, filed a writ petition in 1996 against the finding and sentence of the CM. He had been tried by a GCM on four charges under AA s 52 (f) for fraudulent act. Initially he was acquitted of three charges but was convicted of one charge with certain exceptions. On revision, the CM revoked its finding of "Not guilty"

283 AR, r 69 and AA, s 164 r espectively. The pr ovisions were imported into the I ndian military law with the IAA, 1911 and the IAR, 1911 and have since been adopted for the current statutory mechanism under the Army and Air Force laws. NA of course provides for a mandatory judicial review by the JAG Navy in the presence of the accused and his counsel, if any; NA s 160. The report of such review together with such recommendations as may appear just and proper is required to be transmitted to the CNS for his consideration and such action as he may think fit. This would apparently include all such actions as a confirming of ficer has the power to tak e under the AA and AF A.

284 A right of appeal, as a rule, can only be conf erred by a statute; Sal igram v Emper or, ILR (1943) Al l 238 (FB) and Minakshi Naidu v Subr amanya Sastry, 14 Ind App 160 (PC). This gener al principle of criminal jurisprudence also stands reflected in Cr PC s 372 which states that no appeal shall lie from any judgment or order of a criminal court except as provided by that code or any other law for the time being in force. Since no such right is provided in the three Services Acts, no appeal would lie against a CM decision. This is in sharp contrast with the situation obtainable in the ordinary criminal jurisdiction under the Cr PC. The Supreme Court had strongly highlighted the travesty while pronouncing in PPS Bedi's case, op cit n 30, and the Law Commission of India recommended in its 169th Report in 1999, for the amendment of the AA to pr ovide for the cr eation of an Armed F orces Appel late Tribunal. Pursuant to this, an Armed F orces Tribunal Bill, 2005 was introduced in Rajya Sabha on 20 Dec 2005. The B ill was thereafter referred to the Standing Commi ttee on Def ence. The T enth R eport of said Commi ttee was pr esented to Lok Sabha and laid in Rajya Sabha on 23 May 2006. The revised Bill with certain amendments suggested by the said Committee, and approved by the Union Cabinet on 08 Nov 2007; has since been enacted as Armed Forces Tribunal Act,2007.

285 Consti tution of I ndia, Arts 136 and 227 .

in respect of one more charge and recorded a finding of "guilty" on that charge with certain variation. The sentence was also converted from 5 year forfeiture of service for the purpose of pension to six month RI and cashiering. The sentence of cashiering was finally commuted to dismissal and the unexpired portion of RI remitted by the confirming authority after consideration of the accused's pre-confirmation petition. The respondent, in his writ petition to the Allahabad High Court, challenged the validity of the revision proceedings on the grounds inter alia that the revision was not ordered by an authority who was required to confirm the sentence. It was further added that the officer performing the duties of JA was not duly sworn as the proceedings were continued with a new JA who was not sworn till the fag end of the proceedings when the illegality was pointed out by the defence counsel. The writ petition, apparently with a strong case, took 10 years to provide relief to the petitioner. Another respondent A-186-A-7 had challenged the very legality of the provisions of revision under the AA, held in his case on 15 May 1972 by an order of officiating GOC 23 Mountain Division, when 2 year RI was added at revision proceedings to the earlier sentence of cashiering. The legal ground was that the confirming officer, having no power to enhance the sentence could not do it circuitously by ordering revision in such terms that the CM was left with no alternative but to enhance the sentence. It was also urged that the proceedings were vitiated by violation of principles of natural justice as the accused was given no hearing in the revision or confirmation. The petition was dismissed by the Supreme Court, holding that under Art. 32, the court only considers whether any of the rules of procedure had been violated and that in the case of the petitioner there was no doubt that the procedure established by law, as required by Art. 21, had been completely followed. As regards the principles of natural justice, they do not supplant the law but supplement it.[286] Respondent A-208-A-2 approached the Allahabad High Court for stay of his impending CM trial, on grounds of some illegalities of jurisdictional nature at pre-trial investigation stage. However, pending decision on the petition, he was tried and convicted by a GCM from 23 Nov 05 to 16 May 06. The findings and sentence of the CM have since been confirmed but the petition still lies unheard. Respondent A-207-A-11 was tried, from Dec 05 to Feb 06, and convicted on two charges of murder and attempt to commit suicide, and sentenced to imprisonment for life coupled with dismissal from the Service. A writ petition was filed on his behalf in Allahabad High Court, bringing out inter alia a complete absence of motive, absence of eye witnesses and a 180 degree volte face by prosecution from its stand in the FIR that the deceased had died of an accidental fire from his own rifle while attempting to change magazine, is awaiting its turn in the High Court, while the respondent is suffering rigors of the imprisonment, which according to him is based on illegal verdict of the CM. Lastly, the writ petition of respondent A - 183 - A - 5 against the finding and sentence of GCM, filed some time in 1997 is still pending for decision.

---

286 Capt. Harish Uppal v UOI, AIR 1973 SC 258 paras 4 and 5.

7.15 Satisfaction Level

Q. No. 2.11 of the Interview Schedule was intended to seek the data on the satisfaction level of the respondents (50 in number) tried by CM as to their perception whether justice had been done in their respective cases. Their responses in this regard along with further action, if any, taken by them are tabulated in Table – 32.

TABLE - 32

Whether Satisfied that Justice was Meted out at CM Trial

<table>
<tr><th>Srl No.</th><th>Satisfaction Level</th><th></th><th>Response Frequency</th><th>Percen--tage</th><th>Result of Action Taken</th><th></th></tr>
<tr><td>1.</td><td>Satisfied</td><td></td><td>22</td><td>44</td><td></td><td></td></tr>
<tr><td>2.</td><td>Not satisfied and action taken:</td><td></td><td></td><td></td><td></td><td></td></tr>
<tr><td></td><td>(a) filed pre and post confirmation petition</td><td>12</td><td></td><td></td><td colspan="2" rowspan="7">(i) Petition rejected - 05
(ii) Result awaited - 07
(iii) Relief granted - 03
(iv) No response on result - 08</td></tr>
<tr><td></td><td>(b) filed only pre-confirmation petition</td><td>02</td><td></td><td></td></tr>
<tr><td></td><td>c) filed only post confirmation petition</td><td>02</td><td></td><td></td></tr>
<tr><td></td><td>(d) still planning to file petition</td><td>01</td><td></td><td></td></tr>
<tr><td></td><td>(e) sent petition to President of India</td><td>01</td><td></td><td></td></tr>
<tr><td></td><td>(f) no action taken</td><td>05</td><td></td><td></td></tr>
<tr><td></td><td>(g) No response about action</td><td>01</td><td></td><td></td></tr>
<tr><td></td><td>Sub-total</td><td>23</td><td>23</td><td>46</td><td></td><td></td></tr>
<tr><td>3.</td><td>No response as to whether satisfied or not</td><td></td><td>05</td><td>10</td><td></td><td></td></tr>
<tr><td></td><td>Total</td><td></td><td>50</td><td>100</td><td></td><td></td></tr>
</table>

As may be seen from the data in Table – 32, almost equal number of respondents are satisfied (22 or 44%) as those who are not (23 or 46%). Even though it may not be very high percentage, yet it needs to be appreciated against a backdrop of only two acquittals as reflected at Srl No. 1 of Table – 30. Further, 37 (74%) of the respondents had pleaded "Not guilty", as may be seen from Table – 24, to the charges framed against them. Lastly, out of those 23 respondents who reported not satisfied, only 17 took some action for redressal of their grievances. Out of the remaining 6, five have expressly stated to have taken no action against the adverse CM order and the remaining one kept mum. There may, of course, be various reasons for the inaction on the part of not satisfied respondents, including but not limited to the absence of legal support, financial constraints, punishment being inconsequential on career and individual circumstances.

The satisfaction level may be affected by a number of factors which may broadly be grouped into two: one, the efficacy of the systemic mechanism and secondly, the execution of the 'due process' requirements of that mechanism. The latter kind of state would be registered negatively in the wake of an insincere, perfunctory, inefficient or dishonest performance by the concerned individuals entrusted with the responsibility of putting into effect the relevant provisions of the law. This stands picturesquely illustrated in the comments of Prof. Bishop on the plurality of opinions given in Burns v Wilson[287]:

> " ... the plurality opinion in Burns v Wilson seems to contain serious internal contradictions. It is very well to say that constitutional due process protects soldiers from 'crude injustice', but what if the crude injustice takes the form of a finding, in the teeth of the evidence, that a coerced confession was voluntary and admissible? There may be no more injustice in a naked refusal to listen than there is in a patient, if bored, hearing of the accused's allegations, followed by an arbitrary finding either that they are untrue or that they do not amount to a denial of due process. Yet Mr. Chief Justice Vinson's opinion may be interpreted as meaning that anything short of refusal to consider allegations that due process has been denied is equivalent to dealing with them fully and fairly."[288]

In tune with the observations of Prof. Bishop, this discussion may be concluded with what the Supreme Court had to say of the CM procedure, the systematic limitations of the constituents and a possible way out: "the procedure to be followed by a court-martial is quite elaborate and generally follows the pattern of the procedure under the Code of Criminal Procedure. There are, however, material differences too. All the members of the court-martial are military officers who are not expected to be trained Judges as the presiding officers of criminal courts are. The authorities to whom the convicted person can represent against his conviction by a court-martial are also non-judicial authorities. In the circumstances, a trial by an ordinary criminal court would be more beneficial to the accused than one by a court-martial" in the case of an offence

287 B urns v Wi lson, 346 US 137.

288 Bishop, op cit, Ch 6, n 102, pp 58-59.

triable by a CM as well as a criminal court of ordinary criminal jurisdiction. However, it would be better for the purpose of discipline that offences which are not of a serious type be ordinarily tried by a court-martial."[289]

289 Ram Sarup v UOI, op cit, n 119, p 252.

CHAPTER - 8

EFFICACY OF COURT MARTIAL PROCESS

"And my response to any critic of system, both to the civilians who cry 'drum-head justice' and to military members who cry that the system is too civilianized is that you are wrong. The system functions and functions well. Yes, there may be technical errors and an occasional injustice as the system malfunctions, but grand strategy is sound."[1]

- Hon'ble Walter T Cox III
(Judge, US Court of Appeals for the Armed Forces)

During World War II, about 20,00,000 CsM were convened under the US Articles of War, with 45,000 Servicemen imprisoned under sentences adjudged by the CM and 142 executed by the time the war ended.[2] The courts often had hurried proceedings such as the accused being served with the charge at 1240 hours on 03 Sep 1943, notified that he would be tried at 1400 hours the same day and by 1730 hours that afternoon, he was convicted, sentenced to dismissal from the Service and promptly redrafted.[3] The war being over, hue and cry arose for reform of the military justice system, which led to the enactment of the UCMJ in 1950 that "contained procedural reforms and due process safeguards not then guaranteed in civil courts."[4] Further revolutionary improvements

1 Walter T Cox III, "The Army, the Courts and the Constitution: The Evolution of Military Justice", Military Law Review, Vol 118, 1987, pp 1-30 at 30.

2 Statistical Abstract of the United States, U.S. Deptt. of Commerce, Table No. 385 at 256 (1970).

3 Shapiro v United States, 69 F Supp 205, 207 (Ct Cl 1947). Second Lieutenant Sidney Shapiro was appointed to defend at a GCM, a soldier charged with rape. Thinking that his client could not be identified as the attacker, he substituted another person for his client at council's table. The substitute accused was identified as the perpetrator and indeed was 'convicted' by the CM. Shapiro then revealed his scheme. Not only was his real client thereafter brought to trial and convicted but Shapiro himself was put on trial for delaying the orderly progress of his client at CM, for which he was convicted and sentenced to dismissal. His ordeal, however, did not end there. After being dismissed as an officer, he was promptly drafted back as a Private. Alleging his dismissal to be wrong, he later successfully sued for back pay as Second Lieut minus the salary received as a Private.

4 Lieut Col PPS Bedi v UOI, op cit Ch 5, n 45, at p 1438 (para 46).

were made therein in 1968 with an avowed insight that "the man who dons the uniform of his country today does not discard his right to fair treatment under law".[5] And yet, despite the extraordinary reforms in the system having been in place for full two decades and further the ameliorating steps introduced by the Military Justice Act of 1968, by which "military justice attained virtual parity with civilian criminal justice"[6], the perception of some critics still was that "military justice is to justice as military music is to music."[7] Further, the criticism was seen by the US media as a "chilling analysis of what can pass for justice in military."[8] Commanders of men, on the other hand, felt that the system had become too civilianized[9] and that it was destroying the ability of the commanders to command their troops.[10] Some Generals, however, had a different view.[11]

8.1 Nature and Object of Military Justice

These widely varied opinion statements made by different people from different strata of the US community in respect of their contemporary military justice system apparently reflect their attitudinal response developed in their socio-professional environment and a failure to properly appreciate the nature and object of military justice system, which is essentially, though not accurately, identified with the CM. In the context of the CM as a justice delivery mechanism, two oft quoted critical statements include the observation of Justice Douglas that the "very expression 'court martial' generally strikes terror in the heart of the person to be tried by it"[12] and that of Justice Black about

5 President Lyndon Johnson on the occasion of signing into law the Military Justice Act, 1968 on 24 Oct 1968.

6 Sam J Ervin Jr., "The Military Justice Act of 1968", Military Law Review, Vol 45, 1969, pp 77-98 at 77.

7 R Sherril, Military Justice is to Justice as Military Music is to Music, 1969, cit in Cox, "The Army, the Courts and the Constitution: The Evolution of Military Justice", op cit n 1 p 17 . The title of the book is based on the similarly worded famous quotation from French statesman Georges Clemenceau.

8 Mike Wallace of CBS News, cit in Cox, ibid.

9 The Military Justice Act of 1983 Advisory Commission Report, 1984, (minority report) at 155.

10 Cox, loc cit, n 7, p 28; cf General Hamilton Houze, "Military Discipline and National Security", Army Magazine, Jan. 1971 at 11, 13, cit in Cox, loc cit, n 7:

> "The requirements of military justice are now so ponderous and obtuse that a unit commander cannot possibly have the time or the means to apply the system. "

11 General John Galvin, then Commanding VII Corps of the Army, felt that UCMJ was a "very fine code" under which he had "full authority to do things" but not "absolute authority. That authority is reserved by the United States of America that gave my commission ... I command 85000 people. There isn't a soul in those 85000 people that does not have to obey my legal command. "; report cit supra n 9, p 186.

Major General Hodson, the JAG of the US Army, similarly held a view that if any commander wanted more authority in the area of military justice, it could be only for one reason, and that is that he wanted to have the opportunity to influence the scales of justice when it suited him; please see Hodson, "The Manual for Courts Martial: 1984", Military Law Review, Vol 57, 1972, p 1.

12 Justice William O' Douglas, "Tough Test for Military Justice", supra, Ch 3, n 5.

the Courts martial having "always been subject to varying degrees of 'command influence'," being "simply executive tribunals whose personnel are in the executive chain of command."[13] It may not be out of place to point out here that Justice Black had joined Justice Douglas in his Burns dissent,[14] and voted together in several cases, expressing misgiving about the process in military courts[15] and applicability of the Bill of Rights to soldiers.[16]

Justice Black's view about the CM being simply an executive tribunal, however, draws support from Colonel Winthrop who also feels that, "Strictly, a court-martial is not a 'court' in the full sense of the term, or as the same is understood in the civil phraseology. It has no common law powers whatever, but only such powers as are vested in it by express statute, or may be derived from military usage ...." He draws this conclusion from the fact that a CM does not belong to the judicial branch of the Government and hence it follows that the CM must pertain to the executive department. In view of this, Winthrop would describe CsM as "simply instrumentalities of the executive power, provided by Congress for the President as commander-in-chief to aid him in properly commanding the army and navy and enforcing discipline thereon."[17]

It may be noted that the observations of Winthrop were primarily purported to describe the position of the American court martial in the scheme of their constitutional law. Under the US constitution, the Congress has the power "to make rules for the Government and Regulation of the land and naval forces" (Art I, Cl. 14) in addition to its power to raise and support Armies (Art I, Cl. 12) and maintain a Navy (Art I Cl. 13) and to "make laws necessary and proper". It is under these powers that Congress provides for the trial and punishment of military and naval offences unconnected with Art. I, which provides for the "judicial Powers of the United States" that "shall be vested in one Supreme Court, and in such inferior courts as the Congress may from time to time ordain and establish".[18] When the Constitution and the Bill of Rights were drafted, little mention was made of military justice. However, surveying in detail the practices of the CM in the period during which the Bill of Rights was written, with a view to

13 Reid v Covert, (1957) 1 Law ed 2d 1148: 354 US 1 (1957)

14 Burns v Wilson, 346 US 137 (1953) at 150-155

15 See generally Toth v Quarles, 350 US 11 (1955):

16 He believed that the Bill of Rights was generally applicable to soldiers except when any of the provisions such as grand jury were expressly excluded in application to Naval and land forces. Contrary to this, see Col. Wiener, "Courts Martial and the Bill of Rights: The Original Practice", Harv L Rev, Vol 72, 1958, pp 266-298 at 302 convincingly demonstrating otherwise and Gordon D Henderson, "Courts Martial and the Constitution: The Original Understanding", Harv L R ev, op ci t, Ch 5, n 80, pp 293-324 , also dr awing the same conclusion.

17 Winthrop, Military Law and Precedents, op cit, Ch 1 ,n 1, pp 49-54.

18 Dynes v Hoo ver, 61 US (20 How) 65 (1857).

examining whether those practices conformed substantially to the procedures and rights granted by the first ten amendments of the US constitution, Henderson concluded that the "contemporary practice of courts-martial was such that the application of the bill of rights to them would not have been considered a major reform."[19] The observations of Winthrop about CM belonging to the executive branch of the Government, though made in the context of the American system, hold good equally to the CM under most of the military systems the world over, including the British and the Indian systems. In England, formerly the Sovereign, who is historically identified with the executive[20], constituted the CM by an exercise of prerogative and formed all the laws for the government of the army. The first Mutiny Act, passed on 03 April 1689 and a series of its successors expressly provided that Her Majesty "may from time to time, in like manner as has been heretofore used, grant commissions under the royal-sign-manual, for the holding of courts-martial...".[21] In pre-Independence India, the status of a CM was on the same line, initially being held under the East India Company's Acts and later under the IAA, 1911. The current position is that under the Constitution of India, the Executive power of the Union is vested in the President and the supreme command of the Defence Forces of the Union is also vested in him.[22] There is no mention of CM anywhere in the Constitution. It occupies no place in the scheme of the Union judiciary and of State High Courts or subordinate courts of the States, except that it expressly excludes any court or tribunal constituted by or under any law relating to the armed forces from the purview of special leave to appeal by the Supreme Court and the High Courts' power of superintendence over all courts within their territorial jurisdiction.[23] CsM are also not covered under Articles 323A and 323B of the Constitution dealing with administrative and other tribunals.

The position of the CM as an instrumentality of the Executive not forming part of the Judiciary is, however, not universally true today. In several countries like China, Cuba, Ecuador, France (which can boast of possessing the oldest known document on military jurisdiction in the form of the Montdidier order dated 01 May 1347) and Germany now form part of the mainstream judiciary of the country.[24] Further, in the present age,

19 Henderson, "Courts Martial and the Consti tution: The Original Understanding", op cit, Ch 5, n 80, at 316-321.

20 Wade and Phillips, Constitutional Law, 9th ed, 1983, ELBS & Longman, p 44

21 Simmons, The Consti tution and Pr actice of Courts Martial, op ci t, Ch 7, n 46, pp 2 and 4

22 Constitution of India, Arts 52 (1) and (2).

23 Ibid, Arts. 136 and 227 .

24 "Military Jurisdiction and Domestic Legislation" in Federico Andreu-Guzman, Military Jurisdiction and International Law, op cit, Ch 5, n 159, pp 219-220 (China), pp 254-256 (Cuba), pp 258-261 (Ecuador), pp 263, 273 and 275-277 (France) and p 280 (Germany) , available on web wwc.icj.org of International Commission of Jurists, Columbian Commission of Jurists.

the notion of welfare state and increased governmental intervention in the economy have led an unprecedented upsurge in the quantity and complexities of legislation. The task of the settlement of disputes arising out of such legislation is given to the tribunals in preference over the ordinary courts for the reason of cost, expedition and expertise.[25] In such a scenario of administrative law, the judicial status of a tribunal, whether civil or military, is no more open to challenge as a court merely on the ground of its being an instrumentality of the executive. Then, it may be seen that over more than a century long period since the first publication of Col. Winthrop's celebrated treatise in 1886 and a period of six full decades even since the times of Justices Black and Douglas' disparaging remarks, the system of military justice has undergone significant positive changes. The authority to convene the court being shifted from military commanders to a Defence Council appointee administrative officer in the British system, the military judge having been given the power to preside over the CM under the US military laws, the provisions for effective legal assistance being extended to the accused at all stages of the military jurisdiction, an independent appellate body being created to hear appeals against CM decisions and an attitudinal change in the scope of judicial review of CM convictions are the developments which would impel one to join Justice Cox III to say that "the system has continued to change and evolve into a modern, generally efficient system which tries to serve the delicate balance between the needs of the commander to have an expedient method of administering punishment for serious breaches of the law and the rights of an accused to a fair and impartial trial.[26]

It is undeniable that the changes introduced in the military justice system in the recent times are not evenly spread the world over. In PPS Bedi's case, the Supreme Court, for instance, pointed out the need for having a re-look at our system which is still antiquated and hoped and believed that the changes all over the English speaking democracies would awaken our Parliament to the changed value system[27] and yet twenty years later, the apex Court had to lament in Charanjit Gill's case that except amending Rule 62, no action in that behalf had been taken.[28] However, steps have now been taken in India to have an Armed Forces Tribunal, inter alia for appeals against the CM decisions and related matters. The amendments made in the Army Act in 1992 are also proposed to be soon incorporated in the Air Force and Naval laws. The point to be reiterated is that the institution of the CM today is not what it used to be in the ages gone by. Instead of indulging in any juristic name-calling of the institution of the CM, what is therefore

25 PP Craig, Administrative Law, op cit, ch 7, n, Ch 1.

26 Cox III, "The Army, the Courts and the Constitution: The Evolution of Military Justice", op cit, n 1, p 18

27 PPS Bedi's case, op cit, n 4, p 1438-1439 (paras 45-46).

28 UOI v Charanjit S Gill, AIR 2000 SC 3425 (paras 9-10); cf Nirmal Lakra v UOI, 2003 (3) AISLJ 151 (Delhi) at 162

required to realize is, that the civil courts and the CM belong to totally different systems of jurisprudence. The object of the civil law is to secure to every human being in a community all the liberty, security and happiness possible, consistent with safety of all. The object of a military law is to govern armies composed of strong men so as to be capable of exercising the largest measure of force at the will of the nation. These objects are as wide apart as the poles and each requires its own system of laws, statutes and common.[29] Thus, a CM is a peculiar court which is sui generis and may, in a way, be said to be adjudicating upon the responsibility of persons subject to military law for the military discipline related offences, the same way as any other quasi-judicial tribunals with the matters placed under its jurisdiction. Functioning within its field of action, however, the CM is "fully a court of law and justice as any civil tribunal. As a court of law it is bound, like any other court, by fundamental principles of law, and in the absence of special provisions on the subject, it observes in general the rules of evidence as adopted in the common law courts. As a court of justice, it is required, by the term of its statutory oath, to adjudicate between the United States (read 'State' in Indian context) and the accused without partiality, favour or affection, and according not only to the laws and customs of the Service but also its conscience, i.e., its sense of substantial right and justice unaffected by technicalities". As for the class of courts, the CM is "strictly a criminal court".[30]

8.2 Command Influence

The trial by CM may not strike terror in the heart of the accused any more than his counterpart under the ordinary criminal jurisdiction but an accusation of the CM having always been subject to varying degrees of command influence cannot be straightway denied as unfounded altogether. "The process of maintaining discipline yet ensuring fairness requires a 'delicate balance' in an area filled with perils for the unwary."[31] When this balance is upset, unlawful command influence results.[32] In 1970, Newsweek featured a cover story discussing several sensational cases of the era and concluding that the number one evil with military justice remained command influence.[33] Thirty years later, "concerns over the excessive involvement of command" are now being

29 Sherman (General William Tecumseh), Military Laws, 1880, p 780, cit in Cox, op cit, n 26, pp 17-18.

30 Winthrop, ibid, pp 54-63: cf AA, s 152 for a CM trial deemed to be judicial proceeding and CM to be a court within the meaning of the IPC, ss 193 and 228 and Cr PC, ss 345 and 346. The wordings of the oath prescribed under AR r 45 for the members of the CM are also comparable with Winthrop's observation here as to the statutory oath with which a CM is bound as a court of justice.

31 US v Treakle, 18 MJ 646, 653 (ACMR 1984)

32 Major Martha Huntley Bower, USAF, "Unlawful Command Influence: Preserving the Delicate Balance" Air Force Law Review, 1988. pp 65-96 at p 65.

33 "Military Justice on Trial", Newsweek, 31 Aug 1970.

expressed all over the world, the phenomenon having surfaced in the UK and drawing hammer blows from the European Court of Human Rights, New Zealand Court Martial Appeal Court and Australian Judge and occupying significant space in periodical writings on military justice.[34]

The concept, unlawful command influence is divided into two categories: one, actual command influence cases, and two, apparent command influence. The first one would cover such cases as the case in which the accused may have been denied a fair and impartial hearing or potentially beneficial witnesses by the exercise of command influence and so on. The second category, i.e., apparent command influence, is related to the erosion of belief of the Service members and the public at large in the accused having received a fair trial. Even if a case was not actually affected by unlawful command influence, it may appear to have been, and in that event, it would be a case of the second category. The concept of the apparent command influence was formulated in the case of Navarre. The court held in that case: "We are concerned here with much more, I believe, than the protection of an accused person .... A judicial system operates effectively only with the public confidence - and, naturally this trust exists only if there also exists a belief that triers of fact act fairly and without undue influence."[35] In the case of first category too, it is not necessary that the command influence was intentional. It could occur unintentionally, if, for example, a participant in the military justice system misperceives the commander's desires. An often cited example of such unintended command influence was the effect of the message of "consistency" by Maj Gen Anderson of 3rd Armored Division given in various commander's calls to his subordinates, which was mistaken for his "discouraging favourable character testimony in courts martial," whereas he was trying to suggest in fact that a commander should recommend a lower level CM if he did not believe that the accused should be discharged, and the commanders and NCOs should not testify that the accused was a good soldier or recommend retention if they believed that the accused should be discharged. The General's comments caused widespread litigation that went on in the appellate system for years.[36] .In view of this, it is not sufficient for the military justice system to merely find and fix unlawful command influence - unlawful command influence must be preventive. Because the area is treacherous, commanders and common subordinates should be systematically educated the bedrock principle of military justice that "every person tried by court martial is entitled to have his guilt or innocence, and his sentence, determined solely upon the evidence presented at trial free from all unlawful influence exerted by military superiors or others.[37]

34 Eugene R Fidell, "A World-Wide Perspective on Change in Military Justice", Air Force Law Review, Vol 48, 2000, pp 195-209 at 203.

35 US v Navarre, 5 CMA, 32; 17 CMR 32 (CMA 1954)

36 US v Treakle op cit, n 31.

37 US v Rodriguez, 16 MJ 740 (AF CMR, 1983).

In the present study, one of the hypotheses was that the entire system of the DPCM is fraught with command influence at all stages. A question on this aspect was accordingly included in Parts I and III of the Interview Schedule. In Part I, Q. 1.6 included 'wishes of the superior' and 'views of the superiors' respectively as one of the optioned responses, of the 50 respondents of member category and 50 of the JA category, to the question as to what factors determined their decision/advice at various stages of the tribunal. Q 3.4(a) in Part III sought response of each of the 200 respondents, by way of their agreeing, partially agreeing or disagreeing, with the statement that decision making process of court martial is fraught with command influence at all stages. There was also Q. 3.3(c) which had a bearing on this issue. It sought the reaction of the 200 respondents as to the authorities of the same army command convening the CM, appointing the members and the JA, reviewing the proceedings of the CM and in most cases, confirming the finding and the sentence, as well as dealing with the pre-confirmation and post-confirmation petitions. The data collected in response to Q. 3.4(a) may, therefore, be taken up here and the discussion thereon will also take into consideration the relevant data collected through other questions. Table 33 displays the data collected through Q. 3.4(a):

TABLE - 33

Whether DPCM Fraught with Command Influence

Ser No.	Response	Response Frequency					
		M	J	A	G	Total	%
1.	Agreed	02	04	20	14	40	20.0
2.	Partially Agreed	16	12	04	16	48	24.0
3.	Disagreed	29	30	14	17	90	45.0
4.	Can/t Say	00	00	04	03	07	3.5
5.	No Response	03	04	08	00	15	7.5
	Total	50	50	50	50	200	100.0

Before interpreting the data of Table 33, the data on Q. 3.4(j) carrying a statement that "the decisions of CM are foregone conclusion may also be tabulated as follows:

TABLE - 34

Whether CM Decisions are Pre-determined

Ser No.	Response	Response Frequency					
		M	J	A	G	Total	%
1.	Agreed	01	02	13	12	28	14.0
2.	Partially Agreed	02	04	08	08	22	11.0
3.	Disagreed	44	38	12	27	121	60.5
4.	Can/t Say	01	00	07	03	11	5.5
5.	No Response	02	06	10	00	18	9.0
	Total	50	50	50	50	200	100.0

The data displayed in Table 33 reflect that 40 (20%) respondents were in agreement with the statement of command influence working at all stages of the CM. Half of these 40 respondents, i.e., 20 (50%) were from the category of the accused persons. The least number of 02 (5% of these 40 and just one percent of the total) of those who agreed with the presence of the command influence in CM process was from the member category. The response of both the accused and the member category respondents could possibly be carrying a group bias. As against this, the response of 14 (35% of those agreed) respondents from general category may be said in a way to be generally displaying an unbiased attitude or opinion response. Whereas these 40 respondents fully agreed with command influence affecting CM process at all stages, another 48 (24%) partially agreed with the proposition. Thus, a total of 88 (44%) of the respondents saw CM process as being under the command influence to whatever extent it might be. In this, the maximum number was from the respondents of the general category, their number being 30 (14 + 16) out of 88, i.e., 34% whereas the corresponding data from the accused category respondents was limited to 24 i.e., 27% of those in agreement with the proposition, whether fully or partially. However, this comparison cannot be taken as representing the true state of things since the accused category of respondents also had 8 non-responsees while the number of non-responsees in the case of general category was nil. But then, the non-responsees can be counted neither in favour of, nor against, the proposition. Be that as it may, an unequivocal disagreement of 90 (45%) respondents with the proposition of command influence affecting CM process is there at Srl 3. If we take away the total number of 22 no-option responses (with 7 'Can't say' responses and 15 noresponses), the percentage of those in agreement (88) and those disagreeing (90) would respectively stand at 49.44% and 50.56%. This means that the number of the persons who generally feel that CM process is fraught with command influence and those who feel otherwise is almost equal, but for the fact that the former include, in a sizeable number, such respondents who only partially agree with the presence of command influence in CM process. It is also significant to note that among those who disagree with the presence of command influence, there were 29 (14.5% of total and 32% of those disagreeing) respondents from member category, 30 (15% of total and 33.3% of those disagreeing) from JA category, 17 (8.5% of total and 18.9% of those disagreeing) from general category and also 14 (7% of total and 15.6% of those disagreeing) from the category of those who were tried by the CM. It is interesting to see that out of 38 respondents who did give their opinion on the issue (12 being 'can't say' or no response) from the last mentioned category, 24 (63%) agreed with the presence of command influence, fully or partially, and 14 (37%) disagreed.

The additional remarks given by 18 respondents, along with their individual responses to the question, are also worth noting. Seven (39% of them) only partially noticed the presence of command influence. Respondents M-6 found no command influence at the CM level but did notice it sometime at preliminary stages like C of I. More or less the same was the view of M-15 and J-55, M-14, J-65, G-140 and G-141 who felt the presence of command influence only in some cases. Three of the respondents, M-27, J-77 and G-110 had some suggestions to make to eliminate command influence. These would include matters relating to the appointment of members of the CM, reasoned decision to be given by the CM and establishment of an appeal court. Two of the respondents had to reiterate their responses more emphatically and elaborately to the effect of non-existence of command influence, but one of them adding that "In the question, 'command influence' be changed to JAG's influence", suggesting thereby, as also elsewhere in his other responses, that the JAG representative is the villain of the piece in the entire scheme of things related to DPCM. The remark of this respondent, (A-188) seems to prove the theory that although a belief on a specific issue tends to suggest an attitude, a particular individual's belief on that issue may be heavily weighted by an idiosyncratic component which makes belief integral of his non-general position[38]. In the present case, this respondent generally disagrees with command influence affecting CM process but his belief in respect of the way of working of the JAG's Department colours his attitude towards the role of command influence in the scheme of CM process. Moving further, it is noticed that one respondent (G-124) found the matter being beyond

38 Moser & K alton,Survey in Social In vestigation, op cit, Ch 3, n 17 , p 351. The authors also state elsewhere (p 317) that a person's opinion on virtually any issue is many sided. The answer the respondent actually gives will depend on the aspect of the issue that is uppermost in his mind. In the present context the opinions of the accused category and member category respondents were likely to be affected by their positions vis-à-vis the CM which would be uppermost in their minds while answering DPCM related questions.

his understanding level, whereas the remaining out of the 18 respondents unhesitatingly conceded the command influence but three of them justified its presence. G-138 outrightly states that command influence is needed in a system like the CM, G-118 upholds the requirement of command influence in some particular cases in the interest of the organization, and G-117 brings out the inevitability of command influence in the discipline oriented services, for reasons such as own career prospects and civil-military relationship. Illustrating his viewpoint with the case of a particular high-ranking accused officer, the respondent concluded that the cause of justice may thereby get short-shrift but there is no deliberate intention on the part of any one to sabotage the course of justice. In another context, another respondent, G-106 suggests that the present ad hoc system of CM be changed to quasi ad hoc tribunal consisting of three permanent members and two members appointed freshly by military authorities so as to reduce the play of command influence in the CM trial.

These details of data and the remarks added by the respondents stand interesting comparison with the data collected through Q. 1.6 of the Interview Schedule, which may be displayed in Table – 35 below:

TABLE - 35

Wishes/Views of Superiors as Determinant of Decision by Members and Advice by JA

Sr. No	Response	Response Frequency			
		Members		JAs	
		Number	Percentage	Number	Percentage
1.	Wishes/ views of superiors determined decision / advice	00	00	02	04
2.	Wishes/views of superiors did not affect decision/advice	50	100	48	96
	Total	50	100	50	100

The data in Table 35 reflect that in the case of all the 50 (100%) member respondents, their decisions were not determined by the wishes of the superiors. Similarly, the views of the superiors were not determining factor for the advice rendered by 48 (96%) respondents from the category of JA. Before juxtaposing these percentages with the percentages of the data displayed in Table 33, it will be useful to recall the data displayed in Table 33. The data at Srls 2 and 3 in that Table disclose that 34 (17%) respondents only were in favour of any change in respect of the matters relating to the convening of the CM, whereas 88 (44%) at Srl 1 wanted the present system to continue. It may be inferred that they perceived no existence of command influence entering into the CM as a result of the CM being convened, RT or RAT being rendered, CM functionaries being appointed and post trial review and petition being dealt, within the same command.

Before proceeding further, it will be useful to recall that an attitude is a more general concept than can be accurately determined from the answer to a single question. Therefore, to measure the attitude more accurately, a sample of beliefs covering a range of aspects of the attitude needs to be obtained and a set of answers combined into some form of average. For this purpose, from all the possible statements that could be made about the object of the attitude, a representative sample is required for putting to the respondents. However, the analogy must not be pushed too far; with attitude there is the obvious limitation that the universe content from which the sample of statements is drawn cannot be determined.[39] The scaling method is employed to achieve precise results in measuring attitude. The method, however, is more useful for sociological surveys involving large samples. Further, such method being complicated in statistical terms, is difficult to handle in legal research since lawyers are generally not at ease with complicated statistics.[40] To examine in this light, the percentages relating to the data fetched in response to questions 3.4(a), 3.4(j), 3.3(c) and 1.6 may be compared, combined and averaged in Table 36.

39 Ibid, p 351 and earl ier discussion in 3.5 (on ' Attitude').

40 P M Bakshi, "Legal Research and Law Reform", JILI, Vol 24, 1982, p 391

TABLE - 36

Responses on Different Aspects of Command Influence

Srl. No	Related Question	Percentage		
		For	Against	Others*
1.	Q. 3.4(a) - DPCM fraught with command influence.	44.00	45.00	11.00
2.	Q. 3.3(c) - Command Influence inferred from responses as to convening of CM etc. within same command as of accused.	17.00	44.00	39.00
3.	Q. 1.5 - Command Influence related problems faced by members and JA	18.00	82.00	00.00
4.	Q. 1.6 - Members decision/JA's advice determined under command influence	02.00	98.00	00.00
5.	Q. 1.8 - Command influence contributing to Conviction.	06.00	94.00	00.00
6.	Q. 2.10 - Command related factor resulting into non-production of witnesses or inadequate examination thereof	09.00	91.00	00.00
	Average Percentage	16.00	75.67	08.33
* Includes no-response, can't say and response other than Yes/No				

It is seen from Table 36 that in 75.67% cases the attitude of people towards DPCM is favourable from the point of view of command influence affecting DPCM. Only in 16% cases, people believe that DPCM is affected by command influence, while in 8.33% cases people are either equivocal on the issue or have no opinion to offer. The results worked out here are certainly not as precise as could be achieved if Thurstone, Likert, Guttman or any other scale method had been adopted. Nonetheless, these results do present broad picture on the much talked about command influence as the 'mortal enemy of military justice'.[41]

As noticed earlier in the additional remarks of respondents G-117, 118 and 138, command influence is at times found justifiable in the case of a jurisdiction like that of CM. Often "cloaked in ignorance and the good intentions of commanders and members of their command", command influence may be classified into two: unlawful and lawful. Unlawful command influence is prohibited, expressly in some systems such as, the US system where UCMJ Art. 37 is devoted to prohibition of "unlawfully influencing action of court" and tacitly elsewhere. On the other hand, command influence, "in the sense of lawful participation in the process is necessary and predominant feature of the military justice system".[42] The latter issues from the lawful authority and responsibility that the military commanders have to ensure the timely and fair disposition of charges. However, sometimes the same power and authority is used to influence decisions that should be independent of command prerogatives and policy. Such unlawful command influence is not limited in scope to the actions of commanders alone and would include the objectionable actions of staff officers, JA or even personnel other than officers. One common scenario where unlawful command influence is exercised in command subordinates presents itself, when they make comments or take action to prevent witnesses from testifying on behalf of the accused. In an American case, for instance, while several drug cases were under investigation, an air force First Sergeant told the NCOs in his hospital that any one, who testified that a drug offender was amenable to rehabilitation, might anticipate adverse career impact; and at a post-trial commander's call of the same unit, the hospital administrator criticized those who had testified on behalf of the accused drug offenders.[43] In the present study, respondent A-197 stated that he pleaded "Guilty" to the charge under AA s 69 read with IPC s 304A at his trial by SCM because his CO had told him that he was likely to get away lightly if he pleaded guilty.

In a bid to keep CM proceedings free from command influence, various measures have been introduced in several military systems[44]. However, in India, the issue of undue command influence has not attracted due attention from any quarters; the commanders,

---

41 US v Thomas, 22 MJ 388, 393 (CMA 1986).

42 David A. Schluetter, Military Criminal Justice: Practice and Procedure, 1992, p 255, cit in Capt Teresa K Hollingworth, USAF, "Unlawful Command Influence", Air Force Law Review, Vol 46, 1996, pp 261-276, at 262; cf Major Deana M C Willis, "The Road to Hell is Paved With Good Intentions: Finding and Fixing Unlawful Command Influence", op cit, Ch 7, n 40.

43 US v Sullivan, 26 MJ 442 (CMA, 1988)

44 Please see, supra Ch 7.1(a)

the courts or the consumers of the military justice themselves. Certain precepts[45] are found lying scattered in the legal provisions, the authoritative guidelines thereon in the Notes, the administrative instructions and so on, which have indirect relevance to the notion of command influence but as a specific jurisprudential concept, it is missing altogether. Barring a few cases, it has hardly ever been raised directly in the pleadings before a CM, in any petition before the superior military authorities or while seeking relief through judicial review. This, however, does not mean that the malice is non-existent in the Indian military justice system context. The additional remarks made by certain respondents of JA category along with their response to Q. 1.5 are very much suggestive of efforts having been made to influence their performance. As may be seen from the data at Srl 4 of Table 37, most of the respondents from the members and JA category faced no problem in this regard. However, the related details in the Interview Schedules disclose that 18 (36%) out of 50 JA category respondents did face some problems, which inter alia included command influence related problems too[46]. Thus, it is felt to be very much there physically but all concerned were found to have a passive attitude towards it, in sharp contrast to the situation in the USA. There as early as the

---

45 Examples:

(a) CO not to hold SCM without reference to superiors for an offence against himself (AA s 130);

(b) CM not to include as member the CO of the accused or the Officer Commanding the Corps to which the accused belongs (AR r 39);

(c) Oath taken by members to try the accused well and truly according to the evidence and administer justice without partiality and according to conscience in the event of doubt (AR r 45);

(d) The opinion of members to be taken in succession, beginning with the member lowest in rank (AR r 87);

(e) While considering the sentence to be awarded the court not to presume that the convening authority in sending the case f or trial took a mor e serious view of the f acts (MML, Vol 1. p 42);

(f) Finding of sentence not to be confirmed by an officer who has acted as a member or prosecutor (AR r 74).

46 Instances of command influence as narrated by respondents:

(a) An attempt to win favour for the accused (J-54, 56, 61, 63, 65, 96); J-56 recalls how in the rape case of a foreign woman by NSG officers in late 1980s,, pressure was exerted on him from senior officers in the Dept. for recommending remission in the sentence awarded by the CM to an accused officer. The r espondent did not yield. The r emission was, however, granted by the Arm y Commander despite the advice of the respondent to the contr ary.

(b) Dy JAG was annoyed on acquittal even though the verdict was supported by evidence (J-58, 74);

(c) Pressurized by convening officer to act against the accused but the respondent did not allow his performance to be influenced thereby (J-99);

(d) The administrative military authorities wanted less time to be given to the accused, also interference by convening authority and his staff officers (J-74, 87);

(e) Some members being superseded were anti-establishment and were unduly favouring the accused (J-90, 91, 92, 94).

years soon after World War I, the civilian community began to express concern over command interference in CM proceedings,[47] with the conviction rate of close to 97%[48] in Army CM and the experience of two million CsM during World War II. It was brought out in the report that a significant number of COs was found to have so influenced the CM proceedings that the capacity for a fair and impartial trial was lost and the sentences awarded bordered on the fantastic, with 75 years sentence being not unknown and 50 or 25 year sentences awarded for infraction of discipline.[49]

Instances of command influence in different forms have been frequently brought up in our case at various levels. At USI Seminar Number Ten held at Vigyan Bhavan on 26 Feb 1986, Colonel A C Mangala (Later Maj Gen as the 9th JAG in the post Independence era) pointed out to a letter, issued several years ago, saying that if a CM arrived at a finding of 'Not guilty,' the censure of the COAS would be conveyed to the presiding officer and the member of the CM. Further, at the same seminar, a question was posed as to whether it could be said without hesitation that the members of the CM were free from command influence. In reply, it was brought out by Brig. A B Gorthi (Later Maj. Gen as the 8th JAG) that the number of acquittals pronounced by CM over the years, which they adhered to even on revision, would clearly indicate that the so called command influence was more of a myth than reality. Brig. Gorthi had quoted the statistics bringing out year-wise number of acquittal in the officers cases from 1971 to 1980, totaling to 62 acquittals in 470 (13.19%) cases of GCM trials.[50] Apparently, such a small percentage of acquittal does not seem to prove the point intended to be made. Further, the statistics quoted in his paper were only in respect of officers which would be just about 5% of the total number of CsM in respect of all ranks.

At the Supreme Court level, the issue came up in PPS Bedi's case when it was contended for the petitioners that the interpretation of AR r 40 (which required a GCM to be composed of officers from different corps or departments) must be informed by the underlying intendment that officers comprising the CM must be independent of command influence. The apex court, however, did not go into details on "a loose expression like command influence" and restricted itself to the interpretation of the term "corps" occurring in the said Rule 40. Again, in Major Hussain's case, the issue was brought in indirectly when it was argued that the accused had been denied a reasonable opportunity to defend himself but the Supreme Court, after considering

47 Johnson, "Unlawful Command Influence: A Question of Balance" , The Judge Advocate Journal, Navy, March-April 1965, at 87-88.

48 Powell Report, at 251, cit in Capt Willis, "The United States Court of Military Appeals: Its Origin, Operation and Future", Military Law Review, Vol 55, 1972, pp 39-93, p 41, footnote 3.

49 Vanderbilt Committee Report, at pp 6, 7 for CO's influence and p 3 for excessive sentence.

50 USI Seminar Number Ten, 26 Feb 1982 Report, pp 16, 17 .

various related provisions and administrative instructions, concluded that the CM was properly held.[51] In Lt. Col. Duggal's case, it was contended that a discussion among the members in the closed court, during deliberation on sentence, had influenced the opinion of the members on the sentence and thus the issue of command influence was obliquely raised. The Supreme Court, however, ignored it along with certain other points raised, stating that "these are all internal administrative matters."[52] Then there is the case of Ranjit Thakur[53], in which the command influence may be said to have improperly affected the SCM proceedings in the sense that the appellant had fallen out of favour of the CO who held the trial by SCM. The appellant had complained against the CO and had been sentenced to 28 days RI by the CO for violating the norm of representing to higher authorities and making a complaint. While serving the sentence, he was tried by SCM held by the same CO, for disobedience of superior's order by refusing to eat food when ordered to do so by Orderly Officer Sub. Ram Singh. Convicting him of the charge the CO holding the SCM awarded him the sentence of dismissal and one year RI. The sentence was set aside by the apex court as being against the principle of proportionality and the accused having not been given an opportunity to object to trial by the CO. In the cases of Sep Mahabir Singh and L/Nk Inder Pal Singh of 8 JAT, they were sentenced to death for committing the murder of their CO, Col. S S Sahota on 16 Jun 1987. The existence of command influence was contended in their case, at a somewhat unconventional stage of committing the offence which was abetted by three officers Maj R S Budhwar and two others. It was urged before the Supreme Court that initially Sep. Mahabir Singh and L/Nk Inder Pal Singh declined to take any step towards the commission of the offence but ultimately they succumbed to the "threat, command and influence (sic, command influence)" of their seniors. The Supreme Court commuted their sentence of death to life imprisonment, observing:

> "In our considered view in a case of the present nature which relate to a disciplined force as the Army, the offence committed by the officers who conceived the plan, was more heinous than that of the appellants who executed the plan as per their orders and directions. It is of course true that those orders being not lawful, the appellants, even as disciplined soldiers, were not bound to comply with the same, nor their carrying out such orders minimize the offence but certainly this is a factor which cannot be ignored while deciding the question of sentence."[54]

51 UOI v Major A Hussain, AIR 1998 SC 577 .

52 Lt. Col. S Duggal v COAS, AIR 1991 SC 1617 (para 31). The petition was decided along with that of Major S S Sodhi with same citation.

53 Ranjit Thakur v UOI, (1987) 4 SCC 611; r eviewed at 1989 (1) SL J 109 SC.

54 Mahabir Singh v UOI, AIR 1996 SC 2000 at 2005, disposing together the three appeals of Maj. Budhwar, Sep Mahabir Singh and L/Nk I nder Pal Singh.

The case of Capt Ram Kumar was one in which the allegations of the accused, though not directly speaking of command influence, were very close to such assertions. At his trial he objected to the presiding officer, Brig Bilimoria, and the junior most member Maj Sarabjit Singh Dhillon, on the ground of Brig Y S Tomar's influence being on them. Brig Y S Tomar Commander 330 Inf. Brigade, had directed Lt Col Badhwar the CO of Capt Ram Kumar to put him under arrest. Brig Bilimoria was a course-mate of Lt Col Badhwar who, along with Brig Tomar, had thrown a drink party on the arrival of Brig Bilimoria in station as presiding officer of the CM. Maj Dhillon, the other objected member, was from the Regiment of Brig Tomar and was also serving under his command in 330 Inf. Brigade at the time of the trial. The CM, however, rejected the objections and proceeded with the trial, since Maj Dhillon had stated that Brig Tomar or Lt Col Badhwar had never spoken to him about the case. Brig Bilimoria had also clarified that though he was in fact a course-mate of Lt Col Badhwar but was meeting him for the first time since 1953 when they were together at the Indian Military Academy as cadets. Based on these facts, Delhi High Court did not find any bias in the minds of the two objected officers against the petitioner and dismissed the petition. The appeal was also dismissed for the reason of the procedure followed by the CM being in accordance with the requirement of the related Rule 44.[55] The issue of unlawful command influence was most vigorously, though again indirectly, raised in the cases in which a revision of finding or sentence had been ordered by the confirming authority. In Capt Harish Uppal's case[56], for instance, it was contended that the confirming authority having no power to enhance the sentence cannot indirectly achieve that aim by ordering revision – the CM verdict should be unfettered. In the case of the petitioner, on the contrary, the revision order was in such terms that the CM was left with no alternative but to enhance the sentence, in violation of the principle of natural justice, from the initial sentence of cashiering to 2 years RI and cashiering. Thus, the revised sentence passed on the petitioner was not the free act of the court martial but one forced on them by the officer commanding (General Officer Commanding 33 Mountain Division). The apex Court, however, ruled that the confirming authority himself having power to mitigate or remit the punishment to any lower punishment, the exercise of power of ordering of revision would "necessarily mean that the confirming authority considers that the punishment awarded by the court martial is not commensurate with the offence and it should therefore be revised upwards. To object to this is to object to the provision of section 158(sic 160) itself.... Instead of baldingly stating so, the confirming authority in this case has given reasons as to why he considers that the punishment awarded to the petitioner was wholly inadequate .... The procedure established by law ... has been

55 Capt Ram Kumar v COAS, AIR 1985 Delhi 374 at pp 380-381 para 36.

56 Capt Harish Uppal v UOI, AIR 1973 SC 258.

completely followed in this case." In a comparatively recent case[57], the apex Court again reiterated that the ordering of revision by the confirming authority "could not be said to be a fetter on the exercise of power of GCM. It casts duty on GCM to reconsider its earlier finding or sentence but it was not obliged to change its earlier view". The Supreme Court also overruled the decision of Delhi High Court in Nb Sub Avtar Singh's case that where the confirming authority had given directions to the CM to revise the findings of not guilty into guilty, the order of the confirming authority was bad and liable to be quashed.[58]

In the context of command influence, it is important to distinguish a deliberate act of sabotaging the cause of military justice from an inadvertent or well intentioned act that may upset the balance between the command need to instill discipline and good order, or the compelling military interest of maintaining a fair, impartial system of military justice. The former is outrightly an offence while the latter is what would be termed as unlawful command influence that may turn the natural course of justice to the detriment of the accused or may, within the perception of a reasonable person, appear to have the tendency to be so. A confirming officer, for instance, may legitimately order a GCM to reconsider its finding or sentence or both under the current Army and Air Force laws but will upset the aforesaid balance when the order is couched in a language that impels the members of the court to effect a revision against the dictates of their conscience for whatever reason. Similarly, one should realize that every time the presiding officer tries to influence the court or the Judge Advocate gives unrecorded advice in a closed court, violating the requirements of the laid down procedures, "he puts a nail in the coffin of military justice, for the officers who agree to be influenced or even those who resist it, lose faith in the system. One may achieve one's immediate aim but it is at the cost of the system."[59] Command influence, however, condemnable, does not prompt judicial action in response where an appellate court is convinced beyond reasonable doubt that the proceedings are free from prejudicial influence.[60] To properly raise the issue of unlawful command influence, the accused must show some causal connection between the unlawful command influence and the prejudice or unfairness in the proceedings.[61] The concept of apparent unlawful command influence notwithstanding, generalized or unsupported claims of command control will not suffice to a justifiable issue[62] of the writ prayed for. Irrespective of this the interest of the

57 UOI v Capt A P Bajpai, AIR 1998 SC 1214 (paras 9,13 and 14).

58 Nb Sub A vtar Singh v UOI, 1989 Cr L J 1986.

59 USI Seminar Number Ten, op cit, n 50, p 32 (paper r ead by Col NS B ains)

60 US v Reynolds, 40 MJ 198 (CMA 1994)

61 US v Levite, 25 MJ 334 (CMA 1987), Cox J concurring.

62 US v Serino, 24 MJ 848, 852 (AF CMR 1987)

organization will demand that any precautionary measures required to prevent influence and any action in the nature of restoration or recompense to remedy the ill effect, in individual cases or in general, should not be spared. Under the US system plenty of guidance is available from judicial pronouncements in a large number of cases decided there on the contentious issue of command influence. In our case, the measures will have to be tailored to suit the requirement with a genuine concern for justice and clear understating that in the ultimate analysis, the command need is best served by fair and impartial administration of military justice.

8.3 Structure of Military Justice System

A marked feature of military justice is the presence of commander in every nook and corner of its structure. This has been so, as a functional necessity, ever since the Roman Empire enunciated the principle, "he who gives the orders sits in judgment."[63] However, the famous Ciceronian phrase 'silent leges inter arma' (the laws are silent amidst arms) coined sometime contemporaneously has constantly been on the ebb, though at a rather snail pace. As noted earlier in Chapter 1, CsM of the British model (from which originated several present military justice systems, including ours own) have succeeded to the name, and for the most part to the jurisdiction, of the Marshal's Court but their existing constitution is essentially different. Instead of a judge sitting alone, or with a single assessor, their modern form, which ensures the benefits of trial by jury, was adopted from the 'Articles and Military Lawes to be observed in the Warres' of Gustavus Adolphus[64].

(a) CM as an Ad Hoc Body

The very need of setting up a court martial every time a trial is to take place, as pointed out earlier, arises from the fact of the CM being an ad hoc body, with its constituting element selected on case-to-case basis and carrying an in-built potential of command influence being injected thereby in the decision making process. The result is that "Courts martial more closely resemble a judicial event than that which they are in reality - a court with power and jurisdiction to deal with the most serious of offences under the criminal law, including murder."[65] Justice Lamer, quoting from a decision of the Canadian Supreme Court that the "status of a tribunal must guarantee not only its freedom from interference by the executive and legislative branches of government but also by any other external force, such as business or corporate interests or other pressure

63 Francisco Jimenez y Jimenez, Introduccion al Derecho Penal Militar, Editorial Civitas,SA Mardid, 1987, p.178(Spanish original, free translation), cit in Federico Andreu-Guzman, Military Jurisdiction and International Law, op cit, n 24, p 153.

64 Simmons,The Constitution and Practice of Courts Martial, op cit, n 21, p 1.

65 Lamer,The First Independent Review ... of Bill C-25, op cit, Ch. 7, n 8, p 26.

groups"[66], recommends that "the most efficient way of dealing with the myriad of difficulties faced by military judges as they cry to contort the current system of ad hoc courts martial into an independent judicial institution would be to create a permanent Military Court."[67] It has often been suggested by some members of the Indian Armed Forces too that if military tribunals were established on permanent basis at Formation levels, it would not only save administrative problems involved in the convening of a CM on case-to-case basis but will also add to the quality of military justice by reason of the court functionaries and judges developing expertise. Q. 3.3 (b) was designed to seek the views of 200 respondents on the issue of CM as an ad hoc body as distinguished from static courts under the civil law. The data collected in response are reflected in Table 37.

TABLE - 37

Whether CM be Changed from Ad Hoc to Static Body

Ser No	Response	Response Frequency					
		M	J	G	A	Total	%age
1.	No Change	42	36	37	12	127	63.5
2.	Static Court Required	05	08	13	11	37	18.5
3.	Can't Say/No Response	03	06	00	27	36	18.0
	Total	50	50	50	50	200	100.0

As reflected against Srl 1 of Table 37, 127 (63.5%) respondents had no inclination for any change in the present state of CM being an ad hoc body. This figure included 42 respondents out of 50 (84%) from members category, 36 (72%) from JA category and 37 (74%) from general category. The number of accused category respondents, like the corresponding figure in the earlier tables, was comparatively much smaller, being just

66 R v Genereux, (1992) 1 SCR 259 at 283-284 (canada)

67 Lamer,The First Independent Review ... of Bill C-25,loc cit, n 65, pp 26, 28.

12 (24%) and 27 (54%) non-responsees. The additional explanations offered by various respondents in favour or against any change in the status quo may be juxtaposed in Table – 38 as under:

TABLE - 38

Explanation to Response in Favour or Against Ad Hoc Nature of Court Martial

Sr. No.	Ad Hoc Body	Permanent Static Body
1.	Should be no change since static courts-	There should be static CM which -
	(a) may bring in illegal practices as happens in the civil (b) will result into delay in disposal and accumulation of backlog which will be against the interest of the individual and the organization both (c) will be prone to unlawful influence (d) will lead to its members losing touch with their soldierly profession	(a) will bring in more experience on the part of members; hence static courts be there at least in cases for 3 years or more Rigorous Imprisonment (b) will cut down delay, expenditure and manpower wastage.
2.	No Change, the present system being more supportive to the idea of command which will be lacking in static CM.	Should be static courts who are commanders of troops as at present. This will make the members of the CM more responsible and accountable to the performance of duties in the administration of justice.
3.	CM and civil courts are two different systems which can't be equated; hence no need to follow the suit of static court as in civil.	Could be established to deal with cases like vehicular 'accidents' only.
4.		All courts were initially on ad hoc basis but since the army is not on move now all the time, there should be static courts

Various remarks of the respondents analysed and collectively put together in Table 38, both in favour of continuing with the present system of ad hoc system and those recommending the change to static CM, do represent trepidation of the concerned respondents. The respondents opposed to any change are apprehensive of static courts leading to degeneration in the standards of the dispensation of justice by favouritism and corruption, as in the civil judiciary at lower level static courts. This is in accord with the recent report of Transparency International on world-wide corruption. It slams the Indian judiciary, the lower tier in particular, with an accusation of a whopping sum of Rs. 2,630 crore being paid every year to the court officials and inappropriate influence on the impartiality of the judicial process, by such actors within the system as advocates.[68] Further, the respondents are also conscious of the command needs which, they feel, are better served by the present ad hoc system. A respondent equipped with the vision and experience of a retired High Court Judge seeks to render a mature advice of not going for a change simply with a view to bringing the military justice system at par with the civil system, since the two systems are meant to serve the needs which are conceptually different. This would remind one of General Sherman's words about the objects of the military law and of the civil law being pole apart[69]. However, it should be appreciated that the command need is not a static content. The improvement of the intellectual standards of an average soldier in comparison to that of his distant predecessors, the change in his aspirations brought about by socio-political movements of our times, and conceptual developments in the sphere of modern warfare, would call for rethinking on the contents of the command need itself. Moving with the time, the conditions of the military service have also changed from an ever hectic life to the probability of most of the men and women in uniform not seeing combat, leading to "an increased similarity between military service and skilled civilian occupational pursuits".[70]

Thus, where respondent G-106, a lawman, remarks that all courts were initially on ad hoc basis but now the army too should change to static courts, being not always on the move, he probably had in his mind a long spread change from the assemblage of the people of primitive communities enforcing old customs as courts of Shrines and Hundreds to the establishment of Royal Courts in England after the Conquest, or perhaps Panchayats at community or village level held in our system too in the olden days. This respondent also recommended that there should be static court with three permanent members, including one trained in law and two members appointed by the command authority.

---

68 Transparency International Global Corruption Report, 2007, cit in Dhananjay Mahapatra, "Rs. 2630-crore bribe paid yearly to lower judiciary", TOI, 26 May 2007, p 11

69 Supra n 29.

70 Joseph Di Mona, Great Court Martial Cases, op cit, Ch. 7, n 6, pp vii-xi

A case for establishing static military courts, even though not favoured by 63.5% respondents in the present study would otherwise find support in the structure of the military jurisdiction presently obtaining in several countries. In the military systems of Argentina, Belgium, Cameroon, Central Africa Republic, Chad, Chile, China, Columbia, Congo, Cuba, Italy, Peru, Spain, Switzerland, Uruguay and Venezuela, some or all the military tribunals are of permanent or static nature, with different designations in different systems, such as, Permanent Courts Martial, Standing Military Courts, Military Tribunals, Permanent Military Court, Institutional Courts, Territorial Military Courts or simply as military trial judges.[71] In some systems, they function independently whereas in some other systems they are attached to Formations, Regiments or Corps. Further, there is yet another pattern of permanent military jurisdiction. In some countries like France, Germany, the Netherlands, Norway, Austria, Japan, Sweden, Denmark, Slovenia, Estonia, the Czech Republic, Senegal and Guinea, where military personnel committing any offence in peace time are tried by ordinary courts of criminal justice which are all permanent courts. To cater for proper adjudication on the military aspect of the offence, suitable legal mechanism is provided. For instance, in the Netherlands, armed forces send a representative to sit on Full Bench Divisions, both at district courts and at courts of appeal.[72]

(b) Judicial Competence of Courts Martial Constituents

The concept of impartiality and independence of the judiciary postulates individual attributes as well as institutional conditions. Further, impartiality and independence of judiciary is more a human right of the consumers of justice than the privilege of judiciary for its own sake[73]. It is, therefore, axiomatic that irrespective of whether CM continues to remain ad hoc or made a permanent tribunal, the quality of the individuals who comprise a Service tribunal is of paramount importance. The attributes of such individuals may be examined from four different angles: (i) command related features; (ii) impartiality related requirements; (iii) professional qualities for a judicial duty and, (iv) personal character traits.

---

71 Andrue-Guzman,Military Jurisdiction and International Law, 2004, op cit, n 24, pp 175 (Argentina), 183 (B elgium), 186(Cameroon), 202-203 (Centr al Africa R epublic,) 204-205 (Chad), 210(Chi le), 220 (China), 235-240 (Columbia), 248-249 (Congo), 255 (Cuba), 291 (Italy), 311 (Peru), 332-333 (Spain), 338 (Switzerland), 363-365 (Urugua y) and 371-375 (V enezuela).

72 Ibid, pp 273-274 (France), 280 (Germany), 294 (the Netherlands), 295 (Norway), 157-159 (Austria, Japan, Sweden, Denmark, Slovenia, Estonia, Czech Republic, Senegal, Guinea)

73 United Nations Document E/CN. 4/Sub.2/1985/18, para 75.

(i) Command Related Features

At the outset it may be noted that all CsM under the Indian system, including Naval disciplinary court and the Army SCM, consist exclusively of officers subject to the Service Act under which the CM is convened, except in certain prescribed conditions[74] in which inter-Services command is inevitable, though it is normally preferable even then that the accused be tried under his own Service law. Further, the number of officers appointed and the length of service of each such member officer should not be less than what are required for the kind of the CM in question. Certain additional requirements of rank and services are laid down in the related Rules, Regulations and administrative instructions in respect of the presiding officer and the members vis-à-vis the rank and command status of the accused in the cases of officers. One of these requirements is that for the trial of an officer, the members shall be of a rank not lower than that of the officer accused unless, in the opinion of the convening officer, the officers of such rank are not (having due regard to exigencies of the service) available. Such opinion, when applicable, is required to be recorded in the convening order. Further, in no case, shall an officer below the rank of Captain be a member of a CM for the trial of a field officer.[75]

The issue related to the equation of ranks between the members of the CM and of the accused directly came for consideration in the case of Maj Charanjit S Gill, who was tried by a CM with the JA holding the rank of a Captain. A Division Bench of the Calcutta High Court quashed the convening order of the CM and the consequent verdict by the CM on the ground that "a Judge Advocate being lower in rank to an accused should not be able to take part in the general court martial proceedings". The apex court upheld the decision, observing that "a combined reading of rules 39, 40 and 102 suggests that an officer who is disqualified to be a part of court martial is also disqualified from acting and sitting as a Judge Advocate at a court martial. It therefore follows that if an officer lower in rank than the officer facing the trial cannot become a part of the court martial, the officer of such rank would be disqualified from acting as a Judge Advocate at the trial before a GCM. Accepting the plea to the contrary would be invalidating the legal bar imposed upon the composition of the court in sub-rule (2) of Rule 40." The Supreme Court then elucidated that the "purpose and object of prescribing the conditions of eligibility and qualification along with the desirability of having members

---

74 AR r 188; AFR r 158; NA s 7 .

75 AR r 40 (2), (3); AFR r 46 (2); NA s 97 (restrictions of rank in the case of president only since only the president is appointed by the convening officer and other members are chosen by the president). cf Army Headquarters Letter No. 35418/PS-1 Dt. 21 Jul 1971 about the rank of presiding officer at an Army CM. Please also see UCMJ Art. 25 (d)(1) stating that when it can be avoided, no member of an armed force may be tried by a CM any member of which is junior to him in rank or grade.

of court martial of the rank not lower than the officer facing the trial is obvious. The lawmakers and the rule framers appear to have in mind the respect and dignity of the officer facing the trial till the guilt is proved against him by not exposing him to humiliation of being subjected to trial by officers lower in rank….." The apex court also ruled finally that the "provisions of sub-rule (2) of Rule 40" giving discretion to the convening officer to appoint a member or JA who is lower in rank, subject to a condition that his opinion as to non-availability of an officer of the higher rank be recorded in the convening order, "are not mandatory" but rule 39 having no exception "is mandatory"[76].

No data collected in the present study disclose any infraction of the prescribed requirements of the rank held by the respondents. Table 39 displays the data as to the rank held by the respondents when they attended a CM for the first time as a member or a JA.

TABLE - 39

Rank of Respondents at Their First CM

Srl	Rank	Response Frequency			
		M	%	J	%
1	Lieutenant/-Captain	13	26	41	82
2	Major	21	42	09	18
3	Lieutenant Colonel	04	08	00	00
4	Colonel	08	16	00	00
5	Brigadier	03	06	00	00
6	No Response	01	02	00	00
	Total	50	100	50	100

76 UOI and another v Charanjit S Gill and others, AIR 2000 SC 3425 (paras 7, 16, 18 and 19). However, earlier in Manohar Lal v UOI, (1971) 1 SLR 717 (P&H), a retrial ordered by GOC-in-C after declaring the proceedings of the GCM null and void, for want of recorded opinion in terms of rule 42 (2), was held to be wholly illegal as the petitioner had no say in the constitution of the GCM and had suffered the trial. Please also see Capt Ravi Kumar v UOI, AIR 1985 Del 374, ruling that rule 40, sub rule (1) could be departed from when it was not practicable to comply with it. The question of practicability being a question of fact could not be allowed to be raised for the first time at an appeal.

The data disclose that 13 (26%) respondents attended their first CM trial as members while holding the rank of Lieutenant or Captain. These respondents would have attended CsM with accused persons either below the rank of officers or the accused officer below the rank of field officer in view of restrictions under AR r 40 (3) as discussed earlier. Rest of all respondents attended CsM in different higher ranks from Major to Brigadier as displayed in the Table. On the contrary, as many as 41 (82%) of the JA category respondents were Lieutenant or Captain when they first attended a CM and 9 (18%) were Major. None of the respondents from this category attended a CM in the rank of Lieut. Col. or above. This is due to the fact that the officers from the JAG's Department, who are appointed as the JA, start attending CM as JA soon after their joining the Department on passing out from the Officers Training Academy in the case of direct entry officers or on joining on attachment or their transfer to the JAG's Department from other Corps or Regiment. Generally, it is only before their promotion to the rank of Lieut Colonel that they perform the duty of JA. Thereafter, they are appointed as Assistant Judge Advocate General and go for a CM duty only for complicated cases or when the accused is holding a sufficiently senior rank of Brigadier or above. After the earlier referred case of Charanjit S Gill, any disparity between the rank of the JA and the accused is covered by a certificate by the convening authority in terms of AR r 40 (2). Such a certificate reflects a factually true position since the number of senior officers in the JAG's Department is very small, there being only one Major General and seven Brigadiers. Accordingly, at the trial of respondent A-208 who was tried in the rank of Major General, a Brigadier performed the duty of the JA. While appointing a member, however, there are no such constraints since wider choice is available for selection. Further, regulations insist that an officer will not be nominated as a member of CM even if otherwise qualified, until his CO deems him competent to perform so important a duty. The state of the length of service in the case of the respondents from the members and the JA category in the present study is reflected in Table 40 as follows:

TABLE - 40

Length of Service of Respondents at Their First CM

Ser No	Years of Service	Response Frequency			
		M	%	JA	%
1	01-05	08	16	28	56
2	05-10	07	14	12	24
3	10-15	13	26	08	16
4	15-20	08	16	01	02
5	20-25	09	18	01	02
6	25-30	04	08	00	00
7	No Response	01	02	00	00
	Total	50	100	50	100

The data at Srl 3 show that most of the respondents, i.e., 13 (26%) were within the service group of 10 -15 years when they were first appointed as members of a CM. The 9 respondents who were within the service group of 20 – 25 years when they attended CM were those who attended only one CM in their entire service career. On the other hand, 28 (56%) respondents performed JA duty for the first time when they were within 1 – 5 years service group, this was due to the length of service and ranks restrictions being not considered to be applicable for JA duty before Charanjit S Gill's case.

The data in both these Tables 39 and 40 bring out that the rank and service length requirements are generally adhered to while appointing members and JA for CM.

(ii) **Impartiality Related Requirements**

The impartiality related requirements of members and JA of CM would include disqualification on the ground of personal interest[77]. This being a seminal requirement for the performance of a judicial duty, even a very small or remote interest would attract disqualification. In a charge relating to theft of money belonging to an Officers' Mess or

77 AR r 39 (2)(e); AFR r 45 (2)(e).

Club, every officer of the Mess or the Club may be said to have a personal interest and is, therefore, disqualified to sit on a trial for such charge.[78]

This category would also include the requirement that a GCM shall be composed of, as far as seems to the convening officer practicable, of officers of different Corps or Department and in no case exclusively of the officers of the Corps or Department to which the accused belongs.[79] The intendment underlying Rule 40, as the Supreme Court perceived in the PPS Bedi's case, is to take "note of a possible bias or a personal bias on account of close association. If officers belonging to the same Corps have to try a brother officer, either there might be possible indulgence towards the brother officer or familiarity in working together might have bred some contempt that bias is inevitable. To decry any such possibility and to put personnel of general court martial beyond approach to make it unbiased and objective, composition of court martial is to be so devised by statutory rules to make it an ideal body having all the trappings of a court ... People drawn from different Corps and avoiding officers of the same Corps composing the general court martial would ensure an objective, unbiased body"[80]. Keeping in mind the vertical hierarchy with horizontal equation obtaining in the Army, the apex Court observed that in view of this intendment, the expression 'corps' should not be confused with 'army corps', the two having different and distinct connotation. Going through the relevant provisions, the Supreme Court concluded that "the expression 'corps' in R 40 must be given the same meaning as set out in sub-rule (3) of R 187 and it would mean that every battalion in the infantry and regiment in the cavalry would by itself be a corps". It will be relevant here to note that the British military law requires to select officers from outside the accused's chain of command while appointing members for his trial by a CM and also insists that certain persons who are likely to have a personal bias or to have formed an opinion about the case, by reason of their association with it at pre-trial stage or any previous trial, or have pro-prosecution inclination considering the nature of their appointment, are also disqualified for selection as members[81]. This corresponds almost squarely with AR r 39 (2) under the Indian military law. The US military law also similarly instructs against detailing, as a member of a CM, any person who is, in the same case, an accuser, witness, investigating officer or counsel for any party, or any person who, in the case of a new trial, other trial or rehearing, was a member of any CM which previously heard the case.[82]

78 MML Vol III, p 288, Note 3 to AR r 39. cf Major RS Cheema v UOI, Delhi High Court, W .P. No. 345 of 1985 wherein the High Court interpreted the disqualification to be r estricted to 'every of ficer', i.e., office bearer of the insti tute and not ev ery member of ficer.

79 AR r 40 (1); AFR r 40; NA s 97 (11).

80 PPS Bedi v UOI, op cit, n 4, pp 1427 – 1429 (Paras 25 and 26).

81 Rant, Courts Martial, Discipline and the Criminal Process in the Armed Services, op cit, Ch 5, n 24, p 9 (s 1.20). The Armed Forces (Court Martial) Rules,2009, have introduced no change in this position.

82 MCM, p II -47, Discussion under RCM 5 03: cf UCMJ , Art 26 (c)(1), (d)(1)&(2).

In the present study some respondents suggested the need to adopt the system of random selection for the appointment of members. However, as observed by an eminent US military jurist, in a similar context, random selection may not necessarily produce better results than a careful selection by an impartial convening authority determined to sincerely avoid the potentials of command influence. Further, a system of random selection of members may be administratively cumbersome and disruptive of operational commitments.[83]

(iii) & (iv) **Professional Qualities and Personal Character Traits**

In addition to the statutory provisions of AA and AR, there also exist certain administrative instructions issued with a view to ensuring that no personal bias is allowed to interfere with the need of an unprejudiced and fair decision by the members. Some letters of the Judge Advocate Generals from vintage years, for instance, cautioned against appointing any technical officer as a member[84] or any medical or veterinary officers as the senior most members of the CM.[85] In sharp contrast of this will, however, stand an expertise in legal or judicial field acquired before or after joining the Service. If some officer with such expertise, in the form of a pre-commission qualification or experience or a law course during service, is available, he should be preferred for appointment as a member of CM. As a part of general training of duty as member of a CM, an officer is required, on first joining a service, to attend CM for instruction at least for two years and for such further period as his CO may consider necessary for him to act as a member of courts martial and such an officer will not be nominated as a member until his CO deems him competent.[86] The need to appoint well competent officers as members of CM also figures in the US law which lays down that the authority convening the CM "shall detail members thereof such members of the armed forces as, in his opinion, are best qualified for the duty by reason of age, education, training, experience, length of service and judicial temperament."[87] In the present study Qs. 1.1(d) and 1.2 were intended to collect data on the legal qualification and experience of the member and JA category respondents, in military law, at the time of their first assignment at CM. The data collected is displayed in Table 41.

---

83 Brigadier General John S Cook e, "The T wenty-sixth Annual K enneth J Hodson Lectur e: Manual f or Courts Martial 20X", Military Law Review, Vol 156, June 1998, pp 1 – 29 at 25.

84 JAG of the Forces Letter No. 2081/2/43-44/AA dated 18 Oct 1944:

In the case of a tribunal such as a CM, I hold the view that any special technical knowledge which is required to be put before the tribunal should come from a specialist in the witness box and not from a member of the court. In principle, I do not like the presence of a specialist on the court, since his view, whether sound or not, will carry undue weight with his non-technical colleagues and will of course, not be known to the defence.

85 Army Headquarters New Delhi Letter No. 47588/JAG dated 29 Jun 1949.

86 RA para 457.

87 UCMJ Art 25 (d)(2).

TABLE - 41

Legal Qualification and Experience of Members/JA at First Assignment

Srl No	Legal Background	Response Frequency			
		M	%	J	%
1.	University degree in military law	00	00	00	00
2.	Univ. degree in law with study and experience in military law	09	18	50	100
3.	No degree in law but study and experience in military law	40	80	00	00
4.	No degree nor experience in law or military law	01	02	00	00
	Total	50	100	50	100

The data reflect that no respondent, whether from member category or the category of JA, had a university degree in Military law. This is due to the fact that military law is not included in the syllabi of the universities for the law graduate courses. In the olden days, even the UK universities did not have military law in their teaching scheme. Respondent M-19 passed LL.B in 1942 from Agra University and J-55, who was the first Indian JAG, after Independence, had passed out from King George College, London, in 1939 as a law graduate to become Barrister-at-Law from the Middle Temple in 1940 but neither of the two had studied military law before they joined the Army. However, 9 (18%) respondents from member category and all the 50 (100%) respondents from JA category had university degree in law. Further details of the respondents bring out that they had studied military law and acquired practical experience in military legal proceedings at various stages of their service career, from initial training as cadet to subsequent stages, including promotion examination, staff duty, recording of S of E, being member of C of I and so on. It may be clarified here that a prospective JA invariably attends CsM as an 'officer-under-instruction'. An officer-under-instruction sits with members of the court and remains present throughout the proceedings even in closed court, without actively participating in the proceedings. He is sworn or affirmed not to disclose vote or opinion of any particular member the same way as a member or JA. In the present study, 47 (94%) respondents from JA category had attended CM in such capacity. Two of the remaining three had attended CM as members before attending as

JA and one had the experience of civil courts along with the awareness of the CM proceedings as a witness.

(c) **Increased Role of Law Qualified Element**

It appears from the data analysed in the preceding sub-paragraph that almost all the respondents from both the member and JA categories were equipped to discharge their respective duties. Although legal awareness and functional experience may be no guarantee of their application in a given situation with judicial objectivity, those would certainly influence and urge the mind of the concerned individual in a positive way for a fair discharge of duty at a judicial forum. This would account for an increasing trend, since 1950, towards a process what John Gilissen, the Judge Advocate General of Belgium, describes as 'civilianization' of military courts,[88] moving towards a situation in which civilians and in particular civilian judges, have an increased role in the composition of military courts[89]. Even where there is no civilianization as such, the modern times have witnessed a trend of increasingly greater say being assigned to the members of the Judge Advocate Corps or Department in the dispensation of military justice or a greater number of civilian judges or law qualified members of armed forces being co-opted in the structure of military tribunals. Under the British military law, for instance, the JA is now a member of the CM with his directions being binding on the court.[90] He also participates in the voting for sentence though not in the voting for findings.[91] JAs at the Army and the Air Force CsM, under the British law, are civilian barristers-at-law, advocates or solicitors of not less than seven years standing and are appointed by the Lord Chancellor as full time Assistant Judge Advocate General to perform duty as JA at CM and other duties under the JAG. In a British Naval CM, the JA is a serving officer who has qualified as a barrister. At a CM, he wears uniform, unlike a JA at the Army or Air Force CM who wears the gown[92]. The position of military judges (JA equivalent) under the US system has been much elevated - he now presides over the CM proceedings and there is also a provision for a trial by military judge alone when requested by the accused[93]. In this

88 John Gilissen, "Evolution actuelle de la justice militaire – Rapport general" in Huitieme Congres International, Ankara, 11-15 Oct 1979, L ' Evolution actualle de la justice mil itare, 1981, R ecueils de la societe international de dr oit penal mi litare et de dr oit de la guerr e, VIII, B russels, Vol 1, (Fr ench original free translation) cit in Andrew-Guzman, Military Jurisdiction and International Law, op cit, n 24 pp 11 and 158

89 Francisco Jimenez y Jimenez, I ntroduccion al der echo penal mi litary, op ci t, n 64 , p 158.

90 Br AFA '6, s.154(a). The Armed F orces (Court Martial) R ules, 2009, which came into f orce on 31 Oct 2009, assign JA still greater say in CM proceedings.

91 Dennis L B ird, "The B ritish Court Martial", op ci t, Ch 7, n 246, p 49.

92 Rant,Courts Martial Discipline and the Criminal Process in the Armed Forces, op cit, n 82, pp 9 and 20 (ss 1.21and 1.50).

93 UCMJ Art 26. For similar provisions under the Canadian system, please see Lamer,The First Independent Review ... of B ill c-25, op ci t, Ch 7, n 8, p 18.

context a mention may also be made of certain other military systems such as Central African Republic, Chad, Columbia, Congo, Peru and Spain. Briefly speaking, the first four of these countries have developed, during the past two decades, military tribunals with a 3:2 ratio of military officers and civilian judges and the last two with a JA as member or presiding officer.[94]

In the present study, Q. 1.12 of the Interview Schedule had a direct relevance to the judicial competence of the CM members and JA. It invited from the respondents their suggestions as to qualification, disqualification or eligibility of a person to serve as a member or JA. The data collected through this question were also supplemented with the data collected through Qs. 2.12 and 3.6 calling for suggestions in general, respectively from the 50 respondents of the accused category and from all the 200 respondents. Out of the 200 respondents only 51 made recommendations with a bearing on the constituents of CM, some of them making more than one suggestion, the total of suggestions being 65. These are displayed in Table 42 below.

TABLE - 42

Suggestions for Improvement on CM Constituents

Srl No	Suggestions	Response Frequency	Percentage out of 65
1.	Members should be law qualified	17	26
2.	Bias Related Measures	08	12
3.	Structure Related Suggestions	09	14
4.	Impartiality Related Suggestions	03	05
5.	Selection Related Suggestions	02	03
6.	Experience Related Suggestions	05	08
7.	JA's power Related Suggestions	04	06
8.	Procedure Related Suggestions	06	09
9.	Civilian Judges/JA as member	07	11
10.	General Suggestions	04	06
	Total	65	100

94 Andre-Guzman, Military Jurisdiction and International Law, op cit, n 24, pp 202 -203 (Central African Republic), 204-205 (Chad), 235 (Columbia), 248-249 (Congo), 311(Peru) and 332-333 (Spain).

In Table 42, the maximum opinions (26%) are in favour of legally qualified or trained members being appointed for CsM. Bias related measures (12%) include suggestions that any one who has dealt with the accused in any earlier case should not form part of the CM, or that the officers having a reputation of being conviction oriented should not be appointed as JA, or that an officer convicted by a CM should not, as a policy, be detailed as a member[95]. Another suggestion of this nature was that the JA for a CM should be drawn from a different Service, i.e., at a trial under the Army Act, the JA should be from the Navy or Air Force. The suggestions connected with the structural aspects were of conflicting nature in some cases. For instance, while two respondents suggested that the JA should be the member of a CM and not merely an adviser, one respondent was of the view that justice could be imparted only if the JA was not allowed to sit next to the presiding officer or other members. Some other suggestions include that CM must comprise of members from JAG's branch only. One respondent also suggested that all CsM, trying an accused other than an officer, should have 40% representation of JCO in the case of an accused of JCO rank and of NCO in other cases. If it is not possible or suitable JCOs or NCOs are not available for appointment as members, the officers risen from the ranks should be appointed in their place. It may be noted here that both under the US and the UK systems, a WO may be appointed as a member of the CM trying any person other than a commissioned officer.[96] In fact the US and Canadian military laws allow even an enlisted person (NCOs and below) to be appointed a member of General or Special CM if the accused is an enlisted person. While the British law would not allow more than two WOs as members of a GCM and one as member of a DCM, no such limit is fixed under the US law. Military judge in the case of an American CM, however, has to be a commissioned officer.[97] Under the British law, there is no such express restriction on the appointment of a JA if he otherwise possesses the requisite qualification. The recommendations for the appointment of a JCO or NCO as a member of CM are also in accord with the spirit of earlier discussed Army Rule r 40 and general spirit of a CM being a trial by own peers, which spirit is best reflected in the provision of the regulation that where the accused has been the commanding officer of a unit, as many members as possible should be such as have held similar appointment.[98]

---

95 Please see n 46(e) for adverse view of the performance of permanently superseded officers as CM Members.

96 Br AFA '6 s. 155 and UCMJ Art 25 (b).

97 UCMJ Art 26 and RCM 501 (c).

98 RA para 460. This will also take care of an accusation that the CM system was all about "the officer class" sitting in judgment and w as "social snobbery , not justice"; please see Dr . John Reid' s (Labour) comments on Armed Forces Act, 1996, before a Special Select Committee of the House of Commons, as quoted in Dennis L B ird, "The B ritish Court Martial S ystem", op ci t, n 92, p 49.

If accepted, the recommended change will be a desired relief to respondents who have made such suggestions as "too harsh attitude of superiors" and that "the attitude of superiors must change sympathetically towards the offender to understand his problems" (A-158 and A-159). Further, on the issue of the constitution of the CM, J-100 would like experienced civilian judicial officers to be included in CM as members so as to exclude thereby the influence of superiors. Similarly, respondents G-106 and G-108, both lawmen, suggest that there should be semi-static courts with three permanent members, including one trained in law, and two members be later appointed by the command authority, along with the JA as a member with power to vote and be responsible for all the acts of the CM as any other member. It may be noted here that these suggestions are generally in accord with certain foreign military justice systems. The Armed Forces Courts Martial in Peru, for instance, are permanent bodies separate for each of the three Services but all subordinate in the hierarchy to the Supreme Council of Military Justice and each one consists of three officers of the concerned active service branch, a Colonel or Captain to preside and two other members with the rank of Lieut Col or equivalent thereto one of whom must be from the Judge Advocate Corps[99]. Some other suggestions include a suggestion from respondent J-72 that the minimum service of an officer to be a member of GCM should not be less than five years and according to J-80, it should be between 10-18 years. For JA, the minimum length of service, according to J-74 should be eight years. Presently, a GCM is composed of officers each of whom has held a commission for not less than three whole years. No length of service is prescribed for an officer to be appointed as a JA. Some suggestions were also made for certain changes to be brought about in the role of the JA at CM. These may, however, be best taken up while discussing the data on Qs. 3.3(b), 3.4(k), 3.4(l) and 1.7, which are all related to JA and JAG's Department.

Q. 3.3(b) sought the view of all the 200 respondents about the role of the JA as merely an adviser at a CM, with no power to decide any question of law or fact and his presence with the members deliberating on the findings in the closed court, under the AA and AFA. The data collected in response are presented in Table - 43.

99 Constitution of the Republic of Peru, 1993, Arts 139, 141 and 173 read with related Arts of Basic Law, i.e., Decree Laws no. 23201 of 19 Jul 1980 and no . 23214 of 24 Jul 1980.

TABLE - 43

JA's Role at CM - Whether any Change Required

Srl No	Response	Response Frequency					
		M	J	G	A	Total	%
1.	No Change	30	10	20	07	67	33.5
2.	JA be empowered to decide all questions of law	03	26	16	02	47	23.5
3.	JA be not present during deliberation on findings	07	00	02	02	11	05.5
4.	Combination of 2 & 3 above	05	08	08	12	33	16.5
5.	Any other suggestion	01	00	02	01	04	2.0
6.	No Comments/No Response	04	06	02	26	38	19.0
	Total	50	50	50	50	200	100.0

The data in Table 43 has close links with the questions of the JAG'S Department being amalgamated into one autonomous body so as to insulate CM process from non-judicial pressure and command influence as stated in Q. 3.4(l) and also with the present functioning of the JA. It is believed by some people that almost all decisions at CM are practically made by the JA, the members merely authenticating them and that there is much to desire in the style of functioning of the JA with overbearing attitude and inadequate professional competence. These three aspects formed the themes of Qs. 3.4(l), 3.4(k) and 1.7, the related data being displayed in Tables 44, 45 and 46 respectively so as to facilitate an integrated approach on the discussion on the issue.

TABLE - 44

JAG's Departments of the Three Services be Amalgamated

Srl No	Response	Response Frequency					
		M	J	G	A	Total	%
1.	Agree	01	02	12	15	30	15.0
2.	Partially Agree	02	04	08	08	22	11.0
3.	Disagree	45	40	27	13	125	62.5
4.	Can't say	00	00	03	04	08	4.0
5.	No Response	02	04	00	09	15	7.5
	Total	50	50	50	50	200	100.0

TABLE - 45

Decisions at CM Practically made by JA, Members Merely Authenticating

Srl No	Response	Response Frequency					
		M	J	G	A	Total	%
1.	Agree	01	02	11	17	31	15.5
2.	Partially Agree	01	05	04	02	12	06.0
3.	Disagree	43	38	27	15	123	61.5
4.	Can't say	00	00	08	07	15	07.5
5.	No Response	05	05	00	09	19	09.5
	Total	50	50	50	50	200	100.0

TABLE - 46

JA's Attributes as Experienced by Members

Srl No.	Response	Yes	No	Total
1.	Professionally Sound	44	06	50
2.	Poor Professional Acumen	02	48	50
3.	Pro-conviction	04	46	50
4.	Under Command Influence	03	47	50
5.	Thrusting own view on members	04	46	50
6.	Harsh, Rude, Power-drunk	04	46	50
7.	Unduly favouring accused	00	50	50
8.	Merely rendered advice, leaving decision to members	43	07	50
9.	Respectful, polite, firm	46	04	50
10.	Any other	01	49	50

The data in Table 43 reflect that a good number of the respondents, i.e., 67 (33.5%) was in favour of no change in the present position of the JA in a CM where, under the Army and Air Force laws, he merely renders advice to the court on legal issues and sums-up evidence for their consideration. On the other hand, 95 (47.5%) suggested different changes, 80 (40%) opting for the JA to decide all questions of law at an Army or Air Force CM the way his counter part trial JA does under the Naval system. On the question of the JA's presence with the members, during deliberation on findings under the existing Army and Air Force provisions (under the Naval law he is not so present), 44 (22%) voted for the Naval provisions in this regard to be adopted in the Army and Air Force systems. Interestingly and somewhat untraditionally in the Indian context, were however, the suggestions of four respondents. G-106, a high ranking officer in the Ministry of Law, and G-152, a retired High Court Judge, were in favour of the JA being made a member of the CM rather than merely being a legal adviser. This suggestion is in accord with the present position in the military justice systems of the UK, the USA, Spain, Peru and Canada as noted earlier.[100] Respondent A-207 goes still further and

100 Supra nn 90-95

suggests that the JA should be the sole judge in all matters. According to him, the members cannot do full justice, having no legal knowledge. It may be noted that the US and Canadian military justice systems do provide for a trial by military judge alone in certain cases.[101] It may also be recalled here that the Indian Naval law and the British military justice system in all the three Services allow the JA to hear and decide legal questions all by himself in the absence of the members of the CM[102]. Respondent M-30 suggests that the JA be empowered to decide all questions of law but not to remain present with members during deliberation on sentence though he may be present during deliberation on findings. The second limb of the suggestion is opposed not only to the existing position under the Army and the Air Force laws but also the position under the Naval law where a trial JA is present to assist the court in the determination of the sentence. However, in the context of the suggestion of M-30, it is interesting to note that sentencing, according to Wade and Phillip, is not essentially a judicial function though traditionally undertaken by judges.[103] On the other hand, a dissertation based inter alia on two surveys on attitude to sentencing brings out the need of eliminating court members from sentencing altogether and to turn the entire process over to military judges.[104]

An overall picture that emerges from the analysis displayed in Table 43 seems to carry a favourable attitude of the respondents towards the role of the JA in the military justice system, Most of the respondents would assign to him still greater role and responsibility under the Army law in line with that prevailing under the Naval law in India and some other military law systems. This should be due to the opinion they have about the professional competence of the JA and his style of functioning. Such an opinion may be reasonably inferred from the views of the 50 respondents who attended CsM as members and had thereby a first hand opportunity to watch from close quarters the JAs at the CsM attended by them. There 44 (88%) respondents stated to have found the JA to be professionally sound and restricting himself in 43 (86%) cases merely to rendering advice, leaving decision to the court. 46 (92%) respondents also carry an impression of the JA being polite, respectful and firm. The negative picture of a JA emerges only in 2 (4%) cases with poor professional acumen, in 3 (6%) cases with JA being under command influence and 4 (8%) finding the JA being pro-conviction, rude or power-drunk and thrusting own views on the members. Similarly, the data in Table 45 bring out that 123 (61.5%) of the 200 respondents disagreed with the statement that the decisions at CsM are practically made by the JA and the members merely put their seal of approval thereon

101 RCM 903(2) and Lamer, The First Independent Review ... of Bill c -25,op cit n 66, pp 34 and 35.

102 NA s 114(2); (British) Court-Martial (Army) Rules, 1997, r 43.

103 Wade and Phillips,Constitutional Law, op cit, n 20.

104 Major James Kevein Lovejoy, "Abolition of Court Member Sentencing in the Military", Military Law Review, Vol 142, 1994 , pp 1-66, at 3.

for the sake of procedural formality. It is a different thing that in response to another question, i.e., Q. 1.6 of the Interview Schedule, 29 (58%) of the 50 member category respondents admitted that their decisions were influenced by the advice of the JA. In fact, this has to be since the law requires the court to be guided by the opinion of the JA on any point of law or procedure that arises before it and that his opinion in such matters is not to be disregarded except for very weighty reasons.[105] Majority of the respondents, i.e., 125 (62.5%) out of 200 also do not see any thing objectionable in the existing system of each of the three Services having a separate identity of their legal department. Only 30 (15%) respondents voted for the amalgamation of the JAG's Departments of the three Services into an autonomous organization with a view to insulating the CM system from outside pressure and command influence. It will be relevant to recall here that 90 (45%) of the respondents, as reflected at Srl 3 of Table 38 had disagreed to the statement (hypothesis) put in Q. 3.4(a) of the Interview Schedule that the entire system of DPCM is fraught with command influence. Respondent G-116, a retired Lt. Gen. and now the Governor of a Union Territory was, however, of a view that the JAG's Department should be self- sufficient and be organized on the line of the High Court/Supreme Court set up in matters of appointment, leave and promotion and be divided into three wings managed by three independent JAGs, each regulating the advice at one of the three stages of pre-trial, at the trial and post-trial. Even though this suggestion is somewhat at variance from the view reflected in the responses of 62.5% respondents on the question of the amalgamation of the JAGs Departments of the three Services into one autonomous organization, it does seem to accord with the spirit of judicial independence insisted upon, in the modern times, in respect of all bodies related to the imparting of justice, whether under the civil system or military system. Further, it may be seen that the entire history of the office of 'judge advocate' under the British system, which may be described as the mother of the corresponding present legal support mechanism in India at the trial by CM, is marked with a constant struggle to secure judicial independence for that office.

8.4 Jurisdiction Related Attitudes

The literal meaning of 'jurisdiction' and its judicial concept in terms of original and lost jurisdiction having been explained in the preceding chapter[106], it may be noted here that the issue of the jurisdiction of the DPCM may be examined from three angles: firstly, as to who all are amenable to such jurisdiction, secondly, in what all circumstances, they are so amenable and lastly, to what extent such amenability attracts judicial reviews. The second aspect may be further sub-divided into the offences covered, the extent of

105 Supra Ch. 7, n 187

106 Supra Ch 2.2, Ch 7 , nn 102, 105-109 and r elated text.

the liability in terms of time and place, the procedural prerequisites and the available systemic relief channels.

(a) **Jurisdiction ratione personae**

Briefly stated, all uniformed personnel of the regular Army, Air Force and Navy are subject to CM jurisdiction[107] under their respective Services Acts, "wherever they may be". The expression 'wherever they may be' was interpreted by P & H High Court to cover, though slightly in a different context, i.e., while occurring in the Gazette Notification on persons deemed to be on active service, "not only persons actually engaged in performing duties of their respective offices on the date of commission of offence alleged against them but also the persons on leave at relevant time. Serving would mean holding employment as distinguished from actually performing duties of service."[108] In s 2(1) of the three Services Acts, the expression "wherever they may be", without the word 'serving', seems to exclude the consideration of the place of presence with still greater force. Other personnel subject to the Acts will attract liability for being dealt with under the concerned Act only in the specified circumstances such as being called up etc. in the case of Reserved Forces or Territorial Army. In the case of the civilians like camp employees, contractors, followers, press correspondents etc., their liability to DPCM arises only on active service, in camp, on the march or at a notified frontier post. However, on the entire Indian Army being placed on active service in 1962, it was decided as a matter of policy that the civilians might be dealt with under the Army Act only when they committed in forward areas specified serious military offences like the offences in relation to the enemy, mutiny etc. and civil offences in respect of which it is not reasonably practicable to have the offender tried under the ordinary criminal jurisdiction[109]. The military legal systems of the UK[110], Australia[111] and certain other countries like France[112] etc. have more elaborate special provisions, for the reason of their specific national requirements, to deal with the civilians accompanying their Armed Forces abroad and also to deal with their service personnel in foreign territories at times differently from their counterparts within their national frontiers. On declaration of martial law, the jurisdiction of CM is extended to the whole population of the proclaimed district so long

---

107 AA, s 2(1); AF A, s 2(1); NA, s 2(1).

108 Ajit Singh v State of Punjab, AIR 1970 P&H 351.

109 Army Headquarters, New Delhi, letter AG's Branch No. 54551/PS1 dated 1 Jan 1964.

110 Br AA, s 209; cf Armed Forces Act, 2006, s 51(1) for the Service Civilian Court to try any service offence committed by a civilian outside the British Islands.

111 Defence Force Discipline Act, 1982 (Cth) s 3 (1).

112 French Senate Document "No. 226-Senat, Session ordinaire de 1998-1999, annexe au proces verbal de la séance du 17 fevrier 1999" on webpage http://www.senat.fr/rap/a98-226/a98-2260.html

as the civil jurisdiction is not in force.[113] The Indian Constitution does not have a provision of authorizing proclamation of martial law[114]. However, the conditions of law and order in disturbed areas such as Nagaland, Manipur, Assam and J & K, and more particularly the menace of terrorism, sometimes provoke the question of desirability to extend the jurisdiction of CM process to such areas and to the people indulging in terrorist activities. On the other extreme would be the position of having all military offenders tried in ordinary criminal courts for any civil offences charged against them. The response on the former question will depend upon one's belief as to the efficacy of CM process as a justice delivery mechanism and justifiability of adopting it vis-à-vis human rights concerns. The response in the case of the latter question will have to take into consideration the needs of military discipline as well as the dictates of justice. Questions 3.4 (g) and (h) in the Interview Schedule were designed to probe the mind of 200 respondents on these issues. The data collected in response are presented in Table - 47.

TABLE - 47

Desirability of Extending the CM Jurisdiction to Civilian Offenders in Operational Areas and Foreign Terrorists in All Parts Of India or Having All Military Offences Tried in Ordinary Criminal Courts

Sr No.	Proposition	A	PA	D	CA	NR	Total
1.	Extension of CM process to civilians and terrorists	86	19	65	14	16	200
2.	All Military offenders to be tried in criminal courts	15	12	144	16	13	200
A = Agree PA = Partially Agree D = Disagree CA = Can't say NR = No Response							

The data disclose that 105 (52.5%) respondents agreed fully or partly to the proposition of CM process being extended to deal with civilian offenders in operational areas like J & K and foreign terrorists wherever they may be in India. However, 65 (32.5%) of them disagreed with the proposition, while 30 (15%) of them either expressed their inability to comment or simply remained non-responsive. Further details of the data (not reflected in the Table but available in the Interview Schedule) show that the

113 Simmons,The Constitution and Practice of Courts Martial, op cit, n 21, p 14 (s 34).

114 ADM Jabalpur v Shukla, AIR 1974 SC 1207 (para 535)

86 respondents, agreeing with the proposition, comprised in almost equal proportions of the members category (28), JA category (23) and general category (24) but in less than half of each of them (12) was from the accused category. Amongst the 65 respondents who disagreed, some of them did so on the ground of impracticability of the proposition in our present politico-legal set-up, while a few of them were emphatically against it, one of them explaining that the purposes involved in the civil and military jurisdictions are different altogether. It would be relevant to state here that in Peru, military courts do have jurisdiction over civilians suspected of "betraying the motherland", terrorism or offences against the Military Service Law. In wartime, the jurisdiction can be further extended by orders of the executive of the military commanders[115]. Similarly, Pakistan is also amending its Army Act to allow military courts to try civilians for offences like terrorism, abduction and so on[116]. This suggests that the disagreement with the proposition has nothing much to do with the merit of CM process as a justice delivery mechanism but is based on ideological or practical considerations. Such an inference gets support from the data in this Table on the other proposition of having all the military offenders tried under ordinary criminal jurisdiction. As many as 72% of the respondents, by disagreeing with the proposition, seem to have expressed their faith in the efficacy of CM process.

(b) **Jurisdiction ratione materiae**

Some of the respondents who partially agreed with the above discussed second proposition suggested that all civil offences should be tried by civil courts except when the accused is located at field or the offence was committed at field. As brought out earlier, the Indian military law presently excludes from the CM jurisdiction only three offences and that too in specified conditions[117]. The related provision is antiquated, having been first incorporated in the Indian military law in 1911 from its British model of the Act of 1881, which was further traceable back to the British Articles of War, 1765, which required military commander to turn over to local authorities, upon application by the latter, persons accused of "a Capital Crime, or having ... committed any offence against the Person or Property of Our Subjects."[118] Things have immensely changed over the years in other systems of military justice with the expanding horizons of fair play in action, the universal declaration of human rights and revolutionary developments in juristic thinking in the aim and reach of the justice mechanism. In several countries,

115 Andreue Guzman, Military Jurisdiction and International Law, op cit, n 24, p 314.

116 TOI, 2 Nov 2007, "Pak may try civilians in military courts".

117 Supra Ch 7.4(b), n 93.

118 The Articles of War, 1765, Section XI, Arts 1 and 2. However, Section XX, Art. 2 required a GCM to be convened by commanders to try murder, theft, robbery, rape and coining, if the British troops were located in a country or garrison with "no form of Our Civil Jurisdiction in force".

military jurisdiction has been abolished altogether and in several other countries it has been restricted to wartime or to troops located abroad or only to purely military offences or personnel other than civilians accompanying the troops[119]. In the USA, the Supreme Court ruled in 1969 that a soldier committing an offence which was not 'service connected' was "entitled to trial by the civilian courts" and "could not be tried by court martial"[120]. The decision was based on the reasoning that a CM is "not an independent instrument of justice but remains to a significant degree a specialized part of the overall mechanism by which military discipline is preserved" and hence "singularly inept in dealing with the nice subtleties of constitutional law." The decision was, however, overruled 18 years later on constitutional grounds.[121] The question as to whether or not a conduct that is an offence under civilian law be tried by a court martial was also addressed in some English cases.[122] It may be appreciated that the restoration of military jurisdiction to all offences, whether service connected or otherwise, is not in any way adversely consequential from the viewpoint of a fair trial in the present military justice environment of the USA. There are, in addition to the much progressive original provisions of the UCMJ along with the existence of the US Court of Military Appeals for Armed Forces, the Military Justice Acts of 1968 and 1983 which have greatly extended the role of the lawyers and the powers and responsibilities of the Judges, limiting the role of the commanders in the same proportion. The changes to the MCM have paralleled this process and drawn the rules of procedure and evidence closer to those followed in the federal courts. As a result, CsM under that system "looked a lot like their civilian counterparts."[123] On the other hand, ours is still an antiquated system. It would be but meet to adopt in our system a "service connection" criterion for the offences to be tried by the CM, all other cases being assigned exclusively to the jurisdiction to the criminal courts. The adoption of such an approach as also its rejection later, under the US system were both effected by the US Supreme Court interpreting differently the related provisions

119 In Japan, the Armed Forces personnel are subject to ordinary criminal law and ordinary criminal courts. In Germany, Austria, Norway, Sweden, Denmark, Slovenia, Estonia, France, the Netherlands, the Czech Republic and Senegal, military courts do not exist in peace time. Please see Andreu-Guzman, Military Jurisdiction and International Law, op cit, n 24, pp 158-159; (Australian) Defence Force Discipline Act, 1982, ss 101-101zc restrict military jurisdiction to only service offences.

120 O' Callahan v Parker, 395 US 258 (1969) at 265 and 274 . Mason CJ, Wilson and Dawson JJ, of the High Court of Australia held, similarly that tribunals can validly exercise judicial powers if the exercise is "sufficiently connected with the regulation of forces and good order and discipline of defence members"; please see Re Tracey, Ex parte Ryan, (1989) 166 CLR 518 at 545.

121 Solorio v United States, 483 US 435 (1987)

122 Johnson v The Queen, 4 CMAR 433 (CMAC 1987) in Canada, appeal dismissed vide (1989) 2 SCR 1073; Brown v The Queen, 26 CLR 2d 325 (CMAC 1995) in Canada; Re Nolan, Ex parte Young (1991) 172 CLR 460 (Australia).

123 Brigadier General John S Cooke, "The Twenty sixth Annual Kenneth J Hodson Lecture: Manual for Courts Martial 20X", Military Law Review, Vol 156, June 1998, pp 1 – 29 at 9.

of the US Constitution. There is little possibility of the same situations arising under the Indian Constitution, there being no division of powers to legislate for the Armed Forces and for other subjects as is under the US Constitution and under the British conventions[124]. In the case of India, after the constitution came into force, the power to legislate in respect of any item must be referable to an entry in the relevant list - entry 2 in List I: "Naval, military and air force ..." would enable Parliament to enact the Army Act to the same extent as to enact in respect of the jurisdiction of the Supreme Court and all other courts.

The wide jurisdiction ratione materiae presently assigned to CM process in respect of all but three civil offences attracts yet another constitutional angle. The civil and militarized civil offences being much more severely punishable under the military system than under the ordinary criminal jurisdiction, and that too while "a trial by an ordinary court would be more beneficial to the accused", as the Supreme Court observed in Ram Sarup's case, does this not violate the Fundamental Rights of military men, more particularly the rights guaranteed under Articles 14 and 21? The issue was examined in Ram Sarup's case itself, wherein the apex Court ruled that "each and every provision of the Act (AA) is a law made by Parliament and that if any such provision tends to affect the fundamental right under Part III of the Constitution, that provision does not become void, as it must be taken that parliament has thereby in the exercise of its power under Article 33 of the Constitution, made the requisite modification to effect the respective fundamental right".[125] The decision was referred in several subsequent cases[126] and was criticized in academic circles as "too broad"[127]. However, without going into the merit of the decision, it may be pointed out that the apex court, in PPS Bedi's case, held that "Article 33 did not obligate that Parliament must specifically adumbrate each fundamental right ... and to specify in the law enacted ... the degree of restriction or total abrogation of each right," and that "it is not possible to accept the submission that the law prescribing procedure for trial by court martial must satisfy the requirement of Article 21 because to the extent the procedure is prescribed by law and if it stands in derogation of Article 21, to that extent Article 21 in its application to the Armed Forces

---

124 Supra, related texts referable at nn 18 and 21.

125 Ram Sarup v UOI, op cit, Ch 7, n 119, pp 251 (Fundamental Rights) and 252 (trial by ordinary criminal court more beneficial).

126 Lt Col M L Kohli v UOI, AIR 1975 SC 612; PPS Bedi's case, op cit, n 4; Hazara Singh v UOI, 1982 Lab IC 208 (Del); R Viswan v UOI, AIR 1983 SC 658; Lt Col Amal Sankar Bhaduri v UOI, 1987 CLT 1 (Cal); UOI v L D Balam Singh, JT 2002 (4) SC 364; UOI v Ex Flt Lt G S Bajwa, (2003) 9 SCC 630.

127 O P Sharma, Military Law in India, op cit, Ch 1, n 4, p 290; Paramjit Kaur, "Article 33, Armed Forces and the Judicial Attitude: An Appraisal", op cit, Ch 3, n 35, p 179; USI Seminar Number Ten Report, op cit, n 50, p 31 (Paper read by Col N S Bains, retired, advocate, describes it as a dicta "too widely worded apart from the fact that this particular dicta was obiter".)

is modified by enactment of the procedure in the Army Act itself." This, however, cannot be taken to imply that the procedure so prescribed cannot be given a relook since the Supreme Court itself, despite rejecting the challenge to the prescribed procedure of the CM under the Army Act, on the ground of the violation of Fundamental Rights, did vigorously urge for a review of the current provisions of our military law. In that context the apex court stated with reference to the Army Act that "Three decades of its working, with winds of change blowing over the world, necessitates a second look so as to bring it in conformity with liberty oriented constitution and rule of law ..."[128] In the present context it should not be difficult to see the need of seeking inspiration from other progressive military justice systems striving to promote the cause of military justice without losing on command needs. Accordingly, it would be desirable to consider whether the twin grounds of the "proper discharge of their duties" and the "maintenance of discipline" in the case of the members of the Armed Forces, as perceived under Article 33 of the Constitution, do necessarily require that the Armed Forces personnel charged with civil offences should be tried in all cases by the CM, with its inherent limitations in comparison to a criminal court. In the absence of any manifest military command or discipline imperatives, this will discriminate military personnel from their counterparts committing the same offence and tried under the CrPC, in violation of the dictates of equality before law under Article 14, which otherwise cannot be "cribbed, cabined and confused"[129] in the matters of the right to fair trial which, after Maneka Gandhi's case,[130] is taken as a Fundamental Right of protection of life and personal liberty. It should be realized that though discipline is the soul of an army, as George Washington would say,[131] discipline is "not fear of punishment for doing something wrong but faith in the value of doing something right ... that discipline ultimately flows from within – it is that quality which motivates an individual and an organization to do the right thing even when the right thing is very very hard to do."[132] To do the right thing when the chips are down, depends upon morale. The unfailing formula for production of morale is patriotism, self respect, discipline and self confidence within a military unit, joined with fair treatment and merited appreciation from without ... it will quickly whither and die if soldiers come to believe themselves the victims of indifference or injustice.[133] Further, we should also realize that the commander's interest in morale and discipline in the

128 PPS Bedi's case, op cit n 4, p 1438.

129 E P Royappa v State of Tamil Nadu, AIR 1974 SC 555.

130 Maneka Gandhi v UOI, AIR 1978 SC 597 , para 56.

131 D S Freeman, Washington, 1968, p 116, cit in Brigadier General John S Cooke, "The Twenty sixth Annual Kenneth J Hodson Lecture: Manual for Courts Martial 20X" , Military Law Review, Vol 156, June 1998, pp 1 – 29, at 5.

132 Cooke, ibid, p 6.

133 General George Marshal, cit in Cooke, ibid, p 6, n 13.

unit, important as it is, is not the only consideration in deciding how to dispose case. Specially as our case load involves more common law crimes, the civilian society's interest in disposition becomes greater.[134] On ideological plane, in this regard, some jurists think that there is "no valid reason, from the moral or legal point of view, to remove from the jurisdiction of the ordinary courts, a member of the military who has committed an offence defined as such under ordinary criminal legislation".[135]

An appropriate decision on the issue would involve two questions; (1) whether or not the considerations of military discipline, the world-wide increased expectations from military justice and their relationship with the morale in general, and the interest of society in suitable disposal of civil offences charged against military personnel, demand that the offences which are triable by the CM as well as criminal courts should, in all or most cases, be allowed to be tried in ordinary criminal courts and (2) if the answer to this question is in the affirmative, what legislative mechanism should be adopted to effect the decision.

Under the first question, a comparative study by random sampling may be made in respect of the civil offences committed by military personnel and tried over a period of five years in the courts of ordinary criminal justice and the civil offences tried by CsM, through suitable questions covering the aspects of discipline, morale, workload, logistical arrangements, expenditure and manpower involvement, operational commitments and public relations probed through media reaction. Prima facie, the allocation of trial of all civil offences to ordinary criminal jurisdiction should be a preferable option from administrative angle. Much larger number of officers and men stands committed along with transport and accommodation, much bigger amount of financial resources is to be devoted for funding the stationery and preparing the court complex and much more attention and working time is to be directed to administrative arrangements, when a CM trial is to be held just for one accused person, irrespective of his rank, than the action to be taken, in terms of the requirements of the Regulations, when a JCO, WO or OR is charged before the civil court. In the latter case, just an officer is required to be detailed to attend the court to meet its requirements regarding any service documents etc. and necessary consultation with the concerned authorities to be made and other connected actions to be taken for the defense of the soldier as contemplated in the Regulations.[136]

---

134 Cooke, ibid, p 16.

135 Dalmo De Abreu Dallari, "Jurisdicciones nacionales y derechos humanos", in Jornadas Internacionales contra la Impunidad, 1993, op cit, Ch 5, n 161, p 213.

136 RA paras 417 and 421.

As for the military discipline, it may be brought out that there is perceptible change now in the attitude of all concerned about the extent to which the cause of justice may be compromised for the sake of discipline. Darling Committee constituted by the Army Council in 1919 to "Enquire into the Law and Rules of Procedure Regulating Military Courts Martial" had observed that the need of discipline is fundamental in any army. Without its enforcement "such forces are but a mob - dangerous to all but the enemies of their country."[137] This was in conformity with the old judicial pronouncements for non-interference in decisions of military tribunals assigning all consuming status to military discipline and military duty.[138] As late as 1977, Lord Denning MR, similarly stated, "our history shows that when the state itself is endangered, our cherished freedoms may have to take second place." The U.S. Supreme Court too conceded that the "fundamental necessity for obedience, and the consequent necessity for imposition of discipline, may render permissible within the military that which would be constitutionally impermissible outside it.[139] The advent of the modern times, with the soldiers more awakened to their place in democratic society and possessing higher standards of intellectual attainments as well as the socio-political movements of the new age, has, however, marked a gradual shift on the issue. Lewis Committee Report of the Army and Air Force Court-Martial Committee, manifestly reflect this shift, stating that "in the matters of legal safeguards, citizens should be no worse off when they are in the Forces than in civil life unless considerations of discipline or other circumstances make such a disadvantage inevitable."[140] The same thought process, albeit more relevant to the present context, is discernible in the remarks of Senator Wayne Morse:

> *I do not like this idea, in the new era in which we are living, of building up one justice system here for men in uniform and another one for so called free citizens. You cannot keep a civilian Army, in my judgment, under two systems of justice. Differences, I recognize there will be, but I think the military has gone entirely too far in the direction of a system of justice we cannot reconcile with what I think are some basic guarantees of a fair trial.*[141]

This may be further strengthened with the argument of amicus curiae in support of the petitioner in Solario v United States, who collected authorities from the UK, the USSR, Canada, Australia, New Zealand, Israel, Philippines, Pakistan, France and South

---

137 Darling Committee, Report of the Committee, Comnd No. 428 at para 108 (1919).

138 Sutton v Johnson, 1 T erm Rep 493 (1786); Da wkins v Lor d Paulet LR 5 QB 94 (1869).

139 Parker v Levy 417 US 733, 758 (1974).

140 Lewis Committee Report, Comnd No. 7608 at para 138 (1946).

141 Senator Wayne Morse at Hearings on s. 857and HR 4080 before Subcommittee of the Senate Committee on Armed S ervices, 81st Cong, 1st S ess 84 (1949) ci t in Co x III. "The Arm y, the Court and the Consti tution: The Ev olution of Mi litary Justice", op ci t, n 1, p 18.

Korea and submitted that "the experience of other countries teaches that a service connection requirement is workable and appropriate".[142] Further, this is based on another proposition that "military personnel because of their training and experience may be especially competent to try soldiers for infraction of military rules..... where an offence charged against a soldier is purely military, such as disobedience of an order, leaving post etc,"[143] but such expertise is apparently not needed to adjudge civil offences, which can therfore be tried in ordinary criminal court, with greater standard of a fair trial by trained judges and uninhibited time-tested trial procedure, except when the twin conditions of Article 33 require otherwise.

Keeping in mind all these considerations, if it is decided to pass on to the criminal courts exclusively or in most cases the jurisdiction of civil offences charged against soldiers, the right way to do so will be suitably amending or replacing AA s 70 and the corresponding provisions in the Naval and the Air Force laws. However, until this is done, a policy decision may be taken by the Central Government and promulgated through the Army, Navy and Air Force Instructions, for the general practice to be adopted along with the specific exceptions, if any, contemplated, for handing over the civil offence cases to criminal courts under AA s 125 read with AR r 197-A and the corresponding provisions of AFA and AFR, along with the Criminal Courts and Court-Martial (Adjustment of Jurisdiction) Rules, 1978. Since the Navy Act, 1957 has no provision corresponding to AA s 125, N Regs Pt II (s), reg 115(3) maybe suitably amended to put the decision into effect. Even a letter from the Services headquarters, on the pattern of the earlier referred letter issued to restrict the CM trial in respect of the civilians subject to the AA may meet the requirement for the time being. If considered desirable, an escape-route maybe left open for any particular case of civil offence to be tried by CM, as an exception, for the reasons to be recorded in the convening order.

(c) **Jurisdiction ratione loci**

Unlike the ordinary criminal jurisdiction, the sway of military justice system is not restricted by any considerations of territoriality. For the armed forces of a country, no foreign territory was inviolable before the advent of international law. Even in the present times, the limits are practically set only by the armed capabilities of the forces and the will of the commander, despite the existence of the law on the state liability codified by the International Law Commission. The various events of the Iraq War II leave little room for doubt in this regard. However, a speedy disposal of the misdemeanour or offensive act charged against a soldier, being a functional necessity, cannot wait for the offender to return to his national boundaries to be amenable to military justice. The

142 Eugene R Fidell, "A World-wide Perspective on Change in Military Justice", op cit, n 34, p 198.

143 Toth v Quarks, 350 US 11, (1955) at 17 – 18.

principle enunciated in this regard by the British law is that the military code operates against offenders, not as inhabitants of this or that particular district, but as soldiers in His Majesty's Service, having as such no stated commorancy; therefore His Majesty's Force maybe considered, however dispersed, as members composing one body, regulated by peculiar laws and altogether distinct from the province in which they are eventually stationed.[144] In the U.S. context, this was similarly stated by Chase CJ:

> "wherever our army or navy go beyond our territorial limits, neither can go beyond the authority of the President or the legislation of Congress."[145]

The general law accordingly developed is that when the armies of one nation enter, or pass through, the territory of another friendly nation, the laws of their own nation continue to apply to their forces. The privilege is extended to the armies in their permitted transit through foreign territory. In the event of a transit without permission, the entry would be per se unlawful but an offence committed there would be cognizable by a CM convened within the United States if the offender, at the time of the offence, was a member of an organized detachment or other force under military command and discipline. If the offence was committed while in a foreign territory in a private capacity, the jurisdiction will depend upon the nature of the offence. The offence against an inhabitant of the foreign country would be amenable to local law but an offence like unbecoming conduct would be cognizable under the U.S. law.[146] However, much will depend upon the understanding between the governments of the concerned countries. The determination as to which nation, state or agency will exercise jurisdiction is a matter for the nations, states and agencies concerned and is not a right of the suspect or accused. Under international law, a friendly foreign nation has jurisdiction to punish offences committed within its borders by members of a visiting force, unless expressly or impliedly consents to relinquish its jurisdiction to the visiting sovereign. The procedures and standards of determining which nation will exercise jurisdiction are normally established by treaty[147] such as NATO Status of Forces Agreement, 19 Jun 1951. The provisions of the Geneva Convention are also to be followed in such matters whenever applicable.[148] The basic provision on the subject, however, is in the Services Act which states that any person subject to this Act who commits any offence against it may be tried and punished for such offence in any place whatever.[149] Under the present project

144 Sir Charles Gould, in 1753, cit in Clode, Military and Martial Law, 1874, p 103.

145 Ex parte Milligan, 71 US 2 (1866): 4 Wallace 123(141).

146 Winthrop, Military Law and Precedents, op cit, n 17, p 81.

147 RCM 201(d)(3) and discussion thereunder. cf Wilson v Girard, 354 US 524 (1957).

148 Geneva Convention Relative to the Protection of Civilian Persons in Times of War. of 12 Aug 1949, Articles 4, 64 and 66.

149 AA, s 124; AFA, s 123; NA, s 78(1).

the case study of the trial of Acting Naik/Dvr MT Baldev Singh briefly discussed at 7.4(d) represents the legal position of the jurisdiction ratione loci.

(d) **Jurisdiction ratione temporis**

Under the three Services Acts, jurisdiction ratione temporis stands distributed on two counts which may be broadly conceived as parts of the jurisdictions ratione persone and ratione materiae respectively. Under the former, a CM shall have no jurisdiction to try a person who has ceased to be subject to the concerned Service Act, unless the trial commences within the statutorily fixed time duration computed from the date he has so ceased. Under the latter, every person subject to the Act carries the time-bound liability of trial by CM for all offences under that Act. The time limitation in both of the cases, however, excepts certain specified offences. In a case which attracts both the time limitations, the liability will end on the expiry of either of the two limitations, whichever terminates earlier.

(i) **Limitation for Post-release Liability**

Originally the limitation period of six months was uniformly applicable, under all the three Services Acts, for trial to commence after a person had ceased to be subject to the Act. Under the AA, duration of the liability has, however, been since increased to three years.[150] Further, in computing such period of three years, one would have to exclude the time during which the offender has avoided arrest by absconding or concealing himself, or where the institution of the preceding in respect of the offence has been stayed by an injunction or order, the period of the continuance of the injunction or order, including the day on which it was issued or made and the day on which it was withdrawn, shall also be excluded.[151] The amendment seems to have been inspired by the cases like that of Maj Gen ML Yadav[152] who attempted to dodge the commencement of his trial within the period of limitation by going into hiding and resurfacing on the expiry of that period only. However, it may be appreciated that the subjection of an individual to military law is need-based and it depends upon the individual having surrendered to it by joining the military forces. On his release, neither the military need nor his surrender to the subjection of the military law survives anymore[153]. His trial by

150 Supra Ch 7, n 146.

151 Supra Ch 7, n 135.

152 UOI v Maj Gen Madan Lal Y adav, op cit, Ch 7, n 57, para 21.

153 R v Governor of Warmwood Scrubbs Prison ex parte Boydell, (1948) 2 KB 93; habeas corpus writ issued to discharge on ground of being no more subject to military jurisdiction when tried 3 months after release. However, the writ was refused in R v S ecretary of State f or War, ex parte Price, (1949) 1 KB 1; where Price was on release leave at the time of trial.

the CM after his release may be justified only as a deterrent or retribution. We have authority of the Supreme Court about "retributive justice being relegated to the uncivilized days,"[154] and of a Chief Judge of the United States Army Court of Criminal Appeals, who urged that "the coercive power of the law requires only the minimum, the lowest common denominator: it impels the lazy, the indifferent, and the cowardly to do what is required of them on the battlefield, in order to avoid defeat and disaster."[155] Pitted against the outmoded considerations is the imperative of having a released soldier restored as soon as possible to his full status as a member of the civilian community and that in keeping with that status, he should be amenable only to its law.[156] In such a context what Winthrop argues is most pertinent:

> "... the general rule is that military persons - officers and enlisted men - are subject to the military jurisdiction so long as they remain such; that when, in any of the recognized legal modes of the separation from the Service, they cease to be military and become civil persons, such jurisdiction can, constitutionally, no more be exercised over them than it could before they originally entered the army, or than it can over any other members of the civilian community."[157]

In any case, a period of six months should be good enough for the military authorities to sort out the matter and take appropriate decision in this regard, without extending the post release limitation period of trial. This approach will also accord with original policy adopted in such matters, under which it was emphasized that the provision of AA s 123 be involved only when prima facie case had been established against the offender and that it was "not desirable to keep a retired officer or discharged soldier on tenter hook merely because there is an enabling provision in the Act".[158] If it has not been possible for the Service authorities to investigate the matter and commence trial within six months from the release of the accused, the offence may be tried under the ordinary criminal jurisdiction or the case may be closed where the offence is not very serious or is of purely military nature not triable by a criminal court, in the latter case the military needs existing no more as discussed earlier. Serious offences of desertion, fraudulent enrolment and mutiny are, in any case, triable at any time within the framework of the provisions and so was the case ealier too.

---

154 PPS Bedi's case, op cit, n 4, p 1438.

155 Cooke, "The Twenty-sixth Annual Kenneth J. Hodson Lecture: Manual for Courts-Martial 20x" op cit, n 132, p 6.

156 Bernard Starkman: "Canadian Military Law: The Citizen as Soldier", Canadian Bar Review, Vol 43, (1965), p 420 at 422.

157 Winthrop, Military Law and Precedents, op cit, n 17, p 89 (s 118)

158 Army Headquarters Letter AG No. 01086/PS 1 dated 03 Sep 1976.

It may be relevant to note here that in the British law there has been a gradual softening of the continued liability for a pre-release offence. An express provision was first made in the British military law by the Mutiny Act, 1815 for the trial and punishment of officers and soldiers after they had ceased to be subject to the Act provided the charges were delivered within 6 months from the date of so ceasing and within 3 years from the commission of the offence. However, there is also an earlier record of Lord George Sackville having been tried by a GCM on 27 Feb 1760, at his repeated request to give him an opportunity of justifying himself before a CM. The trial took place within 6 moths from his dismissal on 10 Sep 1759 for his conduct at the battle of Minden as Lieut Gen. He was eventually found guilty of disobedience of orders and adjudged to be "unfit to serve His Majesty in any military capacity whatever." The sentence was executed by the King (George II) erasing with his own hand the name of Lord Sackville from the roll of Privy Councillors.[159] By the times of Pratt, the limitation period of 6 months was reduced to 3 months.[160] However, Armed Forces Act, 2006 lays down a time-limit of 6 months for charging a person formerly subject to service law.[161] Finally, it is also worth mentioning that the US Supreme Court held invalid a provision in Art 3(a) of the original UCMJ which purported to provide jurisdiction for the CM to try persons for certain crimes committed while in military status but who had since been discharged.[162] The new provision of UCMJ s 3(a) provides for jurisdiction of CM in respect of a person who <u>is</u> subject to the code and who <u>had</u> committed an offence within the meaning of the code while formerly so subject and is thus not relieved from amenability to such jurisdiction by reason of a termination of that person's former status. His liability is revived subject to time limitation under Art 43 of UCMJ which varies in different circumstances from 6 months (termination of hostilities) to 5 years. Winthrop, however, is of the view that discharge etc. after offence during the first enlistment, without trial, should be taken as a waiver of the right to prosecute him therefor and a re-enlistment into the army would not revive the jurisdiction for past offences, but the same would properly be considered as finally lapsed.[163] In accord with such a view, the British and the Indian military laws, have no provision for such revival after the prescribed period of continued liability is over.

---

159 Simmons, The Constitution and Practice of Courts Martial, op cit, n 21, pp 23, 24 (s 57).

160 Lt Col Sisson C Pratt,Military Law – Its Procedure and Practice, op cit, Ch 1, n 10, p 44; cf BrMML, 1951, p 377. Note 2(b) to AA s 158 and please see f or Rant, Courts Martial, Discipl ine and the Criminal Process in the Armed Services, op cit ch 3, n 21.

161 (British) Armed F orces Act, 2006, s 57 .

162 Toth v Quarks, 350 US 11(1955).

163 Winthrop,Military La w and Pr ecedents, op ci t, n 17 , p 93 (s 124).

(ii) Time Limit for Trial of Offences

A three year limitation as to time for the trial of offences under the military law had been introduced by the Mutiny Act of 1760[164]. The period for which the accused absented himself, or during which he had not been amenable to justice for the reason of some other manifest impediment, were to be excluded from such period of limitation under section 97 of the Mutiny Act in force during the times of Simmons, who further observes, in the context of Lieut Col James Blake, that the concurrence or acquiescence of the prisoner would affect neither the law of the question nor the jurisdiction of the court.[165] The related data collected in the present study and Winthrop's view along with the Indian military law provisions and judicial pronouncements have been examined earlier.[166] It may be noted that AA s 122, as amended in 1992, has widened the reach of the provision. The three year period of limitation will now commence not only on the date of the offence but also, in the alternative in certain cases, on the first day on which the offence comes to the knowledge of the person aggrieved by the offence or to the authority competent to initiate action, or the first day on which the identity of the offender is known to such person or the said authority. Such an open-ended scope for the commencement of the period of limitation is antithesis to the very objective of the concept of limitation, leaving much room for its misuse to the disadvantage of the accused. It would very often encourage laxity in the efforts to speed up the pre-trial investigation, with such consequent ill effects as compromising the need to secure evidence, lengthening the misery of the accused, extra load on administrative agency, embarrassment to the decision making military authorities and enhancing the potential for the miscarriage of justice, adversely affecting thereby the purpose of CM process itself. This is what happened in the case of respondent A-207 who, a very senior officer of the rank of Maj Gen., was tried on 18 charges out of which as many as 15 had the obnoxious clause to justify a trial to be held on 23 Nov 2005, more than four years after the offences allegedly committed on some unspecified dates between April 2001 and January 2003. The trial culminated into the accused being found not guilty of 11 of those charges and sentenced to 3 year service for pension along with severe reprimand. It is possible to imagine, at least theoretically, a case of GCM trial ten or even more years after the commission of the offence, under this open ended limitation period, simply to settle a score against the accused, though the charge involved be of a trivial nature, contrary to the legislative intention of excluding only serious offences like desertion or mutiny from the operation of the time limitation. It is not difficult to think of such frivolous use of the CM forum in an organization like armed forces where CsM were essentially "the backbone of

---

164 The Mutiny Act, 1760, (1 George III, c. 6) s 71.

165 Simmons,The Constitution and Practice of Courts Martial, op cit, n 21, pp 23-24.

166 Ch 7.4 (e) (ii).

discipline" but could also be "outlet for jealousies and animosities". Col Butler, a Pennsylvania Revolutionary War Veteran, was tried by a CM in 1803 for disobedience of General Wilkinson's order that he cut his hair and was sentenced to a reprimand on conviction. He, however, still refused to cut his "queue" and was again court-martialled in 1805. This time he was sentenced to a year's suspension of command, pay and allowances. Before the sentence went into effect, however, he died of yellow fever, still wearing the queue.[167] Reverting to the context of stretching of the limitation period, it may be noted that while seeking an exception to 2 year limitation under "manifest impediment" clause in an old American case, the Government was held to be estopped from claiming that because "not informed of an offence, it could not prosecute".[168] Another case where the prosecution had similarly claimed the benefit of this clause on the ground that the Government did not know of the offence early enough to bring the accused to trial within two years (the limitation period under the then US Articles of War Art, 103), the reviewing authority General Mc Dowell held, "The accused cannot be deprived of his legal right by the inattention, delay, neglect, oversight or any other fault or failing on the part of the Government. He is not responsible for them and cannot be made to suffer by reason of them."[169] Attorney General Black in that context said that the party, if he is to be tried, is entitled to a "trial within the two years; he cannot be deprived of that right at the option of those who have the power to try him. If ... his superior officers could create impediment which would justify a delay beyond the prescribed period, the time of limitation would be a mere matter of discretion".[170] Winthrop, while opposing the relaxation of the limitation provision for desertion in peace, emphatically argues that "... it is business of the Government, supplied as it is with the forces and facilities for the purpose, to follow up a deserter with such delegence as to preclude, if practicable such a result.[171]

It may be seen from the discussion in the foregoing, that the provision of limitation which, generally speaking, is military justice specific, has lately been subjected to dilution under legislative innovations and executive practice. This has been done ignoring the historical development of the provision and the custom of the Service established over the centuries long stretch of time. The attitude reflected in the entire exercise is opposed to the spirit of our times marked with great emphasis on the preservation of human rights and fair play in imparting justice.

---

167 Coffman, The Old Arm y, A Portrait of the American Arm y in Peacetime, 1784– 1898, 1986, p 32, ci t in Cox III, "The Arm y, the Courts and Consti tution: the Ev olution of Mi litary Justice", op ci t, n 1, p 8

168 US v Kirkpatrick, 9 Wheaton 720.

169 GO 33, Dept. of the East, 1869.

170 Attorney General Black, 9 Opins 184 , cit in Winthrop , Military Law and Pr ecedents, op cit, n 17 , p 257.

171 Winthrop, ibid

8.5 Residual Procedural Matters

The pre-trial procedures and the procedural requirements of CM trials have been covered in the preceding chapters. However, greater elaboration seems to be required in respect of certain procedural matters of CM process which are its peculiar characteristic features.

(a) Procedure of Findings

The finding of any judicial forum, being its end product should be, not only clear but also fully convincing in its procedure and form. However, in the case of a CM, there are grave limitations in both these respects. Being designed to meet the specific needs of the Service discipline, the CM is composed of commanders who are expected to be most suited to judge the disciplinary aspect. Nonetheless being lay military officers with no special qualification or training to perform a judicial duty, they need the guidance of a lawman so as to avoid any slip on the requirements of justice. Since the finding is eventually a reflection of the mind of the commanders on the liability of the accused, it has to suffer the absence of any rationalization of the facts, though still obliged to adopt the modicum of a format carrying a judicial verdict. For all these considerations, the military law required the JA to be present with the members in the closed court during their deliberation on the finding and the finding being "recorded simply as a finding of 'Guilty' or of 'Not guilty'". As noted earlier from the data at Srls. 1, 3 and 4 in Table 43, as many as 67 (33.5%) out of the 200 respondents favoured no change in the current provision of the Army and the Air Force Rules requiring the JA to be so present, while 22% recommended that the JA should not be present. It may be brought out here that, under the British system, the role of the JA at an early 17th century CM trial was of a judicial nature but the Articles of War, 1673 required the JA to "inform the court and prosecute" and thereafter during the 18th century and the early part of the 19th century, he performed this duty, combining at the same time with it the function of a legal adviser. In the latter capacity, he was required to retire with the members when they considered finding and sum-up in closed court. Even after the Articles of War omitted the requirement for the JA to prosecute in 1929, he continued to retire with the court for finding until Sep 1947, when the Rules of Procedure were altered, as a result of the recommendation of the Lewis Committee to exclude the JA from the court's deliberations on findings. The current provisions of the (British) Courts Martial (Army) Rules, 1977 r 70(1) lay down that after the summing-up, the JA "shall withdraw and the court shall close to deliberate on its finding on each charge before it". Similarly, RCM 921(a) of MCM – 2000 states that after the military judge has instructed on findings, "the members shall deliberate and vote in a closed session. Only the members shall be present during deliberation and voting." This is based on UCMJ Art 39(b) requiring that when the members of a CM deliberate or vote, only the members may be present. Our own NA s 116(2) also unambiguously mandates that the trial JA "shall not sit with the court, when the court is considering the finding". It may be of some interest to note here that Lord Roskill Committee, appointed in the UK in 1987 to consider how the trial of fraud cases could be conducted, favored a judge sitting with lay members down from a panel of persons experienced in the world of business and finance. The committee inter alia recommended that the judge and lay members should retire to consider their decision without any prior public direction from the judge on the law, and that, once they have reached their decision, he should express it in a publicly and fully reasoned judgment of the court. The judge should be the sole judge of law, but on matters of fact, each would have an equal vote, and a majority of any two (read "absolute majority" in the context of CM in terms of AA s 132) could suffice for[172] conviction. A CM trial being the trial by a specialist forum like the one envisaged in the Roskill Committee Report, these observations of the committee should be relevant for consideration in the present context, more particularly when the majority of respondents in the present study favour the current procedure to continue without any change. There should be really no valid ground for suspecting the JA's bona fides during the deliberation on the findings. It is only the members, and not the JA, who would be, if at all, interested to tilt the balance in favor of conviction for the reason of their concern, genuine or misplaced, for the effect of finding on military discipline in general or on the state of discipline in the concerned unit. The JA with the legal training and comparatively being at a greater distance from such concerns, is likely to be more objective in his approach. Further, by adopting desired measures for judicial independence of the JAG's Department, as suggested earlier in the context of the question on amalgamation of the JAG's Departments of the three Services into an autonomous body, any probability of the JA unduly influencing the findings of the court during deliberation by the members may be ruled out altogether. On the other hand, the JA's presence during such deliberation may work as a deterrent against any senior member trying to exert influence on any junior in such matters, or any misgiving on any facets of law or evidence likely to adversely affect the cause of justice, may be avoided by his presence there.

The other aspect of the matter relates to the format of the finding. The question of a reasoned decision by CsM has been discussed earlier at 7.11. Response was sought from all the 200 respondents included in the present study on the desirability or otherwise of the verdict of CM to be given in the form of a fully reasoned decision on the pattern of the judgments of a civil court. The data collected may be reflected in Table - 48.

172 Fraud Trial Committee Report, Chairman, Lord Roskill, PC (HMSO, 1986) para 8.69

TABLE - 48

Whether CM Verdict be given on Pattern of Criminal Court Judgments

Srl No	Response	Response Frequency					
		M	J	A	G	Total	%
1.	Agree	17	16	23	19	75	37.5
2.	Partially Agree	14	14	11	05	44	22.0
3.	Disagree	17	16	11	01	45	22.5
4.	Can't say	00	00	05	16	21	10.5
5.	No Response	02	04	00	09	15	07.5
	Total	50	50	50	50	200	100.0

The majority of the respondents (119 or 59.5%) agreed (75, i.e., 37.5% fully and 44, i.e., 22% partially) that the CM verdict should be given in the form of a fully reasoned decision in the form of the judgment of a civil court of ordinary criminal jurisdiction. The traditional view has been that CsM are not expected of giving a reasoned decision and yet brief reasons are now required under the amended AR r 62(1). In practice the requirement is met only half-heartedly. Possibly this may be due to the responsibility for the recording of such reasons being with the presiding officer who is a lay military officer. In their additional remarks, the respondents have generally tried to emphasize the need of a CM giving the reasons for its decision which, within its limitations of comprising of lay commanders, should be easily understandable and explicit, though may not follow the pattern of a judgment of the ordinary criminal court. However, some of the respondents having suggested the desirability of co-opting the JA as a member with full voting rights were of a view that fully reasoned decision should then be given by a CM so constituted. This will be in line with the suggestion of Roskill Committee Report in the context of trials of fraud cases brought out earlier that the judge constituting a quasi judicial set-up within lay businessmen members should give a fully reasoned judgment. In the case of a CM, the JA should be able to write a majority judgment on the pattern of ordinary criminal court, with a little training at the Institute of Military Law, Kamptee, in liaison with a civil judicial officers academy, if need be. In the event of the JA not being with the majority, he should be expected to write a dissenting judgment in detail and the majority decision should carry brief reasons as at present. The only legal impediment in such a course would be that the JA will be disclosing his own vote or opinion in that case, in violation of his oath currently taken by him. The prescribed wordings of the oath will, therefore, have to be suitably modified to meet such eventualities.

(b) **Sentencing Procedure**

A reasoned judgment at the CM trial discussed in the foregoing will cover not only the finding but also the sentence. In respect of the sentence, however, yet another debatable question is as to who, whether the lay members or legally trained JA/military judge, would be a better choice for sentencing in the best interest of military justice. For this, the CM sentencing is often compared with jury sentencing which in some circles, is criticized as "sanctified guessing"[173]. Further, to gain insight into the current attitudes and opinions of those affected by the sentencing process, the relevant data were collected by Major James Kevin Lovejoy from 277 respondents of such categories as defense counsels, prisoners, law course students, convening officers, military judges and staff JAs and also took into consideration the related data from the survey conducted by Advisory Commission to the (US) Military Justice Act of 1983. He found that with the focus of sentencing having shifted in military justice from simply retribution for the offence to an individualized sentence, and the goals expanded to include discipline, individual and general deterrence and rehabilitation of the individual offender, additional information about the accused becomes necessary for the sentencing body to consider. This increases in the same proportion the risk that the lay court members, untrained in the laws and the principles of sentencing, will, during the sentencing deliberations, be prejudiced unduly by what they hear, or will not know how to properly account for the information. In view of this, he reached a conclusion that the military judge, who had attained his present heightened status in the American military justice system, through a process of transformation from court JA to law officer and was now the focal point of the CsM, would much more effectively meet the challenges of the present day requirements of military sentencing, if the court members role in the sentencing is eliminated altogether and the sentencing process is turned over exclusively to military judges.[174] He is supported by the view expressed by General Samual T Ansell, the father of modern American military law, who had suggested that the military court JA determine and impose an appropriate sentence.[175] The same view is ascribed to Maj Gen Kenneth J Hodson, the Judge Advocate General of the U.S. Army, 1967 to 1972 as

173 Charles W Webster, "Jury Sentencing – Grab-Bag Justice", SW L J, Vol 14, 1960, p 227.

174 Major James Kevin Lovejoy, "Abolition of Court Member Sentencing iry, op cit, n.104, p 65

175 Terry W Brown, "The Crowder-Ansell Dispute: The Emergence of General Samual T Ansell", Mil Law Rev, Vol 35, 1967, p 23.

having been expressed in his testimony before the Advisory Commission to the Military Justice Act, 1983.[176]

It may be seen that the proposition for divesting the members of the power to adjudge sentence and transferring the task to the legal adviser of the court has its own limitations. The fact that this has not yet been adopted in the American system, in spite of its almost a century long history since Gen Ansell's time (1920s), itself speaks for the need of a cautious approach in this regard. The reason is not far to see. The very concept of military justice being based on the need of the justice being imparted in the related matters by their commanders will be made to stand on its head by any such move. Further, in the case of serious offences involving capital punishment, sentencing is a matter far too grave to place on the shoulders of one person, no matter how well trained he may be in the related field; and it would be ridiculous to have two separate procedures, conceptually altogether different, for CM sentencing, one for cases involving grave offences and the other for comparatively less serious ones. In fact, in the case of offences carrying a mild penal liability, it is not consequential enough to call for a radical change of the institutional nature on an aspect which is the very essence of the whole exercise of a trial by the CM. Lastly, the justifications given in favour of the proposition for the change in question under the U.S. system would not apply to our system. Under the U.S. system, the members are left alone for a struggle to arrive at a decision on the matters connected with the sentencing which, as discussed earlier, may, in the present times, be too complicated for them to understand without any help of a legally trained person. This makes a tricky situation. The members involved in the sentencing at present, have commander's experience but no legal training and, after turning over the sentencing to the military judge, the incumbent will have legal training but no effective experience of the commanders of men even though formally he is commissioned as an officer after being picked up from the legal profession.[177] Further, the U.S. military justice system for its historical reasons, has developed into a system that is swayed by the expectations of its citizens who are much more vocal in this regard than the Indian citizens, after WW II experience. In the case of Indian military justice system, there has neither been such experience nor such vocal public concern. The system, having thus remained almost static over a century long period since 1911, cannot digest a conceptual change of the CM sentencing being transferred to the exclusive domain of the JA. Further, unlike the U.S. system, the JA at an Indian CM is present with the members to "assist the court in

176 Russel WG Grove, "Sentencing Reform: Toward a More Uniform, Less Uninformed System of Court Martial Sentence", Army Law, July 1988, p 28 n 23.

177 Military Justice Act, 1968, s 2(9): UCMJ, Art 26(b): A military judge shall be a commissioned officer of the armed forces who is a member of the bar of a Federal court or a member of the bar of the highest court of a state and who is certified to be qualified for duty as a military judge by the Judge Advocate General of the armed force to which such military judge is a member.

the determination of the sentence"[178] without, of course, any power to vote or even sway the mind of the court. If a JA is made a member of the CM, as suggested earlier, he will have not only full authority to actively participate in any discussion on the issue during deliberation by the members but also be able to bring in a happy mix of the soldier and the lawman in the sentencing procedure.

There is yet another aspect of the CM sentencing which needs a close examination. The worldwide trend in civilian jurisdiction is in the direction of mandatory sentences with little discretion for the sentencer. The military justice system, by contrast, affords the CM almost total discretion in sentencing except for a very few offences, like civil offences such as murder or gang rape. There is no offence under the AA, other than such a civil offence which does not carry in the penal clause a discretion of awarding "or such less punishment as in this Act mentioned". As a result, the CM sentencing is infested with "the problem of unwarranted sentence disparity"[179]. Some of the examples of such a disparity include the cases of Private Looney and Private Saulisberry who were both convicted of impremeditated murder, the former stabbing a good friend and killing him as a result during an argument, after drinking at several clubs, and the latter similarly stabbing a fellow soldier during an argument while watching television in the barracks room. The sentence awarded to Looney by a military judge sitting as GCM was 120 months of confinement[180] whereas the latter was awarded 240 months confinement by a GCM composed of officer and enlisted members[181]. Seaman Kirkman and Hospital Apprentice Iberra, both of the US Navy, were awarded, by different GCM trials by panel of officer and enlisted men, 89 days and 48 months of confinement respectively for raping victims who were drunk but retained consciousness at the time of their rape[182]. In India, it was argued before the Supreme Court on behalf of the petitioner Maj G S Sodhi that he was awarded the punishment of removal from service whereas other officers were awarded lesser punishment.[183] Even though the apex court did not find the contention to be tenable, holding that "it is for the CM to decide as to what sentence should be awarded in the given circumstances of the case", the fact

178 NA, s 120(2).

179 Major Steven M Immel, "Development, Adoption, and Implementation of Military Sentencing Guidelines," op ci t, ch 6, n 64 , p 160.

180 US v Looney, 48 MJ 681 (Arm y Ct Crim App 1988) at 683.

181 US v Saulsberry, 47 MJ 493 (1998).

182 US v Kirkman, NMCM 9801264, 2000 CCA LEXIS 61 (NM Ct Crim App 2000) and US v Iberra, 53 MJ 616 (NM Ct Crim App 2000) r espectively.

183 Major GS Sodhi v COAS, AIR 1991 SC 1617 (para 22) on the contention that Major SC Mehra tried for similar offence was awarded only severe reprimand and Major Senverma was awarded only 6 month loss of seniori ty.

remains that the disparity in the sentence awarded by different CsM to different accused persons in similar circumstances is not infrequent. In the present study, for instance, such disparity is clearly visible in the case of the thirteen respondents tried in each case on a charge under AA s 39 for illegal absence, as may be made out from the data displayed in Table – 49.

TABLE - 49

Disparity of Sentence Awarded for Illegal Absence

Srl No	Sentence	Number of Respondents	Percentage out of 13
1.	Dismissal	3	23.08
2.	RI for 89 days	5	38.46
3.	RI less than 1 month	3	23.08
4.	Reduction to ranks	1	7.69
5.	No punishment, being acquittal	1	7.69
	Total	13	100.00

It may be brought out here that all the respondents were from different units and of different ranks including NCOs, Sepoys, and anonymous respondents. In the three cases of dismissal, the sentence was awarded, on a plea of "Guilty" in two cases, and on a plea of "Not Guilty" in one case. The sentence of 89 days RI in each case was awarded by SCM, possibly keeping in mind the desirability of retaining the individual in service by having him to undergo the sentence in military custody for which the maximum limit is three months.

One of the factors responsible for the disparity in the CM sentence may be the absence of any effective guideline for sentencing by CM in some systems. In the US system, for instance, the Articles of War, 1795, granted great latitude to panel members in fashioning a sentence and until the Manual for Courts Martial, 1951, there did not exist a separate sentencing hearing as a formal part of the CM proceedings - the evidence presented on the merits was used to form the sentence in the event of conviction. Under the Indian system, however, the Forms of Proceedings of Court Martial (IFAD-906), developed under the Indian Army Rules, 1911 r 147 (pari materia to present AR r 64), provided for the accused to address the court after the court had received evidence as to his previous conviction and character as a part of the proceedings on conviction. The present legal requirements in this regard have been discussed earlier in sections 7.12 (a) and (b). Interestingly, the US Manual for Courts Martial, 1928, did require the members to consider former discharges, previous convictions and circumstances that tend to mitigate, extenuate or aggravate either the offence or collateral consequences of the offence. The 1949 version of the Manual directed the members to keep in mind the accused's background, uniformity in sentencing, general deterrence and discipline. The 1969 Manual, however, removed sentence uniformity as a sentencing goal, after the Court of Appeal had ruled that the law officer's instructions to the members as to sentence uniformity was inappropriate and advised Congress to delete from the related Art 76(a) any mention of sentence uniformity. The court explained that the CM members did not have exposure to a wide enough spectrum of cases to sentence uniformity and CsM have little continuity and therefore confusion would result if they sought to equalize sentences without being fully informed.[184] Irrespective of the reason for inapplicability of uniformity to CM sentencing, the concept of uniformity, wherever it can possibly be applied, has to be qualified as subject to variation on the same consideration as the right to equality admits reasonable classification, including one individual case being classified as a separate class if so required. Any such varying decision apparently will involve some element of discretion and subjectivity. The problem of regulating discretion or subjectivity may be reasonably handled by devising some objective criteria to guide the CM sentencing, such as the one developed for the US federal sentencing.

The statutory maximum sentence was the only limit imposed on sentencing power of the American federal judges before 1984[185]. The Brown Commission appointed to suggest reformative measures for the federal criminal system stated inter alia that the unfettered sentencing authority of federal trial judges was the primary cause of sentence disparity. The Sentencing Reform Act, 1984 and the US Sentencing Commission created thereby have the mission to satisfy the sentencing objectives of honesty, uniformity and proportionality by using sentencing guidelines. These guidelines, which were published by the Commission in Nov 1987 to be effective from Jan 1989 were created by studying

---

184 US v Mamaluy, 27 CMR 176 (CMA 1959).

185 Charles J Ogletree, "Commentary: The Death of Discretion: Reflection on the Federal Sentencing Guidelines Har L R ev, Vol 101, 1988, p 1938, at 1940-41.

10000 pre-sentence investigations, the differing elements of various crimes as distinguished in substantive criminal statutes, the United States Parole Commission's guidelines and statistics, and data from other relevant sources. The sentencing guidelines are encapsulated in a sentencing table where the differing elements of various crimes as distinguished in substantive criminal statutes are placed in the vertical axis of the table which relates to the seriousness of the offence. The Federal Sentencing Table's axis lists the 43 offence levels from minor offence to most serious offence. The horizontal axis lists the six criminal history categories and applies to the criminal history of the accused. Proportionality, which allows different sentences for criminal conduct of varying severity, is secured by combining offence levels, sentence adjustments and criminal history. The specific offence characteristics work to increase or decrease the base offence level. The specific offence characteristics, such as the use of fire-arm in robbery or merely showing the gun but not discharging during the robbery, are distinguishable from 'adjustments' which may be applicable to any offence and not only to a specific offence such as the age or mental/physical soundness of the victim; or the admission of the guilt by the offender and so on. A sentence range can be determined from the intersection of the criminal history category and the offence level. Once the intersection is determined, the sentencing range in months is reached. An adaptation from the US Sentencing Commission, Federal Sentencing Guidelines Manual, 1998[186] is given below to illustrate the point.

CHART 8.1

SENTENCE TABLE EXTRACT

Offence Level	Criminal History Category (Criminal History Points)					
	I	II	III	IV	V	VI
1	-	-	-	-	-	-
19	30-37	33-41	37-46	46-57	57-71	63-78
20	31-41	37-46	41-51	51-63	63-78	70-87

Based on the figures in Chart 8.1, if the offence level is twenty, and the criminal history category were IV, the sentence range would be 51 – 63 months. Under rare circumstances, the trial judge may depart from the guidelines, stating reason for departure.

186 United States Sentencing Commission, Federal Sentencing Guidelines Manual, 1998.

On similar lines, Major Immel prepared Military Sentencing Guidelines with a basic premise that the sentencing goals of the federal system and the military system are alike, that is, just punishment, deterrence, incapacitation and rehabilitation, along with an added goal of maintaining good order and discipline in the case of the military as a necessity of efficiency and effectiveness of the military. And the aim is to cut down disparity in military sentencing except where disparate sentence is required by any of these goals. For example, an aircraft mechanic who illegally takes drugs may receive a sentence more severe than the sentence received by an administrative clerk, who does the same offensive act. The guidelines developed by Major Immel are intended to suit the needs of the U.S. military legal system. Since there are significant differences between the U.S. and the Indian military legal systems, Major Immel's design guidelines cannot be imported for the Indian system. We will have to develop our own military sentencing guidelines. The work would require an independent research project. We can, however, adapt his research experience and design to our use. The sentencing matrix, in our case too, may similarly consist of a vertical and a horizontal axis, the former listing separately the offences and sub-offences defined in the penal sections of our service Acts and the horizontal axis may contain as many categories as warranted, say five, six or seven categories that allow the sentencing agency to weigh extenuation, mitigating and aggravating factors, category I being the least severe and offering the most lenient option and the last category being the most severe and offering the most stringent option of punishment. The sentencing matrix will be established when the categories (horizontal axis) are combined with the punitive concepts in the vertical axis. It may be noted that Major Immel's model of guidelines have limited application, being restricted to the sentence involving imprisonment. For our purposes the guidelines may as well cater for other punishments by suitably assigning different statistical values to different punishments like cashiering, dismissal, reduction to the ranks or even different quantum of forfeiture in terms of the length of service.

Any such military sentencing guidelines, however, cannot be treated as a panacea for all sentencing related ills. In fact, some of the military writers like Cooke "do not advocate anything as comprehensive and cumbersome as the Federal Sentencing Guidelines for our system" in spite of recognizing the need to "provide more guidance to sentencers and to promote greater uniformity in sentencing".[187]

---

187 Brigadier General John S Cooke, "The Twenty-sixth Annual Kenneth J Hodson Lecture: Manual for Courts Martial 20X", op cit, n 83, p 27.

8.6 Judicial Attitude towards Military Justice

(a) Position in the UK

A person does not, by enlisting in or entering the armed forces thereby ceases to be a citizen so as to deprive him of his rights or to exempt from liabilities under the ordinary law of the land.[188] To put it differently, when a person joins the army, he assumes all those particular duties and responsibilities imposed by military law but he does not thereby relinquish all those rights and duties possessed by other citizens. In any democratic society, therefore, there must be means available by which a convicted soldier can test, outside the military legal system, the legality of a finding against him.[189] This line of reasoning should have been in the mind of Lord Loughborough, while enunciating years ago, the general principle that the CM "being established in this country by positive law, the proceedings of it and the relation in which it will stand to the courts of Westminster Hall must depend upon the same rules with all other courts which are instituted and have particular powers given to them. Naval courts martial, military courts martial, courts of Admiralty, Courts of Prize are all liable to the controlling authority which the courts at Westminster Hall have from time to time exercised for the purpose of preventing them exceeding the jurisdiction given to them".[190] Thus in England, where all courts derive their original authority from the Sovereign, as the fountain of justice, and a relation exists between civilian and military tribunals, a power to review the proceedings and sentences of courts martial appear to have been at one time specifically recognized by the Mutiny Act as passed by the superior courts of common law. No such provision, however, was contained in the later Acts. But independent of statute, it has been held, as may be seen from just referred Grant v Gould, that " the writs of petition and certiorari may legally issue from the High Court of Justice to the courts martial; prohibition to forbid the court to proceed on the ground that it is without authority and jurisdiction; and certiorari to require it to certify up the record with a view to the quashing of conviction or sentence if found illegal but not on account of irregularities or informalities or excessiveness of sentence, or when the rights affected were of military character such as atached to military rank etc as distinguished from civil rights. As for habeaus corpus, it may be availed .... on the ground of being illegally detained....,'entailing an inquiry..... into the jurisdiction of the court or illegality of sentence."[191]

This attitude of the superior courts in England to treat CsM almost at par in the matters of judicial control, however, registered a gradual erosion with the passage of time. Lord Chief Justice Goddard's pronouncements in the cases of Martyn[192] and Elliot[193]

---

188 Burdett v Abbot (1812) 4 T aunt 401 at 449-450, per Sir James Mansfield, CJ .

189 Mr. Peter J Rowe, "Military Justice Within the British Army", op cit, Ch 5, n 43, p 101.

190 Grant v Gould, 2 Hy Bl 69 (1792).

191 Winthrop, "Military Law and Precedents", op cit, n 17, p 51 (s 57).

may be taken as the representative decisions of the changed approach that came to be adopted by the middle of the twentieth century. An interference by the superior courts with "military courts and military law" was restricted to the cases " in so far as the civil rights of the soldier or other person whom they deal may be affected", holding unambiguously that once the status of the petitioner as a soldier was conceded, a CM "had jurisdiction to try him", and if the CM, while trying him, "has not observed the proper rules of procedure, that is a matter for the convening officer, and if necessary, the Judge Advocate General to deal with."[194]

Similar approach had been adopted earlier, 91 years ago, when the court had refused to interfere in Capt. Mansergh applying for a writ of certiorari to quash the proceedings of the CM on the ground of the jurisdiction. Captain Mansergh was on duty with his regiment, the 6th Foot, at Calcutta, when on 19 Feb 1858, he was gazetted to a Majority in the 15th Foot in England. The notice of the appointment having been transmitted to India and notified by the Commander-in-Chief in general orders at the headquarters and the regimental orders of the 6th Foot, Mansergh ceased to belong to the 6th Foot. Mansergh felt that his posting out had been engineered by his CO, Col Barnes, so as to prevent him from going with the unit to active service and he accordingly wrote to Col Barnes expressing his views for which he was arrested and tried by a CM at Calcutta, found guilty and sentenced to dismissal from the Service. Three years later, he approached for a writ of certiorari on the ground that the CM had no jurisdiction because at the time of the offence, he was not in the Indian service, being posted to the 15th Foot located in England. The court refused to issue certiorari, holding that the court ought to interfere where "the civil rights of a person in military service are affected by the judgment of a military tribunal, in pronouncing which the tribunal has either acted without jurisdiction or has exceeded its jurisdiction ... Here, however, there was nothing of the sort and the only matter involved was the military status of the applicant - a thing which depends entirely on the Crown, seeing that any person who enters into the military service engages to be entirely at the will and pleasure of the Sovereign."[195]

The approach adopted by the High Courts in these cases, may be briefly summarized in three propositions: one, that the question of jurisdiction of a CM maybe answered simply on the basis of the fact as to whether or not the accused was a soldier; two, if any order or decision of the CM which had jurisdiction did infringe a right of the said soldier, the High Court would not interfere in case it was a right conferred by military law, because it could interfere only on a civil right being infringed; and three, the High Court could not interfere where a remedy existed under military law, such as a remedy by

192 R v S ecretary of State f or War, ex parte Mart yn, (1949) 2 Al l ER 242.

193 R v Of ficer Commanding Depot B attalion RASC Colchester, ex parte El liot, (1949) 2 Al l ER 373.

194 Martyn's case, op cit, n 192, p 201.

195 R v Manser gh, (1861) I B ands, 400, at 406-407 .

way of application to the JAG.[196] It is not difficult to see the fallacy involved in the approach. The narrow interpretation of the CM jurisdiction identified with the soldierly status alone, for instance, does not take into consideration the jurisdiction ratione materiae at all. Similarly, in a number of cases the superior courts intervened on the violation of military rights and procedures as well. For instance, private Brown succeeded to have a certiorari issued in 1892 to quash his CM conviction on the ground of the charge having been previously dismissed by the CO who later succumbed to the pressure of his military superiors to remand the accused for trial by a CM.[197] Without going into any further details in this regard, it may be brought out that the rigid attitude adopted by the superior courts in the UK in the matters of judicial review has since been relaxed considerably in the wake of various developments of the present times. The CO's powers to discipline the new recruit under his command may now be successfully challenged in national and international courts. Such an intervention might be sought directly by an appeal from a CM to the Court Martial Appeal Court, through an application for judicial review under Order 53, Rules of Supreme Court. Before 1977, applications were made for one of the prerogative writs which may now be covered within the term 'judicial review'. To prove the point, the case of Lance Sergeant Alexander Findlay of Scots Guards may be cited. He lost control of himself while in the barracks in Londonderry (Northern Ireland) and held members of his unit at gunpoint. He was tried by the CM in 1991 and sentenced to two year imprisonment for his act, which in fact, was sparked off when the noise of a beer can being opened reminded him of a bullet whizzing past his head at the battle of Mount Tumbledown in Falklands war. At that battle, he had witnessed the death and mutilation of several of his friends and later suffered psychiatric problems. The Army Psychiatrics who examined him had confirmed that he was suffering from post-traumatic stress disorder. He took his case to the High Court. A settlement of Pounds 100,000 was reached out of court, without any admission of liability on the Ministry of Defence. The case, however, finally reached the European Court of Human Rights. A nine Judges bench at Strasbourg, including 80 year old Sir John Redvers Freeland of Britain, heard the case in Feb 1997. Their unanimous verdict was: "A trial by court-martial, governed by the procedure laid down in the Army Act, 1955, did not constitute a fair hearing by an independent tribunal, as guaranteed by Article 6.1 of the European Convention of Human Rights."[198]

196 Holland, DC, "The La w of Courts-Martial", Curr ent Legal Pr oblems, 1950, V ol 3, p 174 , cit in O P Sharma, Military Law in India, op cit, Ch 1, n 4, pp 215-216.

197 Ex parte Brown, (1892) 37 Sol JO 27

198 Findlay v The United Kingdom, Judgment dated 25 Feb 1997 in Reports of Judgements and Decisions, 1997-1: (1997) 24 EHHR 221. Some other similar decisions were in the cases of Coyne v The United Kingdom (judgment date 24 Sep 1997 in case No. 124/1996/734/942) and Cable and others v United Kingdom (judgment dated 18 Feb 1999, communication 24436/1994) both available at http://www.echr.coe.int/eng/judgments.htm. The decisions wer e kept in mind whi le introducing the r eforms in the mi litary justice system b y Armed F orces Acts 2001 and 2006. Howev er, it may be noted that the

(b) Under the US System

Unlike the imprecise beginning of the British military legal history, the U.S. system had a clean start on 14 Jun 1775, when the Second Continental Congress resolved that a military force should be immediately raised to march and join the army near Boston and appointed the same day a committee with George Washington and four others to prepare rules and regulations for the government of the Army. A code of 69 articles was accordingly reported on 28 Jun to the Congress that adopted it on 30 Jun 1775. These articles were copied directly from Massachusetts Articles, which in turn were a copy of the British Articles of War adopted on 5 Apr 1775 by the Provisional Congress of Massachusetts Bay for its own troops. Thus, the two opposing armies were, at this point, governed by similar military codes. The next year, these articles were revised by the committee on spies comprising of another five historical personalities like Thomas Jefferson. The revised articles agreed by the Congress on 20 Sep 1776 and with various amendments made thereto from time to time, were expressly recognized later by the First Congress, on the adoption of the Constitution, and made to apply to the then existing Army, in an enactment of 29 Sep 1789. The U.S. military legal system, in these circumstances, was bound to be one inspired by the contemporary British system and yet was to meet the democratic aspirations of a nation which had several states united together with a common goal and colonial history but was determined to found new traditions different from those of a monarchical system having an all powerful monarch. An independent constitutional power invested in the Congress under Article III, sec 8, to govern the army and make laws therefor without any connection with Article III of the constitution defining the judicial process of the United States, may be seen in a way as a mark of separation from the British legal history of all courts having derived their origin from the Sovereign as the fountain of justice. Ironically, this only contributed on the same constitutional ground, to the superior courts in the USA, distancing themselves from collateral review from CM convictions practically in the traditions of the British superior courts. CsM of the USA, although their legal sanction is not less than that of the Federal courts, being equally with those authorized by the constitution, are, unlike the Federal Courts, not a portion of the judiciary of the USA and are thus not included among the "inferior courts" which Congress "may from time to time ordain and establish"[199]. This would prevent collateral review of a duly confirmed sentence adjudged by a CM. "If it were otherwise ... the civil courts would violently administer the rules and articles of war ..."[200] Classical decisions in Mills v Martin,[201] ex parte Milligan,[202]

European Court of Human Rights has no legal power over the British Government unlike the European Court of Justice, Luxembourg,which has such jurisdiction since Britain is a member of the European Union.

199 Winthrop,Military La w and Pr ecedents, op ci t, n 17 , pp 49-52.

200 Dynes v Hoo ver, 61 US 56 (1857).

201 19 Hons Rep 30.

Chambers v Jenninge,[203] Runke v US,[204] Dynes v Hoover,[205] Smith v Whitney,[206] Johnson v Sayre[207] and the Contested Election of Brig Gen[208] have been cited by Winthrop to show as to how the superior courts in the USA declined to interfere in the decisions of CsM and refused to issue writs of prohibition, certiorari or even habeas corpus where no illegality was exhibited in the proceedings upon their face presuming them to be regular and valid. There was a nearly monolithic harmony within and beneath the US Supreme Court prior to 1944 or thereabouts, as that the federal courts, having no appellate jurisdiction over military tribunals, would, in collateral proceedings attacking the validity of a military sentence, most strictly limit themselves to "ascertaining whether the military court had jurisdiction of the person and subject matter, and whether ... it had exceeded its powers in the sentence pronounced".[209] It was considered to be "the salutary rule that the sentences of courts martial, when affirmed by the military tribunal of last resort, cannot be revised by the civil courts, save only when void because of an absolute want of power, and not merely voidable because of the defective exercise of power possessed".[210] In brief it was held that "no mere errors in their proceedings are open to consideration. The single inquiry, the test is jurisdiction".[211] In the case of Second Lt. Keyes of the 5th Cavalry, the Court of Claims dismissed the petition for pay by the cashiered officer, holing the illegalities to be "mere errors" even when the Colonel commanding the regiment who had preferred one of the charges had appeared as a prosecution witness, and sitting as a member of the CM had voted on the finding and the sentence. The Supreme Court also affirmed the dismissal of Keyes's petition, observing that since "the court martial ... had cognizance of the charges made, and had jurisdiction of the person of the appellant ... whatever irregularities or errors are alleged to have occurred in the proceedings, the sentence of dismissal must be held valid when it is questioned in their collateral way."[212] On the same reasoning, Captain Oberlin Carter failed, despite having devoted a very long period of nearly 40 years in pursuing his mission to prove personal prejudice of the AJAG and the member of the CM, intimidating

---

202 71 US 2 (1866): 4 Wallace 123.

203 7 Mod 125.

204 22 US 556.

205 61 US 56 (1857).

206 116 US 168.

207 158 US 109 (1895).

208 1 Strob 198.

209 Carter v Roberts, 177 US 496 (1900) at 498.

210 Carter v Mc Claughry , 183 US 365 (1992) at 401.

211 In re Grimley, 137 US 147 (1890) at 150.

212 Keyes v United States, 109 US 336 (1883) at 340.

the defence witnesses, known false prosecution evidence, and abstraction of defence documentary evidence.[213]

During World War II, CsM were conducted in the U.S. armed forces in a huge number out of which 90,000 convictions were pronounced by GCM alone. Despite large scale post-war clemency, there remained in Federal penal institutions a great number of men undergoing sentences of Army or Navy CsM. They took to the courts by squads and platoons. Few of the petitioners could adduce the orthodox grounds of collateral attack, for practically in every case, CsM had jurisdiction over the person and the offence and the power to impose the sentence. However, many of them had to tell startling, and some times apparently truthful tales of unfairness of a nature that a Federal judge of average fair mindedness would chafe, under the restrictions of the traditional rules and be receptive to the heterodox propositions that even soldiers were entitled to some sort of due process, whether by virtue of the Constitution or the Articles of War, the denial of which could cause a CM to lose the jurisdiction that it would otherwise have had. As an early example of the emerging thought process, in contrast with the then on- going old approach of restricted collateral review in CM convictions, may be cited the twin cases of Anthony and Arnold who sought habeas corpus separately from their respective prisons in the District of Kansas and the Northern District of Texas. They had been convicted on 03 Apr 1945 at a joint trial by CM on the charges of raping three German nationals about a month ago. Both took the plea of lost jurisdiction because of the mandatory pre-trial investigation being neither adequate not fair and the due process of law having been denied to them thereby. While Anthony was granted the writ and set free for the defects in the pre-trial investigation,[214] with reliance being placed on Hicks v Hiatt,[215] Arnold's petition was denied[216], taking support of Hurse v Caffey,[217] on the spacious ground of the CM having been properly convened, having jurisdiction over the petitioner and the sentence being within the law. These two decisions place in stark contrast two basic approaches to the problem of collateral review of military justice – a problem which had bedeviled the lower Federal courts since World War II and one which the Supreme Court conspicuously failed to resolve for long.[218] No appeal was made by the Government against the decision in Anthony's case, which in any case, was in line with the gradual development inaugurated in civilian criminal proceedings

---

213 In re Carter, 97 Fed 496 (CCSD) NY. 1899.

214 Anthony v Hunter, 71F. Supp 823 (D K an 1947) at 831.

215 64F Supp 238 (MD Pa 1046).

216 Arnold v Cozart, 75F Supp 47 (ND T ex. 1948) at 48.

217 59F Supp 363 (ND T ex. 1945).

218 Bishop, "Civilian Judges and Military Justice: Collateral Review of Court Martial Conviction", op cit, ch 7, n 3, p 43.

by the decision in Johnson v Zerbst,[219] the proposition being that jurisdiction, though existed when the trial began, evaporated because the defendant was somehow denied the constitutional due process. The development was more pronounced in the later cases in civilian criminal courts, but the Supreme Court in military cases simply ignored the due process issue, despite vociferous reaction from the Federal judges against "empty and farcical compliance only" with the Articles of War by a "court ... saturated with tyranny"[220]. In Humphry v Smith, the petitioner sought to impeach a CM verdict on certain grounds, including that the CM was deprived of its jurisdiction by inadequate pre-trial investigation. Though the District Court found no merit in any of his allegations, the Court of Appeals ordered the writ granted. However, the Supreme Court reversed that on the ground that the requirement of pre-trial investigation was not jurisdictional.[221] Hiatt v Brown, with the lower courts directing the petitioner's release, for the reason of the record being so "replete with highly prejudicial errors and irregularities" as to amount to "denial of due process in violation of the fifth amendment", presented a still greater opportunity to the Supreme Court to intervene, but it again simply reversed unanimously, reminding the lower court that it was "in error in extending its review, for the purpose of determining compliance with the due process clause, to such matters as the proposition of law set forth in the staff judge advocate's report, the sufficiency of the evidence to sustain respondent's conviction, the adequacy of the pre-trial investigation and the competence of the law member and the defense council ... 'The single inquiry, a test, is jurisdiction'. In re Grimley ... the correction of any errors (the court martial) may have committed is for the military authorities which are alone authorized to review its decision."[222] In later cases, a gradual shift in this approach was noticed in the pronouncements of the Supreme Court towards the principle enunciated in Johnson v Zerbst. However it was not before Burns v Wilson[223], that an express recognition of the application of the principle to CM convictions was made. Burns and another soldier had been convicted by a GCM of the charges for rape and murder and sentenced to death. They sought habeas corpus with allegations of coerced confession, denial of effective assistance of a counsel, suppression of favourable evidence and the conduct of trial in an atmosphere of hysteria and terror. The allegations were ignored and petitions rejected by the district court on the traditional grounds. The court of appeal affirmed on the ground that the allegations had been resolved by the military authorities upon

219 Johnson v Zerbst, 304 US 458 (1938) cf Pollak, "Proposals to Curtail Habeas Corpus for State Prisoners: Collateral Attack on the Great Writ," YALE LJ, Vol 66, (1956) p 50 at 52

220 Beets v Hunter, 75F Supp 825, 826 (D K an 1948).

221 Humphrey v Smith, 336 US 695 (1949) at 696.

222 Hiatt v Brown, 339 US 103 (1950) at 110.

223 Burns v Wilson, 346 US 137 , rehearing denied, 346 US 844 (1953).

substantial evidence. The Supreme Court could not arrive at a majority opinion, but the case was disposed by the largest faction of four Judges, ruling that the record showed that the military court had heard petitioners out on those allegations and therefore nothing remained for the civil courts to do. Before concluding, they had added that "had the military courts manifestly refused" to consider the petitioners' allegations of fundamental unfairness, the district court might have evaluated for itself the question of due process. In this context, they had also stated in general that the "constitutional guarantee of due process is meaningful enough, and sufficiently adaptable, to protect soldiers - as well as civilians - from the crude injustices of a trial..." and that nonetheless "in military habeas corpus the inquiry... has always been more narrow than in civil cases" for the reason of the UCMJ provisions that the determination of military tribunals shall be final and binding on all courts which "would mean that when a military decision has dealt fully and fairly with an allegation..., it is not open to a federal civil court to grant the writ simply to re-evaluate the evidence"[224] Mr. Justice Frankfurter was unwilling either to affirm or reverse without more and fuller argument on the questions that the case presented but made it clear that he did not agree with the traditional approach of restricting a military habeas corpus to the question of jurisdiction over the person and the crime nor with the view that the scope of inquiry is the same in military cases as that open on review of State convictions and nor with the duty being taken as met simply on finding that the military sentence had been reviewed by the military hierarchy. Lastly, he saw no reason for treating the principle of Johnson V Zerbst - the principle that jurisdiction may be 'lost' by a denial of whatever process is due in the circumstances - as any less applicable to military than to civil courts."[225] Justices Black and Douglas flatly dissented on the issue of military due process,[226] in line with their well known views against the system of military justice. In fact, no discussion on American collateral review of military conviction can be completed without a mention of their earlier referred land-mark decisions of Reid v Covert and O'Callahan v Parker.[227] The variety of opinions expressed by the American Supreme Court and the lower federal courts has been so rich that it would not lend itself to facile taxonomy. Some of the allegations dealt with in the decision include the admission of coerced confessions,[228] errors in the Law Officer's instructions on the law, appointment of incompetent or indifferent defence counsel,[229] conduct of trial in an atmosphere of public hostility and prejudice,[230] no Negro sitting

224 Ibid, pp 139 and 142-144.

225 Ibid pp 149 and 851 (rehearing).

226 Ibid, p 150.

227 Supra nn 13 and 120 r espectively.

228 Rushing v Wilkinson, 272 F2d 633 (5th Cir 1959).

229 Kubel v Minton, 275 F 2d 789 (4th Cir 1960).

230 Day v Wi lson, 155 F. Supp 469 (DDC 1957).

on the CM trying a Negro accused[231] and so on. From such pronouncements, it was clear that the gradual edging away from the orthodox doctrine and toward a practical homologizing of military and civil sentences for the purpose of collateral reviews was very much to be desired and one hoped, after Burns v Wilson, that the "manifest refusal" language would be allowed quietly to fade away and that increasing stress would be put on the requirement of being full and fair. O' Callahan and Solorio[232] decisions may both be appreciated in the light of such hope. The later decisions do keep this hope alive. For instance, the court of Military Appeals had made it clear that the Fourth Amendment (right against unreasonable search and seizure) applied with equal force within the military as it does in the civilian community.[233] The Supreme Court, however, added that the protection offered may be modified somewhat to meet the particular requirements of the military situation.[234] Similarly, the question whether personnel be allowed to refuse summary (non-judicial) punishments was addressed in 1997.[235] Finally, the US Supreme Court reversed 54 years of precedence, on 28 Jun 2004, by answering in the affirmative the question whether aliens detained outside US sovereign territory may invoke habeas relief and challenge the basis of their detention, opening the federal court system to detainees currently being held at Guantanamo Bay, Cuba,[236] contrary to the earlier decision by which the US Supreme Court had denied any such right to twenty-one German nationals convicted by a Military Commission in China for violating laws of war by engaging the American forces after surrender of Germany.[237]

(c) **Judicial Control of CM Process in India**

The attitude of the superior courts in India, towards the military justice system, has been moulded by the facts of the Indian legal history. The English legal system was introduced in the three Presidency towns founded by the British to facilitate their trades there. This was done under the Charter of Queen Elizabeth I, which authorised the East India Company, firstly, to make, ordain and constitute laws, orders and constitution for the good government of itself, of its servants and for the better advancement and continuance of its trade and traffic; and secondly, to devise and impose simple punishments for infringement of laws not deviating from the English legal principles.

231 Wilson v Wi lkinson 129 F. Supp 324 (MD P a 1955).

232 Supra nn 120 and 121 r espectively.

233 United States v Ezell, 6 MJ 307 (CMA 1979).

234 US v Middleton 10 MJ 123, 127 (1981).

235 US v Edwards 46 MJ 41 (1997).

236 Rasul v Bush, President of the United States, 159 L Ed 2d 548 (2004).

237 Johnson v Eisentroger 339 US 763 (1950) at 765-66.

The legislative powers of the Company being inadequate to prevent lawlessness and disorderliness among its servants, while on high seas, the Company had to involve the crown prerogative to secure a commission to the commander-in-chief of each voyage empowering to inflict punishment for capital offences like murder or mutiny by putting into execution the "law martial". The first of such commission was issued on 24 January 1601 to Captain Lancaster and the first trial was held on 28 February 1616 on board the Ship Charles. The offender was one Gregory Littington who was convicted, on his own confession, for the murder of Henry Barton at Surat and was condemned to death.[238] It may be noted here that the jurisdiction of a CM under the then British military law extended in India at a distance of 120 miles from the Presidency cities and on declaration of 'marshal law' it extended to persons not ordinarily under it.[239] When the British landed in India, the Moghul Emperor, being very liberal, obliged the Englishmen in their wish to be governed by their own law in their internal affairs. The Englishman's desire to administer justice to themselves according to the English law proved to be a very important single factor to exert a profound effect on the growth and development of the Indian legal system. When Warren Hastings introduced, in 1772, a scheme of judicial administration, which inter alia included higher judiciary courts of Sadar Diwani (Civil Jurisdiction) and Sadar Nizamat (Criminal Jurisdiction), at Calcutta, the plan laid the foundation of the anglo-Indian judicial system on which the later administrators built super structure. In the context of the judicial control of CM convictions by the superior courts, this translated into the superior courts adopting attitude similar to that adopted by the High Courts in England. The prayer for the writ of habeas corpus, for instance, was turned down in the case of Captain AW Meads v. Emperor, where the findings and sentence of a CM were challenged on the grounds of, firstly, the want of the consent of the Governor General under the Government of India Act 1935, s.270; secondly, the procedural errors resulting into denial of justice, thirdly, the absence of evidence on which a conviction could be based and lastly, the lack of jurisdiction. The Lahore High Court held that the jurisdiction was the main issue on which it was satisfied that the petitioner was subject to the jurisdiction of the CM.[240] As to the procedural errors, the courts relied on Rex v John Suddis[241] that while reviewing CM's decisions it was not sitting as a court of error to review the regularity of their proceedings nor was

238 M.P. Jain,Outlines of Indian Legal History, 3rd ed, 1972, Bombay, NM Tripathi, Ch II.

239 Simmons,The Constitution and Practice of Courts Martial, OP cit Ch 1, n.6, p 13.

240 Capt. AW Meads v Emperor, AIR1946 Lah 112; please also see Kartar Singh S. Jit Singh v Emperor, AIR 1946 Lah 103 and Burhanuddin v. Emperor, SC 224 Ind Cas 608.

241 Rex v. Suddis (1801) 1 Est 306, cf in ex parte Reed, 100 US 23, and ex parte Parks, 93 US 18, holding that "a writ of habeas corpus cannot be made to perform the function of a writ of errors. To warrant the discharge of the petitioner, the sentence under which he is held must be not merely erroneous and voidable but absolutely void".

it to hunt for possible objections. Quoting from Grose J, in the same case, the court added that it was enough to find that such a sentence was pronounced by a court of competent jurisdiction to inquire into the offence and with power to inflict such a sentence. As to the rest, the court must, presume omina rite acta. The decision was in line with Rex v. Murphy,[242] in which the King's Bench had held that a CM in the exercise of jurisdiction which it possessed was called upon to decide questions not only of fact but also of law including the admissibility of evidence; its jurisdiction was not ousted because it happened to give an erroneous decision; and it cannot be denied to exceed or abuse its jurisdiction merely because it misconstrues a statute or admits illegal evidence or rejects legal evidence. The Allahabad High Court, however, granted a writ of habeas corpus under Cr PC 1898 s.491 where the petitioners belonging to the Military Estate Service were held to be not on active service and consequently not answerable to the jurisdiction of the military authorities.[243] The contention of conductor Alfred Beedham was also accepted by the Lahore High Court that he could not be subjected to arrest and trial under IAA s.158(1) after the expiry of the period of 3 months (increased to six months under AA 1950 and now it is 3 years after an amendment in 1992) of his ceasing to be subject to the Act.[244] The Allahabad High Court ruled that the offence of desertion being not triable by the criminal courts, the mere fact that he was arrested by police, put up before a Magistrate and the cases proceeded to some length does not make Section 70 (of the IAA 1911) applicable. Hence, where a military servant commits criminal breach of trust and absconds, it rests with the military authority to decide whether the accused should be tried by CM or not.[245] In the case of Evelyn Betty Vivian Perry v Emperor, a whole-time regular nurse in a Military Hospital, under voluntary aid attachment condition, was held to be subject to military law and liable to be taken in military custody, if she absented herself without leave from the duty.[246] In the case of Feroze Din, the Lahore High Court ruled that it would not go into the matters which were at the discretion of the military authority.[247] Similarly, it was ruled in another case that the High Court had no power to interfere with matters of military conduct and purely military law, observing that the High Court has no jurisdiction to sit in judgment on the findings of any CM where a person has been tried under the Army Act, particularly when a more appropriate remedy was open to the applicant.[248] The Lahore High Court

242 Rex v Murph y, (1921) 2 I r R190.

243 Fazullur Rehman and Mohd. Akhtar v Commander Al lahabad Area, Cr. Misc. Cases No .396 an 397 of 1941 decided on 2 June 1941.

244 Re Alfred Beedham, AIR 1934 Lah 845.

245 Emperor v Lachmi Dat t. AIR 1928 Al l 672: 29 Cr L J 803.

246 Evelyn Betty Vivian P erry v Emper or, ILR (1946) 1 Cal 25.

247 Feroze Din v Emper or, High Court of Judicatur e at Lahor e, Cr Misc case No .218 of 1945.

248 GRFX Monteserrat v Maj Gen Hammond, AIR 1945 Oudh 217: 46 Cr L J 756.

pronounced on the effect of non-confirmation of the CM proceedings, holding that non-confirmation does not amount to acquittal and the accused could be tried by another CM for the same offence.[249] All these decisions by superior courts in pre-Independence India clearly reflect a tendency to restrict judicial control on CM convictions, essentially to the exclusive ground of jurisdiction as was being done by the civil courts in England and the USA in those times.

At the outset of any discussion on the judicial attitude towards CM process in the post-Independence era, it will be useful to point out three important relevant facts: one, non-appealability of CM decisions; two, the judicial control being confined to writ jurisdiction of the Supreme Court and High Courts, and lastly, the constitutional permissibility of restricting Fundamental Rights of soldiers. On the first issue, it may be brought out that the military need of a speedy disposal of the breaches of discipline would conceptually admit no elaborate post-trial review procedures like an appellate jurisdiction for a CM verdict. As a result, the military systems all over the world, before the emergence of the human right consciousness in the modern times, had post trial reviews restricted to the requirement of confirmation by superior military authority and a right to petition by the affected person to such military authorities. Before the Court Martial Appeal Act of 1951 in the UK and the Uniform Code of Military Justice, 1950, in the USA, there was no appeal in the true sense of the word, against the finding and sentence of a CM in those systems either. In the case of India, the Indian Army Act, 1911 similarly intended the findings of a CM as and when confirmed by the proper confirming officer, to be final, subject only to the power of revision for which that Act provided. There was no room for an appeal to His Majesty in Council consistently with the subject matter and scheme of the Act.[250] The position remained the same even after the change of guards in 1947, and continued to be so till 2007, despite the Supreme Court having lamented one-fourth of a century ago, the "absence of even one appeal with power to review evidence, legal formulation, conclusion and adequacy or otherwise of punishment..." in the case of soldiers, in a country "where a counter civilian can prefer appeal after appeal to hierarchy of courts", and observing further that "review of finding and or sentence in conformation proceeding ... is poor solace." In these circumstances, the judicial control of any proceedings of the military justice system in India remained confined to the writ jurisdiction. Under the US system, one may approach a District Court for intervention against a CM verdict, the Court of Appeals and finally the Supreme Court as seen earlier in the context of specific case like Burns v Wilson. This is in addition to a layer of automatic appeals including the one to Army, Navy/

249 Sardar Singh v The Crown High Court of Lahore Misc. Case 1026 of 1945.

250 Mohammad Yakub Khan v King Emper or, AIR 1947 PC 87(88): 43 Cr L J 514; please see Ch 7, n.289 for a right to appeal being not available unless expressly conferred by a statute.

Marine Corps and Air Force Courts of Appeal[251] and an appeal to the US Court of Appeal for the Armed Forces. The Indian system empowers the Supreme Court and the High Courts to issue "directions or orders or writs, including writs in the nature of habeas corpus, mandamus prohibition, quo warranto and certiorari," for the enforcement of Fundamental Rights in the case of the Supreme Court, and for such enforcement or any other purpose in the case of High Courts.[252] These powers may be exercised in respect of CM decisions irrespective of the restrictions imposed on the power of the Supreme Court in the matters of special leave to appeal under Article 136, and of the High Courts in the exercise of the power of superintendence over all courts and tribunal within their territorial jurisdiction under Article 227, in respect of any judgment, determination, sentence or order passed or made by any court or tribunal constituted by or under any law relating to the Armed Forces.[253]

While providing any relief under these provisions to any Armed Forces personnel, the Supreme Court and the High Courts, however, do have constraints of whatever restrictions are imposed on the Fundamental Rights of such persons under the authority of Article 33 of the Constitution by or under the related Act of Parliament. A blanket clearance given by the Supreme Court in Ram Sarup's case in 1965, to every provision of the AA from the angle of the violation of Fundamental Rights, will, however, have to be appreciated in the light of later developments in the judicial and academic thinking on the subject.[254] In a paper read at a recent similar on Human Rights and Armed Forces, Justice V S Sirpurkar of Madras High Court stated about the matters of Armed Forces and more particularly in the matter of CM that "what was once considered as an inapproachable area does not any more remain so and the Supreme Court of India as also the other High Courts have been narrowing the gap between the military law and the civil law. In a number of cases, the Supreme Court came to the rescue of those who were tried under the Court Martial on various grounds such as 'jurisdictional errors' committed at the trial; procedural lapses and at times even the 'factual errors' committed while appreciating the evidence. Very recently, in a landmark judgment in Union of India and others v L D Balam Singh, the Supreme Court went on to hold that where a member of the Armed Forces was being tried for an offence under the ordinary criminal law, the safeguards available under that law would also be available to the said member even during court-martial... this is undoubtedly a very big step, perhaps realizing the

251 During the fiscal years 1998-2002, such Service Courts reviewed 158000 cases; please see Major Jeffery D Lippert, " Automatic Appeal under UCMJ Article 66; Time f or a Change", Mil Law Rev, Vol 182, Winter 2004, pp 1-48, at 2.

252 The Constitution of India, Articles 32(2) and 226(1).

253 Major Subhash Chandra Sarkar v UOI, AIR 1973 MP 191.

254 Supra nn 125-128 and related text.

special position of a soldier."[255] In fact, in Balam Singh's case, Justice Umesh C Banerjee, while pronouncing on his own behalf and on behalf of Justice Y K Sabharwal, begins with a poser: "While it is true that army personnel ought to be subjected to strictest form of discipline and Article 33 of the Constitution has conferred powers on to the Parliament to abridge the rights conferred under part III of the Constitution in respect of the members of the armed forces, but does that mean and imply that the army personnel would be denuded of the Constitutional privileges as guaranteed under the Constitution? Can it be said that the army personnel form a class of citizens not entitled to the Constitutions benefits and are outside the purview of the Constitution? To answer above in the affirmative would be a violent departure to the basic tenets of the Constitution." Quoting the text of the Article, and pointing out the extent of restrictions necessary to be imposed as the plain reading thereof would suggest, the Judge rules that such extent "would necessarily depend upon the prevailing situation at a given point of time and it would be inadvisable to encase it in a rigid statutory formula. The constitution makers were obviously anxious that no more restrictions should be placed than are absolutely necessary for ensuring proper discharge of duties and the maintenance of discipline amongst the armed forces personnel."[256] Extracting from the observations in PPS Bedi's case, that the process of restricting Fundamental Rights "should not be carried so far as to create a class of citizen not entitled to the benefits of the liberal spirit of the Constitution", Justice Banerjee answered in the affirmative another poser in the context of Balam Singh's case on the "availability of substantive and procedural safeguards under a specific legislation" to the armed forces personnel at CM "since such procedural safeguards are said to be mandatory in nature" even though specified in a statute other than the AA, i.e., the Narcotic Drugs and Psychotropic Substances Act (hereinafter to be described as 'NDPS Act'). An accomplice of the petitioner was tried under the NDPS Act and acquitted for the reason of such safeguards having not been made available to him but the petitioner was convicted in the same situation merely because he was tried by a CM under AA s.69 read with NDPS Act s 18. Irrespective of the admirably refreshing interpretation given to the requirements of Article 33 by the Hon'ble Supreme Court to seek parity between the military and civil systems in the matters of investigation and trial of serious civil offences like the one under NDPS Act, it is respectfully submitted that the pronouncement seems to be jurisprudentially questionable. L D Balam Singh was tried for an offence under the Army Act. The charge had a reference to NDPS Act s 18 for the technical requirement of AR r 30(3) that in the charge, a civil offence "shall be stated in such words as sufficiently describe that offence, but not necessarily in technical words".

255 Hon'ble Justice V S Sirpurkar, "Protection of Human Rights of Armed Forces Personnel in International Scenario", in the Report of Seminar on Human rights & Armed Forces, 28 Nov 2003, organized by Dy. Judge Advocate General – HQ Central Command pp 21-29 at 22.

256 UOI v L D Balam Singh, JT 2002(4) SC 364, at 366.

Further, the punishment for the offence had to be awarded in terms of AA s 69, i.e., any punishment assigned for the offence under NDPS Act s 18 or imprisonment for a term which may extend to seven years, or such less punishment as in the AA mentioned. Beyond these two requirements, there was nothing else to be followed for the investigation or disposal of the case in a manner other than that required under the AA and AR. The said Act and Rules are designed to meet their objectives and are kept free from technicalities so as to ensure speedy disposal of an offence thereunder with a view to promoting military discipline and morale. To inject therein the principles and practices of the civil law, without any legislative deliberation thereon, may frustrate the very raison detre of the military justice system. In the words of General Sherman, the objects of the civil law and the military law are "as wide apart as the poles, and each requires its own separate system of laws, statute and common… Every enactment, every change of rules which impairs the principle weakens the army, impairs its value and defeats the very object of its existence".[257] In the instant case, the conviction of the petitioner by the CM was set aside by the High Court, which setting aside was upheld by the apex court, mainly on the ground of the search and seizure of the illicit opium in question having not been made in the presence of a gazetted officer or a magistrate as required by NDPS Act and the accomplices of the petitioner having been acquitted at the criminal court on the same ground. Even if any discrimination was involved in this, the same is inevitable and justifiable on the principle of reasonable classification under Article 14 of the Constitution. The Supreme Court upheld such discrimination in Ram Sarup's case, on the contention of AA s 125 (choice between ordinary court and court-martial) being discriminatory. The apex court observed that "It is not disputed that persons to whom s.125 applies do form distinct class but there is nothing in s.125 to guide the discretion, discrimination between different persons guilty of the same offence is likely to take place in as much as a particular officer may decide to have an accused tried by a court-martial and another by a criminal court for the same offence, the procedure in such two trials being different."[258]

Reverting to judicial attitude in India on the review of the CM decision, the data have been collected from all the 200 respondents on the propositions, one, that "the supervisory and appellate jurisdiction of high courts should be extended to CM" and, two, that a "court of military appeals should be established and the existing writ jurisdiction of high courts and the Supreme Court be barred in respect of CM decisions". [Questions 3.4(c) and (d) of Interview Schedule]. The data so collected are presented in Table 50 on the next page:

257 Supra n 29, p 251 (para 16).

258 Ram Sarup's case, op cit, n 125.

TABLE - 50

Extension of HC Supervisory & Appellate Jurisdiction, Establishment of CM AC and Bar of Writ Jurisdiction

Response Type	Proposition I		Proposition II		Proposition III	
	Number	%	Number	%	Number	%
Agree	42	21.0	123	61.5	03	1.5
Partially Agree	11	5.5	10	5.0	02	1.0
Disagree	109	54.5	36	18.0	84	42.0
Can't say	23	11.5	17	8.5	97	48.5
No Response	15	7.5	14	7.0	14	7.0
Total	200	100.0	200	100.0	200	100.0

Legend:
Proposition I = Supervisory and Appellate Jurisdiction of HC be extended to CM.
Proposition II = Court of Military Appeals be established
Proposition III = Writ Jurisdiction be barred in respect of CM decisions.

The data displayed here reflect that 109 (54.5%) of the respondents disagreed with the proposition of the need to extend supervisory and appellate jurisdiction of HC to the CM and 53 (26.5%) agreed with it fully or partially. Some of those who partially agreed were opting for the extension of the supervisory jurisdiction but not the appellate one. The reasons given by some respondents for disagreeing, included the likely delay to be caused thereby or excessive interference in military justice to the detriment of the cause of military discipline. One of the respondents (G-152) also pointed out that there is no need for this since effective relief can be granted by the High Court in the exercise of the jurisdiction under Art 226. This is in line with what Dr. Ambedkar had stated at the Constituent Assembly in the context of Clauses (2) of Articles 136 and (4) of 226 of the Constitution:

> "... Clause (2) does not altogether take away the powers of the Supreme Court or the High Courts... and ... notwithstanding Clause (2) of Article 112, it would still be open to the Supreme Court or to the High Courts to

> exercise jurisdiction, if the court-martial has exceeded the jurisdiction given to it, or the power conferred upon it, by the law relating to the Armed Forces. Secondly, if the court-martial were to give a finding without any evidence, then again, it will be open... to find out whether there is evidence... Similarly, ... it would be open for a member of the Armed Forces to appeal to the Court for the purpose of issuing prerogative writs.... This article is a necessary article. It really does not do anything more but give a statutory recognition to a rule that is prevalent and which is recognized by all superior courts."[259]

The US Supreme Court had also made it clear in Hiat v Brown that "the civil courts exercise no supervisory or correcting power over the proceedings of a court-martial. The single inquiry, the test, is jurisdiction: The correction of any errors it may have committed is for the military authorities which are alone authorised to review its decision."[260]

Reverting to the data in Table 50, it is further noted that 67.5% respondents were fully or partially in agreement with the requirement of a Court of Military Appeal; only 18% disagreed. As for the ouster of the jurisdiction of the Supreme Court and High Court to interfere under Articles 32 and 226, 48.5% of the respondents were unable to say anything about it, stating that they were not aware of the legal implications but 42% of the respondent did not fovour such jurisdiction being barred after the establishment of a Court Martial Appeal Court. Some of them, particularly, those from the JA category and the law officers in the general category, rightly stated that this would be constitutionally not feasible. This is in accord with the decision by a seven judge bench of the Supreme Court. Reconsidering their earlier decision of upholding the exclusion of the jurisdiction of High Courts under Articles 226 and 227 by Administrative Tribunals as "effective alternative institutional mechanism" under s. 28 of the Administrative Tribunals Act, 1985[261], the apex court held that the judicial review being essential feature of the Constitution, could not be altered through amendment; the Supreme Court and the High Courts are entrusted with the task of upholding the Constitution and it is the power and duty of judiciary to ensure that Legislature and the Executive do not, in discharge of their functions, transgress constitutional limits. In this light, s 28 of the Administrative Tribunal Act, was ultra vires and so were Art. 323-A, Cl.2(d) and 323-B Cl 3(d) inserted by the Constitution (42nd Amendment) Act, 1976 and thus Administrative Tribunals could be set up but only for a supplemental as opposed

259 Dr. BR Ambedkar in Consti tuent Assembly Debates,V ol 10, pp 376-380, (6-17 Oct 1949); cf Major Sarkar's case, Supra n 253.

260 Hiatt v B rown 339 US 103 (1950) at 110-111; Cf I n re Grimley, 137 US 147 at 150 (1890).

261 Sampath Kumar v UOI, AIR 1987 SC 386: (1985) 4SCC 458.

to a substitutional role.[262] Likewise, the Armed Forces Tribunal Act, 2007 does not exclude the judicial review of CM cases by the Supreme Court or the High Courts under Articles 32 and 226 of the Constitution respectively, though it does exclude jurisdiction of lower civil courts in respect of any jurisdiction, powers and authority exercised by the Tribunal. Further, it provides for an appeal to the Supreme Court against the decision of the Armed Forces Tribunal.

An important aspect of the judicial review in India by the Supreme Court and the High Courts is that unlike the assumption of such a power unto itself by the US Supreme Court, under the cover of the Fifth and the Fourteenth Amendments, which has faced persistent criticism of being undemocratic, the Superior Courts in India have the benefit of our Constitution containing express provision for judicial review of legislation and such a task is performed by the courts "not out of any desire to tilt at legislative authority in a crusader's spirit but in discharge of a duty plainly laid down upon them by the Constitution... Specially as regards the fundamental rights as to which this court (Supreme Court) has been assigned the role of a sentinel on the qui vive."[264] It may be noted that when the framers of our Constitution set about their monumental task, the power of civilian courts in judicial review had already acquired a history of nearly a century and a half. In this regard, the position in American Constitutional law in respect of courts created under Article III of the US Constitution is that the judicial review in the United States comprises the power of any court to hold unconstitutional and hence unenforceable any law, any official action based upon a law or any other action by a public official that it deems to be in conflict with the Basic Law in the United States, its Constitution. There the highly significant power of judicial review is possessed, theoretically by every court of record, no matter high or low on the judicial ladder. Though it occurs only infrequently, it is quite possible for a Judge in a low-level court of one of the 50 States to declare a Federal law unconstitutional.[265] Article III, Section-1, itself contemplates the conferment of such judicial powers there by the US Congress, in addition to the power vested in the Supreme Court, so long as the independence of the Judge is ensured in terms of the said Article III, Section-1. Thus, there is no blanket prohibition on the conferment of judicial power upon courts other than the US Supreme Court. The position in our case is different. In an Administrative Tribunal related case the Full Bench (5 Judges) judgment of the Andhra Pradesh High Court,[266] delivered by

---

262 L Chandra Kumar v UOI & others, AIR 1997 SC 1125; cf Justice C K Thakkar , "L Chandra Kumar v Union of India, AIR 1997 SC 1125: Restoration of Jurisdiction of High Courts" , AIR 1997 Journal 177 .

263 The Armed Forces Tribunal Act, 2007 , ss 30,33.

264 State of Madras v V G Rao, AIR 1952 SC 196 at 199.

265 Henry I Abraham,The Judicial Process, 4th ed, 1980, OUP p.296.

266 Sakinala Harinath v State of AP , 1994 (i) APL J (HC)1.

MN Rao J, embarks on a wide ranging quest, extending to the American, Australian and British jurisdictions, to ascertain the true import of the concepts of judicial power; 'judicial review' and other related aspects and concludes that under our constitutional scheme, the Supreme Court and the High Courts are the sole repositories of the power of judicial review. Such a power, being inclusive of the power to pronounce upon the validity of statutes, action taken and orders passed by individuals and bodies falling within the ambit of the expression 'State' in Article 12 of the Constitution, has only been entrusted to the constitutional courts, i.e., the High Courts and the Supreme Court. For this support may be drawn from Kesvanand, special reference No.1 of 1964, Indira v Raj Narain, Minerva Mills, Kihoto Hollohan and certain other decisions.

With such exclusive powers of judicial review, the Supreme Court and the various High Courts have been approached by service personnel in a fairly large number of cases. A 2005 edition of a compilation containing important excerpts from service law related cases[267] includes 1171 such cases out of which 209 are those pronounced by the Supreme Court of India, 35 decided by the Indian, American and the British courts before 1947 and the rest are the decisions by various High Court in post-Independence era before 04 May 2005. Most of these cases have been referred earlier in this study. The judicial attitude reflected in those cases may be broadly classified in three categories: one, constitutional position of the service personnel and the service law with reference to Fundamental Rights, two, scope of judicial review under Article 32 and 226 in respect of proceedings of CM process, and lastly, the legal validity of specific individual cases.

Constitutional position of the Service personnel and the Service law has been mainly considered by the superior courts with reference to Article 33, which may be described as the Constitutional grundnorm of the Indian Armed Forces, and the powers of the Supreme Court and the High Court under Articles 32 and 226 along with the exceptions carved out in Articles 136(2) and 227(4). The judicial attitude adopted in this regard stands out from earlier discussion in the present and the preceding chapters. Briefly speaking, the apex court had initially held that every provision of the AA (and by analogy, the provisions of the other two Services Acts) being made by Parliament would be unchallengeable on the ground of the violation of any Fundamental Rights since any such violation should be taken to be the result of abrogation or abridgement of the related Fundamental Right in terms of Article 33. In later cases, a gloss was added that the process should, however, not be taken so far as to have the Service personnel denuded of all their Fundamental Rights since even prisoners were entitled to enjoy Fundamental Rights other than those necessarily curbed by the requirements of incarceration. How

267 Kumar and Chaturvedi, Law Relating to the Armed Forces in India, op cit, Ch 3, n 22, pp x/vii to/xxx (Table of cases)

much relaxation has been given to the originally adopted attitude in this regard has already been brought out in the context of L D Balam Singh's case.

The Supreme Court made it abundantly clear in several cases, in respect of their powers of judicial review of CM convictions that though the CM proceedings are subject to judicial review by a High Court under Article 226, the CM is not subject to the superintendence of the High Court under Article 227 of the Constitution. Therefore, if a CM has been properly convened and there is no challenge to its composition and the proceedings are in accordance with the procedure prescribed, the High Court, or for that matter, any Court, must stay its hands.[268] There are number of other cases wherein the apex court and High Courts explained the scope of their intervention in the proceedings related to the CM process.

Among the specific matters of CM process dealt with in judicial review may be mentioned the pre-trial investigation (PPS Bedi, Major A Hussain, Flying Officer S Sunderajan, and so on) as discussed earlier at length. Other such matters included the revision proceedings (Capt. Harish Uppal[269] and Capt. A P Bajpai's[270] cases), quantum of the sentence passed by the CM (Ranjit Thakur[271] and R.K. Sharma's[272] cases) applicability of natural justice to the CM and C of I (S N Mukharji's case[273]) and several other matters related to CM process. Without coining any principle like that of 'lost' jurisdiction, the judicial attitude in respect of the pre-trial procedure has been that "judicial" review, generally speaking, is not directed against a decision but is directed against the decision-making process" (Ranjit Thakur's and R.K. Sharma's cases). The court accordingly, adopted an attitude of non-interference in the verdict of a CM challenged on the ground of any irregularities at the pre-trial investigation unless the irregularity violated any mandatory provision.[274] Further, while conceding that a body charged with a duty to act judicially must comply with the minimum requirements of natural justice, the Supreme Court pointed out that "in a trial which is likely to result in deprivation of liberty, the body which has ultimately the power to make an order which would result in the deprivation of liberty must hear the offender, offering full participation and that principle cannot be diluted... It is the decision of the court-martial

268 UOI & Others v. Maj A Hussain, AIR 1998 SC 577 .

269 Supra n 56.

270 Supra n 57.

271 Supra n 53.

272 Supra Ch. 6, n 125.

273 Supra Ch. 7, n 235.

274 Maj. GS Sodhi v COAS, AIR 1991 SC 1617 , (paras 14 and 15).

which would result in deprivation of liberty and not the order directing that the charge be heard..."[275] As for any irregularity at a CM trial itself, the judicial attitude may be best described in words of the Punjab and Haryana High Court which, in a recent case, clarified that "ordinarily there is a finality to the finding arrived at by the competent authority in the Court Martial proceedings. The jurisdiction of the High Court... under Article 226... is for a limited purpose of finding out whether there has been infraction of any mandatory provisions of the Act prescribing a procedure which caused grave miscarriage of justice or for finding out whether there has been a violation of the principles of natural justice. The said power of judicial review is not a power of appellate authority and thus, the Court cannot re-appreciate the evidence in coming to the conclusion."[276] The Supreme Court had also conveyed substantially the same thing while stating in Major Hussain's case that "user of restraint in the matter of interference is the hall-mark of judicial control over administrative action, more so when law courts would be dealing with the members of disciplined forces."[277]

The superior courts in judicial review, however, have not hesitated to interfere where they felt the demands of justice to do so. In the cases of Ranjit Thakur,[278] Sub Dev Singh,[279] Maj Gen D S C Rai,[280] Sheel Kr Roy,[281] Nirmal Lakra,[282] L D Balam Singh[283], Capt. Charanjit S Gill[284] and several other cases, the court suitably intervened and gave appropriate relief to the petitioner, including a cost of Rs.5000 in Lakra's case. On the other hand, the courts came heavy handedly in a case like that of Maj Gen M L Yadav who had absconded to defeat the post-retirement liability and surfaced after the limitation period was over.[285]

Unlike the hostile attitude shown by some US Supreme Court Judges, like Justices Black and Douglas towards military justice system, the superior courts in the post-Independence era have held a very balanced attitude towards the CM, the procedure prescribed for its trial and the Service personnel as a class. The earlier referred cases of

275 Supra Ch.6. nn 90-91, related text.

276 Mithilesh Kumar v UOI, 2003 (3) SLR 667 (P&H).

277 UOI v Maj A Hussain AIR 1998 SC 577;(1998) 1 SCC 537 (para 23 of SCC).

278 Supra n 53.

279 UOI v Subedar Dev Singh, Supr eme Court decision dated 23 Apr 2003in CA No . 5978 of 1997 .

280 Supra Ch 6, n 34.

281 Supra Ch7, n 156.

282 Supra n 28.

283 Supra n 126.

284 Supra n 28.

285 Supra n 152.

Ram Sarup v UOI, UOI v Major A Hussain, PPS Bedi v UOI, Major G S Sodhi v COAS and Bimla Devi v Capt G L Bakshi stand testimony to such attitude of the superior courts, which may be pithily summarized by the pronouncement in Mithilesh Kumar's case:

> A Court Martial has also the same responsibility as any Court to protect the rights of accused charged before it and to follow the procedural safeguard. Procedure prescribed for Court Martial is equally fair if not more than a criminal court provides to the accused... Proceedings of a Court Martial are not to be compared with the proceedings in a Criminal Court under the Code of Criminal Procedure where adjournments have become a matter of routine... It has been rightly said that the Court Martial remains to a significant degree, specialized part of overall mechanism by which the military discipline is preserved. It is for the special need for the armed forces that a person subject to Army Act is tried by Court Martial for an act which is an offence under the Act. Court Martial discharges judicial function and to a great extent is a court where provisions of Evidence Act are applicable.[286]

Similarly in Bimla Devi[287] and PPS Bedi's[288] cases, the courts spoke highly of military authorities and military officers respectively.

The judicial attitude towards the proceedings of CM process, however, may at times appear as not based on proper understanding of the military law and incompatible with military ethos. In Ranjit Thakur's case, for instance, the Supreme Court set aside the verdict of the SCM inter alia on an erroneous ground.[289] Similarly, in several cases the pronouncements of the Supreme Court and High Courts have exhibited an embarrassingly inadequate awareness of the terminology relating to the subject being dealt with. For instance, in Sheel Kr Roy's case, it has been stated that "a Court of Inquiry was held in terms of Army rule 22"[290] whereas the said rule provides for the hearing of the charge by the CO and not the C of I which is held under AR rr 177 to 185. In Maj Gen Yadav's case, the Supreme Court, summarizing the scheme of the AA and AR speaks of "the preliminary report recorded after summary trial" and that "the need for adduction of evidence arises only where the accused pleads not 'guilty'. In that

286 Supra n 276.

287 Supra Ch 5, n 34, p 148.

288 Supra n 4, p 1434.

289 Supra , n 53.

290 Sheel Kr Roy v Secretary M/o Defence, JT 2007 (7) SC 485, at p 488.

situation, the members are required to take oath."[291] The correct position is that there is no summary trial during the course of a trial by a GCM and that the members take oath much before the accused pleads "guilty" or not "not guilty" to the charge. Irrespective of these minor flaws, the superior courts, however, have a very considerate attitude towards military justice and military personnel as is evident from the pronouncements in the cases of Sheel Kr Roy and Nirmal Lakra that it "is now well settled legal principle which has firmly been accepted throughout the world that a person merely by joining Armed Forces does not cease to be a citizen or be (sic is) deprived of his human or constitutional right."

8.7 General Attitude towards Efficacy of CM Process

Four questions were in the Interview Schedule designed to seek data from all the 200 respondents in respect of their general attitude towards the efficacy of CM process. The respondents were to agree, partially agree or disagree to statements included in Q. 3.4 (e), (f) and (j). A similar statement in three parts was to be put vide Q.1.11 to 100 respondents comprising of member and JA categories. The data are reflected in Table - 51 on the next page:

291 Supra n 152, par as 20 & 21 r espectively.

TABLE-51

General Attitude of Respondents to Efficacy of CM Process

Q No.	Statements	A	PA	D	CS	NR	Total
1.11	(a) Conviction at CM necessary to maintain discipline;	11	22	64	03	00	100
	(b) Acquittal by CM adversely affects discipline	01	13	84	01	01	100
	(c) Conviction or acquittal whichever warranted best serves discipline	95	02	02	01	00	100
3.4	(e) CM decisions are discipline oriented caring for justice only incidentally	43	43	89	12	13	200
	(f) Requirements of military discipline are served in a balanced manner along with cause of justice by CM trial of military offenders	140	22	17	08	13	200
	(g) Decision of CM are foregone conclusion, compliance with procedure is mere formality	28	22	121	11	18	200
A = Agree; PA = Partially Agree; D = Disagree; CS = Can't Say; NR = No Response							

As reflected from the data in Table-51, 95% of the respondents believed that conviction or acquittal by a CM, whichever warranted on merit of the case, best served the cause of military discipline even though 11% of them also were of the view that conviction at CM was necessary for the maintenance of discipline and 1% saw acquittal as adversely affecting military discipline. On the face of things, there may seem to be some sort of conflict or contradiction in these three sets of response but in fact there is none. Military discipline is the prime mover of the military justice process but the pre-trial investigation should be conducted so thoroughly that a case reaches the trial stage only when the facts really needed conviction. The US military law seems to have the same aim in providing for a pre-trial investigation by a court-martial convening authority so as to ensure that no charge or specification may be referred to a GCM for trial until a thorough and impartial investigation of all the matters set forth therein has been made.[292] If this is ensured, conviction would be the natural outcome of the trial and acquittal would be a sort of miscarriage of justice. In such a scenario conviction would be considered as necessary and acquittal would adversely affect the cause of discipline. However, perfect pre-trial investigation may not always be possible to achieve and the outcome of the trial may then be unpredictable. In that event, whatever may be the verdict, whether conviction or acquittal, depending upon the evidence, will be in the best interest of military discipline. There is no conflict between the needs of discipline and the cause of justice. However, a short-sighted view of the two or of either may lead to an erroneous perception in this regard, which may at times give a defective impression that decisions of CM are pre-determined and that the trial is merely a farce. However, majority of the respondents (121, i.e., 60.5%) did not have such an impression. They disagreed with the proposition that CM decisions are foregone conclusion. Similarly, majority of the respondents (89 out of 200, i.e., 44.5%), which though not a very big percentage but greater than that of any other responses involved in the question, did not agree with the proposition that CM decisions are discipline oriented, caring for justice only incidentally. However, 43 (21.5%) respondents agreed with it and another 43 partially agreed while the remaining 25 respondents made no contribution, some giving a response of 'can't say' and others simply abstained. In 1919, an American Commander had stated that "the prime object of military organization is victory, not justice.... If it can do justice, well and good, But justice is always secondary, and victory is always primary".[293] Victory still remains the primary objective of the Armed Forces. However, the military justice system has undergone tremendous change since Wigmore's times. There is an increasing realization among the commanders themselves now that "morale and discipline are enhanced when the troops understand that they are being treated with dignity, fairness and equality under the law."[294] As a result it is not only the American system which has become "more sensitive to due process concerns"[295] and their Cs M as "real Courts - independent judicial bodies, with procedures that have many more similarities than differences with civilian courts"[296], but also even a comparatively antiquated military justice system, like ours, now enjoys a reputation of the requirements of military discipline being served in a balanced manner along with

292 RCM 405 read with UCMJ Art. 32.

293 Colonel John H Wigmore, "Address Before the Maryland State Bar Association, (28 June 1919)" in 24 MD State B ar Association T ransaction, 1999 at 188.

294 Cox III, "The Arm y, the Courts, And the Consti tution: The Ev olution of Mi litary Justice," op ci t, n 1, p 30.

295 Weiss v United States, 510 US 163, 194 (1994), Ginsharg J, concurring.

296 Cooke, "The T wenty-Sixth Annual K enneth J Hodson Lectur e, Manual f or Courts-Martial 20X", op cit, n 83, p 10.

the cause of justice. As may be seen from the data in Table -51, as many as 140 (70%) respondents believed so. Such a reputation would have accrued to the system from commensurate attitudinal posture adopted by its functionaries, particularly those constituting its judicial bodies. With a view to examining this aspect, the data collected in the present study about the belief of the 200 respondents as to the factors determining CM decisions is presented in Table 52 below:

TABLE - 52

Factors Determining CM Decisions

Sl. No.	Determining Factors	Response Frequency	Percentage out of 164*
1.	Wishes of Superiors	42	25.6
2.	Conscience of Members	55	33.5
3.	Natural Justice	66	40.0
4.	Evidence and law	115	70.0
5.	Legal advice	82	50.0
6.	Need of Discipline	35	21.0
7.	Can't say/No response	36	22.0
* Calculated by excluding 'can't say'/no response (36) from total of 200			

As may be seen from the data here, 36 respondents did not express any view. Out of remaining 164, as many as 115 (70%) respondents believed that the CM decisions are based on evidence and law. The second largest responses, i.e., 82 (50%) contained a belief that legal advice rendered by the JA made a significant contribution to the decision taken at CM trial. The consideration of discipline occupied the lowest niche in this. Such a position of discipline in the consideration of the CM decision, however, does not reflect any adverse attitude towards this factor. The military discipline being an inbuilt consideration in the system itself, the CsM perhaps do not separately consider it while arriving at their finding. However, in the matters of sentence where the members of a CM have much more discretion, the factor of discipline is a very important consideration.

The attitudinal analysis of several matters related to CM process, in the foregoing, generally brings out that military justice establishes the basic standards of conduct for all men and women who wear the inform, and it establishes the procedures by which those standards are enforced. It does not simply impose discipline through deterrence and punishment. It inculcates and reinforces discipline by consistently applying two fundamental principles; each person regardless of rank, is responsible and accountable for his or her actions; and each person, regardless of circumstances, is entitled to be treated fairly.[297] On the last stated principle, however, we in India have yet to go a long way to catch up with other modern systems by updating our antiquated military justice system to enable it to rise to the yuga dharma, i.e., the dictates of our age of human rights and the high ideals of Justice, Liberty, Equality and Fraternity which are our constitutional aspirations.

297 Cooke, Ibid, p 6.

CHAPTER - 9

EPILOGOUS SUMMATION AND SUGGESTIONS

> *Obviously, there have got to be major differences between soldiers and civilians, including differences in their respective systems of criminal justice. But our policy should not be to maximize these differences so far as that can be done without outraging the court's sense of justice, but rather to minimize them so far that can be done without impairing military efficiency.*[1]
>
> — Professor Joseph W Bishop, JR.

9.1 Introduction

Military justice is often said to have existed ever since the armies came into being. Some military historians believe that what constitutes military criminal law today grew in Rome while others would ascribe the origin of military justice to Ancient Greece where the military court condemned General Filotas to death for conspiring against Alexander the Great in 330 BC. However, many military jurists do not find it possible to talk about military justice existing before the 15th and the 16th centuries.[2] Resisting the lure of going into this any further, it may be noted that the system of military justice would have started with a view to meeting the needs of the Army as a "separate community" having "a separate system of government"[3]. However, such a concept is now considered to be one whose "time is long past"[4]. Further, the system has also attracted criticism in much conflicting terms, with Sir Mathew Hale and Blackstone

---

1 Joseph W Bishop , Jr, "Civilian Judges and Military Justice : Collateral Review of Court -Martial Convictions", op cit, Ch 6, n 102, p 71

2 John Gillissen, "Evolution actuelle de la justice militaire", op cit, Ch 8, n 88, p 48.

3 Carter v Mc Claughry, op cit, Ch 7, n 2, p 389.

4 Bishop, "Civilian Judges and Military Justice : Collateral Review of Court-Martial Conviction", op citn.1, p 70.

describing the related law as "no law, but something indulged rather than allowed as law" for the sake of "order and discipline in an army"[5], and jurists like Justice Cox III finding, on the other hand, the "grand strategy" and the system functioning well.[6]. The present author, having been associated closely with the system for three decades, considered it to be his bounden duty to make his humble contribution in the direction of dispelling the confusion by undertaking an empirical study of the attitudes that the concerned people may be having towards military justice system, so that remedial measures, if any, required to improve the system, could be suggested as a follow-up action.

9.2 Summation

Even though possessing fairly a long first-hand experience of the subject, this author made a wide ranging consultation with senior military commanders, serving as well as retired ones, legal luminaries in the field like Rear Admiral Dr. O.P. Sharma, the first Ph D degree holder in India on a military law topic, judges like Chief Justice V K Gupta who had had a stint with CM trials as an advocate before his elevation to the Bench, and academicians like Dr. K. L. Bhatia of the University of Jammu, who had read a paper at Northern Command Legal Seminar, 1991, on the "Role of Civil and Military Judicial Systems and the Maintenance of Discipline in the Armed Forces". Additionally, the available related literature was also reviewed. Based on the understanding of the subject so acquired, the topic of the study was formulated as 'Decision Making Process of Court Martial : An Attitudinal Study' (referred in this work as DPCM), the objectives of the study were decided and hypotheses developed as brought out earlier in sections 3 and 4 of Chapter 3. In the prevailing circumstances of the universe of the study and the population to be targeted, there was no alternative but to settle for quota sampling for the reasons explained in section 6(b) of Chapter 3. Further, the sample size was fixed as 200 units from four strata, ie,of the accused, CM members, JAs and assorted civilians and armed forces personnel likely to be interested in the subject of study. It was decided to collect the primary data from the sample by personal interview through an Interview Schedule with mostly structured questions. The Interview Schedule was accordingly prepared in consultation with the Research Supervisor, Prof. Dr. S.C. Raina and with active assistance of an expert, Dr. S.K. Gupta, who had the experience of working in the UNESCO in the field of social survey and research. The Interview Schedule had three parts, with 12 questions in each, meant respectively for the respondents of the members/ JAs, accused and in general categories. A total of 208 respondents were interviewed by

---

5 1 Black Com 413, cit in Winthrop, Military Law and Precedents, op cit, Ch 1, n 1, p 47 .

6 Cox III, "The Army, the Courts and the Constitution: The Evolution of Military Justice" , op cit, Ch 8, n 1, p 30.

the reseacher, ie., the author himself and by the interviewers selected for the purpose. While editing the returned Interview Schedules, the researcher found some of them irretrievably deficient, which had to be discarded. The data from the remaining 200 Interview Schedules were subjected to the process of coding and tabulating. The data were then analysed, interpreted and finally presented in the preceding chapters. It may be mentioned that the total number of responses expected from the questions, including sub-questions, in 200 Interview Schedules was 22050, with the break up of 3950 responses from 50 respondents of JA category (79 responses from each), 4350 from members category (87 responses from each), 3550 responses from the accused category (71 responses from each) and 10200 from all the 200 respondents on general questions in Part III of the Interview Schedule which were addressed to all the respondents. This number does not include responses as to personal data and the suggestions made by the respondents.

As explained in Chapter 2, the CM process sets in motion when an offence committed by a person subject to military law, or suspected to have been so committed, comes to light. On the identity of the concerned military offender becoming clear, through initial investigation, conducted formally by a C of I or otherwise, the accused may be taken into military custody. However, such a course is by no means mandatory. The question of placing or not placing a person under arrest, close or open, is pragmatically decided on the basis of certain general considerations such as, nature of the offence, safety of the accused himself and of others, likelihood of his absconding or of tempering with the prosecution evidence and so on. Certain safeguards are laid down to ensure that the period of custody remains restricted to the requirements of the case. Chapter 5 examines in detail the issue of the pre-trial custody and the related data in respect of the respondents who had been accused for offences triable by the CM. The data in Table 13 reflects that 22 (44% of the 50 accused respondents) were not placed in military custody at all before their trial by the CM. The remaining accused respondents underwent pre-trial custody, ranging from less than one month in 16% cases to military custody between 24-30 months in one (2%) case. The majority of those (12%) who remained in pre-trial military custody underwent such custody for 18-24 months. This is in sharp contrast of the practice under the ordinary criminal jurisdiction to arrest the suspects routinely almost in every case. At times, even those against whom charge-sheets are not filed keep languishing in pre-trial custody. Under the present study, those (22 respondents) who were not at all kept in pre-trail custody included 13 (59% of the 22) charged with offences punishable with 10-14 years RI. The discussion, immediately following Table 13, deals with the possible reasons for no custody in such cases of serious offences. As for the offenders placed under military custody, they included personnel of all ranks from an ordinary Sepoy to a Major General. However, officers are usually placed under open arrest. The JCOs and ORs are also placed under open arrest, if desirable. Considering the nature of restraints imposed upon a person under open arrest, this kind of arrest "is something like bail on certain conditions"[7], as observed by Madras High Court. This is one of the reasons why the provisions of bail have never been known to military law. In the context of the Eighth Amendment of the US Constitution providing against 'excessive bail', Henderson points out that the "only problem of construction created by the amendment is caused by the fact that bail has never been granted to members of military awaiting trial by courts-martial."[8] It may be seen that the purpose of bail is to allow an accused to remain free until and unless he is convicted. The individual in military having no such unguarded freedom of movement and being at all times subject to control of his superior, the bail is not applicable to him, argues Henderson.[9] Thus, the provision and practice relating to pre-trial military custody seem to be quite favourable to the accused as compared to his civilian counterpart subject to ordinary criminal jurisdiction. However, there are some drawbacks too, which call for legislative and administrative remedial measures. In Ram Sarup's case, one of the contentions was that the relatives of the petitioner had been refused permission to see him; and the petitioner was thus denied an opportunity to engage a lawyer "through the resources and help of his relatives"[10]. The contention was rejected by the apex court on factual ground but it does bring out a need to incorporate in the military law a provision to implement the direction of the Supreme Court made in this regard in Joginder Kumar's case[11]. The other requirement, in the context of military custody is to have some mechanism of greater control on pre-trial custody by providing for custody hearing on the pattern of the British and American systems, as discussed in Chapter 5.7(c).

Since the military justice system is need based, it encompasses within its scope all the stages of the disposal of a military offence, the pre-trial, at the trial and the post-trial proceedings, with a dominant role assigned to the commander at each stage. Even though the commander's role is considerably eroded in the present times of human rights revolution, in most of the modern systems, the military justice still remains command oriented all over the world, except in the countries where it has merged in the ordinary criminal jurisdiction. Accordingly, the pre-trial investigation of an offence initially takes place at the concerned company level unless the identity of the offender is not yet made out. In the latter case and otherwise in the cases of specified offences, the facts are

---

7 Lt Col SP Sharma v UOI, Madras High Court unreported decision dated 06 Feb 1990 in Cr WP No. 754 of 1990; cf United States. Watkins v Vissering, Misc No. 722 ED va June 10, 1960.

8 Tytler, An Essay on Military Law and the Practice of Courts Martial, 1800, p 202 and Ady e, A Treatise on Courts Martial, 1799, pp 139-140, cit in, Gordon D Henderson, "Courts-Martial and the Constitution : The Original Understanding", op cit, Ch 5, n 80, p316.

9 Henderson, ibid.

10 Ram Sarup's case, op cit, Ch 7, n 119, para 7.

11 Supra, Ch 5, n 2, p 1354.

thrashed out by a C of I, which may be ordered by any officer in command of the concerned body of troops. The procedure of C of I is governed by the instructions of the commanders in the specific case and the general related provisions of the concerned Act and rules or regulations made thereunder. However, an infringement of any such instructions or provision relating to a C of I is not treated as jurisdictional for the legal validity of subsequent CM trial, unless it was an infringement of a mandatory requirement or was otherwise of a serious nature. In the case of Sheel Kr Roy[12], for example, where the petitioner was tried by SCM for absence without leave, ignoring the recommendation of the C of I for regularizing his absence in view of the psychiatric state of his mind, the apex court conceded that in a psychiatric case "the opinion of the Court of Inquiry is only recommendatory" but insisted that the CO holding the SCM was "required to take that fact into consideration." The apex court also found fault with the quantum of the punishment awarded, citing the doctrine of proportionality from Ranjit Thakur and Ex Naik Sardar Singh's cases[13] and held the SCM sentence to be unsustainable. Under the present study, a C of I was held in 42 (84%) cases, which included 64% cases of mandatory requirement and 20% where it was optional considering the nature of the offence involved. It apparently suggests that military commanders do order a C of I in almost all the cases where it is so required by the related provisions and also when considered to be desirable otherwise. However, certain shortcomings have been noticed in practice. AR r 180 (and corresponding provisions of the Naval and Air Force laws) requires that the affected person shall be afforded an opportunity to be present at the C of I proceedings, cross-examine the witnesses and produce witnesses in his defence if he so desired. Though an Army Headquarters letter, misinterpreting the views of the Supreme Court in certain cases, advises that non-compliance with Rule 180 will not affect subsequent disciplinary proceedings, this researcher is of the opinion that the word "shall" occurring in the said rule is suggestive of its application being mandatory and accordingly a scheme has been suggested in Chapter 6 to give effect thereto in the consideration of the finding and sentence at the trial stage.

Irrespective of the nature of the offence and the rank of the offender, every charge against a person subject to military law is required to be heard in his presence by his CO. Before 1992 amendment of the related provision of the AR, this was not a mandatory requirement in the case of officers, as held by the Supreme Court in PPS Bedi's case, but was mandatory in the cases of JCOs and OR[14]. The amendment has made it mandatory in all cases falling under the Army Act. The power of the CO to hear the charge is on the same footing as that of a magistrate under the ordinary criminal jurisdiction to conduct

12 Sheel Kr Roy v Secretary M/o Defence, JT 2007(7) SC 485, at p 490.

13 JT 1987 (4) SC 93 and JT 1991 (3) SC 1.

14 AIR 1982 SC 1413, at 1433-1435.

preliminary investigation and himself dispose minor charges brought before him.[15] Under the military law, the CO is required to dismiss a charge if, in his opinion, the evidence does not show that an offence under the Act has been committed and also has the power to dismiss the charge where he is satisfied that the charge ought not to be proceeded with, in a case other than the one to be dismissed for lack of evidence. However, where the CO decides to proceed with the case, he may summarily dispose it, if permissible within his limited legal powers to do so, order S of E to be recorded, or refer the case to superior authority for further guidance or with an application for trial by a CM. Whereas the hearing of the charge is essentially an oral proceeding, the S of E implies that the evidence is formally reduced into writing in the presence of the accused, giving him due opportunity to cross-examine the witnesses, make a statement and produce evidence in defence if he so desired. Under the present study, there was only one case in which the charge against the accused was not heard in his presence. It was a pre-1992 case of an officer when such hearing was not mandatory unless the accused officer so required. The data in Charts 6.1 and 6.2 further disclose that the charge was properly heard and S of E properly recorded in 72% cases. However, in 24% and 26% cases respectively, the respondents reported that the hearing of charge and the recording of S of E were not conducted satisfactorily. In the context of such irregularities, the Supreme Court's observations in the cases of Major Hussain and Major Sodhi are significantly relevant. In the former it was held that the "requirement of proper and adequate investigation is not jurisdictional and any violence thereof does not invalidate the court martial unless it is shown that accused has been prejudiced or a mandatory provision has been violated."[16] The court observed that the proceedings of the GCM were quite immaculate. In the case of Major Sodhi too, the Supreme Court found no 'flagrant violation' of any of Rules 22 to 25 and observed that even otherwise if there are some "minor irregularities, they do not in any way, affect the proceedings in the general court martial during which a regular trial was conducted".[17] The apex court also quoted from their earlier decision in PPS Bedi's case that the procedure prescribed by these rules is at a stage anterior to the trial by a CM. It is the decision of the CM which would result in the deprivation of liberty and not the order directing that the charge be heard or that summary of evidence be recorded. However, where the hearing of the charge was not conducted by the CO, despite a request by the accused officer under Rule 25 (since omitted by the amendment of 1992), the subsequent trial was held to have been vitiated."[18] The Delhi High Court similarly allowed a petition, holding all further proceedings to be null and void, when

15 James Stuart-Smith, "Military Law, Its History, Administration and Practice", Law Quarterly Review, Vol 85, 1969, pp 478-504 at 493.

16 UOI v Major A Hussain, AIR 1998 SC 577 : (1998) 1 SCC 537 .

17 Major GS Sodhi v COAS and Lt Col S Duggal v COAS, AIR 1991 SC 1617 (para 14).

18 Major Gen DSC Rai v GCM Fort St George, Madras HC unreported order dated 25 Apr 1984 in WP No. 3067 and 3068 of 1984.

the CO had dispensed with the mandatory hearing of the charge under the newly added proviso to Rule 22(1) as amended in 1992, on the ground of the matter having been investigated at a C of I at which Rule 180 had been complied with whereas it was not in fact so complied with in the case of the petitioner.[19] Under the US system, the question of inadequate pre-trial investigation was tackled in two different approaches of collateral review of CM convictions followed at Federal Courts. In the cases of Private Anthony and Arnold, who were jointly tried by a GCM in April 1945 and convicted for having committed rape against three German women, Anthony was granted the writ by the US District Court of Kansas on the ground of an inadequate pre-trial investigation whereas Arnold was denied this by the District Court of Texas under whose jurisdiction he was undergoing the sentence. The latter court refused to intervene, holding that the CM was properly convened, it had jurisdiction of the offence and of the parties and the sentence was within the law. Those facts being irrefutable, the civil court may not inquire any further.[20] The Texas court, in fact, adopted the approach that the US Supreme Court had been adopting all along, prior to 1944 or thereabout, that the federal courts, having no appellate jurisdiction over military tribunals, would, in collateral proceedings attacking the validity of a military sentence, most strictly limit themselves to "ascertaining whether the military court had jurisdiction of the person and subject matter, and whether ... it had exceeded its powers in the sentence pronouncements. No more errors in their proceedings are open to consideration. The single inquiry, the test, is jurisdiction."[21] A break through came only in Burn v Wilson[22], presenting, on its facts, the question whether and to what extent the principle of Johnson v Zerbst[23] ought to be applied to collateral review of CM proceedings. The plurality (not majority) opinion of four judges inter alia held that the constitutional "guarantee of due process is meaningful enough, and sufficiently adaptable, to protect soldier", even though in military habeas corpus inquiry, the scope of matters open to review, has always been more narrow than in civil cases". Justice Frankfurter, though not voting either way without more argument on certain questions, made the position still more clear in his opinion that the inquiry in such cases could not be restricted as to "whether the tribunal was legally constituted and had jurisdiction", and that he saw no reason for treating the principle of Johnson v Zerbst – the principle that jurisdiction may be lost by a denial of whatever process is due in the circumstances – as any less applicable to military than to civil courts."[24] The British Courts also had adopted on most occasions the same attitude of non-interference in CM

19 Major Sarup Singh Sidhu v UOI, Military Law Journal 2000 Delhi 34.

20 Anthony v Hunter, 71F Supp 823(D K an 1947) and Arnold v Cozart, 75F Supp 47 (ND T ex 1948).

21 In re Grimley, 137 US 147 , 150 (1890).

22 Burns v Wilson 346 US 137 (1953) at 142.

23 Johnson v Zerbst, 304 US 458 (1938).

24 Ibid, p 149 and 851 (petition for rehearing).

decisions, except on the ground of jurisdiction and power to award the sentence it has awarded, though nonetheless had issued writ in some cases like that of Private Brown.[25]

Judicial attitude apart, the pre-trial investigation under the Indian military system apparently needs to be updated in the light of the world-wide change in the society. Some suggestions in this regard will follow later.

The pre-trial investigation is only a stepping-stone to the CM trial, except in a case where the charge is dismissed or disposed otherwise. Generally an ad hoc body under most of the systems and composed of a panel of military officers, a CM is often erroneously seen as conducting a jury trial. However, it is important to note that a CM panel is in fact "not a jury; it was never designed to be a jury.... It was designed to be a blue ribbon panel. They are picked up because of their expertise and their knowledge ... the people who were mature; the people who knew how to make decisions; the people who were aware of the military requirements ... They represent the decision-making level of the Army."[26] The officers to serve as members of the CM are appointed by the convening officer under the AA or AFA while the NA provides only for the appointment of the president of the court by the convening officer and the president picks up a panel of the members from among the available officers. No JCO, WO or NCO is presently eligible to be a member of a CM under the Indian law, though the British, the US, Canadian and several other military systems now allow some WOs or NCOs to be members of the CM in the case of an accused of the same rank. Considering that the quality of justice depends more on the quality of the men who administer the law than on the contents of the law they administer,[27] the views of all the respondents in the present study were solicited inter alia on the practice of the members of the CM being appointed by and from the same command in which the accused is posted for duty or attached for trial. The data collected on this aspect are displayed in Table 23 and discussed under section 7.1(a). The need for any change in this regard and in regard to certain other structural aspects of the CM system has been examined in Chapter 8 in the light of the data in Tables 37 and 38 (ad hoc or static CM), and Tables 41 and 42 (legal qualification and other areas of improvement in the constitution of CM). A CM trial being a command function by lay military officers with no professional qualification or training in the administration of justice, a legally qualified officer with the designation of Judge Advocate is also appointed by the convening officer to assist the members in the matters of law and procedure. He, however, has no decision making power under the Army and Air Force laws but the NA empowers him to decide all questions of law himself. There is a global

25 Ex parte Brown, (1892) 37 Sol J 27.

26 Advisory Commission to the Military Justice Act of 1983 Report, p 39, Colonel Garner's testimony.

27 Evan Haynes, "The Selection and Tenure of Judges", National Conference of Judicial Councils, 1944, p 5, cit in Henry J Abraham, The Judicial Process, 4th ed, 1980, OUP, Ch. 1.

trend in the military justice systems to assign a greater say to law officers in the CM trials. One of the reasons for this is a world-wide trend that "the nature of our case load has continued to swing towards crimes against society, not just against the military" as stated by Brigadier General Cooke while suggesting the need for adopting "Judge Alone Sentencing"[28]. In the present study too, the nature of the offences charged against or dealt by respondents is suggestive of the same trend as may be seen from the data in Chart 9.1; the total number of military offences being 111 while that of civil and militarized civil offences being 138.

Chart 9.1
Nature of Offences Charged against/ Dealt by Respondents

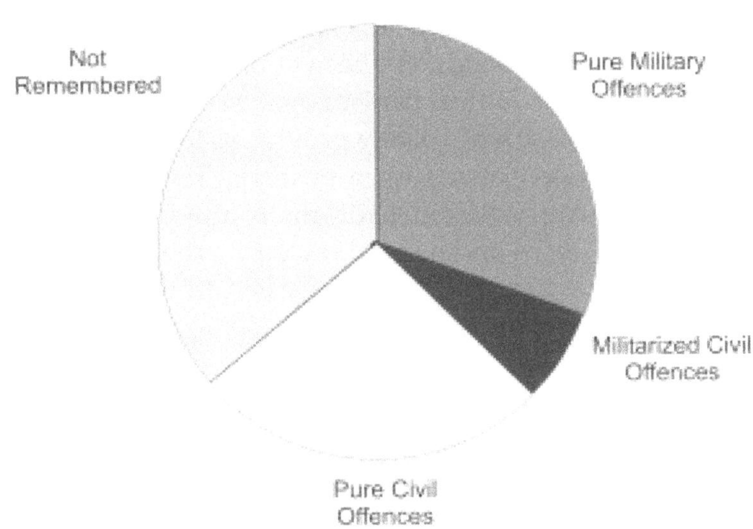

Returning to the legal cover , Tables 43 to 46 reflect the data collected on the quality of the legal cover provided in the administration of military justice and discussed in Chapters 3, 6, 7 and 8 in the light of the said data, along with the general provisions relating to the role of the JA and the entitlement of the accused to legal assistance and legal representation.

---

28 Brigadier General John S Cooke, "The Twenty-sixth Annual Kenneth J. Hodson Lecture : Manual for Courts-Martial 20X", Mil Law Rev, Vol 156, June 1998, pp 1-29, at 20.

The procedure followed by CsM is laid down in the related Services Acts, rules and regulations, as the CsM being tribunals of special laws, the provisions of the Cr PC governing the ordinary criminal proceedings before the civil courts are not applicable. The procedure governing the proceedings of a CM has been held to be quite elaborate and as fair as, if not more, than that under the Cr PC. Certain special features of the CM procedure include the right of the accused to object to any members or waiting members appointed for trial, special plea to general jurisdiction and pleas in bar on such grounds as the offence having become time-barred or double jeopardy, or the charge having been dismissed by the CO, or the offence having been condoned or pardoned. The witnesses are examined in accordance with the Indian Evidence Act, subject to certain modifications made by the Services Acts. The accused or his defending officer or the counsel for defence has practically the same rights in the matters of defence of the accused as available to his civilian counterpart under the Cr PC. There are, however, certain differences too, in the CM procedure, in comparison to the procedure under the Cr PC. For instance, the verdict of the CM is not given as a speaking order. The related provision of the AR has been lately amended in 1992 requiring the CM to give brief reasons for its finding. No such amendment has yet been incorporated in the Naval and Air Force laws. Further, an appeal mechanism against the decision of a CM has been introduced very recently. In the absence of any provisions for appeal against the decisions of CM, the only avenues opened earlier for a post-trial review of such decisions were pre-confirmation and post-confirmation petitions to the Central Government or the Service authorities under AA s 164 and judicial review by the High Court or the Supreme Court under their writ jurisdiction as discussed earlier. In the present study, 124 (62%) respondents were in full agreement and another 11 (5.5%) were in partial agreement of the need for establishing a CM appeal court as discussed in Chapter 8. The recent enactment of the Armed Forces Tribunal Act, 2007, providing for adjudication of the service matters of the personnel belonging to the Army, Navy and Air Force and for hearing appeals against CM decisions is a welcome development in this regard. [29]

9.3 Conclusion

To conclude this study on the attitudes of the concerned people a fleeting glance may be cast over the entire data in Tables 1 to 52 so as to assess whether the overall attitude towards CM process is favourable or unfavourable. For this purpose, total responses in each Table will be assigned a numerical value of 2 for positive response, 2 for a negative response and 1 (one) for neutral. While the classification favourable or

29 The Armed Forces Tribunal Act, 2007, received the assent of the President on 25 Dec 2007 and the Tribunal located at New Delhi and its Benches set at Chandigarh, Chennai, Guwahati, Jaipur, Kochi, Kolkata, Lucknow and Mumbai have started functioning from mid-2009.

unfavourable will be based on an assessment objectively made by common logic and reasoning, the classification neutral will be reserved for a response of 'can't say' or no response. For example, Table 17 on C of I shows that a C of I was held in 42 (84%) cases and not held in 7 cases with no response in one case. C of I is not sine quo non in every case except when it is mandatorily required in such cases as illegal absence etc. The data analysis in section 6.4(d) brings out that military commanders order a C of I almost in all cases where it is a mandatory requirement and also use C of I as a management tool to investigate the cases even when they are not legally obliged to do so. On the basis of these facts, Table 17 would win 2 points towards favourable attitude, and no point towards unfavourable. Since there was one case of no-response too, from among 50 respondents, a value of 0.1 will be assigned to neutral attitude. Similarly, in Table 18, as many as 31 respondents out of 50 having been given due opportunity for cross-examination of witnesses deposing against them, and making a statement and producing witnesses in defence, at C of I in their cases, the data in this Table too will be assigned 2 points for favourable attitude, none for unfavourable attitude and 0.1 for one case of no response. In Table 19, however, there being 40% responses for feeling aggrieved and 22% for not aggrieved with 38% (19 in number) no response cases, the Table will get 2 points for unfavourable, none for favourable and 1.9 for neutral attitudes. Thus, a total of 4 points for favourable, 2 for unfavourable and 2.1 for neutral attitude will be assigned to C of I proceedings in CM process. The points earned at all the Tables will be averaged to arrive at the over-all inference on the attitude towards a the CM process. This may be presented in a Master Table on DPCM Attitudes with reference to the five hypotheses developed for the present study. As stated in Chapter 3.4, the five hypotheses related to; one, the CM procedure being equally fair to the accused, if not more than the procedure followed by ordinary criminal court; two, the CM system with speedy justice being suitable not only for Armed Forces but also for civil administration of justice in terrorism struck areas; three, CM procss being fraught with command influence at all stages; four, CM decisions being predetermined and trial being mere formality; and five, the built-in checks and balances of the CM system sufficiently making up for the absence of appeal against the CM decisions. In the Table given below, these hypotheses will be referred by their serial number stated above. For the purpose of this Table, the expression 'CM procedure' include the pre-trial custody and procedures, and the expressions 'Favourable', 'Unfavourable' and 'Neutral' stand represented by 'F', 'U' and 'N' respectively.

MASTER TABLE - 53

Favourable or Unfavourable Attitude to CM Process

Hyp-othes-is		Referring Table Numbers	F	U	N	Remarks
One	1	T 09-14: Pre-trial custody	02	00	0.1	60% accused respondents suffered 'nil' or below 1 month pre-trial custody.
	2	T 15: Awareness of related law.	00	02	0.1	74% accused being unaware.
	3	T 16 and Chart 7.3: Confession whether extracted by force etc	02	00	0.3	Only 10% accused stated to have confessed under threat.
	4	T 17-19: C of I.	04	02	1.9	C of I held in 99% cases of mandatory requirement and also in 56% cases where it was not obligatory but compliance of natural justice safeguards was not satisfactory in several cases and 40% felt aggrieved, 22% not aggrieved, 38% neutral.
	5	T 20-22 and Charts 6.1 to 6.3:Irregularities at Hearing of Charge and S of E; action taken by the aggrieved ; absence of legal assistance.	02	00	4.6	Held in all cases except one which was not a case of mandatory requirement. Irregularities in 25% of cases only; 90% did not respond to the action taken by the aggrieved. Legal assistance not considered required at pre-trial stage by 64% of all respondents.

Contd/-

Hyp-othes-is		Referring Table Numbers	F	U	N	Remarks
One	6	T 28: General attitude of CM in decisions on prosecution and defence submissions.	00	02	1.0	Prosecution submissions being accepted in 42% and defence in 20%; decided on merit in 36% and 34% cases and not heard in 2% and 6% cases respectively.
	7	T 29: Natural justice safeguards	02	00	1.2	Cross-examination, making statement and producing witness, opportunity given in 72%, 68% and 66% cases respectively.
	8	T 30-32: Whether CM decisions served cause of discipline and justice in a balanced manner	02	04	2.5	66% conviction but sentence above one year, and cashiering or dismissal in 40% of cases, 46% not satisfied and 44% satisfied.
Two	1	T 14: Ten main offences tried by CM (1985 - 1989), Chart 9.1: Nature of offences charged with or dealt by respondents	02	00	00	6 out of 10 offences being purely civil offences or militarized civil offences, shows that CM can well deal such offences. In the present study out of 250 offences charged, 103 pure civil offences and 36 militarized civil offences.
	2	T 37: Ad hoc CM or static CM.	02	00	0.9	63.5% voting for no change.
	3	T 38: Explanation of T 37 data.	-	-	-	No bearing on attitudes
	4	T 39: Rank of members and JA at their first CM.	02	00	0.2	72% members Major or above but JA only 9% Major.
	5	T 40: Quantum of service of members and JA at 1st CM.	02	00	0.2	68% members 10 yr or above service but only 20% JAs with that much of service.

Hyp-othes-is		Referring Table Numbers	F	U	N	Remarks
	6	T 41: Legal qualification and experience in military law.	02	00	00	98% members and 100% JA had legal qualification or/and military law experience.
	7	T 47 (a) extension of CM jurisdiction to operation areas and to terrorist trials everywhere (b) All military offenders be tried by ordinary criminal courts.	02	00	0.78	52% agreed fully or partially agreed with 1st proposition; 72% disagreed with the 2nd proposition.
Three	1	T 23: Convening of CM outside accused's command.	02	00	0.9	44% for no change; 39.5% for certain changes and 17% neutral.
	2	T 33: DPCM fraught with command influence.	02	00	0.55	Only 20% agreeing fully and 24% partially while 45% disagreeing.
	3	T 35: Wishes of superior influencing decision/advice.	02	00	00	96% saying 'NO'.
	4	T 36: Different aspects of command influence affecting.	02	00	00	75% positive responses.
Four	1	T 34: CM decisions being pre-determined.	02	00	0.73	100% said 'NO' to decisions being pre-detemined.
Five	1	T 25: Plea to charges.	00	00	00	
	2	T 26: Documents given for preparation of defence.	00	02	0.5	All documents given only in 26% cases.
	3	T 27: Preparation of defence by calling witness at Govt. exp.	02	00	1.83	44% positive responses; 19% negative, rest neutral.
	4	T 43: JA's role, whether change required.	02	00	0.9	Majority (though 33.4%) said "No"
	5	T 44: JAG's Deptt's merger.	02	00	0.1	'No Change, by 62.5%.

Hyp-othes-is		Referring Table Numbers	F	U	N	Remarks
	6	T 45: Whether CM decisions are made by JA.	02	00	0.8	61% disagreed.
	7	T 46: JA's attributes.	02	00	0.1	88% found them profession -ally sound, 92% polite and 86% found them leaving decision to court.
	8	T 49: Disparity in sentence.	00	02	00	Undesirable disparity in sentence on same charge by different CM.
	9	T 50: Establishment of CMAC	00	02	00	61.5% respondents felt CM process to be deficient in absence of appeal court.
	10	T 32: Factors determining CM decisions.	02	00	00	70% said that evidence and law determined CM decision
	30	**Total**	**48**	**16**	**20.19**	

The data summarised in Table 53 on 30 counts of the five hypotheses disclose 48 (160%) points for favourable responses and 16 (53%) unfavourable. The data also bring out 20.19 (69%) points for neutral responses. Thus, the present study suggests that the population generally has favourable attitude towards CM process though a substantial part of the population is either not aware of or not interested in CM process related matters.

9.4 Hypotheses Tested

To test a hypothesis means to tell, on the basis of the data collected, whether or not the hypothesis seems to be valid. In hypothesis testing the main question is whether to accept or not the null hypothesis. The testing of a hypothesis in statistical terms would consist in making a formal statement of the null hypothesis (Ho) and also of the alternative hypothesis (Ha), selecting a significance level (generally, in practice, either 5% or 1% level), i.e., the 'a' value, deciding the correct sampling distribution, sampling a random sample and working out an appropriate value of the same, and calculating the probability that sample result would diverge as widely as it has from expectations if Ho were true[30]. However, within the limitations of this author, in statistical techniques, the hypothesis testing is being undertaken here through observation and deduction. This is in line with precedents in legal research.

The first hypothesis in the present study was that the procedure prescribed for the CM trial is equally fair if not more than a criminal trial provides to the accused. As noted earlier, Justice DP Wadhwa was of the view that the "proceedings of court martial are not to be compared with the proceedings in a criminal court under the Code of Criminal Procedure where adjournments have become a matter of routine" and that if "one looks at the provisions of law relating to court-martial ... it is manifestly clear that the procedure prescribed is possibly equally fair if not more than a criminal trial provides to the accused."[31] The data displayed in Tables 9 – 22 and 28 – 32 as summarized at Srls 1 to 8 in Table 53 above seem to be in accord with the view of the Honourable Judge. To give a concrete example, the data in Table 25, reflect that 10 respondents had pleaded 'Guilty' to the charges framed against them. The procedure adopted by the respective CM in all such cases was the one prescribed (in AR rr 52 and 54). Comparison with the corresponding procedure in the Cr PC ss 229 and 230 would show that much greater care is provided under the military law in proceeding on the plea of guilty than under the Cr PC where the Judge is required simply to record the plea and "in his discretion" to "convict him (the accused) thereon".[32] Similarly in the matter of pre-trial custody, the data in Table 9 reflect that 44% accused respondents were not placed in pre-trial custody at all, whereas every accused is taken into custody in the ordinary criminal procedure. Further, by the requirement of a trial by the CM to continue on day-to-day basis, the military justice system is known for its speedy disposal. At the same time, there are also certain noticeable negative aspects of the procedure prescribed for the CM. All the members of a CM are military officers who are not expected to be trained judges as the presiding officers of criminal courts are. No judgment is recorded. Even after the related provision of AR r 62 has been amended to require brief reasons to be recorded by a CM for its finding, the reasons so recorded generally leave much to desire. Lastly, the punishments prescribed for civil or militarized civil offences under the Services Acts and the sentence in fact awarded by CM are much harsher than under the ordinary criminal jurisdiction. For instance, respondent A-175-A-10, who was tried by CM for an offence under the Official Secrets Act was awarded 14 years RI, whereas out of the

30 William A Chance, Statistical Methods for Decision Making, 1969, Illinois, Richard D Irwin Inc, p 48, cit in CR Kothari, Research Methodology : Methods & Techniques, 2nd ed, 2004 , New Delhi, New Age International (P) Ltd. Publishers, p 192.

31 Major Hussain's case, supra, n 16, para 23 in SCC.

32 Supra, Ch 7, n 155 and related text.

five civilians who were arrested practically at the same time with secret documents of an Army Regiment and tried by POTA judge, two have been sentenced for 4 years under the OSA and acquitted under the POTA.[33] Thus, the first hypothesis may be partially accepted to the extent that the procedure to be followed by a CM is quite elaborate and generally follows the pattern of the procedure under the Cr PC. However with some material differences too which, in some circumstances, make a trial by ordinary criminal court more beneficial (not necessarily fair) to the accused as compared to the CM. However, the trials in ordinary criminal court are bound to take longer on account of trial procedures, appeals and revisions than trials at the CM.[34]

The second hypothesis starts with the merit of speedy justice obtainable in CM trial and asserts its suitability not only for the Armed Forces but also for the civil administration of justice in terrorism struck areas. The data displayed in Tables 14, 17 - 41 and 47 bring out that a trial by CM is presently conducted in respect of persons subject to military law only. However, it does adjudicate not only upon the acts constituting purely military offences but also upon acts constituting purely civil and militarized civil offences, except murder, culpable homicide and rape committed in respect of a person not subject to military law unless such offences were committed while on active service, at any place outside India or at a notified frontier post. This suggests the capability of CM system to deal with civil offences. As an ad hoc body, the CM has the advantage of being convened at any place to try accused persons in terrorism struck areas. In view of speedy justice, which is the hall mark of CM trial, and the experience and intellectual level its members generally possess, the cause of deterrent punishment without sacrificing the cause of justice in general may be achieved by adopting CM trial for civil administration too in terrorism struck areas, thus contributing to successful fight against terrorism. These might be the reasons for 52% respondents having agreed, fully or partially, to a statement in Q 3.4(h) in the Interview Schedule designed to cover the second hypothesis. The hypothesis, thus, seems to stand proved. However, emphatic disagreement of some respondents with the proposition, mainly on ideological ground, needs also to be noted. Further, a notice may also be taken of the fact that some countries like Peru are already convinced of the desirability of such a move.[35] Pakistan, under the Prime ministership of Zulfikar Ali Bhutto, had also amended her Army Act to bring the civilians under the purview of the said Act. The amendment was later struck down by the Lahore High Court. Now again Pakistan Government proposes to soon issue an Ordinance that will

---

33 Dainik Jagran (Hindi) 24 Oct 2007 , "***pota main paanch aaropi bari***"(Five accused acquitted under POTA).

34 Ram Sarup's case, op cit, n 10, p 252.

35 Supra, Ch 8, n 115 for Peru's military jurisdiction over civilians "betraying the motherland".

allow military courts to try civilians for offences like terrorism with sweeping powers to security and intelligence agencies.[36]

The third hypothesis was on DPCM being fraught with command influence. The matter has been dealt at length in Chapter 8 (s 8.2). As many as 45% respondents categorically disagreed, while only 20% agreed fully and 24% partially with a statement in Q 3.4(a) covering the hypothesis squarely, as may be seen from Table 33. The data in Table 34 also show that all the respondents (100%) in JA category and 96% respondents from the members category did not feel influenced in their advice and decision respectively by the wishes/views of superiors. Table 36 contains the data on certain other aspects of the issue, which reflect that 75.67% of the related responses do not favour the statement that DPCM is fraught with command influence. Thus, the third hypothesis stands rejected.

The fourth hypothesis that the decision by CM is pre-determined and the procedure followed is mere legal formality is in a way connected with the preceding hypothesis as well as the first hypothesis. The primary data collected in the present study as well as the secondary data from the legal provisions, judicial pronouncements and the scholarly expositions by jurists, as discussed in Chapters 2, 5, 6 and 7, however, seem to unambiguously disprove this hypothesis. In the present study, the data in table 34 show that 60% respondents disagree with the proposition that CM decision are pre-determined. Further Table 30 brings out that 4% of the accused were acquitted of all the charges and in one (2%) case, the finding of "Not Guilty" recorded by the court originally was adhered to at the revision proceedings as well. The very fact that there were findings of "not Guilty" in some cases, however small be their percentage, suggests that the findings were not mechanically recorded by the CM based on a pre-determined decision. The same may be also inferred from the percentage of conviction that the member and JA categories respondents had at the trials they attended, as displayed in Table - 54 on the next page.

36 TOI, 02 Nov 2007, p 25, "Pak may try civilians in military courts".

TABLE - 54

Percentage of Convictions at CM Trial

Srl No.	Percentage of Conviction	Response Frequency		Total	%
		Members	JAs		
1.	1 - 50%	00	03	03	03
2.	51 - 75%	04	14	18	18
3.	76 - 100 %	44	33	77	77
4.	No Response	02	00	02	02
	Total	50	50	100	100

As may be seen here, in the case of 21% respondents, the conviction percentage was 51-75% or less. The hypothesis will, therefore, have to be rejected.

The last hypothesis primarily concentrates on the need for an appeal being available against CM decisions. Until recently there was no appeal against a CM decision. A post-trial review of such decisions was traditionally restricted, in all military justice systems, the world over, to in-house reviews at hierarchical levels of military authorities and judicial review in writ jurisdiction. The latter confined usually to the issues of military jurisdiction and legality of the sentence passed. With a gradual change in the attitudes towards the right to justice as applicable to soldiers, an appeal mechanism has since been incorporated in most of the modern military justice systems. In the case of India, a felt need for some similar provision had been voiced from time to time in and out of Parliament. In PPS Bedi's case, the Supreme Court made a very strongly worded recommendation for providing at least one appeal against CM decisions. The Law Commission of India also recommended in its 169th Report that the "Army Act, 1950 be amended providing for the creation of an Armed Forces Tribunal which shall entertain appeals against the sentence/finding/order of the courts-martial under the Army Act" and that the "Navy and Air Force Acts may be so amended as to adopt the Appellate tribunal created by the Army Act for their purpose as well..."[37] However, there were also people who opposed the idea mainly with a two-fold argument; firstly, that any such mechanism would work against the special needs of the military system by eroding the authority of the military commanders and weakening the cause of speedy justice, and secondly, that the in-built checks and balances in the CM system sufficiently made up for the absence of an appeal against CM decisions. Q 3.4(d) in the Interview Schedule sought response of the 200 respondents to a statement that CM appeal court should be established and the existing writ jurisdiction of the High Court and the Supreme Court be barred in respect of CM decisions. The responses to the question have been presented in Table 50 and discussed in Chapter 8.6(c). It may be seen therefrom that 62% respondents felt the need for establishing an appeal court for hearing appeals against CM decisions but majority of them opposed the idea of barring the existing writ jurisdiction of the Supreme Court and High Courts in respect of CM decisions. Even though the procedure prescribed for CM system has been judicially scrutinized and found quite elaborate and practically similar to the one laid down under the Cr PC, as discussed earlier, the existence of certain important differences, including absence of an appeal, has also been highlighted by the Supreme Court. The existing provisions of the military law, despite being quite elaborate, are apparently no substitute for an appeal mechanism. In view of this, the fifth hypothesis stands to be rejected by the data collected from the respondents as well as the secondary data.

9.5 Suggestions

The data spread over 52 Tables and sumarised in Table 53 generally reflect a favourable attitude on the part of all concerned, including those tried by CM, towards CM process. The attitudes reflected in the secondary data from the judicial pronouncements, the reports of concerned committees, the papers read at seminars and the writings of the jurists are also favourable. However, three significant drawbacks in this regard are: one, archaic and antiquated nature of the current military law, with hardly any effective attempt having been made so far for review of the Army Act, 1950; two, general disinterestedness towards the military justice system on the part of those subject to the system, when not immediately concerned with it; and lastly, a general apathy towards, and consequent lack of awareness about, the system on the part of the civil intelligentsia, including the judges of the superior courts and the media. These factors translate into the Indian soldier being deprived of the benefit of world-wide developments brought about in the field of human rights, jurisprudential thought and judicial thinking. Keeping these facts in mind, some suggestions based on the present study are being listed out in the paragraphs to follow.

---

37 Law Commission of India, 169th R eport, April 1999, Ch. VII, "R ecommendations", 7.1(a) and (e) at p 12.

(a) **Pre-trial Custody**

(i) **Custody Review**: The Checks against unreasonably prolonged pre-trial custody, as discussed in Chapters 2 and 5, presently consist only of 8-day delay reports which, in practice, are routinely filed by the dealing staff, at times without even being noticed by the military authority to whom the report is addressed, until a requirement to the contrary arises in connection with a writ petition or a query made by some higher headquarters. The checks introduced in the British and the US military laws to prevent unnecessary prolongation of pre-trial military custody, in the form of custody review, as discussed in section 5.7(c) may be imported into our system, with necessary adaptation, including legal assistance provided to the accused at such reviews.

(ii) **Information to Kin**: Respondents A-178 and A-175 in the present study groused about nobody from their family or friends circle having been allowed to meet them. As a result, though a civil counsel was engaged by the Central Government for the defence in the case of the former who was facing a charge (of murder) punishable with death, the lawyer was neither of his choice nor did the lawyer listen to the accused. Similarly, according to the latter respondent, he could not make any representation against certain irregularities in pre-trial proceedings since he was not allowed to meet anybody. Those irregularities stand documented in the form of memorandum later by the Presiding Officer of the GCM under AR r 92(5). An officer respondent A-186 too had experienced similar difficulties at pre-trial investigation stage. These may not be representative cases of military custody, being only 6% of the accused category respondents (50), yet do illustrate the violation of important rights "inherent in Articles 21 and 22 (1) of the Constitution", as held by the Supreme Court in Joginder Kumar v State of UP[38] and DK Basu v State of Bengal[39]. AR, AFA and N Regs II (s) should be amended to expressly provide materialization of these rights as directed by the apex Court. Necessary measures discussed earlier in 5.7(d) may be adopted in the Indian system of military justice so as to ameliorate the present inadequacy.

(iii) **Right against Torture**: In the present study, the data in Table 16 bring out the use of threat, etc. to extract confession only in 4 (8%) cases but quite a few cases have come to light involving the use of force in military custody under the AA as well as such custody under the Armed Forces (Special Powers) Act as discussed in Chapter 5.7(f). A mechanism is needed to fight the menace as discussed in detail therein. A suggestion made in 5.7(f)(ii) may be incorporated in the Indian military justice system. It will also be desirable for this purpose that the pre-trial investigation of serious cases be assigned to a specialized agency like the Corps of Military Police.

38 Supra, Ch 5, n 2.

39 Supra, Ch 5, n 132.

The current role of the Military Police may be reoriented to include the investigation of offences through modern scientific aids to investigation. A separate sub-organization as Investigation Wing may be formed in the Corps of Military Police for the purpose, with necessary statutory powers and functional infrastructure.

(b) **Structural Reforms**

(i) **Jurisdiction ratione materiae**: As noted earlier, there is no justification, "from the moral or legal point of view, to remove from the jurisdiction of the ordinary courts, a member of the military who has committed an offence defined as such under ordinary criminal legislation".[40] It will, therefore, be desirable to amend the three Services Acts to provide for purely civil or militarized civil offences to be triable exclusively under the ordinary criminal jurisdiction, except where, in any particular case, the exigencies of the Service, for the reasons to be recorded in details by a General Officer Commanding an Army Corps or equivalent Service Organization, require that the offence be tried by a CM.

(ii) **Role of Commanding Officer**: The role of CO in respect of an offence committed by a person belonging or attached to his unit should be re-defined. The investigation report of the military police should be binding on the CO except for the purpose of dismissal of the charge by the CO, when he decides to do so despite the evidence on the record making out a prima facie case against the accused. In all such cases, however, the CO should be required to record his reasons for dismissing the charge.

(iii) **CM to be Semi-static Body with Certain Other Structural Improvements**: General Sir Charles Napier criticized the CM system for turning "the members that compose it, into attorneys-at-law: they lose the frank soldier-like sense of their duty as members of a court-martial with one grand conscientious duty to perform - that of acquitting the prisoner against all legal rules of evidence, if they conscientiously believe him to be (not) guilty. In short, the business of a court-martial is not to discuss points of law, but to get at the truth by all means in their power."[41] In view of such inherent weakness of the CM trial, several military justice systems have established permanent CM with increased say of legal constituent thereof in the decision making process. Based on the data discussed in Chapter 8.3, it is suggested that the Service law be suitably amended to provide for the establishment of semi-permanent CM, at Command or Corps or equivalent level, with three permanent members, including one law member from the Department of the Judge Advocate General, and two members appointed by the

---

40 Supra, ch 8, n 136.

41 Clode, Military and Martial Law, 1874, p 129 cit in OP Sharma, Military Law in India, op cit, Ch 1, n 4, p 311.

command authority on ad hoc basis for each case. The law member should have the same powers as any other member with additional power to exclusively decide all questions of law and procedure. The members should preferably be drawn from other two Services or at least from outside the command of the accused. While appointing the officers to constitute a CM, it should be ensured that the members, other than the law member, also possess sufficient understanding of the related law and procedure by virtue of having attended a course at the Institute of Military Law. Further, "to look at the rank of an accused as one of the factors governing the type of court-martial to be convened is contrary to the modern-day spirit of equality before the law[42]". It is accordingly suggested that there should be only one kind of the CM designated simply as "court martial", composed of 5 to 7 members, depending upon the nature of the offence or the complexity of evidence involved. This is also now contemplated in the British Armed Forces Act, 2006, the Disciplinary Court provided by Naval Discipline Act, 1957, s 52G having already been omitted by the Armed Forces Act, 2001, s 18. Lastly, a CM trying a person other than an officer should have at least one or two members from the class of the accused, depending upon whether the CM is going to consist of 5 or 7 members respectively.

(c) **Procedural Reforms**

(i) **Role of Judge Advocate**: The JA should be empowered to decide all questions of law and procedure as currently under the NA s 114, irrespective of whether he retains his status as a JA under the present system or is a law member to be appointed in accordance with the suggestion vide para (b) (iii) above.

(ii) **SCM**: The suggestion made at sub-para (b)(iii) will also take care of the criticism for the military justice system having, under the AA, a kind of court like SCM where the presiding officer of the tribunal also conducts prosecution and the accused has no right to be represented. Even though the US system of military justice too has a court of the same designation, but its jurisdiction, constitution, procedure and power of punishment are much different from the corresponding features of the SCM under the Indian system. In the present study, Q 3.3(f) of the Interview Schedule was addressed to all the 200 respondents on the issue of desirability of retaining the SCM in the Army. As many as 130 (65%) respondents, including 80% of respondents of general category did not favour a change and only 14.5% recommended for abolition of the SCM. Irrespective of this, the SCM in its present form is apparently not in conformity with the modern notions of dispensation of justice. Considering the utility of the SCM for the Army, as evident both from the data collected during the study and the number of trials for seven years provided

42 Lamer, "First Independent Review of ... Bill c-25", op cit, Ch 7, n 8, p 36.

by the Army, the institution of SCM may not be scrapped till the suggestion for having only one kind of the CM is implemented. It will, however, be absolutely necessary that reformatory steps are expeditiously taken to confine the role of the CO only to presiding over the Court, de-linking him from the prosecution. Further, the accused should be entitled to be legally represented by a law qualified officer. The two officers/JCOs, who presently attend the CM without in any way being involved in the proceedings, should be drawn from outside the unit of the accused and be made answerable to the Formation Commander for submitting an objective and impartial report of the trial proceedings, with an oath to be taken by them to this effect.

(iii) **Plea Bargaining**: Plea bargaining has recently been introduced in India through the Criminal Law (Amendment) Act, 2005 passed in the winter session of Parliament to bring changes in Ch. XXI A of the Cr PC. It is applicable only in respect of offences not punishable with more than 7 years RI and is not applicable to the cases involving an offence committed against a woman or a child below 14 years of age. Under the US military system, an accused and the convening authority may enter into a pre-trial agreement which includes a promise by the accused to plead guilty to, or to enter a confessional stipulation as to one or more charges and specification and a promise by the convening authority, in return, to refer the charges to a certain type of CM, or refer a capital offence as non-capital or withdraw one or more charges or specifications from the CM and certain other similar terms. There are detailed provisions as to the procedure to be followed to implement such an agreement.[43] The rule on the pre-trial agreement is intended to prevent informal agreements and protect the rights of the accused and the interests of the Government[44] and to ensure that certain Fundamental Rights of the accused are not bargained away by some informal understanding.[45] In the present study, one respondent of the accused category, on the question of general plea of Guilty or Not Guilty, added to his response that he pleaded "Guilty" at his SCM trial on an informal indication given by his CO that by pleading "Guilty" he was likely to be given lighter punishment. This suggests a need for incorporating a provision in the AR on the lines of the provision in the MCM in this regard. Irrespective of any such move being in accord with the recent development in the law of the land, it should, however, be considered that the aim of military law is not only to impart justice but also to strengthen the conditions of military discipline and morale. This author is of the view that any plea bargaining goes against the military ethos which would lay stress on soldierly attitude and courage to bear the consequences of one's commission or omission rather than entering into a bargain on such matters.

43 RCM, 705 and 910(f).

44 Grey, "Pretrial Agreements", Federal Bar Journal, V ol 37, 1978, p 49.

45 US v Mills, 12 MJ 1 (CMA, 1981).

(iv) **Civil Counsel for Defence**: Since the trial by the CM is based on the Service necessity, the accused should have the right to a civil counsel for his defence, at the Government expense, in all cases irrespective of the nature of the offence.

(v) **Time Limitation**: The limitation period provided in AA s 122 as amended by the Army (Amendment) Act, 1992, has become open ended after the newly introduced clauses (b) and (c) to the great disadvantage and prejudice to the defence, as explained in Chapter 8.4(d)(ii). These new clauses may, therefore, be repealed. The limitation period of three years under s 122 may, however, be so computed as to exclude any period of time for which the case remained stayed by a judicial order, illegal absence of the accused and the like circumstances. The limitation period under AA s 123 may be brought back to 6 months for the reasons explained in Chapter 8.4(d)(i), with a proviso for excluding in its computation the period of judicially granted stay or the period during which the accused made himself unavailable for trial by going into hiding, improperly admitting into hospital or in any other way.

(vi) **Revision and Confirmation**: Despite a CM being admittedly a command instrumentality, its status as a tribunal would necessitate that its judicial independence should be manifestly visible. The provisions for its finding and sentence being subject to confirmation by a superior military authority, as the confirming officer, with power to order the CM to reassemble to consider its finding or sentence, seem to militate against the concept of judicial independence. The issue of revision has been discussed in the light of the related data in Chapters 7.13 and 7.14 and also in the context of command influence in Chapter 8.2 with special reference to the cases of Capt. Harish Uppal and Capt. AP Bajpai[46]. It may be appreciated that no difficulty has ever been reported under the Naval system from the absence of revision and confirmation of the CM findings and sentences and thus no problem should likewise be apprehended to arise from their absence in the Army and Air Force laws either.

(vii) **Mechanism for Objectivity in Finding and Sentence**: As discussed in Chapter 8, in the context of AR r 180, it will be desirable to develop some sort of mechanism to compensate an accused person at his trial by the CM for any handicap he suffered as a consequence of the non-compliance or inadequate compliance of the mandatory requirements of the said rule. A scheme may be devised for this purpose to quantify various conviction quotients and sentence determinants in statistical terms as well as the values of different possible pre-trial handicaps, in a digital scale. An appropriate finding on the charge, and the sentence, if any required, may be calculated by setting of

---

46 Supra, Ch 8, n n 56,57 .

the points of handicap values from the statistical values of the related conviction quotients and sentence determinants in a given case. Based on the same principle, sentencing guidelines may be developed on the pattern of the Military Sentencing Guidelines suggested by Major Immel.[47]

(viii) **Reasoned Decision**: Sufficiently elaborate reasons should be recorded to clearly support the finding of the court and the sentence awarded irrespective of the kind of the CM. This may not necessarily be done on the pattern of the judgment of a criminal court but should reflect the reasons which led to the finding and sentence in question. AR r 62(1) may be amended to provide for this requirement.

(ix) **Miscellaneous**: Some other suggestions were earlier made in Chapter 5.8. For instance, in the context of bail, it was suggested that the provisions be made in the military for the grant of bail to an accused facing charges under the AA after he has since been released. Similarly, suggestions were also made for consolidation of the law of arrest and incorporation of provisions in the military law for all torture related offences being made exclusively triable under the ordinary criminal jurisdiction. A suggestion was also made for having mandatory provisions under the AA for the release of an offender, without prejudice to re-arrest, when he has been in custody for 90 days and his trial has not yet been ordered. An amendment was also suggested in 7.8, in the text of AR r58 vis-a-vis the questioning of the accused by the court so as to save him from falling into a catch-22 situation. All these suggestions may also be considered for implementation in the light of the discussion in Chapter 5.7 and 5.8.

(d) **Organizational Changes**

(i) **Court Martial Appeal Court**: The need for appeal against the CM decisions, the history of the demand made therefor and the grounds on which it has so far remained illusive are well documented in the record of the legislative debates of our Parliament, the post-Independence military legal writings, judicial pronouncements and the related reports of the Law Commission of India.[48] The data collected on the issue in the present research have also been discussed in Chapter 8[49]. As may be seen from the data in Table

---

47 Supra, Ch 8, n 180.

48 VK Krishna Menon in Lok Sabha on 22-23 Jul 1957; Law Commission of India, 169th Report of 1999; Armed Forces Tribunal Bill, 2005, Standing Committee on Defence (2005-2006) Tenth Report of May 2006; PPS Bedi v UOI AIR 1982 SC 1413 at 1437-38; OP Sharma, Military Law in India, op cit, n 40; Wing Commander UC Jha, "Appellate Court for Military", Civil and Military Law Journal, Vol 38, 2004, pp 225-239; AK Upadhyay, "Appeal under Law of Armed Forces – An Analysis", Journal of Indian Law Institute, Vol 45, No. 2, April June 2003, pp 275-287.

49 Ch 8, s 8.6(c).

50 as many as 67.5% respondents in the present study agree, fully or partially, with the requirement of establishing a court for appeal against the CM decisions. The requirement has already been met, with the Armed Forces Tribunal (hereinafter to be referred as 'AFT') being established[50] at New Delhi and its eight Branches set up in Chandigarh, Jaipur, Lucknow, Guwahati, Kolkata, Mumbai, Chennai and Kochi, under Armed Forces Tribunal Act,2007, (hereinafter to be referred as 'AFTA'). The AFT consists of a Chairperson and Judicial and Administrative Members (hereinafter to be referred as 'CP, 'JM', and 'AM' respectively). A Bench of the AFT consists of one JM and one AM. The CP is required to have been a Judge of the Supreme Court or the Chief Justice of a High Court and a JM to have been a High Court Judge. An AM should have held the rank of Maj Gen or above, or equivalent Naval or AF rank, for not less than 3 years, or should have served for not less than one year as the JAG in the Army, Navy or AF. The Tribunal has all the jurisdiction, powers and authority which were exercisable, immediately before the day it has been established in 2009, by all courts except the Supreme Court or a High Court under Art 32 and 226 of the Constitution, in relation to 'service matters' defined in AFTA s 3(o), including summary disposal and summary trial, and in relation to appeals against the order, finding and sentence passed by CsM. The decisions of the Tribunal are required to be made by the opinion of the majority. In the event of the Members being equally divided, the point of difference will be referred to the CP who shall either hear the point himself or refer it for hearing by one or more Members. The point shall then be decided according to the opinion of majority of the Members who have heard the case, including those who first heard it. An appeal may be made to the Supreme Court against the decision of the Tribunal in accordance with the procedure and the conditions laid down in the AFT in this regard[51]. A cool appraisal of the AFTA will bring out deficiencies in some of its provisions. Considering that a full length discussion of all these matters will be beyond the scope of the instant project, the need of a re-look on the AFTA will be presented by taking up the issue of the existing provisions on the qualifications of an AM[52], just by way of illustrating the point. To begin with, it may be pointed out that military justice being essentially a support mechanism of the military necessities, any decision in appeal against a CM verdict will remain one-sided, if based merely on the abstract principles of justice at large, without an in-depth insight in military life and principles of military law evolved over centuries from the soldiering related requirements. In view of this, a truly judicious decision in a CM appeal will involve the interplay of three elements, namely, proper understanding

50. The Armed F orces Tribunal Act, 2007 ,s.4.

51. AF TA, ss. 3,5,6,15,28 and 30.

52. AF TA,s.3 (a).

of military law provisions, a lived experience of military ethos including clear awareness of the customs of the Services, and, of course, duly internalized general principles of law and justice. Keeping this at the back of mind, it should not be difficult to visualize, under the existing provisions, an AFT Bench hearing a CM appeal with an inadequate representation of one of these three elements. Such situation may arise when the Bench comprises a retired High Court Judge and a Maj Gen from medical, dental, remount corps or nursing service or any other officer of that rank from elsewhere, who has been appointed as an AM being qualified as such under the existing provisions of the AFTA, even though has never been exposed to GCM/ SGCM procedure and practice. The Bench will be handicapped, in that event, the same way as was the apex court in some earlier discussed cases of faux pas[53]. Even the presence of a High Court Judge as the JM on that Bench may not be enough to save the situation, because he too, like the said Maj Gen, may not be sufficiently equipped with the understanding of military law and practice. To argue in this context that the persons appointed as Judges of the British Court Martial Appeal Court and of the US Court of Appeals for the Armed Forces are all ordinary judges of the court of appeal or of the Queen's Bench Division[54] etc in the former case, and 'from civilian life' in the later[55], will hold no ground in our case. Almost all of those judges of the UK and the US courts of military appeals have had experience of military law and military ethos at some stage or the other of their life. Unlike them, however, the Judges of the Supreme Court and the High Courts in India have no such experience and therefore cannot make up the deficiency of CM related experience, if any, on the part of an AM. Instead of insisting upon the rank of Maj Gen or above, in the concerned provision of the AFTA, the laid- down requirement of the qualification for the appointment of an AM should, have been the experience of, say at least 10, GCM/SGCM trials, preferably added with academic distinction in military law. The AFTA may be accordingly amended, along with any other amendment as may be felt desirable in respect of its other provisions, on their critical study or based on the functional experience thereof.

(ii) **Autonomous Department of Judge Advocate General**: An autonomous Department of the Judge Advocate General should be established to provide legal and judicial covers to all the three Services. A uniform military justice code for the Army, Navy and Air Force, on the pattern of UCMJ, will be a pre-requisite for such an arrangement. Earlier, the Government of India, by the Ministry of Defence UO No. 9/ 1/6/D/AG-1 dated 01 Apr 1965, had set up a committee which had drafted a uniform

---

53. Infra. 9.6 54.

54. Court Martial (Appeal) Act, 1951, as amended by The Court Martial (Appeal) Act,1968, and Armed Forces Acts,1996, 2001 and 2006.

55. UCMJ Art 142 (b).

code for the three Services in the shape of a Bill titled as the Armed Forces Code Bill, 1978, in accordance with the recommendations of Sir Arthar Trever Harris Committee Report 1964. However, the draft Bill did not find favour with the Directorate of Personnel of the three Services and was shelved by the Chiefs of Staff Committee on the ground of the working conditions of the three Services being different. It may be noted that the efforts to have a unified code for the three Services had similarly been made earlier but failed in the UK. However, the pending task has now been completed by the (British) Armed Forces Act, 2006, and shall hopefully inspire the Indian Armed Forces to similarly have one uniform code to govern them.

The autonomous JAG's Dept. for the three Services may nominally remain in the Ministry of Defence but should be insulated from all outside influence, direct or indirect, by providing for it a functionally independent system in all respects of appointments, postings, promotions and so on. The Department should have nothing to do with the pre-trial decision on charges, which task, alongwith the convening of the court, the appointment of members and JA and administrative arrangements for the trials and conduct of prosecution at CM, should all be organized under a separate legal service directorate. The appointment of defending officers and defence counsels, in addition to the appointment of trial JA, should be assigned to the JAG's Department alongwith the post-trial review of the CM proceedings. The JAG's Department may be bifurcated into three semi-independent sub-departments, under an additional JAG in each case, to deal with these tasks with officers and necessary staff to meet their respective requirements. The co-ordination of the sub-departments should be undertaken at the headquarters alongwith the preservation of the record of the CM trial. The details will have to be carefully worked out, keeping in mind the need to achieve judicial independence, fair administration of justice and smooth organization of pre-trial, trial and post-trial requirements. However, two basic requirements may be slightly elaborated here. The most important requirement relates to the quality of personnel to be appointed as the trial JA (as member or otherwise). Accordingly, the intake of officers for the JAG's Department should be carefully arranged only from among the advocates with not less than 5 years of practice in criminal courts. They should remain attached to Infantry Units for one year and thereafter at a six months course at Institute of Military Law, before they are appointed as JA at any CM trial. Similarly, the officers being kept on the panels for the duties of the prosecutors and defending officers, along with young advocates willing to take on the duty of defence counsel, be imparted training on short courses of ten weeks at the Institute of Military Law. It will be necessary to devise suitable incentives of career prospects and military benefits to attract the right material for these duties.

(iii) **Review and Research**: Both the British and the US military laws are subjected to periodical mandatory review at fixed intervals. In the UK, the Mutiny Acts from 1690 onward, and the Army Act in place thereof after 1881 to 1955, were passed with one-year life-span, for certain historical reasons. The Army Act, 1955, though still with a requirement of expiry after one year, provided for its continuance for five years by Orders in Council. The latest Armed Forces Act, 2006 is to similarly expire "at the end of five years beginning with the day on which it is passed"[56]. The US MCM has similarly been revised from time to time in 1917, 1921, 1928, 1949, 1951, 1969, 1984 and its latest edition of the year 2000 (relied upon in the present study) being a complete revision of the 1984 MCM, incorporating all Executive Orders (EO) through 06 Oct 1999 (EOs of 1984, 1986, 1987, 1990, 1991 1993, 1994, 1995, 1998 and 1999). Under the Statutes of Canada, 1998, c. 35 too, the Ministry of National Defence has the requirement of arranging for an independent review of the provisions and operation of Bill C-25 (an Act to amend the National Defence Act 1998) every five years. Such necessity of periodical review affords an opportunity of amending the military law, which, in the case of India, has remained unaffected by the wind of reforms in the military justice systems all over the world. It is high time that a statutory provision is made under the Services law for its mandatory review every five years. It will be useful to remember in this context what Major General William A. Moorman, the US JAG Air Force said, "No legal system can remain static, each must change to reflect the needs and demands of society or risk becoming an anachronistic relic of a dead or dying society."[57]

Similarly, very little research has been conducted in the sphere of military law in India. The total number of research studies in military law in India may not go beyond counting on the fingers of one hand. On the other hand, a large number of military scholars outside the country have been pursuing research on various aspects of military law. Some of their works find mention in this and earlier chapters. Though some research work is now being done in the sphere of military law under the aegis of the Institute of Military Law, Kamptee, and at the JAG's office at the Army Headquarters, as a part of their routine duties, no systematic research can be conducted unless a regular research wing operates with officers assigned full-time duty for research. It is suggested that research scholars may be encouraged, both from within and without the three Services, to carry out research in the field of military law with proper guidance and facilities of reading material being made available to researchers, along with financial aid to meet related expenses.

---

56 Armed Forces Act, 2006, s 371 (3).

57 Moorman, "Fifty Years of Military Justice: Does the Uniform Code of Military Justice Need to be Changed?" Air Force Law Review, Vol 184, (2000), p 185.

9.6 Media Management

The importance of media management is self-evident for a justice system which sometimes proves to be slippery ground, even for a Supreme Court judge who will quash the proceedings of an SCM for non-compliance of AA s 130(1) which is not even applicable to such CM[58], or a judge who will speak of "a court of Enquiry ... in terms of Army Rule 22"[59] which in fact provides for hearing of the charge by the CO and not the C of I provided under AR 177,or a judge who uses the expression commanding officer, Central Command" for General Officer Commanding in Chief, Central Command"[60] or a judge who confuses "summary trial" for "Summary of Evidence"[61]. This lack of awareness about the military matters is much more pronounced in the case of media where a national daily publishes the news of a 'first ever open court' with the photograph of a signboard in the background for a Summary of Evidence. The matter acquires further importance because the Indian media, though presently going through a "golden era", the "quantitative growth witnessed by it had outpaced the qualitative growth".[62]

In the context of media management and military justice, Cooke, writing about "the so-called information revolution", highlights the problems it poses and observes that "the satellites and computers simply mean that one person's bad idea or bad facts can now be shared with millions ... almost instantly ... the net effect of all this is to put decision makers under much greater pressure... This is not conducive to calm, deliberate, dispassionate decision making. ... We also see an increase in attacks on judicial independence ... there has been a recent upsurge in efforts ... to call judges to account for their actions. Given the increased scrutiny of judicial decisions ... it is important that we ensure that judges are, and are seen to be, independent of the public furor ... "[63]. The public attitude and the role of media in shaping it have direct relevance to command influence of 'apparent category', i.e., the cases in which the command influence does not focus on the actual effect on the accused's case but instead asks "whether a responsible member of the public, if aware of all the facts, would have a loss of confidence in the military justice system and believe it to be unfair". Such command influence is of great

58 Ranjit Thakur's case, supra, n 13.

59 Sheel Kr Roy v Secretary Ministry of Defence, JT 2007 (7) SC 485 at 486

60 Maj Gen Inder Jeet Kumar v UOI, AIR 1997 SC 2085 at para 12.

61 UOI v Maj Gen ML Y adav, AIR 1999 SC 1340 in par a 20.

62 TOI, 4 Oct 07 , p 7, "PM asks media to act r esponsibly".

63 Brigadier General John S Cook e, "The T wenty-sixth Annual K enneth J. Hodson Lectur e : Manual f or Courts-Martial 20X", op ci t, n 28.

64 US v Gr andy, 15 MJ 275 (CMA 1983).

significance since a judicial system operates effectively only with public confidence, as the US Court of Military Appeals observed.[64]

At the USI Seminar held at New Delhi on 28 Feb 1982 on "Relationship of Military Law and Discipline with the Judicial System of the Country", the sensationalistic, partisan and apparently motivated publicity given to military cases in civil courts came in for severe criticism. Mr. Surinder Nihal Singh, Editor-in-Chief of Indian Express, however, stated that in a democratic set up, the free Press had a vital role to play, and in doing so fearlessly, some errors of emphasis in reporting could be there. He stressed the need of the Press being more objective in dealing with matters pertaining to the Armed Forces but this was possible only when the representative of the Public Relations Organization of the Armed Forces is fully equipped to issue to the Press, on his own responsibility, as much information as he should and refuse what he should not. Mr. Sahay of the Statesman was also of the view that 100% accuracy was not sometimes possible. The representatives of the Press were pleasantly surprised to learn that a CM which they thought was a forbidden forum was in fact an open court. Considering all these facts, the Seminar Report recommended that the Armed Forces Public Relation Organization should be under the Chiefs of Staff and not the Ministry of Defence and it should be headed by a senior officer associated with policy decisions at the highest level.[65]

In the recent times, some cases like those of Siachin fake encounter, Flying Officer Miss Anjali Gupta of Indian Air Force, Colonel Anil Sehgal of Tehelka fame, 'booze brigadier' RP Singh, Major Rehman of 31 Rashtriya Rifles, Lt Col HS Kohli [66] for cheating by sprinkling tomato ketchup to show citizens killed in terror activity and recently the cases of Lieut Gen Avadesh Prakash[67] and other senior Generals in Sukhna land scam have attracted much media attention. However, the reporting of these and some other cases left much to desire in the interest of objectivity and accuracy. It is suggested that the Public Relation Organization should be placed under a person who has been associated with some prestigious civil media organization. Two senior Service officers may be appointed to run the show under his supervision, along with, of course, other necessary staff. Further, the publication of Sainik Samachar, the Armed Forces tabloid, may be accorded greater attention than at present.

---

65 USI Number Ten Seminar Report, 1982, pp 50-51.

66 TOI dated 10 July 2010, " Army Tribunal rejects 'ketchup' colonel's plea" p 11.

67 TOI dated 5 Jun 2010 "Tribunal turns down Lt -Gen's plea" p 9.

9.7 Justice to Promote Discipline

Some of the suggestions offered here are not statistically borne out from the primary data of the present study, even though squarely fitting into the secondary data comprising of judicial pronouncements, juristic enunciations and academic expositions. Further, some of those may also cause concern in the mind of protagonists of the traditional scheme of law and military discipline relationship. However, any one who may have any apprehension of military discipline being adversely affected from any military justice reform could seek comfort in the words of Westmoreland:

> *A military trial should not have a dual function as an instrument of discipline and as an instrument of justice. It should be an instrument of justice and fulfilling this function it will promote discipline.*[68]

---

68 William C. W estermoreland, "Mi litary Justice – A Commander' s Viewpoint ", 10 A M Crim L R ev, 21 (1971).

Appendix 'A'

INTERVIEW SCHEDULE FOR RESEARCH STUDY AT UNIVERSITY OF DELHI

SUBJECT:- DECISION - MAKING PROCESS OF COURT MARTIAL: AN ATTITUDINAL STUDY.

Research Fellow:

Brigadier R.G. Vidhu

C-36, Defence Colony, Meerut(U.P.)

Research Guide:

Professor Dr. S. C. Raina

Faculty of Law, University of Delhi

Note:-

1. The information sought here is meant only for Research purpose. Should you, however, prefer anonymity, you need not disclose your identity. Similarly, any question in entirety or in part may be skipped in the event of your having any reservation thereon.
2. Parts 1 to 3 are for the categories of respondents specified in each case. However, questions 3 and 4 of Part 3 are to be answered by the respondents of Parts 1 to 2 as well.
3. Multiple choice questions may be answered by tick marking the item of your choice from the suggested answers in each case. However, the answer 'Any other' may please be specified further with your intended answer. If the space provided for the answer falls short, a separate sheet or slip of paper may be used to cover the answer and attached to this schedule.

PERSONAL DATA OF RESPONDENT

Name Address with Telephone Occupation/Profesion

Part 1- *(For those who have been a member of a court martial (CM) or a Judge Advocate (JA) thereat.)*

1.1.(a) Please furnish your personal particulars on the following counts, except on those which you would like to skip:

(a) Age ...... (b) Sex ....(c) Religion ....(d) Caste ....
(e) Marital Status ...... (f) Regional Background (urban or rural) ....

1.1. (b) What was your legal qualification and background knowledge of military law when your first attended a CM as a member or JA?

Ans. (a) Graduate/ post graduate university degree in law with (without) military law as a paper,

(b) Military law studied as a subject during training at the National Defence Academy (NDA) / Indian Military Academy (IMA) / Officers' Training School (OTS) / any other institution (– – – – – – – – – – – – – – – – – –),

(c) Military law as a paper at promotion examination Part 'D' / Pre-Staff College Examination / Judge Advocate General's Departmental Examination,

(d) Any other (...)

1.2. What was your legal, judicial or civil court / CM procedural experience before you attended a CM as a member or JA?

Ans. (a)Was member of a court of inquiry (C of I) once / twice / more than two times;

(b)Recorded summary of evidence (S of E) once / twice / more than two times;

(c)Attended CM as officer-under-instruction/prosecutor / defending officer / witness / friend of accused / counsel;

(d)Held Summary Court Martial (SCM) as Commanding Officer (CO);

(e)Attended civil court as ....;

(f)Any other ....;

1.3. How many CM have you attended as a member or JA? Give their details as to the kinds of CM, the total number of the accused tried, the nature of charges disposed?

Ans. (a)Number of CM: GCM........, SGCM....,DCM...,Any other.........,Total.....,
(b)Number of Accused:Officer ..., JOCs ....,OR ......,Any other...., Total......,
(c)Nature of Charges: Mutiny ......, Desertion ....,Illegal absence, Disboedience, ...Spying...., Murder......, Rape........,Any other........ ,Total......................,

1.4. What rank, length of service and position did you have at the first and the last CM you attended?

	Rank	Length of service	Position
Ans. (a) First CM	....	....Years	Presiding officer/JA/ member No.1,2,3,4
(b) Last CM	....	....Years	– Do – –

1.5. The task of the administration of justice being like a walk on the razor's edge, did you face any problem, or were you, before or during the course of trial, ever approached or pressurised to act in favour of or against the accused? If yes, what was the problem or approached by whom, for what and to what effect?

Ans. (a) No

(b) Yes, the problem was ....

or / and approached / pressurised by own CO / accused's CO / other superior (specify) .... /colleague/any other person (specify)– – – – – – – – – to act in favour of / against accused: it did (did not) influence my decisions.

1.6. What factors determined your decision / advice at various stages of the trial?

Ans. (a) In The Case Of Members:-

(i) The advice of JA;

(ii) The pleading of the prosecutor (prosecution counsel) / defending officer (defence counsel);

(iii) The facts presented by witnesses;

(iv) The facts of the case as learnt outside the court;

(v) My own notion of natural justice;

(vi) The relations with the accused;

(vii) The likely effect on my own career;

(viii) The wishes of the superiors;

(ix) The interest of service;

(x) The needs of discipline;

(xi) Any other ....,

(b) In The Case Of JA

(i) The provisions of law;

(ii) The interest of organization;

(iii) The views of superiors;

(iv) The interest of justice;

(v) The effect on my own career

(vi) The case law enunciated by the Supreme Court or any other superior court or ruling from the departmental 'Blue Book' or any CM precedent.

1.7. (a) For Members Only- If the trial was attended by a JA, what is your impression about (i) his professional competence, (ii) impartiality and (iii) personal conduct?

Ans. (i) Professional Competence- Sound / poor knowledge, confident/shaky/ ambiguous while advising, any other ....

(ii) Impartiality- Merely advised the court, leaving decision for members; appeared to be pro-conviction /unduly favouring accused; seemed to be under command influence; acting against conscience/course of justice.

(iii) Personal conduct - Was respectful / polite / firm / harsh/ rude/ power-drunk, virtually controlling the court, thursting own views, seeking undue favour from ....

(b) For JA only- What factors, according to your experience, practically determine the decision-making at a CM?

Ans. (i) The facts of evidence and law;

(ii) The concern of the members for their service career;

(iii) The wishes of the superiors as conveyed in private or in documents such as reply to a reference by CM or revision order;

(iv) The fear of adverse comments by civil courts in writ jurisdiction or suit;

(v) The interest of organization/the prestige of the Regiment/unit;

(vi) The relations with or bias in favour of/against the accused or the accused's CO;

(vii) Arguments in addresses;

(viii) The views of the JA/presiding officer;

(ix) Rumour in station about the cases;

(x) The need of discipline;

(xi) Any other..,

1.8. What approximate percentage of trials that you attended as a member or JA resulted into conviction and what all factors were responsible for conviction and what accounted for acquittal in the other cases, if any?

Ans. (a) Percentage: nil - less than 10%, 11-20%. 21-50%, 51-75%, 76-100%.

(b) Reasons/factors responsible for conviction:

(i) Evidence on record;

(ii) Incompetence of defence representative;

(iii) Command influence;

(iv) Belief that conviction is needed for maintenance of discipline;

(v) Fear that acquittal would incur the wrath of the superiors;

(vi) Any other...;

(c) Reasons for acquittal:

(i) Evidence before the court;

(ii) Inadequate understanding of the members /JA vis - a - vis complicated nature of facts / law;

(iii) Accused being unduly favoured by members/JA;

(iv) Clever manipulation by the defending officer /defence counsel / accused;

(v) Prosecution failure to properly present the case;

(vi) Non-availability of some important witnesses / document;

(vii) Witnesses turning hostile;

(viii) Any other ....;

1.9. Was any of the CM that you attended dissolved or adversely commented upon by any superior civil court for any of its decision or failure? It yes, briefly state the related facts.

Ans. No/Yes, the facts being that ....;

1.10. Are you satisfied that the accused received justice at the CM trial (s) that you attended as a member or JA? If not, why?

Ans. (a) Yes (b) No; reasons being:

(i) Inadequate attention by some members because of their other commitments;

(ii) Limitation of presentation by prosecution / defence /JA;

(iii) Non- cooperative attitude of administrative authorities;

(iv) Biased attitude (pro or anti accused) of witnesses / some member / JA / superior commanders/ medical authorities;

(v) Any other;

1.11. Do you agree ('A'), partially agree (PA) or disagree (DA) with or have no comments(NC) to offer on the statements that-

(a) Conviction at CM is necessary to maintain discipline in the armed forces;

(b) Acquittal by CM adversely affects the cause of discipline;

(c) Conviction or acquittal which ever is warranted by the evidence best serves the ultimate interest of discipline;

Ans. (a) A/PA/DA/NC (b) A/PA/DA/NC (c) A/PA/DA/NC

1.12. Do you have any recommendations to make for the improvement of the CM system with reference to the following:

(a) Qualification, disqualification or eligibility of a person to serve as a member or JA at a CM.

(b) The power of the CM to compel attendance of civil witnesses and punish own contempt of court;

(c) Measures to ensure that no member, JA or other person associated with the CM system suffers in his career prospects in matters of posting, promotion or otherwise for any of his consciencious decision taken in variance with the wishes of his superiors;

(d) Any other point relating to CM system.

Ans. (a)

(b)

(c)

(d)

(e)

Part –2 *(For those who have been or are being tried by a CM.)*

2.1. Please furnish the requisite information on the following counts for research purposes,

skipping those which you do not consider desirable to disclose for any reason

whatsoever:

(a) Age…….. (b) Sex ………. (c) Parents family whether joint or nuclear …………

(d) Religion and cast at birth ……... (e) Regional background (rural/ urban)……….. (f) Place where you mostly lived before joining the Service …………………………..

(g) Your father / guardian's (i) occupation ………. (ii) educational background …… (iii) monthly income……. (iv) size of family within 5 years before joining the Service ……………………………………………………………………

(h) Your age at the time of the death (if applicable) of your mother……….. and / or father ……………..……… and/or the re-marriage (if applicable) of your mother ……………………… and / or father ………..…………………..)

(i) Your marital status before joining the Service:Unmarried / married / divorcee

(j) Your type of entry in the Service such as: / IMA / NDA / NCC / ACC / EC / S.S. /direct JCO, NCO/Recruit along with the year of joining………………………

(k) Institution of initial training ……………………………………………………………

(l) Important courses attended such as: NDC / LDMC / DSSC / Tech Staff / any other ……………………………………………………………………………………

(m) Distinction / award, if any ……………………………………………………………

(n) Foreign terms / assignments if any, along with year ……………………………

(o) Your monthly income from all sources

....

2.2. Before your trial by a CM, were you aware of the provisions of law and procedure relating to CM? If yes, how had you acquired such awareness?

Ans. (a) Was not aware:

(b) Was aware because I had-

(i) Studied military law for a university examination / promotion examination/departmental examination / pre - Staff College examination / during pre-commission training / as part of a course / for academic interest / as need of a professional appointment.

(ii) Attended a C of I / recorded a S of E / attended a CM in the capacity of...

(iii) Acquired awareness in any other way..

2.3. Were the pre-trial procedures of C of I, hearing of charge by CO, recording of the S of E adopted in your case? If yes, were you given an opportunity to cross-examine witnesses, make a statement in your defence and produce witnesses in support of your version?

Ans.	**Held**	**Cross-Examin**	**Make Statement**	**Produce Witnesses**	**Addl. Remarks**
(a) C of I	Yes/No	Yes/No	Yes/No	Yes/No	....
(b) Hearing of change	Yes/No	Yes/No	Yes/No	Yes/No	....
(c) S of E	Yes/No	Yes/No	Yes/No	Yes/No	....

2.4. Did you in any way feel aggrieved in relation to C of I, hearing of charge and S of E? If yes, why and did you bring it to the notice of any superior authority and with what result?

Ans. Did not feel aggrieved / felt aggrieved for ....but made no complaint/ ....and I brought this to the notice of ....

.... as a result of which ..../ but nothing happened.

2.5. Did you make a confessional statement before or during trial? If you did, was it made as a result of any threat, inducement or promise and did you bring this fact to the notice of any superior authority and with what result?

Ans. (a) Confessional statement was made/not made

(b) It was made as a result of .... but I made no complaint / and I

brought this to the notice of .... as a result of which

.... / but nothing happened.

2.6. Before your trial-

Ans. (a) For how along, if at all, did you remain in custody?

(b) What all documents were you given to enable you to prepare your defence and when?

(c) Were you allowed to call your witnesses at the Government expense and provided free access to them to discuss your defence?

(d) Were you informed of your right to engage a civil counsel of your choice at your expense (at Government expense in case of a charge punishable with death) and have a defending officer assigned to you to represent at the CM?

(e) Were you given due notice of an intended joint trial so as to enable you to claim a separate trial if so needed for your defence?

Ans. (a) .... Years(s) .... Month(s) and ....Day(s)

(b) A copy each of C of I proceedings/S of E/charge-sheet/names of officers proposed to constitute CM/ any other .... given......... day before the commencement of CM trial.

(c) Yes / No (d) Yes / No (e) Yes / No /NA.

However, I wish to add ....

....

2.7. What charge(s) were you tried for and did you plead 'Guilty' or 'Not Guilty' thereat? Briefly state the procedure followed by the CM on your pleading 'Guilty'/'not Guilty'

Ans.	Charge		Plea		Procedure
		------		------	
		------		------	Consequences explained/ witnesses examined
		------		------	
		------		------	
		------		------	

2.8. At the trial did you/your defending officer or counsel object to any charge(s), raise a plea to general jurisdiction of the court, challenge any member, put a plea in bar of trial or make any other submission before the examination of witnesses? If yes to what result? If not, why not?

Ans.	Made and	Accepted/Rejected	Not made because (i) had no ground (ii) was not aware of it (iii) considered it futile (iv) any other reason.			
(a) Objection to charge(s)	M	A/R	(i)	(ii)	(iii)	(iv)
(b) Plea to jurisdiction	M	A/R	(i)	(ii)	(iii)	(iv)
(c) Challenge to member	M	A/R	(i)	(ii)	(iii)	(iv)
(d) Plea in bar	M	A/R	(i)	(ii)	(iii)	(iv)
(e) Any other submission	M	A/R	(i)	(ii)	(iii)	(iv)

2.9. During the course of trial-

(a) What was the general trend of the CM about defence pleas / submissions being heard and accepted or rejected?

(b) What was the general trend about the prosecution submissions being heard and accepted or rejected?

(c) Did you / your representative get sufficient opportunity to cross-examine prosecution witnesses, make a statement and call defence witnesses?

(d) Was there any defence witnesses who could not be called or satisfactorily be examined? If so, why?

Ans. (a) Not allowed /heard: mostly rejected/accepted

(b) Not allowed /heard: mostly rejected/accepted

(c) (i) Cross-examined Yes / No / Can't say

(ii) Made statement Yes / No / can't say

(iii) Produced witnesses Yes / No / can't say

(d) No/Yes (i) Could not be called because of service conditions/his high status/being abroad/non cooperative attitude of staff officers /my pecuniary limitations / any other reason ....

(ii) Could not be satisfactorily examined because of (aa) the frequent interference / interruption by the members (s) JA / prosecution (bb) witness being won over, (cc) any other reason ....

2.10. What was the out - come of your trial?

Ans. (a) Acquitted of the charge/all charges

(b) Acquitted on some but convicted on remaining charges and sentenced to

....

(c) Convicted of the charge/all charges and sentenced to

....

....

(d) Acquitted initially of .... charges (s) but, on revision ordered by the confirming authority, convicted of ....and sentenced to...

Additionally, I wish to say that ....

2.11. Are you satisfied that justice has been duty meted out in your case? It not, what factors contributed to injustice and what have you done / are doing about it?

Ans. (a) Satisfied/not satisfied the factors involved being:

(i)

(ii)

(iii)

(iv)

(v)

(b) (i) Filed a pre-confirmation /post confirmation /writ petition as a result of which .... /the result is still awaited.

(ii) Did nothing about it, considering it futile / resigning to my fate/ my pecuniary circumstances not permitting it / any other reason ....

2.12. Based on your experience or otherwise, do you have any suggestions to make to ensure that justice is duly imparted at all stages of the CM system?

Ans.

Part –3 *(For those associated with CM as Commanders, Staff counsels witnesses judges, academics, free-lance thinkers, journalists, social workers or in any other capacity.)*

3.1. Please furnish information, as much as you consider desirable on the following counts.

(a) Your age .... sex .... religion .... caste......... regional .... background ....

(b) Your academic and professional qualification....................................

(c) Your monthly income from all sources ....

(d) The place(s) where you lived up to the age of 18 years and its (their) approximate population at that time ....

(e) The religion of (i) your parents.............. (ii) your own ....

3.2. How many CM approximately have you dealt with? Please state the name(s) of the accused person(s) and the nature of charges involved therein and your approximate duration of association therewith.

(a) Nil-1/2-5/6-10/more than 10.

(b) (i) Accused ....

(ii) Charges..

(c) Duration of association ....

3.3. What are your views about the following aspects of the CM system:

(a) Impermissibility of the assistance of civil counsel at the

(i) C of I (ii) Hearing of charge (iii) S of E

(iv) Summary Court Martial (SCM)

(b) Role of the JA as merely an advisor at a CM with no power to decide any questions of law or fact and his presence with the members deliberating on findings in the closed court under the AA;

(c) The authorities of the same army command convening the CM, appointing the members and JA for the CM, reviewing the CM proceedings and in most cases confirming the finding and sentence as well as taking on the pre-confirmation and post confirmation petition except when confirmation is required by the COAS or the Central Government;

(d) CM as an ad hoe body as distinguished from static courts under the civil system;

(e) The power of the confirming officer to once reassemble the CM under the AA to reconsider and revise its findings and sentence;

(f) The desirability of continuing with the SCM in the Army.

Ans. (a) (i) C of I : Counsel be allowed / not allowed

(ii) Hearting of charges : – – – – do – – – – / – – do – – –

(iii) S of E : ---- do ---- / -- do ---
(iv) SCM : ---- do ---- / -- do ---

(b) No change/ JA be empowered to decide question of law and not remain present with members during deliberation on findings.

(c) No change / different Command Headquarters should be involved to issue pre-trial advice/ appointing members and JA/ reviewing proceedings/confirm or not confirm proceedings /deal with the petition relating to CM.

(d) No change / standing CM should be established at Area or Command level.

(e) No change / No revision / Revision only in case of finding (s) of guilty.

(f) No change / SCM should be scrapped.

Note:- Additional observations, if any, may be made on any of these aspects using a separate sheet.

3.4. How far do you agree with the following propositions? A graded response may be expressed by 'A' for agreeing, 'PA' for partially agreeing and 'D' for disagreeing; adding thereafter any further observation if need be:

(a) The decision making process of CM is fraught with command influence at all stages;

(b) The verdict of CM should be given in the form of a fully reasoned decision on the pattern of the judgment of a civil court;

(c) The supervisory and appellate jurisdiction of high courts should be extended to CM;

(d) A court of military appeals should be established and the existing writ jurisdiction of high courts and the Supreme Court be barred in respect of CM decisions;

(e) CM decision are discipline oriented, caring for the cause of justice only incidentally;

(f) The requirements of military discipline are served in a balanced manner along with the cause of justice by trial of military offenders by CM;

(g) The cause of military discipline and justice may be better served by having all military offenders tried in civil (criminal) courts;

(h) The CM system can be usefully extended to trial of all civilian offenders in operational areas like J & K and foreign terrorists in all parts of India;

(j) The decisions of CM are forgone conclusions and compliance with procedural provisions at the trial is a mere formality;

(k) Almost all decisions at CM are practically made by the JA, the members merely authenticate them;

(l) The Judge Advocate General's Departments of the Army, Air Force and Navy be unified into one autonomous institution so as to insulate the CM system from outside pressure and command influence.

Ans:- (a) A/PA/D...... (b) A/PA/D...... (c) A/PA/D...... (d) A/PA/D.........

(e) A/PA/D...... (f) A/PA/D...... (g) A/PA/D...... (h) A/PA/D.........

(j) A/PA/D...... (k) A/PA/D...... (l) A/PA/D.........

3.5. What factors, according to your view, essentially determine the decisions of CM?

Ans. The wishers of superiors/the conscience of members/the requirements of natural justice/the facts of evidence and law/the advice of the JA whether right or wrong/the needs of service discipline/any other..

3.6. Please enumerate briefly the suggestions, if any, you would like to offer for the improvement of the CM system. You may add a separate sheet of paper, if need be, to cover your answer.

Ans.

BIBLIOGRAPHY

A. Books

(1) Classical Treatises

Adye, A Treatise on Courts Martial, 1779.

Atharvaveda

British Articles of War, Richard II, 1385.

British Articles of War, 1765.

Brihdaranyaka Upanishad

Capt. John Williamson, 'The Elements of Military Arrangements', 1783.

Clode, 'Military Forces of the Crown', vols I & II, 1869.

Clode, 'Administration of Justice under Military or Marshal Law', 1874.

Victor Foucher, 'Commentaires surl le Code de Justice Militaire pour l'Armee de Terre', Paris, 1858

King Gustavus Adolphus of Sweden, 'Code of Articles', 1621

Mathew Sutcliff, 'The Practice and Lawes of Armes', 1593.

Satpatha Brahamana

Sukracharya, 'Sukraniti'

Tytler, 'An Essay on Military Law and the Practice of Courts Martial', 1814.

Von Molitor, Kriegsgerichte Und Militarstrafen Koppmann, Militarstrafgestzbuch (German)

Vyas, Mahabharata, Santiparva

(2) Reference Material

Aiyer's Law Lexicon, 2nd ed, 1997, Nagpur, Wadhwa & Co.

The Compact Oxford Reference Dictionary, 6th Impression, 2003, New Delhi, OUP

Hornby AS, The Advanced Learner's Dictionary 2nd Ed, 1965, London, Oxford University Press

Encyclopedia Britannica, 1973, Vol 22

DK Illustrated Family Encyclopedia, 2005 (Reprint 2007)

Halsbury's Laws of England, 3rd Ed, 1955

'Legal Glossary', 1988, Ministry of Law and Justice, Government of India

(3) Constitution, Principal and Subordinate Legislation

(i) India

The Constitution of India, 1950

Air Force Act, 1950

Air Force Act Rules, 1950

Air Force Rules, 1969

Armed Forces (Special Powers) Act, 1958

Armed Forces Tribunal Act, 2007

Army Act, 1950

Army Act Rules, 1950

Army Rules, 1954

Army (Amendment) Act, 1992

Army (Amendment) Rules, 1993

Border Security Force Act, 1968

Criminal Procedure Code, 1973

Defence Services Regulations (Regulations for the Air Force), 1964

Defence Services Regulations (Regulations for the Army), Revised Edition 1987,

Defence Services Regulations (Regulations for the Navy), 1965 Part I & III (Non-statutory) and Part II (Statutory)

Defence Services Regulations - Travel Regulations (TR) 1976

Human Rights Act, 1993

Indian Army Act, 1911

Indian Army Act Rules, 1911

Indian Evidence Act, 1872

Indian Penal Code, 1860

Manual of Indian Military Law, 1912 (MIML)

Manual of Military Law, 1983 (MML)

Navy Act, 1957

Official Secrets Act, 1923

(ii) Other Countries

Constitution of The United States, 1787

(Australian)The Defence Force Discipline Act, 1982

(British) Air Force Regulations 2000

(British) Armed Forces Act, 2006

(British) Army Act, 1955

(British) Army Custody Rules 2000

(British) Board of Inquiry Rules

(British) Custody and Summary Dealing (Army) Regulations, 2000

(British) Human Rights Act, 1998

(British) Manual of Military Law, 1972, 12th Ed, P&I

(British) Mutiny Act, 1689

(British) National Defence Act,

(British) Naval Discipline Act, 1957

(British) Police and Criminal Evidence Act, 1984

(British) Code of Practice

(Canadian) National Defence Act, 1950 (as last amended 1998)

Criminal Code of Canada

The Dutch Military Discipline Act, 1903

US Articles of War, 1920

US Uniform Code of Military Justice, 1950

US Manual of Court Martial, 2000 Edition (MCM), Pt II,

US Rules for Court Martial (RCM)

(4) Other Books

Abrham, Henry J., The Judicial Process, 4th ed, 1980; Oxford University Press.

Acharya, Dr. Deva Vrat, 'Dhanurveda', 1999, New Delhi, Vijaya Kumar Govindram Hasanand.

Asch, Solomon E., 'Social Psychology', 1959, New Jersey, Prenctice Hall.

Charkravarti, PC, 'The Art of War in Ancient India', 1941, Delhi, Low Price Publications.

Charles Dickens, 'Oliver Twist'.

Cohen Morris R and Ernest Nagel, 'An Introduction to Logic and Scientific Method', 1934, New York, Harcourt.

Craig, P.P. 'Administrative Law', 1983, London, Sweet & Maxwell.

Drechster Carl T., Henry C Lind, et al editors, American Jurisprudence, 2nd Vol, 1971; New York, The Lawyers Cooperative Publishing Company, Rochester.

Dicey, A V, 'Law of Constitution'.

Dwivedi, S.P. 'Jurisprudence and Legal Theory', 2nd Ed 1985, Allahabad, Central Law Agency.

Federico Andreau-Guzman ' Military Jurisdiction and International Law; Military Courts and Gross Human Rights Violation's' (International Commission of Jurists, 2003), Vol 1

Franklin Charles, 'Third Degree', 1970, London, Robert Hale.

Goode and Hatt, 'Methodology in Social Research', 1952, New York, Mc Graw-Hill Broke Company.

Gopal, M.H., 'An Introduction to Research Procedure in Social Science', 1964, Bombay, Asia Publishing House

Francisco Jimenez y Jimenez, Introduccion al deracho penal militar, 1987, Editorial Civitas, Madrid.

Holdsworth, Sir William, 'Essay in Law and History' 1946,

Jain, M.P. 'Outlines of Indian Legal History', 3rd ed, 1972, Bombay, NM Tripathi

Joseph Di Mona, Great Court Martial Cases, New York, Grosset & Dunlop, 1972

Keir and Lawson, 'Cases in Constitutional Law', (5th ed) 1967, Oxford University Press

Kiralfy, A.K.R., 'Potters' Historical Introduction to English Law', 4th ed, 1958, London, Sweet & Maxwell.

Kohli, Atul, 'India's Democracy : An Analysis of the Changing State & Society Relations', 1998, Princeton Press.

Kothari, CR, 'Research Methodology : Methods & Techniques', 2nd ed, 2004, New Delhi, New Age International (P) Ltd. Publishers

Kumar, Maj Gen Nilendra, "Case Studies in Military Law", 1st ed, 2003, New Delhi, Universal Law Publishing Co. Pvt.Ltd.,

Kumar, Maj. Gen Nilendra and Rekha Chaturvedi, 'Law Relating to Armed Forces in India', 4th ed, 2005, New Delhi, Universal Law Publishing Co. Pvt. Ltd.

Mangla, A.C., 'Commentary on Military Law in India', 1992, New Delhi, Eastern Law House.

Mc Arthur, 'Principles and Practice of Naval and Military Courts Martial', 4th ed., 1805, London, Butterworth.

Mangla, A.C., 'Regimental Officers Handbook on Military Law', 1976, New Delhi, Army Law Publishers

Moser & Kalton, 'Survey Methods in Social Investigation', 2nd ed, 1971, London, ELBS and Heinmann Educational Books Ltd.,

Nayudu, C. Sanjeeva Row, 'A Handbook of Military Law', 1st Ed 1951, Delhi, Metropolitan Book Company Ltd

Paton, George Whitecross, 'A Textbook of Jurisprudence', 4th ed, 1972, London, ELBS, Oxford University Press.

Pratt, Lt Col Sisson C, 'Military Law - Its Procedure and Practice', 9th ed, 1915, London, Kegan Paul, Trench, Trubner & Co.

Priyavrat Vedavachaspati Acharya, Veda Martanda, 'A Study in Vedic Polity', Vol 3, 1999, New Delhi, Meenakshi Prakashan.

Rant, Judge J W, 'Courts-Martial, Discipline and the Criminal Process in the Armed Services', 2nd ed, 2003, Oxford University Press

Rant, Judge J W, 'Court Martial Handbook: Practice and Procedure', 1998, New York, John Wiley and Sons.

Ratanlal Ranchohoddas and Dhirajlal Keshavlal Thakore, 'The Law of Evidence', Bombay, 16th ed, 1973, Bombay Law Reporter Pvt. Ltd.

Raza, Maroof, 'Low Intensity Conflicts", 1995 Meerut, Kartikeya Publications

Raichoudhary, H.C., 'Political History of India', 1938, Calcutta,

Rama Jois, 'Legal and Constitutional History of India', 1984 Bombay, NM Tripathi

Sanan, Maj Gen S.K., 'The History of the Department of Judge Advocate General', 2001, New Delhi, Lancer Publishers

Seervai, H. M., 'Constitutional Law of India', 1983 Ed (Supplement 1988), Bombay, NM Tripathi

Sills, David L., 'Encyclopedia of the Social Sciences', Vol. 1, 1960, New York, MacMillan Co. and Free Press

Singh, Sarva Daman, 'Ancient Indian Warfare', 1st ed. 1965, Delhi, Motilal Banarsidass

Sharma, Col G.K. and Col M S Jaswal 'Study and Practice of Military Law', 6th ed, 2006, New Delhi, Deep & Deep Publications, Pvt. Ltd.

Sharma, Rear Admiral O.P., 'Military Law in India', 2nd ed. 1990, Bombay, NM Tripathi.

Simmons, Thomas Frederick 'The Constitution and Practice of Courts Martial', 6th Ed, 1873, London, John Murray

Vas, Lt Gen E.V., 'Fools and Infantry men', 1995, Meerut, Kartikeya Publications

Weston, Paul W. and Kenneth M Wells, 'Criminal Investigation – Basic Perspective', 1974, New Jersey, Prentice Hall Inc. Englewood Cliff

Wade & Phillips, 'Constitutional Law', 9th ed, 1980, London, ELBS & OUP.

Winthrop, William 'Digest of Opinions of the Judge Advocates General (1895-1912)'

Winthrop, William, 'Military Law and Precedents' 2nd Ed, 1920, Washington, Government Printing Office

Young, P.V., 'Scientific Social Surveys and Research : An Introduction to the Background, Content, Method, Principles and Analysis of Social Studies', 1966, New Jersey, Prentice Hall

B. Published Articles and Papers

Abhichandani, Justice R K, "How to Groom Better Lawyers and Better Judges", AIR 2003 Journal 20.

Anand, Justice A.S., "Torture-Negation of Human rights and Dignity", JIMA (Journal of the Indian Medical Association) Vol 98, Number 6 (June 2000), pp 296-298.

Balsara, "Bail and not Jail - Empty the Prison", Journal of Indian Law Institute, Vol 22, 1980, p 341.

Bakshi, P.M., "Legal Research and Law Reform", Journal of Indian Law Institute, Vol 24, 1982, p 391.

Baxi Upendra, "Socio-Legal Research in India – A Programshrift", Journal of Indian Law Institute, Vol 24, 1982, p 416.

Bird, Denius L., "The British Court Martial System", Contemporary Review, Vol 271, (Sep 1997) p 47

Bishop, Joseph W., JR "Civilian Judges and Military Justice: Collateral Review of Court Martial Convictions", Columbia Law Review , Vol. 61, (1961), 40

Bower, Major Martha Huntley, "Unlawful Command Influence: Preserving the Delicate Balance" Air Force Law Review, 1988. pp 65-96

Brown, Terry V "The Crowder-Ansell Dispute: The Emergence of General Samual T Ansell", Mil Law Rev, Vol 35, 1967, p 23.

Cooke, "The Twenty-sixth Annual Kenneth Hodson Lecture : Manual for Courts Martial 20X", Mil Law Rev, Vol 156, Jun 1988, pp 1-29.

Cox III, Honorable Walter T., "The Army, The Courts and the Constitution - The Evolution of Military Justice", Mil Law Review, 1987 Vol 118, pp 1-30.

Dallari, Dalmo De Abreu "Jurisdicciones nacionales y derechos humanos", in Jornadas Internacionales contra la Impunidad, 1993, Comision Internacional de Juristas y Comision Nacional Consultiva de Derechos Humanos de Francia, Geneva, p 209.

Droddy, Lieutenant Colonel J. D. "King Richard to Solorio: The Historical and Constitutional Bases for Court Martial Jurisdiction in Criminal Cases", The Air Force Law Review, Vol 30, 1989, pp 91-133.

Fidell, Eugene R, "A World-Wide Perspective on Change in Military Justice", Air Force Law Review, Vol 48, 2000, pp 195-209

Gangrade, K.D., "Empirical Methods and Tools of Research", Journal of the Indian Law Institute, Vol. 24, 1982, p 635

Gillissen, John, "Evolution actuelle de la justice militaire - Rapport general", Huitieme Congres International Ankara, 11-15 Oct 1979.

Grove, Russel W.G., "Sentencing Reform: Toward a More Uniform, Less Uninformed System of Court Martial Sentence", Army Law, July 1988, p 28

Haynes, Evan, "The Selection and Tenure of Judges", National Conference of Judicial Councils, 1944, p 5.

Healy, Wg Cdr Frank B, "Australian Military Justice System", Air Force Law Review, Vol 52, 2002, pp 93-136.

Henderson, Gordon D., "Courts Martial and the Constitution: The Original Understanding", Harv L Rev, Vol 71, 1957, pp 293-324.

Hodson, "The Manual for Courts Martial: 1984", Military Law Review, Vol 57, 1972.

Hollingworth, Capt Teresa K., "Unlawful Command Influence," Air Force Law Review, Vol 46, 1996, pp 261-276.

Immel, Major Steven M., "Development, Adoption, and Implementation of Military Sentencing Guidelines," Mil Law Rev, Vol 165, Sep 2000,p 160

Jain, S.N., "Doctrinal and Non-doctrinal Legal Research", Journal of the Indian Law Institute, Vol. 24, 1982, p 341

Jha, Wg Cdr UC, "Appellate Court for Military", Civil and Military Law Journal, Vol 38, 2004, pp 225-239

Jha, Wg Cdr (Rtd) UC, "Military Law needs reform", AIR 2003 Journal 108.

Jha, Wg Cdr (Rtd) UC, "Military Justice System in India", USI Journal, April-June 2006, pp 220-232.

Johnson, "Unlawful Command Influence: A Question of Balance", The Judge Advocate Journal, Navy, March-April 1965, pp 87-88.

Jones, Earnest, "Some Current Trends in Legal Research", Journal of the Indian Law Institute, Vol. 24, 1982, p 197.

Kaur, Paramjit, "Article 33, Armed Forces and Judicial Attitude : An Appraisal", Civil and Military Law Journal, 1988, p 175.

Leonard, Doob, "The Behaviour of Attitudes", Psychological Review, Vol. 54, 1947, p 135.

Lermack, "Summary and Special Courts Martial : An Empirical Investigation", St Louis University Law Journal, Vol 10, Spring 1974.

Lippert, Major Jeffery D. "Automatic Appeal under UCMJ Article 66; Time for a Change", Mil Law Rev, Vol 182, Winter 2004, pp 1-48.

Lovejoy, Major James Kevein, "Abolition of Court Member Sentencing in the Military", Military Law Review, Vol 142, 1994, pp 1-66.

Moorman, Major General William A., (US JAG Air Force) "Fifty Years of Military Justice: Does the Uniform Code of Military Justice Need to be Changed?" Air Force Law Review, Vol 184, (2000), p 185.

Mukherjee, Justice Chittatosh, (Chairman, WB Human rights Commission) "Torture from Legal Viewpoint in the Eyes of Human Rights Commission", JIMA Vol 98, Number 6 (June 2000) pp 327-331.

O' Douglas, Justice William, "Tough Test for Military Justice", Time Magazine, 3 Oct 1969, pp 42-43.

Ogletree, Charles J., "Commentary: The Death of Discretion: Reflection on the Federal Sentencing Guidelines," Har L Rev, Vol 101, 1988, p 1938.

Pollak, "Proposals to Curtail Habeas Corpus for State Prisoners: Collateral Attack on the Great Writ," YALE LJ, Vol 66, 1956, p 50.

Rowe, Peter J. "Military Justice within the British Army", Mil Law Rev, Vol 94, 1981, pp 99-134.

Sam J Ervin Jr., "The Military Justice Act of 1968", Military Law Review, Vol 45, 1969, pp 77-98.

Saraf, D.N., "Reference and Utility of Empirical Research in Law", Journal of the Indian Law Institute, Vol. 24, 1982, p 611.

Sobti Jagdish C, BC Chapperal, Eric Hoist "Study of Knowledge, Attitude and Practice Concerning Aspects of Torture", JIMA, Vol 98, Number 6 (June 2000) pp.334-339.

Sirpurkar, Hon'ble Justice V. S. "Protection of Human Rights of Armed Forces Personnel in International Scenario", in the Report of Seminar on Human rights & Armed Forces, 28 Nov 2003, organized by Dy. Judge Advocate General - HQ Central Command p 21-29.

Starkman, Bernard, "Canadian Military Law: The Citizen as Soldier", Canadian Bar Review, Vol 43, 1965, p 420.

Stephen Cohen " The Military in India Democracy"' in Atul Kohli, ed, India's Democracy: An Analysis of the Changing State & Society Relations, 1988, Priceton Press.

Stuart-Smith, James, "Military Law : Its History, Administration and Practice", Law Quarterly Review, Vol 85, 1969, pp 478-504.

Thakkar, Justice C. K., "L Chandra Kumar v Union of India, AIR 1997 SC 1125: Restoration of Jurisdiction of High Courts", AIR 1997 Journal 177

Tomas Martin "Carrots or Sticks? - Experiences of Human rights Education by the Subordinate Staff of an Indian Prison", JIMA, pp-309-311.

Upadhyay, A.K., "Appeal under Law of Armed Forces - An Analysis", Journal of Indian Law Institute, Vol 45, No. 2, April June 2003, pp 275-287

Vico, Capt De, "Evolution of Military Law", the JAG Journal, Dec. 1966 - Jan. 1967.

Vidhu, Lt Col R. G., "Common Service Offences", Sainik Samachar, Vol 37 (1990).

Webster, Charles W., "Jury Sentencing - Grab-Bag Justice", SW LJ, Vol 14, 1960, p 227.

Westmoreland, William C. "Military Justice - A Commander's View Point," 10AM Crim L Rev, (1971), p 21.

Wiener, Colonel, "Courts Martial and the Bill of Rights: The Original Practice", Harv L Rev, Vol 72, 1958, pp 266-298.

Wigmore, Colonel John H., "Address Before the Maryland State Bar Association, (28 June 1919)" in 24 MD State Bar Association Transaction, 1999.

Wilde Oscar, " The Ballad of Reading Gaol".

Willis, Capt., "The United States Court of Military Appeals: Its Origin, Operation and Future", Mil Law Rev, Vol 55, 1972, pp 39-93.

Willis, Major Deana M. C., "The Road to Hell is Paved With Good Intentions: Finding and Fixing Unlawful Command Influence", The Army Lawyer, 1992.

C. Reports

(1) Official

Advisory Commission to the Military Justice Act of 1983 Report, CMD 7608, 1949 The First Independent Review by the Right Honourable Antonio Lamer, PC.CC.CD, of the provision and operation of Bill C-25, An Act to amend the National Defence Act and to make consequential amendments to other Acts, as required under section 96 of Statutes of Canada 1998, C-35, submitted to the Minister of National Defence, 03 Sep 2003

Committee on the Uniform Code of Military Justice, Good Order and Discipline in the Army (Powell Committee) Report, 18 Jan 1960.

Constituent Assembly Debates,Vol 10.

Darling Committee Report, (1919) Comnd No. 428

Fraud Trial Committee Report, Chairman, Lord Roskill, PC (HMSO, 1986)

French Senate Document "No. 226-Senat, Session ordinaire de 1998-1999, annexe au proces verbal de la séance du 17 fevrier 1999"

Geneva Convention Relative to the Protection of Civilian Persons in Times of War

Government of India, Ministry of Home Affairs, Notification No. 488 dated 09 Feb. 1978

Report of Justice BP Jeevan Reddy Committee on abuses of Armed Forces (Special Powers) Act, 1958 after the sexual assault and death in custody of Ms Thangan Manorama in Imphal, June 2006.

Law Commission of India, 152nd Report (1994)

Law Commission of India, 14th Report 1958, on Reforms of Judicial Administration

Law Commission of India, 35th Report, 1967

Law Commission of India, 41st Report 1969.

Law Commission of India, 78th Report, 1979, on Congestion of under-trial prisoners in jails.

Law Commission of India, 169th Report of 1999- Recommending CM appeal mechanism.

Lewis Committee (Army and Air Force Court Martial Committee) Report, 1948, CMD No. 7608,

The Military Justice Act of 1983 Advisory Commission Report, 1984,

National Police Commission, Third Report, January 1980

Pilcher Committee Report (CMD 8094), 1950, London, HMSO.

Report of War Dept's Adivsory Committee (Vanderbilt Committee Report) 1946.

Roland Oliver Committee Report 1938 (CM review).

Standing Committee on Defence (2005-2006) Tenth Report of May 2006

Statistical Abstract of the United States, U.S. Deptt. of Commerce, Table No. 385 at 256 (1970)

UN General Assembly, Resolution No.39/46 [annex, 39 UNGA OR Supp (No.51)

UN General Assembly Resolution No.52/149

United Nations Document E/CN. 4/Sub.2/1985/18

The Vienna Declaration, 1993

(2) Unofficial

Centre of Strategic and International Studies Report, 2001.

Northern Command Legal Seminar, 1993 - Report

Report of the Workshop on Conditions of Women in Detention organized at Penang by Asian Women's Fund, January 2003.

Seminar on Human rights & Armed Forces, 28 Nov 2003, organized by Dy. Judge Advocate General – HQ Central Command - Report

Transparency International Global Corruption Report, 2007.

USI Seminar Number Ten, 26 Feb 1982 Report

D. News Papers and Magazines

'Dainik Jagaran' (Hindi Daily), 15 January 2006, p 16, "Jharokha" (25 female officers first inducted in the Army, on 06 Mar 1993).

'Dainik Jagaran', 17 Dec 06, editorial, "Hirasat mein maut ki saja".

'Dainik Jagran', 24 Oct 2007, "Five Accused Acquitted Under POTA".

Hindustan (Meerut ed.) 27 Nov 2007, p 15 regarding 450 years imprisonment by an Israili Tribunal to a member of Hamas.

Newsweek, 31 Aug 1970, "Military Justice on Trial".

Outlook, 13 Jun 2005, Sugatha Srinivasaraju, "Flight of the Dove".

TOI, 31 Dec 2001, p 9, "India has military edge over Pakistan".

TOI, 11 Nov 2002, Editorial "Bail for Gilani".

TOI, 19 Jan 2003, Soli J. Sorabjee, "Women prisoners & whistle blowers".

TOI 17 Mar 2003, "Amend Official Secrets Act, MPs appeal to Advani",

TOI, 02 Feb 2004, p 5, "Avoid arrest until very necessary, rules HC".

TOI, 05 Apr 2004, p 5, Rakesh Bhatnagar, "The Bail - Acquittal Syndrome".

TOI, 22 Jul 2004, p.7, "Bail Trial : Siwan Judge loses job".

TOI, 16 Jan 2005, p.1, "US soldier found guilty in Abu ghraib prison abuse case"

TOI 20 Apr 2005, "IAF harassment case; Gupta put in custody".

TOI, 22 Sep 2005, p.6, "SC: Follow directions while granting bail".

TOI, 10 Dec 2005, p7, "Anjali Gupta : First Woman Officer court-martialled".

TOI, 21 Feb 2006, p.10, Maroof Raza, "Headcount in Army: Petition filed in SC".

TOI 07 Mar 2006, p.8, Maroof Raza, "Petition on Muslim headcount withdrawn".

TOI 30 Mar 2006, p 16, Maroof Raza, "Limits of Representation".

TOI, 06 Oct 2006, p 7, Dhananjaya Mahapatra, "SC : No easy bail for serious offences".

TOI, 16 Oct 2006, "Kartikeya Undertrial goes insane waiting for case to end".

TOI, 17 Oct 2006, p 6, Gitesh Shilke, "Innocent man freed afgter 11 years in jail".

TOI, 29 Nov 2006, p 16, Editorial, "He's No Khalnayak- Apply Sanjay Dutt yardstick to all TADA, POTA accused".

TOI, 16 Dec 2006, "Retired top cop to hand".

TOI, 20 Dec 2006, p.16, Editorial, "Ardh Satya".

TOI, 26 May 2007, p 11, Dhananjay Mahapatra, "Rs. 2630-crore bribe paid yearly to lower judiciary".

TOI, 08 Aug 2007, p 02, Nikhila Pant and Pallavi Pasricha, "Serves them right".

TOI, 04 Oct 2007, p 7, "PM asks media to act responsibly".

TOI, 02 Nov 2007, p 25, "Pak may try civilians in military courts".

TOI, 11 Nov 2007, p 6, "Approval for armed forces tribunal from cabinet"

TOI, 5 Jun 2010 p9, "Tribunal turns down Lt Gen's plea.".

TOI, 10 Jul 2010 p11, "Army Tribunal rejects 'ketchup' colonel's plea".

E. Web sites

Amnesty International http://www.amnst.org

Canada, Department of National Defence http://www.dnd.ca

Canada, Minister of National Defence http://www.forces.gc.ca/site/reports/review/en/report_e.pdf

Columbia Judiciary http://200.21.19.132/publico/publico/inicio

Columbia Encyclopedia, 6th ed, 2000 http://www.bartleby.com/65/millas.html

Death Sentence - 187 Report of Law Commission of India, http://lastmile.inftykitten.com

Death Sentence http://www.deathrowbook.com

European Court of Human Rights http://www.echr.coc.int

Indian Law Institute - www.ilidelhi.org

Google India http:www.gogle.co.inenat.fr/rap/a-98-2260.html French Parliamentary report on the draft legislation to bring general criminal law and military law together. http:/www.

International Commission of Jurists http://wwc.icj.org

International Society for Mil Law and the Law of War http://wwc.soc_mil_law.org

Law Commission of India http://lawcommissionofindia.nic.in

UK Parliament Research Papers http://www.parliament.uk

OP Sharma, Rear Admiral (Dr.) bigdady@bol.net.in

Newzealand Military Justice System http://www.aflanz.org/intro_mil_law. htm

Peru, Conscjo Supremo de Justicia Militar http://www.mindef.gob.pc/conscjo.htm

Spain Military Law http://derechomilitar.metropoliglobal.com

Journal of Indian Medical Association www.doctoranywhere.com

UK Armed Forces Act, 2006, http://www.opsi.gov.uk/acts/acts2006/ukpga-20060052_en_1

UK Commanders Guide to Sentence http://www.army.mod.uk/militarylaw/command_sentencing.htm

UK Military Law http://www.army.mod.uk/militarylaw/

UK Parliament Research Papers http://www.parliament.uk

United Nations http://www/un.org

Uniform Code of Military Justice http://www/militaryedu.com/studyguide/

United States of America http://www.adtdl.army.mil

University of Delhi, Faculty of Law lawfaculty@vsnl.net

University of Delhi, Law Review delhilawreview@gmail.com

F. Unpublished Literature

Col SS Bedi, "Accidenta Destinalis"

Guide on Naval Law, 1990, JAG, Naval Headquarters, New Delhi

Harish Uppal, "The Law of Armed Forces in India and the Need for Reform", a thesis submitted for Ph D to Faculty of Law, University of Delhi, Library (Th: 12125)

Makhan Singh, 'Police and Custodial Violence', (Sep. 2000), a thesis submitted for Ph D to Faculty of Law, University of Delhi

RK Yadav, 'Judicial Behaviour towards Personal Liability : A Study in Attitude of Contemporary Trial Courts in Delhi', a thesis submitted for Ph D to Faculty of Law, University of Delhi, Library (Th: 10554)

VK Singh and AB Bajela, 'Military Justice System in Dock' 1993, Lucknow, Institute of Judicial Training and Research

INDEX

O

P

Q

R